WILD
STORIES

Also by the Editors of *Men's Journal*
The Great Life

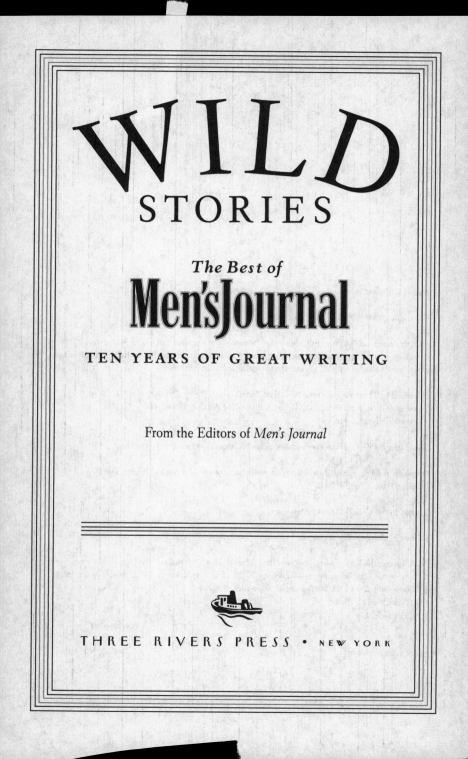

WILD
STORIES

The Best of
Men'sJournal

TEN YEARS OF GREAT WRITING

From the Editors of *Men's Journal*

THREE RIVERS PRESS • NEW YORK

Published by Three Rivers Press, New York, New York.
Member of the Crown Publishing Group, a division of Random House, Inc.
www.randomhouse.com

Three Rivers Press and the Tugboat design are trademarks of Random House, Inc.

Originally published in slightly different form in hardcover by Crown Publishers, a division of Random House, Inc., in 2002.

Printed in the United States of America

Library of Congress Cataloging-in-Publication Data

Wild stories : the best of Men's journal / the editors of Men's journal.
    1. Adventure and adventurers—Anecdotes.   2. Travel—Anecdotes.   3. Travelers—Anecdotes.
I. Crown Publishers.   II. Men's journal (New York, N.Y.)
    G525.W464   2002
    910.4–dc21

                                                                            2002001649

ISBN 1-4000-4830-3

10 9 8 7 6 5 4

First Paperback Edition

Contents

THE SPORTING LIFE

MEN'S LIVES

THE REPORTING

Introduction

A perennial lament among editors of glossy travel-and-adventure magazines such as *Men's Journal* is that they rarely get to leave the island of Manhattan. It's the writers, they say, who have all the fun. But this isn't exactly true. While no one on the staff of *Men's Journal* has ever driven across India on the treacherous Grand Trunk Road or hassled Colombian rebels with "The World's Most Dangerous Places" author Robert Young Pelton, or ridden a dogsled a thousand miles through the interior of Alaska, we definitely know what it's like to do those things.

That's because writers as talented as the ones gathered here don't just fly off to a place and then come back with a story. In the act of writing artfully about what has happened to them, they manage to embark again—only this time they take us along. Here's P. J. O'Rourke, who really did drive across India on the Grand Trunk, describing the thoroughfare's hazards: "Jeeps bust scooters, scooters plow into bicycles, bicycles cover the hoods of jeeps. Cars run into trees. Buses run into ditches, rolling over on their old-fashioned rounded tops until they're mashed into chapatis of carnage. And everyone runs into pedestrians. A speed bump is called a 'sleeping policeman' in England. I don't know what it's called in India. 'Dead person lying in the road' is a guess."

Tim Cahill was the lucky soul (although he didn't necessarily see it that way) who spent several weeks in Colombia with the danger-jaded Robert Young Pelton. Reconstructing a high-profile government raid on a cocaine-making lab "twenty-five minutes into the boonies," Cahill writes, "Two planes flew over and sprayed the coca field with herbicide, while below, the drug lab itself exploded in picturesque billows of flame and black smoke. Pelton was filming all this with a small digital camera about the size of a box of Cracker Jacks. 'Good stuff?' I asked. 'Dog-and-pony show,' he muttered."

And while training for the Yukon Quest Sled Dog Race in Alaska, John Balzar had to learn how to harness a team of dogs, a task, he writes, "that's something between rodeo wrangling and diaper changing. You grab a collar tightly in one fist, unclip the dog from its chain, and with your free hand raise its powerful front legs off the ground. (People who underestimate the brute-muscle force of these creatures have been surprised to discover their fingers broken when they've pulled away.) Trying to move a dog whose four feet are planted would permit it the advantage of traction, and you would likely find yourself being dragged on your face."

This is what great writing does. It takes you to a place you've never been and makes it real, even unforgettable. It introduces you to compelling characters and paints vivid scenes, whether they are funny, sad, or hair-raising. It even changes the way you think about the world. Writers who can do all this without preaching or bragging or resorting to clichés are exceedingly rare. Not only must they possess the passion and the curiosity to get "out there," they must be able to arrange some essential truth out of the beautiful yet bewildering puzzle that is the English language. Mark Twain said that the difference between the right word and the wrong word is the difference between lightning and a lightning bug, and the great ones know how to strike.

These are the kinds of writers whose work is anthologized in this celebration of *Men's Journal*'s tenth anniversary. The magazine has been publishing their brand of ambitious feature writing since Jann Wenner launched *Men's Journal* in 1992. "Men have always been oriented toward action and accomplishment, a perspective that life is, or should be, an adventure," he and John Rasmus, the founding editor, wrote in the premiere issue, vowing to define the magazine's mission "in the broadest sense." Among the feature stories that ran in that first issue were David Roberts's hard look at the climber Jeff Lowe, who, in the depths of personal crisis and financial disaster, believed he could redeem his life by scaling the Eiger, the most dangerous rock face in the world; Roy Blount Jr.'s hilarious account of his bumbling attempt to learn how to drive a race car; a memoir by Charles Gaines of the summer he and his family built their dream cabin on the shore of Saint George's Bay in Nova Scotia; and Chip Brown's ode to the Mid Ocean Club in Bermuda, a story that contained what I consider to be among the best paragraphs ever written about golf. "But just as golf cannot be defined by the segments of society commonly associated with it, so its spirit is not solely embodied in players who know where the ball is going when they hit it. Golf has less to do with sport than with religion, and what makes a golfer is not talent per se, but faith—faith that a better day, or a better hole, or at least a better shot, is coming. Drain a putt, tag a drive, knock a wedge stiff to the pin and suddenly you will have captured all the glory of the game. What other sport offers so many chances for redemption or is so quick to lift the gloom of ineptitude with a moment of grace?"

There weren't many magazines back then that could pull off such a diverse, compelling, and authentically male mix of feature stories. There still aren't. In fact, only a handful of magazines even publish the kinds of long, ambitious feature stories that are called—sometimes with a hint of derision—"reads." Most people don't read anymore, the myth goes; their attention spans have been neutered by television, the Internet, and "fabloid" magazines specializing in splashy photos and inane articles. The new crop of men's magazines, which thrive on today's crowded newsstands by putting scantily clad women on their covers and promising to instruct readers on how to have the abs of a welterweight and the sex life of a Roman gladiator, isn't helping matters. Admittedly, *Men's Journal* borrows from the lad mags' bag of tricks from time to time. But the soul of the magazine has always been its feature well, and reading great stories for the first time has always been when the fun kicks in for us editors. Not only do we genuinely like getting struck by lightning, we enjoy passing the thrill on to *Men's Journal's* readers.

In between that first read and publication, however, comes a vital, delicate, and occasionally alchemic step: the editing process. Back when David Remnick was just a writer (not the editor of *The New Yorker* as well as a writer), John Schulian, a sportswriter in Chicago, once warned him that editors were "mice training to be rats" after someone took too sharp a pencil to his prose. But plenty of writers enjoy happy, productive, even irreplaceable relationships with their editors. When William Langewiesche was working on "American Ground," his 90,000-word account of the "unbuilding" of the World Trade Center for *The Atlantic Monthly*, he and Cullen Murphy, his editor, met several times at a restaurant in Midtown to map out the piece and carve a narrative from the massive amount of material

Langewiesche had gathered at Ground Zero. "Without that map, provided to me by my beloved editor," Langewiesche said, "I would've been incapable of making any sense." It's fair to say that each of the stories reprinted here was improved by some good editors working under a sort of self-imposed Hippocratic oath: respect the art, do no harm, cut with care, and invest yourself into making things better.

In that same spirit, we improved this edition of *Wild Stories* by adding three pieces that were published in 2002, after the book came out in hardcover but still during *Men's Journal's* tenth anniversary. In "The Survivors," Hampton Sides weaves together the harrowing experiences of three men who made it out of the World Trade Center on September 11, only to find that their troubles had just begun. "Fliers Like My Father" is Stephen Rodrick's account of growing up the son of a Navy pilot, and of the month Rodrick spent aboard the USS *Kitty Hawk,* the aircraft carrier from which his father took off for the last time. And "The Big Game" is Jonathan Miles's rollicking profile of a former floor-covering salesman from Arizona who may just be the best marlin fisherman alive.

We divided this book into four chapters simply because that's the way the stories fell. "The Adventures" is a series of razor-sharp travel narratives from around the world, from O'Rourke's Grand Trunk road trip to Rick Bass's search for grizzlies in post-Ceauçesu Romania. "The Sporting Life" is a look into obscure corners of the sports world, where golf's bush-league wannabes try to make it to the PGA and a group of cyclists out-suffer one another in pursuit of the mythic Hour Record. "Men's Lives" includes profiles of singular adventurers such as Yvon Chouinard and Ned Gillette and captures the rewards of such quintessentially male traditions as building a cabin in the woods. And "The Reporting" collects definitive accounts of the most newsworthy disasters, as well as dispatches from Ground Zero, from war zones in Somalia and Sudan, and from environmental hot spots in Alaska and Montana. We began the editing process with more than 500 stories. To winnow those down to the thirty-five choices in this book, we swallowed hard, limited ourselves to one story per writer, and broke our rule only twice. (Never trust an editor who's unwilling to break the rules.)

Men's Journal has been edited by five of the most talented editors in the business, and I've had the privilege of working for all of them. Although Sid Evans was the fourth to take the reins, this book was his idea, so I'd like to thank him first. He edited several of the pieces anthologized here and was relentless in his desire to make everything that appeared in the magazine memorable. John Rasmus, *Men's Journal's* founding editor, laid the blueprint for an ambitious, distinctive magazine, setting the bar high for everyone who's ever written or edited a single sentence that appeared in its pages. Terry McDonell saw limitless new possibilities for the magazine and enhanced its literary ambitions (it's no accident that almost half of the stories in this book were published on his watch), and Mark Bryant brought many new talented writers into the fold. Thanks to all of them for their passion and vision—and to Bob Wallace, the magazine's current editor in chief, as well as the remarkably talented and hardworking editors who produce *Men's Journal* every month: Mark Cohen, Ben Court, Josh Dean, Robert Firpo-Cappiello, Tom Foster, Peter Frank, Tyler Graham, Kelly Griego, Mark Horowitz, Leslie Lewis, Yeun Littlefield, Claire Martin, Christine Penberthy, and Lucas Zaleski. I'd also like to acknowledge the former features editors who helped craft many of these stories: Joe Angio, John Atwood, Will Blythe, Jon Gluck, Peter Griffin, Mark Jannot, Corey Seymour, and Jack Wright. I'm especially grateful to David DiBenedetto, a longtime editor at the magazine who began the huge task of winnowing down a decade's worth of stories to the ones published here, and to Taylor Plimpton, whose help in seeing things through to the end was invaluable. Likewise, this book would never have gotten off the ground without the work of Sarah Lazin, our literary agent; Evelyn Bernal, Wenner Media's contracts-and-permissions expert; and Doug Pepper at Crown.

Thanks, above all, to Jann Wenner for starting the magazine in the first place, and to all the talented writers who've taken us along for the ride. They are magicians. If you doubt it, or if you're one of those people who think the art of the magazine "read" is dying, I hope this book will change your mind. Great writing has a way of doing that.

David Willey
Executive Editor, *Men's Journal*
February 2003

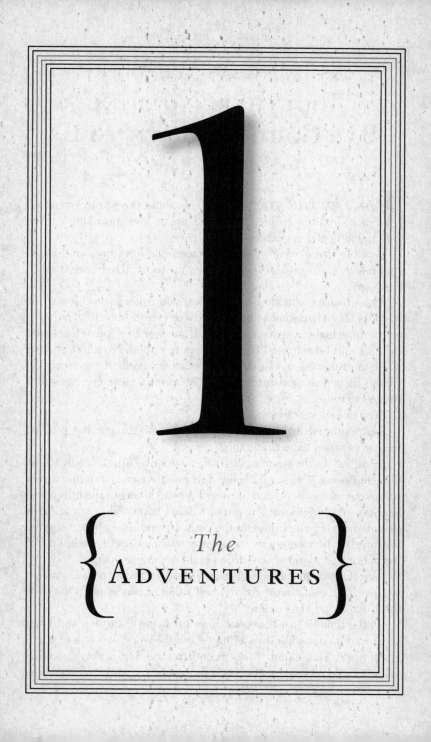

1

{ *The*
ADVENTURES }

As Long As We Were Together, Nothing Bad Could Happen to Us

by Scott Anderson

J ON SAW THE STACK of articles about the war in Chechnya on my coffee table and looked up at me appraisingly. "You thinking of going back?"

"Oh, I don't know," I said, glancing around my living room, "not really." But my older brother knew me too well to believe that. "I guess so."

As journalists who always seemed to cover dangerous places, Jon and I had both had some close calls over the years, but a high percentage of mine had come during a single three-week period in Chechnya in 1995, and I'd returned from there quite rattled. Now, in February 2000, the Russians and Chechens were at war again, it was at least as vicious as before, and for reasons that weren't clear even to me, I wanted to return.

"You think it's a bad idea?" I asked.

Jon pondered this. "Remember Sarajevo?" He saw the puzzled look on my face. "The land mine?"

I laughed. In the summer of 1996, I'd done an astonishingly stupid thing in Bosnia. The war had ended six months earlier, but there were still mines everywhere, and one day I'd gone hiking in the hills above Sarajevo. Walking down a dirt trail I didn't know, I'd nearly stepped on a partially exposed mine in the path. On trembling legs, I'd spent the next two hours gingerly making my way back up the trail. I'd told Jon about it as a kind of humorous, embarrassing anecdote.

"But that was just idiotic," I said. "I got careless."

"Yeah, but you almost got yourself killed in peacetime. Don't you think that's kind of an omen?"

By the time of that conversation in my living room, Jon and I had spent most of our adult lives writing about the worst people and places in the world. That month, I had recently returned from northern Albania, where I'd reported a story on blood vendettas, while Jon was about to head off for war-ruined Angola. When we got together—which, given our schedules, was only about every six months—we talked of where we had just been, where we were thinking of going next.

What we did not talk about—at least not directly—was how any of this affected us. Instead, we had developed a kind of verbal shorthand with each other, the sharing of anecdotes, like mine about the ill-advised hike in Bosnia, that had no real punch lines: "And then I walked back to the hotel," or, "For a while it looked like they were going to shoot us, but then they waved us on and we drove to the capital." We didn't need punch lines; we'd both had enough of these moments to know what the other had felt.

Yet the sharing of these oblique stories served a purpose. My brother and I had both become increasingly superstitious over the years, convinced that all the narrow escapes in our past made it less likely that we would escape in the future, and we relied on each other to tote up the odds. "Is this bet too risky?" "Do I walk away from this story now?" And the reason we sought this guidance from one another was because, in a peculiar way, our stakes were joined, rooted in a secret fear that had held us all our adult lives: that something would happen to the other when he was off in the world and alone, that one of us would die on the other's watch.

The seed of this, I believe, had been planted twenty-five years earlier, in the first great journey my brother and I shared. Whether coincidence or not, that journey also marked the first time we began to regard each other with anything more than contempt.

Summer afternoons are always brutally hot in Gainesville, Florida, but this one, in the middle of June 1975, had been downright perverse. I'd come home from soccer practice wanting nothing more than to lie in front of the air conditioner, only to find my parents huddled close together at the dining-room table. I was surprised to see my father there—my parents had recently divorced, and he came around less and less often—but then I noticed that they were poring over a postcard.

"It's from your brother," my mother said, handing me the card. "He's had a bad accident."

The photo showed some mangy-looking beach in Honduras. On the back, Jon had crammed about eight hundred tiny words—economical, perhaps, but mostly incomprehensible. Something about building a rock wall, collecting coconuts, meeting a witch doctor. The salient details were in the postscript: "P.S. Writing this from hospital. Accidentally kicked a machete and sliced open right foot. Swollen up to three times normal. Doctors say infected, maybe gangrenous, might have to amputate. Ah well, *c'est la vie.* Much love, Jon."

"Gee, that's a damned shame," I said, and faked a somber look for several seconds. "Well, gotta go take a shower."

While it was something our parents had refused to acknowledge, Jon and I were not close. If I really tried, I could dimly recall some pleasant moments in our early childhood, but not many. Much stronger was the memory of the day Jon decided to teach me how to catch by heaving a large rock at my head, leaving a jagged scar through my upper lip. I was six then, Jon eight, and it was a harbinger of the violence to come; from then on he beat me up almost daily. By the summer of 1975, though, I'd barely seen Jon for two years and was quite happy to keep it that way—and if he lost a foot, well, it might just even the playing field in our next fistfight.

But I also saw precisely where this little gathering in the dining room was headed, for on the table next to my father was a small pile of papers: plane tickets, a thin vinyl folder of traveler's checks, and, on top, a half sheet of thin paper that I recognized as a telex record. Somebody was being press-ganged into rescuing Jon in Honduras, and from the way my parents stared at me, I had a pretty good idea who.

This might require a bit of explaining about my family. My brother, my three sisters, and I had spent most of our childhoods being bounced from one Third World country to the next, the result of our father being a foreign-aid officer for the American government. That upbringing, combined with our parents' hands-off approach to child rearing, had instilled in most of us a fiercely self-sufficient and adventurous streak. Jon, for example, had hitchhiked across East Africa by himself at thirteen. Our oldest sister, Michelle, had solo-trekked the Kalahari Desert on horseback at seventeen. At fourteen, I had spent two months on my own in Bangkok.

The catch to all this freedom, though, came into play whenever something went awry with one of us kids. Rather than directly involving themselves in the problem, our parents felt far more comfortable casting another of their children into the fray, and it was with Jon that problems most consistently arose. The previous year, he had dropped out of high school and, after announcing that he was off to the Spanish Sahara to join the Polisario guerrillas in their independence war against Morocco, promptly vanished somewhere between England and North Africa. Our parents had dispatched Michelle, then twenty, to search for him, and she'd eventually found him in the Canary Islands, living on the beach as he tried to repair an old boat he was planning to sail to the war zone. She'd hauled him back to the States, but it hadn't been long before Jon had set out once more, this time to Honduras to help build a friend's house on the Caribbean coast. That's where he had been for the past six months, and now he was in trouble again.

"You're sending Michelle, right?" I asked hopefully, reaching for the telex slip. My parents shook their heads.

My father loved sending telexes. They were charged by the word, with a maximum of ten characters per word, and he could spend hours devising messages that gave him his money's worth. This one was addressed to the main post office in La Ceiba, the town in Honduras where Jon got his mail, and he'd obviously put a lot of effort into it: SCOTTCOMES TOHONDURAS TOMORROWPM. NOREPEATNO AMPUTA- TION BEFORETHEN LOVEMOMPOP.

This was aggravating. My sophomore year in high school had ended a week earlier, and I had big plans for my summer vacation. It was more than that, though. I had always been the good son, the duti- ful one, while Jon had always been the hellion, the one who'd started having run-ins with the law at age eleven. It was he who had intro- duced me to the fine art of shoplifting at eight, and, as he constantly reminded me, we never would have been caught if I hadn't started stealing expensive cigars to give to our father to assuage my guilt.

"Look," I said to my parents in the dining room, "Jon has been nothing but trouble to you people for years; did you stop to think that losing a foot might be just the thing to straighten him out?"

I think that for the briefest of moments my parents actually consid- ered the idea. Then my father shook his head. "Let's not make a big deal out of this. All you have to do is go down there, get him out of the hospital, and put him on a plane home. You'll be back before you know it."

The Paris bar was one of the only places in La Ceiba with air- conditioning, and it felt pleasingly arctic compared to outside. Jon and I sat at a window table, sipping from beers and staring out at the plaza. I was not in a good mood. An hour earlier, I'd been sitting on the front steps of the tiny airport terminal in La Ceiba, contemplating how to find the hospital, when a small blue pickup truck raced up the drive-way and came to a skidding, sideways stop. From out of the passenger seat leapt my brother. He was wearing a straw hat and had a sheathed machete dangling from one hip, and as he nimbly loped up the steps toward me, I couldn't help but notice that he still had both his feet. As it turned out, Jon had sent his fateful postcard nearly a month earlier, and, with the aid of penicillin injections, his foot was now fine.

"So why the hell didn't you call to say you were okay?" I asked.

"Well, I thought about it, but . . ." Jon shrugged lamely. After about a three-second pose of remorse, he grinned and gave a dismissive little backward flip of his hand—a new gesture. "Ah well," he said, "*c'est la vie.* Now that you're here, we'll just make the best of it. Come on, let's go into town."

I didn't have a lot of choice in the matter; the plane that had brought me had just taken off for the return to Miami, and there wouldn't be another one for two days. Angrily grabbing my rucksack, I followed Jon down to the pickup and climbed in for the ride to La Ceiba and the Paris bar.

Our conversation so far had been desultory, with lots of long silences and me staring fixedly out the window. Despite my bad mood, I was struck by how much my brother's appearance had changed in the six months since I'd last seen him: He was deeply tanned and muscular beneath his white T-shirt, and his blond hair had turned even blonder in the tropics. With his machete and his battered straw hat tilted to a rakish angle, he seemed like some Hollywood prototype of a jungle explorer. I fell to studying the machete, hanging from his belt to brush the floor.

"So, what's with the knife?" I asked.

He drew the machete, handed it to me by the black plastic handle. "Whacking things. Down here, you've always got to whack something."

It felt good, heavy, in the hand. The blade was nearly three feet long and razor sharp. I tried a couple of short wrist-flick swings in the air before giving it back.

"You know," Jon said, sliding the machete into its sheath, "now that you're here, you should stay awhile. My job just ended, and we can knock around, have some fun."

Beyond the dirty plate-glass window was La Ceiba's main square, a bedraggled little plaza with some rusting statue in the middle. I hadn't seen anything in Honduras so far that resembled fun. "Maybe you've forgotten," I said, "but we don't really like each other."

He seemed surprised by this. "I always thought we got along pretty well. Oh, sure, we had our little spats every once in a while, but all brothers go through that. It's not like I gave you any permanent scars or anything."

I leaned over the table, pointed to the thin scar in my lip where Jon had hit me with the rock ten years before. Throughout growing up, I'd been rather self-conscious about the scar, a self-consciousness Jon had done his best to promote by constantly referring to it as "the harelip." He squinted to see where I was pointing. "Oh, Christ," he said, "are you still on about the harelip? I apologized for that years ago." He sat back in disgust, motioned to the waitress for two more beers. I returned to staring out the window.

"So how are things in Florida?" Jon asked after a while.

A hard question to answer. Our family had disintegrated exactly two years earlier. My father had taken me out of school, and we'd spent a year traveling together across Europe and the Middle East, but then he'd left me in Florida with my mother and taken to the road again. I'd spent the next six months there plotting my escape: hitchhiking to wherever my father might be, heading to the Yukon to pan for gold with a Scottish guy I'd met on a ship crossing the Atlantic. It had only been very recently that I'd tried to adjust and settle into a normal high school existence. At the Paris bar, I told Jon only about that part—about my friends, soccer, girls I was interested in—but I could tell he wasn't buying it.

"It's not going to work, you know. Fitting in, becoming an American—it's not going to work. We started too late to belong anywhere. The only thing we'll ever belong to is this family, each other."

He looked out the window, his eyes darting over the plaza. It was late afternoon, and the streets of La Ceiba were gradually coming back to life, couples strolling through the plaza, lottery-ticket sellers calling for customers in strange, bullfrog voices.

"And we're always going to end up in places like this."

I imagine that everyone's childhood, no matter how unconventional or exotic, seems absolutely normal while it's being lived. By the time I arrived in Honduras, I was only beginning to comprehend the downside of how we had grown up, the hidden cost that comes with not being from anywhere in particular. Jon, it seemed, had figured it out a little bit sooner. In the years ahead, we would both be caught up in a seemingly endless cycle of trying to fit in, failing, moving on. In a funny way, I think we both drew a certain comfort in the other's inability to settle down—proof that there was at least one more misfit in the family.

At least initially, it appeared that I made a better go of things. By force of will, I actually managed to stick it out through high school and, pushing off college to some indistinct future, took a job with the federal government in 1977. By my nineteenth birthday, I was a full-fledged civil servant inching my way up the bureaucratic ladder, living with my fiancée in a nice Washington, D.C., apartment. Jon, by contrast, continued his errant ways. Having dropped out of school at seventeen, he talked his way into the University of Florida for a couple of quarters, but then signed on as an instructor with some high-school-at-sea schooner and jumped ship in South America. When I next saw him, he was passing through Washington on his way to Nunivak Island off Alaska to make a fortune collecting musk-ox wool, and I could tell he viewed my well-ordered, conventional life with a mix of envy and reproach. When that enterprise failed—it seemed the musk ox were a lot quicker than he was—he headed back down to South America.

By 1982, though, our roles had come full circle. That winter, Jon moved to Washington with his Peruvian wife to take a cub-reporter job, wore a tie, and went to an office every day. By then, I had long since quit my engagement and my government job to spend three years drifting around the country while writing a bad novel. I was rootless, unmoored, so the day after Jon moved to Washington, so did I, becoming a bartender in Georgetown. Jon would occasionally come by to sit at my bar. It was a weird turn of events; now he was the one with the stable home life and a real job, while I was the wastrel, the one the others in the family worried about.

But I'd always been a bit suspicious of this new-and-improved Jon, and when he stopped by my bar one afternoon after work, his mask finally slipped. After staring darkly out at the shoppers on Wisconsin Avenue, he suddenly pointed to my tie, pointed to his own.

"Look at us," he said with disgust. "Look at what we've become." He violently wrenched off his tie and slapped it on the bar: "This is not the way we're supposed to live."

Most people probably wouldn't have understood the source of his discontent, but I did. One thing our upbringing had bestowed on us was a powerful sense of entitlement, a belief that we did not have to live by the rules—college, careers—of most everyone else.

Jon's solution was to head off for the civil wars of Central America. Mine was a five-month ramble across Europe and then to the free-fire zone of Beirut. For both of us, these were our first experiences in war zones, and in them we saw a way to have the lives we wanted, that we were "supposed" to have. We would be writers, together and apart, exploring the darker corners of the earth.

"The Mosquito Coast, man—think of it!" I had already been light-headed when we left the Paris, but now I could barely focus on the small, tattered map of Honduras that Jon spread on the table of the dockside bar. He kept jabbing his finger at the top right corner, a vast stretch of green broken only by the spindly blue lines of rivers, the names of a few towns, and, across its breadth, the single word *Mosquitia.*

"The last great jungle in Central America," my brother went on. "No roads, no telephones. People have gone in there and never been heard from again. We have to go!"

Our stroll to the La Ceiba docks had seemed innocuous enough at first, but I soon discerned a pattern to the people Jon was engaging in conversation: sailors coming off the boats, the captains up in the pilot-houses. There'd been at least a half dozen of these little chats before we came to *El Platanero,* a crude wooden coastal hauler of about thirty feet. Upon learning that it was leaving that very night for Brewers Lagoon, a town in the middle of the Mosquito Coast, Jon had grabbed hold of my arm, gazed at the string of ramshackle bars lining the waterfront, and marched me in their direction.

Now, with more beers before us, he was pulling out all the stops to convince me that sailing off on *El Platanero* was not just a good idea, but a kind of destiny. "So we get to Brewers," he said, "take a steamer upriver until we hit this highway, take a bus over to the capital, and then fly back to Florida. We're talking a week—ten days tops." He looked to me. "What do you say?"

This was a pattern that had been established over our lifetimes. Jon was the confident one who never saw obstacles until he came to them. I was the doubter, the questioner—and in his breezy imagining of our path through the Mosquitia, there was a lot to question. It was interesting, for example, how the forty-mile path out of the jungle had become a "highway" in Jon's telling, when the map indicated that a dotted black line meant "foot trail."

But for some reason—perhaps it was the cozy somnolence of the tropics, perhaps it was all that beer—I found I was reluctant to assume my traditional role. I was tired of being the cautious one.

And maybe something more. Sitting in the bar on the La Ceiba docks, I realized Jon was trying to establish a bond between us that had never existed before. I thought back to what he had said at the Paris, that all we would ever belong to was the family, each other. I wasn't convinced this was true, but on that evening it suddenly seemed a risky thing to chance.

"Okay," I said. "Let's do it."

With a great grin, Jon ordered more beers, then rose from the table and announced that he had to run a few errands. In his absence, I slid the map over and fell to staring at the great green void of the Mosquitia. I was in a happy mood, a happiness that deepened the longer I studied the map and fully grasped what a remarkably bad idea this was. When Jon returned, he was carrying a long, narrow object wrapped in newspaper—a present, he explained. I tore off the paper. It was a machete in a carved-leather sheath, some goofy tassels hanging off the bottom. I slid it out, tested its feel in my hand.

"I also let Mom and Dad know there's been a change in plans," he said, taking a folded sheet of paper from his back pocket. It was a copy of a telex message. Jon had clearly inherited our father's telex-writing style, if not his brevity:

> MOMANDPOP: SCOTTWANTS GOMOSQUITO. METHINKS SOMEKINDOF ADOLESCENT SELFESTEEM DEALSOMAY BENEFITALL INLONGRUN. BACKHOMEIN ELEVENDAYS 1MONTHTOPS. PSFOOTFINE.

Beyond the condescending tone, I was irked by how this had suddenly become my idea.

"Come on," my brother said, and shrugged. "You're the sensible one. If they thought I was behind it, they'd just worry."

Jon came slowly down the rotting wooden dock at Brewers Lagoon, rubbing the back of his neck and staring at the ground as if stupefied. This was a gesture I recognized, and it had a twofold meaning. First, something was amiss. Second, it was not Jon's fault in any way; whatever misfortune had befallen us was completely unavoidable, a simple act of fate.

"Well," he said, "it appears there might be a problem."

Indeed. Rather than the constant flow of traffic up the Patuca that Jon had envisioned, there was precisely one boat, a motorized dugout canoe, that made the run, and it had left just that morning. It wouldn't be back in Brewers for a week, which, funnily enough, was right around the time that *El Platanero*—now a mere dot at the far end of the vast lagoon—would return.

I looked at the Brewers Lagoon waterfront. It consisted of about two dozen outhouses built on stilts over the mud flats, each reached by its own little gangway, and my main source of entertainment while waiting for Jon had been watching the Brewers residents trooping back and forth to perform their bodily functions.

Jon continued to rub his neck. "I found a room we can stay in for two dollars a night. It's got a couple of hammocks, and the woman will cook for us." He followed my gaze over the sprawl of outhouses. "Anyway, I'm sure there's a lot of interesting things to do around here."

This, too, was in error. Rather, Brewers Lagoon was a collection of rude shanties in mosquito-infested swampland, its torpor broken only by the daily three-o'clock rain. We passed the days examining ourselves for ticks and reading—then rereading—the paperback novels we had brought. When we heard that the dugout canoe was finally back in town, I practically cried tears of gratitude.

It was a surprisingly long boat, with an outboard motor in back and room for four or five passengers in its hollowed hull. We set off early in the morning, the two boatmen slowly poling their way through the dense jungle marshes at the far end of the lagoon, charting a course through the maze of water hyacinths and mangrove trees. After a couple of hours, the trees and vines suddenly separated, and before us was the wide, muddy expanse of the Patuca. The captain fired up the outboard and we began to race up the brown, barely moving river.

I watched the riverbanks as we passed. There were no towns, no other boats on the river, but every once in a while I glimpsed a crude wooden shack amid the jungle, a wisp of wood smoke above the trees.

"Miskito Indians," Jon said. "They're the only ones who live in here."

Our destination that first day was the trading town of Awas. According to Jon's interpretation of the map, it was a fairly large town and probably the best place to cash some traveler's checks and stock up on supplies before continuing our journey upriver to the jungle "highway." Of course, it wasn't as if we'd made any actual inquiries in this regard.

By late afternoon, the Patuca had narrowed to just fifty or sixty feet across, and it had been a very long time since we'd seen any signs of settlement. At last, we rounded a bend in the river, and there on the riverbank before us were several Miskito women washing clothes, a couple of crude rafts hauled up onto the mud. The captain killed the outboard as we coasted toward shore.

"Awas," he announced.

"I guess the commercial center is inland," Jon said, trying to sound confident.

For some time, we stood on the Awas riverbank, unable to fully grasp our predicament, a source of amusement for the Miskito women washing clothes on the river rocks. The "commercial center" of Awas, we had quickly discovered, consisted of a single trading-post store, a tiny wooden hut built on stilts at the edge of town. What's more, the river above Awas was studded with rapids, so no boats went any farther. The two little rafts pulled up on the riverbank had been built by upland Miskitos to bring their goods to the Awas trading post and then abandoned, their builders walking home through the jungle.

At first, all this seemed a mere logistical glitch to Jon—his new idea was to emulate the Indians and trek overland—but there was now a practical problem standing in the way of lunacy: money. Between us, we had about six dollars in Honduran lempiras; all the rest of our money was in traveler's checks, and despite Jon's painstaking tutorial on the workings of international finance, the trading-post owner simply stared at the brightly colored slips of paper in confusion. Finally accepting that we had no choice but to take the dugout back to Brewers, we returned to the riverbank, only to learn the boat had left fifteen minutes before.

"But don't worry," an old man said upon seeing our consternation. "It should be back in a few days—two weeks at most."

I tried to imagine spending that much time waiting in Awas, cadging off the Miskitos for food and a place to stay. Given the poverty of the place, and our own stupidity in getting stranded, that seemed indecent, the shame of those long, slow days intolerable. Then my gaze fell on the rafts. They were clearly built for short-term use, rough-cut balsa logs lashed together with jungle vines. One sported a cute little shed, about three feet wide and four feet deep, with its own thatched roof, like a miniature house. The beginning of an idea came to me.

Considering that we had made the trip up to Awas in six or seven hours, I estimated that we were about ninety miles from Brewers; without a motor, drifting along on the Patuca's scant current, our return could take days. I tried to envision a voyage down the river, what dangers might lie along the way, how we would ever know where to turn into the mangrove swamp before we reached the open sea, whether the raft would even hold together that long.

I think most of all, I wanted to impress Jon. So far on this journey, we had played out our traditional roles: he the creator of plans, the pursuer of adventure, me the cautious one, the follower. I think I wanted to show him, for the first time, that I, too, could come up with truly bad ideas.

I pointed to the raft with the miniature hut. "Let's float down."

For both Jon and myself, getting out of tight spots has always been largely a matter of dumb luck. Of course, that's not quite the way we see it; before going to report on a war, for example, we can spend weeks trying to calculate the odds of something bad happening. It's an odd exercise—superstition, really—because the chief characteristic of such places is that their hazards can't be calculated, and all is random. But underlying our superstitions is something a bit more complex, something rooted in our experience in the Mosquitia and reinforced by our subsequent travels together: the belief that, so long as we are together, nothing bad can happen to us.

In the mid-1980s, Jon and I teamed up to write a book about the World Anti-Communist League, an international right-wing terrorist organization. For two years, we investigated death squads in Central America and Nazi war criminals living in the United States and Europe, tracking their trails of murder around the globe. After that, we set off to compile an oral history of modern war, spending a year going from one battlefield to the next across five continents. The journey was exciting, it felt important, but it also came at a high personal cost: for Jon, his marriage; for me, a three-year relationship. By the end of that year, we were like an old married couple, keenly attuned to each other's moods and silences, and there was the sense that, in our rootlessness, in our twin predicaments of having no one or nowhere to go back to, we were more joined than ever.

Afterward, we continued on our own: Jon headed out to do a book on guerrilla groups worldwide, while I investigated a murderous religious cult in the American Southwest and the underworld of organized crime in Northern Ireland and New York. In phone calls from Pakistan and Belfast and Burma, we kept each other posted on our progress, our setbacks, and, in the cryptic, half-spoken way we had cultivated, our close calls. And there was no getting around the fact that for both of us, these incidents were becoming more frequent. In Afghanistan, a Russian tank fired on Jon's jeep, missing it by a few yards. In Burma, he scrambled across a battlefield to interview a shell-shocked Karen guerrilla commander who refused to leave a position that was about to be overrun by government troops. In one four-day span in Chechnya, I was confronted by firing squads from both sides and barely managed to negotiate my way out. By the time of our get-together in Brooklyn this past February, we had probably been to twenty-five wars between us and, if I truly did have nine lives, I calculated I'd now pissed away six of them. Now, when I thought back to that trip in the Mosquitia, our innocence and incompetence there, the simplicity of the hazards we faced, it was with a kind of longing.

While I spread banana leaves over the raft floor, Jon went back to the trading post with our last twenty lempiras to buy food—"provisions," he insisted on calling them—for the journey. He returned with two plastic bags and proudly displayed the contents: three bottles of Colonial rum, one tiny can of Vienna sausages, a kilo of beans, and another of cornmeal. He noticed me wincing.

"What, you think you could have done better?"

"No, it's fine," I said. "I just figured you'd get things we could actually eat." I thought of explaining to him that beans and cornmeal had to be cooked, but decided against it; after all, we were going to be stuck together on this raft for the next two or three days, so harmony was going to be pretty essential.

Evidently, word had spread through Awas of the folly being planned down on the riverbank, so that by the time we poled away, a good two hundred Miskitos had gathered on the bluff to see us off. It occurred to me that we were probably one of the strangest sights they had ever seen in their televisionless lives, these two white teenagers showing up one day, having journeyed all the way up from the coast just to take one of their rafts and float back down again. They waved good-bye to us as if we were sailing off into the abyss, and I suppose, from their perspective, we were.

It was a three-day voyage, endless hours of imperceptible progress along great looping bends, nothing but the sky and the brown water and the dark jungle around us. The Vienna sausages lasted only that first night, the rum not much longer, and after that we were kept alive with the help of the few Miskitos who lived along the river. In the strange way that news travels in the jungle, the Indians seemed to know of us ahead of time. One man, noticing we had only sticks and the bamboo rudder with which to steer, threw us his hand-carved oar as we passed. Others paddled out in their dugouts to give us tortillas or motioned us ashore to share a meal of beans and grilled monkey. These encounters were infrequent, though; there were no other boats on the river, no real settlements along the way. Leery of what animals might lurk along the banks, we poled through the nights, dozing in shifts in the little hut.

Along with the tedium were moments of crisis. On the first day, a sudden burst of wind tore the thatched roof off the hut and squarely into me, knocking me into the water; for what seemed a very long time, I struggled to free myself from the vines pulling me down into the murk. A few hours later, a low-hanging branch got caught on our rudder housing and sheared it away. And throughout was the slow-motion crisis we could do nothing about, the knowledge that we were gradually sinking, the balsa logs becoming steadily more saturated, the brown water sloshing ever higher.

But there was one moment, late in the afternoon on the second day, that stood out. Rounding a bend in the Patuca, we saw a patch of whitewater ahead and, amidst it, a newly fallen tree, its leaves still green, stretched across nearly to the far shore. We'd already been snared by at least a half dozen fallen trees and expended a lot of energy getting free, but this time, with an actual current pushing us, getting out might be impossible. Excited to finally have something to do, Jon and I got to our feet, took up our long poles, and began levering off the river bottom, steering toward the narrow passage the tree had left. We were doing well, nearly in position, when I felt a shudder pass through the raft, heard a small splash behind me. I turned, and for a moment I couldn't make sense of what I saw. On the far side of the raft, Jon was sitting, his left leg stretched out before him; he was using his arms to hoist himself up a few inches, then back down, as if performing some odd calisthenic.

"What the hell are you doing?"

He looked to me then, and I saw that his face was pale. "I'm stuck."

I hurried over. The spread of banana leaves had obscured a narrow gap between two of the balsa logs. Jon's right leg had found the gap and gone through; it was now wedged in tight, clamped just above the knee. I glanced downriver. We were almost to the rapids. "You've got to get out," I said pointlessly.

Jon tried again, his arms trembling with the exertion, pulling so hard that the skin around his knee came off in a broad swath. The logs held him fast.

I looked downstream again and now saw that the fallen tree didn't end where we had thought, but rather extended on across the river just beneath the surface; the raft would clear it, but Jon's pinioned leg wouldn't.

"You've fucking got to get out," I shouted.

"I can't!" he yelled back, still trying, his knee now covered in blood.

I had one of those moments in which the mind seems to skip over to a different plane, one that is less about conscious thought than simple instinctive clarity. I knew exactly what was going to happen if Jon didn't get free. Not the specifics—I didn't know whether the tree was going to break his leg, or slice it open, or take it off completely—but I did know that we were all alone on this river, and I understood the Mosquitia well enough by now to know that once things started going bad out here they just kept getting worse. In the remnants of the shed I spotted my machete. I scrambled over to it, pulled it from its sheath.

The raft consisted of eleven logs lashed together in front and back. Jon had fallen between the fourth and fifth logs on the right side, and I went to the bow and began furiously hacking through the vine roping. We were already in the rapids now, but it took only a few seconds, the last vine producing a snapping sound when it broke. The outer four logs immediately started to part, and Jon swung his leg out and got to his feet. When we scraped over the fallen tree a moment later, the half-separated logs caught on a branch and the force of the current ripped them away. I tried to imagine that force being directed against my brother's leg, and then I didn't want to think about it anymore.

Afterward, the Patuca returned to its usual brown calm, and I poled to keep us out of the shallows while Jon sat and examined his cuts. His leg was red from the knee to the ankle, but I couldn't tell if it was mostly blood or water.

"Just little scrapes, it looks like," he said after a while. He looked up at me. "Quick thinking; thanks."

I shrugged. "Sure."

On that day in February when Jon found the Chechnya articles on my coffee table, we had dinner at a little place in my Brooklyn neighborhood. He was leaving in the morning for his home in Spain, and from there would go on to Angola; I probably wouldn't see him again for four or five months.

"So, if you don't go to Chechnya," he asked, "what'll you do?"

"I don't know. Maybe start on the micro-nation story."

Jon scowled. "That's such a dumb idea. I can't believe anyone wants that."

I shrugged, tried to mask my smile. For years now, we had maintained a competition of who had been to the most foreign countries, updating our lists whenever we got together. Jon had always managed to stay about six countries ahead, and even though my total was now in the high sixties, his was in the mid-seventies, and Angola would give him one more. To keep his gloating to a minimum, I'd recently told him that a magazine wanted me to do a comprehensive report on the micro-nations of the world, a project that not only would mean traveling throughout the South Pacific and the Caribbean, but would add another thirty or so countries to my list. Jon found this prospect so disturbing that he now tended to avoid the country competition topic altogether. On that night, I saw no reason to tell him it was a joke.

Over the course of the evening, we eventually ended up talking about that summer in Honduras. "Can you believe it's been almost twenty-five years?" Jon said. He shook his head. "Jesus, we were such idiots."

We had, of course, eventually made it back to Brewers Lagoon, and the raft trip proved to be only the first of our misadventures as we wandered through Central America that summer. A few weeks later, there was the near knife fight in a bar in El Salvador when Jon decided that a group of four *campesinos* were disrespecting us and drew out his machete; I quickly followed suit, but so did the *campesinos,* and when it occurred to us that we were about to be sliced to pieces, we backed out of the bar like characters in a spaghetti western. Then there was the volcano in Guatemala that had begun erupting so violently that the area had been evacuated—reason enough, in Jon's opinion, for us to climb to the rim for a closer look. When the vapor cloud suddenly shifted direction and came over us, the sulfur dioxide knocked me out, and Jon had to drag me to safety. Thirteen weeks later—or about twelve and a half weeks after I'd originally planned to get back to Florida—we turned up, filthy and penniless, at our grandmother's house in California. After that came our years of wandering, of trying to settle into some place or some job and giving up, of heading off to the wars of the world.

But whatever else was drawing us to this life—the adrenaline rush of danger, morbid curiosity, some poorly conceived notions of the power of journalism—I'd come to suspect that at least part of it was a desire to recapture the sensation we'd had floating down the Patuca, that peculiar mix of excitement and dread we'd felt, the sheer exuberant, innocent naiveté of it all. The problem was, we were no longer innocent or naive. We'd been scared—and scarred—by what we'd seen out there. We didn't trust in dumb luck anymore. My brother had remarried, he had three little kids now, and even though he was away from his family a great deal, he had a compelling reason to get home, to play it safer. For me, it was maybe more cerebral and selfish. I had a number of snapshot images floating around in my head from places I'd been, unpleasant ones, and I wasn't sure how many more I could or should take.

In the Brooklyn restaurant, Jon brought the conversation back to my talk of returning to Chechnya. "Look," he said, "you've had a good run—we both have—but our luck can't hold forever. It's already turned, don't you think?"

I stared at him. I remembered my first time in Chechnya, the land mine outside Sarajevo. I nodded.

"So don't go back," Jon said.

So I didn't.

A few days later, after Jon had left for Spain and Angola, I found myself pondering why I had so willingly accepted his advice. I suddenly realized that part of the reason was rooted in the Mosquitia, in my most distinct memory of that voyage down the Patuca. It was from our second night on the raft, maybe three or four in the morning, during my turn as captain.

For two hours, a lone bat had been my companion, endlessly flitting within inches of my head, and from the surrounding blackness came the sounds of birds, the light rustle of wind in the trees. It was both frightening and thrilling to be on that river in the darkness, and I looked down to see Jon sleeping in the remnants of our little wind-shattered hut. His bare legs were stretched over the logs, and in the faint moonlight I saw the scrapes and dried blood around his right knee.

What would he have done without me? I thought. *He would die out here without me.*

For the first time I saw that my brother was just as lost and helpless and alone as I was on that black river, and that for as long as I stood at the helm and let him sleep, I was his only protector. And in a short time, whenever I imagined that my three-hour shift was up—because, of course, we didn't have a watch either—I would wake him and we would switch places, and then it would be my turn to lie down and sleep on this slow-sinking raft somewhere in the jungle, his turn to stand over me, to carry me down the river.

AUGUST 2000

WEIRD KARMA
by P. J. O'Rourke

I NEVER WENT TO India in the old days, when people were going there to get mystical, meditate their heads off, and achieve the perfect state of spirituality that we see embodied even now in George Harrison and Mia Farrow. I guess I wasn't evolved enough to follow my bliss. And, come to think of it, I don't have the kind of bliss you'd care to tailgate.

I never went to India at all until this past summer, and then, instead of meditating, I took a daft, relentless road trip organized by Land Rover as part of an around-the-world test of its new Discovery sport-utility vehicle. Four journalists, three Land Rover employees, and a photographer were put into two vehicles and sent seventeen hundred miles over six days from Islamabad, Pakistan, to Calcutta, through the most populous part of the subcontinent at the hottest time of the year.

The equivalent would be to drive U.S. Route 1 from the outlet shops of Freeport, Maine, to downtown Miami in August. Consider if the driver had never been to America before. What would he think, after being Blockbustered, Safewayed, Chevroned, Shelled, Dodged, Nissaned, Wal-Marted, Dress Barned, Gapped, Burger Kinged, Dairy Queened, and Taco Belled? Would he have a good impression of the United States? No. Would he have an accurate impression? That's another matter.

Yet even the most accurate impressions may be deeply confusing. You can come back from India in tune with the godhead, I suppose, or you can come back realizing you know nothing about India—or, possibly, anything else. I attained reverse enlightenment. I now don't understand the entire nature of existence. My conscious mind was overwhelmed by a sudden blinding flash of . . . oncoming truck radiator.

Nirvana, from the Sanskrit word meaning "blow out," is the extinction of desires, passion, illusion, and the empirical self. This happens a lot in India, especially on the highways. Sometimes it's the result of a blowout, literally. More often, it's the product of a head-on crash.

We did our driving mostly on the Grand Trunk Road, the "river of life" and "Backbone of all Hind" made famous in Kipling's *Kim*. The Grand Trunk begins near the Khyber Pass, ends just short of the Bay of Bengal, and dates back to at least the fourth century B.C. For the greater part of its sixteen-hundred-mile length, the Grand Trunk runs through the broad, flood-flat Ganges plain. The road is straight and level and would be almost two lanes wide if there were such things as lanes in India. The asphalt paving—where it isn't absent—isn't bad. As roads go in the developing world, this is a good one. But Indians have their own uses for the main thoroughfare spanning their nation. It's a place where friends and family can meet, where they can set up charpoy beds and have a nap and let the kids run around unsupervised. It's a roadside cafe with no side—or tables, or chairs—where the street food is smack-dab on the street. It's a rent-free function room for every local fête. And it's a piece of agricultural machinery. Even along the Grand Trunk's few stretches of tollbooth-cordoned "expressway," farmers dry grain on the macadam.

The road is a store, a warehouse, and a workshop. Outside Chandigarh, on the border of Punjab and Haryana states, a blacksmith had pitched his tent on a bridge. Under the tent flaps were several small children, the missus working the bellows, and the craftsman himself smoking a hookah and contemplating his anvil, which was placed fully in the right-of-way. The road is also convenient for bullock carts, donkey gigs, horse wagons, pack camels, and the occasional laden elephant—not convenient for taking them anywhere, just convenient. There they stand, along with sheep, goats, water buffalo, and the innumerable cows sent to graze on the Grand Trunk. I watched several cows gobbling cardboard boxes and chewing plastic bags. There may be reasons besides sanctity that the Indians don't eat them.

With all this going on, there's no room left for actual traffic on the Grand Trunk. But here it is anyway, in tinny, clamorous, haywired hordes—Mahindra jeeps made with machine tools used on World War II Willys, Ambassador sedans copied from '50s English models, motorcycles and scooters of equally antique design, obsolete Twinkie-shaped buses, and myriads of top-heavy, butt-spring, weaving, swaying, wooden-bodied Tata trucks, their mechanicals as primitive as butter churns.

India's scientists had, just before our arrival, detonated several nuclear devices, yet everywhere around us was Indian technology that seemed more akin to the blunderbuss than to the A-bomb. The Tatas, Ambassadors, Mahindras, and whatchamacallits were coming right at us, running all day with horns on and all night with lights off, as fast as their fart-firing, smut-burping engines would carry them. The first time I looked out the windshield at this melee, I thought, *India really is magical. How can they drive like this without killing people?*

They can't. Jeeps bust scooters, scooters plow into bicycles, bicycles cover the hoods of jeeps. Cars run into trees. Buses run into ditches, rolling over on their old-fashioned rounded tops until they're mashed into chapatis of carnage. And everyone runs into pedestrians. A speed bump is called a "sleeping policeman" in England. I don't know what it's called in India. "Dead person lying in the road" is a guess. There's some of both in every village, but they don't slow traffic much. The animals get clobbered, too, including the sacred cows, in accidents notable for the unswerving behavior of all participants. Late in our trip, in Bihar state, the car in front of us hit a cow—no change in speed or direction from the car, no change in posture or expression from the cow.

But it's the lurching, hurtling Tatas that put the pepper in the *masala* and make the curry of Indian driving scare you coming and going the way last night's dinner did. The trucks are almost as wide as they are long and somewhat higher than either. They barrel down the road taking their half out of the middle, brakeless, lampless, on treadless tires, moving dog fashion with the front wheels headed where the rear wheels aren't. Tatas fall off bridges, fall into culverts, fall over embankments, and sometimes just fall, flopping onto their sides without warning. But usually Tatas collide with one another, in every possible way. Two Tatas going in opposite directions ahead of us snagged rear wheels and pulled each other's axles off. And Tatas crash not just in twos but in threes and fours, leaving great, smoking piles of vaguely truck-shaped wreckage. Inspecting one of these catastrophes, I found the splintered bodywork decorated with a little metal plaque: LUCKY ENGINEERING.

In one day of travel, going about 265 miles from Varanasi to the border of West Bengal, I recorded twenty-five horrendous Tata wrecks. And I was scrupulous in my tallying. Fender benders didn't score; neither did old, abandoned wrecks or broken-down Tatas. Probable loss of life was needed to make the list. If you saw just one of these pileups on I-95, you'd pull in to the next rest stop—clutch foot shivering, hand palsied upon the shift knob—saying, "Next time, we fly." In India, you shout to your car-mates, "That's number nineteen! I'm winning the truck-wreck pool for today!"

As we drove from Lahore, Pakistan, to the Indian border, it was clear that we were approaching a land of mysteries. We went down the only connecting road between two large and important countries and, suddenly, there was nothing on the Grand Trunk. No one was going to or fro. They can't. "Pakistani and Indian nationals are only allowed to cross the border by train," says my guidebook. This utter lack of traffic has not prevented the establishment of fully staffed customs posts on both sides of the border.

Getting out of Pakistan was a normal Third World procedure. A customs official explained the entire system of Pakistani tariff regulation and passport control by rubbing his thumb against his forefinger.

"Fifty dollars," he said. I opened my wallet, foolishly revealing two $50 bills. "One hundred dollars," he said.

Things were very different on the Indian side. The rules concerning the entry of two Land Rovers and a trailerful of spare parts into the country occupy a book large enough to contain the collected works of Stephen King and the unabridged *Oxford English Dictionary.*

The Land Rovers had already passed the customs inspections of thirteen nations, including Bulgaria and Iran, without hindrance, delay, or more than moderate palm-greasing. The Indian officials, upon hearing this, clucked and wagged their heads in sympathy for the hundreds of brother customs agents from London to the deserts of Baluchistan who had lost an opportunity to look up thousands of items in a great big book. Everything had to come out of the cars and the trailer. Everything had to go through a metal detector, even though the detector didn't seem to be plugged in. And everything had to come back through an X-ray machine that the customs agents weren't watching because they were too busy looking up items in a great big book.

All this took four hours, during which the seven or eight agents on duty met each hint at bribery with the stare you'd get from an octogenarian Powerball winner if you suggested the twenty-five-year payout option. The fellow who was recording, in longhand, everything inside our passports did take two cigarettes, but he wouldn't accept a pack.

None of the cases, trunks, or bags—unloaded and reloaded in 105-degree heat—was examined, except for a wrench set. Perhaps there is

one wrench size that requires a special permit in India. Our tire pres-
sures had to be checked, however, in case the all-terrain radials were
packed with drugs. The Indian government tire gauge wasn't working,
so we offered ours. We were halfway through checking the tires when
we realized that nobody was accompanying us. I walked around behind
the customs building to take a leak and found drugs to spare. I was
pissing on $1,000 worth of wild marijuana plants.

By the time we left customs it was late afternoon. The staggering
traffic and whopping crowds of India materialized. We still had 250
miles to go that day to stay on schedule. A brisk pace was required.
Think of it as doing sixty through the supermarket parking lot and the
school playground.

This is the India ordinary travelers never see—because they're in
their right minds and don't drive down the Grand Trunk. And we didn't
see much of it ourselves. The scenery was too close to view, a blur of
cement-block shops and hovels in unbroken ranks inches from the
fenders. But my map showed only open country with occasional villages
meriting the smallest cartographic type size. There are a lot of people in
India, some 970 million. I don't know what they want with the atomic
bomb; they already have the population bomb, and it's working like a
treat. And yet India, with a population density of 745 people per square
mile, is not as crowded as the Netherlands, which packs 940 people into
that same space. But nobody comes back from Holland aghast at the
teeming mass of Dutch.

Indian crowding is not the natural result of baby-having but the
unnatural result of too many people tied to the land by tradition, debt
bondage, caste, and illiteracy. Business and industry are pushed into
the road by subsistence agriculture, which takes up a lot more room
than making a living with a laptop, a phone, and a fax.

Life is jammed tight in India to keep it out of the picnic-blanket-
sized rice field that's the sole means of support for a family of ten.
Every inch of land is put to purpose. At the bottom of a forty-foot-
deep abandoned well, which would be good for nothing but teenage
suicides in America, somebody was raising frogs. Public restrooms in
Calcutta employ the space-saving device of dispensing with walls and
roofs and placing the urinal stalls on the sidewalk. No resource goes to
waste, which sounds like a fine thing to advocate next Earth Day,
except in the real world of poverty, it means that the principal household fuel of India is cow flop. This is formed into a circular patty and

stuck on the side of the house, where it provides a solution to three problems: storage space, home décor, and how to cook dinner.

Therefore, what makes a drive across India overwhelming (and odoriferous) isn't population, it's poverty. Except it's even more complicated than that. It always is in India. The reason for those ranks of shops and houses along the Grand Trunk—and for the cars, trucks, and buses bashing into one another between them—is the money from an expanding economy that people now have to buy and build these things. And the reason for the great smoldering dung funk hanging over India is that people now have something to cook over those fires. The chaos of India is not just poverty's turmoil, it's also prosperity's stew.

When India gained its independence in 1947, the nation's political elite instituted an economic system that combined the perplexities of the capitalist old-boy network with the intricacies of socialism and then added the extra something we'd experienced going through customs. (Britain has a lot of paperwork and is a rich country, so if India has a lot of paperwork, it will be a rich country also.) The result was known as the "license-permit-quota raj." *The Economist* once said, "This has no equal in the world. In many ways it puts Soviet central planning to shame." Indian industries were trapped and isolated by the government. Like an aunt locked in the attic, they got strange. Hence the Tata trucks, the Ambassador sedans, and the motorcycles that Evel Knievel would be afraid to ride.

But by 1992 India had begun to surrender to free-market reforms. Imports were allowed, foreign investment was encouraged, and customs regulations were (amazing as this seems after having been through Indian customs) simplified. The Indian economy has been growing at about 7 percent a year ever since. As many as 200 million people now make up the Indian middle class—a number roughly equal to the total middle class of the United States. There are plenty of flat bellies in India but few of the distended kind that announce gross malnutrition. And the beggars, whom Western visitors have been taught to expect in legions, arrive only in platoons. A kid selling trinkets in Agra was irked to be mistaken for such. "I'm not a beggar," he said. "You want to buy, you get. Eighty rupees."

The quaint, old India is still there, however, just beyond the clutter of the Grand Trunk Road. In West Bengal we visited a beautiful farm village full of amusing thatch architecture and cute peasant hand-crafts. Here the handsome patina of tradition glowed upon lives that were quiet, calm, and as predictable as the lifelong poverty, semi-annual famine, and the dowry needed to marry off the ten-year-old daughter.

The villagers were friendly enough. But what if carloads of French tourists pulled into my driveway and took happy snaps while I scrubbed down the barbecue? I preferred the messy hopes on the Grand Trunk.

Maybe—on a brief trip, anyway—it's better to make no attempt to understand India. Just go to the beauty spots like the rest of the inter-national rubberneckers and stand agape, getting your tonsils sun-burned. We tried that, too. (Land Rover needed PR photos with something other than wrecked trucks in the background.)

We took a side journey into the Himalayan foothills, to Shimla, the colonial hill station that was the summer capital of British rule. It's built at a higher elevation than Katmandu. The road up was like the Grand Trunk except at the same angle as your basement stairs and in the shape of used gift-wrap ribbon on Christmas morning.

Shimla is a mulligatawny of concrete and roof tin, with the only charming parts being the leftovers of colonial oppression. Along the Mall there's a row of dusty shops that the British—seeing mountains all around them and not knowing what else to do—built in Alpine style. The parade ground has views to die for (or die of, if you lean against the flimsy railings). Atal Bihari Vajpayee, the prime minister of India, was headed to town. Preparation consisted of a minor govern-ment functionary's loudly testing the PA system:

HELLO HELLO HELLO HELLO HELLO HELLO HELLO
HELLO HELLO HELLO HELLO HELLO HELLO HELLO
HELLO HELLO HELLO ONE TWO THREE FOUR FIVE
SIX SEVEN EIGHT NINE TEN MICROPHONE TESTING
HELLO HELLO HELLO HELLO HELLO HELLO HELLO
HELLO HELLO HELLO HELLO HELLO HELLO HELLO

For an hour. This was the crowd warm-up. The speech must have been a dilly. Meanwhile, behind handsome batik curtains, tribal women in full native dress with nose jewelry the size of baby shoes were repairing the pavement.

Back on the Grand Trunk, we visited the Taj Mahal, an impressive pile built with public funds in Agra while a famine scourged the countryside. The Taj was commissioned by Shah Jahan to memorialize his favorite wife, who died in 1631 giving birth to their fourteenth child. If Jahan had really wanted to show his love, he could have cut back on the Viagra.

And we saw the holiest place of all, Varanasi, where millions of pilgrims descend the ghats into the Ganges, using its waters to purify themselves of sins, as well as to carry away the funeral pyres of friends and relatives. Everybody but me made a sunrise trip to see these sacred rites. I stayed in bed. No death before breakfast, please. Plus, there's the matter of barging in on other people's religious ceremonies: Yo, is that the Holy Eucharist? Cool! Can I taste?

And once you got started looking at religions in India, how would you know when to stop? There are Buddhists, Muslims, Sikhs, Jains, Parsis (Zoroastrians), Christians, Jews, and 800 million Hindus.

I am confused enough by the material surface of India without delving into its metaphysical foundation garments. Hinduism is said to have 330 million gods, which is fine by me if folks want that many. But such multiplication of divinity can't help but add to the profound obscurity of Indian culture, as do the seventeen officially recognized languages and the intricate caste system that somewhat resembles American ideas about social class, except you can't touch Wayne Huizenga because he founded Waste Management, Inc.

Everything in India seems to be a brainteaser. Just getting dressed is a riddle. This is how you put on a sari: Take a piece of cloth four feet wide and twenty-five feet long and tuck one corner into your underpants. Turn around clockwise once. Tuck the upper hem into your underpants. Make a pleat by holding the fabric between your thumb and little finger, spreading your hand, extending the fabric around your forefinger and bringing it back to your thumb. Do this eight times. Tuck the top of the pleats into your underpants. Turn around clockwise again, and throw everything that remains over your left shoulder. (And I still looked like hell.)

Each little detail of India is a conundrum. Painted above door frames you see the Sanskrit character for the sacred, meditative *om,* bracketed by a pair of swastikas. The swastika is really just a Hindu symbol for self-energization and the accomplishments of life (the

Nazis swiped it for the Aryan look). Nonetheless, the message over the doors seems to read *"Sieg heil inner peace sieg heil."*

Which isn't too far wrong at the moment. The current coalition government in India—the one that likes atomic bombs—is headed by the Bharatiya Janata Party. The BJP is avidly nationalistic and espouses Hindu fundamentalism—sort of like Pat Buchanan and Ralph Reed but with 330 million Jesuses. And the BJP believes in rigid observation of the caste system, so it's like Pat and Ralph have gotten together with the people who do the Philadelphia social register. Or worse, because the most influential support for the BJP comes from the Rashtriya Swayamsevak Sangh, the RSS, a secretive, hard-line Hindu brotherhood that was almost certainly responsible for the assassination of Mahatma Gandhi, and whose half million members wear matching khaki shorts to early-morning rallies and make funny, stiff-armed salutes. One reputed RSS leader, K. S. Sudarshan, has said, "We don't believe in individual rights because we don't think we are individuals."

Modern India is, in ways, an unattractive place. But things could be worse. And the BJP seems determined to make them so. The country has a population greater than those of North and South America combined. Its land area exceeds France, Germany, Great Britain, Iraq, Japan, Paraguay, and Ghana put together, and its citizens are that similar. They get along as well as everybody at the U.N. does. India is as complicated as the earth. Indeed, if a person were to announce his nationality as "earthling," there would be a one-in-six chance that he was Indian. To all this, the BJP responds with a slogan: "One nation, one people, one culture."

Just when you think you're not getting India, you start to get it even less. East of Varanasi, in Bihar state, we encountered a Communist rally. Hundreds of agitated-looking agitators waved red flags and brandished staves. We were a ripe target for the anger of the masses—eight capitalist prats in fancy Land Rovers with a trailerful of goodies protected by only a tarp. We were ignored. It seems the ideological fury of the Communist Party of India (Marxist-Leninist) is directed primarily at the Communist Party of India (Marxist).

The latter runs Calcutta. According to my guidebook, "they have somehow succeeded in balancing rhetoric and old-fashioned socialism with a prudent practicality. . . . Capitalism is allowed to survive, but made to support the political infrastructure."

Not that you'd know this by driving into Calcutta, where the infra-structure doesn't look like it could support another flea. Certainly the Howrah Bridge over the Hooghly River couldn't. It carries sixty thou-sand motor vehicles a day, and they were all there when we tried to get across at 5 P.M.

I spent the next four days trying to accomplish something in India. If you're going to be confounded by the country, you can't go as a tourist. Tourism is a pointless activity. Pointless activity is a highly developed craft in India. You could spend months touring the coun-try, busy doing fuck-all. Meanwhile, the Indian government and busi-ness bureaucracies are busy doing fuck-all of their own. You could accidentally come back thinking you'd caught the spirit of the place. If you intend to be completely baffled, you have to try to accomplish something. Any task will do. For instance, the Land Rover Discoverys and the trailer had to be put into a cargo container in Calcutta and shipped to Australia. This should take twenty minutes. Adjusting the clock to official Indian Daylight Wasting Time, that's four days.

First, the port was closed. Well, it wasn't really closed. I mean, it *is* sort of closed because the Port of Calcutta has silted in and is nearly useless. Only about three ships were there. This doesn't keep hun-dreds of stevedores, shipping clerks, and port officials from coming to work, of course. But there were city council elections that day, with attendant rioting. So the police had to suppress voters and weren't available for harassment at the port.

Then the port was closed because it was Sunday.

Then our shipping agents got into an argument about when to pick us up at the hotel the next day. Not that they disagreed with one another.

"We will go to get them at nine-thirty in the morning," one said.

"Oh, no, no, no, no," said another. "It must be nine-thirty in the morning."

"How can you talk like this?" said a third, stamping his foot. "The time for us to be there is nine-thirty in the morning."

We had about ten shipping agents. There's no such thing as hiring an individual in India. In a Bihar village it took the services of two shops, four shopkeepers, and a boy running for change for me to buy a pack of cigarettes.

While I waited for the port to open, I wandered the streets of Cal-cutta. The city is a byword for squalor, but parts of Washington, D.C., are dirtier (Congress, the White House), and Calcutta smells no worse than a college dorm.

The poverty is sad and extensive, but at least the families living on the streets are intact—talking to one another instead of to themselves. I did see some people who seemed really desperate, addled and unclean. But these were American hippies getting mystical at Calcutta's Dum Dum airport. I was standing in the ticket line behind an Indian businessman, who stared at the hippies and then gave me a stern look, as if to say "These are *your people*. Isn't there something you can *do*?"

Calcutta's pollution is more visible than it's fashionable for American pollution to be—smoke and trash instead of microwaves and PCBs. The food sold on its streets may be unidentifiable, but it's less likely than New York City hot dogs to contain a cow asshole. The crowding is extreme, but you get used to it. You get used to a lot of things in India— naked ascetics; a hundred sheep being herded through downtown traffic; costumed girls parading in single file linked by electric wires, one carrying a car battery and the rest with blue fluorescent tubes sticking out of their headdresses.

I was waiting to cross the busiest street in Calcutta when a four-story temple complex on wheels went by, complete with high priest, idols, acolytes, clouds of incense, blazing torches, and banging gongs. And what I noticed was that I hadn't noticed it. Imagine the pope (and quite a bit of St. Peter's) coming down Broadway at rush hour and you thinking *Should I wait for the walk signal?*

There's a certain pest factor in Calcutta, caused mostly by roving market-bearers who double as shopping touts. But it's not without its entertainment value. Bearer number A49 from New Market told me to avoid the other bearers because they would get me into their shops and cut my throat. Lesser merchants, squatting on the street, sell everything from new Lee jeans to brightly colored pebbles and pieces of broken mirrors. The poster wallah's selection included photographs of kittens tangled in balls of yarn and a rendering of the goddess Kali holding a severed human head by its hair.

In the midst of this was the Oberoi Grand Hotel, its guards stationed at the gate with sticks to use on touts and beggars. At the Oberoi everything was efficient, crisp, clean, pukka (except when the electricity went out). The Indians inside seemed as perplexed by the India outside as I was. I told Alex, the restaurant manager, about the muddle at the port. "Oh, this country," he said. "There are no two ways around it."

We had parked the Land Rovers and trailer in the hotel's court-yard. The shipping agents came by to inform us that everything in the vehicles had to be clean and packed exactly as described on the customs documents. We set about amending seventeen hundred miles' worth of dirt and equipment disorder. It was a hundred degrees in the courtyard. Removing the trailer tarp, we discovered an ax had come loose from its lashings and punctured a container of beef stew and a can of motor oil. The trailer bed was awash in oil and what Hindus euphemistically call "brown meat."

On Monday we went back to the port, where the customs inspectors ignored everything about our cleanliness and packing except the ax. "What is this?" asked the chief inspector.

"An ax," we said.

The officials conferred at length and decided it was so. Then there was a seven-hour delay because of an engine serial-number discrepancy. The customs inspectors were worried that we'd stolen one of the Discoverys from Land Rover. *"We're* from Land Rover," we said. "These are the only Discoverys in Asia, and they can't be stolen because they're both right here." The inspectors returned to their office cubicles to ponder this. We sat on the dock.

I asked one of our shipping agents why so many of the Tata drivers had decorated their front bumpers with one dangling shoe.

"Oh, for the heck of it," he said.

Finally, the Land Rovers were rolled into the cargo container. I stayed on in Calcutta for a few more days, in awe at a dundering flux of a place that seemed in total disarray but where I couldn't even get lost because everyone with a clean shirt spoke English. In the midst of the street stampede (not a figure of speech, considering the sacred cows), there are young hawkers with what look like shoeshine boxes. What's offered for sale, though, isn't a wingtip buff. The youths crouch in the hubbub, juggling the tiny wheels and springs of wrist-watches, setting timepieces running again. There is a whole street in Calcutta lined with tiny stalls where artisans with soldering irons rearrange the logic on the latest computer circuit boards.

Indian journalist and novelist Gita Mehta says her country produces 5 million university graduates a year. That's four times the number of bachelor degrees awarded annually in the United States. Yet nearly 48 percent of all Indians are illiterate, and almost two-thirds of Indian women are. It is the smartest country in the stupidest way.

You walk by a newsstand—a "newssquat," to be precise—and see the *Calcutta Telegraph,* the *Calcutta Statesman,* the *Asian Age,* the *Times of India,* and stacks of newspapers in Hindi, Bengali, and other languages. A *Telegraph* feature section contained a "KnowHow" pull-out on particle physics. A *Statesman* op-ed page had an article on energy efficiency: "The heat rate of the power plant, in layman's terms, refers to how much kilo calorie of heat is required to produce 1 kwh of power." You think you're in a nation of Einsteins. Then you look up from your newspaper and see a man walking along wearing a bucket upside down over his head.

DECEMBER 1998/JANUARY 1999

CREATURES OF THE DICTATOR

by Rick Bass

WE DRIVE NORTH FROM Bucharest, three Americans in a black Citroën crammed with backpacks and camping gear, in a country where we do not know the language, heading for Transylvania on the beautiful edge of spring and riding just behind the fall of Communism in Romania—so soon behind its wake that perhaps, underground, all the flesh has not even finished rotting off of Nicolae Ceaușescu's skull. Romania was the only Communist country to overthrow its regime with bloodshed, and I sense a bit of that capability—that irksome human affinity for applying steel to flesh, blade to bone—still lying latent in the centuries-old air outside. Only it isn't latent: It, the violence, has just been expressed, and the still-lingering echo of it, the *feel* of it, seems as recent as the upturned furrows of bare soil that are soaking in the spring fog and rains. Cherry orchards line the hilly roads, petals float everywhere like snowflakes. Old women walk to and from the spring fields carrying instruments of cutting and ripping and gouging: machetes and axes and sickles and scythes. They are beautiful old women, and I do not know where the men are. Ceaușescu and the *Securitate,* the secret police, killed tens of thousands of Romanian citizens, leaving an orphan population of forty thousand. Over a quarter of the populace was either in jail or had a close relative behind bars at one time or another.

We don't see other cars, just horse-drawn carts that we swerve to miss, coming around blind corners in the little towns. Steaming horse turds, true navigational hazards, lie in mounds up and down the rain-slicked roads. White chickens run clucking in all directions at our approach, and we can barely take our eyes from the orchards, they're so beautiful in the mist. Ray, the photographer, is crammed into the backseat, making moaning noises as we pass orchard after orchard, churchyards, cemeteries, all that pretty-picture stuff. Sue, our guide—she was a Fulbright scholar here last year, but, upon returning to her cabin outside Fairbanks, Alaska, has forgotten nearly all of the Romanian words she learned except the two biggies, "thank you" and "please"—looks worried. She's concerned that we don't have a phone number for the man we've come looking for, Peter Weber, the only grizzly bear biologist in Romania. We have only a street name in the city of Mediaş. And we're not sure Weber knows we're coming. A friend of a friend—Joachim—was supposed to alert Weber to our arrival and ask if he'd take us up into the mountains—into grizzly country—but the phones haven't worked reliably in Romania for years, not since the December 1989 revolution.

The reason we want to go looking for grizzlies is that Romania has so many of them: about twelve times more than Montana, and Romania is only two-thirds the size of that state. And most of Romania's bears are concentrated in the north, in the Carpathian Mountains and Transylvanian Alps. It's estimated that there are more than six thousand grizzlies up there, and if we can't find Weber, or if he's not willing to take us, then we're going to just park the car and start hiking until we see one.

The reason there are now so many grizzlies in Romania—back in the 1940s, for example, there were only about nine hundred—is that Ceauşescu liked to shoot them, sometimes killing eight or nine a day. He brought bears in from Poland, and had a very active captive-breeding and propagation program, raising scores of zoo bears and then turning them loose near his favorite "hunting" spot. He would bait the area with dead animals, horse meat and vegetables to keep the bears close, and each dusk when they came in to eat, he'd shoot the shit out of them. Then he would have his picture taken next to the carcass and, if the bear was large enough, apply to have his name entered in the record books. This practice ultimately led to a large overall population (though, like Communism, it was hell on individuals) because Ceauşescu forbade anyone else to kill a bear, even if it was raiding crops or livestock—although he'd allow wealthy foreigners to pay thousands of dollars for the privilege.

I've always believed that how you treat animals, and how you treat the land, is how you'll treat people. I've noticed that either you have lots of respect, have it in spades, or you generally don't have any at all.

Ceauşescu, obviously, did not have it; he just kept shooting. Blood just kept pouring into the soil. New bears kept springing up out of that soil. Of course, he's gone now—the bears outlasted him. It's new blood that's being turned over now, the old blood that's soaked into that soil being furrowed and spaded and chopped and graded, and there's a new government, new hope and it's springtime. Maybe this time it will all be different.

As we drive north toward the mountains, driving through the sinking, misty dusk, the cherry orchards grow more luminous until they seem to blaze in the gloom. The old women are still coming in from the fields, talking to one another, axes and sickles slung over their broad shoulders, and they're all dressed in red and black, vampire colors, the colors of blood and death, although we are not yet into vampire country.

It's so lonely to be in a foreign country, lost at night, not knowing the language, directions or anything; it's as if you cease to exist. All I want to do is get into Transylvania—the north-central part of Romania, just below the Hungarian and Ukrainian borders—where the language of the woods and the bears, I feel sure, is universal.

We reach Sibiu after midnight and check into the Hotel Bulevard, in the center of that big city. It looms gray and prisonlike on the edge of a hill, but inside it is funky and musty in an elegant sort of way: huge high ceilings, chandeliers, worn red carpets, tarnished-brass art deco fixtures.

We drift into the cavernous dining room/ballroom, ravenous, bleary-eyed and overstimulated. The tables are set with immaculate white linens; it's as if we're two hours early for a wedding reception. Sue calls her friend Joachim to meet us there and fill us in on the agenda, if there is any. Over at the far end of the dining room—where, of course, there are no other diners—stands a huddle of cooks, waiters and waitresses, half hiding behind the grand piano. They're watching us uneasily, and they're definitely refusing to wait on us.

We sit for five minutes until Ray goes over and politely harangues the workforce. They grumble, but disperse to their stations. We have two hot American dollars burning holes in our pockets—dinner is about seventy-five cents each, and a bottle of wine is fifty cents—and we can order pork, or pork.

It's good pork, though; it's some of the best I've ever eaten. Romanian pigs range free through the countryside, like deer, and the pork loin, salted and peppered and cooked with a little butter, tastes like the finest, leanest venison. I could eat five pounds of it. The wine is delicious.

The grand clock on the high ceiling above us strikes 1 A.M. Joachim comes in through the big, glass double doors. He is a small, dapper, precise man with short dark hair and a trimmed beard—he looks a little Faustian. He doesn't mince words.

"They have killed a horse for you," he says when he sits down. He studies the menu. "It was not a very good horse. I told them not to buy one for over two hundred fifty U.S. dollars. It made the farmer very happy; it was an old horse. I'll have the pork."

It turns out Weber knows we're coming. But Joachim says he told Weber we'd be at his house bright and early in the morning, and that Weber would be able to spend three to four days with us in the mountains. That's why they killed the horse—to bring all the bears in.

Still, no one really knows where Weber lives. Never mind that we're supposed to be on his doorstep—wherever that is—in a few hours, in a city fifty kilometers away. Joachim bids us good night, slips mysteriously back out those double doors, disappears into the night, and we never see him again.

The day is not flattering to Sibiu. There are too many people, too many buildings, too much carbon in the air and too many lingering diesel clouds. Driving behind the large transport trucks, we breathe in so much diesel exhaust that we have to cover our mouths with napkins; and when we pull the napkins away, there are black circles outlined on them, lithographs of what's been strained out. God knows what went in.

It calls for whiskey—even if it's only 9 A.M. We've got a lot of it, from the airport customs shop in Frankfurt. Sue was going to give it to friends in Sibiu, but there isn't time for any of that. In the backseat, she starts mixing us drinks. We stop at a market and buy a two-liter bottle of some green glowing liquid, some Cactus Cooler–, Gatorade-looking fluid, and pour that into the mix. It's vile, like barium, but the scenery demands it. We pass through the factory town of Copşa Mică, where crude coal is processed alongside the river. Crumbling smokestacks spew plumes of ebony into the sky. The streets, the buildings, the dead trees are all cloaked in black, as are the people and the animals—the dogs, the cats—even the children. People are cruising down the sidewalks in grimy wooden wheelchairs—people without arms and legs. It's too much. I pass on the driving duties to Ray so that I can really slug down the medicine. I am crying. Just over the border, to the west, the Serbs and the Croats are killing each other, cutting one another into pieces, while up in the mountains, perhaps, the bears hide deeper in the forest and watch.

In Weber's bustling town of Mediaş, we drive around aimlessly for a while, then park and get out to hunt for him on foot. We reel up and down the busy streets—it's Saturday, market day—in the bright sunlight, inquiring of everyone we meet how to find Weber. I, for one, am staggering drunk. We've written down Weber's name and address on a scrap of paper and are showing it to people, who keep pointing us in different directions, convoluted hand-chopping sequences of lefts and rights, so the effect, I think, is that we must gradually, in a spiraling fashion, be getting closer to Weber, but damn, are we lost. I'm not even sure where the car is. We reel down cobblestone alleyways, calling for Weber to come out and show himself.

It is gypsies who save us. They are coming up the steps of a dungeonlike place, a young boy and two women dressed in bright clothes and jewelry, and our paths intersect.

They can't understand a word we're saying, but their eyes show that they're concerned. I've been warned to watch out for the gypsies, and I remember that in the past some of them have not been particularly kind to bears. One gypsy tradition, I've read, involves training a bear to dance whenever music is played by forcing him out onto a red-hot sheet of metal. After a few such training sessions, the bear hops and moans and dances anytime it hears music, remembering the incredible pain. The gypsies then take such a dancing bear from town to town, and while the village folk gather in a circle applauding the bear, the gypsies pick their pockets.

But these gypsies look nice; they peer at our scrap of paper with genuine concern. They take us by the arm and lead us down the busy street, and then down an alleyway. They point to a big stockade gate, the kind that could protect a fortress during wartime. It has Weber's name on it, in tiny print, and his street number! The gypsies back away, pleased with our exuberance.

We pound on the door to the compound. It is a brilliant, blue-sky day, and the alley is swarming with people and bicycles. A wild, stocky, bearded, redheaded, *troll*-looking man throws open the gate and peers at us. He is dressed in hiking shorts with suspenders, and is wearing heavy boots with knee-high stockings held up by garters. He has on a long-sleeved wool shirt and one of those funny little Robin

Hood caps with a feather stuck in it. He looks like he can yodel. It is
Weber!

"We must go now, if we are to go," he says. I'd been told he didn't
speak English, but he gets his message across fine: We're late and
we're drunk.

Weber hurries us toward his garage, in which the world's smallest
car is hidden—a small, brown job like the ones you see the clowns
and poodles spilling out of in the circus. He rolls his eyes like a Chinese dragon when he sees all the gear we've brought. "We can take
nothing," he says. "Sleeping bags okay. One pair of underwear. A
toothbrush. Nothing else."

"My camera gear!" Ray cries, and Weber scowls, and says finally,
"Okay."

Somehow we jam ourselves into the little shitbox. We rocket out of
Weber's driveway like messengers in the king's employ. Anicka, Weber's
beautiful girlfriend, slams the double gate shut behind us, throws the
crossbar deadbolt in place. We're off for Transylvania: for the dark
woods, the high mountains, the rushing rivers, the misty valleys.

The little car smashes and shakes over the potholed roads. Weber
grins a mad grin and drives faster, as if to punish us for being late and
for not knowing the correct foreign languages; in this case, German
and Romanian. Along the way he points out places where he's had
wrecks as he swerves around hay wagons and blares his shrill little
horn at bike riders. We're into the country now. "I was watching wolf
up there," Weber says, pointing to the foothills—I want to look, but
cannot turn my eyes away from an oncoming bicycle as Weber occu-
pies the center of the turtlebacked, one-lane, rain-slicked road—"and
pow!! I go off the road, roll car many times, break very many bones. A
very heavy thing." He is still watching the foothills as the cyclist shouts
and at the last second swerves his bike off the road and down the deep
roadside drainage ditch.

American politeness precludes us from asking him to slow down.

He cuts a swath through village after village, and finally after we start
to get up into some high valleys (which he pronounces as "wallys"), he
begins to relax and grow more affable. He drops his speed to under 140
kilometers per hour. I've been trying feebly to converse with Weber,
to compare notes about bears, science—but he won't have any of it.
Everything I say, it seems, is incorrect or bad science. It's like he's on

some superstrict kick to adhere *ferociously* to the scientific method. He's denying utterly, it seems, the individuality—the intelligence, spirit and soul—of grizzlies, and instead keeps talking about them as if they are bacteria in a petri dish. "If a bear lives or if it dies—to me, it makes no matter," he says. "As a scientist, I am interested only in"—he pauses, groping for the English—"social interactions within population."

It's classic Communism, I think smugly—and then I remember that Romania has more than six thousand grizzlies, while the entire grand old lower forty-eight has far less than a thousand. Still, it becomes my goal to try to get Weber to admit that, yes, he loves the bear.

I look out at the marvelous woods, the mixed conifer and oak-beech, hornbeam forests—the latter producing rich mast crops, so important to bears during the fall predenning period—and prepare not to see a bear. I know how secretive they are. In my valley in Montana, the population is down to about ten individuals. In seven years of hiking almost every day, I've seen two. Dozens, hundreds of black bear—but only two grizzlies.

Their presence must be more visible in Romania, however. Evidently the frequency with which they come down into villages to steal pigs or chickens or sheep is high. I had read a recent account of a farmer who fought off a bear with a pitchfork. (For the most part, they don't have guns in the countryside, but most farms have four or so formidable dogs to scare off bears.) And Weber tells me about the case a few years ago of a schoolteacher who tried to take a shortcut through the woods. He says that he can take us to visit with "peoples who have good bear stories."

The people up in this part of Transylvania—the Harghita Mountains within the complex of the Carpathians—are direct descendants of the Magyars, wild mountain Hungarian stock who still view this area as Hungary, not Romania. All they speak—all they *acknowledge*—is Hungarian. But that's okay, Weber knows that language, too.

Everywhere I went in Romania, people would fill me in on which ethnic groups to avoid: how the mountain people were different from the village people, were different from the coastal (Black Sea) inhabitants, were different from the flatlanders . . . how the gypsies were horrible people, and how, above all, the terrible, blood-lusting Magyars were the worst. All this ethnic tension in a country two-thirds the size of Montana.

Transylvanians, especially, have a history of hiding out in the dark forests, battling back invasions by the Daco-Roman/Vlachs, the Ottoman Turks, the Russian steppe rabble-rousers and just about anyone else who carried a sword. (It was Vlad Ţepeş—also known as Vlad the Impaler—who saved the region from the Turks in the 1400s, spearing his enemies' heads on iron spikes and providing the legendary basis for Count Dracula.) Then in 1952 came the Communist Gheorghiu-Dej, practicing a nationalistic isolationism; and lastly, in 1965, the dictator Ceauşescu, the son of an abusive father, and the blood continued to flow.

Everywhere we went, there seemed to be a kind of frightened, hesitant, half-passive, half-aggressive sense of waiting for the other shoe to drop; waiting for the vaporous combustion of latent hate to flash into being again. You would think that having just pulled together to overthrow Communism there would be a glowing national harmony, but that kind of community feeling seems to exist only within the borders of individual villages. On the face of it, Romania is now a democracy, but political scientists question how much power the government will ultimately return to the people. The new leader, Ion Iliescu, is considered by many to be nothing more than a "Communist retread" who, to preserve his own power, may have little interest in pulling the country out of its blood cycle.

What I think is that there are too many people over there, more than what is biologically sane for the social dynamics and evolution of our species, and that individuals within the human populations do not have enough space, and cliques are a defensive response. Small bands gather closer and closer together because there is nowhere else to go.

Weber, pointedly apolitical, sees this same thing happening to the high bear populations. He says that can be fixed by shooting some of them.

He is grim-faced and unapologetic. Now an official at the Municipal Museum in Mediaş, Weber used to be Ceauşescu's biologist; he was there, I guess, while the dictator squeezed off the rounds. And his government still sells permits to shoot the bears—up to four hundred a year—charging wealthy Germans and other foreigners up to $20,000 a kill.

This money, Weber explains, is used to help the forest.

But his explanation sounds feeble, and I think he knows it.

o   o   o

We'll be staying in a log cabin along a creek, high in the little valley of Varság. Weber insists that I am mispronouncing it.

"*Voar-shawwgg,*" he says, wagging his thick finger.

"*Voar-shawwgg,*" I say, and he grimaces, shaking his head. Weber is flirting with Sue—telling us, in broken English, about the superiority of males over "ze femuls." And he's talking about feces, too—calling them "fay-cees." Talking about ze wally of Voar-shawwgg.

Good biologists know that people are the largest factor in any animal's life, and, like a good biologist, Weber knows almost everyone in the little village (population twelve hundred) of Varság. They don't hesitate to tell him what the bears are up to, how many pigs they've taken in the last week.

We stop at an ancient stone farmhouse with a brook trickling past it. There's a water wheel outside the kitchen window. The barn is made of hand-hewn spruce logs. There's a wooden gate around the farmhouse. It's neat as a pin. All the wood is split and stacked perfectly, and even the barnyard animals—the chickens, the sheep and the dogs—appear to have a preciseness to them. A small old man who looks like he could be running a dry cleaners in New York comes out and hails Weber with affection.

The farmer's name is Ferencz Szabó, and he has plenty of bear stories. One grizzly in particular likes to play a game with Szabó's stock: The bear hides up in the woods, watches and waits until he and his dogs head into the fields with the sheep each morning. As soon as they're a few hundred yards from the cabin, the bear will run down the hill, jump the fence, grab a young pig and then run back into the woods with it.

Such stories are common in Varság—there is no one who does not have a bear story—but there doesn't seem to be any real loathing on the part of the villagers when they talk about them. When I ask Szabó through Weber how he feels about there being so many bears in the woods, his face grows thoughtful. He says something serious to Weber. Szabó compares it—the bears' occasional depredations—to the nature of humans. "Sometimes we go into the bear's woods to take his berries," he says. "It is only fair that sometimes he comes and takes a sheep or a pig. As long as we do not take too many berries, and he does not take too many sheep, it is fair."

We ask Szabó about Ceauşescu, what it was like in the days when he came here to kill things. I listen closely as Weber translates, and notice that he does not use Ceauşescu's name. (Romanians generally refer to him only as "the dictator," or, sarcastically, "our leader," and I don't know whether this was a subtle, psychological way of disempowering his violent memory or an aftereffect of the days when it was dangerous even to say his name, when there were spies everywhere.)

Szabó points to the table where we're sitting. "He came through here in his limousine once," Weber translates. "He came in with his bodyguards and sat right there and asked if Szabó had seen any animals.

"Szabó told him there had been a stag feeding on his neighbor's field. Ceauşescu finished his drink, got up from the table and left with his bodyguards, got back in his limousine and drove off.

"About three minutes later, Szabó heard a gun—*piff! poof!*—go off three times." Weber shrugs.

Szabó says something. Weber stares back at him for a second but Szabó's old face looks firm.

"He says," Weber interprets for us, "that Ceauşescu was a small man with a big gun."

On our way out the gate, Szabó's dogs come trotting over to investigate. They're friendly but tough-looking, with nails driven through their leader collars, points sticking out to create spiked collars.

"For their fights with the wolves," Weber explains. "Sometimes the wolves come out of the woods and try to kill the dogs and eat the sheep."

The next morning we cook a fine Romanian meal on the woodstove. The cabin fills with smoke. More wild pork loin, bacon, fried eggs, potatoes, pancakes and thick Turkish coffee. Weber makes hash browns. It reminds me of Montana.

Except that I'm a little puzzled by the way Weber allows all the odors to get in his clothes—especially the bacon. How are we going to sneak up on wild grizzlies when we smell so strongly? They can smell an elk carcass at a distance of at least seven miles; how are we going to get Ray and his cameras, for example, within a hundred yards?

Instead of bears, what we sneak up on that day is a wonderful old woman called Giza-nèni, and her tiny, wiry husband, Feri-bácsi. They're on the hillside raking and burning leaves from their sloping field. They rake them with a wooden tool they made themselves, load them into a huge straw basket they wove themselves and carry them down to one of the smoldering leaf fires, smiling all the while.

Giza-nèni and Feri-bácsi, the terrible old blood-sucking Magyars, put down their rakes and baskets, seize us by the arms and escort us down the hill into their yard. We wade through chickens and dogs, past an old horse, and they all but force us into their tiny home. We feel hugely guilty, arriving at midday like this—it's the spring planting season, and here we are, coming in unannounced, robbing them of their hand-to-mouth work time—but Giza-nèni is glowing like an angel, and Weber makes signals with his eyes and face that we are *not* to hurt her feelings, that we are to abide by her wishes *precisely*.

Giza-nèni stands up on a stool—she's well under five feet tall—and pulls down her fancy shot glasses and a dusty, two-gallon glass jug of what appears to be gasoline. Its contents glow orange as she carries the jug with reverence over to our table, passing through shafts of sunlight and wood smoke. Weber, standing in the open doorway, grins like a wolf. So does Feri-bácsi, and I know what is expected of us.

Giza-nèni pours each of us a glass and motions to us to down it. *"Pálinka,"* she says, and points out the one tiny, dusty window toward the peach blossoms floating on the hill below. In the golden sunlight, I can see the fumes rising from the glass, as when you're filling your car at the gas station. *"Savee-vi-shen,"* Giza-nèni says, or something like that—she clasps both hands to her bosom and smiles at us—"From the *heart*," Weber translates—and it is time to face the music.

It is hot and vile and it hurts. It makes us cry and shiver and wretch and jump up and down in our seats. Weber and Feri-bácsi are laughing. Giza-nèni watches us with a concerned look, as if it would crush her heart were we to say we didn't like it.

"Good," I try to say, but the word doesn't come out; the lining of my esophagus in gone.

But Giza-nèni knows what I'm trying to say. She smiles and pours us all another round, even though we have not gotten down more than perhaps an eyedropperful. Feri-bácsi laughs, shakes his head, gets up and goes out to water the animals. Finally, Weber saves us, grabbing us by the collars and pulling us from the *pálinka* table, which delights Giza-nèni to no end. She is blowing kisses and calling out *savee-vi-shen* as Weber hauls us away.

Farther back in the mountains, even among the smaller villages, there is an autumn sport in which the men, after a bit of *pálinka*, roll up their trousers and wade barefoot into the icy stream, looking for trout. They sneak up on the trout, which they see resting behind a boulder, slip their hands slowly under the trout's great white belly and begin to tickle it, almost as lightly as the water current itself, until the fish becomes strangely paralyzed—but only for a moment or two—and the fishermen are able to snatch the great fish up, clutch it to their chests with both arms and stumble back to shore to the cheers of the villagers, the winner being the one with the largest fish.

And not far from here, up in the high Alps, there is a monastery where monks raise Lipizzaner stallions. I picture the monks in their robes the color of dried blood, barefooted or perhaps in sandals, riding the great animals in lunges through the fresh powder to wear them down, to gentle them. Then monks sitting around sipping tea, each in his room alone, talking to *Cristos*, while down in the cities below, in the flatlands, Ceauşescu and the *Securitate* were laying the corpses out in long rows to be photographed, cutting the fetuses out of pregnant women.

We fall asleep to the sound of wolves howling at the full moon.

When morning arrives, Sue and Ray go through the village on foot, while Weber takes me to talk to people who've had bear experiences. The people are friendlier than any I've ever seen. We stroll down a dirt lane and pass a cheerful old woman who's casting seeds into her rich, black, fresh-turned furrows. She's dressed in blue and green—many houses here have these colors throughout—and she puts down her metal bucket of seed, and comes running across the field, waving to us to stop walking. It turns out she wants me to be her guest, to stay in her home for however long I'm in Varság and she wants me and Weber to come in for a meal—is it lunchtime?—*right now.*

We tell her no, but thank you very much (*"Ko-sho-nem"*), and leave her standing there in the field looking mournful.

The bear stories are relatively tame, more tales of pig-thieving, a lamb every now and then. But nothing like you'd expect—not with six thousand of them roaming the mountains.

That night, as we eat the stew Weber has prepared, I try to steer the conversation back to bears. But Weber has still got that wall up. "Why do you study the bear, then?" I ask. "Surely there have been moments when you've felt the bear's magic, a hugeness of spirit, a kind of grace?"

Weber is as stiff as a board. He chooses his words carefully, as if someone is listening just outside the door. "What I like about this job," he says slowly, "is that it allows me opportunity to be out-of-doors. To go into the woods.

"I am only bear biologist in Romania," he says. "Only one." He looks away. "It is a good job."

And so I back off. It's so easy to be an eco-warrior in the States. But I wish to hell we had six thousand grizzlies, big trout to tickle and monks on stallions in the high snowy mountains.

"This is good stew," I tell Weber, ladling out seconds. "What is it?"

"Oh," Weber says, smiling. "I thought you recognized the taste. You are eating grizzly bear."

All three of us stop eating and freeze, and Weber laughs.

The next day we stroll through the woods—Weber shows us a couple of bear dens—and wander through the village. Then, later in the afternoon, Weber takes us to see the bears.

It's a bigger deal than I'd realized; I'm still thinking in American terms, where the wildlife does not belong to anyone but the forest itself. Here, however, the grizzlies are like ten- and twenty-thousand-dollar bills roaming the forest.

We meet the local game warden and his wife, who is wearing an ermine stole and jewelry. The game warden is one of the darkest, most frightening people I've ever seen. He is not intimidating physically—he looks like the actor Burt Young, with a five-o'clock shadow—but he appears to have a heartlessness to him that strikes me as dangerous.

We ride in a big limousine into the woods. Neither the warden nor his wife will look at us. I feel badly for Weber, who's in the middle. The warden and Weber are chatting, but it is a serious chat—I get the sense that Weber is defending us. The wife, the ice queen, stares out the window at the passing countryside, which is still barren and bleak higher in the forest, still only on the edge of spring. I get the feeling that it was better for her in the old days, when there was *real* power, power fueled by the fear of others, fear of the government, and that she is angry now, that her lot in life—the warden's wife!—has been reduced such that she is now having to ride in the backseat with three American journalists.

We ride quietly down red-clay roads, across meadows, past giant beech trees and into the dark forest. The limousine crosses a wooden footbridge—a beautiful brook rushes beneath us—and then we park and get out at the base of a little knoll. Another car is already parked there. The dusk is gathering fast, I want to linger, to walk by that brook, but Weber hurries us up the steep flight of steps to the little cottage at the top of the knoll.

As we climb the steps, Weber explains that this was Ceauşescu's main hunting cabin. "He was a small man, and not in good shape," Weber whispers. "He had trouble climbing these steps. They had to build this handrail for him."

It's chilling, even macabre, to be walking in his footsteps. Fog begins to rise from the Transylvanian woods, from the dark firs. Steam rises from the creek. No one would ever find us back here.

We step inside the little two-room hunting cabin. The ceiling is low. It's cold at first, but the warden's wife—who is now suddenly excited—busies herself lighting a fire in the woodstove, and sweeping the carpet with a straw broom. She seems at least ten, fifteen years younger. Two young Czech women have also come to see the bears. They're distant relatives of the warden's wife.

We move into the front room, which has two beds in it, and little windows that you slide open to shoot through. There's a clearing at the top of the knoll where bears often appear. There are feeding troughs and a big, heavy apparatus, a cage with iron bars. "Is that for the really bad shots?" I ask. "Do they lock a bear in there for the people to shoot at, to keep the bear from running away?" I ask, and Weber looks embarrassed for both of us.

"They put the *bait* in there," he explains. "It keeps them from pulling the bait off into the woods."

Where is the horse? Our horse?

It didn't exactly work out, Weber says, and I'm not sure what he means by that, but I'm greatly relieved and I tell him so.

I tell him something else, too: "It feels *bad* being here." My heart is splitting, and I'm whispering to him not like a guest or a fellow scientist, but as a fellow lover of the woods: For I'm convinced he is one, too, even if he can't show it.

Weber looks uncomfortable, edges away from me, squints out of the window. I turn and see that the game warden is sitting on one of the beds in the far corner, hidden in the shadows, studying me.

The two young women are giggling; they've brought video cameras. They're hogging the seats in front of the little windows. I feel an incredibly black depression, and I do not try to fight it. I walk back into the rear half of Ceauşescu's little sin parlor, which houses a big double bed decorated with cheap, red-tassel fringe like a backwoods whorehouse, and examine the gun cabinet and the pantry with all the expensive liquors and canned goods. Anchovies, for Chrissakes, in bear country.

The sin parlor is getting hot from all the people; I feel like I'm roasting in hell. I step onto the back porch, into the cold spring evening air, and look at the tops of the dark forest beyond. *This is no way to kill bears*, I think. I'm not even as upset about the fact that the bears are being shot, for once, as I am about the method, the incredible steps that have been taken to avoid an engagement with nature. We could be anywhere, I think—it doesn't have to be in Romania, at the edge of the old, crumbling Communist empire. We could be at a game farm in California, Texas or Illinois, in a hunting blind—a shooting gallery—set up for some rich industrialist to come and do his thing. I've seen plenty of it: the alligator "hunts" by jet boat, where the $3,000 fee includes a pair of boots made from your very own gator. The pathetic need to kill, to erase the large, grand and the magnificent—to kill and bury it. How terrifying, this example of how the far ends of Communism and Capitalism meet in a circle.

In a while, the warden's wife pours shots of vodka into little jiggers and carries them around on a silver serving tray. Everyone accepts a drink with great bonhomie, but I refuse mine. This troubles her, but it's the only way I have of making sure they all know exactly what I think, that I can no more accept her liquor than I could shoot one of those tragic bears.

Then people jump up from the beds as if electrified, bumping their heads on the low ceiling, and hissing and whispering as four bears come gliding in from out of the dusk.

They are huge, and they are so close. Their claws, their muscles, their giant heads—all of them. They're right in front of us; you could almost kill one with a javelin. Everyone's scrambling around to see— the two Czech women elbowing to the front, and cackling like hens—"Sssh!" Weber cautions, and the game warden and his wife stand back, like proprietors, and watch us watch the bears.

Their movements are identical to those of Montana's grizzlies, ten thousand miles away—the tiniest nuances, the pauses and head swings, the way they *move*. Watching them there on the knoll, I know that they all come from the same spirit, deep within the core of the earth: molten wildness, muscled beauty.

I am almost unable to look at the bears—it feels pornographic. I concentrate on watching Weber. Between 1979 and 1981, he spent over three thousand hours watching bears from this blind, hidden in the sin parlor, but still he leans forward quickly, lips moving, mumbling to himself, as if this is the first bear he has ever seen.

He loves the grizzlies.

I peek under one of the Czech women's underarms and see that a huge bear, with a head the size of a tractor tire, is standing over the feed, swinging his head left and right, looking and sniffing for the whereabouts of other bears and for the possibility of a trap.

"We have to keep feeding them or they will stop coming," Weber says.

"Is that a male?" I ask.

Weber turns and looks at me crossly. "Why do you ask that?"

"Because of his coloring," I say, "and the size of his head. Back home, the darker grizzlies are males, more often than not, and their heads are sometimes larger."

"Yes," says Weber. "It is a male."

More bears come out of the gloom: a forest of bears, a village of bears. Weber's excited, talking fast, pointing out subtle body movements that indicate where each bear lies in the social hierarchy.

"We call that one Money," he says, pointing to the largest one, weighing, I'd guess, close to six hundred pounds.

"How much would it cost to shoot that one?" Ray asks.

"About twenty thousand dollars," says Weber, watching the animal through binoculars. "He would be a trophy."

Ceauşescu and his wife, Elena, are dead. Yet his name is still in all the record books of Asia and Europe, not just for killing the biggest and most bears, but also wild boars, stags—anything.

And people.

They say that when they executed him, on Christmas Day in 1989, more than three hundred soldiers volunteered to be on the firing squad, that they began shooting as soon as they saw him.

They say . . .

I feel as if I have sinned against my nature by even drawing this close to such a spectacle. I feel as if I am as guilty as Ceauşescu himself, or any of the old party bosses—being in the sin parlor and spying on those bears, those bears who are waiting to be shot. I feel like it's worse, for me, because I love the bears and the woods, wildness and freedom, and Ceauşescu probably hated these things. I cannot get away from there quickly enough.

That night, by lantern light, and downing that wine, Weber and I go over it again. *Say it, Peter: You love the bears. What they're doing up there on that knoll is wrong.*

He won't admit it. But—after about the fifth or sixth glass of wine, after Ray and Sue have gone to bed—he suddenly stops defending the operation and the money it brings in to a bankrupt government and admits that he has an idea, something he's been thinking over.

It turns out Weber doesn't like the foreigners coming in and shooting "his" bears like that *(piff! poof!)* after all. Weber would like to see some kind of rule in place where a person could still pay $20,000 to kill a bear, but would have to spend a week or two in the woods first, learning a little bit about the bears and the forest. Maybe even doing a little physical labor that would somehow benefit the bear. Erosion protection, or something like that.

Weber sighs. It would never work, he says—people who have and spend that kind of money don't generally like to do physical labor— and besides, he, Weber, is just one man.

It's Weber's goal to someday come to the United States and learn how to do telemetry tracking of animals—how to use radio collars to study movements of individual bears. His government won't buy even one collar and radio. I don't have the heart to tell him that in the States, biologists are moving away from a reliance on radio collars, since the individual's movements may not be entirely natural (while being chased by trackers, for instance). I don't tell him that biologists in the United States are trying to rely more on habitat protection for the overall population rather than just hounding a few individuals.

His goal is to go to Alaska and study those grizzlies and learn about radio tracking, he says, and for me, the grand, spoiled inquisitor, I guess that's enough. It says the same thing. *I love the bears.* It just says it in a different kind of woods code, a different language.

I have hundreds of memories from Varság, the valley of bears, the friendliest valley I've ever visited: from the dark, spooky mountains of Transylvania that seem like a second home, a place of comfort.

A hawk's wing in the carpenter's shop, used for brushing away wood shavings. Giza-nèni's girlish kicks and her bright dress. The high, short beds in the cabins, high off the ground, because at night as the cabin cooled, that's where cold air settles, close to the floor.

Woodcutters of all ages: boys, men and old men, standing on the side of the road with axes, tying up ricks of firewood to sell for a few fractions of a cent. Strong arms and backs from a lifetime of endless chopping at the edge of the dark forest, the American myth—that no forest, no wilderness, is endless—not yet revealed to them.

Walking through the ancient hillside cemetery in the rain, looking for the grave of the schoolteacher, the one who got it from the bear, when there were so many thousands who got it from the hands of their fellow man, the hands of Ceauşescu.

Watching the bears feed at that trough outside Ceauşescu's sin parlor, so far back in the woods, where so many bears had been shot, and wondering what the culture of bears had to say about the history of such a violent place; wondering if they could smell all the blood that must have leached through the soil there, wondering if the bears, like any intelligent being, could feel the still-lingering echoes of terror bouncing around on that strange knoll. Wondering if they know that Ceauşescu's gone. Wondering if the Romanians know it, *really* know it. I think that they do.

Weber showed me the stump of an apple tree in Feri-bácsi's yard. He explained to me that the bears loved the apples from this tree more than any other, and kept coming into his yard to get them, and kept making trouble. This went on for a few years, and so finally Feri-bácsi cut down the apple tree and made a beautiful picture frame out of the wood. The bears moved someplace else. And I see then what I have always suspected: It doesn't take any real patriotism or courage to kill a bear. It takes patriotism—love of the homeland—to let them live. To think of ways that will allow them to live. And to just plain *think*, rather than merely react, like sheep, like mindless masses with no concept of free thought.

Varság showed this to me.

Thousands of countrymen butchered over a quarter of a century, and I get all hot and bothered about a few bears?

But that's exactly where it all began—the domination and oppression of the voiceless, of the supposedly "lesser" beings: the bears and the wolves, the forests and the rivers, the gypsies and "ze femuls." It is out there in the woods, I think, where it all went wrong first, and I believe that is one of the ways and one of the places where we must learn, all over again, how to do it right: how to remember the quaint ancient notions of tolerance, freedom and respect.

We say our good-byes to Weber, thank him again and again for his hospitality. We leave Transylvania, home of wolves, bears and vampires, and return to America the bloody continent, where there are very few bears, very few wild things whatsoever, except for our own lonely species.

APRIL 1994

X-RATED

by George Plimpton

THE LAS VEGAS CONVENTION hall was packed with lines of men moving slowly toward the booths in which the porn stars were waiting: Tiffany Mynx, Kristi Myst, Misty Rain, Candy Apples, Sindee Coxx, Shyla Foxx, the Xs a salute to the X-rated industry in which they serve. The women were heavily made-up with scarlet lips, mascaraed eyelashes, hair carefully coifed and piled high, tight-fitting pants of black leather, some girls with tattoos (a butterfly, a black rose on a bare shoulder), and the shoes, of course, with the spikelike stiletto heels—hardly the girl-next-door look. Odd, because it seemed to perpetuate the concept that the porn star is only a notch or two up the social scale from the street prostitute. The stars came out of their booths and had pictures taken with their fans—the men's faces quite solemn, as if they were about to be handed a certificate for good citizenship. What they got was a poster. The girls rolled the posters into tight cylinders and then slid a rubber band up their length between thumb and forefinger—"like they're putting a condom on a guy," as someone in line pointed out.

I paid a visit to the booth of *AVN* (*Adult Video News*, the industry magazine that was sponsoring the 1997 porn-awards gala that would take place that evening), where I was introduced to a young woman who reviews porn movies for the publication (her nom de plume is Lily White). In addition, she has the gargantuan job of helping the staff select three hundred nominees—from the staggering total of seventy-two hundred porn films made over the year—for the silver statuettes that would be awarded later on. She was wearing a stud in her tongue and a ring in her nose. Sometimes, she said, she wears a silver spike through the septum of her nose. Her husband does her better—a big ring in the septum, a labret on either side of the lower lip, a ring in his right nipple, and the upper part of his body covered in tattoos. "In the supermarkets we kind of freak people out," she said.

"A certain amount of clashing when you kiss," I suggested.

"We feel quite uncomfortable without all that stuff on," she said. "It's like you lose your ballast."

We began talking about the night's awards ceremony. One hundred and one statuettes were to be given out. There were categories satisfying almost every imaginable delectation. She described the "Specialty" videos for those who like big-breasted women: *Big Boob Bikini Bash, The Duke of Knockers.* There was bondage, naturally: *The Punishment of Little Red Riding Hood.* Spanking: *Sweet Cheerleaders Spanked.* Bizarre Videos, which produced the spanking film, was also responsible for a nominee in what Lily referred to as the "Other Genre" category—*Waterworld: The Enema Movie.*

I remarked how numbing it must have been for her to plow through all this. Since the number of sexual positions and combinations is limited, wasn't pornography doomed to ultimate monotony? Lily agreed that the fast-forward button on the VCR is the essential piece of equipment in judging pornography . . . and that judicious use of it actually allowed her to get through a hundred or more films a day, since the sex acts themselves (often called "commercials") were invariably filmed at close range and unremittingly, as if the cameraman had set his camera onto a small tripod at the foot of the bed and gone off to have himself a beer. Fast-forward time.

"The formula is two minutes between commercials," Lily was saying.

I mentioned that I'd learned of a nice sixteenth-century word for "commercial": a "flourish."

"A what?"

"A 'flourish,' as in, 'Let's have a flourish on the tilting green.'"

Lily laughed and said that whether it was a "commercial" or a "flourish," it was still fast-forward time.

I was surprised to learn later that an *AVN* compatriot of hers named Jim Holliday (who's famous around the magazine's offices for outfitting himself entirely in white, including his moccasins, and who bears the title "senior historian") would have been horrified at Lily's use of the fast-forward button. A porn-film anthologist as well as a director, he writes in an introduction to his *Adult Video Almanac and Trivia Treasury* that he never fast-forwarded once during his viewing of almost two thousand films while researching material for his book. He claims that "[a]ll sex scenes are not the same, and fast forwarding can cause you to miss a milestone of erotica found in an otherwise dreadful film. I will put up with the dreary agony just to find those gems."

When I met Holliday, he mentioned a number of times that he had the mind-set of an Ohio farm boy, which was his upbringing: "Quite normal," he said. His insistence was that the intent of pornography, whether written or pictorial, was to arouse sexual feelings—not to entertain. He makes up for a lack of plot by populating his films with large numbers of stars—ergo, more couplings. He specializes in eighteen-to-thirty-girl epics with such titles as *Sorority Sex Kittens* and *Car Wash Angels*. He makes a lot of what he calls "double-vocational-adjective" movies—as in *Cheerleader Nurses, Sorority Nurses,* etc. The success of these has led predictably to "return" films . . . *The Return of the Cheerleader Nurses*. He mentioned a possible ne plus ultra in this field: *The Return of the Black Anal Sorority Cheerleader Nurses*. His *Car Wash Angels* would be in contention that night.

He took me over to another booth and presented me to a slight, middle-aged man, Alex de Renzy, considered one of the titan film-makers of the porn industry. I knew something about him. In 1969 he had gone to Denmark with a two-man crew and filmed Copenhagen's sex fair, where there was considerable flaunting in public of what hadn't been seen anywhere before. De Renzy spent eight days mak-ing a documentary about the Danish porn industry, which eventually showed in mainstream movie theaters in the United States. We had met before. In fact, jokingly, I had asked him at the time if he could slip me into one of his films, an interesting participatory exercise. He seemed so agreeable that I stammered about and told him that if he happened to be filming in Egypt, I'd be glad to oblige.

"Do you remember that?" I asked. "I specified it had to be Egypt."

"I never understood that."

"I don't either," I said.

Shouts rose from down the aisle; porn stars were tossing condom packages to the men waiting in line. I wandered over to look at some of the booths featuring bondage and S&M devices—leather whips, paddles, ankle restraints, studded halters, love cuffs, stiletto-heeled boots that looked more like weapons than footwear, women's edible undies (retail price: $1.75), biker caps, bitch-goddess bras, chokers, leashes, harnesses. The most alarming device was on display in the Paradise Electro Stimulations booth—the Auto Erotic Chair, a grim, skeletal black-leather structure that at first glance suggested an off-shoot of an electric chair. A flier I was handed announced that it was "a new apex in bondage gear . . . four top-quality leather restraints, which with the fully adjustable arm and leg horns will get you or your other 'spread eagle' in no time." Two "electro stimulative devices" come with the chair—the Vaginal Plug (which can be "aimed for a perfect fit") and the Micro Acrylic Anal Plug (no mention of whether this could be "aimed" or not).

As I was walking away, a gentleman leaned out of a booth and called out my name. He introduced himself as Bill Margold and quickly announced himself as a Detroit Lions fan. His calling card, which he pressed on me, was trimmed in blue and silver, the Lions' colors. It read WILLIAM MARGOLD CREATED HIMSELF. We talked about the Lions. He's worried about their defense. We could have been chatting in the Silverdome in Pontiac. Margold is such a fan that he has incorporated mention of the Detroit Lions into most of the three hundred porn films he told me he has made to date. "Is there anything better than sex?" a girl asks him as the two lie exhausted on a bed in one of his early films. "Yes," he replies. "Watching the Detroit Lions play." In one film, Margold used the stage name Lem Lary, derived from Lem Barney and Yale Lary, two of Detroit's stars in the '60s and '70s. "Do the Lions know this?" I asked, wondering how William Ford, the team's owner, a mild-mannered family man, would take to this symbiotic relationship.

"Oh, yes," Margold said. "I get fine seats for the games. Hey, you know what?"

"What?"

"You're responsible for my getting into the porn industry."

I looked at him, dumbfounded.

"That's right. You were my inspiration." He went on to say that in 1968 he had reviewed my book *Paper Lion* for the Santa Monica *Evening Outlook*. He looked at me and laughed. He said, "I knew *you* weren't going to get into the business." (I was tempted to interrupt and tell him about Alex de Renzy and Egypt but refrained.) "So I said to myself, *Why not try it?* If I failed, it would be a comic tragedy and I'd have a great story. If I succeeded . . . if I could pull off the three *G*s . . ."

"The three *G*s?"

"Get up, get in, get off . . . and do this on cue. I succeeded. My first film was *The Goddaughter*. Others followed. *Weekend Fantasy*. *Lust Inferno*. I went into the playpen of the damned. That's right. Once you do this, you're damned forever. But I didn't want to get out.

I knew I could become the leading authority. I didn't come into it for the sexual activity. That's mechanical. I came into it for the glory."

I was to learn that Margold is not only committed but also a substantial figure in the porn industry—known as "Papa Bear" for his efforts to help his "kids" work out their personal problems, especially concerns of self-esteem. His apartment in West Hollywood is overrun with stuffed teddy bears sent to him in gratitude. He has been in all aspects of the industry. As an agent, he discovered one of the most famous of porn stars: Seka. "I told her, 'I'm starting you off as hamburger. You'll end up filet mignon.'" He is fond of aphorisms. His most famous is probably "No one ever died of an overdose of pornography."

That evening, the ballroom of the Riviera Hotel filled with people. The men in the orchestra onstage wore dinner jackets. The master of ceremonies was Bobby Slayton, a stand-up comedian, who after each joke would turn to the orchestra and motion to the drummer for a rim-shot—ker-*boom*. Slayton shared the stage with a number of "co-hostesses," including a tall, graceful porn star in a white sheath dress named Nici Sterling, who is from England, where the pornography industry is a shadowy presence—no adult stores; clerks in dingy Soho alleys keep unmarked videos under the counter. She warmed up the crowd by remarking that there was more to the English than a stiff upper lip. Slayton later countered this with the comment "Englishwomen don't come; they arrive." Ker-*boom*.

The awards procedure involved as many as seven porn stars, almost always women, walking out in single file from the wings to a microphone at center stage. Each in turn would read out a nominee's name from a list. After the envelope was opened, the seven girls would lean toward the mike and attempt to call out the winner in unison—very rarely successfully. It was not easy for them to sing out as one, "And the winner is . . . *Buttslammer 2!*"

Unlike at the Oscars, no film clips of the award-winners were shown on a giant screen—predictable enough, I suppose, since no matter how jaundiced, or how supportive of the X-rated industry, it is hard to imagine that the audience members viewing, say, the Best Spanking scene would not have erupted into a bedlam of hooting and catcalling.

The award, held high in triumph by the winners, was a "Winged Victory" statuette of a woman holding aloft a wreath—a trophy that could just as well have been bestowed upon the champions of the local girls' softball league. The female winners, perched on their stiletto heels, moved for the podium in staccato strides. Once there, they found that they had very little to say . . . a "gosh," often followed by a fit of giggling. Out front we were spared what Oscar audiences are forced to suffer—the list of people "I would like to thank," on and on. It occurred to me that because of the vast number of films in which each winner had performed over the course of a year, much less the number of lovers, it was hopeless to sort out a few names for special mention.

A male star named T. T. Boy received an award for his performance in a video called *Shock*. Often called simply "the Boy," he is a legend in the business, not only for being able to maintain an erection indefinitely (which in the industry is known as "sustaining wood") but also for producing an ejaculation (referred to as a "money shot," a "cum shot," a "money pop," etc.) on cue—and, amazingly, for being able to do a number of them in succession. In *Sorority Sex Kittens,* he produced five money pops in one scene. T. T. Boy does not look at all glamorous—he's a small, tough-guy, assistant-mobster type; sometimes he chews gum during his lovemaking scenes. He pounds his partners. From the podium he said he hadn't seen *Shock* (he plays a gargoyle) but heard it was interesting. Once memorably described as "nothing more than a life-support system for his penis," he got the kind of admiring, solid applause reserved for a large artillery piece going by in a parade.

My friend Holliday didn't think much of T. T. Boy's gargoyle footage. "I'm a midwestern farm boy from Ohio," he told me again. "Gargoyles? They're to jump down and slit someone's throat, not make love. Gargoyles belong in horror films."

"What about T. T. Boy himself?"

"One of a kind. In the whole business there are only about sixteen or twenty men who can perform—the paladins of Charlemagne!" he said grandly.

The big winner of the night was a cute young star named Missy, sometimes referred to as the Shirley Temple of the industry. She won both the Best New Starlet and the Female Performer of the Year awards—a "historic event," as it was reported later in *AVN*. Missy, who seemed to me more a healthy-cheerleader type than a Shirley Temple, thanked her husband, Mickey, for his support during her "sexual adventure." I wondered if Mickey didn't deserve an award for Most Open-minded. At our table we worked it out that, in the forty films she had made in her first year in the business (given that she had performed in, say, four commercials, or flourishes, in each), Missy had been unfaithful to Mickey 160 times. Someone at the table pointed out that Mickey was a porn star himself. Out came a pad and pencil. If Mickey had made as many films as his wife, averaging two partners per, the total number of acts of infidelity would amount to 240, a figure surely of *Guinness Book of World Records* proportions.

Missy stayed onstage and was joined by all the evening's winners and performers. A comedian arrived and, quite off-key, sang, "Thank heaven for grown-up girls." This was followed by the porn stars doing a lively macarena (announced as a "cockeranal"), in which the hand movements included a move from the crotch to the mouth. The dancing became disorganized, a lot of kissing and mock lovemaking. Many of the principals were not wearing anything under their dresses. Then everybody clustered together and, arranging themselves like a family portrait, sang "We're a lovely horny porno family." The lights went up and it was over.

I left for the Hotel Rio, where I was told there was going to be a cyber-orgy. I had no idea what that was, but I went anyway. The party was held in a duplex suite on the twentieth floor. The place was crowded with men. I didn't see any women. But they were expected. From the second floor of the suite, I could look down over a balcony at the crowd milling below. Not far away was Paul Thomas, the porn star and director, sitting alone. One of Charlemagne's paladins!

It was my chance. I thought I'd ask him why the female stars invariably wear high-heeled shoes during the flourishes in X-rated movies. In the early days of pornographic films, the men often wore calf-length black stockings and the women wore high-heeled shoes, as if both partners felt they had to maintain at least some shred of dignity. But in present-day films, only the high heels remain; the stilettos, pitch-black, wave above the male performer's back like a set of antennae. The insistence on heels leads to rather improbable scenes—the female star tottering on spike heels as she heads for a liaison in a forest glade, or a poolside cabana, or a barn, or a garage (a favorite venue) to perform with a guy against the flank of a motorcycle. The shoes never come off.

I went over and introduced myself. We sat and chatted. He told me something about himself. A graduate of the University of Wisconsin, he had gone to New York seeking a career in acting. Blessed with movie-star good looks, he had appeared onstage in both *Hair* and *Jesus Christ Superstar.* He said he had been attracted to the porn world because he liked the exhibitionist factor. He liked being watched.

"So I got a chance to be in the Mitchell Brothers' X-rated *Autobiography of a Flea.* I didn't know what I was doing. I was a drugged-out hippie. I wanted to show my penis to everybody, and it was a perfect opportunity. I was a swinger. My generation had a much larger range of sexual experience—swapping partners, tripping on acid, watching your girlfriend with a bunch of people in the balcony, and partying all night in Polk Street in San Francisco and everybody having sex . . . that was what was going on."

I said I didn't remember that part about the guys up in the balcony. . . .

"Oh, yes."

He got up and looked down at the crowd, and then turned back and shrugged.

"No sign of the cyber-orgy?"

"Nope."

He sat down and continued. "I'm telling you that in all likelihood I might have made it in the mainstream as an actor or a director. But doing X-rated films will ruin your chances in the mainstream. You'll never enter big-time corporate America. You'll probably never run for president."

Playpen of the damned, I thought. I asked if he was recognized on the street.

"Every day. I like it."

Thomas made hundreds of films. Now he works as a director for Vivid Video, which since 1987 has had a subsidiary contract with Playboy Enterprises. He is able to make $150,000-budget X-rated films because of the edited versions—removal of any sight of male genitalia or penetration—which appear on pay-cable networks and on hotel-bedroom TV screens.

Thomas is one of the few people who still shoots on film rather than with video. "I tell a story," he explained. "I try to involve the audience in the characters of the story so that when it comes time for them to have sex, it means a bit more to the audience. They have some emotion invested in what's going on. I'm also wary of porn conventions," he said. "Big hair, big breasts. We don't have a makeup person on the set. We hire girls with natural breasts."

"What's your take on having girls wear high-heeled shoes in bed?"

To my surprise, he liked the convention.

"They extend the leg," he said simply.

"I talked to a guy, a porn star named Nick East, who said he got gouged."

"His problem."

We gazed on the men milling about below, many of them facing the door through which the stars were expected to appear.

I stirred and said, "Paul, did you know that back in the sixteenth century having sex was sometimes called having a flourish?"

"Is that right?" he replied. "A flourish."

"It turns up in the diaries of the time. 'We had a flourish on the settee.'"

"I like it. I'm going to use it."

Think of that, I said to myself . . . I had made two contributions to the porn industry—Bill Margold and now "flourish."

It was getting late. It didn't look as though the cyber-orgy was going to take place, certainly not in our suite, or even that any of the porn stars would show up for a drink.

I thanked Thomas for taking time to chat with me. Out in the hotel corridor I spotted T. T. Boy walking by, moving swiftly, a small entourage crowding around him . . . like a prizefighter on the way to the ring. On his way to the cyber-orgy? I didn't hasten after him.

In my hotel room, the TV set was on. I could watch an adult film for $9.95. It would have been appropriate enough, I suppose. But I didn't. The next day I heard that a girl at the party had performed with a beer bottle and danced naked on a table. At the time I was sound asleep.

The Cajun Road

by Charles Gaines

W E PULLED INTO THE parking lot of Prejean's Restaurant in Lafayette, Louisiana, just after noon on December 2—three dusty, road-hardened blood-sportsmen with appetites. We had not had a single unforgettable meal since dinner, sixteen long hours before, at Frank Harris's Pecan Brake Lodge, and we were understandably impatient for our next one. This was, after all, the heart of Cajun country, where even the alley cats eat brilliantly. Moreover, one of my traveling companions, photographer Tom Montgomery, and I had learned long ago that you cannot bring all you have to this sapping business of fishing and hunting and dancing and eating and drinking your way across an entire state without regular sustenance of a high order.

We meant business, Jody Bright, Tom, and I. Our plan was to get in and out of this lunch, prepared specially for us by one of the best Cajun-Creole chefs in Louisiana, as quickly as possible—thirty minutes, max—and on into the nearby Atchafalaya Swamp, where we faced twenty-four grueling hours of bird-watching, bass fishing, and more great eating. By this ninth day of a thirteen-day sporting road trip, Tom and I had already fished for redfish in two locations, hunted ducks at three shooting camps and geese at a fourth. We had labored through a Cajun Thanksgiving, at which the good food was knee-high; grazed the oyster bars of Abbeville; drunk Frank Harris's "bogsuckers" until we went silly; and stuffed ourselves with fried alligator while doing the Cajun two-step at Randol's here in Lafayette. There was more hard work coming up: more redfishing after the Atchafalaya, maybe another duck hunt, and a long night of partying in New Orleans. This was Jody's first road trip. He had joined Tom and me only four days before, and we were teaching him a little about pacing. As we entered the restaurant, I reminded him gently that this was a job like any other. All we had to do was keep our eyes on the ball.

We were at Prejean's to meet an old friend of Jody's mother's,

Becky Stokes, her boyfriend, her son, her secretary, and a person named Rebel Kelley. Becky, a native Louisianan, had been helping us organize our trip. Rebel Kelley, the assistant director of the state chapter of the Coastal Conservation Association, was coming down from Baton Rouge to fill us in on the CCA's redfish-conservation work. And for our dining pleasure, Becky had enlisted the help of her friend James Graham, the executive chef at Prejean's and at his own Fish and Game Grill, also in Lafayette. Graham has been called in print "the most innovative master of wild-game cookery in America," and he was about to demonstrate those very skills for us in a special presentation, for which the others were already waiting at the table.

We greeted Becky, her boyfriend, her son, and her secretary. Staring at a delicious young blonde woman whom I took to be the son's wife, I asked, "Where is the guy from the CCA?"

"I'm Rebel Kelley," said the blonde.

"You're not."

"Rebel *Anne* Kelley, really." She grinned up at me, and my old heart just flopped right over.

I met the late poet and novelist James Dickey at an academic party one night in Wisconsin when I was in my early twenties and he in his late thirties. We got drunk together on red whiskey and then lay down on somebody's living-room floor and arm wrestled. I beat him, whereupon he grabbed my head in both of his big hands and whooped, "You're one of *mine*, goddamnit! Boy, you're one of my own!"

Periodically throughout my life, maybe once or twice a decade, I see in a female face a particular shining mingling of beauty, wit, and unabashed appetites, and I just want to pop a straw in that person and drink her. This cannot properly be called a crush. I am a very happily married man, and I get pretty much the same feeling every time I look at my daughter, Greta, and at my seventy-two-year-old quail-hunting friend, Peggy Meyer Pepper. I just happen to have a strong affinity for lovely, unafraid women with a sweet tooth for life. And here, in Prejean's Restaurant, was clearly such a woman.

Over the next two hours we drank a few bottles of wine and we ate: shrimp wrapped in applewood-smoked bacon, pepperjack cheese, and grilled tasso, then deep-fried; a gumbo of pheasant, quail, and andouille sausage that won the state championship six years in a row; southern Texas blackbuck antelope with black-butter crawfish; and Acadian bread pudding with a coconut, caramel, and pecan sauce.

Rebel Kelley—with smart, inquisitive eyes and an unhidden disdain for regulations—is thirty-two, the age of one of my sons. "We educate and legislate" is all I remember of what she told me, professionally and at length, about the CCA. My own professionalism, case-hardened as it usually is on these trips, was already weakened by the wine and the food when Rebel finished it off completely over dessert.

"You know, my two favorite things in the world," she said, "are fishing and cocktail dresses."

I didn't grab her head and cry, "You're one of my own!" but I might as well have. "Come with us, Rebel Anne," I said, sealing my fate and that of my fellow road-trippers. "Come with us into the Atchafalaya!"

"Okay," she said, "but I have to go get my fly rod first."

"Hey, Chuck," said Jody when we were back in our rented Pathfinder, his two big coolers tied messily on top. "I'm still learning the ropes here, so I need you to fill me in on something."

"Anything, my boy. Just ask."

"What kinda ball is it exactly we gonna be keepin' our eye on out there in the swamp with Rebel?"

Redfish Heaven

The thing is, you have to be light on your feet in this road-tripping business, as well as beautifully organized. You have to leave yourself open to a certain amount of serendipity. You can't be afraid to paddle onto a good wave when it comes along, whether you're ready for it or not. But it would have taken too long to explain all these principles to Jody, so I decided to let the road be its own hard tutor, as it had with Tom and me.

"Sportsman's Paradise" is what the state of Louisiana calls itself on its license plates. Being sportsmen chronically in search of paradise, Tom and I had taken that as a challenge to mount one of our patented sorties of exploration, camaraderie, self-indulgence, mishap, passion, and revelation. Our previous trips, reported in the June/July 1995 and November 1996 issues of this magazine, were taken in Montana and Florida, respectively, both of which might legitimately advertise themselves as sportsmen's paradises; but it is only Louisiana that actually does so. The boldness of that appealed to us, and we were determined to put the claim to a fair test.

We began this trip, as we had in Florida, in the company of Jimbo Meador. A regional business manager for the Orvis Company and out of Point Clear, Alabama, Jimbo is my generation's true Natty Bumppo.

A lifetime devotion to the outdoors has rendered him curious, digni-
fied, skilled, incorruptible, and funny (as such devotion reliably will if it
is long and pure enough and the man is good enough to begin with).

"You know why white pelicans have those black feathers on the
ends of their wings?" he asked me on the first morning of the trip.

We were in a custom-built Go-Devil mud skiff with guide Mark
Brockhoeft, afloat in a marshy estuarial basin of the Gulf of Mexico
near Myrtle Grove, Louisiana. The basin is less than a forty-five-
minute drive from the French Quarter of New Orleans but might as
well have been two days from civilization for all the signs of it there.
We were stopped for lunch, gunwale to gunwale with the skiff holding
Tom and Bubby Rodriguez, who, along with Brockhoeft, operates Big
Red Guides & Outfitters. Mild winter sunlight lay over everything like
a blessing. In the air and on the water were thousands of birds: ibises,
herons, egrets, widgeons, teals, white pelicans. . . .

"No," I said. "Why?"

"'Cause black feathers have more melanin. They're stronger. The
pelicans need the strength down there to get their lift." Jimbo grinned
at the gentle noon. "Nature's really got things figured out," he said.
"She dud'n miss a trick."

We spent the afternoon as we had the morning, poling through
clear, shallow water amid islands of golden coontail and widgeon grass,
looking for redfish to throw flies to. And finding them. Due to recent,
stunningly successful Gulf Coast conservation efforts, redfish are now
present from Texas to Florida in good-old-days numbers. The marshes,
bayous, and flats that constitute the coastline of Louisiana have become
the nation's largest fishery and a gigantic nursery for redfish, where the
reds fatten on blue crabs, shrimp, and baitfish until they are large
enough (at twelve to fifteen pounds) to move offshore. It's also a fly fisherman's playground. At almost any time of the year, except during the
coldest snaps, Brockhoeft and Rodriguez can put a fly rodder on redfish
weighing six to eight pounds—waking, finning, tailing, even "crawling"
after food in water so shallow their whole backs rise out of it—so many
of them that forty to fifty "shots," or casts, to individual, sighted fish is
considered an average day.

We drifted and caught fish and watched the clouds of ducks trading the bright, empty marsh; and that first day's mellow, easy abundance seemed a good omen, a promise of largesse to come.

"Dck Capitl of America"

The next morning, Jimbo went home and Tom and I drove through Baton Rouge into Cajun country. Traveling west on I-10, you encounter the landscape as if through a looking-glass around the town of Henderson. Suddenly, all the men seem to be wearing camo. There are hand-lettered signs advertising catfish and gaspereaux, lots of dead dogs and nutria along the roads, alligator-skin stores, raised cemeteries, little roadside crosses commemorating fatal crashes, dual Rottweilers in a few front yards, bass and jet boats in others. The names on the mailboxes are Tibodeau and Boudreau, Pettipas and Breaux. A bumper sticker on a camo-painted monster truck said COONASS AND PROUD.

"Coonass" is a self-embraced nickname for Cajuns. It derives from *cunaso,* a Caribbee Indian word (via Spanish) meaning a man who lives simply on and with the land. "These are my *people,*" I gushed to Tom. What I meant was that I love the Cajuns. I wish I had been born a Cajun. The Cajuns are descendants of (and their name a rough abbreviation for) the Acadians, who were among the first Caucasians to settle North America, emigrating from France in 1604 to Nova Scotia. In 1755, most of them were gathered up and thrown out of Nova Scotia by the Brits, and many of those refugees wound up in southern Louisiana, where their ancestors today number 700,000-plus strong and happy souls.

Outside of Gueydan, a sign missing the *u* in *duck* and an *a* in *capital* proclaims the town the DCK CAPITL OF AMERICA. This is flat country: live oaks and pines, miles of yellow rice fields, some of them flooded. And ducks. Finally, the road just ends some thirty marshy miles from the gulf, and there stands the Florence Club.

The columned main building was built in 1911 by a Wisconsin entrepreneur named Arsene L. Arpin, who intended to use it as the central office for a rice-farming town named for his daughter, Florence. When the town went belly-up, the building and the fifty-one hundred acres of rice fields and marsh around it served as a private hunting camp. In 1951 it became an exclusive oil-business duck club, specializing in sixteen-ounce rib-eye steaks and porters who woke the members before dawn with trays of strong coffee and news of temperature and wind direction. After languishing during the '60s, '70s, and '80s, as waterfowl populations and shooting seasons and limits dwindled, the place was bought in 1995 by a Metairie businessman and turned into a commercial operation at pretty much the same time North Atlantic ducks began making a show-biz comeback that made hunting for them fun and guiltless again. With plenty of water on the nesting grounds and with the long-term conservation efforts of Ducks Unlimited and similar organizations paying off in spades, 1996 was a stellar year. And '97 was even better: The fall migration on all American flyways was up to nearly 100 million birds, the most since the salad days of the club, in the late '50s. All that plenty made the Florence Club a very upbeat place to be during duck season. It was also everything your sporting nostalgia tells you a southern Louisiana hunting camp should be: the fine old virgin-cypress building with its red-oak floors and brick piers; its mounted ducks and racks full of twelve-gauges, and the bar bristling with single-malt scotches; the camo jackets hung in the hall and the black and yellow Labs wandering the grounds; the shallow-draft duck launches, some of them dating from the '40s and '50s, rocking in the boat shed. "This," whispers your nostalgia, "is what it was like to be Nash Buckingham." And at $7,000 per day for your party of up to fourteen guns (the club does not mix groups), any such little historical evocation is welcome.

The next morning we were waked by two gentlemen who worked in the kitchen, one toothless, the other with a toupee. The toothless one carried coffee and little cups on his tray; the other had the sugar and cream. "It's four-thirty in the mawnin', boys. Forty-six degrees. Wind out of the southeast at about five," said the man with the toupee.

"Interesting touch," said Tom when they left. I—who had waked with a start, staring up at the grinning, toothless one—was not sure how I felt about it. After more coffee with biscuits in the dining room, we departed the boat shed at 5:30 with a young Cajun guide named Chad Bertrand and his retriever, Goldie, and by shooting time we were seated in a pit blind sunk into the lightening marsh and surrounded by a couple dozen decoys.

It was a windless, beautiful morning. The new light, white and yellow on the marsh grass, sneaked up on the decoys, then suddenly illuminated them like a nice surprise. Chad blistered his lip on a colorless Haydel duck call, and lots of mallards and teals came in, and we shot some of them and Goldie retrieved them, and for a while out there on the Florence Club marsh it was just about as fine as duck hunting gets. By eight o'clock we had ten ducks, and we went in shortly after that to the good crumping noise of twelve-gauges coming from the club's other blinds.

On Highway 14, from Gueydan through Abbeville and New Iberia, and then on 90 East, through Franklin and Morgan City, I began my Cajun-music-appreciation initiative for Tom's benefit. I stopped at a Wal-Mart and surprised him with Wayne Toups, Waylon Thibodeaux, the Cajun Playboys, Nathan and the Zydeco Cha Chas, Beau Jacque and the Zydeco Hi-Rollers, and Fernest Arceneaux. With shrewd, joyful, land-loving music pouring out the windows of the Pathfinder, we sped past cane fields, rice fields, and oil wells.

Then we were in Houma, where everyone seemed to have a Ram 1500 with an ATV in the back. We were there to go out with a redfish guide named Danny Ayo, who owns and operates the Shallow Minded Guide Service, but not until the following day. For that afternoon, Danny's wife's brother-in-law, a shrimper, would take us with him on his boat.

Vincent Menge, his wife, Anna, and their seven-year-old son, Opie, live in Chauvin, south of Houma, in the middle of bayou country. They greeted us when we arrived in their driveway, loud with Cajun music, as if they'd been hoping for months that we would come. Vincent is short and stocky with brushy black hair and friendly hazel eyes. He and his son took us out for a couple of hours on their twenty-nine-foot shrimp trawler, the *Captain Opie*.

Vincent, forty-one, shrimps for six months and does carpentry work for the rest of the year. When the shrimping season ends, in late November or early December, he shoots ducks, geese, and deer and traps nutrias, minks, muskrats, and otters until the end of February. Then, until mid-April, he and Anna crab. Pretty much year-round Vincent fishes—for bass, speckled trout, and redfish inshore, and for bull reds, cobias, and tuna in the gulf. This past December and January alone, he landed eighty-six speckled trout off the boat dock forty feet behind his house.

"The good Lord's been kind to me. I'm a very, very, very happy man, bru," he said.

All we caught in the nets that afternoon were a few jellyfish. Though the white-shrimp season had three more weeks to run, Vincent thought they had already moved back into the deep water of the gulf. He'd had a pretty good season, grossing close to $28,000. In order to take home $20,000 from that, he does his own engine work, weaves his own nets, welds his own A-frames and skimmers. He earns another $10,000 or so from his carpentry. On $30,000 or $35,000 a

year, he and Anna and Opie "have everything we want, bru, and money
in the bank," said Vincent. How could this be? you might wonder, as I
did: "We live off the land as much as we can. We eat what we catch
and trap and shoot. We don't buy much."

It was almost dark when we tied up back at Vincent's pier. Anna
was waiting for us. The next day was Thanksgiving, and she and Vincent invited Tom and me to eat dinner with their family after we finished fishing with Danny Ayo. "We have plenty food, bru," said
Vincent. "No end of food."

"Lache Pas la Patate"

It was early on a calm, cool, flawless Thanksgiving morning, and we
had just run from a boat launch to the mouth of the first bay we were
going to fish somewhere in the enormous system of marshes and bayous that extends for more than thirty miles south of Houma to the
gulf. We could hear the guns of duck hunters around us, but there was
not another angler in sight. I had just stood up on the casting platform
in the bow of Danny's skiff and was stripping out line, with the fly
lying dead in the water twenty feet away, when a thirteen-pound redfish ate it. After we released the fish, Danny poled into the bay, and
redfish scattered like rats off the shallow bottom.

The pug-nosed, blue-collar, toe-to-toe-fighting redfish can go from
piggishly indiscriminate to confoundingly picky in its eating habits.
Occasionally, one will munch any old fly dumped right on its head, or
even its tail. More often, they are easier to spook than even bonefish
are, and the *only* productive cast drops the fly two feet in front of a
cruiser—and a foot beyond him—so that it can be retrieved virtually
into the fish's mouth.

I blew a few fish; we ran over some; several more wouldn't eat.
Then Tom took the push-pole and Danny got on the casting platform
with his Orvis one-weight fly rod. When asked why he prefers to use a
fly rod designed for quarter-pound bream while fishing for six- to
twenty-pound redfish, Danny answered, "Why be normal?" But there
is also the fact that he would like to break the current fifteen-pound
world record for redfish on a two-pound tippet, and he believes the
one-weight is the rod he is divinely intended to catch that fish on.

Danny devoutly worked a few fish with no appetites: "That's the
one, that's the cast . . . God *wants* me to have this fish!" After one of
the reds gave us the fin and swam off in a huff, Tom, on the pole, said,
"I'm afraid in my apostasy I'm not helping you."

Then Danny caught a six-pounder, very nicely, on his one-weight. Then I caught one, an eight-pound tailer. Then Tom hooked a monster of maybe eighteen pounds, and his leader broke at a knot. The fish had turned on a little bit, and there were thousands of them. In a lifetime of redfishing, I'd never seen so many in a single area.

Ducks were flying, and ibises and terns and pelicans. We pushed up a flock of roseate spoonbills and watched them ignite in the new sun. The sky was a speckless blue dome, and under it we worked and caught about a dozen fish, having the pure fun that even impure men can have at fishing. At 11:30, we ran back in for Thanksgiving dinner.

Danny's wife was there, and Anna, as well as Sonny and Rosabelle Arceneaux's other two daughters and one son, and all their children and spouses—everybody crammed into Sonny and Rosabelle's little house across the highway from the Menges'.

As if we were old friends suddenly returned home, the twenty-plus relatives and one poodle welcomed Tom and me with something different, richer, and more comforting than hospitality—something more like passing around the big platter of their intimacy and pleasure for us to share as we did their food.

As for that, there was gumbo, turkey, a roast from a deer that Vincent had killed, pork, turnip greens, macaroni and cheese, potato salad, fried French bread, pies, and cakes. There was also cold beer, and football on the tube, and the young cousins playing games in the front yard, and everyone laughing at Sonny's jokes. He and Rosabelle had lived in this two-bedroom house ever since they were married. Their four daughters had grown up sharing the extra bedroom; their son had slept in the washroom.

"Do you know what the Cajun motto is?" one of the daughters asked when she brought me a piece of pecan pie. She was smiling. She had wonderfully calm and affectionate eyes.

"*Laissez les bons temps rouler!*" Let the good times roll! "You Arceneaux really know how to do it."

"There's another one," she said, "for other kinds of times. '*Lache pas la patate*'—'Don't let go of the potato,' it means. Hold on; keep going. We know how to do that, too."

Goose Hunting with Bubba

The next day, we picked up Jody Bright at the New Orleans airport and headed west again, after tying Jody's two big coolers to the roof of the Pathfinder. Jody had flown in from Kona, Hawaii, where he's a big-game fishing captain. He was planning to hunt and fish with us for a week and then go on to southern Texas, where he's from, for more hunting with family and friends. He had packed his clothes and an empty duffel bag in the coolers. As all the ducks and deer and redfish and quail and what-all he had promised to folks back in Kona went into the coolers, the clothes would come out and go into the duffel. The plan left us looking like a bunch of Okies with a beer habit, but that (and most anything else you can think of) would never bother Bright.

Hammy Patin's duck-hunting operation just outside of Abbeville announces the final turnoff to itself with the words ACE HUNTING CLUB and an arrow spray-painted on the side of a Dumpster. Like that sign, the place gives you everything you need without frills and doesn't sweat the presentation. The central meeting/dining room looks like a southern Louisiana roadhouse, with a big-screen TV that's on all the time, a pool table, a Bud Light sign over the bar, photos of Huey P. Long on the walls, and burly guys in camo named Blue and Rodney sitting outside around metal pails full of beer on ice.

The man who gives this place its particular Elks Club/fraternity-house/juke-joint tone and its generous, effusive *bon temps rouler* spirit is a three-hundred-plus-pound, ex-Golden Gloves heavyweight state-champion boxer with a Cajun accent, an indefatigable sense of humor, and an unlit, filter-tipped cigar never out of one of his husky hands: Hammy Patin.

He was waiting for us. "You boys picked a good time to come. Them birds are flyin'," he said. Before long there were appetizers of crawfish étouffée, sausage rolls, and chicken wings, followed by a dinner of guinea-and-sausage gumbo, then homemade pies. The big dining room was full of high-humored hunters from all over the Southeast, most of whom return to Hammy's every year and many of whom stayed up late over liquid refreshments that night.

Jody and I hunted together the next morning with a very good guide named Bubba in a pit blind sunk between rice fields in an area that specklebellied geese had been using heavily off and on all season. "It'll likely be feast or famine," said Bubba.

As it happened, no one at the camp had very good hunting except us. A few ducks and hordes of geese worked our decoys slowly but steadily all morning, and we came back in around nine with six mallards and the limit of specklebellies.

On the concrete apron of the cleaning shed, the guides laid out all the birds that had been shot that morning—the big handsome speckle-bellies, the snow and blue geese, the elegant pintails and dapper little teals and beautiful northern mallard drakes with their iridescent green heads and red feet. All that wildness and speed and navigational instinct, the feathers still redolent of the north, of potholes in Alberta. A few people took pictures; Jody got it on video—and as soon as the birds were cleaned, the first of his clothes came out of the cooler.

Ayouuuuu!

Abbeville is a charming town where you could easily eat yourself to death. We took a couple of lay days there, staying a few miles outside of town at a camp on the Vermilion River graciously provided to us by Becky Stokes. The spunky Miss Becky fairly fizzes with optimistic energy. The oil-related company she owned and ran with her sons was turning a wonderful profit. She had a good-looking boyfriend named John and a brand-new purple Jag with a license plate that read EZ2ENJOY.

Abbeville may be more serious about good food than any town its size in the United States. Even the local Texaco station advertises shrimp stew on a sign underneath the gas prices. At Black's Oyster Bar, Shucks!, Pupuy's Oyster Shop, and the River Front, we ate shrimp, oysters, gumbo, frog legs, crawfish, catfish, and alligator. Then Becky suggested we get serious about our Cajun chow and go up to Lafayette with her and John for a meal and a *fais-do-do* at Randol's. A *fais-do-do* is a Cajun dance. They have them every weekend at Randol's and, believe me, you haven't done that until you've done it.

At Randol's we met Becky's friends Virginia and Dayton, and all of us sat at a table on the edge of the big dance floor, drinking pitchers of beer and eating Cajun-fried crawfish tails and alligator bits. Out on the floor were thirty or forty couples doing the Cajun two-step, the Cajun waltz, and the Cajun jig to the impossibly lively music of a band called File. Moving counterclockwise as they danced were old folks and kids, snappy young hotshots with bandannas on their heads, full-figured guys in John Deere caps, and a popular seventy-seven-year-old gent named Leopold who looked under fifty and never missed a dance.

"There's everyone from gas-station attendants to doctors out there," said Virginia. "Hairdressers, lady lawyers. Cajun dancing's a great equalizer."

Women were asking men to dance, boys asking fine women, old men asking girls. "Aren't you guys ever going to dance?" a woman finally asked Tom and me.

"We're watching," I told her.

"We don't understand watching," she said. "We'd just flat wither up."

After a while, I did dance a two-step for fun with Virginia to a tune called "Matilda," then a waltz, then a jig. And I wanted never to leave the floor. I wanted to learn how to yell *"Ayouuuuu!"* the way the Cajuns do.

On the road again—headed north through Lafayette, Opelousas, Gold Dust, and Lone Pine—Tom and Jody and I, for lack of anything better to do and inspired perhaps by the raunchy music of Nathan and the Zydeco Cha Chas, invented a character named Buck Boudreau, who despite our best efforts to control him kept gesturing rudely and shouting salacious things in a faux French accent to pretty Cajun misses as we flew past them.

Not really. Really what we did was talk about fishing, like the simpletons we are. When we had all thoroughly tired of the ear-exhausting Cajun music, I turned on NPR, hoping for some soothing Liszt or something. What we got was Purcell's opera on King Arthur. I turned it up, hoping to upgrade my young friend Bright's musical taste. I drove and from time to time helped Sir Somebody conduct. Sitting in the passenger seat, Jody listened disinterestedly for a while, then with growing animosity.

"That can't be the same Purcell who played in Willie Nelson's band," he said witheringly at one point. "Ned Purcell?"

"Hush," I told him, "and listen to this sublime plethora of horns."

"Would you *please* turn that shit *off*?" he asked a little later.

"Not right now. We're coming up to Guinevere's magnificent aria."

"Uh-huh. Yeah," Jody said after a moment and looked out the window. "That's always been one of my favorite parts, too."

Just before we arrived at Frank Harris's lodge, he said, "Hey, Chuck, idn't a plethora somethin' like a nutria?"

"Not really," said Tom. "I think it's a little bigger."

Land of the Bogsuckers

Frank G. Harris III is as unadulterated an example of the true gentleman sportsman as it is still possible to find in these ungentlemanly times. He is a sixty-three-year-old petroleum geologist from Shreveport, and the owner, manager, and entire staff of an elegant little shooting lodge called Pecan Brake, near Jonesville. Frank built the lodge with his son in 1975 and opened it commercially in 1994—to only two paying hunters at a time—as an excuse for spending the entire shooting season at his camp.

The lodge is in east-central Louisiana near Catahoula Lake, a shallow, twenty-thousand-acre body of water that is one of the state's major wintering areas for ducks. Frank has land on the lake and puts his hunters into excellent duck shooting out of three-man blinds. But his real passion, and Pecan Brake's signature offering, is woodcock hunting. I happen to be in love with woodcock, and have been for two decades. They are my favorite game bird, both to pursue with pointing dogs and to eat, though—as their populations are in decline throughout much of North America—I kill fewer of them every year, and may soon wind up hunting them with my setter just for his sake, and to watch them tower in the alders and hear the flushing whistle of their primary feathers.

We arrived too late that afternoon to gear up and go for ducks, and the woodcock season was not yet open. We had to leave the next morning at ten, and since I wanted to spend the hours before then seeing Frank's woodcock covers rather than duck hunting, we never uncased our guns at Pecan Brake. But I didn't have to hunt with Frank Harris to know what hunting with him would be like.

He is a tall, slim, deliberate man with gray hair and a pencil mustache, and his lodge is a showcase of his preoccupations: Outside is a kennel holding five Brittanys and a Chesapeake; inside are polished wood surfaces, leather couches, the skins of zebras, bears, and wolves, and mounted ducks and wild turkeys. On the walls are photos of camping trips and horse-packing elk hunts. His two beautiful Parker shotguns, which were his father's and will go to his son, and a meticulous journal of every day he's spent at the lodge since August 1975 are in there, too.

"Bogsucker" is a fond if unflattering name for a woodcock. The recipe for "Frank's Bogsucker Cocktail" is posted in his kitchen: "Four parts of good gin, one part dry sherry served on rocks with a crisp olive. To be enjoyed by gentlemen of the hunt prior to dinner. The olives, with seeds in, are first dipped in Tabasco sauce and are served in the libation impaled on a black locust thorn which is properly dressed with woodduck and woodcock feathers."

After driving us down to see Catahoula Lake in the near dark, Frank served us and himself premixed bogsuckers out of the freezer, prepared as the recipe called for in Mason jars made in 1858. The presentation was a velvet glove for an iron fist of a drink that had Jody, Tom, and me, all experienced tipplers, saying even dumber things than usual after two of them.

Then Frank went into the kitchen, put on an apron, and tended to three pintails and a canvasback that had been roasting in a clay cooker, and an onion pie. He made rice, a comely fruit salad, and a gravy out of beef broth, white-truffle oil, and the pan drippings from the ducks. Eaten with good red wine, it was a meal to make you long for the company of Ivan Turgenev. Later, it seemed to me it was also something more than that. As I lay in bed, following a late evening with Cuban cigars and good talk, it seemed to me that few things I've seen in more than forty years of pursuing the sporting life were as truly and affectingly emblematic of the best of that life as Frank Harris. Here was a man at an age when very little time should be wasted—laboring in an apron over a dinner fit for his children or his very oldest friends but going instead to three strangers who only instinct could tell him would enjoy it enough to make that labor worthwhile.

The next morning, after flushing five woodcock over his two Brittanys, Frank asked us to stay and hunt ducks with him, and I couldn't think of a thing I would rather have done. But a job is a job, so Tom, Jody, and I put on our game faces and headed south to the Atchafalaya Swamp and the redfish flats near Slidell. But first we had to stop for lunch in Lafayette with Becky Stokes, her boyfriend, her son, her secretary, and some guy from the CCA named Rebel Kelley.

Into the Swamp with Rebel

Rebel met us at the Butte La Rose landing on the Atchafalaya River with her fly rod and a rain suit. The sky was bruised and stormy, but she looked up for anything, as bracing and blonde as a bank of daffodils in the fog.

"You travel light," I said. "Most women would have at least two suitcases for a night in the swamp."

"What do you mean 'a *night* in the swamp'?"

"We're spending the night. Didn't I tell you that? In a cabin."

"Get *out*," said Rebel. "I don't even have a toothbrush."

"You can use mine," Jody said with southern Texas charm.

"Coerte, are they kidding?" she asked Coerte Voorhies, our guide.

He shook his no-nonsense head. Rebel shrugged. "Well, what the hell. I just hope somebody brought some red wine."

"We gotcha covered there," Jody told her.

Coerte had driven Jody, Tom, and me out from Lafayette to the landing, where his son, Kim, was waiting with a boat. Coerte and his wife operate a bed-and-breakfast called Bois des Chenes in an 1820 plantation house in Lafayette, out of which Coerte and Kim run a swamp-tour company called the Atchafalaya Experience. Coerte is sixty-eight, a burly, energetic, well-spoken ex-military man who still wears a camo uniform every day and carries a nine-millimeter automatic on his hip. His family has been here for two hundred years. His grandfather lived to hunt and fish, he told me; so did his father; so do his son and grandson. And him? "Are you kidding?" he said. "What else is there?"

Kim Voorhies, who looked to be in his early thirties, has a *bon temps* face. Retired from the military with a bad back, he also wore camo, causing Tom to wonder if there might be some kind of survivalist action going on back there in the swamp. I don't think so. I think the Voorhieses' outfits are part of the way they represent their business—a way of announcing that when you leave the landing at Butte La Rose, you are heading into serious Tarzan country.

For almost two centuries, a small community of Cajuns lived in the Atchafalaya Basin—860,000 acres of swamps, lakes, bayous, and water prairies—in cabins and on houseboats, visiting floating grocery stores for what little provender they couldn't take from the swamp. Now, by law, residents keep their permanent homes outside the levees, but they can have cabins in the basin, and boats. Some still make a living there; many more, like Rennie and Barry Serrette, brothers who work and live in town, would tell you they still *do* their living in the swamp.

As soon as she walked into their camp and introduced herself, Rennie and Barry recognized Rebel from her appearance a few months before on the cover of *Louisiana Sportsman*. It was a cover they remembered well: Rebel had been wearing a bikini top and holding a fish. Rennie and Barry were very happy, if a bit surprised, to see her dropped mysteriously into their camp in the swamp.

Barry and Rennie's camp was just upriver from the Voorhieses'. It was bigger, with a few more amenities, so Coerte and Kim had arranged for us to take our meals there. After a dinner of alligator sauce picante and Cajun navy beans, we drank the George Dickel I'd brought (almost as well received as Rebel had been), smoked cigars, and talked about being Cajun.

"It's not an ancestry, it's an attitude," said Rennie. "A Cajun gives you everything he has. He never holds back. Drink hard, sleep hard, cook hard, hurt hard."

Jody wondered if Cajuns liked opera—guys like Ned Purcell. There was a long silence. Then Kim offered, "Well, I love the smell of opera in the morning."

Back in the little Voorhies cabin, with Tom soundly asleep, Jody, Rebel, and I lay in our bunk beds considering conservation. Rebel had borrowed not only Jody's toothbrush but also his sweatpants to sleep in, and he promised her, with more southern Texas charm, that he would never wash them again. The great swamp was soughing outside in the black night, Pink Floyd was playing on the boom box, and the music mixing with the moist air felt weirdly liberating and expanding.

Jody's brother had served as the executive director of the CCA. Jody had been so impressed by the group's work in bringing back inshore sport-fishing along the Gulf Coast that he had founded the Hawaii Conservation Association, which now plays a major role in billfish conservation in that state.

Rebel said that though the Louisiana CCA had had good success with many of its efforts, the state's coastal marshes, which comprise a full 40 percent of the nation's coastal marshlands, were being lost—due partly to the erosion that results from the dredging of more and more oil-access and shipping canals—at the terrifying rate of up to twenty-five thousand acres per year. Unless something was done, Rebel said, it wouldn't be too long before it was all over but the shouting for the kind of inshore fishing and waterfowl shooting we had been enjoying. Then Louisiana would just have to change its license tag.

Lying in her lower bunk, Rebel talked with heart and good sense about Louisiana conservation. Because I wanted to hear more, and not at all because of her general luster and verve, I felt disinclined to quit Rebel's company when we left the Atchafalaya. So the next day—after some early-morning bird-watching and bass fishing, followed by a breakfast of venison, Cajun sausage, and eggs—I said: "Why don't you meet us over in Slidell tonight? We have a house this time, with a shower and a toilet and everything. You can go fishing with us, and maybe somebody'll hook a big fish for you and let you reel it in." That is Alabama charm.

We were back at Butte La Rose landing; Coerte was there with our Pathfinder.

"Get *out*," said Rebel.

"Why not?"

"Okay," she said. She had to see her boyfriend, Charlie, in New Orleans, but she would meet us in Slidell the next morning before we went out fishing. There are two things you learn about Rebel after very little time: She is not an amateur at life, and she is a woman who will never be down for long.

"Good job, Chuck," said Jody when we were headed east. "I sorta thought we needed to keep our eye on the ball a little longer, too."

Playing the Inner Game with the King of the Road

We slid into Slidell, forty minutes northeast of New Orleans, around 4:30 and went to Gary Taylor's house. Gary is a wiry, enduro-motorcycle-racing fishing guide, who for the past nine years has owned and operated Go for It! Charters out of Slidell. His wife, Viki, met Tom, Jody, and me at her door and told us "the best fisherman in the South" was down in the garage.

He was checking over the sixteen-foot Hewes Bonefisher skiff and one of the twenty-two-foot catamarans that we'd be going out in the next day. With him was Jimbo Meador, who had driven back from Alabama to join us on this last leg of the trip. Gary had arranged for us to stay at a friend's weekend house outside of town, and after we rigged some plans for the next day, he led us over there. Parked in the driveway—as unmistakable as Elvis's gold Cadillac—was Paul Bruun's van.

Bald, bearish, sensitive, and courtly, Paul is the sort of uniquely inspiring example to road-trippers everywhere that Jimi Hendrix was to guitarists. He is a trout guide, writer, gourmand, and raconteur extraordinaire from Jackson Hole, Wyoming. Every November and December, Paul leaves Wyoming for a nomadic ramble of sport, country-music appreciation, and gourmandizing. He drives first to Texas for bass fishing, quail hunting, and dove shooting. Next he goes to Louisiana for redfish and speckled trout; then on to Florida, his native state, for the angling smorgasbord down there; Alabama for the smallmouth fishing in Pickwick Lake; and, finally, to Nashville for the Grand Ole Opry. All along this route, Bruun chases down food, music, and fishing leads: buying hams in an Alabama country store some-where; visiting somebody in Tennessee to learn about a "revolutionary jig-head system with a straight worm"; pilgrimaging to the Meridian, Mississippi, home of Jimmy Rogers, the Singing Brakeman.

In his home on wheels are a half dozen dress shirts on hangers, shotguns and shells, hip boots, a dozen bait-casting, spinning, and fly rods with two or three reels for each, and close to ten thousand lures and flies. It is the van of a passionate and tireless bloodhound, who chases down and brings to earth along the highways of America what he calls "the inner game" of the things he cares about.

I asked Paul what he valued most from his lifelong obsession with fishing, the inner game of which few people know or play better. "The spiritual return, and the getting there," he said without hesitation. Spoken like a king of the road.

We left from Butte La Rose landing at dawn the next morning, with Rebel meeting us exactly on time and ready to *rouler*. We made up an imposing fish posse: Gary, with his Hewes skiff and two big-engine, shallow-draft cats; Jimbo, with a 14.5-foot kayak; Rebel, Tom, Jody, Paul, and me; and three friends of Gary's—Ralph Smith, Jim Lamarque, and Dave Hall, the legendary Louisiana game warden.

The Biloxi, or Louisiana, Marsh is a vast off-coast system of grass islands, creeks, and ponds that is chockablock with redfish and speckled trout. We didn't catch anything that morning, but after an early lunch, the sun came out and the fish got hungrier. Rebel got in one of the cats with Jim, Dave, and Jody, and fielded those boys' attentions like a major-league shortstop. They also got serious about putting some trout in Jody's coolers, keeping twenty-two of the forty they caught.

And Jody got to show off his road-trip-improved vocabulary. Late in the afternoon, he and one of Gary's guides and I were poling a little pond, casting to occasionally finning redfish. A nutria swam by.

"There goes a nutria," said the guide.

"Naw, his back's too big," said Bright. "That's gotta be a plethora."

After a considering pause the guide said, "Maybe. But we haven't seen many of them lately. The commercial trappers liked to got them all."

We ate our penultimate road-trip dinner at Gary's house. Viki made the best gumbo we had yet eaten, and it preceded a wonderful

Greek vegetable casserole and redfish fillets cooked skin- and scales-down on the grill. With more than a little wine, we all toasted the meal, the trip we were finishing, and the paid-off promise of richness and plenty that I had felt on the first day.

One Last Dance

I hugged Rebel as she was leaving the Taylors' house and told her I would miss her, that she had sort of been to our trip what one of those carved female heads was to the bow of a nineteenth-century whaling ship, and the comment seemed to make some sense at the time.

"Y'all aren't through with me yet," she said. "You and Tom and Paul are *mine* tomorrow night when you're in New Orleans. You know I told you about my *two* favorite things? Well, I left one out."

Could I be hearing this right? I wondered. Was it the wine? Did Tom and Paul have to be in on this? I tried to smile casually. "Get *out*," I said.

"Y'all have been taking care of me in the swamp and all, now I'm going to take care of you. Charlie has to work, so I'm going to take y'all to dinner and then we're going *dancing*."

The next morning, after telling Jimbo and Gary good-bye, I left Tom and Paul to explore Slidell and dropped Jody and his coolers off at the airport, wishing him well with his new vocabulary. Then I drove on to the Hotel Monteleone, the oldest hotel in the French Quarter and my favorite in all of New Orleans. There I took a workout and a nap, and after that I felt ready for pretty much anything Rebel Anne Kelley could come up with.

At eight o'clock we all met in the hotel lobby and walked over to the G & E Courtyard Grill. Paul was attired like an English squire, in a tweed cap and jacket; Tom and I were in old fishing clothes two weeks from a washing; and Rebel was dressed, all in black, simply to kill. We had a good Creole-meets-Asian meal at the G & E, then, around 10:30, we turned ourselves over to Rebel.

Driving her Explorer with dispatch, she took us up St. Charles past the Camellia Grill to a joint called the Maple Leaf, where Rockin' Dopsie Jr. and the Zydeco Twisters were playing.

Rockin' Dopsie Jr.—a stringy guy wearing a black cowboy hat, an apron, and a metal washboard called a *frotoir* on his chest—could strictly make music. Zydeco is Cajun soul music, Cajun dirty danc-ing—a beat rather than a melody—and Rockin' Dopsie Jr. and his band owned it. The dance floor was cheek-to-jowl with bodies shaking and clapping and shouting and high-fiving, and every face had a grin on it. Rebel was the queen of the place. She tore it up—dancing on the bandstand with Dopsie, pulling me and Tom up every time we tried to sit down, and dancing with us both, clapping and pointing at the ceiling and whooping, "Ain't life fun or *what*?" her yellow head bobbing like a beacon.

We danced until the place closed at two. Then we got back into Rebel's Explorer and she whipped it down the weekend uptown streets, past all the decorated-for-Christmas dowager mansions on St. Charles, through stop signs and over curbs, anywhere she wanted to, finally pulling up in somebody's yard to park in front of the F&M Patio Bar—where things were just getting going.

We danced there, too, on a floor so crowded with *bon temps roulers* that some of them were dancing on the pool table. Later Rebel and I found ourselves at the bar eating cups of red Jell-O marinated in 151-proof rum while she told me, with her hard, clear, bright good spirits, about an imperfect childhood. I told her about meeting James Dickey. Then I took her face between my hands, kissed that child on her forehead, and broke the news to her that she was now one of my own.

We finally said good-bye to Rebel in the Hotel Monteleone parking lot just after 4:30, two and a half hours before my plane left. She backed away down the street, waving and blowing kisses. I stood watching her, realizing that she would have walked on coals that night to show the geezers in her charge a good time; that in her untiring gaiety and readiness for anything, in her generosity and inattention to the regs, in her death grip on the *patate,* Rebel belonged on the cover of *Louisiana Sportsman's* every issue. If Tom and I and our various hearties had learned anything about Louisiana after two weeks and sixteen hundred miles, it was that the place goes for broke whether it has a toothbrush or not. And if that's not a working definition of a sportsman's paradise, I don't know what is.

NOVEMBER 1998

ALONE

by Philip Caputo

INDING CONNECTIONS BETWEEN APPARENTLY disconnected facts or events is a sign of genius or of madness. Isaac Newton linked the rise and fall of tides to the gravitational attractions between Earth and the moon. At the loony end of the scale is the right-wing militiaman who weaves the federal government, the United Nations, and the helicopter he heard fly over his house into a conspiracy to land saboteurs in preparation for a U.N. takeover of the country. I'm no Isaac Newton; therefore I wonder, as I sip whiskey beside a campfire deep within New Mexico's Aldo Leopold Wilderness, if I'm a little gone. For several days, something has been causing my brain to see conjunctions between things that any normal person would say have nothing to do with one another. Maybe it's too much solitude: For three weeks before this solo backpacking trip, I was living alone on a remote Arizona ranch, which is when the symptoms first appeared.

One night when a violent storm knocked out the power, I was crumpling newspapers to get a fire going in my adobe cabin. Two horrific crime stories on the front page of the *Arizona Republic* got my attention, and I found myself reading them by candlelight and then clipping them instead of consigning them to the fireplace. As I continued, a few other stories about subjects seemingly unrelated to the homicides also caught my eye. I read them and cut them out, too, and then, without quite knowing why, joined them to the crime stories with a paper clip.

Now, leaning against a log close to the campfire, I'm pondering what relationship the stories could possibly bear to one another. Whatever it is, I sense that it also has something to do with why I am here, alone in one of the vastest and possibly one of the last authentic wildernesses left in the contiguous United States.

The region is called the Gila, a term of convenience that applies to the 5,200-square-mile Gila National Forest in southwestern New

Mexico, as well as to the three wildernesses that form its primitive core—the Gila, the Aldo Leopold, and the Blue Range. Logging, mining, livestock grazing, roads, and motor vehicles are prohibited in the wilderness areas, whose combined territory could easily accommodate Rhode Island. Within them are mountain ranges nearly two miles high—the Mogollon and the Diablo, the Mimbres and the Black. Ancient forests of ponderosa pines, Douglas firs, and Englemann spruces bristle up the slopes, while agave and prickly pear cling to the canyon bottoms. Rare Gila trout hold in the pools of the streams and rivers, waiting for what food the swift currents bring them; elk graze in high alpine meadows, desert bighorn sheep stand poised on steep ledges, black bears prowl remote gorges. All in all, it's territory that at least resembles the America that stretched from sea to sea before the "stern impassioned stress" of Pilgrim feet began to beat a path that appears to have led our civilization to the shopping mall.

It is early spring and, because of the freakish weather stirred up by El Niño, still cold—nighttime temperatures of ten degrees at the higher elevations. The Gila is most heavily visited in summer and early fall, though it draws only a fraction of the mobs that descend on Yellowstone and Yosemite. Now, with the weather nippy and unpredictable, it is virtually unpopulated, solitude all but guaranteed.

Before I'd hiked in, I told John Kramer, the chief wilderness ranger (I'd love to have a title like that), that I wanted to minimize or, if possible, eliminate any chance of running into my fellow bipeds for the next five days. He suggested a route in the Aldo Leopold, which is named for the great conservationist who wrote *A Sand County Almanac*. The Gila Wilderness, twice the size of the Aldo Leopold and bordering it on the west, attracts more people because it contains prehistoric Indian cliff dwellings and its gateway is reachable by a paved road. The Aldo Leopold has no tourist attractions, and New Mexico State Highway 61—a narrow, rutted, washboarded stretch of dirt—is the only way to get to it by car.

Shortly before noon, I started up Route 61. It was posted with two signs that read CAUTION ROAD AHEAD RESTRICTED 4 WHEEL DRIVE AND HIGH AXLE VEHICLE. NO FOOD LODGING OR GASOLINE NEXT 120 MILES. The road turned out to be less formidable than advertised, but the side track to the trailhead for the Continental Divide Trail was a real axle-breaker if taken at speeds faster than five miles per hour. I tucked my dust-cloaked, mud-splashed Pathfinder behind the ruins of a corral, shouldered my pack, and hiked off. In the distance, scraping a heaven scrubbed clean of clouds, was my destination: the 10,100-foot crest of the Black Range, mantled in snow and the dark spruces and firs that, I surmised, give the range its name.

On this night, my first in the boondocks, I am somewhat pleased with myself. I have hauled a sixty-pound backpack through some five miles of wilderness, all of it uphill: a gradual ascent for the most part, but in a few spots fairly steep, the path a treachery of shale and rubble. I have pitched my tent, gathered firewood, strung my food bag high in a tree to avoid presenting bears with an occasion to sin, cooked my dinner of freeze-dried beef stew, and managed to get a good fire going in a woods still wet from the storm that passed through a couple of days ago.

But I haven't come all this way to prove what a manly fellow I am. Been there, done that; bought that T-shirt ten times over as a marine platoon commander in Vietnam, then as a war correspondent in the Ethiopian desert and in Afghanistan's Hindu Kush. I don't regard the great outdoors as a fitness center or an arena for athletic contests. Having hunted, fished, backpacked, and run rivers everywhere from Alaska's Brooks Range to Florida's Everglades, I've learned that merely getting from point A to point B in wild country provides sufficient challenge for anyone.

I have come all this way to take a kind of American walkabout. My reasons are contained in a remark Theodore Roosevelt Jr. made to one of his brothers, expressing his loathing for the sort of holiday we would call a "family vacation." "When I go," he said, "I go hard and I go alone." That should be every backpacker's motto.

I am going hard because I think it's important to test yourself. I am going alone because I wish to follow my own agenda, not a guide's; and because I don't want to deal with the needs, wishes, and complaints of a companion. I am seeking more than escape from the toe-jam of contemporary American society. I seek what wilderness engenders in me—the feeling and state of mind that I am supposed to have in church but seldom, if ever, do: joy. Fulfillment. Happiness. "To be dissolved into something complete and great," as Willa Cather wrote. The natural world is whole and sufficient unto itself; it doesn't need us or want us. It is stunningly indifferent, and yet, to immerse yourself in its completeness, if you can manage that surrender, is to grasp happiness.

Unfortunately, those ugly newspaper stories keep intruding. They hobble my pursuit, reminding me that if I am in a vast and beautiful cathedral, it is one surrounded by a much larger aesthetic and moral slum.

On February 24, 1998, in Phoenix, the *Arizona Republic* reported, a thirty-one-year-old unemployed laborer, John Sansing, high on crack with his wife, Kara, telephoned the Living Springs Assembly of God Church, asking for help in feeding his family. The church sent Elizabeth Calabrese, a forty-one-year-old mother of two, to deliver a box of groceries. According to the *Republic,* this is what happened next: When the good Samaritan appeared at Sansing's door, he pulled her into the living room, threw her to the floor, beat her over the head with a club, and then, with his wife's assistance, tied her to a chair. The couple did this in full view of their four children, ages nine through twelve, who couldn't understand why their parents were hurting the lady who'd brought them food. Their father explained it was for the money and showed them the cash he'd netted from Mrs. Calabrese's purse: $1.25.

Sansing then blindfolded and gagged her, dragged her into the master bedroom, and raped her while Kara watched. When he was through, he got a kitchen knife and stabbed Mrs. Calabrese to death. It had been quite a day for John and Kara; they left the body in the bedroom, went into the living room, and promptly fell asleep.

On March 22, 1998, the *Arizona Republic* reported mixed reactions to the news that Maricopa County, which encompasses Phoenix and its suburbs, was the fastest-growing county in the nation. It even outpaced Clark County, Nevada, where Las Vegas has been spreading like a gigantic oil spot. Between 1990 and 1997, according to the U.S. Census Bureau, Maricopa County welcomed an astonishing 574,097 newcomers. Developers and cheerleaders of laissez-faire growth were elated: "I think it's very exciting," gushed Jan Brewer, the chairwoman of the county board of supervisors. But some residents thought their desert paradise was repeating the mistakes of postwar Los Angeles, subjecting them to urban sprawl, overcrowded schools, polluted air, traffic jams, and more crime.

About the same time that the Census Bureau report was issued, this headline appeared in the *Republic:* MOM TORCHES KIDS. Kelly Blake, a thirty-four-year-old unwed mother of three, telling her children that they were going to play a game, lured them into a shed beside their Phoenix house. Once they were all inside, their mother poured gasoline on the children and set them on fire, then exited the shed. The two boys—John Fausto, fourteen, and Ramon Fausto, twelve—managed to escape. While John was trying to extinguish the flames that engulfed his brother, Blake doused herself in gasoline and set herself ablaze. Firefighters who arrived on the scene saved her life and John's, but nine-year-old Vanessa Fausto burned to death, while Ramon died of his burns the next day.

Meanwhile, back on the growth front, Tucson's *Arizona Daily Star* reported in its March 29 edition that as of 1996 there were 247 golf courses in the state, 129 in the Phoenix area (average annual rainfall: eight inches) and another 35 in Tucson (average annual rainfall: twelve inches). The metastasizing of greens and fairways is devastating the Sonoran Desert's ecology and draining the state's aquifers. It takes 185 million gallons of water per year—as much as is used by about thirty-six hundred people living in single-family houses—to keep the average eighteen-hole course looking lush. Conservationists were gearing up to battle developers and politicians eager to draw more tourists and retirees to the state by building still more links, the *Star* said. But one statistic cited suggested that the conservationists have about as much chance of halting the advance as the Polish cavalry had of stopping German panzers in 1939: Golf in Arizona brings in approximately *$1 billion* a year.

And, finally, this item, reported in the *Arizona Daily Star:* Scattered across a ridge in northwestern Albuquerque—New Mexico's capital and another Sunbelt city busting its seams—are some fifteen thousand petroglyphs that ancestors of today's Pueblo Indians carved into boulders spewed from five now-extinct volcanoes. The figures of horned serpents, masked men, flute players, birds, spirals, and stars are revered by Zunis, Hopis, Sandias, and Cochitis, who believe that the volcanoes link living people to the spirit world and the afterlife.

A six-lane commuter highway abruptly stops at the foot of the ridge, which was designated a national monument in 1990. Beyond it, out in the pristine Chihuahuan Desert, subdivisions for sixty thousand people are going to be built early next century, and the developers and their political allies want to extend the highway through the monument to connect the new communities with the rest of the city. They defend this plan by saying that the extension would slice off only a sliver of the petroglyphs: a little more than 8 acres out of a total of 7,244. To the highway's Indian opponents that is like saying that a proposed widening of Fifth Avenue in New York City will lop off only the front of St. Patrick's Cathedral.

"In Albuquerque, major roads stop at golf courses," a Cochiti Indian leader, William Weahkee, told a reporter. "Are those sacred sites to you guys?" He must have known the answer. A proposed alternative to the route had already been dropped, after residents realized it would amputate a few holes from a golf course in the suburb of Paradise Hills.

So now I am a long way from the places where little white Spaldings soar over the bones of Anasazi shamans, farther still from neighborhoods where sociopaths prompted by drug-jangled neurons rape and murder churchwomen. But I am still no closer than I was days ago to connecting the dots between golf and homicide and Indian petroglyphs.

I stoke the fire, flick on my penlight, and begin rereading *A Sand County Almanac*, both because I like it and because it seems a good way to express my gratitude. June 3, 1999, will mark the seventy-fifth anniversary of the creation of the Gila's wilderness areas. If God was their father and Nature their mother, Aldo Leopold was their midwife; he was working for the U.S. Forest Service in the early half of this century, and thanks to his impassioned advocacy, the wild heart of the Gila National Forest was spared from the ax, the chain saw, and the bulldozer.

The opening of his book, published almost fifty years ago, has always struck me for its clarity: "There are some who can live without wild things, and some who cannot. These essays are the delights and dilemmas of one who cannot. . . . Like winds and sunsets, wild things were taken for granted until progress began to do away with them. Now we face the question whether a still higher 'standard of living' is worth its cost in things natural, wild, and free. For us of the minority, the opportunity to see geese is more important than television, and the chance to find a pasque-flower is a right as inalienable as free speech."

The only thing wrong with backpacking solo is that you have to do everything yourself; the chores involved in pitching and striking camp take twice as long. But the brain-cleansing effects of solitude make it worth the effort. It is past ten-thirty before I am on the trail the next morning. The going is pretty easy, but the sixty pounds on my back make my progress less than Mercurial: a little less than two miles an hour. Because of the weather, I'm carrying more warm clothes than I'd originally planned, and because Kramer told me the springs up ahead have run dry, I've tanked up on water—a two-quart saddle canteen and two one-quart water bottles.

After an hour, I take a short break, faintly hearing in memory's ear a drill sergeant barking, *Take five, troopers. Lamp is lit. Smoke 'em if you got 'em.* Don't got 'em. Quit 'em, though I have brought five cigars: one for each night. I am looking westward, out across Rocky Canyon, at a landscape of such breadth and beauty that it seems to stretch the ligaments of my soul. The tiered foothills and mountains go from dark green to blue to purple at the horizon, where the Mogollons rise and their highest summit, Mogollon Baldy, is so slabbed with snow that it might be in the Canadian Rockies. In the middle distance, a pair of hawks orbit over a side canyon. They ride the thermal until something is revealed to their keen eyes, and they glide down and away, in a line so perfect it's as if they are sliding down an inclined cable. In thirty seconds, they disappear over a ridge that looks to be a mile from where they'd been circling. It would take me half an hour to cover that mile on the ground. Backpacking in rough country revalues the currency of distance; the mile cheapened by the car and rendered almost worthless by the jet plane once more costs something, and so means something.

I set off again. I do not intend to wander aimlessly on this walkabout: My plan is to reach Reeds Peak (now some six miles away and another twenty-five hundred feet up), follow the Black Range crest southward, past Mimbres Lake to McKnight Mountain, and then descend to the South Fork of the Mimbres River, tracing that to the main stem of the Mimbres, which will eventually lead me back to the trailhead. Thirty-five to forty miles altogether. Kramer warned me that I might not make it, however: There is deep snow on the crest, and the drifts could be waist-high on the north faces of the slopes below it.

And they almost are, as I discover around noon, when I reach eighty-five hundred feet. I am following fresh elk tracks, in the hopes of photographing the animal, but for the moment my attention is focused on the impressions its hooves have made in the drifts. I try to walk where the prints are only a few inches deep and to avoid those places where the elk's legs have drilled what look like post holes. As the day warms, the frozen crust thaws fast, and several times I plunge to my thighs. It takes an hour to get around the north face of this particular hill, and I'm chilled from the thighs down, drenched in sweat from the waist up. I've also worked up a raging thirst and emptied one water bottle and half the other. The map says that Aspen Spring is about a mile and a half farther on. Maybe, with all the precipitation, it has water in it.

The hike there is easy and exhilarating at first, but the trail then wraps around the north face of another slope and I am again hobbled by snow. Aspen Spring is dry; I am, too, and I drain my second water bottle. It is now two in the afternoon, and I will have to find a decent campsite in an hour or so. At about nine thousand feet, I encounter more deep drifts. Reeds Peak and the western face of the Black Range loom ahead. A brisk wind has risen from the south, and the sound it makes as it moves through the pines is sometimes like a waterfall, sometimes like the rush of an approaching train. Scanning the crest with my binoculars, I can see only snow, cascading down the slopes. It looks very cold and forbidding up there, and I remember that just last week Kramer and his rangers rescued seven young adventurers who had been trapped in the Gila by a sudden storm. They had run out of food and two were into advanced stages of hypothermia and had to be taken out on packhorses. "That's our best-case scenario in search-and-rescue work, a large group of fit young men," Kramer told me, leaving unsaid what was a worst-case scenario: a middle-aged man on his own. I decide to leave my trek along the crest for the future—maybe the fall, when the aspens turn gold.

I camp for two nights in as flat and sheltered a spot as I can find on a ridge overlooking the named and unnamed canyons that lace their way downward into the Mimbres River valley. I gather pine needles, pine cones, and dry grass, cut shavings from a dead stick of gambel's oak, then make a tepee of twigs over the tinder and strike a match. Advocates of minimal-impact camping frown on fire-making. I carry a backpacker's stove, but mostly for emergencies or for use in places where ground fires are prohibited. I think it's important to know how to make a cooking fire out of what's around rather than relying on a gas bottle. And a backpacker's stove can't keep you warm or provide cheer in the darkness.

At around 8:30 P.M. on my second night at the site, while I am thinking about absolutely nothing and savoring my nightly whiskey ration, I hear the most bizarre noise I have ever heard in the wilderness. It is coming from the east, near where the land falls steeply into a small canyon: a piercing screech with a pulse as regular as a metronome. With my flashlight, I walk toward it, and it never varies in tone, pitch, or rhythm. Could it be some high-tech signaling device used by lost hikers? "Is someone there?" I call out. "Somebody in trouble out there?" The noise stops. "Hello? Anyone there?" Silence. Ten or twenty seconds later, it starts again. Now I can hear that it's coming from up in a tree somewhere. A bird? I cannot think of a bird capable of making such an absolutely unearthly cry. Some sort of tracking collar? But tracking collars don't emit sound. A weather balloon that's fallen to earth and is sending a distress signal? But weather balloons are pretty big; in the bright moonlight, I would see one if it had fallen this close. How about space aliens? After all, this is New Mexico, land of Roswell. Once more I shout, once more it falls silent. All right, to borrow a line from the horror flicks—*it's alive!* I'm sure of that now. It also flies, because in a few seconds the sound starts coming from the south and from high above. Shrill, insistent, not frightening so much as irritating. At one point, I yell, "Shut the hell up!" And it does, but soon resumes and doesn't stop. After a while, I get used to it, so used to it that I actually crawl into my tent and fall asleep to that *screep-screep-screep*.

In the morning, while I'm melting snow for my morning coffee, I scour the woods, looking for bird droppings. I scan the branches but can't find a clue about the night's strange visitor. Two days later, the biologist for the Gila Wilderness will clear it up for me. I will learn that I had an encounter with a famous endangered species. The screech was the alarm cry of the female spotted owl, and I was what she was alarmed about.

If climbing through the snow to the crest would be too much adventure, backtracking to my truck would be too little. I break out my topo map, orient it, and see that the anonymous canyon below me strikes southeastward and joins another, which in turn tumbles down to meet the Mimbres River. On paper, a trek of about two and a half miles, but figure a good three and a half to four on the ground. And a fairly rugged walk for the first two, judging from the crowded contour lines.

Even in a wilderness, following blazed trails dilutes the adventure. The idea of going off-trail, into unnamed canyons, appeals to me. Also, there is sure to be fresh running water in the bottoms—my coffee and breakfast were seasoned with dirt, bark, and bits of leaves embedded in the snow I'd melted. Silencing the memory of the

Robert Service poem that Aldo Leopold quotes in his book—"Where nameless men by nameless rivers wander and in strange valleys die strange deaths alone"—I hoist my pack and start on down.

Soon, I hear the rush of water: A clear, swift stream, no more than a foot across, descends in a series of rocky steps. I fill my water bottles, drop in some iodine tablets, and while I'm waiting for them to take effect I shoot an azimuth down the length of canyon to make sure I've read the map right. Yes, 120 degrees magnetic. There is a lot of satisfaction in navigating cross-country with map and compass. I prefer that to turning everything over to a GPS. For one thing, you never know when the little box of microcircuits will go on the fritz; for another, not knowing where you are right down to the yard creates a certain pleasurable frisson.

The canyon is almost a slot canyon, with nearly sheer walls of sedimentary rock—sandstone, mudstone, conglomerate, ash tuff fused by volcanic eruptions and the collapse of calderas 30 million years ago. I am walking on ground perhaps trod by dinosaurs. I haven't seen any humans for three full days, but I've seen signs of them. Down in No-Name Canyon, however, I don't see a single boot print. The only trail is one blazed by elk and bears. The going is tricky, for the canyon falls in rocky ladders, creating tiny cataracts. There are windfalls and deadfalls everywhere, but I can see where the elk and bears have gone around these obstacles. I follow their lead—what the hell, they live here. Several times, I have to do some nontechnical rock-climbing to find a way around narrow gorges. I am very careful. The surtax for a lack of caution or a lapse in attention could be a broken ankle or leg, and I know Ranger Kramer and his rescue team would have a devil of a time finding me here.

An hour and a half later, I reach the junction of No-Name Canyon No. 1 with No-Name No. 2, which is twice as wide. I come across a recent bear dig, ten feet long by four wide by nearly two deep. To be on the safe side, I call out, "Bear, hey, bear," and make a lot of noise as I walk along. Grizzlies are gone from the Gila; the last one was shot in the 1920s by Ben Lilly, the famous mountain man and hunter. But I am not complacent about black bears; it's a matter of record, I've been told, that they have killed more people than the infamous *Ursus horribilis*.

Another two hours brings me to the Mimbres, which curves southwestward, glittering like a brightly jeweled cord. I make good time for the next three miles. Compared to the side canyons, the river valley is a park. White and violet wildflowers are beginning to bloom in the meadows. Far above rise cliffs fissured by eons of rain, sculpted by millenniums of wind into towers and minarets and spires.

Farther downstream, I have to make eight river crossings within a mile—and that slows me down. Tired, I decide to pitch camp in a trail-tramper's Eden: a knoll above the river, with soft, flat ground and plenty of standing and fallen deadwood. I perform the usual chores, wolf down dinner, and take up *A Sand County Almanac* while there is light enough to read. The line "Now we face the question whether a still higher 'standard of living' is worth its cost in things natural, wild, and free" leaps out from the page and discloses the common thread in the stories I clipped from the newspapers.

It is growth. The one thing our society does hold sacred is growth. Not intellectual or spiritual growth but economic growth; and not stable, sustainable economic growth but let-'er-rip, boomtown, pave-it-don't-save-it growth. Our grail is an ever-higher standard of living that must be sought and grasped at almost any cost: polluted air, a soaring crime rate, a degraded quality of life. But there is this difference between today and Aldo Leopold's day: Then, getting and spending was a big part of what we Americans were all about; now, it seems to be *all* that we are about. Our national religion is a kind of evangelical consumerism. We even consume things that aren't really things—we swallow the salt water of information by the gallon while our throats are parched for the springs of wisdom; we consume violence in computer games and on tabloid TV while we gorge on a home-delivered pizza.

Of course, we pay a price for a consumer culture such as ours, a culture that demands its instant gratifications. It isn't paid only in the coinage of rivers drained dry to irrigate golf courses or of sacred petroglyphs bulldozed to make travel more convenient for commuters. Our bodies pay a price: Study after study has shown that Americans are more obese now than at any time in history; we are the fattest people on Earth. We pay in lowered quality of our moral lives. Heinous crimes like John Sansing's and Kelly Blake's are not anomalies but signs of our spiritual emptiness, signs that what we have built over the past half century is not civilization. It may be development, but it's not civilization. It seems that the more we despoil the land and divorce ourselves from the rhythms, cycles, and beauty of the natural world, the less civilized we become.

Well, I am still no Isaac Newton, so am I crazy for making these connections? Hope not. In the past, this country needed a frontier as an outlet for people seeking to build new and better lives for themselves. I wonder, here beside the Mimbres River, if we need more wild places like this one as sanctuaries in which we can restore and renovate our inner lives. I think we would all benefit if more of us spent more time watching geese instead of television; if more of us devoted more time to absorbing the information wild creatures leave instead of filling our brains with the data-babble on the Internet. Woods and rivers can teach us lessons about patience and humility, about the interconnectedness of all living things, about discerning what is important and lasting and what is trivial and transient. Thoreau said that in wilderness lies the salvation of mankind. John Muir, in one of his essays on the California Sierras, wrote that each alpine wildflower was "a mirror reflecting the Creator." Maybe you don't believe in a Creator; so put it like this: Through that window we can see the grandeur in all creation, from atoms to galaxies; we can catch at least a transforming glimpse of something bigger than ourselves, something ineffable to remind us that consumption isn't the point of being human.

I have spent four nights in the Gila. Tomorrow, I will hike the remaining four miles to the trailhead, get in my truck, and return to what is commonly called the real world. But I'm not so sure it is.

AUGUST 1998

THE MOST DANGEROUS FRIEND IN THE WORLD

by Tim Cahill

YEARS AGO, A FRIEND of mine I'll call John C. took me to a restaurant in New York's Little Italy. When his cannelloni arrived, John asked the waiter, "What are these? Baked Hoffa fingers?" Seconds later the chef was at our table, carrying a gleaming cleaver. The cannelloni, he explained, gesturing vividly with the blade, "are not Hoffa fingers. Everything here is *fresh*-killed." Exit the chef. John was in ecstasy. "I think dinner ought to be fraught with danger," he said.

Few people, I suspect, would agree with John that veiled death threats are an aid to digestion. In fact, most people think my friend John is a jerk.

I found myself contemplating those cannelloni, jerks in general, and the pleasures of mortal peril in the days before I went off to spend several weeks this past summer in Colombia with Robert Young Pelton, author of the bestselling guidebook *The World's Most Dangerous Places*. Pelton, if I understand him correctly, believes that extreme jeopardy can be both life-enhancing and numinous. Billed as an essential guide to "getting into and out of areas sane people dare not venture," the book (and Discovery's Travel Channel show of the same name) combines advice on maximizing one's near-death experiences with quasi-journalistic dispatches from Pelton and his various stringers around the globe. There are impertinent interviews with Afghan warlords, recommendations of hotels in Algeria, and tips on how to contact a rebel group or survive a drive on a mined road (sit on your flak jacket). Most of Pelton's readers and viewers, of course, have no intention of ever putting this advice to use, but simply find it entertaining in a reality-based, *Survivor*-with-more-bite sort of way. Other people, particularly those such as foreign-aid workers and war correspondents who have no choice but to brave danger on a regular basis, are sometimes skeptical that Pelton is ever really in as much peril as he appears to be. They also think he's a macho, voyeuristic jerk.

Now, in my twenty-five-year career, I've traveled constantly and have found myself—always inadvertently—in a number of urban riots, negotiated with rebel factions for my safety, run from areas where various armies were shooting at one another, and been held at gunpoint more times than I care to remember. So my editors figured I could handle whatever Pelton got me into. If the skeptics were wrong about his level of exposure or he acted stupidly in seriously terrifying situations, I'd just make myself scarce. I intended to find out if he was a jerk, not if I was a hero.

Colombia was an easy choice. With a bloody thirty-six-year-old civil war, two major violent leftist guerrilla factions, several even-more-violent rightist paramilitary groups, a reputedly cruel and ineffective military, and a suddenly booming kidnapping business, not to mention the world's most active drug trade, this midsize Andean nation on the northwestern hump of South America was, hands down, the most dangerous destination we could have picked in the Western Hemisphere. Our plan, as Pelton described it, was simple: We'd fly down to the capital city of Bogotá and observe some military "operations" designed to show journalists that the army was competent, committed to human rights, and working to root out corruption. If possible, we would then shake our hosts and slip off into the bush to interview some seriously heinous guerrillas, the kind of "driven, resolute" people who, as Pelton describes in his newly published autobiography, *The Adventurist,* "burn fiercely, but briefly." If all went well, he told me, he should get some excellent footage for an upcoming *Dangerous Places* episode and I'd be back fishing at my Montana summer cabin in less than two weeks.

As Pelton worked out the details, I did some research of my own, usually boring stuff that I suddenly found scintillating when my life was at stake. A few months earlier, for instance, the U.S. State Department had issued an advisory saying that while it's not a great idea for American citizens to travel to Colombia "at any time," recent events presented "additional opportunities for criminal and terrorist elements to take actions against U.S. interests." The risk of being kidnapped in Colombia, the report said, was now "greater than in any other country in the world," with left-wing guerrillas accounting for most of the action and common criminals the rest, although the criminals sometimes made a quick buck wholesaling their richest hostages to the guerrillas.

The civil war had left more than thirty-five thousand dead since 1990, and homicide was now the leading cause of death for Colombians over the age of ten. A nine-year-old leader of a children's anti-violence movement had recently appeared on television pleading for peace. Several days later, three men carrying grenades and pistols dragged the fourth-grader off his school bus and spirited him away, apparently as a warning to any other loudmouthed kids with similar ideas. The next week, prosecutors finally figured out which guerrilla leader was behind the brutal murder of the country's most beloved TV-and-radio satirist, who'd been killed a year earlier when gunmen on motorcycles machine-gunned his Jeep Cherokee. Authorities had still not apprehended the fugitive.

Robert Pelton fired off a number of e-mails to me describing many of these same events. The one he headed "Bring your bank statement" concerned the Revolutionary Armed Forces of Colombia, or FARC, the largest and most powerful of the leftist groups. One of its field marshals, a man whose nom de guerre is Mono Jojoy (pronounced *moan-oh ho*-hoy), had announced a slight change in the organization's kidnapping policy. From now on, FARC would kidnap fewer ordinary people and focus on millionaires, which would be a more efficient way, he said, of countering aggression paid for by the government's own taxes on "Yankee imperialist" interests.

Research suggested that it was the worst possible time to go to Colombia, and Pelton was greatly encouraged by this. "Our timing," he e-mailed me, "is impeccable." You never knew what was going to happen, he continued, but there was every indication that our visit would be exceedingly eventful. There would be five of us traveling together. "Freak-outs," he warned (facetiously, I think), "will be sold to the highest bidder."

En route to Los Angeles on the first leg of my flight to Colombia, I finished thumbing through Pelton's autobiography. The forty-five-year-old author has said that he considers himself "only a passable writer," but the book is mostly compulsive reading. There are gloomy descriptions of his bleak childhood on the plains of Alberta. After his parents' divorce, Pelton, aged ten, was dropped off at St. John's Cathedral Boys' School, once described by Canadian *Reader's Digest* as "the toughest boys' school in North America," a place where boys ran fifty-mile snowshoe marathons and paddled huge freight canoes a thousand

miles in the summer. Later, when his mother and her new husband
decided it was time for Pelton to leave the nest, he bought a $150
Rambler and lived out of the car, picking fruit to make money. He was
sixteen. There are also testimonials to the lessons Pelton absorbed
while clawing his way to the top of the geek-eat-geek world of producing audiovisual presentations for corporate conferences. Of a pivotal
moment, soon after burying his father, when he decided that he was
destined for something more than the AV business, he writes, "It was
time to live like the wind and then to die like thunder."

Such occasional bombast aside, the most perversely satisfying parts
of the book are those in which he details his success with his current
enterprise. In 1993, the minor slide-show tycoon cashed out of projec-
tors and used the proceeds to buy the old Fielding Guides out of bankruptcy. Since then, Pelton has transformed the moribund guidebook
company into a travel-and-danger conglomerate, selling more than a
million books, producing one of the Travel Channel's highest-rated
programs, and hawking untold numbers of *World's Most Dangerous
Places* hats, T-shirts, and stickers, all of them festooned with the logo of
a laughing skull—"Mr. DP"—an icon Pelton designed himself.

Pelton, wearing a black polo shirt sporting the DP logo, picked me
up at the airport in his Mr. DP–edition African-safari-style Land
Rover. He was a big man, six-four, with big hands and feet and a
prominent beak of a nose, all of which combined with a pair of piercing gray eyes to give him the look of a slightly goofy eagle. He had
wanted me to stop off in L.A. to see the "normal" side of his life, but
first we had to drop by a TV studio. Pelton was scheduled to be interviewed on CNN about Sierra Leone, where several U.N. peacekeep-
ers had recently been taken hostage.

The anchor asked whether Sierra Leone was a dangerous country.
"Yes," Pelton said, "especially if you're in the U.N."

"It's not funny," the anchor said. (True enough, though the question was pretty laughable.)

Pelton lives in a spectacular converted 1960s tract home overlooking
the Pacific. He introduced me to Linda, his wife of twenty-five years,
and his blonde, athletic sixteen-year-old twin daughters, then showed
me out to the deck, high above the beach, where we promptly launched
into our first argument of the trip. He asked whether I'd packed appropriate jungle-colored gear. I told him that, in my experience, it was
best for Americans in dangerous locales to wear the brightest-colored

civilian clothing possible, so as not to be mistaken for anything but a dumb tourist. "Oh, no," he said. "We don't know what's going to happen. We could be on patrol with the army, with the guerrillas, and they're not going to want us around if we don't blend in."

This minor altercation called for some lubrication, and Pelton broke off to make us some gin and tonics. While he was inside, I asked Linda if she worried about Robert.

"He always comes back," she said.

"I gather you prefer not to think about it."

"Yeah," said Pelton, catching the tail end of this as he returned with our drinks. "The other night, she was watching my episode on the Travel Channel about Afghanistan, and she said, 'Oh, my God, is that what you do when you're gone?'"

I nodded and considered the fun times ahead.

If it weren't currently Kidnapping Central, we'd probably be seeing Sunday-travel-supplement articles—"Colombia, Country of Contrasts"—full of lyrical prose about "glacier-clad" mountains, vast tracts of pristine jungle wilderness, and stylish cities. The capital, Bogotá, is set at nine thousand feet and has skyscrapers and an abundance of rolling green parkland, giving it some of the feel of Denver, or at least a Denver with more than its fair share of serial killers. We stayed at a rather elegant European-style hotel. On one of our first nights there, the fun-loving desk clerk asked if we had been bombed, kidnapped, or shot. "Not yet," said Pelton, though it wasn't for lack of trying. He was asking people who should know—cops, cab drivers—which areas of the city we should avoid, and that was exactly where we went.

On the city's famed "street of sin" we encountered prostitutes and pimps and gang members engaged in drug deals, but we knew that the terror lay, for the most part, outside the city in various undeclared war zones. To experience that, of course, we were going to need to get our military hosts to trust us. Fortunately, Pelton's contact in Colombia, freelance journalist Steve Salisbury, had already started the ball rolling in this direction. And so, on our second afternoon in the country, the three of us, along with photographer Rob Howard and Pelton's cameraman, an ex–Special Forces operative named Rob Krott, piled into the wood-paneled office of General Fernando Tapias, sort of the Colin Powell of Colombia.

The general was articulate and avuncular, but not much of a source for riveting television material. His main point was that whatever parallels had been noted between the current situation in Colombia and the one in Vietnam circa 1962 were all wrong. "People assume U.S. soldiers are involved in these operations," said the general, as Krott filmed the scene. "There are just two hundred U.S. military advisers here, and none engage in operations. Still, whenever the guerrillas lose a battle, they always claim, 'It was against American troops.'"

In sum, the general said, the army was fighting a leftist insurgency that was less and less about ideology and more and more about drugs, as FARC guerrillas brutally moved to fill the vacuum that had existed since the Medellín and Cali cartels were crushed in the early 1990s. He also briefly condemned the atrocities and drug-trafficking ambitions of the rightist paramilitary groups (which, he failed to mention, are generally believed to be encouraged by the military). The general proudly described recent opinion polls that showed the army having a 69 percent approval rating, compared with a score of just 6 percent for FARC. On our way out he handed us a brochure, in English, that had a list of the names of all the soldiers and civilians who'd been murdered over the past year, plus some horrible full-color photos of the military casualties. One photo showed two brothers who'd been decapitated by FARC guerrillas. The heads, boxed up and sent to the men's mother, were pictured on page 3, followed by photos of dead men with their eyes gouged out, their chests and stomachs slit open, and their skulls pulverized. One soldier—this photo has disturbed my sleep ever since—had had his face sliced off and the underlying tissue melted with hydrochloric acid.

"These are the guys," Pelton said, referring to the face slicers, "we really ought to be talking to."

But first we had to let the army fly us up to the northern town of Cúcuta and watch them blow the hell out of some coca leaves.

In recent years, both leftist guerrillas and rightist paramilitaries have been exacting heavier and heavier "taxes" on coca growers and drug dealers in regions under their control. The government, in turn, has been devoting ever more resources to obliterating coca bushes, drug labs, and harvesting sheds. Cúcuta is a new hotbed of coca growing and its attendant strife. Just months before, fifty-one people had been murdered in Tibú and La Gabarra, two towns directly to the north and west, apparently by paramilitaries and revolutionaries trying to outmuscle each other for growers and distributors, and Cúcuta itself had been the site of frequent bombings by assorted sides.

Our escort, police captain Fernando Buitrago, had secured us rooms in a hotel chosen primarily for its proximity to the local station house. "Do not open your door to anyone," he said as we checked in. "Call me if someone knocks. I can tell, my friends, you are not safe here." I glanced over and saw that Pelton was filling out Rob Howard's registration card:

> *Name:* Howard the Duck
> *Occupation:* Rich American
> *Reason for visit:* Drug bust

This knack of Pelton's for laughing in the face of danger was, frankly, starting to get a little irritating.

Luckily, his humor, such as it was, went unnoticed. The festivities started with a helicopter ride. Thirty journalists were dropped on a hillside about twenty-five minutes into the boonies. Fields of waist-high coca bushes stretched to the horizon. There was also a little three-walled shack with a thatched roof, some plastic bags full of coca base, a bin full of silver-white coca leaves, and a few barrels of gasoline and ammonia. Presently, two planes flew over and sprayed the coca field with herbicide, while below, the drug lab itself exploded in picturesque billows of flame and black smoke. Pelton was filming all this with a small digital camera about the size of a box of Cracker Jacks.

"Good stuff?" I asked.

"Dog-and-pony show," he muttered.

The next day, it was off to the opposite end of the country, to Putu-mayo, the largest coca-growing area on earth. We were ushered into a prefabricated tentlike building, surrounded by razor wire and sand-bags, which Pelton began referring to as the circus tent. There, a Major Muriel laid out the situation for us in an interminable Power-Point presentation, complete with charts, maps, graphs, and many, many words on the army's commitment to human rights. Muriel told us that the country's rivers had become "ribbons of commerce in drugs and arms." Eventually, mercifully, we were led to a large pavil-ion overlooking one of the rivers. A young soldier stood at a lectern, reading from a script. "A narcotics lab is located across the river," he announced, and a helicopter swept out of the sky, strafing some trees on the far bank, while K.C. and the Sunshine Band's "I'm Your Boogie Man" thudded from the pavilion's sound system. Two open boats containing a dozen soldiers each came roaring out of the fog and blasted the same poor trees with .50-caliber shells. The boats landed, soldiers poured into the forest, there were the sounds of light-arms fire, and then silence, except for the disco.

"The drug lab is neutralized," the young soldier announced, and then the army flew us back to Bogotá. Pelton was in a funk for the entire flight. General Tapias notwithstanding, he thought the day's events had been "very Vietnam." The great connoisseur of hazard apologized for the dismal lack of menace anywhere and promised me that, in the very near future, we'd find danger if it killed us.

The next day, there was another one of those hideous crimes that happen with such appalling frequency in Colombia. In the rural town of Chiquinquirá, Mrs. Elvia Cortés, a fifty-three-year-old dairy farmer and mother of a banker, was fitted with an orthopedic collar made of PVC piping stuffed with twelve pounds of explosives. Eyewitnesses heard Mrs. Cortés yelling, "We've paid and paid and paid." A male voice replied, "You won't pay? We'll see about that." Mrs. Cortés was seen coming out of her house wearing the bomb. Police were called, and, along with an army explosives expert, they worked for five hours trying to defuse it. TV cameras were there filming the whole thing: the woman's terror-stricken face, the explosives specialist's caution, his attempts to calm her. No luck. The bomb exploded, killing them both. FARC was immediately fingered for the atrocity, though the authorities would later admit that they couldn't be sure about that. Occurring as the event did on the day after Mother's Day, the Colombian media began calling it the mother bomb.

We were among the first people in the country to hear about the mother bomb, because we were at police headquarters in Bogotá when it happened. The police, finally having tired of Pelton's demands for more "authenticity," were letting us spend the night with them listening in on 911 and riding along on calls. After the mother-bomb report, we watched as detectives took down a couple of armed car thieves, then accompanied an urban intelligence squad on a planned raid. As many as six armed militiamen thought to be affiliated with FARC were holed up in an apartment in northwestern Bogotá. We sped through the city in a six-car convoy. It was about three in the morning when we reached an area with unpaved roads and dim streetlights. The cops parked some distance from the target house, and we scurried through a muddy alleyway to a narrow street of three-story poured-concrete houses. While dogs barked hysterically from the roofs, one policeman—I couldn't believe this—knocked politely on the door of the suspected stronghold.

Pelton, in one of the little bits of advice scattered throughout *The World's Most Dangerous Places,* had suggested people in our situation take positions behind the front wheel of whatever car was parked on the street, where they'd be protected from bullets by the engine block. Naturally, there were no cars parked on the street. But I had a couple of police in front of me and a couple behind, and I planned to use them as my engine blocks. All of us were squeezed up against the wall under the balcony of the house to minimize the chances that any-one would get a clean shot at us. All of us, that is, except Pelton, who was standing out in a muddy field just across the street, filming the whole thing with his infrared-equipped Cracker Jack–box camera.

After some minutes the door swung open, the police swarmed in, and they came face-to-face with . . . a rather stout woman, two small children, and a fit-looking young man in his underwear. After some rummaging, the police unearthed a bunch of .38-caliber bullets and a few military-style backpacks and ski masks, but in terms of a firefight this had pretty much been a premature ejaculation.

Pelton and I, all revved up with nowhere to go, now started arguing about who'd acted more irresponsibly back there. I thought that a field thirty yards from the front window of the house wasn't exactly the best place to stand when you're expecting a firefight. He coun-tered that urban militiamen weren't likely to have rifles—"too con-spicuous"—and that he was out of pistol range, while the insurgents could easily have dropped a grenade on my head.

We were still arguing about this two days later, out in the middle of Colombia, on the Magdalena River, the country's longest ribbon of illegal commerce. The army had finally caved in to Pelton's badgering, so now we were in a gunboat of the sort we'd seen in Putumayo, with Pelton and me outfitted in helmets and heavy flak jackets.

A small ferry carrying dozens of passengers hailed us urgently from a distance. The passengers shouted that a column of guerrillas were stationed on the east side of the river—they were only minutes away.

All the passengers pointed in the same direction: *That way, guerrillas . . .*

Shells were jacked into our big guns, and we coasted slowly— agonizingly slowly—along the east bank of the river, where the grasses grew higher than a man's head.

"They're there," an officer assured me. "They see us. They won't shoot because they know they're outgunned. We're trying to draw their fire."

Good plan, I thought, and not without a certain amount of animosity toward Pelton.

That night, over drinks in the hotel bar, as a large-screen TV replayed the terrible saga of the mother bomb for about the seven hundredth time, I made a point of asking him what he gets out of continually putting himself in these situations.

"I know what some people think," he said, between sips of aguardiente, the anise-flavored drink he favors when in South America. "They think a travel guide to war zones is pathetic. Big-time journalists, for instance, assume that 'little people' should not be attempting their great feats. It pisses them off, because the democratization of information and experience just might contradict the drivel they write from the hotel bar. Journalists," he said, referring to me and my colleagues, "are mostly pompous pussies."

We ordered another round of milky-white liquor. "Look," he finally said, "I try to do an intelligent book for intelligent readers. You've got a guidebook on Colombia with you, right? Now you're here. Does it say anything about murder, kidnapping, war?"

"It's a little irresponsible that way," I said.

"Exactly." Pelton sipped his drink. "My book isn't about seeking danger. It's about finding safety in dangerous situations."

Over a third round, he admitted that, still, he'd probably never be able to find his way home in one piece if not for two critical influences. The first was that bastion of corporal punishment they'd called a boarding school: "That kind of experience affects different people in different ways. I'm actually thinking of making that my next book. I'll go around and talk with my old classmates and see what happened to them. I want to call it *The Breaking*." His other salvation is the daily reality check that comes from having a pair of teenage daughters and a woman you've been married to for twenty-five years. "I'm really proud of that. That's where I'm grounded," he said, and maybe this was the aguardiente talking, but for a moment he did sound it—grounded, I mean. A little, anyhow.

"Of course, the publishers didn't like the last book idea I suggested. It was going to answer all the big questions. You know, like, Why is there poverty?"

"You know?" I asked.

"That was the publisher's question."

"I'm guessing they found the whole idea just a little bit, oh, arrogant."

"Yeah, the imbecilic little shit-suckers."

He paused to drain his glass. Up on the TV, the announcer had turned to the question of who was really responsible for the mother bomb. Was it actually FARC guerrillas—as government prosecutors still suspected—or could it have been some other party intent on sabotaging the peace process and making FARC look bad? Despite the rebels' adamant protestations to the contrary, conventional wisdom seemed to be sticking with the first story. "What do you say," suggested Pelton, "we go down to FARC-land, ask Mono Jojoy and the boys if they're mama bombers?"

Photographer Rob "the Duck" Howard had left for an assignment in Egypt, and Rob Krott had flown to Cuba for his own wedding. So that left just me, Steve Salisbury, and Robert Pelton as the only gringos on the commercial flight to FARC-land.

San Vincente del Caguán, the capital of the region recently awarded to the rebels by the government as a peace gesture, turned out to be an authentic cattle-ranching town where the inhabitants rode around on horses and wore cowboy hats. As we stepped off the plane, we were accosted by Lelo, a forty-two-year-old cab driver who said he'd known the rebels for thirty-five years. Lelo found us a hotel that looked a lot like the cell block at the Bogotá police station, then led us over to the FARC office on the main square. Young, uniformed rebels, some of them in their mid-teens, sat on metal folding chairs out front, drinking Cokes. Each had an assault rifle, a machete, and a grenade or two.

One of the FARC youngsters took us inside and knocked on a door plastered with a poster that depicted an American flag being flushed down a toilet. The woman who answered, a rather sour information officer, explained that interviews with Mono Jojoy or any other rebel leader were out of the question without official permission. We thanked her for her trouble and headed back out to the square to regroup. After a fair bit of prodding by Pelton, Lelo agreed to just drive us to the rebel headquarters himself.

Twenty miles down a gravel road, we pulled up to a neat town of newly constructed buildings. "This is the rebel camp?" Pelton asked. Lelo explained that the Village of New Colombia had been built for FARC by the government in another extravagant peace gesture. Peace talks, in fact, were being held in a nearby building.

Poking our heads into the main complex, we saw rebels sitting at banks of computers, answering e-mails. There was also a public forum between concerned local citizens and the guerrillas' "Thematic Committee." A young man from the private-tourism sector proposed a "Tourist-Friendly Zone" in which no one would be kidnapped and massacres would be frowned upon. The Thematic Committee was taking notes on this idea when a new blue Toyota Land Cruiser pulled up. The driver, Mono Jojoy, was a stout man in a neat green uniform and a black beret. Seldom seen in public, Jojoy was immediately mobbed by civilian autograph seekers. Pelton, who was wearing the vaguely military-looking clothes we'd argued about in Los Angeles, approached to ask for an interview.

"You are CIA," Jojoy said.

"It's just the way he's dressed," I wanted to say, but Jojoy stepped on my best line of the trip, joking in a deadly serious kind of way, "You have a gun in those packs around your waist."

"I have cameras and batteries," Pelton answered. "Are you going to kidnap us?"

Jojoy shrugged and referred us to his provision that only millionaires would be kidnapped. Pelton was the only one of us who might have qualified—a millionaire CIA agent from the Travel Channel— but Jojoy skipped the credit check and disappeared into the crowd.

During the public forum, Sandra, a rebel information officer, asked whether we wanted to meet some FARC women. She said she knew the media always liked to take pictures of armed and uniformed women. We walked down to a tent camp in the trees, where we met several attractive female rebels, some as young as fifteen, poor farm girls whose main attraction to the cause, Sandra admitted, was the promise of regular meals. "Yes, I have killed in war," said one pretty twenty-six-year-old insurgent named Lucero. "I take no pleasure in it. The army is filled with poor people, too. They are just like us."

"Are you married?" Pelton asked.

"It is not permitted."

"Well, do you have boyfriends?" asked Pelton.

Jeez, I thought to myself, get him around a young woman with an automatic weapon and all that boozy family-man stuff goes right out the window. Lucero didn't seem to mind, though. She explained that while female comrades were forbidden from marrying, they could have a companion, or *socio*, if they obtained proper permission.

"And what if your *socio* is on the front fighting?" Pelton asked. "Can you have sex with someone else?"

"Yes, but we have to have permission."

We were approached by two FARC girls who asked if we wanted to hear them sing a revolutionary song. We sat for a long time waiting while they sought permission.

"Permission?" asked Pelton, amazed. "Permission to sing a revolutionary song? These are not my favorite rebels."

Later, back in San Vincente, we were at a cafe drinking coffee at the table next to Lucero's. She was sitting with a young civilian family, and at one point she squatted down to play jacks with their little girl. We all fell silent and watched them play, Lucero with her assault rifle slung expertly over her back. A great sadness descended upon me, and I didn't know why. "There," said Pelton, expressing the thought taking shape in my brain, "is a woman who wants a baby."

"These girls get passed around," he said. "I'm sure of it. They're sex slaves." I could almost see the "Sex Slaves" segment on Pelton's next TV show, but somehow it didn't seem so crass anymore. FARC-ettes are a familiar public relations contrivance, part of virtually every story produced on the guerrillas—the leftist equivalent of staged helicopter raids on nonexistent drug labs. So how come Pelton is the only person I know of who has ever bothered to ask them about the personal heartache involved?

Later the same night, we were invited to a rebel party at a nearby farm kept by the rebel leaders as a kind of country retreat. For the occasion, Mono Jojoy, our host, wore a black beret with a gold star, "to honor Che Guevara," he said. Pelton told me he thought it made him look like a pissed-off Frenchman.

"Should we be afraid?" Pelton asked. Salisbury was translating.

"Afraid?" Jojoy threw down another shot of Absolut, which was being passed around in small plastic glasses. "Ha-ha-ha," he said.

"Ha-ha-ha," we agreed.

"But you don't like gringos," Pelton persisted.

"I like gringos who want to help the people," Jojoy said. "Gringos who don't help the people . . ." He drifted off into an ominous silence.

We were all sitting on new plastic lawn chairs in front of an old farmhouse about five miles down a dirt road from San Vincente del Caguán. It was getting dark, and a rebel named Cristian was sitting across from us, filling the plastic cups. There were, at a guess, a dozen heavily armed guerrillas at our party.

"The gringo human-rights workers FARC killed," Steve Salisbury said, referring to the three Americans FARC had slain in March 1999, "they wanted to help the people, no?"

A thin, intense man with a neatly trimmed beard, named Iván Márquez, said that those gringos had been slaughtered "in error. It was like when your planes bombed the Chinese embassy in Yugoslavia," he said. "It was an error."

Márquez began speaking about tenets of Marxism: how the workers of the world should unite, because the only thing they had to lose was their chains; how religion was the opiate of the masses; how an entrenched capitalist oligarchy exploited the poor. . . . "These are old, tired ideas," Pelton said. "They didn't work in Russia. Why do you think they would work here?"

"It will be different here. It will be Colombian Marxism." Márquez glared at Pelton, and the mood soured.

"Come on," Pelton said. "Don't pump sunshine up my ass. In what way will it be different?"

Steve Salisbury didn't like the turn things were taking and translated the "sunshine" part of the question as: "You are very eloquent. Where did you study these ideas?"

"At the University of FARC," Márquez said. He glanced around fiercely, daring anyone to challenge these credentials. "The University of FARC," he continued, "makes Harvard look like nursery school."

Jojoy said, "Don't take any more notes. This is a party." The vodka was doing its work, and Jojoy had begun slurring his Spanish. "Tell me," he said. "You are really CIA, no?"

"I am making a film for the Travel Channel," Pelton said.

"What do you really want?" Jojoy asked.

"I want to film a real guerrilla camp," Pelton said. "I want to eat guerrilla food. Go on patrol."

"What is the name of your program?" one of the guerrillas asked.

"The World's Most Dangerous Places," Salisbury said—a bit apprehensively, I noticed.

"You think this is a dangerous place?" Márquez asked.

"If you're in the CIA," Pelton said.

"Ha!" Mono Jojoy said. "Ha-ha-ha."

And so said we all: "Ha-ha-ha-ha."

Pelton dug into one of his bags and brought out a half dozen large Mr. DP stickers.

"It's a military symbol," one of the rebels said, handing off the jolly skull to another guerrilla. "Military," the second man agreed. If there is one thing FARC members hate more than American imperialists, it's American imperialist military advisers. "What does this mean?" Mono Jojoy asked in a menacing whisper.

Pelton said Mr. DP was actually a thoughtful kind of fellow and was meaningful to those people who really wanted to know what was happening in places that were being ripped apart by war or rebellion, places from which reporting was spotty or inaccurate or colored by political agendas of one sort or another.

The guerrillas behind us were talking loudly about kidnapping and the sum of one million dollars.

Pelton plowed on, describing Mr. DP's philosophical connotations: Mr. DP wasn't political; Mr. DP didn't take sides; Mr. DP wanted to see for himself, talk directly to the people involved. And if there was danger involved in that, why, Mr. DP laughed in the face of that danger. Mr. DP was a symbol for all courageous, intelligent, fair-minded people.

Pelton, I thought, was veering off into some serious bullshit, a perception apparently shared by Mono Jojoy, who said, *"En realidad, ustedes son los monos"* ("You guys are the real monkeys"). This was a foreboding statement. *Mono,* in Spanish, means "monkey," but in Colombia it also refers to a light-skinned person such as our host. I hoped he meant that our skin was even lighter than his. I feared he meant that we—as obvious CIA military-adviser imperialist lackeys— were dumber than monkeys for coming here.

In an attempt to defuse the situation, Salisbury hurriedly began trying to joke with Jojoy at a furious and not entirely intelligible pace.

"Jojoy," Salisbury shouted, and reached out to shake Mono's hand. The word is also a common greeting in Jojoy's home province of Santander. "Ho-hoy, ho-hoy," Salisbury said rapidly. "In English we have a similar word, *ahoy*. We say, 'Ships ahoy!' Ha-ha-ha! Mono Jojoy, ships ahoy!"

"Shits hohoy?"

"No, no!" Salisbury said, "not *shit, mierde—ships*, ships, *barcos*, boats, ah-hoy, ahoy there, ha-ha-ha." Steve's comedy act was dying, for want of a better word, and that made him try all the harder. Better to have the rebels laugh in your face, I guess, than slice it off.

I picked up on the strategy and turned to Cristian, who was pouring the vodka. "No more for Mr. Steve," I said. "Mr. Steve is very drunk." (Actually, Salisbury had had about a thimbleful of vodka.) "Ha-ha-ha. Look, Mr. Steve doesn't make any sense at all. Ha-ha."

Jojoy, ignoring Salisbury, turned to Pelton and said, "We can show you a real guerrilla camp right now. You can eat real guerrilla food."

Someone else added, "You can cook guerrilla food."

"Stay as long as you like," Jojoy offered.

"Maybe longer than you like," another voice added.

"We can leave right now," whispered Jojoy.

Pelton, Salisbury, and I asked for a moment to confer among ourselves. We walked over to Lelo, who was waiting with the cab, and he suggested we get the hell out of there, fast. Salisbury and I agreed. Pelton said, sensibly for once, "Yeah, well, I think we ought to go."

For a guy who doesn't consider himself a journalist, Pelton did pretty well. We interviewed the heads of the army and the national police; we interviewed or at least met every major FARC leader. Still, when I talk about my time with him, there are those folks of fine sensibility who remain convinced that he is a jerk. Some find his logo, Mr. DP, especially repellent. Massacres and slaughter and human suffering almost beyond imagination are not funny. Of course, neither is nuclear war and the end of civilization as we know it, but that doesn't mean *Dr. Strangelove* is a bad movie.

Sometimes, in defending Pelton, I point out that he thinks volunteer work is one of the best ways to begin to understand a dangerous place. Organizations that do good work are listed in his book. One could assist refugees searching for their relatives in Rwanda, or clean toilets in the Congo, or help clear land mines in about half the countries on earth. But defending Pelton is a thankless task. The guy doesn't really care about what he calls "flatulent political correctness," is congenitally arrogant, and expects his work to speak for itself. I suppose I stand up for

Pelton because we spent some intense time together, working reasonably hard at not getting killed or kidnapped, and that is the basis of at least one kind of concentrated friendship. Still, I wouldn't travel with him again on a bet. Robert Pelton really does go to dangerous places, and he really does do dangerous things. He's not a fraud, and for that reason, I worry about him. A lot. The jerk.

NOVEMBER 2000

Editor's Note
In January 2003, Robert Young Pelton and two American journalists were kidnapped in the Darién province of southeastern Panama by 150 armed men belonging to the right-wing United Self-Defense Forces of Columbia (AUC). They were released to the Roman Catholic Church after four days.

CUTTING HORSE ROAD

by Thomas McGuane

IT WAS A UNIQUELY brutal December in Montana. In my haystack, spaces between bales were filled with dead songbirds, a whole flight that missed the southern migration in an early storm. Our driveway drifted in with snow on a daily basis. On our front porch hangs a wind chime, audible throughout the kitchen and generally pleasant. It became more active in December, but by January it sounded like Lionel Hampton on crank.

We caught a ride to California for four of our horses and began to scheme about getting warm. For a month, they basked while my wife, Laurie, and I fought the good fight and paid their board by U.S. mail. We wanted to join them and go to some cuttings, our customary form of escape.

When we've traveled with our horses, we have often felt uncomfortable leaving them unattended at rodeo grounds while we hunted up a motel, then slept but lightly, imagining hooligans letting them out, throwing firecrackers into their stalls, or stealing them, all things we've heard of happening. Various companies that make trailers have learned how to supply the needs of worriers like my wife and me. They build horse trailers with compact living quarters for the humans. Our children, who see a risible connection to the world of RVs, have, after the Winnebago, dubbed ours the Horseabago. My friend Jim Harrison is more thoughtfully reminded of the French farmhouse wherein folk and livestock are separated only by a wall thinner than those at a Super 8. We simply pictured ourselves in one end, and Delta, Sassy, Zip, and Lena in the other, with wheels underneath.

We wrote the check and drove off with our Labrador, Shelagh, to take delivery in central California and then set out for home by the Great Circle Route to compete in some cuttings and see some country—towing four horses, four saddles, ten bridles, eight saddle blankets, three breast collars, two hoof picks, shoeing tools, equine pharmaceuticals, alfalfa, timothy hay, buckets, brushes, slickers, boots, clothes, a toilet, a shower, a stove, a microwave, a refrigerator, a bed, a table, an awning, a sink, and a color TV. It was a modern farm at seventy-five miles per hour.

We were headed for a cutting at the DLR Ranch in Temecula. To calm my nerves while crossing the cities of southern California, I listened to Arnold Weinstein's audiotape lectures on classic American literature. Laurie suggested at one point that this implied a two-track existence between the cultivated and the moronic, and that sooner or later we would have to choose. *Faw!* as the old fur trappers once exclaimed when faced with sibylline conundrums. The real test, as far as I was concerned, lay not in our capacity to withstand incongruities like cutting-horse contests in Southern California, but rather in our ability, after a quarter century of living on the wide prairie—sometimes just wide enough for our prickly dispositions—to reduce our playing field to what Barbra Streisand would reject as a shoe closet. We would see: Weeks of aluminum-bound intimacy lay ahead.

Years ago, I took a twelve-year-old broodmare that I owned to a cutting-horse clinic in Livingston, Montana. She was out of shape, and I didn't know what to expect. But I knew she had once been a cutting horse. When my turn came, I rode her into the herd of cattle that milled at the end of the arena. All I had to do was cut one cow from the herd. But each one I tried slipped past me.

Already the mare had begun to change beneath me. I felt her heightened alertness, a flow of new energy. The reins with which I guided her required a lighter and lighter touch. Finally, one cow stood in front of us. The mare's attention was riveted, and I no longer needed the reins at all.

When the cow tried to get back to the herd, I knew I would ride cutting horses for the rest of my life. With liquid quickness, the mare countered every move that the cow made. Riding her on slack rein gave me a sense of controlled free fall. Centered between the ears of my horse as if in the sights of a rifle, the cow faked and dodged. Much of the time I didn't know where I was or where the cow was, and I was certainly no help to the horse. But by the time I picked up the reins to stop, I was addicted to the thrilling shared movement of cutting, sometimes close to violence, which is well beyond what the human body can ever discover on its own.

In ranch work, the cutting horse is used to sort out unproductive cows from the herd, to separate bulls, to replace heifers, and to bring out sick or injured cattle for treatment. The herd instinct of cattle is extremely strong, and to drive out an individual cow and hold her against this tidal force a horse must act with knowledge, skill, and precision. Otherwise, the cow escapes and returns to a thoroughly upset herd.

The day of the cutting horse as a common ranch tool is waning, and the training and use of cutting horses has become largely a sporting proposition. To deny this would be like claiming your old bird dog is just another food-gathering device you maintain to keep your kitchen humming. Still, there is beauty and grace in a cutting horse, as well as a connection to a world older than we are. Amazingly, cutting horses can be found in every state in the Union, and competitions sanctioned by the National Cutting Horse Association are held in the lower forty-eight states and Canada.

As a sport, cutting has a low entry level. Anyone who is reasonably comfortable riding can get on a cutting horse, hang on tight to the saddle horn, and feel the satisfaction and excitement of sitting astride a trained cow horse. But the journey to competence can be very long, and the frustration can be extreme. You must learn to ride in a way that does not drag at the motion of the horse. The body language between you and the horse must be bright and clear. A polished cutter sits in the middle of the saddle, holding the saddle horn but not pushing on it, never slinging his weight or dropping a shoulder into the turns. This quiet, eye-of-the-storm riding style is not easily achieved on the back of a sudden-moving, half-ton athlete. But to violate this style is to take the horse's mind off his work and increase his vulnerability to the movements of the cow.

Cutting begins and ends with horses—the minds, bodies, and souls of horses. You have to have a deep love of the animals to endure the training. If you don't sense a kind of magic in watching a horse take two steps, or put his nose underwater, or switch flies, there's no real point. Cow-horse people sometimes can't tell their horses from themselves. You either learn to look at the world through the eyes of a horse or you quit cutting.

We began by renting a small farmhouse for a few weeks near Los Olivos, California. We had stolen guiltily away from our home in Montana. If you leave Montana for so much as one day in January, the neighbors will greet you on return with "Back for the summer?" It's barely worth it. The atmosphere was California agricultural, with an eager rooster who climbed onto a 1974 Oldsmobile Toronado engine block right below our bedroom window and announced the day an hour before dawn. My horse Zip had injured a suspensory tendon, and we were trying to get him treated, if not rehabilitated, before we left to go cutting. Each day we worked all four of our horses, getting them to run straighter, stop harder, turn faster, and read cattle more accurately.

In the farmhouse, I built up the courage to take on the L.A. freeways in my pickup truck and thirty-eight-foot horse trailer. After three weeks, I was emotionally tuned up for the trip. I had watched semi trucks with new admiration. Laurie had prepared for the trip by buying a cell phone with which to stay in touch with everyone. And I had promised that there would be no road rage, a tall order in a state where car dueling is a way of life.

The day of departure arrived, and we loaded our four horses and increasingly worried dog in the dark. We were up even before the neighbor's rooster. We were ready to go. We had everything with us and were prepared for traveling in all kinds of weather. At the moment, it looked like rain. I managed the driveway without mishap, though we required both lanes of the road to pull out. The various running lights on the trailer streaming behind me gave me a vague Casey Jones feeling as I started down our long canyon toward the freeway, eight miles distant. When we reached it, traffic was still moderate and I was able to pull on and get up to speed and take my place modestly in the slow lane. Laurie was doing preliminary map work for the blizzard of interchanges that faced us some hours down the road. Between times, she read the instruction manual for her cell phone.

As the sun began to come up, we passed Point Conception, which lies seaward of the highway and gives the impression of an oak-filled expanse of ranch land that extends to the sea without interruption. After the racehorse farms, we passed vast citrus groves with what appeared to be this year's harvest rotting on the ground. Spinning along in the semidark with us were the laborers in their jalopies, hurrying to pick the food and clean up the messes. Their favored machine was a stylish and utterly used-up compact car whose pert design contrasted morbidly with its current dilapidation. These are often on the highway covertly, having flunked the California emissions test. It is all their occupants can do to keep California from collapsing. But there we all were, heading south with a thousand different missions and obligations, and the urgency of the highway was building fast.

And then we were crossing Los Angeles, part of an infinitely complex symphony of traffic. I found myself, as I always do when driving long distances in California, becoming caught up in the local obsession with the automobile. As we passed car lots, I tried to spot sexy new models, despite the fact that I was hurtling along with a load of hay and horses. "There's the new BMW roadster!" I cried out to Laurie, who was fixated in sensible terror over her map. But I was picturing the wind in my hair, bucket seats, the beach. I was recalling happier days of hot-rod obsession—Deuce roadsters, flathead Fords, magical names like Edelbrock and Iskinderian, speed tuners from deep in my car-crazed memory. Traffic poured into my flanks from either side, until I was part of a southbound river of metal, confined in four directions to the gestalt of a 72 mph traffic jam. It was impossible to know where to place myself. If I picked what I thought was the slow lane, it either turned into a bombardment of oncoming traffic or, worse, it became a nearly inescapable exit lane to Pomona or Palm Springs. Since I could not imagine being swept onto one of these off-ramps with any hope of return, I hit the turn signal and forced my way back into a through lane in a cascade of indignant horn blowing. Most cars would finally yield, but I soon learned to spot the goatees and backward caps of the demented drivers who would rather ram their cars into one of the horse stalls than let me back into their lanes.

At length, we made it to Interstate 15, bound for Temecula, a dizzily evolving small, Western-looking town that is sending out malls and planned hamlets in all directions, up and down the hills into the special California great beyond. A couple of years ago, we had admired a new town surrounding a broad, gentle lake; this year, the lake was gone. "Where's that lake?" Laurie shouted intemperately. As a child of Old Alabama, she is furious at all this moving about of the landscape and is weirdly obsessed with natural features "staying put."

I was still occupied with the real business of being here, playing it as it lays at 3,000 rpm. I had one off-ramp to conquer, followed by a hard left. Laurie was fiddling madly with her cell phone, which had numerous tiny buttons, unparalleled range, more memory than any of our children, and palm-snuggling ergonomics. She had started our trip by buying bulk-rate airtime, which gave me the sense that we were falling off the end of the Earth. Not much had happened with the phone, though I'd heard Laurie cry, "I can't get any reception!" a few times, after our speculations as to whether various of the kids had "gotten there yet" or "heard about that job." The little phone had so far only emphasized our distance, producing affectless recorded messages from a communications empire identified to us only by its acronym. I rather thought that KGB, IBM, CIA, ITT, and so on had begun running together.

The stoplight was out at the bottom of the off-ramp. In its place was a well-groomed police officer, directing traffic. I stopped and awaited his directions. When he noticed me, he furiously waved at me to make my turn, as though I should have known what to do in the first place. I rolled down my window as we passed him and said that I had been waiting for him to signal me. "Fuck you!" shouted the California police officer.

We made it to the fine and expansive DLR Ranch, where I felt liberated to have so much wiggle room for my big rig. I swung around in a circle, cut it too tight, and managed to burst the back window of my truck on a corner of the trailer with a big noise and in full view of everyone. "I'll never live this down," I commented to a cutter from Northern California. "No," he said, "until someone else screws up, you're 'the trailer guy.'"

We picked a nice place to set up our camp. I had never before experienced such a bounty of water and electricity hookups. Laurie and I sometimes fuss at each other about where to park, and parking a rolling home is akin to the selection of a home site. One must form a principle along the lines of "I'm doing the best I can. I know there are no trees, but there's water."

The world of rolling homes is oddly genderless, though the boys who are mechanically inclined try to isolate themselves on an RV Olympus with specialized information about things you can't see, like the insides of motors. In real RV clusters, there is often a soothsayer who treats the big rigs with a laying-on of hands and sacerdotal murmuring: "Bleed the hydraulics now or you'll never get 'er stopped"; "She's losing everything through the intercooler"; "They're all squirrelly at seven thousand feet." And so on.

Laurie and I unloaded the horses, fed and watered them, hooked up power and water, jacked the trailer, and released the truck. Rain started to fall, and soon we were tucked away in the trailer, supper cooking, operation manuals for water pumps, holding tanks, hot-water heaters, microwave ovens, propane tanks, and generators spread out on the dinette table. The rain drummed down.

When we fed our four horses early the next morning, I noted all the horses and trailers that had arrived while we slept. Several had living quarters. There were hundreds of cutting horses, heads sticking out of stall doors, impatient for breakfast. Under the shed roofs, people stumbled in from the rain, wearing boots whose weight had doubled with the masses of mud and a local gumbo called DG, for deteriorated granite— a substance that abrades and ruins shoes in record time. While the horses ate, Laurie and I had a look at the cattle, which were penned about a quarter mile away. They were light, fast-looking Brahma cattle with a lot of ear. We would have to be on our toes to manage these little rockets. You can pretty much tell what latitude you're on in the American West by looking at the cattle. Go far enough south and they will be dewlapped and down-eared; as you head north, the dewlaps disappear, while the ears shorten and angle increasingly upward. Finally, at my parallel, the forty-fifth, you see the customary easygoing English cattle—Angus and Here-ford—with a sprinkling of exotics like Charolais, Simmental, and . . . you back there, bouvier des Flandres is a *dog*, not a cow.

Jimmy Kemp, a cutter from Brady, Texas, who had been cooking for masses of friends at contests all winter, stuck his hand into the rain and said, "I wonder what we ought to eat tonight." No one knows what gustatory windfalls might be found at Kemptown, which encom-passes Jimmy's trailer and the surrounding appurtenances, including a huge propane-fired barbecue and a prep table. Meals in the past have been crawfish étouffée for forty, several dozen wild quail cooked over coals, fresh asparagus, new potatoes, portobello mushrooms, big bacon-wrapped Gulf shrimp, and aged steaks. Jimmy rides a smart gelding he calls Einstein, pronounced "Ahnstahn." We all hope Ein-stein takes him to plenty of pay windows so he can invest his winnings in food. Jimmy Kemp must be an optimist, because I have loped circles with him at daybreak on our horses and listened to him plan the evening menu.

I was already nervous because I had never competed on my horse Lena before. My usual mount, Zip, had been lame for a year, and it seemed like I had talked about nothing but lameness in horses that entire time, hock problems in hard stoppers like Zip, stifle injuries, caudal pain, splints, sweenies. I'd tried everything: radiography, bone scans, cortisone injections, isoxsuprine, butazolidin, break-over aluminum shoes, chiropractors, masseuses, and magnets! But he healed very slowly. So I bought a nice young mare from Jan and Jerry Bob Seago in Oklahoma, beautifully trained by Jerry Bob. When I went down to try her, I got completely lost in the various animal-based interests of the Seagos and nearly forgot why I was there. There were longhorn cattle wandering around the yards, numerous cow dogs, twenty or thirty horses, yearling cattle, and, in an extended yard, an enthralling breeding operation for fighting cocks. Jerry Bob said, "I like coming down here, get away from them goddamn horses." He said it with the same fatalism he had when he'd gestured at his place happily and said, "What can I say, we're Okies."

Looking around at my rather complete rolling home, I considered the example of my friend Don, a single man who rides cutting horses. He enjoys meeting women on his trips and has often said to me that the key is having a good cooler. He keeps his Igloo filled with sophisticated snacks: Black Diamond cheddar, Fuji apples, a crisp Traminer, refreshing lagers, sourdough baguettes, alder-smoked chicken or turkey or ham, red onions, lovely Norwegian sardines. "You run a good cooler," says Don, "and you won't be able to keep them off with a stick." I was not in a position to try to overpower Don's cooler with my Horseabago, but I felt it was in the air that I could if I had to.

Roger Peters and his wife, Lisa, old friends from Nebraska, paid us a visit. Roger and I each had owned a Lucky Bottom horse, and they were two of the best, Roger's Lucky Bottom 18 and my Lucky Bottom 79. They were extremely snorty but talented horses that required infinite understanding. Roger had, at the time, an enterprise in Nebraska called Peters' Wieners, with the motto "Nobody beats our meat." Today, Roger and Lisa, after the usual pleasantries, had something they wanted to take up with us, and I sensed their reluctance to intrude. Finally, Roger spoke: "I don't want to stick my nose in where it doesn't belong, but I hope you are using RV-recommended toilet paper." I assured him that we were. "Because if you don't," Roger went on in a more emboldened fashion, "your waste tank is going to be the most ungodly wreck. I mean, you really don't want to see what happens." This seemed to have been accompanied by the roll of kettle drums.

❋   ❋   ❋

I had a terrible draw on Lena, dead last on wild cattle. I studied the herd, trying to pick out some cattle that I hoped wouldn't run me over. Someone suggested the brindle mot (short for "motley-face"; also called "brockle-face" or "brock"). There was a nice redneck cow with a smeared brand I hoped no one else would cut and a "race cow" that presented itself as workable but that you couldn't hold with a gun. In a herd of seventy-five head, they tended to blur together, and late in the draw it was like a swarm of bees in there. I rode in and couldn't find any of my favorites. I cut a hard-moving Brahma heifer who got right in Lena's face. Lena stopped with such deep smoothness that we were able to handle things at pretty high speed without getting beat. In the increasingly muddy conditions, she was sliding halfway past the cow but still getting back to hold it. I got up over her too much and really had to push off the saddle horn to stay where I belonged. Laurie managed to have a respectable run on Delta in ghastly conditions, and we hung around to see if we might limp into the money. The rain fell harder, and when Jimmy Kemp walked by, he held out his hand, palm up, and said, "This might be a good night for chili." Finally, the footing gave out and the announcer stated, "No sense crippling you or your horse," and called it off for the day.

We put up our horses and fed them early. We went into the living quarters of the trailer, left all the muddy clothes in the tack room, and . . . got into our bathrobes! This seemed too good to be true. The rain beat down on the roof, and Laurie made hot chocolate on the stove. I stretched out on the couch and got so lost in a strange Brazilian novel that I forgot where I was until the cocoa arrived. Laurie lay down in the opposite direction, and we abandoned ourselves to lavishing admiration on our horses. I explained how pleased I had been with Lena's ability to bear down on wild cattle, watch them closely, and take care of the work at hand. I added flourishes about her big eyes and graceful neck, her neat thoroughbred feet and long pasterns. I noted how she passed the loping horses without ever getting out of her smooth, extended trot. And her stop! Montaigne said four hundred years ago, "There is nothing in which a horse's power is better revealed than in a neat, clean stop." Lena stops so deep, I have to bell-boot her front feet to keep them from being hit by her back feet. Laurie listened to all of this patiently. She believes—and I agree—that her little mare, Delta, is the horse of her lifetime. Indeed, they fit together brilliantly. Delta is just a little over fourteen hands and has the personality of a Labrador who has always lived in the house. She follows Laurie around sleepily, checking her pockets for treats, sighs languidly when she's being saddled, and seems too weary to be warmed up and generally unable to decipher what all the excitement is about. Furthermore, she is afraid of cattle. But when Laurie cuts a cow out of the herd, something happens. The sleepy eyes turn into two hot coals and the inner Delta emerges, a blazing-quick cow horse with so much style and precision that Laurie has the ongoing task of fending off importuning buyers.

I felt guilty about all my comfortable lying around the trailer and got up and dressed to water my horses. I stopped to talk to Don Boon, a serious competitor from Texas who rides a terrific gelding he calls Bullet. Bullet has enabled Don to win a tremendous amount of money, despite the gelding's numerous leg ailments. One day, the young man who trained Bullet called Don and said he had another horse just as good. The owners wanted to sell him immediately, and he was moderately priced. Don sent a check, and the new horse was delivered. He was not as good as Bullet. Some months later, Don ran into the trainer—and a fine trainer he is—at a Texas cutting. "How'd you like to show Bullet in the open?" Don asked. The trainer was thrilled. He showed him and won the open. Later, when the two were sitting in the stands, the trainer asked Don, "How is it you decided to let me show Bullet?" "I let you show Bullet," said Don, "so that the next time you call me and tell me you got a horse just like Bullet, you'll know what you're talking about." Interestingly, this was not told as a reproachful tale but rather as something more good-natured, in the manner of a card player describing how he guessed someone else's hand.

By the end of the Temecula cuttings, we were emerging from our winter rust and beginning to move at the same speed as the horses under us. The coefficient of drag was on the decline. We would soon be departing, and there were details of housekeeping to which I, as co-owner of a rolling home, would have to attend. I decided to work with the sewage and wastewater outlets. I use these two terms advisedly, because at the outset I didn't quite know the difference between them. My feeling that sewage versus wastewater was a matter of splitting hairs proved ill-informed. They are also known as black water and gray water. The outlets for these, consisting of capped pipes and knife valves, are under one side of the trailer, and to get a feel for them, you need to slide under there on your back and have a good look. That is what I did. Once in viewing range, I noted that one knife valve was out and one was in. I thought to push the out valve in, but it wouldn't budge. *Am I understanding this?* I wondered, letting my mind wander between "black," "gray," "sewage," and "waste," not to mention the combinations implied by caps and valves. Perhaps I should pull the in valve out; it seemed a logical thing to do. Laurie heard me cry out a complex phrase that was not "Great Caesar's ghost!" When she asked for an explanation, I shouted, "I'm covered with shit!" By then I'd stemmed the tide by pushing the in valve *back* in and was staggering around, shocked into an apelike crouch, trying to think of someone or something to blame.

We bade good-bye to our California friends as we banqueted that night at Roger Peters's trailer. Jimmy Kemp, unable to be merely a guest, arrived with superior bratwurst he had precooked in beer to be finished on the charcoal grill. After dinner, we pulled our big rig east toward Lancaster and Indio and Blythe, a real no-man's-land of battered and forlorn desert; hopeful groves of palms encircling vanished buildings; assaultive high-yield farming facing off with brand-new towns over available water; incongruous golf courses; "Fantasy Springs," a wilderness of wind generators—the kind of landscape I associate with space landings and Captain Beefheart (may he rest in peace). The traffic streams from L.A. to Phoenix past prison off-ramps with huge signs urging you not to pick up hitchhikers; antediluvian tractor-trailer rigs with tall, shrouded stacks; rocketing luxury cars, threading their way through the unlucky jalopies. You quickly take on the local travel mood: that you are fleeing.

At the end of the day, we found a place where we could rent four stalls and park our trailer. The owner, in pajama bottoms and a T-shirt that read HEAVENLY BODIES and depicted '50s hot rods across the expanse of his vast belly, walked past us without making eye contact, tossed four flakes into the stalls, and said, "Sixty dollars." Then he added that it would be all right to turn our ponies into the roping arena for exercise, adding mirthlessly, "That's fifty dollars, ha ha." He and his neighbor, he explained, are very strict about their property lines and have piled their tree trimmings and other moderately obnoxious debris between each other to emphasize that fact. Later, the two big bellies began shouting at each other across the property line, inciting tiny dogs invisible behind concrete walls into sympathetic barking. Laurie and I went for an evening walk, finding, as the closest thing to an appealing vista, a '47 Buick plowed into a gigantic pile of manure sprouting a crown of feral grasses.

We went to bed early, as much from weariness as to psychologically accelerate our time of departure and the outbound crossing of the California line. When we let Shelagh out to relieve herself in the night, she hit an electric fence with her nose, yelped, and launched the tiny, invisible dogs into a clamor that lasted the rest of the night. In the morning, as we prepared to go, the mystery tubbies were glowering at us across the lines of their private property.

We refueled at Flying J truck stops, as they are set up for big rigs like ours. You pull up to the pump, pick up a telephone, and explain your intentions to an unseen cashier. When you're finished, you pull forward into your own fifty-five-foot parking space and go inside for food, showers, television, magazines, money machines, video games, telephones, maps, and so on. With the right cards, you could run a modest-sized nation from a Flying J truck stop. Flying J seems to have forgotten nothing in serving its customers, though from observation, I don't know why it decided to farm out the tattoos. Oddly enough, Laurie found this atmosphere ominous and disquieting. She spotted a small group seated around a table, intently watching a television set that was not tuned to a station but simply displayed a screenful of loud, hissing snow. She felt that people here were casing one another. She felt it wasn't looking good. In retrospect, this was the beginning of our homesickness for the frozen north.

When you first cross into Arizona from California, the scenery is slow to change, and you see things to which you are unaccustomed at home: drive-through zoos, flea markets measured in square miles, pickup trucks hauling Exercycles, a huge automobile junkyard served by a Subway sandwich shop, Liz Claiborne outlets, the Harlem Globetrotters tour bus, airborne garbage bags, the Rooster Cogburn Ostrich Ranch.

We made our way through all of this, out the other side of Tucson, and into the hill country near Mexico, where our friends Peter and Molly Phinny allowed us to pull our trailer onto their land and use their corrals. Laurie walked around in the mesquite trees with her phone, trying to find a signal.

When we put our horses into their spacious cedar corrals, it seemed we were meeting them again, in more appropriate surroundings. They were in the middle of a big expanse best traversed by horse, and as they wheeled happily around their new place, I felt whatever that great feeling is about horses and the country they ought to be in. Today's equestrian contests—whether cuttings, reinings and ropings, or dressage meets—are rather industrial affairs of trucks, trailers, stalls, and wheelbarrows, as well as the continual veterinary attentions appropriate to these physically stressed animals. But horses seem to like new country nearly as well as we do. Ours were overwhelmed by their good feeling and began speeding in circles that cast a long cloud of dust adrift over the scrubland.

The next two nights were spent dining at the home of Linda and Jim Harrison, who live in a nice, cool house sensibly embedded in a wildlife refuge. Jim and I abandoned ourselves to the horseplay of forty years' customary habit until the expression of alarm on the face of his youngest daughter, Anna, encouraged us to moderate. We ate good food and talked eagerly of books and birds. Because Linda suffers from asthma, Jim must pursue his frantic cigarette-smoking by plunging his upper body into the fireplace, where he continues to interject in a voice made sepulchral by the masonry. The door was opened upon a small patio that overlooked a birdy wood, where the elegant trogon or vermilion flycatcher could fall to one's eye. I thought the euphoria I felt on these evenings might be part of the wanderer's grace, in which elements of the past and the present unexpectedly collide, like the Paris saunterings of middle-aged Lakota warriors and ex-cavalrymen in Buffalo Bill's circus.

It's possible that being around people in a wheelless home contributed to further inklings of homesickness. I became more aware that my setter, Gracie, was at home in Montana, as were my kelpie, Pat, and our broodmares. I admired, from this distance, the jays and chickadees at our feeders, who refrained from bolting to warm climes in the winter.

Our decision to set out for a couple of weeks of living in an area not much larger than the mudroom on the ranch was a plunge into the unknown. To our surprise, we were rising to the challenge. I had developed some housekeeping skills I'd not previously possessed, and my faintly obsessive personality found a home in the washing, drying, and storing of dishes. At the outset, we had agreed to view each other's organizational eccentricities in the manner of anthropologists. We tried to take note of these things rather than exception to them. There were new problems of censoriousness, as when one gazed with feigned objectivity at the dirty clothes festooning a doorknob. This was fooling no one, and eventually we gave it up. Our attention turned instead to the curious society of laundromats; the renewability of propulsive fuels for the people of the highway; and that most remarkable of conveniences, the free RV-holding-tank dump station, the sort of thing that really keeps a marriage together.

We now loaded the horses and headed back through Tucson and up to Maricopa, home of several feedlots, including the O.K. Cattle Company. We hauled our trailer into a universe of feeder cattle, hundreds of thousands of them, a genuinely grim scene. The wind howled over this gloomy world, and we resorted to routine as we unloaded horses, buckets, rakes, and blankets, hooked up all our hookups, and stalled the horses. It was a four-day cutting, and we immediately began to win a bit of money, which was heartening; but on the third day the wind died, and the smell nearly took the paint off our truck. There was reason to doubt that having our own home in the middle of this was a real plus. Overhead, an array of high-tension lines prevented Laurie from getting a good signal, though she wandered about with her cell phone like a uranium prospector. I think she wondered whether people who lived like this could really have children and needed electronic confirmation of their existence. At night, nearly everyone left, and we were alone with two hundred horses and eight Porta Pottis.

On the last run either of us would have before starting home, Laurie and Delta were perfect, securing a healthy check. Laurie had been working hard toward this accomplishment, the moment when she and her mare were one. When the cutting was over, we gathered up our winnings, loaded our weary horses, and started balling the jack northward. We were in our shirtsleeves, the windows down in the truck, as we pushed through Phoenix and Flagstaff and on across the sweeping Navajo reservation, one hundred gallons of Number Two Diesel under our belts, past Indian children herding sheep, Navajo veterans' memorials, a museum dedicated to the Navajo code talkers of World War II, a sign that proclaimed CHIEF YELLOW HORSE LOVES YOU!—we're coming, dogs, broodmares, kids!—all the way past the last hogan into Utah, where by a miracle we found comfortable corrals in the heart of the canyonlands. We ate in our coats and made laughing reference to the sunburns we retained from the day before.

The next day, we pulled hard, clear across Utah and into Idaho, then up toward the high country near Montana, whose border crossing we anticipated giddily. By St. Anthony, Idaho, we were driving on packed snow and ice, and I noticed that there were fewer and fewer souls on the road. Near Island Park, it was us and a bunch of snowmobiles. Our doubts were growing as the walls of snow built on either side of us. The light level in midafternoon was so low, the snowmobilers had their beams on as they cavorted among the trees. We passed an accident scene, a helmeted figure stretched out on the ground under a thermal blanket next to a four-wheel-drive ambulance. As we moved into northern winter and sundown, I was grateful for the cell phone and our AAA membership.

By the time we crossed into Montana, losing our light in an intensifying blizzard, pulling thirty-eight feet of house and horses over corrugated ice, I was looking for a place to stop for the night. Laurie crawled into the backseat with Shelagh, her phone, a bowl of water for the dog, her Flying J popcorn, her paperback, and her diet Coke. The Madison Valley seemed snowed in and free of even ranch traffic. Small, distant yard lights glowed through the blizzard, and I was focused on what little of the road I could see through the gusting snow.

"You know," I said, "maybe we ought to call in and get a road report. This is looking tough."

"I don't think so."

"What do you mean, 'I don't think so'?"

"I dropped the phone in the dog water. It's dead."

It was true: No amount of warmth from the heater could resolve the fog in its little window; its chirpy dial tone had become the croak of a raven. Getting stuck was not an option. We would keep going forward or be found later, by probe.

We stared down every crawling mile until the familiar glow of Ennis appeared through the storm. I wheeled my way to the rodeo grounds west of town, where we dragged the trailer until the snow stopped our progress. We double-blanketed the horses and put them in the bronc pens, which were so drifted in we had to shovel their gates loose. The water hydrant was frozen, so we carried buckets from the trailer in biting, snow-filled wind. The horses turned their butts into it and nosed down into their double rations of hay. We were wondering how a couple of empty nesters could get themselves into a place like this. "What were we thinking?" Laurie asked of no one in particular.

A sign at the entrance to the rodeo grounds stated that it was necessary to have permission to stall horses there and gave a phone number. But our phone didn't work. So I climbed a fence and trudged toward a house across a snowy field. I knocked on the door, startling the older couple sitting in the living room. They looked at each other hesitantly before answering. The woman came to the door, and I explained my situation, asking to use the phone. I got permission to use the corrals, and when I hung up, the woman said, "Where are you staying?" I told her about the living quarters in our trailer.

"Not on a night like this," she said emphatically. "You go get your wife and stay here. We have a nice spare bedroom." I explained that we would be very comfortable where we were. "Well, if you're not, you come right back here. I don't care what time of the night it is."

I thanked her and walked back to the trailer. Even the snow felt warm.

AUGUST 1999

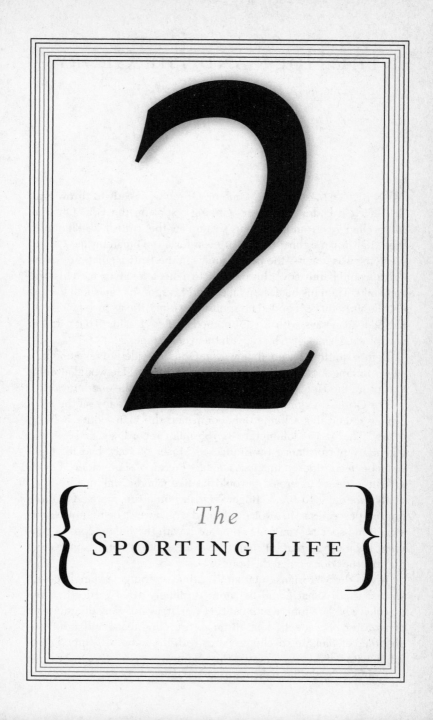

2

{ *The*
SPORTING LIFE }

THE HOUR AND THE GLORY
by John McLaughlin

I N SEPTEMBER 1992, Graeme Obree was ready to throw it all in. He'd had a good year, winning a spot on the U.K. Olympic cycling team and finishing second in the British 25-kilometer time trials for the third time. But even for a top amateur like Obree, the going was tough—the prize money on the British amateur cycling circuit could barely cover his bus fare to a meet, let alone feed his wife and child. Then his bike shop failed and his sponsor vanished, leaving only debts behind: "I ended up sponsoring *him*," the twenty-nine-year-old Scotsman says with a gap-toothed smile. "I said, 'That's it. I'm never racing again. I've had it with the whole game.'"

Before quitting for good, however, Obree decided to take one last, all-or-nothing shot at making his name and fortune. He would attempt to capture the Holy Grail of cycling: the record for the one-hour ride.

For Obree's neighbors in rural Ayrshire and for many on the U.K. cycling circuit, his scheme only confirmed the man's loose hold on reality. The 51.151-kilometer (31.785-mile) record, set in 1984 in a legendary performance by Francesco Moser of Italy, had for eight years been considered unapproachable. For an obscure rider of modest antecedents to break it would be like Candy Maldonado's suddenly emerging to break Roger Maris's home-run mark. As Obree himself describes it, in a voice softened with awe: "The hour record is something special. You can't compare it with the mile record in running. It's more important than that. All the other records in cycling put together don't equal the hour."

It was the Victorians, infatuated with everything newfangled, who started it all. What could be more thrillingly avant-garde than the bicycle? The late nineteenth century was an age of zany dilettantism: of monster bike meets, long-distance tricycling feats, and stout Englishmen challenging cycling records with the same stiff-lipped resolution with which they amassed the colonies.

Unofficially, the heroics began at the dawn of racing history, with one F. L. Doods, who in 1876 hammered round a track in Cambridge, England, for 25.508 tooth-rattling kilometers. The first modern record, though, was set by a Frenchman, the same Henri Desgrange who created the Tour de France. In 1893, on the old Buffalo Stadium bicycle track in Paris, unassisted by pacesetters—who were later banned when a rider broke 100 kilometers drafting behind a motor bike—Desgrange rode 35.325 kilometers on a thirty-three-pound tank of a bike. His record lasted just seventeen months, but it stamped the test as a lone endeavor and launched it into the future.

Since then, a magical aura has settled round the record, thanks to the murderous difficulty of breaking it and the pedigree of those who have. In Europe, to break the record is to become a legend. As the veteran French cycling writer Pierre Chany put it: "The hour record has been a cycling monument reserved only to a few exceptional riders. In the hour, champions of great quality have met with stinging defeat. Others were forced to try and try again before taking it."

Its history is littered with great names. On the eve of World War I, French ace Marcel Berthet and Swiss flyer Oscar Egg leaped over each other four times before Egg's 44.247 kilometers settled things. He would hold the record the longest: nineteen years.

Five-time Tour de France winner Jacques Anquetil took it in 1956; a second record was declined years later when he indignantly refused to take a drug test. And Roger Riviere sped to two records (in '57 and '58) before he broke his back falling down a ravine in the 1961 Tour.

The two riders widely regarded as the best ever are also on the honor roll. Italy's Fausto Coppi took it in 1942 with 45.848 kilometers, but had an awful time of it. Thirty years later, Eddy Merckx, dubbed "the Cannibal" for the ruthlessness with which he devoured his competitors, attacked the record on a high-altitude track in Mexico City, where the thinner atmosphere offered less resistance to his six-foot frame. He pounded out 49.431 kilometers, but vowed "never again" afterward. "It was a Calvary," he would say. "It burned three years off my life."

Unlike those who came before him—whose game plan was invariably "start, then pedal like hell"—Francesco Moser was willing to make a few concessions to the record. He had a wad of sponsorship money and an army of eggheads—led by noted biochemist Francesco Conconi—plotting his every breath: They changed his diet and riding position, analyzed his physiology, and devised a race plan that would keep him working at a high pace for the full hour. And the team gave him a high-tech bike with then-revolutionary disc wheels, the rear one visibly larger.

Attacking Merckx's record in 1984, Moser broke it twice in five days (also in Mexico City), carrying it past the psychological barrier of 50 kilometers, to 51.151. The new mark caused Merckx to sniff that it was "less a sporting record than a triumph for technology." To which Moser retorted, "No science in the world can turn a donkey into a racehorse." Whatever—it was a mark so intimidating it took ten years for the cycling world to challenge it anew.

It was Moser's record that Obree had his eye on, and he now accepts that it must have looked a touch ambitious. "My friend Gordon has a bike shop and I was over at his house and we just thought, 'Let's go for this,'" he says. "Anyone else would have thought it was crazy. Moser's record was considered unbeatable. Plus we're Scottish. Up here they'd say, 'He's just the guy from round the corner. He can't do that.'" But skeptics underestimated him and the pressure he was under: "In February of 1993, we were searching through the drawers to find tuppences to buy a loaf. That's what the situation was like. I knew what the record could do for me."

By 1992 developments in bike technology and training techniques had seemingly brought Moser's record within reach of the pack—and Obree wasn't the only one who had noticed. At least one other top racer had declared his intention to go after Moser, adding urgency to Obree's preparations. Not that his preparations were anything normal to begin with: Indeed, Obree's views on training, diet, riding position, and bike design had won him a reputation as a kind of Caledonian Rube Goldberg, churning out madcap notions and impossible contraptions. The difference is that Obree's notions have a funny habit of panning out, the contraptions of running forever. He is an original, but with a cycling savvy that belies his image. And he has the cussedness of his race. As he says of his drive for the record: "There was nothing obsessive about it. It was very clinical. I knew what I had to do."

He started training by riding flat-out for an hour twice a week on a stationary home cycling trainer, a simple leather pants belt substituting for the original, which had worn out long before. The trainer had no gauges he could monitor, "just that old belt I could tighten. If I wasn't suffering enough I'd turn it up a bit. Mentally," he says of those sessions, "it was incredibly hard." For strength training, he would take to the road, riding big hills in superhigh gears.

Obree has no time for regimented training schedules, preferring to trust the signals his body sends him; he trained when he felt like it. "I'd go out on the bike, hail, rain, snow, or sunshine, and start pedaling and I'd know if it was there or not," he says. "If you feel tired, then you just don't do it. It's either all-out or recovery. There's no in-between."

Meanwhile, strapped for cash, he was cannibalizing his friend Gordon's shop and combing the countryside to assemble his bike. He discovered his bottom-bracket bearings in an old washing machine, fashioned a crank arm from a bit of iron found near his house, and built the handlebar from some rusted BMX aero tubing lying at the back of Gordon's shop. For the hour record, Obree says, factors such as bike weight are secondary to aerodynamics: At such high speeds, any gain in velocity is met with a significant increase in wind resistance that is further compounded by turbulence. The bike and his position on it were designed accordingly.

"The bike was never drawn on paper," he says. "The whole thing evolved in my mind. I tried to drop all the preconceptions I had about riding. I tried to imagine the first time I ever went on a bike, what felt wrong about it. Now, what felt wrong for a start was the width of the [pedal] bracket."

He halved the size of his bottom bracket to 68 millimeters. That drew the pedals, and thus his legs, closer together for a more aerodynamic profile and a pedaling action closer to running. It also reduced tension on the frame as he rode. Obree's outlandish riding position dictated the shape of the handlebars, made of small mountain-bike bars jutting from a thin shaft.

The Obree Position—head pitched far out over the front wheel, arms tucked almost invisibly under his chest, fingers contortedly gripping the handlebars—was, with his ideas on training, the basis of his "mad Scot" reputation. But again, the position, developed over years of road racing, worked for him. He'd use it briefly to break away from the pack. But powering around a velodrome in that unholy crouch for an hour would be something else.

The first real test came in the spring of 1993, when Obree went after his own British record on a blustery, open-air circuit in London. He added nearly three kilometers to it, almost reaching Merckx's mark. "I thought then, 'If you take an indoor velodrome and have Specialized wheels on and really go for it, you could get this,'" he says.

He went for it indoors at the Hamar velodrome in Norway on July 16, riding a souped-up version of his garage bike built by Mike Burrows, a former Lotus bike engineer. Nobody was surprised when he missed it. But instead of staggering off to bed and thence back to Ayrshire and grim reality, Obree rescheduled for the following morning, before the judges would depart. And he pulled out his own bike, dubbed "the washing machine" by *L'Equipe,* Europe's top sports daily. Nobody believed he could recover in time. He was written off.

"France Two [the TV network] was filming, and I told them, 'It's not over till it's over,'" says Obree. "It was the cornered-animal syndrome. I had to get this record or else we're bust, basically. They were coming to take the stuff out of me house."

The next day, he was on the move before the pressure could build up. "I got up at ten past eight, had a bowl of cornflakes and a quick stretch, got my skin suit on. And then it was, 'Where's my bike? Right. Where's my helmet? Right.' Then I did three warm-up laps and I said to [the judges], 'Are ye ready?' And they said yeah and as soon as they did, *bang,* I was away, gone, and I could see out of the corner of me eye them fiddling with their watches, so they weren't *really* ready. But I was into it."

The bike may have been built to accommodate the Obree Position, but the hour took its toll on the rider all the same. Pushing an immense fixed gear of 52 T 12 (measured by the number of teeth on the chain-rings) that propelled him 9.25 meters with each circuit of the pedal, "the last twenty minutes got very uncomfortable. I started to hurt all over—legs, back, everywhere. You're drawing energy from wherever you can get it. Your fingers and toes start going numb because all the blood is going to your muscles. You've just got to go on for one more minute, then one more."

By the time the hour ran out, Graeme Obree had driven his impossible contraption 445 meters past Moser's record, to 51.596 kilometers, stupefying the handful of spectators there to see it and the wider cycling world as the news billowed out from Hamar. By the next day, he was the talk of Europe, even elbowing the Tour de France aside on the front page of *L'Equipe.* And just as Obree had predicted, the record's lure brought sponsors (including Specialized) running, and won him a spot on the top French pro team, Le Groupement.

In the months that followed, the sclerotic grandees of the Union Cycliste Internationale, the sport's governing body, would mount a fierce attack on Obree's riding position and his bike, which they insisted was not a bike at all but a "human-powered vehicle." Ultimately they let the record stand, but missed the point. From Graeme Obree's outlandish machine to his prerace diet of cornflakes and marmalade sandwiches, nothing could be truer to the spirit of the record than his assault on it. What is more, in outracing Moser, Obree not only put a gleam in the eye of every amateur with a bike in his garage but also shattered the notion that the limit had been reached. In saving himself, Graeme Obree brought the record back from the dead.

Fourteen hundred miles away, in the French wine capital of Bordeaux, Chris Boardman's spirits took a perceptible dip as the details of Obree's record seeped down from the north. For a week, he had been holed up in Bordeaux's Le Lac indoor velodrome putting the finishing touches on his own record preparations. Obree had known full well what Boardman was up to and had deliberately scheduled his crack at the hour to come first.

As Boardman says now in his mild Liverpool accent: "It was very annoying. No one had attempted the record for years, and then he wants to do it a week before me. Suddenly, I wasn't taking Francesco Moser's record. I was taking the record of some guy in Scotland who makes his own bikes."

For years, Boardman and Obree had been rivals on the British amateur circuit. Obree says, "It was good for both of us. I'd like to think I put pressure on Chris to do better. He certainly put pressure on me because I realized that to beat him I really had to pull my finger out."

The record, which both men had been pursuing with frightening purpose, gave the rivalry a new edge. Boardman complains now that Obree tried to sneak into Bordeaux ahead of him and decamped to Hamar only after Boardman refused to sacrifice any training time at the velodrome. "It wasn't illegal," Boardman says, "but it was pretty damned cheeky."

Obree counters that "there was a lot of jiggery-pokery about who declared they were going for the record first. And just before I went for it, [Boardman] wrote in a newspaper that Graeme Obree should get himself a good job and just do cycling for fun. I was treated as a bit of a joke.

"It's not personal with Chris," he adds. "He is one of those riders who likes to build up his rival and use the energy to get a better performance."

Boardman had already done wonders for the profile of British cycling, which had languished for years in the less-than-riveting company of lawn bowling and pigeon fancying, by winning gold in the 1992 Olympic 4,000-meter pursuit. In pursuit riding, two cyclists start off half a lap apart, and each tries to gain on the other. Never in Olympic history had one rider caught another in the pursuit. Yet in the final, Boardman, riding a space-age Lotus "super-bike" designed by Burrows, reeled in the German world champion Jens Lehmann like a flailing fish, powering past him off the final bend to take the gold. It made his name. With 1993 empty of major amateur competitions, he turned his sights to the hour.

Boardman, whose father, Keith, was a top amateur rider in the '60s, also saw the record as a springboard for a pro career. "The plan was to do it in Bordeaux just before the Tour de France," he acknowledges, "to cash in on the huge publicity cavalcade that comes with the Tour."

Before Obree shattered the aura of invincibility around the one-hour mark, Boardman, then twenty-five, might have been written off almost as dismissively as the Flying Scot. Peter Keen, Boardman's coach for seven years and a sports scientist at the University of Brighton, had more faith. "The beauty of the hour record," he says, "is that it lends itself to fairly accurate quantification." Simply put: If a rider can generate enough power for an hour, he can break the record.

"I went through it with Chris one day," says Keen, "and the numbers we were getting reassured us it was not a totally lunatic thing to embark on. The record had developed a myth around it that frightened off serious thinking. But when you looked at it on a clinical level, you realized it was not that outstanding."

Early in 1993, Boardman began training, though initial signs were not encouraging. On the Kingcycle, a stationary bike hooked up to a computer, he could not hold 400 watts of power for ten minutes. To outstrip Moser, he would need to maintain 430—for an hour.

But the pair stuck with it, "training the engine to work as efficiently as possible aerobically," in Boardman's words. Keen, the coach of the U.K. cycling team since 1989, says his methods challenge the old idea of pounding out the miles in the belief that the more you suffer, the more you gain. "That may have worked in the past but now there's a level of performance and sophistication where quantity becomes destructive, where you go past the point where it's going to do you any good." He prefers, instead, to "reduce the time spent training, primarily to ensure that once loads are attained there is enough recovery time to do some good."

Boardman started putting in miles on the road and racing in time trials in the high, fixed gear he would use in Bordeaux. He also spent hours hooked up to the Kingcycle, with Keen monitoring his power output and heart rate to tailor, and regularly adjust, his training. "I was doing very short, intense sessions," says Boardman. "I would do ten minutes at one kilometer per hour over the pace necessary for the record. It was all threshold workloads," just below flat-out.

The aim for the record attempt was to get quickly up to threshold and hold that speed lap after lap. As Boardman says, "It's a fine line between hitting it right and producing too much lactic acid to absorb. It's like bailing out a boat. If there's a surge, it might take twenty minutes to recover."

Boardman has never had a problem maintaining an even pace: "I can just switch off and think about the shopping." And he had other advantages. As Keen says, Boardman's maximum oxygen uptake, at 85 to 90 milliliters per kilogram of body weight per minute, "is about as high as has been recorded in cyclists or skiers or runners." And with his slightly rounded back, he had a riding position that was aerodynamically near-perfect.

One advantage he would not have was the Lotus bike. Already irritated by the company's claims for it, Boardman walked away after a Lotus director suggested he could not break the record without it. He tested four others, settling on a carbon-fiber Corima, a sleek vision in canary yellow.

Conditions in the Bordeaux velodrome on that midsummer day were hardly ideal. The humidity was 80 percent by the time Boardman, who is shorter and more compact than Obree, strode into the arena. And the temperature in the metal-roofed stadium, arc lights blazing for the benefit of the television cameras, was also rising fast. Keen sprayed Boardman with ethyl alcohol to cool him down just before the start.

At 10:02 A.M., spurred on by the roar of three thousand voices, Boardman put foot to pedal and was away. "The record attempt is an extremely emotional event, and very fraught," says Keen. "People see the way I work as somehow removing the spirit and human qualities from it. But there's a lot you can't predict or measure, particularly how people will react to pressure."

Boardman, who admits to "hideous nerves" before big events, reacted beautifully. For 5 kilometers he lagged behind Obree's pace, but then surpassed him, relentlessly grinding out laps, winning a second or two with each kilometer, sweeping through the final laps, when he knew he had the record in his hands, on a tide of noise and adrenaline. The distance: 52.270 kilometers. Obree's record had lasted less than a week.

The rivalry between the two British amateurs would have one more flourish, when Obree took a slightly modified machine to Bordeaux the following April to grab back the record, pushing the huge gear for 52.713 kilometers. He continued to stir strong feelings among observers. As Boardman said: "He annoyed a lot of people [in cycling]. Someone with a multimillion-pound team doesn't like hearing people who eat marmalade sandwiches and build bikes out of washing machines say they're going to give them a good kicking." But the press, and cycling fans, were entranced.

Thierry Lacarriere, the director of Bordeaux's small jewel of a velodrome, captured the mood, telling Jean-Yves Donor of *Le Figaro,* "Obree reconciled me with top-level sport. He is an idealist. He approaches his sport like they used to thirty years ago, with incredible passion."

This time, though, Obree's record caused less of a stir. As Mike Burrows told *Bicycling* magazine after assisting Obree during his first record, "Someone has surely got to come back and put us in our place. Otherwise their credibility is shot." In fact, the pros were already warming up, starting with the most feared of them all: Miguel Indurain.

"The Extra-Terrestrial," *L'Equipe* labeled him in 1992, after Indurain had demoralized his rivals by cruising imperiously to a second Tour de France win. In a sport where slight, sinewy bodies are the norm, Indurain used his immense power to dominate the time trials. He also pushed his six-foot-three, 172-pound frame up and down the Alps and Pyrenees ahead of all but the best climbers, and always within sight of his main rivals.

As Keen says, "To be that big and climb that well takes one hell of an engine." By 1994, when he took his fourth consecutive Tour de France,

Indurain had acquired a reputation for invincibility and a psychological dominance over his peers unseen since Eddy Merckx. It was time to go for the hour. "Everyone wanted to see him try," says Indurain's team manager, Jose-Miguel Echavarri. "And it was good for everyone: for the sponsor, the team, Miguel. It was a great spectacle." But it would not be the cakewalk widely, and unrealistically, anticipated.

"I'd had a good road season," says Indurain, "winning the Tour and all, and then the chance came to go for the hour. I thought, 'Why not? I'll take a shot.'" He began training just one month before his attempt. "Preparing for it was very difficult. I was doing shorter, more intense sessions, building up my power and consistency. Instead of riding five or six hours, I'd be doing just one, but very intense. It was all about adapting."

Meanwhile, Echavarri supervised progress on a custom-designed Pinarello bike, which finally emerged in rainbow colors, with a sculpted carbon-fiber frame, disc wheels, and triathlete bar. Indurain chose Bordeaux for the attempt, along with a 59 T 14 gear, each circuit of the pedal propelling him 8.76 meters along the track.

In an analysis of Indurain two years ago, *L'Equipe* noted a pulse rate under stress in excess of 190 beats per minute and a resting rate of less than 30—so slow it is almost comatose. The piece also calculated his oxygen absorption rate at an impressive 88 milliliters per kilo of body weight per minute. Most crucial, it observed that Indurain's dynamo of a heart pumped more than 45 liters of blood a minute, almost double the average. "That's staggeringly high," says Keen, who calls the measure "the most fundamental characteristic of physiology that makes a great rider what he is."

But the hour record required something else. Power is important, but so are aerodynamics, and Indurain's size and the awkward riding position it mandated were enormous handicaps. His attempts to counter with raw power the drag from that massive frame were painful to watch when he mounted his record-breaking ride in September 1994.

If those sixty minutes were tough to watch, they were obviously a torture to ride. Le Lac is a fast track made of Cameroonian hardwood, but at 250 meters it is also fairly small. Indurain's speed seesawed wildly under the pressure. He found himself being dragged up the banking on the curves. And even though he finished in crescendo, he struggled through the last ten minutes, jaw clenched, ravenously sucking in air. He climbed down from his bike, muscles cramping, face scarlet, suddenly older than his thirty years, and began shaking. He had taken the record, though. The new mark: 53.040 kilometers.

Tony Rominger is an unlikely looking athlete. At five foot eight and 143 pounds, he is a slight man, though about average for a pro cyclist. He has a round face, a thin smile, and the satisfied air of a small-town bank manager greeting a wealthy customer. He is Swiss, which might also explain the methodical pragmatism that has taken him to the top of the cycling world. Last year was his best ever. He won his third consecutive Tour of Spain and was No. 1 in the world for the first time. His only real disappointment was the Tour de France, which he had been expected to fight out to the end with Indurain. Instead, he dropped out with eight days and the Alps to go, complaining of stomach problems. He was then almost eight minutes behind the Spaniard, who was all but whistling from the fun of it. Some believed Rominger had simply given up.

As the Tour raced away into the distance, Rominger trudged off into an uncertain future. At thirty-three, his days as a pro were running out, and a six-month layoff before the next season would be tough to overcome. But he dragged himself back. From September on, he entered and won a string of post-Tour time trials that sharpened him up without the drudgery of marathon training sessions. By mid-October, he was ready to attack Indurain again—this time for the hour.

It was Michele Ferrari who persuaded Rominger to go for it. The Italian sports physician had been a key member of the scientific hit-squad that had plotted Moser's assault on the record. In the years that followed, he had lent his skills as doctor and trainer to a string of riders, some of whom went from obscurity to stardom. He was known as a miracle worker.

For all his gifts, though, a shadow has always hung over Ferrari. Rail thin and buck-toothed, abrupt and imperious, he has made an art of deftly evading questions about his methods. Some say his elusiveness is part of the willful cultivation of a mystique that has served him well. To others it is but one end of a crooked path leading to drugs and blood-doping.

Nothing has ever been proved, but Ferrari has done little to dispel the talk. In April of last year, as trainer and doctor of the hot Gewiss-Ballan pro team, he told *L'Equipe* that "the limit of the medical care given to the cyclist is the limit of the drug test. Everything that isn't banned is therefore acceptable." He denied his team's success was chemically assisted but added: "If I were a rider and I knew an undetectable product existed that could improve my performance, I'd use it." Gewiss-Ballan canned Ferrari for speaking his mind. The team would miss him.

Rominger, with Ferrari in close attendance, climbed onto his bike for the first time at Le Lac on October 17. A novice on the track, he promptly fell right off. But he was confident enough of his form to joke to the press that this, too, might be a record.

His confidence was justified. Officially, Rominger was in Bordeaux only to run a few tests, but he felt so good he decided to attack Indurain's mark then and there, after just six hours of practice on the track. He would ride a Colnago bike remarkably similar to his regular time-trial machine and with the same 59 T 14 fixed gear as Indurain's, though it propelled him 10 centimeters farther per pedal-stroke because of its larger back wheel.

On the gray October day of the record attempt, the few fans in attendance were kept outside to prevent their breaking the rider's concentration. The lights of the velodrome were turned on only at the last minute to avoid driving the temperature up. And then Rominger was off, a little wobbly at first, but soon establishing a ferocious rhythm.

An hour later, he not only had shattered Indurain's record by an imposing 800 meters but was bounding off his bike as fresh as a colt. Watched by only the UCI judges, a handful of cycling journalists inside the velodrome, and the few diehard fans outside, noses pressed against the glass, he had ridden 53.832 kilometers for the hour.

As Jean-Yves Donor wrote in *Le Figaro* of this feat in an eerily quiet, near-empty velodrome: "It was phenomenal, almost surreal." Dauntingly for his rivals, Rominger said he would try again, on November 5, this time in public, his sights set on pushing his record past the 54-kilometer barrier.

The rivalry between the pros, Indurain and Rominger, was as intense as that between the amateurs, and the intervening two weeks were marked by the sound of gunfire booming across the sports pages. Indurain sniped that Rominger, who gave the impression he had cruised to the record as an afterthought between visits to his accountant, "must have been working himself pretty hard in secret."

Rominger left the blunderbuss to his wife, Brigitte. "Tony," she said, "is the world Number One and is just as popular as Indurain. He can give interviews in six languages, while Indurain can only express himself in Spanish."

Offstage, Colnago was working to refine the aerodynamics of Rominger's bicycle. The handlebars were lightened and fitted with outriggers, and the fork and rear tubing were flattened. Rominger, meanwhile, took to the road, riding hard in the saddle, attacking big hills in big gears, seeking out head winds and driving through them. And he continued to pound out laps on the track. On November 3, he raced 25 kilometers at a 54.628 kph pace.

Bordeaux was chill and blustery on the morning of Rominger's second attempt, but by 2:30 P.M., minutes before start time, humidity was a nonfactor and the temperature in the velodrome, at sixty-eight degrees, was ideal.

Standing trackside as Rominger glided past on his warm-up laps, the great Irish rider Stephen Roche said: "Tony's right to do it again. The first time, you're always holding back. You're afraid you're not going to make it to the end, that your legs are going to go. He'll be more relaxed, plus he's got the form and he knows it. Form doesn't go away in two weeks."

At almost 2:34 P.M., his gear fixed at an impressive 60 T 14 for a distance per pedal-stroke of 9.02 meters, Rominger powered slowly away from the starting line. Arms parallel to the ground on his triathlete bar, body pitched far over the front wheel, knees grinding ever faster, he soon found his rhythm. By the ninth kilometer, he averaged more than 55 kph.

Surely he couldn't hold that pace. The crowd was entranced as Rominger flashed by, the per-kilometer times hugging the space between 1.04 and 1.06 minutes with hypnotic regularity. As he approached 25 kilometers, all eyes were locked onto the electric scoreboard. Suddenly 27:08.672 flashed up, 41.118 seconds ahead of his previous record pace.

In the crowd perched above the track, there was a sudden shifting forward in seats, a low murmur like the buzz of a high-voltage wire. The tension over what might be coming had the crowd by the throat and the only release was to roar it out. Rominger rocketed through 30 kilometers, then 40, and as each marker disappeared behind him the roar deepened and expanded. Again and again, Rominger shot past, face impassive, upper body flat and still, bike holding tight to the bends. He broke the magical 50-kilometer mark with almost six minutes to go, by which time the entire stadium was up, everyone on their feet, beating hands and stamping to the rhythm of the cyclist's legs. Rominger, riding through that bowl of noise, felt it and responded. Suddenly finding another gear, he accelerated just when he should have been struggling and reeled off the last two kilometers at more than 56 kph. At one hour, the scoreboard, mercifully, froze: 55.291 kilometers.

Rominger's record elicited the same head-shaking incredulity that Moser's had a decade earlier, and with good reason. In crashing through the 55-kilometer barrier that November afternoon, he took the one-hour mark past the point viewed not long before as the ceiling of human ability.

Moser had held the record until just sixteen months earlier, but if they had been racing head-to-head on Bordeaux's 250-meter track, Rominger would have lapped him sixteen times. The new record-holder also scorched 2 kilometers past the record eked out by Indurain just weeks before, a massive advance at this level of performance. As Boardman says in wonder, "It's equivalent to running a 3:35 mile." Adds Obree: "If you can imagine going at a pace to beat Moser's record and someone comes past you at strolling pace, that's the difference. I mean, that is incredible."

Rominger's record, however, is unlikely to have the same paralyzing effect as Moser's on those who come after. Already, veterans of the record and tyros like Yevgeni Berzin of Russia are pondering the next challenge.

Back at his home in Villava, Spain, Miguel Indurain says his priority this year is a record fifth consecutive Tour de France title, but the memory of his painfully won, briefly held record still rankles. He says now that it was "just a test," and adds, "It wasn't the best I could do. The next time I would have to have a better aerodynamic position and two to three months of preparation."

With the Tour de France climaxing in late July, two to three months more would bring him to the world championships, taking place September 26 to October 8, in Duitama, Colombia. Michele Ferrari says a high-altitude assault on the record there could add 1,000 to 1,500 meters to the hour. The top Italian pro, Gianni Bugno, has already declared his intention to try to break the record at a

Colombian velodrome at an altitude higher than 2,600 meters (8,530 feet).

In his living room in Ayrshire, Graeme Obree says, "There's a reasonable chance I'd go again, but whereas the last time I could get away with a few things not right, now everything has to be perfect." As for Chris Boardman: "I didn't think it was attackable, but I've looked at the figures. I can get up to fifty-four kilometers, and even to fifty-five, but not at sea level." Not yet, anyway. But he believes "it's quite feasible to beat it." And he will almost certainly try. The question is when and where.

In any event, this outlandish record will not go unchallenged for long. Bicycle technology is advancing too rapidly. And too many hot young stars have experienced, however vicariously, the transforming power of the hour. It pieced Graeme Obree's world back together. It catapulted Chris Boardman into what should be a glittering pro career. It almost defeated the mighty Miguel Indurain. And it turned Tony Rominger, that most unlikely of athletes, into a legend.

AUGUST 1995

Editor's Note

In 1996, Chris Boardman recaptured the Hour Record from Tony Rominger, riding a stunning 56.375 kilometers. Shortly thereafter, the Union Cycliste Internationale, cycling's world governing body, decided that technology was tainting the record's purity. In effect, the UCI told everyone to start again, using the 49.431-kilometer mark established by Eddy Merckx in 1972 as the new standard to beat, and prohibited potential record-breakers from using aerodynamic helmets, bladed spokes, carbon-fiber frames, or any other technological innovation that Merckx didn't enjoy. So in October 2000, riding a steel-framed bike stripped of its aerodynamic enhancements, Boardman again established a new mark: 49.441 kilometers. Boardman immediately retired, at the age of thirty-two, and at the time of publication his record was still standing.

THEY MIGHT BE GIANTS

by John Paul Newport

THE HARDEST-WORKING MAN on the Space Coast Tour is Gene Jones Jr., a.k.a. Gene the Machine. Granted, that's not saying an awful lot, since many of Jones's peers, especially the youngsters, spend as much time honing their personalities as honing their games. Unlike on the PGA Tour, where wit and colorful behavior are relics of the past, the bush-league professional golf personality counts for a lot. That's because most of the players are just giving the pro game a shot for a few years before moving on to their true life's work, conducting golf seminars for the plaid-pants crowd at backwater clubs or selling universal life-insurance products for Prudential.

Jones is like the nerd in your college lit class who always read every assignment. After a tournament round, he will pound balls at a driving range, go home to videotape his swing in the search for tiny flaws and then practice putting and chipping for an hour or two. On days when the Space Coast Tour doesn't stage an event, he finds another tournament to enter. On Sundays he practices some more and then usually takes his ten-year-old daughter, Amberly, out for a round of golf. What drives Jones to pursue golf so maniacally is a matter of considerable speculation among his fellow competitors. But obviously, he's very serious about the game.

I first encountered him as I was standing near the scoreboard during the first round of the DeBary Plantation tournament, north of Orlando, last fall. Around me, young Space Coast cadets were offering preposterous excuses for why they had scored so poorly. "I'd have shot a sixty-eight if I hadn't triple-bogeyed number eight," a curly-haired fellow from Colorado assured me, explaining his round of seventy-seven. Another player, this one from Georgia, pointed toward the neat, handwritten row of fours, fives, sixes and sevens that appeared after his name on the scoreboard and complained, "How could someone as studly as me have shot a dip-shit round like that?" He didn't seem overly upset, however, as he lounged in his golf cart, feet on the dash, guzzling a Coors. He was young and good-looking, he had a rich sponsor somewhere paying all his bills, and there would always be tomorrow.

This is when Jones drove up, making the turn after nine holes of play, his eyes scanning the scoreboard like antiaircraft sensors. At thirty-five, he is a short, sturdy-looking man, with blond hair, plump cheeks and a forlorn, distracted air. In baggy black shorts, a Nike cap and saddle-oxford golf shoes, he looked more like a schoolboy than the tour's leading money winner. Nevertheless, his arrival silenced the cadets.

"What's the low score?" he asked in a taut North Carolina accent.

The question was precisely worded. Not "Who's in the lead?" because Jones didn't care about the person attached to the score. Not "What's in the money?" because finishing high enough to earn a check is not the issue; Jones almost always does. Rather, simply, "What's the low score?" What number precisely did he have to beat to take the lead?

"Uh, three under, Gene," someone said.

"Thanks," Jones replied and gunned the cart up the path. No one dared ask after his score, which happened to be even par.

After a pause, the banter resumed. "No one can play well *all* the time," my pal with the Coors continued in defense of his dip-shit round. But then he added, with a none-too-friendly edge in his voice, "Unless your name is frigging Gene the Machine."

The Spalding Space Coast Tour is golf's version of Bull Durham baseball. Most of the players are in their twenties, and everyone thinks he is on the brink of big tour stardom. Pitted against them is a handful of cagey veterans and downward-spiraling former tour pros with names like Tony Cerda and Doug Weaver. The latter group almost always cleans up.

The biggest difference between Bull Durham–style minor-league baseball and the Space Coast Tour is that in baseball the players earn a living. On the Space Coast Tour, which operates most of the year except for the hot summer months, probably fewer than a dozen golfers actually support themselves out of winnings. The rest, mostly the young guys, hit up Mom and Dad for cash transfusions, wangle financial-sponsorship deals from wealthy sportsmen who might otherwise back a racehorse, hustle amateurs at the approximately 140 Orlando-area golf courses or work part-time.

The Space Coast Tour is essentially an open-air golf casino: Players put down their bets in the form of $300 to $350 entry fees, and the top few finishers walk off with most of the loot. The Spalding Company, hoping to curry favor with the club professionals of tomorrow, kicks in $100,000 a year to the kitty. And the house—in the person of J. C. Goosie, sixty-four, sole owner and proprietor—sweeps away 12 percent after course expenses. Last year the total purse was about $1.2 million, compared with more than $54 million on the PGA Tour.

"Our operation is simple," Goosie told me over the telephone. (He doesn't show up at Space Coast events when he qualifies for tournaments on the Senior PGA Tour.) "We want ex–college players to come down here and spend about $16,000 to $17,000—that's for everything, entry fees, living expenses, everything—and play for a year. If a guy's good, he's gonna make $12,000 to $13,000 of that back. If he's very good, he may break even. So for fifteen to thirty cents on the dollar, next to nothing, he's gonna get experience he can't buy nowhere else."

J. C. Goosie invented the minitour concept twenty years ago, basically because he and his pals who couldn't get on the regular tour needed a place to play. The idea caught on. Over the years quite a few Space Coast alums have made names for themselves on the PGA, including stars like Paul Azinger and Craig Stadler. Recently, however, the best subtour talent has gravitated to the PGA Tour–sponsored Nike Tour (formerly the Ben Hogan Tour) and the four-year-old T. C. Jordan Tour. That leaves Goosie and a few other upstart minitours, like the Golden State Golf Tour, in California, defending the honor of single-A golf.

Conditions are what you'd expect: spiky greens, sprinkler systems that occasionally burst to life in the middle of a player's backswing, passing motorists yelling "Fore!" as a joke and no sign of a gallery anywhere. The absence of fans has advantages: Players feel free to relieve themselves in the woods whenever they like and to indulge in the same colorful expletives that golfers everywhere enjoy. The day-to-day manager of the Space Coast Tour is a former pro and real-estate agent named Bobby Simpson, who has an odd way of holding his head, like a turtle peeking out of its shell. The starter is an affable Cajun nicknamed Crow, who spends the balance of his week at the dog track. And the rules officials include retired old pros who disperse around the course in golf carts and can often be spotted snoozing.

Such is the sweet narcotic bliss of golf, however, that nobody seems to mind.

I followed Jones around the back nine at DeBary, and it took me a while to identify his value-added as a golfer. His drives, though accurate, were not particularly long, and his swing, though serviceable, was brusque and pared down, pistonlike—not at all the elegant, modern Fred Couples ideal. He did appear perfectly comfortable standing over the ball, which is not always the case with golfers on the Space Coast Tour, many of whom bounce up and down neurotically and back away from the shot so often you begin to wonder if they might be afraid of hurting the ball.

After a few more holes, however, I began to understand that Jones's distinction is not his ball-striking ability so much as his raw animal hunger to score birdies. He works the course like a perpetual-motion machine, darting after his balls with the ferocity of a terrier, swinging extra clubs to groove the right feel, pacing like a CEO in a doctor's office whenever he has to wait, sizing up putts from every angle of the compass. On the eleventh hole he missed a seven-foot birdie putt and stayed on the green for several minutes afterward, inspecting the turf around the hole with the disgust of a surgeon trying to comprehend a botched operation.

Jones's attitude stood in marked contrast to that of his playing companion for the day, D. W. Smith, forty-two, a courtly Mississippian wearing a straw fedora. Smith, a very fine golfer himself (during one seventeen-round stretch last summer he shot ninety under par), lolled about in the cart between shots chatting with other golfers like a pastor at a church social. "Look at D. W.," Jones said derisively, nodding as Smith nonchalantly got up to arch his back like a cat enjoying the sun. "If *I* was two over, I'd be eyeballing down the fairway to see how I could get me a birdie."

During a brief delay on the fourteenth tee, Jones took me aside to apologize for a minor display of temper—he had tossed a club—on the previous hole. "I expect a little more out of myself is all," he said. "When you're playing this bad, it just gets under your skin, that's all. You gotta get after yourself, gotta get a little bit mad." The day before, he said, he had shot sixty-seven in a hurricane to win the $1,000 first prize at a tournament in Lady Lake.

With that he stepped up to his ball, mumbled something like "Come on, now, just gimme a chance," and sizzled a three-iron straight down the center of the fairway. "Whoo-ee, Jethro," Smith cooed in appreciation. Jones acknowledged the compliment with a tight-lipped smile and stood aside, practicing his hip turn as the others hit.

"Personality-wise," I jotted in my notebook, "this guy's a natural for the PGA Tour."

❄   ❄   ❄

I had hoped to talk with Jones more extensively after the round. But before I could collar him, an entertaining golfer named Billy Glisson asked me for a ride to his car. I had met Glisson a few days earlier. He claims to be the World's Leading All-Time Minitour Winner, and he probably is, though many would consider that a dubious honor.

"I come down here for one thing and one thing only, and that's to win," he told me in his hurry-up South Carolina accent as we barreled down a derelict stretch of highway. He was dragging on a Viceroy and blowing smoke out the window. "Coming in second don't cut it. That's why I've won ninety-one-plus minitour events. I reckon it's like Nicklaus."

Glisson, forty-six, is a friendly, lackadaisical mess of a man. He has a broad, blunt nose, longish, dirty blond hair that curlicues out the back of his gold cap and such a monster belly that he never even tries to tuck his shirttail in. He tends to wear the same pair of baggy gray shorts day after day and leaves a butt trail of Viceroys around the course that Hansel and Gretel would envy. I estimate he smokes three packs per round. Glisson also engages in the disturbing habit of popping his ball in his mouth between holes despite all the insecticides around.

If the Space Coast Tour attracted media attention the way the PGA Tour does, Glisson's personal history would be the stuff of legend. During the early years he supported his golf habit by working as the night manager of an Orlando brothel that operated out of a beauty salon. He got so good at golf, however, that by the early '80s he was supposedly winning more than $50,000 a year on the minitours. In 1981 he made it to the big tour and did pretty well. "Got on TV four or five times," he bragged matter-of-factly. Unfortunately, he soon suffered a nearly fatal stroke—"Too much drinking and carrying on, I reckon"—and so, after a couple of years' recovery, it was back to the minors.

Glisson lasted long enough on tour to make a mark, however. He is remembered, among other reasons, for confusing the courtesy-car volunteers with his frequent requests to pick up more than one "Mrs. Glisson" at the airport. At one tournament, the real Mrs. Glisson spotted her husband strolling the fairway holding hands with a Mrs. Glisson not herself and stole his Corvette out of spite, leaving only his street shoes in the parking space.

Despite a too-quick backswing and constant exasperation at slow play,

Glisson still wins his share of minitour events. That's why the seventy-nine he had shot that morning was such a thorn. "Couldn't make a putt," he grumbled as we drove. "When you play golf for a living, you gotta have total concentration. All I could think about was my damn car."

His car, a black 1983 Eldorado with an I'D RATHER BE GOLFING bumper sticker in the rear window, had broken down that morning on an I-40 exit ramp. He had had to hitch a ride, by chance with Gene the Machine, to make it to the tournament on time. We found the car, apparently repaired, tilting half in, half out of a muddy ditch beside the weather-beaten combination garage and sign shop where he'd left it. The proprietor charged Glisson only $35. "Hot damn," Glisson said, beaming like he'd just holed out a pitching wedge from a hundred yards. "I thought they'd take me to the cleaners."

Even so, he had to borrow $20 to make it back to the friends' apartment where he stays, sleeping on the couch, while competing in Orlando. And a few days later the Eldorado broke again. This time the repairs cost $800.

Glisson has a new wife and two children back in South Carolina. I asked him why he still plays tournament golf. "It just gets in the blood, I reckon," he replied, "and you can't get it out."

The next day, back at DeBary Plantation, Gene the Machine failed to win the tournament. He cranked out what for him was another disappointing round of even par to finish three shots off the pace. The winner, in a sudden-death playoff, was Doug Weaver, another former tour pro like Glisson but unlike Glisson in nearly every other possible respect. I realized this immediately when I offered to buy him a drink at the clubhouse bar to celebrate his exciting victory and he enthusiastically accepted by ordering milk.

Weaver, thirty-three, is a solidly built redhead with a deep Southern voice and a lightly pocked face. I thought he was joking about the milk, of course, but he wasn't. He ordered a tall glass of it, took one sip, then dashed off to a telephone to tell his wife the good news of their $4,300 payday. "God must be teaching us to be very dependent on Him," Weaver said when he returned, "because every time we get almost broke, I win a tournament."

Two years earlier, he said, the family had been in a similar pickle. Their bank account was practically zero, his wife was pregnant, his swing was incoherent. And he had just shot eighty-one and eighty-two in a pro-am tournament at Pebble Beach. After the tournament, he and his wife, Patricia, walked down to the beach below the course and prayed. "Dear God," they beseeched, "if we're going to play golf in 1991, You're going to have to put the money in our hands because we're too embarrassed to ask anyone for it ourselves anymore." Sure enough, a few days later Weaver received an offer from a potential sponsor—one of his partners in the disastrous Pebble Beach pro-am, no less—of $30,000 over the next two years. He was back in business.

I asked Weaver what keeps him golfing when the financial abyss yawns. "I realize I could go back to South Carolina and get a good job," he replied. "But the Bible says a young man without vision shall perish. That doesn't mean really perish, but he just won't have a good life." He paused to take his last gulp of milk. "This is the dream God has laid on our hearts."

The shocking thing about the pro-golf scene in Orlando is the sheer number of men, like Weaver and Glisson and all the cadets, who manage to arrange their lives to play golf every day "for a living." Because in addition to Goosie's operation, two other, even lesser minitours operate in the area: the Tommy Armour Tour and the North Florida PGA Winter Tour. Together the three tours qualify Orlando, without a doubt, as the Bush-League Professional Golf Capital of the Universe.

I called on the Tommy Armour Tour one Saturday during its one-day tournament at the Overoaks Country Club. First-place prize money was $1,000, and the second-place check (which went to Gene the Machine for shooting sixty-seven again) was $600. When I arrived, the players who had already finished were standing around in a grove of live oak trees, the branches hung with Spanish moss, sipping beer or soft drinks and chatting amiably amongst themselves. It looked a lot like a big Southern picnic or family reunion. "No offense," a competitor recently arrived from New Jersey told me, "but this is the lamest tour I've ever played on."

The man who owns the Tommy Armour Tour is a perplexed-looking forty-nine-year-old named Terry Fine. Fine plays in his own tournaments as a way of tuning up for the Senior Tour. The day I visited, he shot an eighty-one. "The biggest complaint the players have down here in Florida," he said, "is the blatant stealing out of the purse that takes place on some of the other tours." By "other tours" he was clearly alluding to Goosie's, though Fine later said he did not mean to suggest by "stealing" that Goosie was doing anything illegal—merely that he was keeping too high a percentage of the pot for himself.

No love is lost between Fine and Goosie. For Goosie, the Tommy Armour Tour is "kind of a sore thumb." He claims not to mind the competition—"good, honest competition we can handle"—as much as the way Fine "slipped around behind my back, giving my players his cards, that sort of thing," when Fine was getting his tour off the ground three years ago.

As for Fine, he likes to portray himself as the golfers' true friend. He prides himself on keeping a higher percentage of the players' money in the pot, after expenses and profits, than does Goosie. But since his major sponsor, the Tommy Armour Golf Company, contributes less to his tour than the Spalding Company does to the Space Coast Tour, the players still get a better return with Goosie. To compensate, Fine was working on a deal to offer all Tommy Armour Tour members in good standing a 10 percent discount at Wolf Camera outlets across the South. "One thing we're trying to do at the Tommy Armour Tour is add a little dignity," he said. Earlier, the tour had been known as the Hooters Tour, after a restaurant chain that features busty waitresses in tight T-shirts and hot pants. So dignity-wise, that's progress right there.

I wandered over to the clubhouse porch, where a number of competitors were loitering after their round. They constituted the usual assortment of oddballs one finds in bush-league golf: a bartender and occasional dancer at a Chippendales-like club, a frightened-looking kid from South Africa who appeared to be no older than twelve, a forty-one-year-old tenured Delta pilot who competes regularly by virtue of his eighteen off days per month and a surly, ponytailed, practice-range pro who was griping about how much Fred Couples earned for switching to Parallax clubs (supposedly $4 million) and showing off his own abnormally long driver. This club's head weighed about ten pounds and was made of Kryptonite or plutonium or something and if manipulated correctly could propel the ball, he said, 339 yards. He let me try it on the range. It was like swinging a maypole with several small children attached. My best attempt reached the 100-yard marker.

As I was preparing to leave, a twenty-four-year-old golfer named Joe Shahady took me aside to suggest privately that I might want to mention in the article how much he enjoys eating PowerBars. Power-Bars, according to some information Terry Fine made available, provided delicious, nutritious, *sustained* energy to help golfers maintain the focus required for hitting straight drives and making crucial putts.

I forgot to mention earlier that the PowerBar company is an official sponsor of the Tommy Armour Tour. Any player quoted in the press singing the praises of PowerBars gets a $500 bonus.

I finally had a chance to sit down and talk with Gene the Machine after the first round of the next Space Coast tournament, a two-day affair at the Kissimmee Bay Country Club. He had just shot a sixty-six but couldn't resist complaining about a couple of knee-knocker putts he missed. "I just couldn't get anything started on the front nine," he grumbled.

Off the course Jones is not nearly as daunting as he is when stalking a golf ball. He has a mild, fidgety manner and a hang-dog vulnerability. During the interview, whenever a subject arose that he didn't feel comfortable with, such as the past, he flitted off to something more benign, usually golf. "I used to be down on myself because I didn't have any money and all, but the insight I had was that the more failures you go through, the higher you can achieve," he said. "You can work hard in golf and make it."

Reportedly, Jones was a superstar in high school in Orlando. He won the Florida PGA Junior title and the U.S. Olympic Junior championship before turning pro at eighteen. Then something happened, all the details of which I could not discover. A car wreck was part of it; for five years he wore a neck brace. Apparently, too, he didn't get along with people; he was introverted and, as he puts it, "too hard core" about golf. For a long time he drifted. He sold pots and pans in Fort Worth, cleaned swimming pools in Orlando and mowed the grass at a country club in South Carolina. "I had went as low as I could go," Jones says, "but I won't say I was going crazy, because I still always believed that I could play."

His rescuer was Malcolm McDonald, an Orlando-area surgeon and friend of the family. Dr. Mac, as Jones calls him, remembered what a fine player Jones had been as a youth and convinced him four years ago to move back from South Carolina. To make that financially possible, McDonald bought Jones and his wife a trailer and a few acres of land outside Orlando and encouraged him to reconcile with his dad, a teaching pro.

The turning point for Jones, golf-wise, seemed to come last year when he qualified in a preliminary round to compete in the Greensboro Open, a PGA Tour event. "At Greensboro, you'd hear ten thousand people giving you the clap, and it was really motivating," Jones said. "I'm not gonna say I belong out there on the tour, but that experience made me think I might."

In 1992, by the time we were talking, Jones had already won seventeen tournaments on the minitour scene. "It scares me how well I'm doing," he said. "Right now I'd be afraid to take a week off."

Then he excused himself to go home and practice for the next day's final round. He was tied for the lead.

To get to Kissimmee Bay from DeBary Plantation, you motor down the interstate past the fantasy factory at Universal Studios and the counterfeit reality of Walt Disney World. Then you turn left into a nightmare strip of bogus American roadside attractions. You pass Gatorland, Pirate's Island, Medieval Times and Fun 'n Wheels. By the time you reach the county jail, where you turn right, Long John Silver's seems like a high-class seafood shoppe.

I mention this because it occurred to me as I drove to Kissimmee that it's no coincidence that the Bush-League Professional Golf Capital of the Universe should be in a city like Orlando, which is wholly predicated on the suspension of disbelief. Because that's what golf is all about, too. For ostensibly mature adult men to persuade themselves that the possibility of slicing a dimpled ball into some completely artificial, blue-dyed lagoon is a risk with as dire and pulse-quickening consequences as being eaten by a bear or ambushed by the Viet Cong demands not only the suspension of disbelief but also the collusion of an entire social ecosystem. That the players are engaged in *professional* golf (albeit third-rate professional golf) only adds to the gravitas and urgency of the adventure. The delusion grows that these rounds really matter, that the players' very careers hang in the balance on each and every shot. This, I concluded, could be the ultimate source of professional golf's dark and addictive thrill and possibly the key to understanding why men of the bush league so willingly sacrifice all the nice things that their wives would like them to buy with the money they don't earn, such as new drapes for the living room and higher-quality knickknacks.

That was my thinking, anyway.

For the final round of the Kissimmee Bay tournament, Jones was paired in the next-to-last foursome with three cadets named Scott Pleis, Bo Fennell and Chris Hehmann. Hehmann was a rookie who had apparently never before been so high on the leader board for a final round.

Diluting the potential tension of the round was the observational presence, in a golf cart, of Steve Pleis, Scott's brother, and Brad McClendon, a brawny, crew-cut, good old boy from Louisiana. Steve Pleis and McClendon, having gone out in the first group of the day, had already finished their rounds. They had zipped around the course in near record time—"They played like they were in some kind of hurry to take a shit," one rules official told me—and now had a bad case of the giggles, especially when it came to Hehmann.

"He's playing out of his ying-yang," McClendon chortled at number eleven when Hehmann mishit an approach shot but then chipped in from fifty feet for a birdie. On fourteen, when Hehmann left a forty-foot putt almost fifteen feet short, Steve said, "There's a lot of chicken left on that bone," and he and McClendon sat stifling their laughter like Sunday schoolers in a church pew. Eventually Hehmann self-destructed.

Jones, of course, was having none of it. He continued to play nearly flawless golf, hitting most greens in regulation and rolling his lag putts to within inches for tap-in pars. If Jones even noticed Pleis and McClendon trailing the group, he didn't show it. The Machine was focused, readying himself for what he had told me the day before was his primary focus and favorite part of a tournament: the final three holes. Coming off the fifteenth green, Jones said he figured two birdies out of the three would give him a chance to win. "We'll see what we can do," he said.

He got one birdie at the par-three sixteenth, draining a forty-footer. On seventeen, a 416-yard par four, he parked his approach shot five feet from the pin, and I had no doubt the Machine would hammer home the putt. But he didn't. The ball gave the hole a smell but then lipped out. On eighteen, all Jones could muster was a routine par.

His sixty-nine tied him for fourth. "One of those days," he said tersely and walked off the course.

In the clubhouse bar afterward, a couple of dozen players were waiting around to pick up their prize checks. Roger Rowland, a towheaded cadet from nearby Ocala, was hunched over his beer at the bar and shaking his head from side to side. He had just won the tournament with twin sixty-sixes. "Man, I'll tell you," he was muttering, "you plain gotta play some golf to win one of these things."

Billy Glisson was there, chain-smoking Viceroys and throwing back Seven and 7s as he regaled the Pleis brothers with tales from the good old days. "There was a lot more going on in those chairs than just blow-dries, I guarantee," was one line I overheard, presumably in reference to the beauty parlor/brothel where he used to work. For some reason he was carrying a jumbo driver and waggling it, Bob Hope–style, as he delivered his shtick. The Pleis brothers seemed only mildly amused.

To my surprise Gene Jones walked in and took a stool at the bar. I had the impression that drinking with the boys was not something he did very often.

"Hey, Machine," someone called out. "There's a rumor going around that you're making so much money you don't even cash your checks."

The barroom grew quiet to hear his response. "That's right," Jones said and took a long sip of beer. "I just go home every night and stare at 'em."

The line got a laugh, and that seemed to relax him. When a relative old-timer sauntered by and said, "Hey, Gene, what happened out there? I'm not used to seeing your name that far down the list," Jones smiled and seemed to relish the implicit compliment.

I took the stool next to Jones and offered to buy him a beer, but he bought me one instead. I asked him about his round. "Golf's a tough business," he replied with a shrug. "It's all about making the short ones."

He got out a pencil and calculated on a cocktail napkin that the missed five-footer on number seventeen had cost him $800. "But I still had a $2,000 week. I'll be getting $1,400 from Goosie and another $650 from the Spalding bonus pool. That's pretty good money for a country boy." Then he began pulling jewelry out of a pouch that he carries around in his golf bag: a gold Rolex, a gold pinky ring with a gaudy dollar sign on its face and a key ring hung with a tiny gold golf club and a spike wrench.

Finally, the tour manager, Bobby Simpson, began circulating with the checks: large, yellow Space Coast bank drafts signed by J. C. Goosie himself. Jones folded his neatly into quarters and tucked it in his wallet beside two suspiciously similar-looking pieces of paper. "What are those?" I asked.

He took them out and showed me: uncashed Space Coast checks for $3,000 and $1,000. "I guess I am getting a little behind," Jones admitted sheepishly. But as he returned the checks to his wallet, he held my glance for a moment, and I could see how powerfully proud he was of winning checks that large. He was proud of all that he had accomplished with his life in the last few years. Maybe he does take the checks home and stare at them, I thought.

The instant Jones left the bar, a journeyman pro named Dan Oschmann said: "The son of a bitch. I wish he'd get the hell out of here and let the rest of us make some money." He meant it as a joke, but he was serious, too.

In the PGA Qualifying Tournament, which began two weeks later, Jones obliged. He was one of only forty-two players out of nearly nine hundred entrants—including a large proportion of the Space Coast irregulars—to win a coveted tour card for 1993.

I talked to the Machine by telephone afterward. "I'm looking to earn a million dollars," he said. As of late April, however, Jones had made the cut in just two tournaments, earning a total of $4,340.

Only $995,660 to go.

JULY/AUGUST 1993

Editor's Note

Gene Jones lost his card after the 1993 season and never made it back onto the PGA Tour. There was one unheralded player competing in the tournaments described in this story, however, who did go on to earn Big Tour fame: Steve Stricker, who at last count had won three events and $6.5 million.

STARTING OVER

by Jim Harrison

O N THE SURFACE FISHING is a primitive activity. I mean in the anthropological sense that fishing is included in the hunting and gathering activities of our remote ancestors. It is all about filling the tummy.

In a decidedly comic sense it is hard to stay on the surface. Especially in the past two decades, a legion of men (and some women) have been writing about fishing. It's as if since fish spend their entire lives underwater we try to join them by going even deeper. Except in the rarest cases (for instance, Thomas McGuane's *The Longest Silence*) we utterly fail, because it's as hard to write well about fishing as it is about anything else. Shocking as it might seem, we know even less about fish than we do about women. We even talk about the Zen of fishing with a captious banality. As a twenty-five-year student of Zen I must tell you that fishing is fishing and Zen is Zen. The confusion here is that any activity that requires skill and during which we also manage to keep our mouths shut seems to acquire a touch of the sacred.

Some of us feel particularly good about essentially Pleistocene activities. If I walk a full hour through the woods to a beaver pond and catch a two-pound brook trout on a No. 16 yellow-bellied female Adams I feel very good. The important thing isn't the technique or the equipment but the totality of the experience, of which they are a very small part. There are the hundred varieties of trees and shrubs you pass through, the dozen different wildflowers, the glacial moraines, the stratocumulus clouds, the four warblers and the brown thrasher, the heron you flushed, the loon near the lake where you parked the car, the Virginia rail you mistook for a cattail, the thumping of your heart when you hook a fish, the very cold beer when you return to the car just before dark, even the onion in the baked-bean sandwich you packed along. But above all it is the mystery of the water itself, in the consciousness, not in the skill or the expensive equipment.

Nothing is quite so inexplicably dreary as watching a relatively rich guy who has spent a lot of money on a trip to the Florida Keys or to a big western river like the Yellowstone and can't make the throw. You wonder why he bothered or if he assumed his enthusiasm would some- how allow him to overcome the twenty-knot wind, the moving skiff or McKenzie driftboat. Fly-casting is most often a sport without second chances, and, like wing shooting, it requires the study of prescribed motion and the spirit of repetition. And if you can't afford a guide or, better yet, don't want one, your ultimate chore is understanding habi- tat. Both fish and birds hang out in their restaurants, but there are no signs out front.

So over a period of fifteen years you spent near a month a year on the flats of the Florida Keys fishing for permit and tarpon, your brain relentlessly mapping and remapping the area topographically to fig- ure out where the fish will be, given specific conditions of date, weather, tide, water temperature. Even then you don't have it figured. Why is a school of two hundred tarpon coming in Hawk Channel under the absolutely wrong conditions?

And then one day you don't want to go fishing. You want to go to an art museum or a bookstore. How many times have you gotten up at 6 A.M. to meet the right tide after only getting to bed at 3 A.M. and not necessarily alone? There's nothing like a windless ninety-two-degree day on the flats to tell you exactly how you behaved the night before. The sweat dripping into your eyes and down your nose smells like whiskey and other not necessarily commendable substances.

And, of course, you forgot that you were simply fishing, and that when you had taken it to a magnum level it was still just fishing, despite the fact that you were fly-casting to a 150-pound tarpon, which you can't really extrapolate by trying to imagine a 150-pound rainbow or steelhead. And this is not including stray shots at Pacific sails, striped marlin, and blue and black marlin off Ecuador and Costa Rica, where you had the suspicion that your body parts might detach. You had become not all that different from the humorless and somewhat doltish moguls who Leared into Key West for a few days of flats head- hunting, as if their real quarry were just another form of arbitrage.

So you burned out, and the burnout on magnum fishing also slipped the soul out of the day-to-day fishing in the Upper Peninsula that was a pleasant balm when you weren't running your dogs to get ready for bird season. Burnout is endemic to our culture, whether in a job or in sport.

I think it's actually traceable to brain physiology, if I understand Gerald Edelman's "neural Darwinism" properly, which I probably don't. Your responses become etiolated, atrophied, plain frazzled, and in this case you have quite simply fried your fishing neurons, except for the two weeks a year on the Yellowstone River near Livingston, Montana, floating in a McKenzie boat, which was more a retreat from your work life than anything else, and trotting with tadpoles in Kashmir would probably also do the same thing, except your grandsons were in Livingston.

In July I launch my new Poke Boat, a splendid and slender craft that weighs about thirty pounds and is perfectly suited to hauling into remote, uninhabited lakes in the U.P. You can paddle it like a kayak or install a rowing contraption, which I did—or, rather, a friend did for me, as turning doorknobs stresses the limits of my mechanical abilities. I weigh either 130 or 230. I'm forgetful these days, but it's probably the latter, which makes getting in and out of the boat a trifle awkward. A beastly process in fact.

But it's a crisp virgin boat, and I feel younger than springtime as I fairly slice across a river estuary leading to Lake Superior, the body of water that not incidentally sank the seven-hundred-foot freighter *Edmund Fitzgerald* about seventy miles from here.

The first wave wrenches my bow sideways. The second, third, and fourth waves fill my virgin boat to the gunwales. How can this be? I'm nearly tits high in water and why didn't I leave my wallet in the car like I intended? Luckily my next stop, the Dunes Saloon, will accept wet money.

There's inflatable flotation in the bow and stern of the Poke Boat, so I manage to crawl it to a sandbar. At least I drown a swarm of noxious black flies that were biting my legs. I wish mightily an old couple weren't watching me from shore. As a lifelong leftist I have always considered dignity to be faux-Republican indifference, but then everyone wants to look nifty. With a violent surge of energy and upper-body strength, I turn myself turtle on the sandbar, doubtless looking like a giant beetle from shore.

At the Dunes Saloon an especially intelligent Finn says, "You're wet," followed by a French-Canadian drunk who says the same thing. What's extraordinary about the experience is that I do the same thing the next day. The only excuse, unacceptable anywhere in the world, is that I was working on a novella about a closed head injury and was living in a parallel universe where one doesn't learn from experience.

Luckily I moved inland in the following weeks and had a marvelous time drifting among herons and loons and one lake with at least seventy-seven thousand white waterlilies. It was August and the fishing was poor, though one day on my first cast with a streamer I caught a pike the size of a Havana corona, a truly beautiful little fish that nearly covered the length of my hand. Her (it had to be female) sharp, prickly teeth gave my finger a bite when I was about to slip her back in the water. With the gout of blood emerging from my finger, there was a momentary and primitive urge to squeeze her guts out, but then I am a sportsman. If the pike had been a male, I might have done so.

During all my benighted years as a dry-fly purist I occasionally did some slumming, partly because I was in my thirties and the molecular movement of hormones made any stupid thing possible. If you trek far out on the ice and spend an entire day in a fish shanty with a friend staring down through a large hole in hopes of spearing a pike, you are demonstrating that it's hard to find amusement in the Great North in January. You forgot the sandwiches but you and the friend remembered two bottles of Boone's Farm Apple Wine and two bottles of Ripple made from indeterminable fruit, plus a half dozen joints of Colombian buds. Due to this not-very-exotic mixture the day is still memorable.

When a pike finally made a pass on our dangling sucker decoy, I think we said in unison, "Wow, a pike," and forgot to hurl the spear. We wobbled toward the shore in a blinding snowstorm, our compass the church bells in our small village.

Of course drugs and fishing don't mix. It's fun to mouth truisms that have become inanities. The tendency of boomers to tell older folks to "stay active," as Melvin Maddocks points out, infers the opposite, "stay inactive." It was certainly difficult to concentrate or cast well on LSD, but it made the rattling of gill plates on a jumping tarpon a fascinating sound indeed. And, once, in an altered state Jimmy Buffett revved his engine to the max when it was tilted up. I sat there in a questionable daze as the propeller fired out toward the Gulf Stream, glimmering in the blue distance. Mostly on acid you couldn't fish well because you became obsessive about the improbable profusion of life at the bottom of the shallow flats. A passing crustacean

became as monstrous as it is to lesser creatures, which might have
included yourself.

Recently, a few days before heading to Montana for my annual fishing
vacation, I decided to go north pretending I was an enervated businessman who had been strained through a corporate sheet and was
desperate for a day of fishing. Parenthetically, I was only halfway to
my cabin before I realized that except for my journal and poetry, I had
never written for free, and a dense Martian might actually think I was
a businessman. Many writers are as hopelessly venal as day traders.
This is all the more reason to go fishing, which is a singular way to "get
out of your mind" to where you might very well belong.

A friend of mine in the U.P., Mike Ballard, had consented to act as
a guide. We've been fishing together for twenty years and often have
assumed different names to dispel the ironies involved in adults at
sport. Mike is a consummate woodsman and occasionally refers to
himself as "Uncas," the James Fenimore Cooper hero. In recognition
of my own true character I am just plain Brown Dog. This is all plain-
tively idiotic but to have fun the inner and the outer child must
become the same, which is harder than it sounds. For extended periods of my life I have condemned fishing to death by playing the
mature adult, an illusion most of us live and die with.

It was one of those pratfall days. We boated five miles up the estu-
arine arm of a large lake, the fishing so slow we went ashore and
walked a high ridge, which was delightfully wild. The sour note was
that from the ridge we could see a huge, black rolling squall line
approaching from the west, and by the time we made it back to the
boat Uncas said, "Even our balls are wet." So were the sandwiches
(capicola, provolone, mortadella), but the two bottles of Côtes du
Rhône were secure. We stood under a tree and drank them both,
making our way to the landing in a stiff wind and temperatures that
had dropped from seventy degrees down to forty.

It's dreary to keep hearing that it doesn't matter if you're catching
anything, it's the experience that counts. Well, of course the experience counts and we spiritually thrive in this intimate contact with
Earth, but it's a whole lot better to catch fish than not to catch fish.
You can't fry a reverie, and I like to fry fish in a cabin in the same manner as my grandfathers, my father, and my uncles did before me.

I have supposed that at times you penetrate a set of feelings known intimately to your even more remote ancestors.

Probably 99 percent of the fish I've caught in my adult life were released. I don't say "released unharmed," as a creature's struggle for life is indubitably harmful to it. We should avoid a mandarin feeling of virtue over this matter. It's a simple case that a variety of torture is better than murder for the survival of the species. The old wisdom is that the predator husbands its prey. "Catch and release" is sensible, which shouldn't be confused with virtuous. "I beat the shit out of you but I didn't kill you" is not clearly understood by the fish. This is a blood sport, and if you want a politically correct afterglow you should return to golf. Eating some wild trout now and then will serve to remind you that they are not toys put in the river for the exercise of your expensive equipment.

When you try to start over, you are forced to remember that enthusiasms that have become obsessions burn out rather easily. You think of the talented adolescent tennis and baseball players who withdraw when pushed too hard by neurotic parents. I was pushing myself in my twenties when I, as a dry-fly neurotic on a Guggenheim grant, fished ninety days in a row. Such obsessive-compulsive behavior is supposedly a mental defect, but then I also wrote the title novella of my collection *Legends of the Fall* in nine days, which I view as worth the madness. It can be caused by backpressure in the sense that I had been teaching for two years on Long Island and was longing for my beloved northern-Michigan trout streams, thus the ninety-day binge. In the case of "Legends," I had brooded about the story for too long and had to write quickly or lose it.

Of course, certain fishing behavior is indefensibly stupid. Years of fishing permit and tarpon for thirty days back to back out of Key West naturally sours one, especially when augmented by bad behavior. You need only to check into a hotel when a convention is in progress. Having had my cabin in the U.P. for twenty years, I've been able to study hundreds of groups of men who have come north to hunt and fish. I've had the additional advantage of spending time studying anthropology. There is whooping, shouting, jumping, slugging, and countless manly trips to the toilet to relieve the mighty freight of beer. One could imagine Jane Goodall off in the corner making her primate notes.

This is all an extension of the mythologies of outdoor sport that begin in childhood, when the little brain fairly yelps, "Twelve-point buck! Ten-foot wingspan! Ten-pound brown!" Woods and water might very well be infested with "lunkers" of every variety. Within this spirit of conquest and food gathering I have watched a fishing friend dance with a 350-pound woman so tall he barely nibbled at her chin while trying to kiss her. Early man and later man had become one under the feral pressure of a hunting and fishing trip.

As a language buff I've been curious how quickly speech can delaminate in the face of excitement. Years back, well off the northern coast of Costa Rica with my friend Guy de la Valdéne and the renowned artist and fishing fop Russell Chatham, we managed one afternoon, using a rubber squid and a casting rod, to tease up a black marlin of about six hundred pounds and a blue marlin that certainly approached a thousand. First of all, it is alarming to look closely into a blue marlin's softball-sized eye maybe twenty or so feet away, and when Guy flopped out the fly, the fish sipped it into the corner of its mouth. The ratio would be similar to a very large man eating a very small brisling sardine.

Once hooked (it must have felt like a pinprick), the immense fish did the beginning of a barrel roll, its entire length emerging as it pitched backward away from the boat. And to me the audio was as memorable as the visual; bleak screams, cries, yelps, keening, with each sound swallowed soon after it began.

An hour or so later we nearly had a repeat with the black marlin, but I was doing the teasing and lost the rubber squid to the fish before I managed to get him into casting range for Russell. It took a lot of yelling for me to console myself, but then finally I accepted the fact that we were fishing for the reasonably sized striped marlin, and the encounter with the two monsters, though lunar, was a doomed effort, a case of outdoor hubris similar to trying to take a Cape buffalo with a BB gun.

I have long since admitted that my vaunted maturity is in actuality the aging process. More than a decade ago, in a state of financial panic (fifty years old and no savings whatsoever), I began to work way too hard to allow for spending a lot of time at a sane activity like fishing. Saving money is even less fun than watching corn grow. My sporting life was reduced to a scant month, with two weeks of Montana fishing and a couple weeks of Michigan grouse and woodcock hunting. I don't count my afternoon quail hunting near our winter "casita" in Arizona, which mostly consisted of walking the dog. If your hunting is spliced between a double work shift you're never quite "there" in the field.

Sad to say this thoroughly nasty bourgeois work ethic, taken to my usual manic lengths, quite literally burned down the house of my fishing life. Years passed, and I began to envision my epitaph as "He got his work done," something that fatuous. I think it was the novelist Tom Robbins who said that he doubted that success was an adequate response to life. Saving money, though pragmatically laudable, gets you in the garden-variety trap of trying to figure how much is enough. A straight answer is unavailable during a period in history when greed is not only defensible but generally considered a virtue. When overcome by greed, the fisherman tends to limit himself to head-hunting, a kind of showy trophy search on the far corners of the earth. When living correctly and relatively free from greed, I did not differentiate between my humble beaver-pond brook-trout fishing and the stalking of large tarpon.

On one of my Poke Boat voyages I paddled into a ten-acre mat of white waterlilies to protect my ass from gathering waves. As a lifelong claustrophobe, to me an uninhabited lake is the ultimate relief from this phobia that cannot clearly be understood. I have, however, considered the idea that I might be somewhat less evolved than others are. After a severe childhood injury I quite literally ran to the woods, which has proved to be my only viable solution. When in Paris or New York, the Seine, the Hudson, and the East River present me with immediate relief from my phobia, as do the Bois de Boulogne, the Luxembourg gardens, and Central Park. Even as a wacky young beatnik in New York City in the late '50s I'd have to head up to the Botanical Garden in the Bronx.

Nearly all fishing takes place in a habitat that is likely to make you unable to think of anything but the sport at hand. In late August at my cabin I was brooding about my recent financial collapse and drove out to the gorge of a nearby river, basically a sand-choked mediocre river but nonetheless prepossessing. I sat down on a very high bank with a miniature fly rod and glassed a stretch with my monocular (the only real advantages to being blind in one eye are that I was 4F during

Vietnam and I don't have to carry cumbersome binoculars). Under the shade of an overhanging cedar tree was a succession of decent brook-trout rises. I reflected on the gasping it would take to get out of the gorge, also the number of small grasshoppers in the area, which must be what the trout were feeding on. I had only a small packet of flies with me and a single, small Joe's Hopper from Montana. I made the long slide down the sandy bank on my butt, regathered myself, and took my first throw, only to hook a root halfway up the bank on my first backcast. I didn't yell "Gadzooks!" I climbed up to the root by pulling myself hand over hand on other roots. I detached the fly and managed to catch the smallest of the rising trout, scaring the others away. Now soaked with sweat, I took off my clothes and wallowed in an eddy. I paddled over an exchange, a blurred glance with several trout that seemed curious rather than frightened. Even the predictably gasping trip back up the bank was pleasurable indeed compared to important meetings in offices high above cities that I have experienced. As Thoreau said, "While I sit here listening to the waves which ripple and break on this shore, I am absolved from all obligation to the past."

Every few years I've taken to the idea of worms or minnows as bait or plugs for casting for pike and bass. The mood usually doesn't last and probably emerges from my modest egalitarianism, also an occasional sense of repulsion from being in the company of fresh- or saltwater fly fishermen when they are especially full of themselves, all fey and flouncing and arcane, somewhat like country clubbers peering with distaste over the fence at the ghetto bait types in the distance. However, I have sense enough to blush at my occasional proletarian masquerades at my income level. I still can't bear to "dress up" like the fishermen I see who, with an addition of one more gadget, appear likely to either drown or sink through the earth's crust from the weight of their equipment, or better yet, the outfits—the costumes, as it were—designed for a terrestrial moon walk or perhaps ridding an airliner of Ebola virus.

Of course, this is probably only an extension of my own childhood lust for first-rate equipment after I had judged those fifty-cent, fifteen-foot-long cane poles inappropriate to my future as a great angler. For a number of years, all of my earnings from hoeing and picking potato bugs went to rods, reels, plugs, and flies.

I suspect that I'm a fly fisherman for aesthetic reasons, adding the somewhat suspicious quotient of degree of difficulty. My father fished for trout using only a fly rod, whether with streamers or bait, and so I suppose it was all inevitable. He was a well-read agriculturist and fished incessantly, taking me along on every occasion after I was blinded in one eye at seven. We were rather poor, but he was giving me the woods and the water to console me after a bad deal. Right after World War II, he and my battle-weary (South Pacific) uncles built a cabin on a lake where we lived in the summer, with several trout streams in easy reach. I imagine millions of men are still fishing because they did so as children and it is unthinkable not to continue. And it is still a consolation in a not-quite-comprehensible world.

This quality of intensity in one's personal history can be unbearably poignant. After my father died in an accident along with my sister, I gave his fishing equipment—including a large, immaculately arranged tackle box—to a Mexican migrant kid named Roberto who lived with his family on the farm we rented. Roberto was about twelve and fished a lot in Texas when he wasn't working. There were at least a hundred plugs, antiques now, but I'm sure they were put to good use.

In George Anderson's fly shop in Livingston, you never hear fish referred to as "old fangface" or "waterwolves," euphemisms for northern pike up in Michigan. This shop is as discreet as Armani's in New York. When I annually pick up my license, I ask an old acquaintance named Brant how the fishing has been, and he usually says, "So-so," having doubtless answered the question a hundred thousand times. He can't really say, "As good as your capabilities," which would be accurate.

A few years ago the Yellowstone River suffered serious flooding, but it has begun to recover. I simply love to float it in a McKenzie boat and have booked an expert guide, Dan Lahren, for the past decade. In that I have fished there nearly every year since 1968, I scarcely need a guide, but then it's a great deal more comfortable than stumbling over slippery rocks, and since I'm committed to the fee, I fish six hours every day. Ultimately the cost is nominal compared to evening meals in New York and Paris, where there's little fishing, though striped bass have been reappearing around New York and I've long promised myself the absolute inanity of fly-casting the Seine right in the middle of Paris, particularly the stretch near the Musée d'Orsay. Lest you question my sanity, I should add that I don't value sanity very highly. Besides, we all know that every creature is confronted moment by moment by the question of what to do next, and casting a woolly worm out into the turgid waters of the Seine seems a splendid option.

I fish a total of about seventy miles of the Yellowstone, selecting a piece each day, keeping in mind the specific pleasures of scenery, habitat, the hydrologic shape of the water, the memories each stretch evokes. Tom McGuane moved to the area in 1968, and his friends followed, including Russell Chatham and Richard Brautigan, and in recent years I've fished a number of times with Peter Matthiessen. This year the fishing was mediocre, though I was distinctly more conscious, mostly because I've pulled back from the screenwriting business but partly because I fished a lot in the summer in my attempt to jump-start an old obsession. I had no forty-fish days, as I've had in the past, and no fish over three pounds, but each day was an unremitting delight. During slow periods I'm always reminded of McGuane's essay, the title work in *The Longest Silence,* on how angling is often filled with a pleasant torpor interrupted by truly wild excitement. My friend and guide Lahren likes to remind me of the time I pulled a dry fly away from a giant brown trout, thinking for truly inscrutable reasons that it was an otter trying to steal my fly. Its dense, massive arc seemed too large for a trout. This fall the most noteworthy day brought a squall that turned the river into a long tidal riptide, and when we left the river even the irrigation ditches had whitecaps.

It's now October 22, and there's a gale on Lake Superior, with the marine forecast predicting waves from eighteen to twenty-four feet. Perhaps I should get my beloved Poke Boat out of the shed, but first I'll knock off fifty pounds for ease of maneuvering. As a backup, a friend is building me a classic Chesapeake skiff. Also, I'm planning to go to Mexico to catch a roosterfish on a fly, a rare lacuna in my experience.

I won't say I've reached the location of that improbably banal word *closure.* You don't start fishing a lot in the same place you left for the same reason you can't restart or renew a marriage back to a state of innocent, blissful passion. It's quite a different person baiting the hook or, better yet, tying on the fly. It is, however, fine indeed to know that if you've lost something very good in your life it's still possible to go looking for it.

FEBRUARY 2000

HAIRBALL CARCASS
TOSSING IN THE CHUGACH
by Charles M. Young

I N FOOTBALL, A TEAM loses five yards if its left tackle jumps
offside. But if the left tackle keels over and dies of heatstroke, loss
of his services is deemed sufficient penalty. If a power forward collapses of a heart attack on the basketball court, the referees do not give
the opposition an extra free throw. And in baseball, batters universally
avoid catching fastballs with their foreheads on the theory that being
awarded first base fails to compensate for getting killed. So death for
most athletes and to most rules committees is, ipso facto, bad.

In extreme snowboarding, you lose thirty points if you die.

"Yeah, the days of belly-flopping off a cliff and collecting a prize are
definitely over," says Steve Klassen, the 1996 winner of the King of
the Hill Snowboard Tournament in Valdez, Alaska. It's hard to tell if
he's nostalgic or numb as he nurses a beer at the 1997 opening ceremony in April. A little fall that doesn't alter your line of descent will
cost you one point. If you fall and slightly alter your line but show
good stability in the recovery, you lose two points. If you use your arm
as a stabilizer (doing a "wheelie bar"), you lose three points. And so it
goes for minor, medium, and large falls, down to a minus-ten for three
or more cartwheels (also known as "starfishing"). From minus-eleven
to minus-twenty-nine, the rules mention no penalties. Then, at
minus-thirty, you draw the ace of spades: a major fall that "endangers
rider safety," which is to say "ragdolling," which is to say you flop
uncontrollably for forty-two hundred feet down a seventy-degree
mountainside, contusing all your internal organs on exposed rocks,
starting an avalanche with chunks of snow the size of a bus, and getting buried at the bottom of a glacier in a bottomless crevasse.

"No, I don't feel like *I'm* risking life and limb," says Klassen, once a
business major and an All-American pole-vaulter at USC, now the
owner of the Wave Rave Snowboard Shop in Mammoth Lakes, California. At thirty-two, he serves his young sport as both an elder statesman and a champion, most recently having won the European

Extreme, in Verbier, Switzerland. "To me, only the Downhill Day has any risk. It's unnatural to go as fast as you can. I like going as fast as I want. My thing is more fluidity of line. A lot of guys jump off bigger cliffs. I don't like pushing it so far that I'm risking my life."

The dining room at the Totem Inn, the official KOH headquarters, has a moose head the size of Iowa mounted over the fireplace. To its left is a glass case holding two stuffed beavers and a stuffed wildcat. To its right sits another case, with a stuffed wolverine and two sets of carved walrus tusks. The walls are covered with huge banners advertising the various sportswear and equipment companies sponsoring the event. The room is dominated, though, by a pink coffee can sitting next to the cash register, for donations to Jim and Wendy Burgett, to help pay for the convalescence of their son Myles.

"We were doing a photo shoot for this movie called *Quest,* on Sugarloaf, in British Columbia," Klassen recalls. "There was good snow, good avalanche stability, no reason to think it was unsafe. [Myles] was on a planned route and just made the wrong turn, went off a twenty-five-foot cliff, and landed in a patch of rocks. I was down at the helicopter with the pilot when it happened. The cameraman got to Myles within five minutes, and we were able to fly the helicopter in about seven minutes after that. We didn't have a stretcher, so we stuffed him into the outer shell of a sleeping bag because he couldn't wait. I thought we did a good job with the first aid—repositioning him, getting him into the helicopter with the guide—but there wasn't much we could do. He was unconscious, gurgling. The back of his head was smashed in. He was bleeding from his ear. His jaw was locked. He was still alive—that was all you could say."

He wasn't wearing a helmet?

"No, in general people don't wear helmets when they film. But if you're doing anything around rocks, you should definitely wear one. In Mammoth Lakes, I'm the safety spokesman, and I've gotten a lot of guys to wear them. The way people are pushing it now, I tell them they can push it even further with a helmet, as far as going over cliffs and stuff."

What does Klassen think of Myles?

"I admire his ability, and I'm intrigued with his personality. I've been to college, been around the world, own a business. Myles was nineteen at the time of his accident, and he'd lived almost his whole life in Valdez. He had this simplicity, this childlike curiosity, that you only find in people who have been exposed to almost nothing. He was really shy until he got to know you, and then he could just amaze you with these really powerful insights that could only come from the innocence of his experience—something I'd lost sight of a long time ago. At the same time, he was a hard-partyin' Alaska boy. He drank, he smoked. He was a little closer to death than the rest of us. I think his hero, Jim Morrison, had a lot to do with his wild streak. He was always rattling off quotes from Doors songs. He came to visit me in Mammoth Lakes once—it was his first trip to California—and he wrote a line from 'Roadhouse Blues' on a poster in my shop: 'Keep your eyes on the road [and] your hands upon the wheel.'"

Nick Perata—KOH organizer during the winter and spring, fishing and hunting guide during the summer and fall—stands up in the Totem Inn dining room and calls for quiet. He yells for quiet. He screams for quiet. Lots of people join him in screaming for quiet. Maybe a third of the room glances at him, causing a drop of about five decibels in the din. Perata shouts: "This event is designed to find the best all-around snowboarder, not just the most extremist guy. It's about speed, freestyle, and extreme. All my competitors should be reading the judging sheet. If you don't fall, you win. So don't fall. The whole reason I'm doing this event is so people can snowboard safely."

The background decibel level goes back up. Perata reminds the four or five people still listening that for their $1,100 entry fee, they're getting three square meals a day, lodging, transport up Thompson Pass, and a whole bunch of rides on a helicopter or a ski plane to various backcountry locations in the Chugach Mountains, places with such names as the Cheese Grater, the Python, the Berlin Wall, and the Terror Dome. And if they crash, they *might* get first aid.

"There's not a lot of snow this year," shouts George Ortman, the head of the rescue squad. "That means more rocks, lots of brush. It's bonier than ever. It's manky. And we found a big avalanche today. The mantra is: It's up to you guys not to get hurt. If you do, it's 'cause you went too fast and you hit a rock. We can't control it, and we can't make it safe. If you crash in our domain, we'll try to save your life. If you crash outside our domain, you're on your own. So *listen* when we tell you what's out of bounds. Nobody gets on the chopper without a helmet, beeps [an avalanche transceiver], and a shovel to dig your buddy out. The rescue squad can commandeer anyone. If they need help, listen to them. It's really dangerous, as skinny as I've ever seen it."

Perata announces that there are forty-three entrants this year from all over the world: ten women, who will go down the mountain first, and thirty-three men. The winners, male and female, of each of the three days of competition get $1,000; the two overall winners get $10,000 apiece, a fresh twenty-five-pound king salmon, a bitchin' beautiful broadsword, a crown, and a massive pile of swag from the various sponsors.

The final speaker is a woman named Theresa Ingersol, a friend of the Burgett family.

"Myles has been making a little progress since the accident on February third," she says. "He's coming out of the coma now." Big cheers. "He had an operation to fix his feeding tube, which was causing an infection. He is able to move his fingers, and he recognizes his family. But he can't talk with the feeding tube in his throat. The doctors won't take it out until they're sure he has a swallow reflex."

Silence. Perata seizes the moment to hold up the pink coffee can. "It doesn't matter about the prizes, just put your money in here," he says. The noise starts to build again. "One more thing," he yells. "The Totem Inn has the finest waitresses in the entire world! Tip them, and they'll be stoked to serve you!"

The next morning is declared a weather day, meaning that it's cloudy in Valdez and there are snow squalls thirty miles up the pass where you catch the helicopter. This is why Perata scheduled ten days for a three-day, three-event competition. Back in the Totem dining room, it's also a hangover day. Only a few of the competitors have shown up for their officially allotted biscuits and gravy with unlimited coffee refills.

"I'm the only one in my family who isn't a brain," says Perata, who is originally from La Canada, California, the town next to Pasadena. "My parents got divorced when I was three, and school never interested me much. Me and my friends, we were huge into vertical-ramp skateboarding. In 1983, we made our first snowboard—just a piece of plywood, and the binding was seat belts. We took it to the Angeles Crest National Forest above Pasadena and hiked up about three thousand feet near the Krakta Ridge ski area. I was the first guy to go, and it was just so natural and easy. Waist-deep powder, and I didn't fall the whole way down."

Not quite Saul getting smacked by white light on the road to Damascus, but it was still a life-changing religious experience, against which higher education just couldn't measure up. After a year at the College of the Siskiyous and a year at Boise State, Perata admitted to his old man that he wasn't learning squat, dropped out, and moved to Breckenridge, Colorado, the mecca of snowboarding in the mid-'80s. "The mountains were as good as, maybe better than, Aspen's, and it was so much cheaper," he recalls. "They actually wanted snowboarders in Breckenridge."

In 1989, Perata decided to climb the Moose's Tooth, a mountain near Alaska's Mount McKinley. On the twenty-eighth day—spent mostly above the tree line, where there were no colors except the white of the snow and the blue of the sky, no sound except the rumblings of avalanches, no smells except that of pure air—a plane dropped him a package containing a case of beer, a quarter bag of weed, two tins of chewing tobacco, five packs of cigarettes, and a zillion cookies. Comesting his comestibles, surveying all of Alaska at his feet, Perata had his second religious experience. "I realized what an asshole I was, what a punk asshole snowboarder," he recalls. "And that whatever you do with your life, the mountain doesn't care. It is magnificent and you are nothing. It can kill you, and it is not even trying. No matter how tough you think you are, how bad you think you are, the mountain won't let you do certain things. I was humbled. And I realized that the mountains in Colorado weren't gnarly enough. Colorado had no challenge."

As a competitor in the snowboard wing of the 1993 World Extreme Skiing Championship in Valdez, Perata was standing on a ridge with a group of other entrants and EMTs when he had his third religious experience. A cornice of snow—fifteen feet thick and six hundred yards long—fractured, and the back draft sucked a skier off the ridge and into the avalanche, killing him. As Perata watched him tumble for thirty-three hundred vertical feet, he knew there had to be another way. He would organize his own tournament, just for snowboarders. It would be safer. It would have better rock-and-roll bands. It would be called King of the Hill, and he would incorporate himself as the Alaska Freeriding Federation so he couldn't be sued personally if someone got hurt.

In the annals of Valdez disasters, the inaugural KOH, in 1994, doesn't summon anywhere near the post-traumatic stress disorder caused by the 1927 meteor that shattered the peak of a nearby mountain, the 1964 earthquake that leveled the town, or the 1989 oil spill that besmirched Prince William Sound. But it does hold a very special place in local memory. Perata appointed as his head judge a man named Scott Liska, once an electrician, now the owner of the Boarderline Snowboard and Skate shops in Anchorage, Juneau, and Fairbanks. Liska drove down Richardson Highway from Anchorage in his black Cadillac hearse with its superamplified sound system blaring Dr. Dre and the Geto Boys. His first stop was the Valdez police station, to bail out a recently busted friend. The police wanted cash, however, and at the local branch of the First National Bank of Anchorage, Liska was too drunk to sign his name. Finally, Liska tried the ATM, which unreasonably refused him money when he couldn't remember his PIN. So he pissed on it. The security camera caught it all, so to speak, and the incident made a secondary splash in the *Valdez Vanguard*'s coverage of the tournament.

During the weather delays that year, a number of the entrants built on this public-relations coup by shooting holes in traffic signs. At the awards ceremony, at the new Valdez Convention and Civic Center, a facility that would be the pride of any small town in America, half the dance floor was designated for the underage local youth and half for the overage drinking snowboarders. The local underage youth, however, kept slipping over the line to the bar, then had their morals further corrupted by the punk-rock song stylings of Pennywise and the Offspring, whose language was deemed unfit for minors. The hall sustained a moderate mosh-pit trashing, and Matt Goodwill, the first winner of the King of the Hill title, punched several holes in the stage with his bitchin' beautiful broadsword. The cops shut down the show early, Perata refused to pay the center's rental fee for eight months, and the city of Valdez has declined to rent the building to him ever since.

"Alaska is the best place in the world to snowboard, and I'm trying to support it," says Liska, still the head judge, whose gray hair makes him look older than his thirty-nine years. "The mountains are steeper and the powder is deeper. You go to a ski resort, all you see are the moguls, the tracks of other skiers, the crowds at the tram lines. When you go up in a helicopter, you don't see another track. Just blue sky, untouched snow, perfectly white, with the sparkling crystals."

Seems like aesthetics plays a big part in the thrill.

"Oh, yeah. I made more money when I was an electrician, but once you've experienced this kind of snowboarding, you just want more. When we started King of the Hill, I was worried that if we didn't have a new event and draw in some more people that the local heli-skiing company would go out of business and I wouldn't be able to get to the top of the pass anymore. These mountains are way too big to hike up. I had to get back up there."

What's the difference between snowboarders and skiers?

"Snowboarders are a little more anticonformist, and they're looking for a different thrill. Skiing is more speed; snowboarding is more style: riding the terrain, sliding on logs and rocks, just using everything on the mountain. And you can go backward and forward on the board, which you can't on skis. Judges vary in what they like, but in general you want to avoid stopping and standing and falling. You do want to choose the best line down the mountain and stay in control. The experienced riders take Polaroids at the bottom and look at them again at the top, because everything looks different up there. You've got to memorize your landmarks from the helicopter."

Does Liska know Myles Burgett?

"Yeah, it was really scary to hear about him. I rode with him a lot. When I first got to be friends with him, I thought he had a death wish. It seemed like he was taking incredible risks, like he didn't care if he made it or not. Then I thought, *Well, maybe he doesn't have a death wish. Maybe he has a special gift.* If you were flying in a helicopter and you saw somebody's track that made you think *How did anyone go there?*, you'd just assume it was Myles's. All he cared about was finding the biggest, gnarliest cliff drop. I remember one year I was judging, and Myles traversed the mountain and dropped into a chute, which funneled down to this eighty-foot cliff. The edge was rounded, not a straight drop-off, and I thought it would be impossible for him to generate enough speed to clear it. He made a couple of turns in the chute and started an avalanche, and you couldn't see anything but this big cloud of snow. All you could hear was Myles's board clacking on the rocks. I was pretty scared, with that clacking. Suddenly, the cloud spit Myles out, like a surfer getting shot out of a huge tube, and I heard him yelling. The avalanche actually saved him, gave him enough speed and pushed him out over that rounded cliff. He seemed invincible."

The forty-seven hundred residents of Valdez like to talk about: (1) the time a big RV pulled into the Tesoro gas station and an eagle swooped down and ate the family's poodle; (2) the looming likelihood of another earthquake hitting 9.2 on the Richter scale, as did the one in 1964, the worst in North American history; and (3) the prospect of declining tax revenue from the oil pipeline's forcing the prosperous town to become a tourist trap dependent on snow as a natural resource.

Officially measured at 227 inches through March, the snow—now piled in grayish black pyramids all over the wide, flat streets of Valdez—appears to be an especially abundant resource, even in balmy April weather. Compared with the record of 561 inches in the winter of 1989–90, however, this year has been positively bony, manky, and skinny. The farther up Thompson Pass you go, the more snow you get, but there are still lots of rocks and brush visible at the thirty-two-mile mark, where the sign ALASKA BACKCOUNTRY ADVEN-TURES/ HELI SKIING $65, AIRPLANE $45/FULLY GUIDED beckons snowboarders to a slushy parking lot, two mobile homes, and a couple of Porto-Sans that reek heinously even at subfreezing temperatures.

The vibe is sort of *Apocalypse Snow*, with Perata playing both the Dennis Hopper and the Marlon Brando roles, orchestrating which of the forty-three contestants, twenty media people (mostly on camera crews), eleven rescue-squad workers, eight work-crew members, and five judges get to fly up the mountain in which trip of the Bell helicop-ter and the DeHaviland Beaver ski plane. The Beaver, a model of mid-'50s Canadian vintage much loved by bush pilots, has a little rope tied to each of its wingtips. When the engine starts, creating a hurri-cane of loose snow in its wake, two guys hang on to the ropes and pull in a seesaw motion to rock the plane's skis out of their frozen ruts. Then the plane takes off toward some high-tension wires about a mile down the road, winging up to land on a high glacier. For the non-Alaskan, the scene doesn't inspire confidence.

In the parking lot, Julie Zell, a small blonde who has been Queen of the Hill for three years running, tosses a stick for her retriever, Bamboo. Besides sporting the usual logos for her various sponsors, her snowboard is painted front to rear with a quote from Teddy Roo-sevelt: "Far better it is to dare mighty things, to win glorious tri-umphs, even though checkered by failure, than to take rank with those poor spirits who neither enjoy much nor suffer much, because they live in the gray twilight that knows not victory nor defeat."

"I just found it in some magazine," says Zell, thirty, pulling a string of Tibetan prayer flags out of her car and folding them into her back-pack. "I'm looking for a good place to hang these on the mountain.

They're for my brother Jimmy, who was paralyzed in a paragliding accident. Myles in a coma, my brother fighting for his life in a New York hospital, and this other friend of mine, Trevor Peterson, dead in an avalanche recently. Trevor was a pioneer of extreme skiing. His name was synonymous with 'first descent.' I've been asking myself lately, who had the worst fate? The guy who's in a coma and will have to relearn everything? The guy who's paralyzed but mentally all there? The guy who died? I never thought much about this until my brother's accident. There have been so many accidents, even in this little town. Did we cross a line somewhere? That's why I have that quote from Teddy Roosevelt. It's been hard to motivate lately."

The last of eight children, Zell grew up in Syracuse, New York. She entered her first ski race at the age of five, cried inconsolably when she didn't win, and still wonders why such a young child would care so much. She had a ninety-three average in high school but couldn't buy the undertone that life was predestined to college, job, marriage, kids, and death. She got a ski scholarship to the University of Alaska for one season. She got another ski scholarship, to Montana State, for one season, until that program got cut in a budget crunch. After a stint in Hawaii as a tour guide, waitress, and tie-dyer, she moved to Jackson Hole, where her older brothers Jeff and Jimmy were ski racing.

"I decided to go back to ski racing and see if I was any good, but I hated it," Zell says. "I was still too young, and I couldn't handle the politics. It seemed like the rich kids had all the advantages. They could go to all the camps and ski races, get training and expenses. Lots of times, you'd miss out on things because of political decisions. You'd be following the rules and suddenly there was this exception to the rule, this habit they had of moving the goal posts. In 1990, after a lifetime of bumming out over skiing, I tried this snowboard that was lying around the house. I pulled out of my first turn, and it was so easy and natural and perfect that I started laughing. And that was it. I was hooked. My brothers tried to convince me that I was throwing my life away, but they're proud of me now. If you've been coached all your life, been too regimented and disciplined, the freedom of snowboarding can just grab you. You have to be yourself to get down the mountain. The biggest obstacle is your own nervous system."

How well does Zell know Myles?

"He's a crazy kid, definitely a go-for-it kind of guy. I've heard a lot of people say 'It was bound to happen.' And I feel like clotheslining them. You never know why people take the chances they do. Maybe they see the risk differently."

The Brobowl, site of Downhill Day: a thirty-five-hundred-foot vertical drop, at moderately steep angles; sixteen gates; each competitor gets two runs; only speed counts, with a maximum of around 70 mph possible; so named by Perata because he and three of his bros were the first humans to snowboard the route. One of the bros (Jay Liska, son of Scott) is competing today; one is off filming another event, in Juneau; and one is doing time for handing out a large batch of mushrooms after last year's closing ceremony.

Casualties: two—Julie Zell and a member of the rescue crew. After Zell's smooth first run, the clouds blow in, reducing visibility to dangerous levels during her second run. Coming out of a steep incline at 50 mph, she hydroplanes and hits a bump. She starfishes three times into a snowbank, suffering a moderate concussion and a jammed spine. The rescue-crew guy catches the tip of his ski on something. "He fractured his tibia and fibula," says squad head George Ortman. "It's going to cost twenty-five thousand dollars, and he doesn't have medical insurance. The bones of the mountain are sticking out everywhere. Definitely the most dangerous year I've ever seen."

Later, back at the Totem: "Most of the other Frenchies are assholes, but not Antonin," says Perata with his unerring instinct for political correctness, speaking of the first day's leader, Antonin Lieutaghi. "The other Frenchies won't even talk to you most of the time. Antonin is a good ambassador, and he's the best athlete in the event. He's the only one I know who actually trains, who doesn't get fucked up, who is always first on the bus in the morning. What wins in this sport is your legs. Way before reaching the bottom, your legs are Jell-O. The strongest legs, the strongest will, the strongest route-finding ability—Antonin is best at all three. And every competitor I know likes him."

Lieutaghi, who has dark hair and eyes and is one of a small minority of snowboarders who can do a triple back flip, is also the only competitor with his own press packet, which conveniently identifies him as being twenty-nine years old, a snowboarder since 1986, and a current resident of the French Alps. "His legendary good mood, his passion for mountains and his unceasing foolery are nowadays known in the snowboard family," it says. "The fluidity, the esthetic style and the incredible power to situate himself in space. All that, make of Antonin Lieutaghi a special sportman."

"I was too noisy at normal school," says Lieutaghi. "I always wanted to move. It was difficult to sit at my desk, and I didn't want to make study after school. I wanted to do some sports. They sent me to the Fratellini Circus School, in Paris. I learned acrobatics, trapeze, trampoline, tightrope, juggling, clowning. I learned to handle my body well in the air and some stuff like that. I can live only for snowboarding. What I like is freeriding. I don't like to race. I race only to be recognized by my sponsor and to make some money."

What do his parents do?

"My father is a writer and botanist. My mother is a proofreader. Nobody else skis in my family. My father has too much job. Is very difficult for him to have good organization. He tells me I am a good example for him. He very much appreciates what I did to arrive at my point now. He maybe wants to do something else, but not in sports. I don't tell my parents what I really do. This winter, I fell in a big crevasse and broke my ribs and collarbone. I fell in a big avalanche. I jumped a forty-meter cliff. I try to be careful for myself, but I don't tell them about these things."

"They measure his progress daily with the Glasgow Coma Score," says Wendy Burgett at a table in Valdez's Sugarloaf Saloon. "There are three categories—eye opening, vocal ability, and movement ability—for which they give points and then add them up. On a scale of three to fifteen, Myles is at nine right now, which technically is not even a coma. He opens his eyes and makes eye contact slowly. He has expressions on his face. He's been moving his left arm all along, and he's beginning to move his right arm, which I thought he might have lost the ability to do. He made a sound early this week. They're working on his digestive problems, and his pneumonia is gone. It's a slow process, a year or two of rehabilitation, and he will have to relearn a lot of basic things. But the brain can recircuit. There's every chance he'll be walking and talking and functional.

"I don't know what we'd be doing if the accident hadn't happened in Canada, where they're paying for his rehabilitation. Our Blue Cross didn't cover Myles, and we couldn't find other insurance. His father and uncle are with him in Vancouver now. We have to pay our travel and living expenses in Vancouver, but our friends in Valdez have come through for us. A raffle raised six thousand dollars."

"We have a prayer chain going like you wouldn't believe," says Wendy's friend Sharon Keese.

Why was Myles so drawn to snowboarding?

"It was his art form," says Wendy, a native of Wisconsin who works in the Valdez women's shelter. "He was a quiet person, but he'd get on the board and come alive. I had no idea how motivated he was most of the time. When he came home last year after Extreme Day, I asked, 'How did you do?' He just said, 'Pretty good.' It turned out he was in first place. I was just happy that he'd found something he loved."

"The consensus of his friends is that he would have won the whole thing this year," says Keese. "It never went to his head, though. He was always teaching his friends new moves."

"He's in six videos, has his own poster, and we have a stack of snowboarding magazines with pictures and articles about him," says Wendy. "But he's always been just an ordinary kid. The competitions aren't very competitive, just an excuse to hang out with your friends."

What about school?

"When he applied himself, he was a great student," says Keese, whose own sons are close to Myles. "I think he was bored in class. One of those kids who are a little too smart for school."

"He did well in creative writing and art," says Wendy. "When he did it, he did well. He just had difficulty applying school to his life."

"There were a lot of kids who didn't go to school on good snow days," says Keese.

Was he thinking about another career eventually?

"He was talking about doing something else, planning to study for his GED," says Wendy. "When he would leave in the morning for the mountains, he would say, 'I'm going to work,' so he had a strong sense of professionalism. When Myles was fifteen and considering dropping out to snowboard full-time with a sponsor, the principal of his high school had a long talk with him, tried to convince Myles to stick with his classes. Myles dropped out anyway. Within a year, he had been to Uzbekistan, New Zealand, France, and South America. I don't know how high school could have been any more educational."

"He thought the women in Russia were hairy," says Keese.

"When they went to Bolivia, one of the riders got sick," says Wendy. "They had several days with nothing to do, so Myles went up on the roofs to explore the city. He found this chapel where he rang the bell, just to hear what it sounded like. Well, the bell hadn't been rung since World War II, and the police almost shot him. The priest wanted to throw him in prison until Myles gave him all his travel money."

She must have worried about him.

"All the time. His father would say, 'You don't need to take the risks anymore. You're good enough.' The accident wasn't a harebrained back flip. It was a planned route, and he made a wrong turn. They tell me he wanted to wear his helmet that day, but he forgot it in the closet back home."

"You wanna know what happened?" asks Steve Klassen, deeply embarrassed to have finished twentieth on Downhill Day, carrying a large grocery bag full of junk food back to his hotel room. "I thought I had a smokin' first round, but I used the wrong wax on my board, which really slowed me down. For the second round, I switched to a new board. It was faster, but I couldn't feel anything because the new board was stiffer. And I couldn't see anything in the flat light. You couldn't tell slab from snow. Sometimes you just need luck, and I didn't have any. This will be the first contest in three years that I lost."

"I can't remember anything except pulling my head out of a snow-bank," says Julie Zell, also carrying a bunch of junk food to her room. "I feel like I got two steel bars running from my shoulder down to my ass. Somebody said the light was like riding in a milk bottle."

"In the future I'll be wearing speed suits and shit like that," says Klassen. "A little bit of performance is added every year. And a little soul is taken away."

Nick's Happy Valley, site of Freestyle Day: a thirty-two-hundred-foot vertical drop; so named because Nick Perata loves its wind lips, natural half-pipes, cornices, small cliffs, and other natural features that make snowboarding extreme; competitors are judged for style, aggression, control, and fluidity; ten gates determine the route, so everyone is working with the same terrain; the run is untimed; it's said to get the best powder in the area when snow comes in. Unfortunately, snow comes in while half the competitors are on the summit and half still in the parking lot. Perata spends the morning and early afternoon beseeching the skies, muttering oaths about "bluebirds" (clear skies), "graybirds" (cloudy skies), and "suckerholes" (gaps in the clouds that promise a bluebird but deliver a graybird). With $1,000 out of his pinched budget already spent on flights to the summit, he must decide on a tooth-grinding, minute-by-minute basis whether to pull the riders off the mountain because it's too dangerous or to send more riders up and go on with the show.

A discreet word on dope: A snowboarder's day runs at the same pace as a rock musician's—long periods with nothing to do leading to short periods of intense activity and absolute focus. Some, not all, snowboarders smoke pot to pass time during the long periods and to enhance the flow during the short periods. So whenever a suckerhole blows over the summit of Nick's Happy Valley, all Alaska sparkles down below, all the universe opens up above, and several billion brain synapses in the immediate area go electric with this staggering skunkweed that smells just like Starbucks coffee.

Another discreet word on dope: Riding the features of a mountain with your feet locked to a small board exerts astronaut-level G-forces on select areas of the human body. Kneecaps have been known to shatter without hitting anything, so great are these forces. Of necessity, snowboarders learn to be amateur chiropractors, adjusting their ligaments, tendons, joints, and spinal columns on a nightly basis in their motel rooms. Many find this process more tolerable with a lungful of skunkweed.

Casualties: none. But you can't see much, either. Most of the runs occur during light snow squalls, which give the mountain the look of a Zen painting as the clouds blow in and out. At the first jump, a wind lip reinforced with a man-made snow ramp, the riders do some jaw-dropping spins (180 to 540 degrees) and back flips, then disappear into the gray. Lieutaghi takes second behind a local rider named Jason Borgstede, and Klassen moves up to twelfth.

"Dead last!" moans Morgan LaFonte, rubbing peppermint oil into her bare feet, ostensibly to keep warm. The window of her room at the Village Inn, across Richardson Highway from the Totem, is wide open, creating an access hole of about sixteen square feet for the stiff, chilly wind. "I'm dead last! I can't go to the Totem! I won't go to the Totem! I can't bear sympathetic looks! I'm just not competitive enough. I hate to look at other people and think, *Hey, I'm better than her.* I have no killer instinct."

Despite two lousy days in this competition, LaFonte has done well enough in the past that she has her own production-model snowboard marketed by K2. Her room is strewed with clothes, while her stash of herbs, vitamins, and foodstuffs is scattered in a terminal moraine of Tupperware. Unable to spell the name of her hometown after several tries with pen and paper, she volunteers by way of autobiography that she's from northern Michigan and has been living in Colorado for twelve years.

Her friend and fellow KOH contestant Lori Gibbs grew up in a strict Mormon family on a small farm on the Snake River, in Idaho. She barrel-raced at high school rodeos, hunted, fished, and endured the hard winters. After two years at the University of Innsbruck, in Austria, she ran off to California to live with a surfer who had to hide her skis to get her to try snowboarding, and for much of the next twelve years she ranked among the top three women in the sport. Most recently, she won the European Extreme.

"We're the dinosaurs," says Gibbs. "The kids coming up now, they look at me and say, 'She's old.' It's taken us a lot of years to get where we are, and it's taken a lot out of us."

By way of injuries?

"Well, let's see. I broke the same set of ribs twice. I broke my back. I blew out both my knees. The third time was the clincher. In 1991, I broke my leg in five spots, crushed my ankle. We were guinea pigs for testing equipment in those days. I have a pretty high tolerance for pain, but I had to take a year off for rehabilitation. I did a lot of thinking about the true meaning of snowboarding."

Which is?

"That I do it for my soul, not for a sponsor. That I will still be doing powder runs even if I'm on the pro-golf tour and making real money. It's like finding a drug that you really, really love. It's like sex."

"An injury is not the worst thing that can happen," says LaFonte. "I had a clean record until last winter, when I tore a bunch of ligaments in my knee. It freed me up to take a look at myself. I decided to be kinder to my body if I wanted to live to be an old and happy human being."

So what's next?

"I've been through all the levels of excitement in this sport, and either you get through it or you die," she says. "I'm in the final stages now, and what I really want to do next is surf."

✧ ✧ ✧

The White Room, site of Extreme Day: a forty-one-hundred-foot vertical drop; to the west, a steep ridge about a mile long; to the east,
another steep ridge about a mile long; to the north, a gap; to the
south, a slightly lower gap; in the middle, a glacier that slopes gently
to the south, giving the effect of a football stadium with an opening at
either end zone; named for the Cream song; should be renamed the
Anvil of the Arctic Sun, because under a bluebird, the 360-degree UV
hammers any exposed skin.

Planted in the snow at the bottom of the run is a profusion of banners bearing the logos of several companies. In addition, most of the
best riders have individual sponsors whose insignia are plastered on
their helmets as if they were stock cars at the Daytona 500. When making the yearned-for transition from doing the thing you love to getting
paid for doing the thing you love, snowboarders learn the same hard
lesson as rock musicians: Open the door for capitalism, and suddenly
the thing you love is tainted. Ambivalence replaces that pure sense of
freedom, which is why you got into it in the first place. So while most
pro snowboarders are grateful to get enough of a stipend that they
don't have to wait tables or do carpentry at least part of the year, they
are simultaneously resentful of the boss. A snowboarder who show-
boats to impress a sponsor is known as a "nutswinger."

A discreet word on language: The work crew and the first-aid crew
are not referred to as such. They are called "banner nigs" and "rescue
nigs." In fact, anyone with a job is a "nig." No racism appears to be
implied; it's part of the general atmosphere of taboo tromping.

The word *extreme,* once useful to designate activities requiring both
courage and coordination outside the realm of traditional sports, has
gone through the usual transition to meaninglessness as Madison
Avenue and the entertainment business have applied it to all manner
of insipid crud. Today's truly extreme snowboarder is often described
as "hairball," as in what your cat barfs up every week or two. For
instance: "What we do is pretty hairball," says Morgan LaFonte, "but
they have more injuries in those bogus half-pipe competitions for
television."

To be hairball, one must "huck," which Klassen defines as "throwing yourself off a cliff where you have a fifty-fifty chance or less of
landing it." Head judge Scott Liska barks over his walkie-talkie to the

work crew on a ridge: "Get 'em off of there! I don't want anyone huck-ing off that cornice thinking there's pow underneath!"

Handling one's body well, riding the features of the mountain within an inch of ragdolling—but not ragdolling—is "meat hucking." A synonym for meat hucking is "carcass tossing." Thus Elke Barns, a rider from Girdwood, Alaska, compliments Lori Gibbs on an espe-cially thrilling descent: "That was some hairball carcass tossing, girl!" "Taco tossing," by contrast, means hitting something so hard that you fold your body around it. This is to be avoided.

Casualties: No one actually taco tosses on Extreme Day. Three rid-ers do go down something called the Koch Notch, a narrow chute with little snow ending in a tiny rock ledge that drops off to a sixty-foot rock cliff that descends at an eighty-degree angle. All three riders stop on the ledge and stare down for minutes before making the leap. Two of them more or less huck. One of them breaks his leg. The rescue squad digs him out and carries him to the helicopter for the ten-minute ride back to base camp, pausing first for a snapshot. The rider with the bro-ken leg laughs the whole time. Another boarder finishes his run and pulls off his glove, revealing a pinkie sticking out of his palm at a right angle. George Ortman grabs the finger, while another guy yanks the boarder's shoulder, and they snap the pinkie back into place.

Some forty-one hundred feet up, there's a mile-long ridge to the west. Every ten minutes or so, a boarder starts down from any point of his choosing. On the glacier below, there are clumps of banners, clumps of camera crews, clumps of spectators, and one clump of judges (who sit in a half igloo to shield themselves from the pounding sun). The riders begin as little black dots, discernible from the rocks only because they are moving. As their descent proceeds, the sheer, overwhelming beauty of meat hucking becomes apparent as the rid-ers find routes where there appear to be none, turning every obstacle into an opportunity for acrobatics.

Even to the untrained eye, the two best rides are obvious. Klassen carves the White Room in exhilarating, long, graceful slashes that have an almost architectural geometry. And Matt Goodwill attacks the boulders as if God put them there just to piss him off. At one point, he leaps onto the edge of the chute and jibs the nose of his board back and forth on either side of the spine, drawing cheers and gasps from the clumps below. It's like watching Rembrandt and Jackson Pollock fall off a mountain, Mozart and Motörhead, Laurence Olivier and Jim Carrey. Carrey wins, one hundred to ninety-eight.

"No, he wasn't shy. He just didn't like to talk," says Trevor Keese, son of Sharon. "What was odd about Myles, he never said good-bye. When he was bored, he'd just disappear. You'd look around and he was gone. You never knew what he was going to do."

Was he interested in anything in school?

"He could draw pretty good. But the principal, him and Myles didn't get along. Myles was always skipping to go snowboarding, and he'd never give any explanation. When he got a sponsor and went professional, he was figuring he didn't have much chance of graduating, anyway. But he paid his dues. The principal kept us out of our classes, made us stay in the office and do our work. It was that or suspend us. And a suspension was just giving us another day off to go snowboarding."

"Remember when you asked me about risking life and limb?" says Klassen, across a long table in the Sugarloaf Saloon banquet hall, where the faithful have assembled for the closing ceremony. "When you ask about life and death, I just see snowboarding. Do you see that now, after Extreme Day?"

Well, the appeal is clear. But it still looks like he's risking his life.

"Only in my youth," says Klassen, whose strong second yesterday moved him up to tenth in the overall standings.

"Death—that's a boundary you don't want to cross," says Jason Schutz, a rider from Bozeman, Montana, who finished sixth. "Even I get scared watching some of those guys. I saw Myles risk his life several times, but I only saw him frightened once, when he had a big exposure and not much powder. Even he had his limits. In the year before his accident, Myles was talking about getting safer, taking fewer risks."

"Whenever anything's exposed, I wear a helmet now," says Eric Klassen, Steve's younger brother. "I saw a guy rag all the way down in Tahoe recently. You could hear his helmet clacking on the rocks. That could have been his skull."

"I just got a new motorcycle, and I'm going to wear my helmet all the time," says Goodwill, the winner of Extreme Day, sixth on Freestyle Day, eighth on Downhill Day. Once a carpenter, Goodwill has long reddish blond hair and listens to Pantera and Biohazard on a

Walkman for maximum aggro when he snowboards. "It's boring without the tunes," he says. "This is as close as you can get to being a rock star without having any musical ability."

After a raucous food fight between the Americans and the Frenchies, Perata assumes emcee duties and thanks the competitors, the sponsors, the Totem Inn, the Village Inn, the work crew, the rescue squad, the judges, the media, and last year's King and Queen of the Hill—Steve Klassen and Julie Zell.

Klassen climbs onstage and stands with his back turned to the audience, staring into the microphone. Zell whispers in his ear. "'Far better it is to dare mighty things, to win glorious triumphs, even though checkered by failure. . . ,'" he mumbles, as Zell whispers to him again, "'. . . than to take rank with those poor spirits who neither enjoy much nor suffer much because they. . . ,'" she whispers yet again, "'. . . live in the gray twilight that knows not victory nor defeat.'"

"I think that about covers it," says Zell, grabbing the mike, "except to say that I'm glad no one got whacked too bad this year."

Perata calls Goodwill, the new king, and Karleen Jeffery, the new queen, to the stage. They kneel before their predecessors, who present them each with a robe, a crown, heli-lift passes, a not-entirely-fresh king salmon, and a bitchin' beautiful broadsword.

"My brother Goodwill," Klassen says, "your victory is one of triumph."

Goodwill punches several holes in the stage with his broadsword, which he then holds aloft. "This shit's going to look good on my wall!" he shouts.

With the king and queen looking down from their thrones, Perata hands out a mound of lesser swag to the competitors, giving each an introduction that falls somewhere between generic and personal: "And at number five, Elke Barns! She's a badass woman, she does it all!"

Finally, a band called Freedom 49 sets up and starts playing long, slow, mournful blues. "This is dedicated to a brother we lost on the slopes," says the singer. "A friend of ours who died last year." The room clears in minutes as everyone is driven to the bar, where they drain the entire stock of hard liquor in an hour.

"We were friends since the age of five or so," says Justin Taylor, who lives near the Burgetts. "We were twelve when we got into snowboarding. It seemed like he was at least a year and a half ahead of everyone else when we started, and he just got better. We were in the same classes until he dropped out in the tenth grade, but he didn't spend much time in school, anyway. He was always up at the pass doing kickers. There wasn't anything else to do until we got old enough to party, a couple of years ago. We'd have bonfires and drink beer until we puked."

Did Myles ever talk about why he hated school so much?

"No, he never talked about anything. He didn't like the principal just 'cause he was the principal. A lot of snotty people went to our high school, and we were never a part of it. We were the antisocial ones who never went to the pep rallies. Everybody else considered us losers."

When he made it to class, how did Myles behave?

"I remember in the fifth grade, this one kid in our class got in trouble, and the teacher wrote his name on the blackboard, which meant you couldn't go out for recess or something. The kid hadn't done anything. But the teacher wouldn't listen, so Myles went up to the blackboard to erase the name. The teacher had to tackle him and hold him down until the principal came and took him away. We all knew it wasn't the kid's fault. Myles was the only one who stood up to erase the name. That was the first incident. He never liked school again. He was a hell of a guy. And he still is."

"Where you going?" says the cop.

"The Tsaina Lodge," says Nick Perata. "There's a benefit for that local boy who's in a coma. I was only doing sixty-nine."

"You know what the speed limit is?" says the cop.

"Sixty-five?"

"That's correct." The cop looks at Perata's license and then back at Perata. "Haven't I seen you before?"

"I'm with the King of the Hill Snowboard Tournament."

"At the auditorium, three years ago. Yeah. You're the one who booked those bands. All night it was 'motherfucker this' and 'motherfucker that'—and my kid was in the audience."

"Well, you stopped the show."

"No, we didn't. We let it go on *a long time.*"

"Okay, but we didn't shoot up any signs this year."

"The people of Valdez would want me to express their heartfelt gratitude for that," says the cop, eyeing the seven snowboarders stuffed into Perata's old Buick. "Tell you what. I'm so grateful that I'm going to let you go with a warning, but if I catch you again going even a hair over sixty-five, you're busted. Awright?"

"Yes, officer."

Perata pulls back onto the highway. "I'm hoping they forget all that shit from the first year and let me rent the Civic Center again next year," he says. "The hall at the Sugarloaf isn't big enough to bring in the good bands." The stars are shining in an almost-cloudless sky, the Hale-Bopp comet hanging out the rear window like a banshee, the mountains looming like ghosts in the blackness. "I lost twenty-two thousand dollars last year. This year, I paid that off, and I lost another thirty-five thousand dollars. I haven't made a nickel in four years. So I don't do this for the money. You know why I do this? I do it for Alaska. I do it for the mountains. And the moment somebody dies in my tournament, that's when I pull the plug."

DECEMBER 1997/JANUARY 1998

BLUNDER ROAD

by Roy Blount Jr.

THE NORTHERN CALIFORNIA COUNTRYSIDE was a vibrant blur, and my car and I were alone, moving together, *vehhhhhhhn,* knowing each other, as I squeezed and feathered the brake—chirp, my back Goodyears sang to me, chirp—with one side of my right foot, blipped the gas—*VUM*—with the other side, moved my left foot from the dead pedal to the clutch (not that I was conscious of all this footwork, for it had become second nature), slipped smoothly into third, checked the tach (holding steady at five grand) and swept round the blind downhill corner as if the pavement were packed snow and I were lying back on a Flexible Flyer powered by one hundred invisible horses, *vahhhhhhn . . .*

"Unless you're sure that the car is in neutral, Roy, I just can't talk to you anymore," said Kelly Collins, one of the Skip Barber Racing School's Three Day Competition Course instructors, as he crouched down next to the Formula Ford race car I found myself elaborately strapped into all by myself on the morning of the first day.

Evidently the car had been in second, fourth or some other forward gear when I coasted to a stop, feeling rather pleased with my coasting. After Kelly crouched close by the car to instruct me, I had let my foot off the clutch and the car had lurched, causing Kelly to jump and then give me a look.

"Because this wheel," he continued, pointing to the right rear one, "will run over me."

I looked at the wheel. Rather than being where it ought to be, under the car, it was way out on the side. And so were the other three. That much wasn't my fault. The car was designed that way. It was also designed so that I was lying down in it, and my ass was only three inches off the pavement.

Several other things, however, were my fault, apparently, because Kelly went on to make several helpfully withering comments about the lap I had just driven around blind and S and hairpin and up- and downhill curves at speeds that struck me as already breakneck and that were going to be doubled by the end of the course.

And I determined that this would be one of my goals: to make it through the three days of the course without running over any of my instructors, even Kelly.

But I was also up for some speed, for some whipping around corners. What I didn't reckon with was being expected to do these things *right*.

My instructors were professional race-car drivers. They had been racing motorcycles and snowboards and various other vehicles since childhood. With a diploma from the Skip Barber Competition Course you can actually drive in serious professional auto races. After hurtling some 250 miles over the Sears Point International Raceway track (one of the most technically demanding tracks in the world), in Sonoma, California, I have been awarded that diploma, on one condition: that I never even think about using it.

Fair enough. It's not as if I aspire to be the next Mario Andretti. But sometimes now on the road I remember that big round G-feeling, the force of a sweeping downhill curve pushing me and that little shell of a car away while I lean in and squeeze power through the arc I want—like a running back digging and torquing to turn a corner while a big linebacker tries to shove him out of bounds—and . . . and then I remember the time I determined to really show 'em some rotation on this turn, and I locked up the brakes and plowed way off the track, ninety degrees from the direction I was supposed to go, and I thought, "Well, I didn't quite nail that one," and I came around to be critiqued by Kelly, who said, "There's no excuse for that."

No excuse?

Maybe I should have worked my way up to the Competition Course by way of Advanced Driving and Introduction to Racing. The other seven guys in the course were an airline pilot, a professional skateboarder, an Olympic steeplechase rider, a graduate of Go Kart school, a car wash magnate whose lifetime dream was to drive a race car, a graduate of another competition course in Europe and a professional golfer whose father used to be an official of the Indianapolis 500. All of whom spoke familiarly of Porsches, Alfa Romeos and Beemers.

Nothing against my classmates, who were unfailingly cordial when they might have felt justified in feeling infinitely superior to me, car-racing-wise. Nice people. Enjoyed their company. But generally speaking I do not hang out with people who say "Beemer."

For my part, for day-to-day road performance I look less to my engine, suspension and tranny than I do to my tape deck. My automotive pleasure is to move along briskly, with as much space as possible between me and everybody else on the road, in some low-maintenance vehicle that costs less than I paid for my first house, in 1966: $14,750. Lately I drive a Volkswagen Jetta. I like it. But I still have a soft spot in my heart for the Plymouth Horizon Miser I operated between 1981 and 1986, which got forty-two miles to the gallon and had enough headroom that I could wear a hat without getting a crick in my neck. That car could get way over the speed limit, even (if you planned ahead) uphill.

Which frankly I do not think disqualifies me as an American man. I have been making good time and passing people on the highway for thirty-five years. I have driven in forty-one states of the union— receiving tickets in seven—and in several foreign locales, including Senegal (where I got stuck in red sand), Paris, Iceland (where I got stuck in black sand) and London. I have driven a sleeping child through a blizzard, my ex-mother-in-law's Pontiac over the Rockies in an ice storm and a woman in a straw hat and a flowery dress down to Mexico. I have driven with a sick black cat wound around my neck like a steel coil.

Of course, when Mark Epperson, the pilot, told me, "In the navy I flew jets six hundred miles an hour at fifty feet, but this is more *connected*," I hated to come back with "Well, one time in this little yellow Horizon I used to have, I was rushing the cat to the vet's, and . . ."

"Maybe I have been depriving myself," I thought as I sat there in class in my flameproof jumpsuit (with patches saying SKF BEARINGS, BOSCH SPARKPLUGS, KONI SOMETHINGS and also, I hoped not ominously, EASTERN AIRLINES), holding my sixteen-pound visored helmet in my lap. Maybe I drive the way people who read Sidney Sheldon read, the way people who eat Stove Top Stuffing eat, the way people who voted for George Bush vote. Maybe I am not getting what is to be got.

So I tried. I swear I tried. For three days, from eight till five, we'd sit in a classroom for an hour as our instructors drew everything from the pedals we had to heel-and-toe to the envelope one hoped to push, and then, *voom*, we were out in the cars, first driving through a short slalom course (somehow I managed to break my ignition key in that), and then after another lecture taking laps around the actual track, then another lecture and more laps, and after each lap I would pull up beside an instructor, feeling hopped up, and he'd say, "I don't mean to be hard on you, but . . ."

I had imagined the track would be an oval, which I could just sort of lock myself into and zoom. The Skip Barber School operates at more than twenty locations around the country, from Sebring to Seattle International, and of all those tracks, Sears Point is most like a bootlegger's escape route. It's beautiful country around Sonoma, wine country, mostly flat with hills jutting up like the tops of elephants' heads, but a lap around that two-and-a-half-mile track—shaped, from the air, like a highly irregular slingshot—is like a roller-coaster ride through a maze.

"I keep thinking," I told Kelly Collins, "that I'm going to come around a corner and find myself in the middle of traffic on the wrong side of the road with a siren behind me."

"I never heard that one before," he said.

I did in fact manage to get lost a couple of times. Not counting the time a wheel got off into loose gravel and I spun out and, *vwang*, rammed into the bank, which was a common enough error and kind of fun, at least after I sat there for a moment thinking, "Oh, well, this is it, I've torn it now, I'll probably go into shock, and they'll have to use the jaws of life to get me out of here or airlift me and the car together. . . ," and realized that I could just crank it again, back up and carry on.

But two or three times I accidentally got into the pit lane and found myself next to the Media Building, which fortunately did not contain any media representatives. And twice when I was supposed to wind up in the pits I bypassed the pit lane and had to sort of sneak back and around to it as casually (not very) as possible. No one else did either of these things.

Although everybody had trouble (though not as much as I did) finding the optimum line around the track. Since the line was marked by orange cones, you might think it would have been easy to follow, but let me explain what the line is, and while I am at it I will answer the question people most often ask me, a vulgar and uninformed question: How fast were we going?

One of the first things we were told was, "Any fool can go fast on a straightaway." Something I figured out for myself was, this track didn't have any straightaway to speak of. Just to get the speed over with: By the end of the course, when we were going at 5,000 rpm in fourth gear on what passed for straightaway, we were going about a hundred miles an hour. But the car didn't even have a speedometer, so I will call it four hundred miles an hour, which is what it felt like, and that was fun.

What the car did have was a tachometer, and our job was to keep the rpm up as close as we could to our assigned maximum (which was raised from 2,500 to 3,000 to 4,000 to 5,000 as the course went on) while running through four gears and negotiating twelve corners.

Negotiating these corners *correctly*.

What the orange traffic cones marked were the TP (turn-in point), the apex and the TO (track-out point) for each corner. The TP was where you swung to the outside edge of the track to begin the turn, the apex was where you just skirted the inside edge and started accelerating and unwinding the steering wheel, and the TO was where you came out of the turn back on the outside edge and started setting up for the next TP. You were supposed to come within six inches of each of these cones, meanwhile visualizing the cones ahead. Connect the dots—not mechanically, one cone at a time, but smoothly, sinuously tracing the ideal line, the line of least wasted motion, the fastest line.

"You seem like an intelligent person," said Nick Kunewalder, another of our instructors, as he drove me around the track in a Beemer, on a special remedial point-by-point lap. He said it in a tone of genuine wonderment. "Don't you know the turns yet?"

The truth was, I didn't. But since this was probably the fifteenth time I had been through them, I said, "Yeah, sure, well . . ." The truth is, I've been known to make a wrong turn on a route I have been traveling daily for years.

"You get the line right once, but then the next lap, you're way off."

"Yes, well, I . . ."

"Think ahead. Turn your brain on and leave it on all the time."

I felt terrible. I felt like I felt a great deal of the time in adolescence and in the army. On the other hand, whoever said race-car drivers are hitting on all cylinders?

"You can't teach anybody how to make love or drive a race car" was something Kelly said several times. Right. Nor can you get through to a race-car instructor the reasons you are racing-impaired. But here they are, for those who care:

One: I Never Stayed Within the Lines in Coloring Books, Either. If it didn't sound so self-serving, I would give this point the subtitle You

Seem Like an Intelligent Person, Mr. Edison. Why Can't You Match Up Your Socks? It wasn't that my brain wasn't turned on; far from it. I would let a TP slip up on me, which would force me to swerve over toward it and then swerve back in the direction of the apex and then say, the hell with the TO, because I was thinking: "It's because my mother taught me to drive. In a Studebaker. Well, forget the Studebaker angle—am I being sexist? No, the problem is not that my mother was a woman but that she didn't like to drive. She taught me how to read, too, and she liked to read. Of course, maybe I *read* in some kind of gender-tangled way—whoops, missed another one. Damn! What's *wrong* with me? Kris [Wilson, an instructor] was saying in the classroom, 'It's not just a matter of who's got the biggest *huevos*. There's a lot of thought involved.' Maybe my problem is I've never been able to use my *huevos* and think at the same time.

"Or maybe I'm not screwed up, I'm rebelling. I was reading the other day that men's-movement thinkers see male fascination with cars as a symptom of puerility, real-human-relationship avoidance and loss of true organic manhood. Maybe I'm—whoops, *damn*."

Two: It's Hard to Make Love When You Don't Fit In. The only point I scored during the entire three-day course was when Kris (who is not tall) said, "You don't see many tall drivers," and I said, "That's because tall people don't have to be race-car drivers to get the attention of women."

Naked heightism. All right. But in fact I can see that being six feet tall was a great disadvantage for me. With my arms bunched up around that slightly-larger-than-a-CD steering wheel and my legs banging against the side of the chassis (I had big bruises on my knees), I felt quite frequently the way I felt, years ago, when I lived in a trailer with a shower so small that once I got the water way too hot and kept twisting the knobs frantically and thought for a minute I was going to have to run outside *wearing* the shower. Of course, I am also about fifteen pounds overweight. And when they asked me in advance how much I weighed so they could have a car the right size for me, I may have lied slightly, because I figured I would lose a few pounds before I got there, which I didn't. My feeling when I finally got all five or six straps fastened over myself (oh, how I love to fumble with webbing) was that my entire body was in a shoe too tight for it.

Three: I Never Could Make Love With My Feet. Mine are size eleven and a half D, and if they are not entirely flat, they do have trouble staying on key. In racing, you see the cars roaring around, but you don't see all the little feet twinkling inside of them. They've *got* to be little feet. I'm telling you, Mario Andretti must have elfin feet, only very wide in the right ball. Let me explain.

I was dismayed to learn that when I went squealing heavy footedly into a turn like Robert Mitchum in *Thunder Road*, I was met with disapproval. These cars had, as one instructor said, "superduperresponsive brakes," and we were supposed to learn "threshold braking" for maximum efficiency. I found it hard to accept how quickly you could stop that little hornet of a car and by how many delicately distinct degrees of modulation you could slow it. Scary as it got at high speeds, we didn't have to worry, rationally, about getting hurt, because the cars don't flip easily and the roll bar is strong. *Irrationally,* to be sure, I sometimes heard myself saying, "Help me, Jesus."

In racing you don't downshift to slow down into a curve, you downshift just before the curve so that you are in the right gear to come out of the curve at maximum speed. You go into the turn as fast as you can, and as you downshift, you squeeze the brakes down to just shy of lockup (when they lock up, they scream and you lose momentum, but when they are at the threshold, they chirp to you), and if you brake just right while turning you "get rotation": Your rear end swings around to where it pushes you straight through the turn.

Is that clear? It is to me, in principle, but in practice I found that it was like trying to play the flute with your feet. They call it heel-and-toeing, but actually it's not that simple. Your left foot stays to the left of the clutch, on the "dead pedal," until it's time to shift, and your right foot stays on *both the brake and the accelerator.* You have to articulate the ball of the right foot into two instruments ("modulated by the ankle," according to instruction). Going into a turn, you keep firm (but "feathering," or delicately adjusting) pressure on the brake with the left side of the ball of the right foot, and with the right side of the ball of the right foot you stand ready to "blip" the accelerator, rev it enough to get the engine speed up to wheel speed. (In nonrace cars you don't have to blip, because their gears are synchronized.) While keeping your heel on the floor.

That, too, is clear to me in principle. In practice . . .

And here is the sequence you have to go through, to downshift from fourth to third:

Brake.

Clutch in.

Shift to neutral.

Clutch out.

Blip.

Clutch in.

Downshift.

Clutch out.

Ease off brake (unless you want to keep going down to second, in which case you have to go through the entire above sequence again).

No matter how deftly you danced through this little nine-step, the gears would grind somewhat: *ggrrrt*. I tended just to jam the damn thing into something. Occasionally, I would go from fourth to fourth. And meanwhile I would sometimes have forgotten to put my helmet visor down, causing instructors to wave frantically at me (a bug could take out my eye). Every now and then I would weave through a sequence of turns like an otter down a waterfall and get a feeling of ooooo . . . , woooo . . . , woo-*hooo*. But unlike an otter (I assume), I kept wondering in the TO or the TP of my mind: "What am I probably doing, or just on the verge of doing, wrong and why, why, why?"

One lesson I hope I learned is this: The next time I'm with someone who is having a hard time picking up something I find easy (assuming there is such a thing), I will be sympathetic. Or burn in hell.

I did not learn to be a novice race-car driver. And everybody else in my class did. And they loved it. They also misshifted and spun out and knocked over cones, but toward the end they were saying, "I just grabbed my balls and went for it," and things like that. Some of them are thinking of going on to drive in races, finding their line while surrounded by other cars trying to find it and without the aid of cones. "My dad is getting into racing," said Roy Dillon, the professional skateboarder, "and he said, 'You're the perfect little dude to be the driver.'" Good luck to them.

Passing was allowed on our last six-lap run. My aversion to being overtaken was so drastically reduced that I gave a wave-by to everyone who hove into view, praying that I would pick up in my juddering rearviews all who hove. (Did I mention that behind my visor, which kept fogging up, I was wearing bifocals?) By the final lap I was in the clear, in a negative sort of way.

Suddenly I knew a certain peace. Linc Watkins, who runs a debt-syndication desk for a Japanese bank and seemed to be driving faster than anybody else, had told me part of his secret: "Just stay in third all the way around." So I tried this, and as I came through the gentle S curves and hit the longish barely curvy stretch toward the end, I pushed on up to 6,000 rpm, approaching the car's 120 mph capacity, and I finally felt like I wanted to feel—a fool going fast on the straightaway.

Of course, the instructors had stopped watching me by then.

But I want them to know this: The next time I drove my Jetta on the highway, I found that if I concentrated I could look further up the road than usual and plot my course smoothly through a series of turns. Well, two turns. A turn and a half. At one point, as I swung all the way to the far edge of the right lane and unwound smoothly back toward the far edge of the left, I felt something. A fleeting connection with some Platonic vector matrix stretching from Detroit to heaven.

I like to think it was my apex.

MAY/JUNE 1992

CRAZY IN THE DESERT
by Hampton Sides

W HILE I WAS OUT THERE all those days, wandering alone, I
became like an animal, a desert creature that lives by the
rules of the sun and behaves entirely on instinct. I crawled
as a reptile crawls over the ground, hunting for beetles to stab with my
knife, searching for the shade of a tamarisk tree, foraging for roots to
suck. I fell into a hyperalert state. I became attuned to every shift of the
wind, the promising wisp of a cloud building in the east, the sound of
mice running over the sand at night. Every thought, every movement of
my body, was devoted to surviving. I repeated to myself, "Do not surrender." I would climb one ridge and find a beautiful city of stone
spread before me. Temples and citadels, white minarets, the remnants of
a great civilization. But the people were all dead and gone. Time became
the sun and the moon, the crunch of my feet on a cracked riverbed.
Dune. Wadi. Another dune. A camel carcass. A Berber ruin. Salt flats
stretching out for eternities in the shimmering heat. A scorpion clawing
over dried animal dung. Fields of blue boulders under starry skies,
satellites blinking across the night. I imagined that there had been a
nuclear war and that I was walking over the charred remains of the
world. The last one left.

After his dreadful adventure five years ago, the Italian newspapers
called Mauro Prosperi "the Robinson Crusoe of the Sahara." He was
pale and stick-figured when he got back home, shambling off the
plane from Algiers in a loose-fitting robe. Now, it was a bright morning in September 1998 in his hometown, the Sicilian fishing village of
Aci Trezza, and Prosperi was the picture of good health. He turned
heads outside a local cafe as he dismounted from his BMW motorcycle and removed his wraparound shades. A tautly constructed man
whose black hair is flecked with gray, Prosperi was wearing spandex
running shorts, a loud cycling shirt, and a Sector watch that chirped

on the half hour. He was still sweating from a run on Mount Etna, the active volcano that soars eleven thousand feet above the town.

"I brought something for you," he told me as he sat down. After ordering a cappuccino, he unfolded a topographical map of North Africa. "This is the route," he said, pointing to the line of fluorescent ink zigzagging across the blond immensity of the Sahara. "Five thousand five hundred kilometers. From the Atlantic to the Nile."

Prosperi, forty-four, has been planning this expedition for three years: a nonstop and mostly unsupported walk across the entire width of the Sahara Desert, more than three thousand miles, with his running companion, an endurance athlete and former Special Forces commando from Naples named Modestino Preziosi. He intends to finally execute it this year, beginning in early September. Pulling custom-designed carbon-fiber-and-titanium wagons filled with freeze-dried food and other supplies, they will trudge eastward in temperatures as high as 130 degrees. They'll cross the desolate precincts of Algeria and Libya—places with ghostly names like Amguid, Ghat, and Waw an Namus—and pass through the seemingly endless miles of the great *hamada,* the hard, stony desert, following a slightly jagged route to maximize their access to known wells. By mid- to late October, with nothing connecting them to the world but a satellite phone and an emergency position-indicating radio beacon, they will be inching across the dreaded Murzuq—350 uninterrupted miles of rippled dunes. Their plan is to reach the Nile just in time to usher in the next millennium and to celebrate their accomplishment—in a suitably Italian spirit of grandeur—at a rumored Pink Floyd concert to be held among the Pyramids of Giza on New Year's Eve.

Over the centuries, any number of deranged existentialists have crisscrossed the Sahara in any number of ways. But no one has yet had the audacity to attempt the obvious—a full west-east traverse, tracking the whole mother on foot. In terms of mileage, it's the equivalent of walking from San Diego to Nova Scotia. But distance, of course, is not the only obstacle. In a world in which true endurance firsts have become increasingly esoteric, Prosperi's concept, compelling in its simplicity, is also utterly quixotic, given all the things that can go wrong, which include possible encounters with bandits, border guards, genocidal Algerian guerrillas, scorpions, snakes, and zero-visibility sandstorms—not to mention the threat of running out of water. If Prosperi and Preziosi can bring it off, their accomplishment will arguably be on a par with the Norwegian Børge Ousland's 1997 solo crossing of Antarctica.

Poring over the map at the cafe in Aci Trezza, Prosperi offered an elaborate rationale for his trip, saying it would advance the science of desert survival and that it would also help foster goodwill among Saharan nations. Suddenly, he waved his hand dismissively and said, "But screw all of that. The real reason is selfishness. It's something I *want* to do."

Five days a week, Prosperi is a crowd-control cop in the nearby city of Catania. He sits astride a police horse, cutting a proud figure for the tourists in the civic square. But the truth is that police work bores him. He joined the force in 1973, when he was living in Rome—his native city—because Italy's police federation generously subsidizes the training of national-caliber athletes. Day after day, he stares dully at the crowds and the pigeons and yearns for an encore in the desert.

"But why," I pressed him, "would you go back to a place that almost killed you?" For the past few days, he had been telling and retelling the story of what had happened to him when he disappeared for nine days in the Sahara, the story that had made him famous across Italy.

"I feel a connection there," he said. "I love the clarity. And you see, the Sahara spared my life. Those days in the desert were my happiest."

As much as I wanted to believe Prosperi's story, I didn't—at least, not entirely. Lots of people didn't. As with so many tales of survival in the wilderness that lack the benefit of witnesses, there was something fundamentally incredible about his account. The possibility that Prosperi might be a fraud seemed to hover over everything he said and did.

He was one of two things: either the most dementedly obdurate bullshitter the world of endurance sports had to offer or a physiological anomaly whose feats deserved to be written up in medical journals. If his claims were true, he had confounded the laws of dehydration science. There was nothing like him in the literature of the Sahara or in the literature of *any* desert. But whatever had happened out there five years ago, he had never been able to turn loose of it. One way or another, the desert had taken him.

Competing in the Marathon des Sables, a seven-day "self-sufficiency" endurance race held every spring in the Moroccan Sahara, is the equivalent of running six marathons back-to-back in a convection oven. With a severe romanticism on loan from the French Foreign

Legion, the event requires participants to carry their provisions on their backs—everything, in fact, but their water, which is furnished at each checkpoint.

In April 1994, Prosperi was one of 134 entrants in the event. A gifted runner, fencer, and horseman, he had won or placed in international modern-pentathlon contests from Hong Kong to San Antonio. Although the Marathon des Sables was his first competition in the desert, Prosperi was running an exceptional race.

On the morning of the marathon's fourth and longest stage—a diabolical slog totaling some fifty miles—Prosperi was in seventh place and maintaining an impressive clip despite temperatures that were climbing to 115 degrees. It was Thursday, April 14, and the runners were approaching the finish line at Zagora, a Berber village in the palm-studded Draa Valley. Shortly after one o'clock that afternoon, Prosperi briefly stopped at the third checkpoint, twenty miles into the day's route. Giovanni Manzo, a friend from Sicily who was running with him, helped him tape up a festering blister on his foot. Shortly afterward, Prosperi signed for his two-liter allotment of water and then took off.

Some fifteen minutes later, the winds started to kick up, in gusts at first, then in a steady howl that escalated into a blinding sandstorm. Visibility dropped to near zero. Marathoners up and down the course were forced to wrap themselves in sleeping bags to ride out the choking swirls of sand, which stung the skin and caused bloody noses and respiratory-tract abrasions. The organizers formally halted the race for the day.

The winds lashed for six hours. That night, as the storm subsided, officials grew concerned: Manzo had straggled in at the fourth checkpoint, but there was no sign of Prosperi. Manzo didn't understand what could have happened—Prosperi had been running ahead, and even with the storm slowing his progress, he should have come in hours earlier. But the race officials trusted that Prosperi would not have strayed far. The rules stipulated that should a sandstorm occur, runners were to halt in their tracks and await further instruction. The race officials decided they would commence a full-scale search in the morning.

At first light on Friday, race employees were dispatched in Land Rovers to comb the trail, while a pilot undertook a reconnaissance flyover in an ultralight craft. The searchers methodically covered the terrain in a grid pattern. They realized they would have to move fast during the morning, because Prosperi had at most only two liters of water and by noon temperatures would be in the triple digits.

But the searchers found no trace of him. He had simply vanished.

Later that morning, the Moroccan military began assisting with the search. Bedouin trackers were dispersed. A helicopter was sent up. Moving farther afield from the course, the growing search party worked all day and through the night.

The race officials could not believe they had simply lost a contestant to the open desert. Although its promoters liked to bill the Marathon des Sables as "the toughest footrace on Earth," only one person had actually died in it thus far, a young French runner who had suffered a massive heart attack in 1988. The Marathon des Sables' literature spoke of pitting "man against the elements," but that was just a cliché of faux survivalism. For Prosperi, however, the ordeal had ceased to be a controlled simulation of extremity and had become dreadfully authentic. He was an incongruous, Lycra-clad creature loping across the wastelands of eastern Morocco, his marathon bib number meaningless now, a runner struggling to win an entirely different kind of race.

I first heard about Mauro Prosperi in April 1998, while in Morocco for the thirteenth Marathon des Sables. He was back in the Sahara again, running the race for the second time since his disappearance in 1994. He was considered one of the curious sideshows of the marathon, the mad Italian flagellant who'd returned for more desert punishment.

One cool evening early on in the contest, the French founder and director of the race, a ruddy-cheeked former concert promoter named Patrick Bauer, held a meeting with journalists outside the press tent. Bauer had hatched the idea of the Marathon des Sables after he went on a "solo expedition" of some two hundred miles across the Algerian Sahara in 1984. "People thought I must be mad," Bauer said. "It was just a personal quest, something I had to do." He spoke mystically of the prolonged solitude he had experienced, of the shooting stars he had seen, of what the desert had done to him once he was dropped into its vastness. Bauer did *not* mention, until prompted by a French journalist who knew the real story, that he had been accompanied on his so-called solo trek by his brother and girlfriend, who had followed him in a support vehicle.

"Yes, but they did not help me in any way," Bauer insisted. "They were there to document this historic experience."

Later, I asked Bauer about Prosperi. It seemed to me that these two men were kindred spirits, for they had both experienced a transcendental communion with the desert that had changed their lives.

"Don't listen to Mr. Prosperi," Bauer replied. He pursed his lips and exhaled contemptuously. "His story is a fabrication. He will have you believe he is Superman. It is physiologically impossible for a man to travel more than two hundred kilometers in the desert without water. This is a supernatural act."

Was he saying that Prosperi had never really been missing?

"Well, it's possible that he got genuinely lost for a few days. But all the rest rings false. We believe that early on he was picked up by someone. And then he decided to hide out for a while."

Why would he do that?

"He thought he could make a killing out of this if he prolonged his ordeal. He thought he could sell his story to the tabloids. He aspired to be the star of his own movie."

The next afternoon, I went over to the Italian tent to meet Prosperi. He'd come in from a twenty-mile run and was boiling a packet of freeze-dried stroganoff. He was shirtless, and a medallion of blood from a burst blister was seeping through one of his socks. I told him what Bauer had said, and, for a moment, he turned deep red with anger.

"Yes, I know what Patrick Bauer says about me," he replied, tentatively, in a soft, high voice. "We've had our differences. I almost took him to court. But he says those things because he knows that my desert story is better than his. And because he fears that he is the copy and I am the real thing. I didn't have a truck following me every step of the way."

"He said you'd have to be Superman."

"Me, Superman?" he said, looking around at some of the other Italians in the tent. "Well, yes. Precisely." He smiled broadly, and everyone erupted in laughter.

I liked Prosperi instantly. But after what Bauer had said, I was wary of him. I approached him as if he were some kind of human-endurance hustler. "You want to hear the story?" he asked, once he had finished his dinner. Removing his socks, he made little ditches in the sand with his bare feet and stared eastward, toward the Algerian border.

* * *

When the sandstorm started to blow, I lost sight of everybody else. I kept running, though, because I thought I could see the trail. I was in seventh place and didn't want to lose my standing. But the storm was raging with such fury that I had to stop and seek cover. I found a bush and crouched inside it. The sand felt like needles piercing my skin. I wrapped a towel around my face and waited. The dunes were shifting all about me, and several times I had to move to avoid being buried.

It was nearly dark before the winds relented. I started running again, but after a few minutes it occurred to me that I had lost the trail. For an hour or so, I kept backtracking, searching for the flags the French had put out to mark the piste. Finally, it became pitch dark, and I decided that there was no longer any point in wasting my energy. My only thought was that through my stupidity I had forfeited any chance of winning the race. But I knew that I couldn't be more than a few miles from the trail and that the rescuers would come searching for me at dawn. So I prepared a camp and lit a small fire to create light. I slipped into my sleeping bag and fell asleep under the stars.

At dawn, I scrambled to the top of the highest dune. My heart dropped like a stone. I couldn't see anything—no truck trails, no signs of a camp, no Land Rovers. Nothing looked familiar. I realized that the situation was grave. I had drunk almost all my water: There was only one finger of it left in the second bottle.

The race manual had instructed us not to move should we become lost, so I just sat on the hilltop, watching the horizon for any movement. Just before sundown, I heard something that was music to my ears: a helicopter, flying low and angling toward me. I fired my distress flare to make sure the pilot could spot me. He flew directly overhead, so close that I could see his white helmet in the cockpit. I knew I was finally saved. But the helicopter didn't land. It kept on flying past me and vanished. I didn't understand. I was desperate now, crazy with fear. I yelled, "Giovanni! Where are you!"

That night I urinated into my water bottle and saved it. I said to myself, "I will drink this if I need to." I ate a PowerBar and fell asleep on the high dune.

The next morning, my eyes blinked open with a start, and I saw two large birds circling overhead. I pulled together my things and started walking. The sun was bearing down on me like a weight. I glimpsed the outline of a building about a mile away. I hurried over to it and found that it was a small Muslim temple with a stone turret; I later learned that it was a marabout shrine, a religious structure that's common throughout the Sahara. It was a mausoleum, really. An Islamic holy man was buried in one of the walls. Inside, it was cool and dark. Up in the tower, I spied three bird's eggs in a nest and ate them. I found a wooden pole and went outside to hang an Italian flag on it in case someone were to fly over. Then I sat out the day in the shade of the shrine.

By that night, my hunger had grown so terrible that I did something I never thought I could do. There was a small colony of bats living under the eaves of the building. Just before dark, I snuck up there and snatched two of them. I decided I would eat them raw, because cooking them on my portable stove would only dry them out, and I knew that moisture was what I needed most of all. So I wrung their necks off and sucked. It was a repellent thing to do, but I was crazed with hunger. All I tasted was something warm and salty in my mouth. That night I fell asleep on the floor of the shrine.

Just before dawn on the fourth day, I woke to the sound of an airplane. I didn't know if it was a search plane or not, but when I stumbled outside, I could see it was flying in my direction. This is my last chance for rescue, I thought, and so I decided to risk it all. I took out everything from my backpack that was combustible and set it aflame. As the airplane drew nearer, I wrote SOS in large letters in the sand. But when the plane headed away from me, I said to myself, "There goes my life."

All I could think about was that I was going to die a horrible death. I had once heard that dying of thirst was the worst possible fate. From the embers of my bonfire, I removed a piece of charcoal and wrote a final letter to my wife. I asked her to forgive me for not being a better husband and father. I was out of my head, not thinking clearly. I cut my wrist with my knife, but the blood was so thick from my advanced dehydration that it wouldn't flow. I sat there on the floor of the shrine and cried.

After a time, I came to my senses. I realized that the marathon was moving on, that I couldn't rely on the race officials to save me. I decided I must confront the desert myself. They had told us that at the end of the race, in Zagora, we would see a mountain range. As I looked at the horizon, I could see mountains in the distance, some twenty miles away. I decided I would try to reach them. As the sun dropped *low, I pulled together the few belongings I hadn't torched, and I started walking.*

On the morning of Saturday, April 16, 1994, Patrick Bauer announced that the race would resume, a decision that dismayed many of the runners, who were resting in a dusty tent-city encampment some fifteen miles from the area where Prosperi had gone missing. "We hated to leave, because all we could think about was Mauro out there alone, dying," says René Nevola, a British runner who had befriended Prosperi earlier in the race. "Everyone's morale was incredibly low."

The Italian camp was especially devastated, no one more so than Giovanni Manzo. "I felt horribly guilty because I was the one who'd convinced Mauro to sign up for the race in the first place," he said. "Now, all I wanted to do was drop out. I didn't think I could carry on."

Prosperi had been missing for more than two days before his wife, Cinzia Pagliara, heard the news. No one from the race committee had thought to notify her. "Like everyone else in Italy," she said, "I read about it in a newspaper. The story was now in papers all over the world." The following day, Prosperi's brother Riccardo, two Interpol investigators from Rome, and Pagliara's brother Fabio boarded a plane for Casablanca, determined to organize a search party of their own. Because Prosperi was a policeman as well as an athlete of national stature, officials both in Rome and at Italy's embassy in Morocco mobilized with unusual swiftness to provide funds and vehicles. Now that Bauer's staff, the Moroccan military, and the Italian authorities were involved, the search for Prosperi had become the most ambitious rescue operation the Sahara had seen since 1982, when Englishman Mark Thatcher, the son of then-prime minister Margaret Thatcher, was lost for six days after his car broke down during the Paris-Dakar rally.

On Sunday, April 17, the exhausted racers crossed the Marathon des Sables finish line in Zagora, and the following day, a ceremonial banquet was held. But what was supposed to be a party took on the hollow cast of a memorial service. Four days after Prosperi's disappearance, the other runners increasingly spoke of him in the past tense. "The spirit of the race was ruined," said Bauer. "There was nothing to celebrate." On Tuesday, April 19, the racers boarded charter buses bound for Marrakech and said their bittersweet good-byes to the desert.

By now, the Italian volunteers, led by Prosperi's brother and brother-in-law, were the only ones still engaged in a search the authorities were saying was futile. The Moroccan military had never heard of a man surviving for more than four days in the Sahara without water.

The Italians ignored these calls to reason, and on April 20, six and a half days into Prosperi's ordeal, they made a stirring discovery. In a no-man's-land near the Morocco-Algeria border—an area designated as an "archaeological zone"—they found Prosperi's water bottle and his aluminum-coated emergency blanket. In their minds, it was the first compelling suggestion that Prosperi could still be alive. "These are only signs," Cinzia Pagliara told a reporter for the daily *La Sicilia*, "but they feed our hope after all these days have passed without any news from Mauro." A few days later, the searchers found one of Prosperi's shoelaces. But by now, eight days after his disappearance, everyone was beginning to concede that the situation appeared hopeless.

The mountains I was aiming for were not a mirage, but they were the wrong mountains. Instead of bearing northeast toward Zagora, I was heading due east. Of course, I did not know this. My sense of the days, and of precisely how I spent them, was becoming vague. I kept alive by sucking wet-wipes. In the mornings, I licked the dew off the concave surfaces of rocks. I sipped my own urine and boiled it with freeze-dried food. I ate what the desert offered. I improvised a slingshot with a forked stick and a bungee cord and stunned a mouse with a rock. I killed a snake and ate it, too. Mostly, I ate scarab beetles and plants. In a dried-up riverbed I found grasses that had roots dripping with moisture.

I was strict in my regimen. I walked only in the early mornings and in the early evenings. In the harsh glare of the day, I rested in the shade of cliffs or caves or trees. At night, I buried my body in the sand to keep warm. Along the way, I planted clues to my whereabouts. I would leave miscellaneous articles—a T-shirt, toothpaste, socks, a shoelace. On the crests of dunes, I would leave tinfoil and metallic food containers.

On the eighth day, I came upon an oasis. Really it was only a large puddle, a mirror of water in a wadi. I threw myself upon it and gulped with abandon, but I could hardly swallow. I managed to force a mouthful of it down, and almost immediately I vomited. I couldn't hold anything. I found I had to take tiny sips, one every ten minutes.

I lay by the puddle like some leopard at its watering hole. I took larger swallows. By morning, my thirst was slaked.

I looked for signs of life and found nothing. I filled my water bottle and started walking again. I continued on all day and night. The next morning, I spotted the fresh excrement of goats. My spirits grew brighter. Then I saw something that made my heartbeat quicken: human footprints. I crested a hill and beheld an incredible sight. There was a nomad girl, maybe eight years old, tending a flock in the sparse greenery of a wash.

I ran toward her and begged for help. She looked at me aghast, screaming in terror. I beseeched her to stop, but she disappeared over a dune.

I must be a hideous sight, I thought. I took out my signal mirror and turned it toward my face. I was appalled. I was a skeleton. My eyes had sunk so far back into my skull, I couldn't see them. The girl returned with her grandmother, and I stumbled after them, conscious of what a pitiful castaway I'd become. There was an encampment set among the trees. They were Tuaregs, the famous "blue people" of the Sahara, traveling in a caravan. The old woman instructed me to lie down in the shade of a lean-to. She prepared me mint tea and a cup of goat's milk. Then the men came into camp. They loaded me on a camel and took me to the nearest village, a journey of a few hours. There, they turned me over to a patrol of military police, who immediately blindfolded me. As I later learned, they suspected that I might be a Moroccan spy, and they wanted to prevent me from glimpsing the lay-out of any military installations.

I was driven to a military base, where an officer started interrogating me. I told him I was a policeman in Italy, and for some reason this seemed to help. Then another officer burst into the room. He took one look at me and said, "Are you Mauro Prosperi?"

"Yes," I said, astonished to hear the sound of my name.

"Welcome to Algeria, sir. We have received a report about you from the Moroccan authorities. We must get you to the infirmary straight-away."

On the evening of April 24, Cinzia Pagliara had just put her three children to bed when the phone rang. The signal was clear, the voice buoyant and vital. "Cinzia, it's me. Did you have a funeral for me yet?" Pagliara dropped to the floor—*Mauro*. He was lying in a military hospital in a place called Tindouf, in southwestern Algeria. He had traversed a mountain range, the Jebel Bani, and then stumbled across the tense border between Morocco and Algeria, which was frequently patrolled by guards and rumored to be laced with land mines. The Tuareg nomads had found him some twenty-five miles into Algeria and about 130 miles from the area where he'd disappeared. He had lost an astounding thirty-three pounds, about 20 percent of his body weight. Nurses had plied Prosperi with sixteen liters of intravenous fluids. The doctors said his liver had almost failed, but after a day and a half of convalescence, they thought he was going to be okay. Only now were they permitting him to call home.

"My skin is like that of a tortoise," he told Pagliara. "Don't worry, Cinzia. I'm still beautiful."

After recovering for seven days in Algerian hospitals, Prosperi, still gaunt and feeble, was flown to Rome, where he received a hero's welcome. He was photographed with dignitaries, interviewed endlessly, celebrated in newspaper stories from Milan to Palermo. He was a walking miracle, it seemed, the man who had come back from the dead. His very name seemed to sum it up—Prosperi, "the fortunate one."

A few weeks later, however, journalists started to report the doubts expressed by several sports physiologists concerning the medical feasibility of Prosperi's account. It was suggested that Prosperi had faked his own disappearance, that he was the rankest sort of glory hound. One Italian magazine even surmised that Prosperi and Pagliara had staged the ordeal together, from beginning to end. "They said we planned the whole thing so we could make a pile of money," Pagliara told me. "If that was the case, then you've never met two people who are more stupid than we are. We never got any money for this."

Asked what she would do if she found out that her husband actually had invented his story, Pagliara replied firmly: "If his story is not true, don't tell me about it. Because he had me suffering for nine days. I could never forgive him."

Soon after Prosperi's return, the organizers of the Marathon des Sables, perhaps worried about bad publicity, also accused him of fraud. Meanwhile, Prosperi was considering a lawsuit against Patrick Bauer, charging, among other things, that the trail had been poorly marked. But what really rankled Prosperi was that Bauer's race crew had never told Pagliara he was missing. In the end, Prosperi dropped the idea of the suit—"My problems with Bauer weren't legal, they were personal"—but his resentment banked.

Prosperi enjoyed a temporary reversal of fortune when a Roman film crew retraced his steps for a 1995 documentary reenactment of his ordeal. Among other things, the crew located the marabout shrine and found, next to some of Prosperi's belongings, the skeletons of several bats. Nevertheless, public doubt continued to hang over Prosperi like a toxic cloud. The suspicions made him restless and morose; all he could think about was the Sahara.

After speaking with his family and friends and with dozens of other athletes who ran in the 1994 Marathon des Sables, I gradually came to believe Prosperi's story. Although there were still questions about the chronology of events—was it possible that the Tuaregs had found him earlier than he thought?—his was the only explanation that worked. And he'd stuck by his narrative, in every detail, since the day he was found. Prosperi had no prior history of spinning melodramatic fictions. In many ways, he was your basic nuts-and-bolts guy: a cop, a gifted athlete past his prime, a doting father of three. Yes, his passion for the desert was grandiose and arguably demented, but he seemed otherwise pleasantly even-keeled, widely liked, and respected on his home ground.

The main problem with the suggestion that Prosperi invented his ordeal, of course, is that the man suffered profoundly. One would have to go on a hunger strike for weeks to look as he had and to lose the kind of weight doctors in Algeria said that he had lost. Prosperi's health problems continued long after he returned. For a month, he could eat only extremely bland food ground up in a blender. He experienced severe leg cramps for a year, and his liver was permanently damaged.

There are other telltales of his experience. One night, for example, I asked Prosperi if his suicide attempt had left a scar. He seemed pained by the question, but then, reluctantly, he rolled up his sleeve and revealed a one-inch white line running along his right wrist.

"He was never the same after he came back," Pagliara told me on a hike up Etna. "If you want to know the truth, I think all the publicity went to his head a little bit. When he returned, he was *just* a father, *just* a husband, *just* a policeman. Everything seemed so banal to him. Ever since, he's been searching for ways to get back to the desert."

And so his notion of a trans-Saharan trek was born. Although he wouldn't admit it himself, his friends see the adventure as an attempt to restore his good name: Tired of defending himself, Prosperi came up with an epic retort to his critics. By undertaking an odyssey of definitive and unassailable proportions, he hoped to silence his doubters forever. It is a logic that makes sense to many who know him but not to his wife. "I am absolutely opposed," she said. "I am sure that his three children would rather have a living father than a famous dead one."

To help prepare for the trek, Prosperi has returned to the desert many times. Last year, he ran a two-day, seventy-five-mile race in the Libyan desert, and he has run in the past three Marathons des Sables. When he can't train in the Sahara, he works out on the blackened crusts of Etna, a desolate landscape that at least looks and feels like the desert.

As can be imagined, the project has been an all-consuming one for Prosperi and Preziosi. Beyond the usual dance for sponsorship manna, they have had to arrange for emergency food and water drops at strategic locations in the remotest desert, and conduct a considerable amount of diplomacy work in order to persuade the mutually hostile governments of Morocco and Algeria to let them pass unmolested across the border.

As they make their way across the blazing desert for four months, the expeditioners will rely on each other for their survival—and for their sanity. The thirty-seven-year-old Preziosi, who helped in the '94 search, has never wavered in his belief that Prosperi's story is true. He says he has complete trust in Prosperi and great confidence in his skills and judgment.

There is one job Preziosi is not prepared to surrender to Prosperi, however. "I will be in charge of the navigation," he said. "For all his strengths, Mauro never was very good with a compass."

If the two men don't get lost, if they don't expire from heat exhaustion or thirst, if desert thugs don't set upon them, they probably have the disciplined strength and sheer stubbornness to cross an ocean of sand—but who really knows? For Prosperi, though, there is an added personal dimension goading his every step: the sense that the farther he goes, the more he redeems himself, with all the doubts and suspicions of the past five years disappearing in the desert bleach. And when it's over, and he's standing at the reedy waters of the Nile, he'll finally have another story to tell—a better one.

❋ ❋ ❋

I felt as though all I had done as an athlete, all my years of training, had prepared me for this ultimate competition. What had begun as a contest against other people had become a contest with myself. I was in the midst of the greatest athletic performance of my life and I knew it. As athletes, we put on uniforms and cross over to an artificial world we call "sport." But as I moved over the dunes, I felt as though that barrier had been washed away and that the two worlds were now one.

I was desperate and scared. But I had never felt so alive. I decided that I loved the Sahara more than any other land, and that if God should see me through this, I would return to this magnificent place.

OCTOBER 1999

Editor's Note

Mauro Prosperi has not yet attempted his solo trek across the Sahara Desert. However, in April 2002 he completed the sixteenth Marathon des Sables, placing thirteenth with a time of twenty-five hours, thirty minutes, thirty-seven seconds.

FAR NORTH

by John Balzar

D AYS ARE GROWING SHORTER by three minutes every twenty-four hours. Today, just four hours, eleven minutes of sun. The temperature is dropping, and the lake in front of the cabin is frozen. Wind has blown away the snow, leaving a naked rind of glaze-blue ice. There are twenty-three restless working dogs staked in the yard. Two wolves have been seen nearby, one black and the other cream-colored. Their tracks, broad as a man's hand, criss-cross the valley. It is winter in the Yukon.

We have no electricity, no TV, no phone. In the long darkness, we rely on kerosene lamplight. A woodstove crackles with heat, but the old patchwork cabin is drafty still; gaps around the door collect con-densation that freezes as hot air meets cold, and we have to put our shoulders to the door each morning to break a half-inch seal of frost. We draw water in five-gallon buckets from a hole chopped through the ice of a nearby creek and pull it home on a toboggan. Inside, the sagging couch and cast-off chairs are chewed by rodents and stained by years of working men and their working clothes. Damp socks and gloves dry on a clothesline looped beam to beam across the kitchen. We unroll our sleeping bags on raw boards in a loft. The cabin reeks of game meat, dog food, and the moist ammonia-and-shit odor of thawing trail-dog harnesses.

By demographic standards, the four of us are living in conditions of impoverishment and hardship.

Which, as we think about it, calls for a good laugh and another shot of Jack Daniel's. There are oversize baked potatoes cooking in the coals and a creamy ptarmigan stew bubbling on the woodstove. In the shadows of a kitchen shelf, I see two bottles of whiskey in reserve. Cords of dry firewood are stacked just outside. I grab my parka and pac boots and venture out to pee, and the whole night sky is aflame with furious smoky-green belts of luminescence: the otherworldly light of the aurora borealis. Athabaskans say the aurora blazes the trail to heaven. Why not? What better home to imagine for God than at the end of that shivering firmament of pure energy? Spindly spruce trees between cabin and lake are cake-frosted and silhouetted in the greenish shadow-light. Air burns clean and cold in the throat. The night is utterly silent.

Impoverished? Hardly. We envy no one and desire nothing. Only the rich can say that.

"It's always been my thought that money would interfere with the fun I want to have in life," says Joe May, the sixty-two-year-old sourdough who has brought me here to Dezadeash Lake, Yukon Territory, northern Canada, a half-day's drive west of Whitehorse, forty miles from the Alcan highway truck stop at Haines Junction. To this borrowed cabin in the bush at sixty-one degrees north latitude, to a lake valley encircled by handsome, treeless, wind-scoured peaks—a landscape where it is possible to get a hundred miles from a road and just be starting out.

And the fun?

Dogs. This is a dog camp, as in working dogs. May is a dog driver, a former champion of the 1,049-mile Iditarod Sled Dog Race and a respected father figure in the world of dog-mushing. He wears big horn-rimmed glasses now, his teeth are discolored, he forgot to go to the barber this year, and there is some jowl to him; but his muscles are still hard and his caterpillar eyebrows bounce with energy from a life of action. A merchant marine on the Great Lakes, he divorced and came north in a Fiat half a lifetime ago and homesteaded in the interior of Alaska. His ex kept the refrigerator; he didn't replace it for twenty-seven years. Right away, though, he picked up a few dogs to help him get around in winter and drove them along a hundred-mile trapline. He decided to trap only martens (or sables, as in sable coats)—nasty-tempered little scavengers that died fast in the trap and suffered, he told himself, less than the more majestic creatures of the north. Then he was invited to participate in a local sled-dog race, and his trapline dogs, surprise, won. *Why, Christ,* he thought, *I can make a living this way and don't have to kill anything.* "My only regret," May says wistfully, "is that I'm not young again." Pass the Jack Daniel's, please.

Most of the twenty-three seemingly mismatched mongrels outside once belonged to a fur-trapping neighbor, and May is now helping their new owner establish a training regimen for the north's other great thousand-mile dog-mushing epic, the Yukon Quest International Sled

Dog Race. May ran his last thousand-miler in 1986. He stopped in the Quest's finishing chute, built a small fire, and ceremoniously burned his snowshoes. Never again—too grueling. It was reported that tears froze in his eyes. For a few years he went off and indulged himself with a sailboat and long-distance voyaging. But he wasn't able to get trail dogs out of his blood, and he's back kicking around the kennels and wilderness trails again.

Dan Turner is the dogs' new owner, and later this winter he'll be mushing fourteen of the best of them up the Quest trail, from White-horse to Fairbanks, 1,025 miles through some of the wildest, most for-bidding, and remotest country on the continent—the toughest overland trail in the world. A quiet forty-five-year-old native of Colorado, Turner recalls how he used to daydream out loud about Alaska when he was working construction. If it's so damn great up there, his coworkers finally asked one day, why didn't he go? He loaded his tools and was on the road in two hours. That was twenty-two years ago. Like many migrants, he scraped for jobs: liquor-store clerk in Anchorage, taxi driver, engine-shop mechanic. Now he is, of all things, the tax assessor in the coastal town of Haines. He is six foot six, with rangy good looks and a trimmed mustache. This will be his second try at the Quest. Two years ago he made it halfway before the trail broke his spirits.

"When I quit in Dawson City, I said I'd never get on a dog sled again," says Turner. "Then last year, I began having flashbacks, like Vietnam vets. I'd dream about the Quest. So I decided to do it again. There's a lot in just being able to do it. Not just the race but the char-acters, the traditions, the places. The race itself, there's nothing I've done that's been so miserable. . . . I never really realized I was in a race, except maybe at the prestart banquet. But the rest of the time, it's between you and yourself."

Roughly the same distance as the Anchorage-to-Nome Iditarod, the Quest is a colder journey: terrible and exhilarating cold. The mountain passes are higher, the intervals between checkpoints greater, the sled-loads heavier, the isolation more profound, the help farther away—usually impossibly far away. Temperatures frequently plunge to forty below, and even colder snaps must be anticipated at this time of year. Because it occurs first, in the long darkness of Feb-ruary (with the Iditarod in March), the Quest is more of a nighttime odyssey—a frightful prospect to those unfamiliar with the vastness of the subarctic, the chill and the loneliness. A finisher's patch from either race will gain you heaps of respect up here, where respect does not come cheap; but the Quest is undoubtedly the greater challenge. And it's purer: not just a race but a full-blooded winter wilderness camping trip, a rendezvous with adventure, a commemoration of mankind's old bond with working dogs, a private celebration of the values of the Far North without the high-pressure commercialism of the Iditarod.

To prepare the dogs for the extreme climate and terrain, May and Turner established their dog camp in the remote western Yukon. With us, too, is nineteen-year-old Will Rhodes of Crescent City, California, whose summer visit to an uncle in Haines has stretched into winter, plans for college postponed. After arriving in Haines, Rhodes answered a newspaper ad seeking a dog handler.

"The deal was, no money, just food and experience. And beer. The beer's been big," Rhodes explains, grinning. Rhodes, with his reluctant beard and football player's build, shovels dog shit, helps with feedings, administers medicines. He drives the camp "snowmachine" (local patois for "snowmobile"), extending practice trails ever deeper into the bush, and he mushes dogs on training runs. Yesterday a shotgun dislodged from its position along the seat of the snowmachine, whipped around, and hit Rhodes in the back with enough force to splinter the stock. A quick student in the ways of the north, he is treating himself with canine liniment and Budweiser.

And me? I'm spending the winter here because dog-mushing and the Quest got under my skin. I have been traveling through and writing about these parts for a decade. In 1997, I joined the Quest as a volunteer veterinary tech. Events lasted three weeks, but that wasn't long enough. Not enough time to take in the sleepless, hallucinatory exhaustion of perpetual motion through a vast wildness where most of the day is night and the nights are cold enough to frostbite exposed skin in quick minutes; where one's field of vision on a thousand-mile landscape is sometimes only a hundred feet in any direction through the blackness. Not long enough to penetrate a culture in which mushing is not a pastime but a way of life.

The hookup is chaotic: loud, violent, powerful, disturbing, and joyful.

Sled dogs are bred for strength and endurance and, more than that, for heart and enthusiasm. So they scream at the sight of an armload of harnesses, desperate bloodcurdling howls. They lunge and spin on their chains. They dance on the roofs of their unpainted, straw-filled doghouses. *Don't forget me, you bastard,* they say, or the canine equivalent.

Earlier, the dogs were fed a broth made with chopped raw meat— perhaps freezer-burned beef at $15 for a twenty-five-pound block. On the trail they will have a snack, a piece of frozen whitefish. Then, for dinner, a bouillabaisse of salmon, beaver, chicken skins, horse meat, and kibble. A greedy appetite is one of the most desirable qualities in a trail dog: A fifty-pound dog needs to consume at least ten thousand calories each day during the Quest, more when temperatures are really cold.

Now May and I shake the snow from the race sled, made of aluminum and steam-bent wood joined by limber nylon cord. We aim it in the starting direction and affix its snow hook to a pickup bumper. The double-jawed, fourteen-inch stainless-steel hook, attached by a stout rope to the sled's frame, acts as a parking brake for the team. When dogs are fresh and in a fury to bolt, the hook must be secured to something substantial—the trunk of a large tree, say, or a ton-and-a-half pickup left in gear. Later, when the dogs settle in to work, it will be enough to stomp the hook into hardpacked snow to keep them in place.

Today, May is running ten paired dogs, not quite a full fourteen-dog Quest race team. A second sled is tied to his by a six-foot-long polypropylene rope; I'll be riding the double. A fifty-foot-long gangline is unrolled from the front sled. Harnesses are unbundled and spread on the snow, causing complete hysteria: Howling dogs throw themselves against their chains. May has to roar out the lineup of dogs I'm to fetch, one by one: Piggy, Big Dan, Linus, Solo . . .

Harnessing dogs is a task that's something between rodeo wrangling and diaper changing. You grab a collar tightly in one fist, unclip the dog from its chain, and with your free hand raise its powerful front legs off the ground. (People who underestimate the brute-muscle force of these creatures have been surprised to discover their fingers broken when they've pulled away.) Trying to move a dog whose four feet are planted would permit it the advantage of traction, and you would likely find yourself being dragged on your face. But when you hold its front feet aloft, the dog must hop and jerk forward in an awkward dance across the slippery packed snow of the dog yard.

Straddling the squirming, half-berserk animal, you wrestle its head into the harness, then one front foot, then the other. A loop at the back of each harness is clipped to individual three-foot tug-lines that vee off the main gang-line. Finally, the dogs are clipped, two in a row, collar to collar, with foot-long neck-lines to keep each one aligned.

Behind the lead dogs are the swing dogs, which ease the team around corners and prevent the whole group from turning at once. Then come the four team dogs, or pullers, paired off by compatibility, or because one dog acts to motivate its partner, or for any of a dozen other reasons. At the rear are the wheel dogs, bruisers that must absorb the jerk and sway of the sled, which can weigh three hundred pounds when fully loaded.

At first, because of the riotous barking, you may miss another sound—the reassuring words of driver to dog: *Easy. Good girl. That's it. Ready?* A good musher spends much of the day in conversation with his animals, who then come to know his voice, the tics and moods of the one person who speaks to them as God.

Even with two people, hookup takes a half hour. And now, impossible as it seems, the dogs are even more frantic. Their howling is incessant, the primordial delirium of the pack before the hunt. The rope lines holding the team together crack and stretch band-tight with every lunge. The two sleds shudder from the strain.

Standing on the runners of the lead sled, May nods, arching a bushy eyebrow. I wait for slack, then yank the snow hook from the pickup. May says, "Okay." Mushers do not yell "Mush!" Maybe "Hike," or they whistle, but usually it's just "Okay, guys," or perhaps a wiggle of the sled. We catapult forward, zero to twenty in a single leap. At that instant, the howls cease. We whip-snake up the trail in silence. Except for my inner voice: *Oh, shit. Christ. Wasn't it Gus Grissom who said, "Please, God, don't let me fuck up"?*

The first minutes with a fresh team are the most exciting. And the most dangerous. Though each sled is equipped with a boot-controlled hinged brake, which drives two steel chisels mounted underneath into the snow, plus a drag brake made from an eighteen-inch section of snowmachine tread that rides between the runners, you can no more stop these animals now than you could teach them to eat with a knife, fork, and finger bowl. You want your dogs to go, not stop. "Whoa!" is a command usually overlooked in training. So at the start of each day, and after each break, the dogs must be allowed to burn through that first crazy release of adrenaline, a rush that passes through the team in a seeming contagion of emotions: competition, elation, fear, and who knows what else. Hang on. Or, as dog drivers say, don't fucking ever let go.

Earlier, I had this conversation with May:

How do you steer a sled?

"I don't know."

What do you mean you don't know?

"I can't tell you how to ride a bicycle, either."

I have mushed dogs alone before, including big teams, but I still cannot entirely grasp the physics of maneuvering a sled down a winding, hilly, lopsided trail while trees whiz by. At any given time, some dogs are going up a hill, others down—and on S turns, some can be going "haw" while others are already headed "gee," the old mule-skinner terms for "left" and "right," respectively. I know that you lean into some corners and away from others. You can gain advantage by pulling the sled up on one runner and torquing the handlebar. Sometimes it seems natural and other times mystifying. I know you never put on the brake when you're cornering toward a tree, or you'll get pulled right into it. But if you're skidding straight for a tree anyway, what the hell do you do then?

Training for the '98 Quest, Peter Zimmerman, a longtime Swiss musher living in the Yukon, flew out of his dog yard behind a furiously fresh team and was slingshot into a spruce. In a hospital bed four months later, he still could not move his arms or legs.

Uphill now, we dismount and run-push behind the sleds, jumping on the runners for the elevator drop downslope. This particular hill is uncommonly steep and—*oh, shit*—a ninety-degree right turn awaits us at the bottom. I was just relishing the manly sensation of ice growing in my beard and marveling at the frosting on the spruces and aspens that hug the trail, sometimes merging overhead into a branch canopy and sometimes opening up to reveal the faceted faces of the Saint Elias Mountains beyond. I was enjoying the pleasant glow of exertion; the soft, satisfying *shushhhhhh* of runners over the hardpack; the tugging, bouncy-alive feeling of the gang-line ahead; and the low-slung, deceptively easy-footed cadence of dogs shouldering forward.

And now this impossible turn. I ride the drag until the last second to try to control my speed, and then I twist my weight to send the front of the sled around the corner. Harder, with all my might. *Oh, shit* . . .

I'm somersaulting into the shrubbery now; I can feel snow slide down my neck as I tumble along. Over on the trail, my sled is on its side, ricocheting against trees like Crack-the-Whip.

Using his brake and snow hook, May works the team to a stop at the next rise. When I come lumbering and huffing up, I am greeted by dogs looking over their shoulders, puffing little clouds of vapor, quizzical looks on their hairy, frosted faces. I right my sled, brush dry powder off myself, and acknowledge my date with the camp dishes tonight, the penalty for coming off a sled. *And quit staring at me, you wide-eyed, whiskery beasts. Don't you know, Gus Grissom fucked up, too.*

Today we're making only a twelve-mile run, and I will become separated from my sled three more times, each occasion on a corner that called for some shift of weight that I cannot fathom. Dishes for the rest of the week. The most difficult maneuver proves to be turning the team around in the thick spindle forest at the halfway mark. From a stop, the command is "Come haw," a 180-degree U-turn that brings the animals back down the left side of the narrow trail. We try to yank our sleds around into position but are not quite fast enough, as the dogs break into a lope. May's sled leaps across the brushbow of my own, and he is knocked down. When the towrope tightens, I'm spun off my feet, too. The two of us are dragging behind tipped-over sleds, plowing up snow, holding on for dear life. May is barking profanities. I'm muttering the only words left in my vocabulary, *Oh, shit.* Eventually, the whole strung-out apparatus grinds to a stop. May rises, grinning, head-to-toe caked in snow and spruce needles, his long gray hair frozen into a stand-up fan, like Don King's. "See, nothing to it." And those bristly, maniacal faces are once again looking back impatiently. We right the sleds, jump back on the runners, push up the hills, hang on coming down, duck the overhanging branches, lean in to the corners . . . or was it lean out?

I ask myself: Is it enough to say that the rough, twisty, windblown, three-foot-wide trail chopped through the wilderness for the Yukon Quest covers just about the same distance as from Los Angeles to Seattle, or from New York to Daytona Beach?

The experience leaves me uneasy. My plan is to mush one leg of the Quest trail with my own dog team in just three months. *Please God . . .*

We right the sleds, jump back on the runners, push up the hills, hang on coming down, duck the overhanging branches, lean into the corners . . . or was it lean out?

Early afternoon, sundown: chores completed, dogs fed, shit shoveled— time for social hour. If you travel regularly between urban settings and truly rural places, it is no surprise how gregarious people can be in the bush, how self-reliant they are about amusing one another in the absence of television and radio. It is no surprise how pleasant life can be without the numbing distractions of the electronic age.

"Tea or whiskey?" I ask Heinz Eckervogt, who looks to be about seventy, tall and lean, as he kicks the snow from his boots and moves to warm himself at the stove.

"Tea," he answers in his brittle German accent.

"Okay," I say, "and I'll have whiskey."

Eckervogt is a neighbor, more or less. And neighbors drop by. Hardly a night passes without visitors. I'm particularly happy to see this one, because I've been tipped off to his story. Eckervogt eases his lanky frame into the droopy couch, blows on his tea, and begins the ritual round robin of conversation about the weather and things hereabout. Winter temperatures in the Yukon can fluctuate more than eighty degrees in a day, so there is almost always something to say. Right now, it's eleven degrees. "Goddamn winter. Last year it was fifty-four below at this time. Real weather. Snowed yesterday, might snow tomorrow. Could be wind, too. Haven't seen any moose. Damn wolves get them all."

"So, I hear you found a nugget," I say.

Eckervogt nods. It was back in '88. He and his sons had a mining claim up on Squaw Creek, which has since been absorbed into Kluane National Park. At the end of a workday, his oldest son said, "Here," and slipped something buttery-smooth into the old man's hand. Gleaming, it was two inches thick and so big around Eckervogt could barely clasp it. The weight of it was shocking. Another load of gravel had gone through the sluice box, and there it was on the first grate: 76.5 ounces, nearly 5 pounds, 98.6 percent pure, the second-largest nugget ever found in North America. He and the boys went to Haines Junction and kept the bar going until dawn. Eckervogt safekeeps the nugget in some unspecified security storage now, "although we had it home the other night." He has turned down all cash offers. One company wanted to fly him around the world to display the nugget for a promotion. His answer: Don't feel like going around the world just now, thanks.

Art Papineau is a sixty-four-year-old French-Canadian with one heart attack under his belt. He is a neighbor, too. We wander over to his cabin one night, if for no other reason than Papineau swears more vigorously than any man alive, an old potbellied, tobacco-chewing son of a bitch with a half-full, five-gallon spittoon there on his kitchen floor.

He was a gold miner too, until the government made a park of his claim. "Never much on dogs. But did try a couple once. [*Spit.*] Big goddamn brutes. Belonged to some lady. The sons of whores couldn't walk a straight line, but shit-oh-Christ they could pull. Loaded up a toboggan with staples—sugar and flour and tobacco—and they pulled that bastard load all the way up the creek. For meat, we planned on shooting moose. But that year, not a fucking moose anywhere. And nothing to feed them dogs. Had to shoot the first one. [*Spit.*] To tell the truth, they weren't any damn good anyway, them dogs. They were too used to listening to a woman. You know what I mean? My partner skinned it out. Then he came to me. And he said, 'You know, have you taken a look at the meat on that bastard?' Big, red, muscly stuff. . . . Shit, yes, we were hungry. So I put some of them ribs in the oven. Oh, God, they came out as pretty golden-brown as you've ever seen. [*Spit.*] But, fuck. It was just like biting a boot. Couldn't get a tooth into that stringy shit. So we boiled up the whole damn dog for about six hours. It wasn't so bad then. After a while, we still couldn't get a moose. So we shot the second dog, too. [*Spit.*] Goddamn, we were hungry, see? Then one day I got to looking at my partner's dog. I asked him, 'You seen the size of the fucking brisket on that thing?' 'Oh, no, you don't,' he said, 'that's my pet.' 'Why, Jesus H. Christ,' I told him, 'you just ate two of mine. . . .'"

Paddy Santucci, an Alaskan via Azusa, California, first went mushing because he liked to travel to the remote Athabaskan villages of the interior. Sledding was an intimate, quiet, and traditional mode of winter mobility that originated with the Eskimos—their teams splayed out in fans to traverse the shapeless topography of the arctic coast—and then was adopted and modified to in-line hitches for the forest and river trails by missionaries, mail drivers, and gold miners. Perfect for a twentieth-century loner.

I met Santucci last year. He was not racing but following the Quest as dog-handler for Mark May, Joe's veterinarian son and an accomplished musher. He never took off his greasy tent-sized anorak, he never slept, I never saw him eat, he moved among the dogs with command, people were drawn to him but he always seemed apart. He had a pinch of tobacco under his lip and rarely smiled, but when he did he lit up a room. Santucci has a fierce joy about him. He seems to embody and convey the character of the Far North—thirty-seven years old, an accomplished mountaineer with one heroic rescue on Denali to his credit, a hunter, a bush pilot, a construction worker, a dog driver. He doesn't mention that he has a degree in physics from U.C.-Davis. He is smallish but stringy-hard, with shoulder-length hair. He is clean-shaven now because his beard once froze solid and scarred his face with frostbite. He speaks seldom—and never to hear the sound of his own voice. Acquaintances say his word is as solid as gold.

"I'll be racing next time," he told me back then.

"I'll catch up with you."

Somewhere there is an answering machine that Santucci some-times checks. He lives in the bush north of Fairbanks. When he gets my message, weeks in advance, we agree to meet. He arrives at the appointed rendezvous in Fairbanks a half-hour early with his dog-handler friend, John Boyce, an itinerant professor of economics who now teaches in New Zealand and is on his summer break. In locker boxes built into the bed of Santucci's crew-cab pickup are seventeen dogs. On top of the boxes is a sled. We will add a trailer and two snow-machines. Destination: Tanana, an Indian village at the confluence of the Yukon and Tanana rivers, sixty-five miles from any kind of a road. Among mushers, "Tanana" means "dogs." The brood stock for many good teams originated in this village, where sled dogs and racing go back generations. It was here that the U.S. Army once maintained a vast dog yard. It was here that the sleek saluki was introduced into the mongrelized lineage—a mix of husky, hound, malamute, retriever, and other breeds—of the Tanana village dog. The resulting animals—small-hammed and with gracefully arching backs—have proved to be some of the fastest sprint racers in the world, traveling a nine-mile course at average speeds of twenty-two miles per hour.

We head north up the oil-company haul road toward Prudhoe Bay. Partway, we join in a convoy behind another of Santucci's friends, Peter Moore, a state department of transportation worker in charge of plow-ing the treacherous passes we must travel. After seventy-five miles, we turn left into high hills over an icy, windblown single-lane road. After another seventy-five miles, we arrive in Manley Hot Springs, population sixty-five, in darkness at 4 P.M. Santucci stakes out and feeds his dogs.

That night, at Manley's one tavern, I introduce myself to Susan Thomas. "What do you do here?" I ask. "I'm a mail-order bride," she says, beaming. Until two months ago, Thomas tells me, she was an office manager at a dental clinic in Belvedere, Tennessee. She answered an ad in *Alaska Man* magazine, a lonely-hearts publication that owes its existence to the gender imbalance in the Alaskan bush. She received no answer. She wrote a second letter. He called on August 12. "Between then and October 3, I sold my house, sold my car, sold everything I own, quit my job, and came here. The best decision of my life." She now lives without running water but has joined the town's crafts guild and is getting used to the quiet. She couldn't sleep for the first two weeks because of the stillness. She is learning how to can food. Her first chore: canning the meat of a bear. Tonight, her new husband is behind her, shooting pool and listening shyly. "Oh," she confides, "we're not officially married yet. But we will be in about six months."

Long before sunup, we put Santucci's dogs back into the truck, drive to the edge of town, unload and re-stake them, attach harnesses, roll out the sled and gang-line, and hook everything up. Seventeen insanely shrieking dogs are rocking the big pickup back and forth, pulling on the bumper. Something is about to move, or break. Santucci releases the snow hook and catapults, now silently, into the darkness of the trail, his high-powered headlamp barely able to penetrate the ninety-foot distance to his lead dogs. He vanishes.

It is twenty-below here and windless. Ahead, in the low country and river bottoms, it will drop to thirty-below. Here, your breath clouds up in front of you and you find yourself walking through ice crystals of your own making. A rind of ice builds quickly in your beard and in the fur ruff of your parka; to move your head you must crack the ice. These are the temperatures that prompt interior Alaskans to begin talking seriously about cold and its cruel compounding toll: It now takes longer to do a chore because you are numb and slow; consequently, you are exposed to the cold longer. Dogs and humans both dehydrate quickly—as in, freeze-dry—and it is essential to gag down prodigious amounts of liquid, which means building fires to thaw water. Mushers put fleece jackets on some of their more sensitive dogs and affix pile jockstraps, "peter heaters," on the males to guard against frostbite.

For a serious competitor like Santucci, this trek is a complex part of the conditioning of his team. From this group of seventeen will come most of his fourteen-dog starting lineup. By breaking the animals' regular training routine—penning them in the truck and bouncing them along roads, exposing them to strange trails, altering mealtimes, running long distances with minimum rest—he will come as close as possible to duplicating the circumstances that await them after the starting voice of the Yukon Quest announcer echoes down First Avenue, Whitehorse.

Three hours behind, we follow on the snowmachines—Boyce and photographer Stephanie Bradfield riding tandem on one and me on the other. Dog breeder and former racer Fred Jordan, a native of Tanana, has agreed to be our guide—although he is such a notorious speed-freak on his souped-up snowmachine, we seldom see anything but his track.

From town, our route leads north and west, into the heart of the great Alaskan interior: a landscape of only modest vertical drama when compared with the galactic expanse of its horizontal. The first fifteen miles take us down a seasonal mining trail that's no more rugged than a lumpy one-rut road. Then the trail narrows, to barely shoulder-wide in places, and veers left and downhill and we encounter, in succession, the three topographies that will occupy our imaginations and our exertions for the rest of the day—the twisty, hilly forests of stunted spruces and willows, followed by maddeningly dimpled meadows of tundra tussocks, and, last, long-frozen sections of lake, slough, and river. We drop fifteen feet down vertical stream banks and wrestle our way up the other side. We jounce and skid along side hills, sometimes slipping off the trail, having to dismount and hoist ourselves back. Overhanging willows poke at our faces and shower us with clouds of spindrift. Protruding logs grab at steering skis and at our numbed feet. Tussocks slow us to a crawl; we jerk and bounce along. And then we make furious, screeching, full-throttle runs across the ice, blinded by the fine snow crystals churned up by Jordan but unable to slow down for fear of encountering a weak spot in the surface that would send us into the frigid water. No matter how cold the temperatures, ice remains alive—with springs and currents underneath eating away at its bottom, with changing water levels opening gaps between frozen and fluid water, with wind blowing against the surface mass and pushing open cracks which may now be made invisible by snow. Santucci has attested that Jordan is "the finest woodsman I know," yet even he broke through the ice of the Yukon River once with a dog team during a Quest. Jordan and his dogs survived. No mushers have died on the Quest, although former champion Bruce Johnson perished with all his dogs when the team broke through ice during a 1993 training run.

About sixty-three miles down the trail, we catch up with Santucci, who's feeding and resting his dogs. Together, we cross the vast Yukon, the fourth-biggest river on the continent and the last to be explored, the great highway of the Far North. Half of it is frozen, glassy-smooth; the other half is a maze of knife-sharp ice blocks with a rough trail chopped through by ax and chain saw. I blink—my eyelids are beginning to freeze; I blink again, and my right eye will not open. It is at least ten degrees colder down on the river's surface than it is a few feet up the bank. But we are almost to Tanana. We navigate the last of the trail and arrive—me, half-blind—in the village, less than a hundred miles south of the Arctic Circle. Within a few hours, my cheeks and nose will swell and turn chalk-white, then fiery red. Surface frostbite. I have no feeling in my feet, and when I take off my boots, my socks are sheathed in ice. Altogether, a rookie's arrival. Though I will feel better later when I hear one of the locals mention he'd also had cold feet.

Tanana's population of 300 or so is a mix of Athabaskan natives and whites. For the most part, residents live subsistence lives. Fish-wheels along the banks of the Yukon throw out tons of salmon and whitefish during summer. In autumn, the seemingly boundless valley of spruce and tundra, known locally as the Yukon Flats, yields moose for meat; in winter, the fur of lynxes, wolfs, beavers, foxes, wolverines, and martens. Transportation of supplies—via river barges in summer and bush airlines the rest of the year—is a major enterprise. And so are dogs. Insulated by distance and united by the culture of the wilderness, the village has remained fundamentally unchanged in character and ethos for a century.

We bunk at the lofted log cabin of Pat Moore, who came here as a boy when his father worked at a now-closed FAA tracking station. His wife, a native, is the town's postmaster. They have two children and sixty-five racing dogs. The living room of their home is like a hotel lobby, with a constant stream of people in and out—kids wandering through after school, a trapper dropping by from the bush, a few friends over to say hi to Santucci, an village elder or two who heard about some strangers in town, the local state trooper hiding out from his girlfriend, and an assortment of others whose intentions mainly seem to be to warm their hands around the stove and see if anything interesting is happening. As the day ends, pools of meltwater spread across the entryway under the rows of heavy boots and the heaps of parkas hanging from nails driven into log walls. A large wire-mesh screen over the woodstove is covered with drying gloves and socks. For dinner: thick, gamy moose chili with slices of cheddar. The Moores must haul their water from a spigot in town, and it is too bitter to drink. So we choose instead from cases of soda and beer, airfreighted in.

I was exhausted, but refusing sleep seems to be an everyday part of the mushing culture. Maybe it's a habit that comes from the trail, where rest is for losers. Or perhaps it's simply the fear of missing something. Sometime late in the night—while I'm feeling warm, leaden, and drowsy—Pat Moore leaps into his parka and leads us around the side of his house to his dog shop, a building that smells of liniment, sour fish, thawing harnesses, and the smoke from a small, puffing woodstove. He taps a baby-keg of his home-brewed Scotch ale—a beautifully wrought and well-aged beer with a preposterously high alcohol content—and we drink from Kerr jars. Damn good ale, we agree. The shop fills with people, and the haze of cigar and cigarette smoke, and the murmur of conversation—mostly about dogs, training dogs, the pain in the ass of having dogs, the equipment needed for dogs, the latest race results, which dog has a bum foot and which has puppies, how a naturally fermented whitefish aids digestion in a nervous dog, which medicines work . . .

Sam, an old, full-bearded refugee from California, has found a miniature cattle prod and is busy jamming it into his shoulder. *Zzzit.* His head jerks to the side and his boots lift off the floor. Keeps the soreness out of the muscles, he explains. *Zzzit.* Santucci shows the scars on his ropy arms from when he broke up a dog fight. Darwin, drunk already, is trying to focus his eyes, trying to keep from falling down while looking for a stool on which to sit. Best damned snow-go mechanic in the village.

Ken, a trapper, carpenter, and handyman, talks about coming to Alaska in 1972 out of high school in Sacramento. Upriver that summer, he and a friend gathered some empty fifty-five-gallon drums, lashed up some logs, and built a raft. They put Ken's old pickup camper shell on it and floated downstream for two weeks to get here. "That first winter, I never had enough money to leave," he says. "Same the second winter. Then, by the time I made enough to leave, I liked it here." He has gone into Fairbanks once in three years, and it scared him: too big and bustling. He has a rotten tooth. I ask him where he will go to get it fixed. "I'll go to the toolbox and get a pair of pliers when it gets bad."

John, one of the village elders, is not drinking or smoking; he has a quiet, contented dignity that makes me feel loud and coarse. I go outside to pee and see the thermometer at twenty-eight-below. I don't bother looking at my watch.

It's morning. There's commotion in the dog yard. Moore's assistant Soren Lund, an eighteen-year-old musher from Denmark, is hooking up a team for a training run. "Come along," he says. So I climb into the sled "basket," which is roughly like reclining on a wicker chaise lounge strapped onto an F-16, no place for a grown man recovering from alcohol poisoning. If trail dogs are built for a hundred miles of endurance, sprint dogs only know speed, and they run more than twice as fast over courses of just a few miles. The frenzied howls during hookup are like needles jabbed into my brain. Lund pulls the snow hook from its anchor. We slingshot out of the yard, the dogs a blur of fur and feet, the sled whipsawing behind, me gripping the sled with one hand and holding the ugly, sharp snow hook in the other. A quick right turn and then a ninety-degree left onto a long, icy straightaway.

But we do not get to the straightaway. The sled skids through the second turn like a car in a four-wheel drift, the dogs lunging for more speed on the gang-line. Almost sideways, the sled encounters some imperfection in the ice, and we're flipping over. It happens so instantaneously, I cannot raise my hand from the side of the basket to cushion the fall. My forehead smashes into the ice. I think to myself, *That was a hard one.* I am aware of myself clinging to the overturned sled, careening down the ice. *Don't fucking ever let go.* A loose team will crash and tangle and perhaps half the dogs will be injured, some will die. But dogs make no allowance for human mishap, so they're still digging for more speed. Then I remember that somewhere bouncing along with me on the end of a rope is that evil snow hook. Sharp, dangerous, where is it? Later I will see that it has entered my parka, ripped through the front at mid-chest, and emerged at my throat, slicing my neck gaiter in two. I am aware that Lund fell off the sled long ago. I am facedown, holding on, scraping over the trail at twenty-five miles per hour. Then the snow hook is in my hand, and I jam its points into the ice and bear down with all my weight. The gouges in the ice run for more than a hundred feet before the dogs are drawn to a halt, where they look back curiously.

Curtis Sommer, the village nurse, will thaw my forehead to get it to bleed clean before sewing it up. Lisa Penrose, the general manager of Apocalypse Design cold-weather outfitters in Fairbanks, will sew up my parka. I will turn purple with bruises down my legs and chest. I have banged loose the edge of my left retina, and I will see strange white bursts of light in my eye for months, whether it's open or closed. But those things will mend, all except for the empty yearning I cannot satisfy—for those far-off friends, the exhilaration of the cold, the howls of dogs, the elegant simplicity of woodstoves and log cabins, the easy evenings with the storytellers, the phosphorescent dance of colors in a cobalt-black sky, and the long trails into the wild.

Postscript

Thirty-eight mushers started the 1998 Yukon Quest. Dan Turner lasted only 260 miles before he gave up, angry and despondent. Neither he nor his dogs seemed prepared to go past the one-quarter mark. Paddy Santucci had a rough start, crashing his sled into trees and injuring a dog early in the race. Some of his younger dogs, on which he'd banked his hopes, lost their drive and had to be dropped, which is permitted under race rules, although no fresh dogs can be added to the team. Down to only eight dogs at the midpoint, Santucci beat the odds and finished sixth. I came to believe that I'd met a future champion.

Joe May served as a volunteer race judge. But before the trophy banquet, he was on his way home to Trapper Creek, Alaska, where neighbors promised to help him assemble his own new race team. Trapper Creek used to be famous for dogs, and there are some people who want to put it back on the map, he says.

Me? Again I served as a volunteer for the Quest, but I interrupted my work to mush a team of dogs eighty miles over one of the most remote legs of the trail. I frostnipped my fingertips and face trying to roll a cigarette in the wind, but the astronaut's prayer—or perhaps just the savvy of the dogs themselves—got me exactly where I wanted to go: the middle of nowhere.

FEBRUARY 1999

THE BIG GAME

by Jonathan Miles

ALL HIM MOOSE. EVERYBODY else does, and it fits him: He's a big guy with a big voice and a big smile, a supremely regular guy from the Sun Belt who loves his dad, deep-sea fishing, his job, his hometown ball club, Copenhagen snuff, and a medium-well steak, more or less in that order. In short, he's not the sort of man that eats sushi, and that's his current problem.

"*Blech,*" says the Moose, seated at a table near the stern of a sixty-two-foot yacht anchored in Okoe Bay, off Hawaii's Big Island. He takes a deep, pained breath before sinking his face back into the split belly of a small opelu, or mackerel scad, tearing the fatty purplish flesh with his teeth while the fish's head and tail hang limply from either side of his hands. He looks like he's using the fish for a harmonica.

Seated with him, and watching him intently, are four men, two of them legends of Hawaiian fishing. One of these legends, Peter Hoogs, is the very definition of "old salt"; with his white beard and sun-creased face, he looks more Hemingwayesque than Hemingway. He's the only skipper on the planet ever to have caught a thousand-pound blue marlin and a thousand-pound black marlin in the same waters, and he is, according to the Moose, "the Man." The other's name is Kerwin Masunaga, and he skippered his boat, the *Holly Ann,* to the World Cup title in 2000; more recently, he's famous for having landed a 1,140-pound blue marlin *by himself,* reeling in the fish, hour after hour, while at the same time driving the boat. He is also, according to the Moose, "the Man."

And the Men, at this moment, are barely hiding grins. "Now," Masunaga tells the Moose, "you eat the head."

The Moose balks, glaring at the mangled fish on his plate. A few hours earlier, he was using opelu for bait, lacerating the slimy purple mass with a 9/0 chrome Mustad hook and slinging it overboard. It's hard for him to avoid that thought. "No way," says the Moose.

"But the head is the luckiest part," says Masunaga. From a platter at the table's center, he fetches an opelu and, with one swift and the-atrical motion, bites off its head. The Moose recoils at the sounds of bones and scales crunching, scanning the men around the table for reactions, but they are mostly poker-faced, betrayed only by the slightest of smiles, listening to Masunaga chew.

"You eat the head," Masunaga finally says, "you catch a marlin."

And there, for the Moose, is the rub. The Moose doesn't like to monkey with luck, and so far—three days into a four-day high-stakes marlin-fishing tournament pitting the Moose against these old-salt legends—he's done everything right. He's been wearing his lucky shirt. The band on his lucky watch broke, but he brought the thing along anyway. They're even flying the Stars and Stripes on the boat, because, hell, how could *that* be bad luck? No, the Moose is not one to tinker with fishing hoodoo—*kapu,* in the local parlance—but right now, jeez, the Man is telling him to eat a raw fish head, and sure, maybe the Man is jacking with him, because they're always jacking with the Moose here, but what if he's not? What if the Moose refuses—and, repulsed by what's on his plate, he's got "no" on his lips—and then, *bam,* like that, his fabled lucky streak collapses?

No, it's an awful thought, one he can't bear, so the Moose gingerly places the fish head on his tongue, like a pill—just a regular guy with, at this moment, an irregular resolve to win. Or at least to prove that he's the luckiest friggin' man on the high seas, which, considering the com-petition at the table, might well be the very same thing. The Moose's eyes go wide with hope and revulsion as he bites down on luck.

His given name is James Karamouzis ("mouz" = "moose"), and at the age of thirty-eight, he may be the most unlikely big-game-fishing cham-pion in the world. The story goes like this: Two years ago, the Moose was vacationing in Kailua-Kona, Hawaii, with a couple of pals. It was the standard routine—beaches, golf, funny shirts, drinks with umbrel-las. But just as he was about to board a day-trip snorkeling boat, another ship in Kona's Keauhou Harbor caught the Moose's eye. It was a thirty-eight-foot twin-turbo-diesel Uniflite with "Bite Me" painted on its stern, and it was a charter fishing boat. "Wait a second," he told his pals.

The Moose was born and bred in Phoenix, and his fishing experi-ence, not surprisingly, was limited—a few trout pulled from Arizona's White River, the occasional reservoir bass, but never anything you couldn't carry home in a bucket. He can't say what it was about the

Bite Me that grabbed his attention, but he booked it for the next day before scampering back to his snorkel boat. He got skunked that first day out, but it wasn't so bad, and the skipper was persistent, so he chartered the boat for half of the next day, too—right up until his plane was scheduled to leave, to get him back to the floor-covering business he runs with his dad. That morning, he caught a 207-pound blue marlin, and excuse the pun, but the Moose was hooked.

The *Bite Me*'s young skipper, a four-year charter captain named Brian Wargo, convinced the Moose to come back to try his luck in a marlin tournament, so he did, and he won the first day's competition with a 723-pound blue. It was a hell of a big fish for the neophyte angler, and pails of cold water had to be poured over the Moose's head while he rocked in the fighting chair, as startled as anyone. He came back to Hawaii for another tournament, and won one of its top prizes by catching three blue marlin in less than an hour. Those victories were enough to garner the Moose an invitation to the inaugural Championship Event of the Maui Jim Hawaii Marlin Series, the newly instated Super Bowl of Kona marlin-fishing, in November 2000. The seas off Kona are arguably the best big-marlin waters in the world, which means the competition among skippers and anglers here is feral; the championship was founded to ferret out the best of the best, to put up a fence between luck and skill. In short, it's fair to say that by this point the Moose was out of his league.

But damn if he didn't win the championship, too.

It's precisely one year later, the skies over Kona gray and mottled from a storm that has just passed, and the Moose is once again aboard the *Bite Me,* vying to retain his improbable title. "When we're on a fish, I want you to strap me in the chair," he tells the first mate, Tom Siebler, a former charter captain himself. "That's legal, right? Nate"—a mate from a prior tournament—"tried to get me to strap myself in, but I had a couple of fuckups that way. And don't be afraid to tell me what I'm doing wrong. Beat me over the head with it."

Up on the flying bridge, Captain Wargo is piloting the *Bite Me* out toward blue water while the deckhand, twenty-three-year-old John Bennett, readies the outriggers. The championship is a kind of expeditionary tournament; we're at sea the entire four days, even sleeping on board. Dinner and cocktails are served nightly on the *Sunseeker,* a sixty-two-foot Hatteras yacht, the organizers' mother ship; a seventeen-foot

Zodiac shuttles crews from boats to yacht and back. Just four boats are competing in this year's run; a fifth boat was slated to fish, but its skipper didn't want to chance the stormy seas between Maui and Hawaii.

As for the number of entrants, the championship is a small, if select, event, and that smallness is reflected in the purse. (This year's winner will earn roughly six grand, which is chump change in the marlintourney business; side bets typically pump those cash figures up, sometimes jaw-droppingly, though not for the Moose, who ruefully gambles just enough to be polite.) Because there is no supreme governing body for big-game-fishing tournaments, no one can say for sure just how many are held around the globe each year—the safest estimate is around a thousand, ranging from Tahiti to Venezuela to Australia to Mexico to Florida to Maryland, which hosts one of the biggest-money tourneys of them all, the $1.8 million Ocean City White Marlin Open, every August. The number of entrants in any tournament can vary from just a few to a few hundred, but even the vaguest arithmetic makes one point evident: Big-game tournament fishing is a very big game, drawing hundreds of thousands of participants worldwide. Anglers spend minor fortunes—on travel, entrance fees, equipment, etc.—for the chance to make it all back and then some. Or to garner a little prestige, which brings us back to our present venue. The Maui Jim qualifying preliminaries offered respectable winnings—this year's World Cup, for instance, proffered a $135,000 purse—but the championship is about less tangible gains. Bragging rights, dock swagger, the making and breaking of legends. That sort of thing.

"Moosie!" Wargo yells down. Like the Moose, Wargo is a big guy, thick-necked as a linebacker, with a ponytail and an easily provoked, high-pitched laugh. He looks like the kind of guy who'd be into Kid Rock, which he is. "What're you waiting for? Put on the shirt."

"The shirt" is the T-shirt—a plain white Reebok-logo tee—that the Moose was wearing when he caught his first marlin; the shirt attained sanctity that day. It's been tucked on board the *Bite Me* ever since, and because it also hasn't been washed ever since, it's the color of caramel. Some folks would say it's nasty—me, for instance. But nasty luck is luck nonetheless, and the Moose dons the shirt.

"Besides luck," I ask Wargo, nodding at the Moose as we ease into trolling speed, "what separates a good marlin angler from a bad one?"

"Technique," Wargo says. "Part of it is natural, and part of it takes a long time to learn. Moosie is good—he's got the natural part down."

Most of that natural part is stamina; hauling in a giant marlin requires a specific and brawny kind of athleticism, especially near Kona, where anglers have been known to fight fish for as long as thirty-four hours. Adrenaline can get you through a smaller fish, which is how your fat, red-faced cigar smokers pull it off, but a long fight—hour upon hour of heaving the rod up, reeling in line, heaving, reeling, heave, reel—will exhaust the average Rotarian. Yet as with any sporting endeavor (climbing comes to mind as a fair example), brawn will get you only so far. Fishing for marlin, you have to know what to do when a fish is stripping line, for instance, which is a vastly different thing from what you do when a fish is charging the boat. You have to know how to keep the line taut as a guitar string, but also how to crank in the fish without overpowering the reel's drag. Of course, this all comes with experience, or from the well-timed advice of a good skipper and crew—but also, perhaps, from something like instinct. Or even something less quantifiable, like luck, which brings us back to the Moose.

Several hours of trolling later, all of them biteless, the radio crackles. "The *New Horizon* is hooked up," says a competing boat. "We've got a stripey," he says, meaning a striped marlin. It's not a crushing blow by any means, but it's points for the *New Horizon,* and for many on the boat the air goes out of the afternoon like that from a leaky balloon.

Not for the Moose, though. "Last year, we did it all on the last day," he says calmly, sipping from a can of Dr Pepper, his lucky shirt ripening in the twenty-knot breeze.

For the record, the Maui Jim Championship Tournament is scored as follows: Any blue or black marlin weighing less than four hundred pounds is worth three hundred points; those weighing in excess of four hundred can be brought to the scales for weighing, with one point awarded for every pound. A stripey earns fifty; a mahi-mahi, or dolphinfish, earns one point for every pound over twenty. . . . Oh, to hell with it. The idea here is to catch a big marlin; the rest is just fine print for tiebreaking.

On day two, a blue marlin runs through the trolling pattern and knocks down a couple of lures, but that's it. Meanwhile, the *New Horizon* keeps piling on the stripey catches: one, two, three, and damn them, anyway. And then, from the radio, comes a report that the *Ihu Nui,* another competing boat, is hooked up on a fish.

"Be a shark," Wargo whispers. It's a shark. "I wished a shark on them!" he roars. "It worked!"

By the end of day two, however, the *Bite Me* is still scoreless, while the *New Horizon* ends the day with 250 points. It's small consolation that the other two boats—the *Pamela,* skippered by Peter Hoogs (with Masunaga on board as a kind of freelance consultant), and the shark-bit *Ihu Nui*—have been wholly skunked. "This is frustrating," says the Moose, staring out to sea. In two days' time, the *Bite Me* has traveled roughly 130 miles, all of them in circles.

"It's not frustrating," Wargo shouts over the radio's static. "It's fishing."

Those who've never fished for marlin tend to imagine it as much more exciting than it actually is—or rather, as more consistently exciting. They envision hoist and spray and constant epic battles with fish the size of Datsuns. And, true, sometimes it is like that—but rarely, in the way that headboard-banging sex doesn't come along all that often. No, the reality of big-game fishing—at least for the angler—is that it's a lot like waiting, which means that it's closer in spirit to ice-fishing than it is to, say, fly-fishing. You snap on your lures or hook on your bait, and then you ride around in giant loops like someone looking for a contact lens on the sidewalk. For the skipper, of course, the routine is far more complex than that; the skipper is hitting his hot spots, patrolling over undersea drops, monitoring his fish finder and radio, all the while as focused as a jetliner pilot.

But an angler's mind can wander. You stare at the boat's wake, trying to decipher shapes in the geometry of the water, the way you do with clouds, but there isn't much there—an arrowhead, at best. At this point, a lot of fishermen reach into a cooler for a beer, or, more rarely—but not too rarely—fetch a baggie of cocaine and dig in like a boar after a truffle. Not to disclose secrets, but this is one reason why some anglers will return to the dock claiming to have had the time of their lives when nary a fish was even spotted. As with ice-fishing, the hands-free angling, relative isolation, and tick-tocking boredom lend themselves nicely to self-obliteration; mimicking such behavior, your average fly-caster would hook himself squarely in the rump before being swept downstream into a power turbine. I should note, however, that none of this pertains to the Moose. The Moose drinks beer the way a diabetic eats cake: only on special occasions, and then cautiously. And the Moose is never bored while fishing. Even when he's talking, which is always, he's scanning the horizon ten times a minute, looking for signs of baitfish or a telltale feeding bird, looking, looking, though usually it's just horizon: blue sky, blue water, blue sky, blue—

"*Stingerstingerstingerstinger!*" Wargo screams as he revs the engine (translation: a fish is on the stinger rod, the long-line rod at the center of the five-rod pattern), and the *Bite Me* absolutely explodes. On the bridge, leaping from his chair, the Moose throws down his can of Dr Pepper and sprays the deck with soda froth. Stuck to his ass, the seat cushion goes with him, coming straight off of the chair. ("A polar bear on roller skates," Wargo mutters.) The Moose skitters down the ladder while Siebler and Bennett scurry around in a kind of orchestrated chaos, pulling in the other lines, everyone jumping and shouting and grabbing, serious as infantrymen, the boat lurching through the waves, engine roaring, the Moose plopping himself in the fighting chair, wrestling the rod into position, gritting his teeth and biting his tongue as he begins reeling in a . . .

"Mahi," Wargo announces, disappointed.

The Moose returns to the bridge to clean up the Dr Pepper and apologizes for the chair.

"Was it a bull?" Wargo asks.

"It was pretty big," the Moose replies.

"No, I mean was it male or female? The bull has the flat head."

He shrugs. The champ is still learning.

The history of big-game fishing is surprisingly short; long-ago whalers may have taken the occasional harpoon potshot at passing marlin or sailfish, but it wasn't until the mid-nineteenth century that anyone thought to pursue deep-sea fish for their own sake. Back then, big-game fishing was a folly for madmen and wealthy adventurers, for men "who like a dash of spice with their pastimes," as an early deep-sea angler named Charles Frederick Holder once put it. Landing a marlin with a rod and reel was considered as formidable and extravagant as scaling a Himalayan peak, and attracted the same sort of characters: well-postured Victorians determined to subdue another corner of the natural world, or coarser Americans lusting for the zest of new frontiers. By painting the sport with a mythic, primeval brush, writer/anglers like Zane Grey, and later Ernest Hemingway, galvanized the imaginations of thousands. Legendary anglers became legendary guides, and amateurs were soon landing legendary fish; in a relatively short time, what had once been the pursuit of madmen became something to squeeze in between meetings during corporate conferences. You could tussle with nature all day and still make it back in time for the marketing department's luau.

Back aboard the *Bite Me,* anchored in the smooth, twilit, fantasy-land waters of Okoe Bay, the Moose is staring across at the *Pamela,* Hoogs's boat. "Man, I'm scared," he admits. The Moose shakes his head. "When I started all this, I don't think I knew enough about marlin fishing and about Kona to even be intimidated. Now, though . . ."

Surely, I say, some of the old-guard anglers must resent him, this amiable landlubber with outlandishly deep pockets of beginner's luck.

"A couple of the guys wouldn't congratulate me last year, when we won the championship." He shrugs. "But that's changed. After the Okoe Bay tournament, when we caught three marlin in an hour, guys were starting to ask if they could rub me for good luck. So it's gotten better." He nods up toward Wargo on the bridge. "I guess we're like the expansion team," says the Moose.

As a group, marlin anglers have what we might gently term a mixed public image. For one, there's the fish itself: massive, mysterious, noble, and, unless one is fond of fish jerky, flagrantly inedible. Killing any creature for trophy purposes—in order to talk about it later—carries a foul whiff these days, as it should. And the marlin-filled trash dumpsters that tournaments used to leave in their wakes—and still sometimes do (though far less so now that catch-and-release has become de rigueur in most competitions)—never helped matters. But the marlin anglers themselves have also struggled with a sour stereotype: that of the drunken, rich blowhard, fixated on his machismo, whose sporting pursuits strike some as the equivalent of offering one's biceps for a squeeze. Compared with the hushed, contemplative, almost nerdy image of fly-fishermen, big-game anglers can seem like high school linebackers knocking over baby carriages to get to a keg.

Like all stereotypes, this one is occasionally true but mostly false. The best are more like Hoogs, a thoughtful, soft-spoken captain of thirty-some years whose respect for the fish he catches seems limitless. Hoogs believes in karma, not machismo, in gods who reward fishermen for their fealty to the sea.

· · ·

The final day of the tournament dawns gorgeous: the trade winds gentle, the sky dusted with powdered-sugar clouds. On board the *Bite Me*, the Moose changes into his lucky shirt immediately. "No more messing around," he says. He puts the *Gladiator* soundtrack on the CD boom box—for inspiration, he watched the film twice before the tournament—and the morning fills with its hyperdramatic strains. I cannot help but feel we are heading out less to fish for a marlin than to execute one. "Moosimus!" Wargo bellows, and guns the *Bite Me* toward blue water.

Five hours pass. The tension is palpable. If none of the competitors catches a blue, the *New Horizon* will win with its middling run of stripeys, which didn't even qualify for points in last year's championship. December isn't the prime month for Kona marlin, true, but the fishing has been particularly miserable. There are yawns.

The Moose's cell phone rings. It's his dad. "It's good luck when Dad calls," he says afterward.

"Dad calling is good luck," Wargo affirms.

And it's true: Dad calling *is* good luck. Or eating raw opelu is good luck. Or the nasty-but-lucky shirt is good luck. Or maybe just the Moose—the King Midas of marlin—maybe it's just the Moose who's good luck, all 240 landlubbing pounds of him, because just before noon, Wargo screams and the Moose crashes into the fighting chair and the *Bite Me* all but detonates, the rubber band of tension that has gripped the boat for three and a half days snapping in one head-spinning heavy-metal instant. "It's a blue!" Wargo shouts.

Out on the water, the marlin leaps, a gymnast in desperate flight, but the Moose doesn't see it. He's watching the reel, pulling up on the rod, reeling in as the marlin drags it back down, his eyes almost crossed from concentration. "That a boy, James, go to work," Wargo says. "You know what to do." At this point nothing is certain, or even very probable. Marlin can be foul-hooked or bill-hooked, or the hook can just slip out; or the line can snap, or the leader break, or the fish strip all the smoking line right out of the reel; or the fight can go on forever, tiring the fish so thoroughly that it literally dies of exhaustion and becomes unretrievable dead weight, a tragic anvil suspended in the blue. Not this time, though. The Moose winds it in steadily and seriously. The marlin is small, perhaps 125 pounds, and the battle brief—ten minutes at most. Wargo's wife snaps the verification photo with a disposable camera, then deckhand Bennett tags the thrashing fish on the top of its head and, with a quick whip of his arm, releases it. "Good work, Moosie," Wargo says, with a monster of a grin.

"We're the Boston Celtics of fishing!" the Moose shouts to his dad on his cell phone when the day's fishing is finally concluded, with every competitor skunked but the Moose—when the Moose, bless his soul, has won it all again. Then he thanks his dad for the good luck, thanks him over and over again, and tells his dad he loves him.

"Shallow men believe in luck," Emerson once wrote, but then, he never fished for marlin. Following the awards ceremony—at which everyone, so far as I could tell, congratulated the Moose—I walk down to Waterfront Row in Kailua-Kona, to a wall of black-and-white photographs locally known as Grander's Wall. This is where the thousand-plus-pound marlin catches of Kona anglers are immortalized, and this is where the Moose took me on the day we met. He pointed to an empty spot on the wall—number 63—and said, with a boyish dreaminess, that this was where he wanted to be one day, he and Wargo: pictured alongside the legends of marlin fishing and their behemoth catches, up there with the 1,165-pounder Ray Hawkes caught in '93, or the 1,060-pounder Hoogs found for two anglers in '85, or the 1,649-pound giant that Gary Merriman pulled from the sea seventeen years ago aboard the *Black Bart*. I lean in, peering at the faces of the smiling, fortune-crowned men in the photographs. It takes skill to find and catch fish like these, make no mistake, not to mention diligence, money, and a very precise sort of sea smarts. But I've been fishing too long to ever discount the role of luck, never mind Emerson. Perhaps it's trite, but the old saw rings true: We do not take fish from the water; we accept what the water gives us. And the water, it's obvious, likes the Moose. I rub the empty space at number 63 on Grander's Wall like a totem; the Moose will be there one day, I'm sure of it, dwarfed by a grander marlin, grinning his landlubber's grin, amazed as always at his own golden fortuity, just a regular guy who got lucky, again and again and again.

MAY 2002

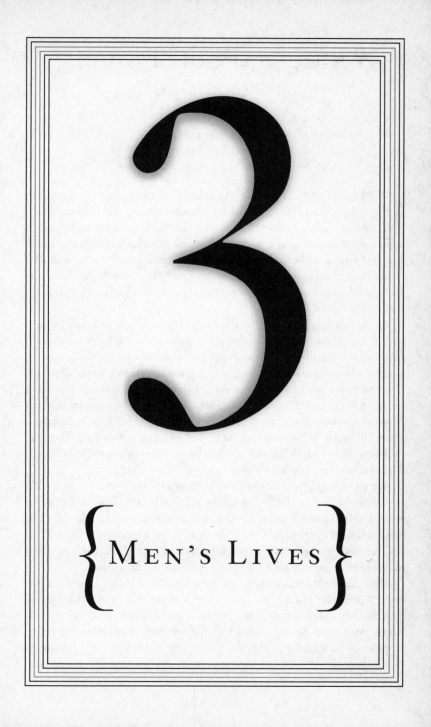

3

{ MEN'S LIVES }

A Mountain of Trouble

by David Roberts

CLIMBING HARD ALL DAY, Jeff Lowe forced the route through a wilderness of false leads and frustrating dead ends, but darkness caught him short of the ledge he had hoped to reach, stranding him in a vertical labyrinth. He was left with no choice but to carve a makeshift cave in a fan of snow plastered against the steep rock, then crawl inside. Wet, cold and physically spent, he lit his balky stove and began the task of turning pot after pot of packed snow into drinking water.

In the middle of the night the storm hit. A heavy snowfall poured out of the black sky, and as the snow gathered, it set loose spindrift avalanches that filled Lowe's cave and threatened to smother him. All night he lay in his sleeping bag, pushing and pounding the walls of his flimsy bivouac sack to maintain some breathing space inside the cave.

A lifelong tendency toward claustrophobia compounded Lowe's distress. As he grew drowsy, he would be seized with panic; ripping open the door of the bivouac sack, he would gasp fresh air, allowing snow not only to spill inside the cave but to fill his sleeping bag, where it melted and soaked his clothes.

By morning, Lowe was in a perilous situation. It was February 28, his ninth day on the north face of the Eiger. He had climbed forty-five hundred feet over those nine days, but in the fifteen hundred feet of frozen limestone that still hung above him, he was sure he would find the hardest passages of all. His food was almost gone. He could not stay warm at night. And he was on the verge of exhaustion.

This, Lowe knew, was how climbers died on the Nordwand. In just such a way the audacious Toni Kurz had come to grief, his rappel jammed on a knotted rope; or Stefano Longhi, left behind by his partner to freeze to death after a bad fall; or Max Sedlmayer, climbing hopelessly toward the avalanche that would pluck him from his life.

Getting down from so high on the north face, in the midst of a storm, would take a desperate effort, if it was indeed possible at all. At the moment, with avalanches thundering over the cliffs above and sweeping the fan of snow, descent was out of the question: Lowe could not even escape his snow cave.

Hunkered inside his claustrophobic hole, alone in a gray universe of nothingness, Lowe brooded on his predicament. During the last few days, with the weather holding, he had climbed so well; at last he had felt in perfect form, as success had dared to whisper in his ears. Now the prospect of failure loomed larger with every hour of snowfall. And if the situation got any worse, Lowe would be in a battle for his very life.

No, things were not going right—and the pattern was all too familiar. For a year now, things had been going wrong for Jeff Lowe. Major things, disastrously wrong. Bankruptcy. The failure of his marriage. Separation from his two-year-old daughter. He had scrambled to hold it all together, but his despair had peaked in late October, just after his fortieth birthday, leaving him sleepless, his antic mind tormenting him with a parade of furious creditors and disapproving friends. Out of the nadir of that depression had come the decision to climb the Eiger. A new route on the north face—a clean, direct vector between the Czech and Japanese lines. Solo. In winter. Without bolts.

If he could pull it off, it would be the greatest climb ever accomplished by an American in the Alps. And at a deeper, more personal level, the Eiger might somehow tame the internal voices howling of failure and loss. It would be a way for Lowe to return to his strength, to the thing he did better than almost anyone in the world.

Twenty-four hours after burrowing into the mountainside, Lowe was still stuck inside the inadequate snow cave. As he prepared to spend a second night there, shivering in a soggy sleeping bag, he got out his two-way radio and warmed the batteries against his body. Rousing his support team at the hotel far below, Lowe spoke slowly, his voice seamed with fatigue. "I've got a decision to make. Whether to go up or down. It's a tough one."

There was a long pause. "I don't know how hard it would be to get down from here," he said. "I figure it'll take three days minimum to reach the summit if I go up. And that's only if the weather's good tomorrow and Saturday."

Another pause. "I guess tomorrow's going to tell. If I go for it, I'll have to pull out all the stops."

The Purist

Had Jeff Lowe been born a Frenchman or a German, he would be a celebrity, sought after for product endorsements, asked to write his memoirs. But in the United States, great alpinists remain as obscure as chess champions.

Lowe, moreover, is a purist. He makes a wry distinction between "expeditions"—large, highly publicized assaults conducted in the spirit of the Desert Storm campaign—and "trips with friends," on which, with from one to three cronies, he can attempt brazen routes on unexplored mountains. From his only Everest expedition, a massively funded attack on an easy route involving fourteen climbers, Lowe came home disenchanted. But on some of Lowe's trips with friends, he has performed splendid deeds on spectacular Himalayan mountains such as Tawoche, Kwangde and Nameless Tower; on his ascents of Pumori and Ama Dablam, the only friend was himself.

Climbs like Tawoche and Ama Dablam, however, do not make headlines in the United States. Since his early twenties, Lowe had been one of the two or three best ice climbers in the world. Names such as Bridal Veil Falls, Keystone Green Steps and the Grand Central Couloir—extraordinary ice routes that Lowe was the first to master—can bring an awed hush over parties of cognoscenti, but they mean nothing to the lay public.

In the last two decades, the cutting edge of mountaineering has become "good style"—and nobody's style has been cleaner, bolder or more prophetic than Lowe's. Says Michael Kennedy, editor of *Climbing* and a frequent climbing partner of Lowe's, "Beyond a shadow of a doubt, he's the most visionary American Himalayan climber who's ever lived."

In a family of eight children growing up in Ogden, Utah, Lowe and his three brothers were pushed hard by their lawyer father to excel in sports. He was climbing seriously by fourteen, quickly developing his skills and managing to survive the usual near disasters of adolescent ambition. After he spent three years at unaccredited Tahoe Paradise College on a ski-racing scholarship, Lowe became a full-time climber; meanwhile, he scrounged a living from the kinds of marginal jobs most American climbing addicts resort to: pounding nails, teaching at Outward Bound and tutoring beginners in the sport.

In 1968, Lowe's older brothers Greg and Mike launched an outdoor-equipment company called Lowe Alpine Systems, which quickly gained cachet for its innovative packs and began turning a robust profit. Fifteen years later, Jeff Lowe started his own company, Latok—named for a mountain in Pakistan that was the scene of one of his most memorable climbs—which sold technical climbing gear. His first full-scale business venture, it began to collapse in 1987, and Lowe's brothers took over the company's debts to bail Jeff out.

Looking back, Lowe says: "I think part of my business problems stemmed from a feeling that I had to be more than a good climber, that I had to do something more 'meaningful.' And that may come from my father."

As if remounting the horse that had thrown him, Lowe soon joined with Texas entrepreneur Dick Bass to organize the first international climbing competition on American soil, at Snowbird, Utah. Contests on artificial walls had become one of the hottest new spectator sports in Europe, and Lowe was gambling that Americans would similarly embrace the spectacle. In the end, Snowbird '88 was an aesthetic success, but far fewer people than anticipated were willing to fork over twenty dollars to stare at the inch-by-inch progress of European climbing stars they had never heard of.

Undaunted, Lowe incorporated himself as Jeff Lowe Sport Climbing Championships Inc., attracted sponsors and investors and laid plans for an ambitious nationwide series of climbing competitions to be held in 1989 and '90. Thus began the downward spiral that in two years sucked Lowe into a whirlpool of failure. None of the events came close to breaking even, and Lowe's debts piled up to vertiginous heights. He began borrowing from future projects to pay off past ones. By the time the final competition of 1990 approached—an event organized by the late Bill Graham, the legendary rock promoter, to be held in Berkeley, California, in August—Lowe was teetering on the brink of financial ruin.

In need of a quick infusion of cash just to pay his personal bills, Lowe concocted a trip with friends to Nameless Tower, a soaring tusk of granite in the Karakoram Range of Pakistan, to be filmed for ESPN. The big draw for European sponsors would be a summit push pairing Lowe with thirty-one-year-old Parisian Catherine Destivelle, the most famous woman climber on the planet.

The Berkeley competition, which took place while Lowe was out of the country, turned into yet another financial fiasco plagued by dismal attendance. Lowe persuaded the North Face, a purveyor of high-end outdoor gear, to lend its name to the event as the leading sponsor. In order to keep the competition from sullying its good reputation, the company claims it was forced to cough up $78,000 to cover Lowe's bills. "We believed that when Lowe went to Pakistan, he'd secured his loans," says Ann Krcik, director of marketing operations for the North Face. "Three days before the event, it became evident that Sport Climbing Inc. didn't have the money." Bart Lewis, an entrepreneur who helped market the competition, claims that when the dust cleared, Lowe owed him $40,000. Lowe counters: "That's absolutely insane. I owe Bart not even close to forty thousand dollars." Other creditors emerged, clamoring for payment. Says Lowe: "I always emphasized the risks involved. Those who were misled, misled themselves."

On the other side of the globe, meanwhile, Lowe and Destivelle managed to climb a difficult route on Nameless Tower. The film was broadcast on ESPN, but several European sponsors had backed out at the last minute. The upshot was that Lowe came home from Pakistan deeper in debt than ever, owing money even to close friends and fellow climbers who had worked as his support party. For two decades Lowe had been one of the most admired figures in the tight-knit fraternity of American climbers; now, around certain campfires, in various climbers' bars, his name began to elicit bitter oaths and tales of fiscal irresponsibility.

By the fall of 1990, Lowe had been married for eight years to a woman he'd met in Telluride, Colorado, where she was a waitress. The couple settled in Boulder, where Janie Lowe became her husband's full-time business partner. In 1988 they had a daughter, whom they named Sonja.

On Nameless Tower, Lowe was deeply impressed by Destivelle's performance. As their teamwork evolved, Lowe realized that with only one or two men had he ever felt so confident climbing in the great ranges. At some point, he and Destivelle began an affair. Because her private life is intensely scrutinized in France, and because she had a longtime partner of her own back in Paris, Destivelle urged Lowe to be discreet about their relationship.

When Lowe returned home from Nameless Tower, "he seemed very angry and distant," says Janie Lowe. "It was as if he wanted nothing to do with me. I asked him if he was having an affair with Catherine. 'No, no, no.' Finally, it came out. I asked him 'Why did you lie to me?' That hurt me so bad. He said, 'I'd promised Catherine.' I said,

'After twelve years, you tell me your loyalty to Catherine is greater than your loyalty to me?'"

On September 13, 1990, Lowe turned forty. He was deep in a whirlpool, clutching for flotsam. At the end of October, Lowe declared bankruptcy. As his business partner, Janie took an equal brunt of the misfortune, and their relationship grew more troubled. As she tells it, "Jeff would come home and go straight into his study and close the door. Sonja would say, 'Mommy, why doesn't Daddy want to talk to me?'" In mid-December, Jeff moved out of the house, and they began the process of getting a divorce.

"I fell apart," Jeff says. "I felt hopeless. All I knew was that I couldn't stand it after a couple of weeks. I had to start dealing with things one by one."

By early February, Lowe was in Grindelwald, Switzerland, staring up at the north face of the Eiger.

Beguiled by the shape of this unfolding drama, Jon Krakauer and I had come to Switzerland as well, to serve as Lowe's support team. Lowe's business woes were common knowledge in the climbing community, and word of his Eiger project had spread far and fast. More than one observer suggested that Lowe might be on a suicide mission. Boulder writer and climber Jeff Long, a loyal friend of Lowe's, later admitted, "With all the pressure he had on him, I was afraid he was going to use the Eiger as some kind of exit."

Suicidal or not, the scheme—a new route, solo, in winter, without bolts, on the most notorious face in the Alps—seemed wildly improbable to most climbers. Destivelle later told Lowe that her French friends were of a single mind: "He'll never do it. It's too cold in winter, and too hard."

Jeff Lowe does not look like a climber: an accountant, you might guess on meeting him, or maybe a viola player. He stands five feet ten, weighs about 150; his slender physique seems more wiry than muscular. Clean shaven, he has an open face, on which alertness struggles against a natural placidity. He wears the wire-rim glasses of a professor. The long, straight blond hair conjures up the hippie he once thought himself to be. Though his hairline is receding, he combs his locks straight back, as if daring them to retreat farther. When he smiles, his eyes crinkle shut, and incipient jowls shadow his jaw. To call his low, cadenced speech a drawl is to suggest a regional twang it does not possess: His voice is rather that of a tape recorder whose batteries are running low.

"For the first five years, we were extremely happy," Janie had told me. "I think our problems had a lot to do with having a daughter. When Sonja came along, things changed."

Now Jeff Lowe commented obliquely on marriage and business. "It's a lack of freedom," he said. "I'm trying to get my freedom back. I could have saved my marriage if I had chosen to. But when I was forced to take a new look, I realized, 'Hey, it's not what I really want.' If I do what I really want—it's a weird thing, but climbing is still at the center."

Lowe paused. "The Eiger—even if I succeed—isn't going to make all the other shit go away. I don't expect this climb to make everything right." A grin spread across his face. "It'll just feel real good."

The Base Camp

The hotel at Kleine Scheidegg near Grindelwald is a rambling Victorian masterpiece, festooned with tiny rooms supplied by elegant if quirky plumbing, with linen wallpaper and richly varnished wood wainscoting, cozy reading nooks, eighteenth-century engravings and oak floors that creak and undulate like a glacier. For fifty-six years the hotel has been the headquarters for Eiger watching. As he prepared for his ascent, it became Lowe's base camp.

The hotel is owned and run by the legendary Frau von Almen. She is a handsome woman of seventy with an imperious manner and a constant frown of disapproval on her brow. Checking in for the three of us, I told her about Lowe's plans. The frown deepened. "This is insane," she announced. "It is more than insane—it is mad." She turned and walked away. "I do not like the accidents," she nattered. "Because they are so unnecessary."

To stay in the hotel is to put up with Frau von Almen's tyrannical regime. There was a lengthy codex of unwritten rules, a good portion of which we managed to break. I wore my climbing boots upstairs; Krakauer and Lowe brought sandwiches from outside and ate them in her cafe; I foolishly asked her to unlock the front door of the hotel before 8 A.M.; and Krakauer had the nerve to wonder if he might move and photograph a portrait of the pioneers who had made the first ascent of the Nordwand in 1938.

There was no way to get on her good side. After dinner one night, I complimented her fulsomely on the four-course repast. "And did your friend enjoy the dinner, too?" she asked ominously.

"Oh, yes," I answered.

"Because he will not eat like this up on the mountain."

Only Frau von Almen's longtime guests—those who had come every winter for more than a decade and skied innocuously each afternoon—seemed to bask in her approbation. The truth was that she was down on climbers. And this was sad, because her husband, Fritz, who died in 1974, had been the climbers' best friend, watching them for hours through his telescope, exchanging flashlight signals with their bivouacs each night. The Frau still had the telescope but would unpack it, she said, "only for emergency." An old-timer told us that a few years ago some climbers accidentally knocked over the telescope and broke it, then ran away.

On February 11, Catherine Destivelle arrived from Chamonix. Five feet four inches tall, with curly brown hair, a conquering smile and a formidable physique, she is a superstar in France, yet fame has left her relatively unaffected. Though they could hardly disguise the fact that they were staying in the same room, at first Lowe and Destivelle maintained a demure propriety. Gradually the handclasps became less furtive, the kisses semipublic.

For a first-rate climber, Lowe seemed woefully disorganized. For days his gear was spread all over his hotel room, but as he inventoried it, he discovered that he was lacking essential items. From Krakauer he borrowed a headlamp, pitons, first-aid supplies and a crucial pair of jumars for ascending ropes; Destivelle brought him foodstuffs (she swore by powdered mashed potatoes) and a two-way radio.

Destivelle was scandalized by Lowe's preparations. "I can't believe he is climbing with equipment he has never used before," she told us again and again. "I would never do this." Lowe dismissed the problem, omitting one of its causes: He was so broke he had had to sell much of his climbing gear and now was dependent on the largess of European companies intrigued with his Eiger project.

On the night of February 18, Destivelle joined Krakauer and me in the bar, where she chain-smoked half a pack of Marlboros. (Ordinarily, she goes months without a cigarette.) At breakfast the next morning, she said she had dreamed obsessively about an all-out war in which everybody was hunting Lowe. She had spent a fitful, miserable night, while beside her Lowe had slept soundly.

In the morning, Destivelle rode the cog railway up to the Eiger-gletscher station, where she kissed Lowe good-bye. He put on his skis and headed for the base of the wall.

The Mordwand

On February 19, his first day on the Nordwand, Lowe waltzed up two thousand feet in only two hours. The going was easy but dangerous, a matter of planting the picks of his ice axes in a steady rhythm, of stabbing the crampon points strapped to his boot soles into brittle ice overlying steep rock. He soloed without a rope: If he slipped, he would die. But Lowe was in his element on this nerve-stretching ground. The speed and precision that had made his technique famous among a generation of American climbers spoke in every swing of his axes.

It was, however, still the heart of winter, and this was the Eiger. Over the last six decades, it was the easy start on the north face that had seduced so many alpinists: Between fifty and sixty of the best climbers in the world had died here, in a variety of gruesome ways.

The names of the Eiger's most storied landmarks—the Ice Hose, the Death Bivouac, the Traverse of the Gods, the White Spider—are canonic touchstones to alpinists everywhere. Whether or not they have ever seen the notorious wall, all climbers grow up with a keen awareness of its history. Eight of the first ten men who set out to climb the Nordwand were killed trying. The first man to attempt a solo ascent backed off prudently, only to die on a subsequent attack with a partner. The second, third and fourth solo attempts all ended in death. Early on, the wall acquired its punning German nickname, the Mordwand.

Accounts of these disasters built up the Eiger mystique. Every climber knows the tales, as visceral as tribal legends passed on around the campfire: Hinterstoisser falling to his death as he tried to reverse his traverse on iced-up rock. Angerer strangled by his own rope. Toni Kurz expiring when the knot jammed in his carabiner, only a few feet above his rescuers, as he spoke his last words, *"Ich kann nicht mehr"* ("I can do no more"). The last words of Longhi, borne on the wind from the ledge high on the face where he froze to death: *"Fame! Freddo!"* ("Hungry! Cold!")

At the foot of a sheer 350-foot rock cliff called the First Band, the climbing abruptly turned hard. As Lowe used his rope for the first time, his pace slowed to a vertical crawl. In three and a half hours, he gained only 110 feet. On the second day, a dogged and ingenious struggle over nine intense hours won Lowe a mere 80 feet more.

On other great mountain faces, clean vertical cracks, good ledges and solid rock abound. The Eiger, however, is notorious for limestone knobs that crumble as you grasp them, for down-sloping ledges covered with ice and for a scarcity of good cracks. The severity of the terrain brought out the best in Lowe, as he used tiny metal hangers and the tips of his ax blades to "hook" his way upward.

But already there were problems. Lowe had what he called fumble fingers, dropping three or four of his most valuable nuts and pitons, and the pick on one of his ice axes had worked loose. He climbed on anyway, adjusting his technique to the loose wobble of the pick, which meant he could never really swing the ax hard and plant the blade securely into the ice. It was a bad compromise, like driving at 30 mph on a flat tire.

Late on his third day of climbing, he had put most of the First Band beneath him, but the climbing was the most frightening yet. The storms of the last few weeks had glued snow and ice onto vertical and even overhanging rock. Lowe had to shift back and forth between rock and snow, from spidering with bulky plastic boots and gloved hands among the limestone nubbins to crabbing his way up the hollow snow with crampons and axes. When he could, he placed protection—a machined nut or piton in the rock or a screw in the ice.

At 2:50 P.M., Lowe clung to a particularly flimsy patch of rotten snow. Two thousand feet of cold, empty air fell away beneath his boots. He doubted whether he could reverse the moves he had made above his last protection eight feet below and had no idea whether he could find protection above or climb through the looming overhang that blocked his view of the rest of the gigantic wall. For all he knew, he was creeping into a vertical cul-de-sac.

The boldness of Lowe's choice to go without a bolt kit was now manifest. Throughout his efforts to surmount the First Band, he had been stymied right and left by blank, unclimbable rock. With bolts, it is possible to drill the rock and build a ladder through the most featureless impasse. Every other new route on the Eiger in the last thirty years had employed bolts; the Japanese who had pioneered the imposing line just to the right of Lowe's had placed 250 of them.

Bolts also bestow a huge bonus in safety. When a climber is "running it out"—leading into uncertain terrain, with bad protection—he never knows whether he can find a reliable anchor before he reaches the end of his rope. With bolts, a solid anchor can be manufactured where nuts and pitons are useless. Without bolts, the process is like creeping farther and farther out on a lake covered with thin ice.

Lacking bolts, Lowe fiddled with a tiny nut, trying to wedge it into a crooked, quarter-inch crack that split the First Band. Suddenly the snow broke loose beneath his feet. He was falling.

In conventional climbing, with two people on a rope, one anchors himself to the precipice and feeds out the rope as the other leads above. If the leader falls, he plunges a little more than twice as far as he was above his last protection, until his partner "belays" or stops him by holding tight to the rope. For a soloist, the belayer is a mechanical apparatus. As one might suspect, solo self-belaying is far less reliable than the kind afforded by a human partner.

As he had started up the wall three days before, Lowe carried a new kind of self-belay device he had never used. Before his first hard pitch, he had not even taken the contraption out of the plastic bag it was sold in. The question now, as he fell through the air, was whether the device would work.

An abrupt jolt gave him his answer: The rig had done its job. Lowe was unhurt. He had not even had time to be scared, but now the delayed adrenaline started to surge. In response, he edged his way back to his high point, where he found another plate of snow to try. Gingerly he moved up it, anticipating another fall with each step, until he stood beneath the rock overhang.

The only way to proceed was to angle left through a weakness in the browing cliff. Lowe made a series of delicate moves on rock, until he could plant the picks of his axes on snow above, the left pick wobbling in its disturbing fashion. But here the snow was worthless, sloughing loose under the slightest touch. For a full hour he struggled in place, patiently probing the terrain for its arcane secrets. At last he found a small patch of more reliable snow. He planted both axes, moved his feet up and stabbed the front points. The snow held. He moved a few feet higher, then surged upward.

He was over the First Band, but by now it was getting dark. Lowe placed three ice screws at his high point, then rappelled back down to the snow cave he had slept in the night before. He crawled into his thin sleeping bag and pulled the frosty bivouac sack over him. Tired though he was, sleep escaped him. His problems danced mockingly in his mind, their shadows darting from wall to wall inside the cave of unhappiness in which he'd lived for a year. The loose pick on his ax nagged at him, and at the rate he was burning stove fuel, he would run out of gas canisters long before he could reach the summit. And he needed those nuts and pitons he had dropped.

In the morning Lowe turned on his walkie-talkie and called down to Krakauer and me at the hotel. "Guys," he said in his slow, gravelly voice, "I'm thinking about a slight change of plans." He had decided, he told us, to leave his rope in place over the most difficult parts of the First Band and, while he was still low enough on the wall to do so, descend briefly to Kleine Scheidegg, where he might fix his malfunctioning ice ax, replenish his supply of food and fuel and replace the hardware he'd dropped. Then, in a day or two, he could go back up the wall.

Lowe reached the hotel before noon. "Why did you not tell me before the weekend that you were coming down?" Frau von Almen complained, fingering her room charts. It happened to be Friday. "Now I have to put you in eighty-eight, way up on the fourth floor."

"That's fine with me," said Lowe.

"I know," said the Frau as she walked away. "But you are very simple."

A stack of faxes was waiting for Lowe at the hotel, most of which were from furious creditors demanding payment. These did not appear to rattle his composure, but a long missive from Janie seemed to trouble him deeply.

Having come to admire and like Lowe, I was puzzling over the vehemence of his detractors. Jim Bridwell, who claims Lowe still owes him $3000 for Nameless Tower, had said: "I think of Jeff as a climber and what that used to mean. You used to be able to trust climbers. But Jeff'll say one thing and do another. I just think he's disturbed. Either he doesn't know he's lying, or . . ."

Janie Lowe thought Jeff's problems had been compounded by his pride. "He can't say he's sorry," she told me. " 'Hey, I really fucked up.' Just a few sentences would resolve his debt with his friends."

One voice in Lowe's defense, however, was that of Jeff Long, who insisted: "These people want Jeff's professional corpse swinging in the wind. I think what they did in investing in Jeff was to invest in his vision. What collapsed, they thought, was a whole vision they shared. The brotherhood of the rope. But what was going on was really just business."

For all her sorrow, in any case, Janie was determined to keep the channels open. "We'll always be parents," she said. "We have a wonderful little daughter. For Sonja's sake, I hope we can keep our own bullshit in the background."

One night in the hotel, Lowe had watched the three-year-old daughter of a guest carrying her plate heaped with food from the salad bar. The sight had brought tears to his eyes. "Yeah. I really miss my daughter," he admitted.

As Janie had pointed out, though: "Yes, he totally loves Sonja. But you know what? He doesn't love her enough to be with her."

In his own way, Lowe acknowledged that stricture. "I think I know now," he said in a reflective moment, "that I can't do this sort of climbing and have a domestic side. You're not a practicing father if you're not there. You're maybe a visiting father."

There had been a snowstorm on the morning of Lowe's descent, but by the following day the precipitation had ceased and the weather had stabilized. The temperatures were strangely warm, however—well above freezing at the six-thousand-foot elevation of the hotel. That was better than brutal cold, except it meant bad avalanche conditions. In the weekend prior to his start on the Nordwand, thirty-one people had died in avalanches across the Alps.

There were, in short, plenty of reasons to give up the climb, excuses lying ready to be seized. But Lowe spent the evening in room eighty-eight, sorting his gear in his slow, fastidious fashion. Early the next morning he returned to the foot of the wall, and by noon he was back at his bivouac cave, at the lower end of the ropes he had left in place. By the time evening fell, he had reascended the ropes and wrestled his hundred pounds of gear up to his previous high point.

Then, boldly, he led on into the dusk. It was not until three hours after dark that he suspended a hanging tent from a pair of ice screws and crawled into his sleeping bag. He was halfway up the Nordwand.

"Good morning, Vietnam," he radioed us in the morning. "I just woke up from one of the best sleeps I've had in a long time." When he started climbing again, his route coincided for a few hundred feet with the classic 1938 line. This section of the route, known as the Ice

Hose, had been a formidable test to most of the expert climbers who had attempted the Nordwand over the years. For Lowe, with his impeccable ice technique, it was almost like hiking. He raced up the Ice Hose and across the Second Icefield and at day's end was bivouacked at the base of the summit head wall.

Only a little more than two thousand feet of climbing remained, but it promised to be severe and unrelenting. And as he inched his way up into the dark, concave head wall, it would grow increasingly difficult to retreat. Somewhere on that precipice, he would reach a point of no return, after which descent might well be impossible, and the only escape would be up and over the summit.

It was Monday, February 25. The forecast from Zurich was for continued good weather through Wednesday; then a warm front bearing heavy snow was predicted to move into the area. A fiendish scenario began to propose itself. With two days' steady climbing, Lowe might well find himself near or at the point of no return, only to get hammered by a major snowstorm.

The Storm

Krakauer and I were using the coin-operated telescope at the gift shop next to the hotel to follow Lowe's progress, but he was so high now that we could tell little about his individual moves. On Tuesday night we took a walk. There was a full moon directly behind the Eiger. We caught sight of a pinpoint of light, impossibly far above us, three-fifths of the way up the wall: Lowe's headlamp, as he dug his bivouac site, a lonely beacon of purpose in the mindless night.

Later, his voice came on the radio, raspy with lassitude. "Watch that forecast real carefully," he said. "It's going to be a strategy-type thing. If it comes in hard and I'm not in a good place, it's not going to be good."

On Wednesday night, the storm indeed came in hard, forcing Lowe to hole up in the claustrophobic snow cave he'd dug in the vertical fan of snow. It was from this pathetic shelter that he'd wondered aloud over the radio "whether to go up or down." After a long, pregnant silence, he confessed: "I don't know how hard it would be to get down from here. I figure it'll take three days minimum to reach the summit if I go up. . . . If I go for it, I'll have to pull out all the stops."

Lowe's miserable snow burrow proved to be a poor place to ride out the tempest. On Thursday morning, he remarked over the radio:

"I've never been so pummeled in my life. There's a big avalanche coming down every five minutes. I couldn't move if I wanted to."

At noon Lowe radioed again. He had managed to get out of his snow hole, but a search for a better bivouac site had been fruitless. The avalanches were still rumbling down, his clothes were soaking wet, and he was cold. It seemed that Lowe had little choice but to descend, and even that would be exceedingly sketchy. Much to our surprise, however, he declared, "I'm going to sign off now and try to get something done." He had resolved to push for the summit.

More than a week before, I had probed Lowe's motives by alluding to the suggestions I had heard of a suicidal impulse. "I think everybody has had thoughts about checking out early," he said. "But I wouldn't do it this way. I'd do it a lot simpler."

Even if Lowe could complete his route, what lasting difference would it make in his life? Magnificent though the climb might be, was it little more than a superstitious gesture, a way of lashing back at the furies that bedeviled his path? The finest climb ever accomplished by an American in the Alps could indeed bring with it a huge bestowal of self-esteem. And in the chaos that his personal affairs had become, self-esteem might be what Lowe needed most.

He had said: "For me there's no future. All I'm interested in is now." In the hotel, that had sounded like wishful thinking. Divorce and bankruptcy turned *now* into a crumbling wall between the flash floods of the past and the future. But up on the Eiger, all that changed. The past was the piton ten feet below; the future was that handhold three feet above and to the left. *Now* was what held him to the world, and the trance of grasping its ledges and cracks gave it a glorious breadth. It expanded and became the ocean of all that was.

Friday, March 1, marked the sixth day of Lowe's second attempt on the Nordwand, his tenth day of climbing overall. A south wind sent hazy wreaths of fog sailing over the mountain, but the favorable weather that had blessed the first week of the climb had returned, although another storm was forecast to arrive by Sunday. If he didn't reach the top before it hit, his prospects for survival might be grim. By noon, Lowe had hauled all his gear up to a distinctive ledge called the Central Band. Only twelve hundred feet remained.

Here the wall was scored with ice-glazed ramps leading up and to the left, most of which led nowhere. The protection was minimal, the climbing nasty. Lowe was aiming for the Fly, a small ice field five hundred feet above. But now, when he needed to move fast, with the threat of the next storm hanging over him, he was slowed drastically by what turned out to be the most difficult climbing yet.

Watching through the telescope, I could gauge how steep the cliff was when I saw him knock loose chunks of snow that fell forty feet before striking rock again. At one point it took him more than an hour to gain twenty-five feet. The rock had turned loose and crumbly; stone towers, teetering like gargoyles, sat waiting to collapse at the touch of a boot, and pitons, instead of ringing home as he pounded them, splintered the flaky limestone and refused to hold. Bolts would have been a godsend.

Yet on these pitches, Lowe's brilliance came to the fore. He thought of one particular stretch of fifty feet as a kind of never-never land: It was the crux of the whole route to this point. A more driven, impatient alpinist might succumb to dizzy panic here, where the slightest misjudgment could rip protection loose and send him hurtling into the void. With his phlegmatic disposition, Lowe inched his way through his never-never land in a cloud of Buddhist calm.

On Saturday, Krakauer started up the west ridge—the easiest route on the Eiger and the path by which Lowe would descend. Krakauer wanted to camp near the top to greet Lowe and, if need be, help him down. As soon as he skied above the Eigergletscher station, however, Krakauer realized the venture was a mistake. A few days before, he had cruised halfway up the ridge in only two hours; but in the interim, the conditions had completely changed. The storm had blanketed the slope with deep, unstable snow; without skis, Krakauer sank in to his waist, and even with skis on he plowed a knee-deep furrow as he zigzagged laboriously upward.

At the fastest pace Krakauer could sustain, it would take days to get to the summit. What was worse, the slopes were dangerously close to avalanching; indeed, as he climbed slowly up the ridge, his skis periodically set off small slides.

At two o'clock Krakauer came over the radio. "I'm getting the hell down," he said in a jumpy voice. "The hundred feet just below me is ready to avalanche. Watch me carefully. If it releases, it's going to be massive." With a series of slow, deliberate turns, he skied down as delicately as he could. The slope held.

When Lowe next radioed, I had to tell him about Krakauer's retreat from the west ridge. He took the news calmly, even though it raised the specter of serious danger for his own descent. For the first time we talked about the possibility of a helicopter's picking him up on the summit.

Lowe climbed on. By early afternoon clouds had gathered around the upper face, where it was snowing lightly, even though the hotel still baked in sunshine. Pushing himself beyond fatigue, again well into the night, he managed to set up an uncomfortable bivouac just below the Fly. His two-day push from the Central Band had been a brilliant piece of work, but the Sunday storm was coming in early, and seven hundred feet still lay between him and the summit. He was well past the point of no return.

That evening he slithered into his dank bivouac sack and tried to sleep. Lowe had two gas cartridges left to melt snow, but his food supply was down to a couple of candy bars. His hands were in terrible shape—the incessant pounding, grasping and soaking had bruised the fingertips until they swelled into tender blobs, and the nails had begun to crack away from the cuticles. Each morning, his fingers were so sore and puffy that merely tying his bootlaces was an ordeal.

Worse, his sleeping bag, thin to begin with, was soaked like a dishrag: It provided almost no warmth at all. That night Lowe got not a wink of sleep. For fourteen hours he shivered, waiting for dawn, as the snow fell outside his cave.

On Sunday morning it was still snowing. "Where I am," he radioed, "it's hard to even peek out of the bivy tent without dislodging everything. I'm going to sit here and hydrate." He faced an acute dilemma. If he hunkered down and waited for the storm to end, he could run out of food and gas and succumb to hypothermia. If he pushed upward prematurely, on the other hand, the storm itself could finish him.

By noon he had not moved. At two o'clock, through a break in the clouds, we saw him climbing slowly above the Fly. As he started to climb, however, he grew deeply alarmed. Something was wrong. He felt weak all over, weaker than he should have from fatigue alone. He had been going on too little food, not enough liquids, insufficient sleep. This was how climbers died on the Eiger. This was too much like what had happened to Longhi and Kurz. After stringing out three hundred feet of rope, Lowe returned to his bivouac hole of the night before and spent the rest of the day resting and hydrating and trying in vain to get warm.

Once more, sleep was impossible. Lowe shivered through another night, even though he lit the stove and burned precious fuel in an effort to heat his frigid cavern. The weather had cleared late Sunday afternoon, and the sky was now sown with stars. There was an odd acoustic clarity: Toward morning he could plainly hear dogs barking in Grindelwald, miles away and ten thousand feet below. And he thought he heard something else: a humming, crystalline, harmonic music in the air. Was it an aural hallucination? Was he beginning to lose his grip?

The Fall

Monday dawned luminous and clear, a perfect day, of which he would need every minute. Good weather had been forecast to last through the evening, but a major storm was due on the morrow. We called REGA, the government-run rescue service, and alerted it to a possible need for summit pickup. Then we watched Lowe climb. At 9:15, he turned a corner and disappeared into a couloir we could not see. Two hours later, there was still no sign of him, no murmur over the radio. Though we did not admit it to each other at the time, Krakauer and I each separately trained the telescope on the base of the wall, where we swept the lower slopes. In just such a way over the decades, the fate of several Eiger victims had been discovered.

Lowe had hoped that once he was above the Fly the going would get easier. But in icy chimneys broken by bands of brittle rock, he was forced to perform some of the hardest climbing yet. Normally he never let himself be rushed on a climb: It was one of the secrets of his sang-froid and his safety. Now, however, he kept looking at his watch, and his brain hectored, *Oh, no, hurry!* Ever so slightly, his technique lost some of its famous precision. He felt less weak than he had the day before, but the sense of struggling to meet a terrible deadline oppressed his efforts.

It was hard to place good protection anywhere. Lowe found himself hooking with front points and ax picks on rounded rock wrinkles that he had to stab blindly through the snow to locate. His balance was precarious, and then, just before it happened, he knew he was going to fall.

The picks scraped loose: He was in midair, turning. Twenty-five feet lower, he crashed back-first into the rock. The self-belay had held, but he was hurt. He felt as though someone had taken a baseball bat and slammed it into his kidneys.

Oddly, instead of panicking him, the long fall calmed him down. *Okay,* he said to himself, *you've done that. Don't do it again.*

He pulled himself together, started up again and found a way through the dicey hooking sequences despite the pain pounding in his back. At last he surmounted a buttress and reached a good ledge, only four hundred feet below the summit.

But here he faced a problem. The warm sun had loosened the summit snowfields. Every chute and depression became an avalanche track. One swept right over Lowe, filling his goggles with powder snow, buffeting his body as it tried to knock him from the wall.

He was moving faster now, as slides shot down all around him. For two hours he climbed doggedly on. During that time, three more avalanches engulfed him. One of them knocked his feet loose, but he managed to hang on with his axes. At 3:20 he called.

"God, Jeff, those avalanches looked bad," I said.

"Yeah, they were pretty horrendous." His voice was ragged with strain. "I got really douched. I'm totally wet. Am I about a pitch from the west ridge?"

"A pitch and a half, maybe."

"I'm going to call for a pickup. I just want to get up this thing."

We signed off and called REGA. They were waiting in Grindelwald, ready to fly the moment Lowe emerged on the west ridge, a few feet below the top. But a stiff wind had begun to blow a steady plume off the summit. The wind could prevent the helicopter from approaching close enough to execute a pickup or even cause it to crash.

To our dismay, Lowe disappeared once more into a couloir. The minutes ticked by. At 4:15 he emerged, fighting his way out of the top of the gully, spindrift hosing him at every step. He was only forty feet below the crest of the ridge.

We prepared to call REGA, then watched in distress as Lowe stopped at a mottled band of rock and snow, only twenty feet below the ridge. For ten minutes he thrashed in place; we saw him grabbing chunks of black limestone and tossing them into the void below.

In the hidden couloir, Lowe had found it impossible to get in any protection. He had dashed upward, aiming at the mottled band, but when he got there, he found only a skin of ice holding together rocks that were as loose as a pile of children's blocks. When he flung stones aside and dug beneath, he found only more of the same. He could engineer no kind of anchor—neither piton, nut nor ice screw would hold.

Only twenty feet short of safety, he had run out of rope. His own anchor, three hundred feet below, was imprisoning him. In despair, he realized that he would have to climb down at least forty feet to the previous rock band, try to get some kind of anchor there, rappel for his gear and jumar back up. He was not sure he could make that down-climb without falling. What was more, he was running out of daylight.

Lowe got on the radio. Krakauer said what we were both thinking: "Jeff, if you just dropped your rope and went for it, could you free solo the last twenty feet?"

"No problem," said Lowe. "But are you sure the helicopter can get me?"

If we urged Lowe to abandon his gear and the helicopter failed, he would be stranded near the summit without ropes, sleeping bag, food, stove or even his parka. He was soaked to the skin. The wind was whipping hard, and the sky had grayed to the color of lead. Tuesday's storm was arriving early.

Krakauer said, "I'm almost positive they can pick you up."

"Let's do it," said Lowe.

He untied his rope and draped the end over a loose rock. He was abandoning all the gear that he had fought for nine days to haul up to the six-thousand-foot precipice and, with it, deserting his own last refuge.

We called REGA; the helicopter took off from Grindelwald. To be picked up on the summit of the mountain was not a true rescue; more than one previous Eiger climber had resorted to flying from the top when he was far less strung out than Lowe was. It would, however, be a kind of asterisk attached to his great deed. It would not be the best style, and that would bother Lowe. But it was survival.

He sprinted up the last twenty feet. All at once, Lowe had escaped the north face. He stood on a broad shelf of snow on the west ridge, just below the summit. The helicopter spiraled upward toward him.

Still talking to us on the radio, Lowe couldn't keep the shivering out of his voice. Krakauer instructed him: The helicopter would lower a cable, which he was to clip on to his waist harness.

Now the chopper was just above him, hovering in the stiff wind. Suddenly it peeled off and flew away toward the Jungfraujoch. For the first time, Lowe seemed to lose it. He wailed, "What the hell's going on?" Nervous about the strong winds, the helicopter pilot, we later learned, decided to drop off a doctor and a copilot who had been on board, so he could fly as light as possible when he made the pickup.

The helicopter reappeared and hovered above the summit, its rotors straining against the wind. The steel cable dangled from its belly. We saw Lowe swipe for its lower end, miss once, then seize it. He clipped in, and the helicopter swept him into the sky. Down at the hotel, the guests and skiers cheered wildly all around us. Lowe was off the Eiger.

The cable wound upward as he rode it toward the open door. The winch man reached out his hand. Lowe climbed through the door and crawled back into the conundrum of his life.

May/June 1992

How It Feels to Be
Yvon Chouinard

by Doug Stanton

THE WIND IS BLOWING at sixty knots, gusting to seventy, and we're walking this broad, yellow plain, and we're going fishing, Yvon Chouinard and I. Ahead of us, a dust storm rises and screws its way upward into the blue sky. Chouinard says, "You can *feel* it." Feel what? "The fishing is going to be *shit-hot* today," he declares, smiling. "It feels like that moment before an avalanche."

Green carnations of foam are exploding across the Río Grande as the river surges through the bare Patagonian hills. Beaten by the wind, it almost appears to flow backward, as if surrendering and retreating to its source in the foothills of the Andes, across the Argentine border in Chile, thirty miles away. This is sacred country to Chouinard, his favorite wilderness, and each year he stays at a lodge called Villa Maria to fish this remarkable river, recognized as the best sea-trout water in the world.

Chouinard punches merrily through cyclonic blasts of wind, his fly rod quivering: He's happy under these conditions—typical of Tierra del Fuego—not because they're inherently dangerous, but because they'll make the fishing more challenging.

"Incredible!" exclaims Chouinard. "You gotta love it! Unbelievable!" He looks back at me, grinning wildly. "What doesn't kill you makes you stronger, right?" And I can't help but grin, too. I hunch over, pull down my hat, and try to keep up with him.

Which is when Yvon Chouinard—supremely fit and tanned at age sixty; a pioneering mountaineer; an expert fisherman, kayaker, and surfer; a blacksmith and a gourmand; a lover of Beavis and Butthead and the poetry of Charles Bukowski; an environmentalist, an entrepreneur, and the founder of the clothing company Patagonia—stops to study the river thoughtfully, and then steps off the bank into thin air, to catch the biggest trout on Earth.

In a world of shrinking horizons, Yvon Chouinard has come to embody something near-mythic: a life lived hard-on-the-edge, perfectly and gracefully. These days, even as supermodels sport Patagonia jackets at art galleries, climbers are still wearing them on Everest. Almost single-handedly, and with just a handful of patents, Chouinard has democratized adventure by inventing and manufacturing outdoor clothing so effective that even your grandmother might survive a journey to the North Pole in it.

In many ways, Chouinard wishes this were not the case. "An adventure is what happens when you screw up," he tells me. He insists that adventure is something you'll never really find on prepackaged trips or by donning one of his mountain parkas. Still, he acknowledges that he's selling a dream: "Everyone wants to play."

He speaks politely, with a tiny drawl—perhaps the way Henry Fonda would have sounded if Henry Fonda had been a California-bred surfer. Now, however, Chouinard is a surfer whose company tallied sales of $180 million last year, and who is quite possibly having as much fun as anyone on the planet. He's climbed in Nepal and Chamonix. He has skied the Alps. Lately, he's surfed in Australia, salmon fished in Iceland, and bonefished off Christmas Island in the Pacific. Next, he's planning a trip to Chile and a forty-six-day trek through China. Between expeditions, Chouinard kayaks rivers in the American West and surfs the point-breaks near his solar-powered house just north of Santa Barbara.

Of course, his life hasn't always been fun. During the '80s, Patagonia's profits soared, but in 1991, recession forced Chouinard to lay off 120 of his 620 employees, a step that he found extremely painful, priding himself as he does on providing a vibrant and supportive work environment. He emerged from the crisis with a bold purpose: He would change American business by using Patagonia as a model of "sustainable industry," one that neither harms the environment nor grows so quickly that its own viability is jeopardized.

Patagonia shirts and pants are now made of organic cotton, its jackets are spun from recycled plastic bottles, and Chouinard annually donates more than a million dollars to eco-groups that otherwise might receive no funding at all. Business schools invite him to lecture; Yale has awarded him an honorary degree (doctor of humane letters); and President Clinton has praised him as a "responsible corporate citizen." He counts Tom Brokaw, Harrison Ford, and novelist Tom McGuane among his friends. Life is good.

Yet the good life for Yvon Chouinard has little to do with the cachet of running a multimillion-dollar company. He has always preferred to categorize himself as a craftsman-turned-businessman. Even now, he refuses to read the business section of a newspaper, so Malinda, his wife of thirty years, peruses it for him. You learn that he doesn't have a savings account because he plans eventually to give everything away. He dreams of living on $200 a month, without electricity and eating whatever he can raise in a garden or catch by fishing. He dreams, in the end, of owning absolutely nothing.

Which is partly why he loves Tierra del Fuego. On the Río Grande, he's in search of what he has always looked for outdoors: the Perfect Moment, a flash of "lucidity, focus, and emptiness," the psychic intensity that hardship brings. But there's a slight problem. Though the fishing has been great—superb, in fact—the Villa Maria, part of the historic Estancia José Menendez, a ranch outside the town of Río Grande, has come to seem, well, too *plush*. Chouinard wants something more. He wants to test himself, even in his favorite place. He wants more hardship, period. His longtime fishing companion Tom McGuane explains it like this: "Whenever he gets comfortable, he gets suspicious of everything, and he sort of smells a rat. We have a camp on the Dean River [in British Columbia] where we have warm beds and where somebody cooks for us, and I know that bothers him." McGuane adds: "He always wants to do things the *hard* way."

So we'll fish the Río Grande in comfort for now, and then we'll do something Chouinard has always wanted to do: We'll disappear up a nearby river that he once glimpsed, for a moment, from an airplane, and whose image has lain in his memory, burning and beckoning. We'll scrounge for food and eat with our fingers; we'll sleep under the stars beside the silver river. Maybe we won't catch anything at all. We'll suffer; we'll know happiness.

It's now midday at a pool called Nirvana, and Yvon Chouinard has just hooked a trout. It's a big one, getting bigger as he reels it in. Chouinard's back is curved like a violin, his knees are braced against the current, and he's not making a sound. The fish's only apparent effect upon him is registered in the flexing of his jaw muscles, in the minute adjustments of his black eyebrows. All morning, we've been blasted by the howling, line-tangling wind, and I've caught zip. Chouinard has landed and released three gorgeous brown trout, none under fifteen pounds.

Then, as if no longer able to stand his own concentration,

Chouinard lets out an invigorating chortle, crescendoing into a cry
that his friends later describe to me as his "cave-man laugh," as in:
"AHHHH . . . HAAAAA!"

It's startling, to be sure, yet so heartfelt that you can't help but love it.

"God, what a trout!" he says. The huge silver fish leaps and then
drops back from its skyward course as if repelled by the sun, descends
beneath the surface, and holds there, trembling, on the river bottom.
Chouinard kneels, cradles the exhausted fish—which he guesses
weighs twenty pounds—and rocks it gently in the current. A fish to
remember.

"You know," he says, after releasing the trout, "fishing this place is
one of the few things in life that keeps getting better. When I first
came here in sixty-eight, I thought I was stepping back in time."

That year, Chouinard—along with Doug Tompkins, the founder of
the North Face; champion skier Dick Dorworth; climber-filmmaker
Lito Tejada-Flores; and an English climber named Chris Jones—
piloted a secondhand van eighteen thousand miles from California to
Mount Fitzroy, about four hundred miles from where we are now.
The journey, which took six months, was a traveling circus of surfing,
skiing, and mountain climbing—a road trip à la Neal Cassady, with a
soundtrack by Mingus. "The whole point of the trip," jokes Chouinard,
"was a search for the perfect flan."

In its scope, the excursion was akin to taking a hang glider to the
moon. The group's successful ascent of the eleven-thousand-foot
Fitzroy—the third ever—took sixty days, many of them spent trapped
in snow caves by hideous weather. On the summit, the men unfurled a
flag that read VIVA LOS FUN HOGS! It was a landmark climb; no American had ever summitted Fitzroy before. "It really opened up Patagonia," says Dorworth. "It really changed our lives."

You might think Chouinard was a bankrolled hippie with a lot of
free time on his hands; actually, he was the son of a French-Canadian
couple of limited means. Chouinard recalls that, as a young boy, he
watched his father sit down with a bottle of whiskey and a pair of pliers and pull his own teeth—all of them—because he felt the dentist
was charging too much for dentures. "Because I inherited some of
these genes," Chouinard wrote years later, "I have a preference for
learning and doing things on my own."

He discovered climbing while pursuing falconry, which he'd taken
up at age twelve, rappelling to the birds' nests high in the mountains

of the San Fernando Valley. By 1957, when he was nineteen, he had already revolutionized mountaineering by creating a piton that could be nailed into and then removed from rock, unlike the European kind, which had to be left in place. He could make two in an hour on his portable forge, and he sold them from the trunk of his car for $1.50 each.

"His first ascent of El Capitán was, in its time, the hardest climb in the world," says Tom Frost, a photographer and fellow gear-head who accompanied Chouinard in 1964 as he pioneered a route up the massive North American wall in Yosemite. In 1968, the year of his epic journey with the Fun Hogs, he finished designing his now-legendary climber's ice ax, one of which is included in the Museum of Modern Art's permanent collection. When he wasn't pushing the limits of his craft, Chouinard would sit around Yosemite's infamous Camp 4, the vortex of America's burgeoning climbing scene, copying aphorisms from books he was reading—Camus, Nietzsche, the poetry of Robinson Jeffers. He was cultivating a lifelong credo, he says, based on Zen-like ideas of simplicity and impermanence.

"Every one of those friends of mine . . . [we] never wanted to work, we never wanted to become stable citizens. All we wanted was to climb, forever. It was as valid a life as anything we could think of."

Some stories people tell about Chouinard: "I remember one time we were on the Kautz Glacier in Washington, and I'd had what I call the 'Three-Minute Yvon Chouinard Short Course in Crampons,'" says Tom Brokaw. (Together, Brokaw, McGuane, and Chouinard constitute a sporting threesome they call the Do-Boys.) "We were [crossing] this *very* treacherous stretch of black ice, and if you slipped, it was at least two thousand feet before you'd stop. So I turned to Yvon and said, 'Shouldn't we rope up together here?' And he said, '*No way!* If you go, I go!' He said, 'This is just like getting a taxi in New York! It's every man for himself!' There's no bullshit factor when you're with him. With Chouinard, you can either do it, or you can't. And I live in a bullshit world," says Brokaw, laughing, "so it's a perfect antidote to that."

"It's Brokaw's stories that have kept me from similar adventures," says Harrison Ford, a neighbor in Jackson, Wyoming, where Chouinard owns a home. This month, Ford will present Chouinard with the Riverkeeper Environmental Excellence Award for his conservation-minded work ethic. "I've gone fishing with Yvon and I've played tennis with him," says the actor, "but I have *not* gone up a mountain with [him]. I don't trust Yvon to know the limits of a natural human being."

"One day he was looking at the magazine *Earthwatch*," says writer Rick Ridgeway, "and it had this picture of a spire on this island, and he said, 'Hey, we oughta climb that sucker.'" It was 1988, and Chouinard, at fifty, had begun to wonder if he still had his edge.

A few months later, Chouinard and Ridgeway, with Doug Tompkins and Jim Donini, a fellow climber, were on a fishing boat steaming from Puerto Natales, Chile, in search of the unnamed peak. They didn't even have a map. The captain steered for the island by looking at the photo Chouinard had ripped from the magazine.

"The boat left us on this uninhabited archipelago with a month's food, our climbing gear, and our kayaks," says Ridgeway. "We didn't even know if we were in the right place." After a few days, the weather cleared—and there was the peak, right above them. But the wind had kicked up, blowing so fiercely that every time the men tried to stand, they were knocked to the frozen ground. They spent two weeks hunkered in tents, waiting.

As soon as the weather broke again, Donini and Chouinard quickly began an ascent, both thinking they'd make a few pitches, look around, and return to camp. Soon, the men passed some mental point of no return. They continued climbing for fourteen hours, hammering pitons and fixing ropes, finally summitting the four-thousand-foot peak in frigid darkness.

Chouinard and Donini were forced to crawl back down the mountain through the night. Ridgeway and Tompkins were lying in their tents, weeping, certain that their friends were dead. In the morning, the two half-frozen climbers reappeared, their clothes shredded. And now they faced a seventy-five-mile paddle to the mainland.

"The winds were so strong," says Ridgeway, "that you had to do everything to keep from flipping over. Chouinard was flipped in one of the worst gusts, and it just held him down." Bobbing in an ocean laden with icebergs, he turned hypothermic but managed to climb back onto the upturned boat and paddle himself to a nearby island, where his friends built a fire to thaw him out. They finally made the mainland the next day.

"I really scared the shit out of myself on that climb," Chouinard tells me. "Before, I'd always had enough to take it right to the edge. I came too close to going over."

"When we pulled the kayaks up on the beach in Ushuaia," says Ridgeway, "we all looked back at what we'd just come from. And I'll never forget it: Yvon suddenly got this big grin on his face. And the first thing he said was, 'Well, that's just what I needed!'"

It's ten minutes to dusk, and I've been watching Chouinard fish, feeling compelled to be better than I am, which is the signature effect of his life. We're standing at a pool called the Secret Spot, waiting for what Río Grande fishermen call the Magic Hour, the silken time just before dark when the fish bite readily. I ask Chouinard for a casting lesson. You catch these capricious Río Grande trout by plopping your fly on a far bank and drifting it into the current in a steady pattern: cast, drift, take two steps downstream, then repeat. But my fly line swims skyward with each thunderous blast of wind. Part of the problem is that, with my smaller eight-weight fly rod, I'm underpowered: *De rigueur* on the Río Grande is the longer power-stick known as a double-handed spey rod—like Chouinard's—which can drive a fly line through a brick wall.

Chouinard proceeds to demonstrate the balletic moves of spey casting, praising me when I nail it. Soon, I halfway have the hang of it. Chouinard told me earlier that rock climbing was about "making links," about finding a zone and wasting no effort. "Fishing," he said, "is like that, too."

As I stand on the riverbank, thinking about this, I start casting in a new rhythm, a new zone, reaching water I haven't reached before. Still, I can't touch the Secret Spot completely, so I cross the river and climb the opposite bank, as Chouinard did that morning. On my second cast, the line comes tight. I can tell the fish is big, but who knows how big? It's dark. The trout sulks on the bottom. Finally, I turn him, and he rises slowly. As he swirls in a blurred pane of moonlight, I see he is the biggest trout I will catch in my life.

Crossing the river, Chouinard calls, "Hey, Doug! Way to go!" And the trout, with a beat of its tail, runs up the stony beach and comes to rest at my feet: a male weighing twenty-five pounds.

"My God," Chouinard says. "Look at that *fish!*" He shakes my hand, telling me maybe twenty people out of the hundreds who have visited the lodge in its ten-year history have caught a brown trout as enormous as this one. That night, Chouinard toasts me over dinner. We seem ready for the river of his memory, for still more unexplored territory.

"Look at these hands!" It's early morning, and we're heading down an empty gravel road into the interior of Tierra del Fuego, to the secret river. "Paper cuts!" Chouinard is saying. "I've got paper cuts! All I do is work!" He can't wait now to suffer, can't wait to sleep on cold dirt under the stars. The road rises past tin houses that rattle in the cold wind. It's a sound that maybe only ten people a year get to hear, the landscape is that empty. Sheep and cattle scatter as we pass. After two hours, we arrive at the fifty-thousand-acre Estancia Marina, southwest of Río Grande.

Yes, he will lead us to the river, the *estanciero*—the owner of the ranch—tells us. "I have no idea if it's got fish," he says, "but, please, be my guest, fish it. And tell me if it's any good."

This idea of an unfished river astonishes Chouinard, and we follow in our rented pickup as the *estanciero* leads us along a path through dense stands of beech trees that seem to close behind us as we pass—I begin to imagine that we'll never find our way back. The sun is warm on our faces, and I look up and see the snow on the mountains and feel the cold wind and hunch down in my jacket and feel lonely and happy all at once. Chouinard says, "Jesus, what country, what country." At a camp on a hill above the river, we build a fire at dusk.

Across the water, we can see a kind of tepee, a forty-foot cone of carefully arranged logs—the former home, the *estanciero* told us, of the last Ona Indian to have lived in Tierra del Fuego, dead for some twenty years now. The story may or may not be apocryphal, but the tall, blackened doorway suggests an uneasy emptiness, as if someone has just stepped back from it into the shadows. Wherever we look, we see it out of the corners of our eyes. "Spooky," says Chouinard.

At the campfire, Chouinard starts making dinner. He lays our steaks—the only food we've brought—directly on the fire's red coals. Even though I am aware that we have no plates or cooking utensils with us, I still can't believe what I'm seeing. I'm certain that our entire food cache is turning to cinders.

It's then that I realize we haven't brought any water with us either. In fact, I have outfitted myself for this three-day camping trip with nothing except a tent and a sleeping bag. Chouinard has brought along even less. "I didn't even buy a tent until I was forty," he explains. "I could always find a cave, or a tree, out of the wind. . . ."

After a while, though, the lack of supplies doesn't trouble me. I start to think, *Who needs all that shit?* Chouinard is squatting by the coals, smiling at the glow. "This will work out great," he says. "I once taught a class about cooking outdoors without pots and pans. You can make bread, you know, just by using a stone." He snatches the steaks from the fire and sets them on a mossy log. They're not burned, and they're not coated with cinders. They're perfect, in fact. We eat in the dark with our fingers, tearing off pieces with our teeth.

At dawn, we find the fish. They're in six inches of water, hovering, as if in a clarifying fluid, along the banks. They seem to look up, unafraid, as we pass by. Maybe it's been years since anyone has walked here; maybe no one ever has. These are rainbows and browns, two, three, and four pounds each, and I catch five of them and keep one for dinner. I walk downriver as I cast, my head feeling as if it's bumping against the sky.

Chouinard, for his part, is being driven to his usual fits of ingenuity. Crouching on the bank in stealth postures, he tries sinking lines, then floating lines. Every few minutes, I hear him: "Ah, shit! Missed 'em!" Then: "Jesus, did ya see that fish!" It's an endearing lecture to himself, filled with wonder, as he catches one glorious fish after another. He walks up to me, smiling, and sits on the bank. "What a day we're having," he says. "We haven't seen another footprint. What a day." Winding up the slack on his reel, he stares at his rod, then finally gives it a jiggle. "This," he says, "is one of the best days of fishing in my life. Fabulous."

Before long, Chouinard is up again, walking and casting. At one point, a swallow lands on his fly rod, mistaking it for a tree branch, then disappears in a frantic burst of tiny purple wings. Chouinard catches so many fish he loses count: forty-five, fifty, sixty-five. . . . I can just barely see him now, walking downstream, bobbing in the waves of heat boiling from the valley floor.

Resting on the bank, I recall something Chouinard read to me, something he'd written about a climbing experience he'd had on El Capitán when he was young: "Nothing felt strange in our vertical world. Each individual crystal in the granite stood out in bold relief. . . . After a period of time, the artist gets caught up in the sculpture, and the material comes alive."

That afternoon, when we are driving out, picking our way down the valley and looking for our hidden passage back up through the beech forest, I point from the car window at the distant silver river threading through the green valley. Chouinard is staring at it, too—he has been glancing at the river the whole time he's been driving, not saying a word.

He turns slowly, as if he has just remembered that I'm in the car. His eyes are bloodshot, his lips are cracked, his face is baked red. He's been wasted by sun and wind. We both have.

"Tempted?" I ask.

Sitting up, he says, "Oh, yeah, I am definitely ready to play."

MAY 1999

MUCH ABOUT THIS WORLD
by Chip Brown

G UY WATERMAN DREW UP the itinerary of his last day as
he had drawn up the daily plan for thousands of less-eventful
days, scribbling his schedule on a three-by-five index card.
For as long as anyone could remember, he had carried a sheaf of the
color-coded cards in his breast pocket. He would pull them out to
make a note of some arresting detail: the song of a new bird, a shift in
the wind, the name of a dog. Hiking an unfamiliar trail, he often
would log every notable bend and cutback. People said his whole life
was in those cards. It was hardly the case of his needing to jog an infe-
rior memory—he could, for example, recite five hours of *Paradise
Lost* with his eyes closed. If some people found his constant scribbling
a touch obsessive, others saw it as an aspect of his exceptional character; not a symptom but a sign of his delight in the patterns that could
be uncovered in compilations of data, of his intense relation to nature,
his aptitude for noticing.

He once went to the library in the village of East Corinth, Vermont, where eccentric requests are not unknown, and asked if he
could photocopy a log his wife had found in the woods. When the
page emerged, the librarians were astonished to see what looked like
a perfect lithograph of a prairie—the trees, the grass, everything but
the sod-roofed house.

"What does this look like?" Waterman asked.

"A prairie!" said one of the staff members, still unable to see in the
wood what had been made so plainly visible on the paper.

"That's what I think, too."

The difference was that Waterman had seen it in the wood. He was
meticulously attentive to detail in most facets of his life. His days usually
began at four in the morning, when he would get up while his wife Laura
was still asleep and work at his desk until seven. They had built their cabin
together in 1973 on thirty-nine wooded acres in east-central Vermont.
They called the place Barra, after the Hebridean island of Waterman's

Scottish ancestors. It was about half an hour's snowshoe from the road to East Corinth, where there was a post office, a Congregational church, and the library with the accommodating copy machine.

They had been back to the land for twenty-seven years now, practicing the stringent economics of homesteading. Their annual budget was about $3,000, the money drawn from a small savings account, their earnings as freelance writers, and, since 1994, the windfall of Social Security. To live at Barra they had become vegetarians. Year after year they lugged their water up from a stream by bucket. They bathed in an old cattle trough. They hauled and sawed and stacked their firewood by hand. They tapped a grove of sugar maples for syrup, and filled the root cellar with fruits and vegetables from their garden. Twenty-seven years without a phone or electric lights. No fax, no computer, no radio, no TV, no motors or mechanical devices of any kind except for windup clocks. It was not an easy life for a younger person, and now they were getting on. Guy had regraded all the trails to make hiking around the homestead easier on Laura's knees. And where he used to bound down mountain trails, balancing on boulder crests, now friends noticed the shuffle in his step.

In those early-morning hours, working by the light of a kerosene lamp, Waterman would often write letters. Mail was the couple's only way of arranging visits, planning trips, soliciting news. Their stationery was standard homestead stock, which is to say any blank scrap of paper they could get their hands on: cardboard candle-box liners, the backside of renewal notices from the Society for American Baseball Research, even labels from forty-six-ounce cans of Grand Union pineapple juice. You could read a Waterman letter and then turn it over and find a solicitation from Sidwell Friends School: "Dear Guy, We've been alumni for more than forty years. I'm not sure that it's great to have been around that long, but it sure beats the alternative!"

He often wrote in first-person plural, speaking for himself and Laura. But the notes that he had been drafting over the last few days were his alone. They were addressed to friends whom he hoped would understand and accept the decision he'd made: John Dunn, a physician with whom he'd once climbed Damnation Gully on Mount Washington when it was thirty-six below and the winds were blowing eighty miles per hour on the summit; Dan Allen, with whom he shared a birthday as well as many backcountry adventures. He wrote the noted climber Mike Young, and Brad Ray and his wife, Rebecca

Oreskes, who would remember that he gave her an especially heart-felt hug after what proved to be their final get-together at Barra the previous fall.

To his young friend Doug Mayer, he wrote: "On a less cheery note, one of us wants to mention what perhaps he's hinted at in conversations over the past couple years. If you hear he's off to the mountains in killer weather, he hopes you may respect that it's his considered preference, and thus not sad news. . . ."

And to Tek Tomlinson, a former diplomat from Ethiopia: "Sorry to be taking this step as I was enjoying the developing friendship with Sally and you. I've discussed this at length with Laura. The prospect of aging with all its discomforts, indignities and limitations were even more than I cared to put up with. And there's much about this world that's too much for me. You've told me you're from a culture which respects decisions of this sort. I hope you can respect my decision."

At Barra he had always been the sort to think things out. He acted with deliberation. He lived by the Yankee ethic of self-reliance and personal responsibility. When he went somewhere, he was almost never late. So there was little doubt in the minds of anyone who knew him that if he had made an appointment, he would keep it. The last stop on his schedule for that Sunday, February 6, was scribbled on the card in his pocket—"5 PM: Summit."

"It Was Painful to Reach the Road"

Four days later, Laura Waterman knocked on the door of the parsonage of the Congregational Church at 9 A.M. and told Reverend Holly Ross Noble that her husband, Guy, had gone into the White Mountains on Sunday morning with no intention of coming back. Reverend Noble showed her to the phone. Laura reached Ned Therrien in Gilford, New Hampshire. Ned called Rebecca Oreskes, who worked for the National Forest Service; Rebecca called Jon Martinson; Jon called Doug Mayer . . . and so Guy Waterman's wide network of friends learned of his death on Mount Lafayette.

The National Guard helicopter dispatched that afternoon failed to locate his body. The forecast was for a storm, which threatened to delay the search and recovery. Mayer and Oreskes informed the state fish-and-game officials and the Forest Service that people who knew Guy Waterman were determined to recover his body themselves.

"It was something we wanted to do," Mayer said. "The forecast

Friday was not good, and we wanted to bring some closure and get this done."

"It was somehow fitting to go up there in a storm," recalled Mike Young. "Guy believed people should rescue themselves, and in a way we were rescuing ourselves—one of us."

And so the following morning, February 11, they gathered at a trailhead in Franconia Notch: Mike Young and his dog, Jamie; John Dunn and his dog, Brutus; Jon Martinson; and Doug Mayer. Mayer also invited Mike Pelchat, who knew Waterman only slightly but was the director of the ski patrol at Cannon Mountain and a veteran of many wilderness rescues and recoveries.

It was an unusually introspective group that started up the Old Bridle Path for the summit of Mount Lafayette around 8:30. They kicked through the new snow on the trail. The temperature was in the low twenties, and the summit winds were blowing at about thirty miles per hour.

"I've retrieved people in the mountains before, but never a friend," said Young. "Intellectually I knew there was no chance that he was alive."

When the group reached Greenleaf Hut, they put on snowshoes to traverse the knee-deep drifts. A short distance later, at treeline, they cached the snowshoes and climbed up into the icy fog in crampons. Visibility was about 100 feet. They followed the cairns. Around noon they reached the summit, 5,260 feet. The party fanned out along the ridge, walking toward the north peak of Lafayette. Mike Pelchat was on the ridge trail itself; after about ten minutes, he whistled that he had found what they were looking for.

"I almost walked right by him," Pelchat said later.

A foot of snow had drifted over the upper portion of the body. Waterman's ice ax, planted like a headstone, was covered with frost feathers. He was wearing crampons on a pair of plastic double boots that Mike Young had given him, wind pants, a blue 60/40 parka over a shirt and sweater, and a balaclava on his head.

"He was lying on his side, legs bent at the knees," Pelchat said. "It didn't look like he'd suffered. It looked like he went to sleep and didn't wake up."

When the others in the party arrived, they were in a little bit of shock. They gathered around their friend and said some quiet prayers. Gently, they removed his dark-green pack, which contained two water bottles, two flashlights, a tin of anchovies, a can opener, two clocks, and two small stuffed bears. They put his body into a bivvy sack and then lashed it to a fiberglass toboggan. The whole business took less than a half hour.

And then they started down, three in front, two in back, hauling the red sled from the front, braking it from behind on steep sections.

"It was very much like a mountaineer's version of a funeral procession," recalled John Dunn. "We were pulling him along quietly in the sled, like it was a casket, each of us lost in our thoughts about the meaning of his life. It was as if he was still with us, as if there were six of us."

They reached the trailhead around 4:30, as day was fading. The hearse arrived a little while later.

"Once we were down, it was over," said Dunn. "It was painful to reach the road, because it broke the spell."

The Great Stone Face

In the weeks to come, many people would find themselves preoccupied by the meaning of Guy Waterman's life. He was a singular man, and the vivid image of him in his trademark tam-o'-shanter singing arias to tentmates at 5 A.M. was not easily forgotten. Nor was his lambent spirit, how he pranced up gullies like a dancer, at a rate that winded hikers half his age. He was an army-surplus guy in a world of Gore-Tex. But his hand-knit sweaters and duct-taped wind pants had served him well enough when he climbed classic rock and ice routes in the Adirondacks, on Cannon Mountain, and on Huntington Ravine, often in the most god-awful conditions, which he referred to in the understated vernacular of British climbing as "refreshing." The worse the weather, the happier he was. Ice climbing had broken most of his knuckles because he never adopted the hand-friendly, high-tech tools of modern practice. He never bothered to thread slings through his axes either, which made for some refreshing moments on frozen waterfalls. His bushwhacking skills were legendary and proved to be the key to his epic achievement as a hiker: He was the first person to make winter ascents from all four points of the compass of all forty-eight White Mountain peaks over four thousand feet.

He wasn't tall, topping out at around five foot six. In his later years he became even more elfin, thanks to his white chin-strap beard and his canted-into-the-wind walk. He was highly intelligent but didn't wear it on his sleeve. He had a playful wit that was expressed in things like the wooden cell phone in Barra's guest cabin, or the notice that certified the outhouse as Y2K-compliant.

"The secret to Guy is that he was a performer," said his nephew Dane Waterman. "His tam was a symbol of that."

He had performed professionally as a jazz pianist in his early days, and remained a lifelong storyteller who could enthrall a hut full of hikers. There was something of Shakespeare's spell-weaving Prospero in him—an association he made himself when he titled his unpublished memoirs *Prospero's Options*. He loved dogs and would often tell them stories that were inaudible to human ears. He would put his arm around the maples in his sugarbush as if he were personally acquainted with their virtues, and vice versa. He could make the woods come alive for anyone who hiked with him. Once, on a walk with a friend's daughter, he planted ceramic elephants along the trail. The figurines were part of a herd he had gathered in the first half of his life when he worked as a Republican speechwriter on Capitol Hill. The delighted girl was drawn from bend to bend, amazed by the cornucopia of elephants, unaware of course that Waterman, who had agreed to carry her trophies, was surreptitiously rehiding the same three.

Despite the isolation of Barra, the Watermans were not hermits. They tried to bring their community into the woods with them, inviting friends and family to visit during the sugaring season, or to join them on hiking and climbing trips. Guy gave jazz concerts to raise money for a church fellowship group in East Corinth. He served on the board of the Mohonk Preserve, which oversees the Shawangunk cliffs near New Paltz, New York. In recent years he and Laura had volunteered three days a week at the local library, doing the thankless work of updating the card catalog. For many years they had maintained a section of trail along Franconia Ridge, which reaches its apex at Mount Lafayette. They built scree walls to protect the delicate diapensia and alpine moss. They shored up eroding embankments.

But their greatest contribution to wilderness preservation was their writing. They wrote exhaustive histories of hiking and climbing in New England, and their two seminal tracts, *Backwoods Ethics* and *Wilderness Ethics,* helped inaugurate the no-trace camping movement in the United States. Asking questions such as what place cell phones and helicopters have in the backcountry, the Watermans became, in the words of Doug Mayer, "the conscience of the New England wilderness."

For the people who knew Guy Waterman, the news of his death prompted the usual range of emotions—sadness, anger, bewilderment. Friends cast about for reasons. They wondered at the almost-never-mentioned grief and guilt he'd felt over having lost two of his three sons, one by the haunting precedent of a suicide in the mountains, the other under even more enigmatic circumstances. They weighed the paradoxes of character and asked themselves whether he had been caught up in the code of the Hard Man, who climbs at the sharp end of the rope and lives or dies by his ability to extricate himself from difficulties without help. It was not Guy Waterman's nature to seek help from doctors, or to mitigate what he called his "demons" with pills and therapists. He owned his demons, until the end at least, when they owned him. He left the people who loved him to wonder whether his choice was the action of a noble figure who withdrew before old age made him an embarrassment to himself and a burden to society, or the action of a tragic figure doomed by his code or something in his nature never to find the strength to be weak: the strength to ask for help, to be a burden, and so ultimately to know oneself in the compassion of others.

"Guy never offered a complete picture of his life," said his friend Tek Tomlinson. "My sense was that he was permanently grief-stricken, but that he did not feel the world deserved his tears. He was an unusually beautiful person. He had a way of getting into your depths." To Mike Young, Waterman seemed like the main character in Hawthorne's story "The Great Stone Face," which was inspired by a famous rock formation in Franconia Notch, just across from the ridge where Waterman died. "There was something in Guy that he couldn't recognize himself," said Young. "I think there are many of us who feel as if we failed, failed to convince him of how much he meant to us, what a good and loyal and true friend he was. I know his death has got to do with depression, and when depression speaks, it can't hear. But there is a collective feeling of 'What more could I have done? What could I have said? Why didn't I tell him: What an amazing person you are. You made my world so much bigger.'"

But if he had a way of getting into someone else's depths, it was almost impossible to get into his. Laura Waterman, in one of her only extended public comments on her husband's death, wrote in a local newspaper, "Guy believed in the uniqueness of the individual. That we are all separate and unknowable in our deepest core, one from one another."

"Warring Tendencies"

He had two lives, really, one before Barra, one after. Where he was impulsive before, he was deliberate after. Where he was a city rat before, he was a country man after. A self-described alcoholic before, a teetotaler after. From the one-time night owl and habitué of jazz dives emerged a man who liked to hit the hay by nine.

A similar polarity defined his sense of self. He was divided by what he called the "warring tendencies" of constructive action and self-destructive behavior. He saw his psychological dynamic symbolized in the characters of Ariel and Caliban from Shakespeare's *The Tempest.* Caliban served as a metaphor for defiance and darkness; Ariel was the sky spirit of moral action and social responsibility. "These impulses are probably in conflict within everyone," he wrote in *Prospero's Options,* "but in me the swings, the vehemence of the contrast, seem remarkable."

How much simpler things were when he was a boy, capering around in a deerskin loincloth and beseeching his family not to close the door on his imaginary friends. He was born in 1932, the youngest of five kids, and raised in a home steeped in science, literature, and music. His mother, Mary Mallon Waterman, was a graduate of Vassar and a former suffragette. His father, Alan Waterman, was a physics professor at Yale and a gifted viola player who eventually became the first director of the National Science Foundation and received the Presidential Medal of Freedom.

Fourteen years separated Guy from his oldest brother, Alan, but the first decade of his life, before his siblings scattered to Vassar and Princeton and Yale, was a prewar idyll of family picnics and adventures. Or so he remembered it. The Watermans called their ten-acre patch of pasture and orchard in North Haven, Connecticut, "the Farm." The kids gravitated to the banks of a woodsy brook, where they could traverse fallen logs and whack the mushrooms that sprang up after a rain. There was a tepee and a horse named Dolly. Mother read aloud to them at night—Shakespeare, Sir Walter Scott. At a young age Guy was besotted with baseball and developed a preternatural command of players' stats. He was also talented musically. He had absolute pitch and was picking out tunes before the age of three.

With summers off, his father took the boys to the Maine woods for canoeing and camping. "His Maine guide's license meant more to him than the Medal of Freedom," recalled Guy's sister Anne Cooley.

When World War II broke out, the family relocated, first to Cambridge, Massachusetts, and then in 1946 to Washington, D.C. The departure from the Farm marked the start of Waterman's tumultuous adolescence. Unhappy terms at prep school. The discovery of alcohol. It also marked his awakening to the glories of ragtime and Jelly Roll Morton's New Orleans jazz.

In the fall of 1948, as a junior at Sidwell Friends School in Washington, he fell for a girl in the senior class named Emily Morrison. In May 1950, they eloped. As Waterman noted many years later in his memoir, the marriage "was not a product of love but of a joint rebellion against the adult world. The resulting relationship was predictable, once there was no adult opposition to join forces against."

They hung on for nineteen years. In Waterman's view, all but the first were strained and unrewarding, but the union produced three sons. Bill was born in April 1951, shortly before his father turned nineteen; Johnny arrived seventeen months later; and Jim came three years after that, in 1955. By day Guy was studying for an economics degree at George Washington University. Three nights a week, he played jazz gigs with a group called the Riverboat Trio. He took his boys to the zoo, but the burden of caring for the kids fell to his wife.

After college, Waterman found work as an analyst with the U.S. Chamber of Commerce, and by the end of the 1950s he had made his way onto Capitol Hill, where he worked for the Senate Minority Policy Committee, writing speeches and reports, and analyzing economic legislation. He had thrown in with the Republicans partly out of a sense of establishmentarian loyalty, and partly out of a defiant refusal to carry his family's liberal standard simply because it was expected. He wrote speeches for Richard Nixon's 1960 presidential campaign, but his days in Washington were numbered, owing to what he saw as the Caliban forces of self-destruction. He was drinking every night. He felt himself to be "borderline suicidal." The night Nixon lost was his nadir: Waterman went on a bender and woke up in jail.

In early 1961, seeking a fresh start, he moved his family to a house in Stamford, Connecticut, and began commuting to New York City, where he had a job as a speechwriter for General Electric. The work proved to be drearier than he had feared. The hopes he'd entertained of entering Connecticut politics unravelled, and the malaise of his marriage deepened. His drinking got worse than ever. And then in the fall of 1963, he stumbled upon a series of articles in *Sports Illustrated* about the history of attempts to climb the North Face of the Eiger in Switzerland.

"Mountains and climbing dawned on my drunken, shamed, lonely life like a beacon of hope," he later wrote. "Here was a whole new world of aspiration and effort, contrasting with the nightmare my life had become." He devoured mountaineering books. That October, he took a climbing course and was exhilarated to make his first forays onto the steep cracks and overhangs of the Shawangunk conglomerate. In November, he packed an old army tent and in lousy weather made his maiden voyage onto Franconia Ridge—the place that he would come to think of as his spiritual home, and that summoned him at the end of his life.

The discipline of climbing motivated Waterman to quit drinking. He reformed his habits with a characteristic display of independence—by will alone, without the help of counselors or AA groups. He began hiking to the railroad station from his house to get into shape. He climbed the twenty-one flights from the street to his office in the GE building, and often ran down the stairs trying to beat the elevator.

Hiking and climbing trips also gave him a way to be with his sons. When they reached their teens, Bill and Johnny began to join him, and eventually Jim did, too, though not to the same extent. Guy took the older boys on long trips to Katahdin and the White Mountains. He and Bill took their first winter trip to the White Mountains, hiking up Lafayette in February 1967, when the temperature was thirty-six below zero. Guy tore his trousers with a crampon and developed frostbite on one of his knees.

After his climbing debut at age thirteen, Johnny quickly emerged as a prodigy. Whereas Bill had a more rounded life—he played the drums; he made friends easily—Johnny poured himself into climbing as if his identity depended on it. He would do four hundred push-ups a night, walk the two and a half miles from school to home just to touch the door of the house and then go back and make the circuit again.

By 1969, the Watermans' marriage was finally over, and the sons had begun to grapple with the dissolution of their family. Guy set up life as a bachelor father. His youngest son, Jim, came to live with him for his final three years of high school, while Waterman went through the motions of his job at GE. He lived mostly for his weekend getaways at the Gunks.

Fresh out of high school in 1969, Bill headed west, hopping freight trains. One night in June, running away from railroad crews at a yard in Winnipeg, he scooted under a boxcar just as an engine gave it a nudge. A steel wheel rolled over his leg just above the ankle, irreparably crushing the bone. The leg was surgically shortened, but its function could not be restored, and eventually it was amputated and a prosthesis was attached. Four years later, in May 1973, when he was living in Fairbanks, Alaska, Bill wrote to his father to say that he was going off on a long trip and would contact him when he got back.

He was never seen or heard from again. To this day, what happened to him is a mystery.

That same summer of 1969, a few months before his seventeenth birthday, Johnny embarked on his first great adventure in Alaska. He joined a party of older mountaineers and became the third-youngest person ever to summit Mount McKinley, the crown of North America. One of the team members, the well-known climber Tom Frost, gave Johnny a pair of wind pants after their ascent, and a couple of years later, Johnny passed them on to Guy, who wore them for the next two decades. In the end Johnny was the son with whom Guy identified most closely; the son whose fate he felt most responsible for. In his memoirs Guy wrote, "Poor Johnny embodied those impulses in me which have been destructive, as they were so finally for Johnny." But it was possible to believe otherwise in the summer of 1969. It was possible to spill over with fatherly pride as Johnny threw himself into a climbing career that over the years encompassed some of the most difficult routes around, climaxing in his masterpiece: an incredible solo traverse via the unclimbed central buttress of the South Face of 14,573-foot Mount Hunter in the Alaska Range in the summer of 1978. Johnny climbed alone, with only the lice that had infested his body for company. He fixed ropes and ferried supplies up a frightnight ridge of crumbling cornices, friable ice, and overhanging rock. He made as many as twelve trips over each pitch in order to haul all the gear and provisions. There were times when he broke down and sobbed as the climb turned into an epic of endurance, stretching on and on for an astonishing 145 days. In the end he triumphed. The noted climber Jeff Lowe later wrote of the ascent: "There is nothing else in the history of mountaineering with which to compare it."

When Johnny returned to Fairbanks, his life began to unravel under warring tendencies of his own. Several friends had died in the mountains. He felt himself to be a social outcast, loveless and isolated. He was prone to bursts of rage. He made obsessive notes of his conversations and encounters with people on the street, eerily echoing the note-taking of his father. But what seemed like constructive idiosyncrasy in Guy was spinning into madness in his son. Political spirit had driven Guy to write speeches for Eisenhower, Nixon, and Ford. In Johnny it inspired a quixotic bid for a local school-board seat on a platform of liberalized drug use. After his defeat, he decided to run for president under the banner of his own Feed the Starving party. Seeking publicity for the cause, Johnny set out to solo McKinley in the winter with only flour, sugar, margarine, and protein powder to sustain him. He trained by immersing himself in a bathtub of ice cubes.

His initial try on Denali failed. He returned to his base in Talkeetna. When his cabin burned down, he checked himself into the Anchorage Psychiatric Institute for two weeks. In 1981 he made a second attempt to solo the mountain, but unlike most Denali climbers, who fly to the base of the mountain, he planned to walk in all the way from Cook Inlet, carrying an enormous pack for about one hundred miles. He got to two thousand feet on the Ruth Glacier, then retreated. In March, he turned toward the great mountain for the final time, telling his friend, bush pilot Cliff Hudson, "I won't be seeing you again." He was last spotted on April 1, walking toward Denali's east buttress. He had no sleeping bag, no tent, no dark glasses, no sunscreen. The route led toward an area known to be seamed with crevasses.

While the circumstances of Johnny's disappearance were hardly as mysterious as those of his older brother, he was—like Bill—never seen again.

The news of Johnny's death would bring to an end what for his father had been the happiest period of his life. For most of the 1970s Guy had been graced by the blessings of a second marriage and the good life that was promised to those who quit the rat race and went back to the land. He was growing his own food and hauling his own water and cutting his own wood. No electricity, no phone. Then came that April morning in 1981. . . . The cabin was half an hour from the road, and some high school kids from the village came running in to tell him there was a ranger calling from Alaska.

The Price of Happiness

Guy Waterman's second act—the half that made his death so compelling to so many people—began with a chance encounter at the Gunks in 1970, when he met Laura Johnson. She was seven years younger, the daughter of the noted Emily Dickinson scholar Thomas H. Johnson. Waterman was smitten and quickly had her on belay. They were perfectly matched—a thirty-eight-year-old Republican rock hound with three kids could have searched a long time before finding someone who not only loved roping up as much as he did, and shared his ardor for books and music, but was also willing to abandon her career as an editor at *Backpacker* magazine to pursue the countercultural dream of a cabin in the woods. They were married in the summer of 1972 and spent their honeymoon night on a Shawangunk belay ledge big enough for a small tent.

On June 9 of the following year, they moved onto land they had bought in Vermont and began building Barra. They poured the foundation on the Fourth of July and trucked in the Steinway grand when the roof was up in August. It was a race to get the sixteen-by-thirty-two-foot cabin finished before winter. Over the years they added a porch, a woodshed, and then a sugar shed where they could boil the syrup drawn from their maples. They built footbridges over streams. They cut trails through the woods that you would hardly notice. They planted pear and apple trees. They bartered their labor for loads of manure, and each year enlarged their garden. The earth erupted with lettuce and kale and Swiss chard, with broccoli, carrots, beets, rutabagas, potatoes, and buckwheat. What they couldn't grow—peanut butter, some flour, cereals, Tang—they bought in bulk. They fashioned a root cellar where they stored carrots and beets in sand, and turnips and onions and potatoes on the shelves. Laura canned rhubarb and rose hips and blackberries. Guy cut firewood—oak and hop hornbeam, ash, beech, and yellow birch—seven cords of wood, winter after winter.

People often asked them why they had moved to the woods, why they lived under circumstances that were closer to life in the fourteenth century than the twentieth. Waterman often demurred, saying he was a "doer," not a "deep thinker," and that his ideas were "full of inconsistencies and doubts." Part of the answer was that he didn't want appliances around if he couldn't fix them. There was a side of him that disliked dealing with people, especially when his mood was sour. But he also sought to exercise mind and body equally. He relished the chore of sawing wood. He counted each stroke. At the outset, he and Laura had avowed their objectives: "To live simply, cheaply, unhurriedly, basically." They drew up a set of principles that included staying out of debt, not using machines, keeping up with friends, creating beauty, and, fatefully, given the forethought that went into Waterman's suicide, "planning all activities in detail and well in advance."

The life itself was the attraction. They lived the way they lived in order to live the way they lived.

So the years unfurled in the rhythm of the homestead seasons. It was impossible for many people to imagine the two of them apart. They wrote their books together. They tented, snowshoed, and climbed together. Laura cooked at home; Guy cooked in camp. In the early years, they played four-handed piano. After supper, he read to her from the library that lined the cabin walls. They devised the best way to clean windows: Laura would wash on the inside while Guy washed on the outside, the one mirroring the other with only a pane of glass between them.

Every morning at 7 A.M., Waterman collected temperatures from three weather stations on the property. He added the data to the immense store of "Barra-stats." He tracked the monthly household consumption of Ben & Jerry's by flavor. He knew which of their bushes produced the most blueberries and followed the yearly variations, from the lean harvests of five thousand to ten thousand berries to crops like the one in 1998, which netted forty-three thousand berries. He knew the number of gallons of maple sap issued by the eighty-eight trees they tapped, all of which had names. Some trees, like Ozymandias, were chronic underperformers. Some were sap issuers of almost heroic enthusiasm. Eight times the tree known as Mad Dog won Waterman's Tree of the Year award.

If there was a Faustian price for the happiness Barra brought Waterman, it was the lingering feeling of guilt that he had abandoned his boys. Particularly Jim, who had graduated from high school just as his father was heading to the woods with his new wife. Waterman had put some money aside for his sons' college educations, but it wasn't nearly enough. As an advocate of personal responsibility, he had to confront his shortcomings on that front. "What it came down to is that I walked away from that responsibility, leaving my sons with a difficult time to finance their own college," he wrote in his memoirs. "My mind was on my own future, from which there was no turning back for me."

When the news of Johnny's death reached him on April 21, 1981, at 4:30 in the afternoon, the happiness of Barra began to crumble from within. For a year Waterman did not play the piano. He buried a pair of Johnny's boots under a cairn off Franconia Ridge, near Mount Lincoln. Each year on the anniversary of Johnny's death, he and Laura hiked up to the memorial to commune with the memory of the lost son. He began to brood about the origins of Johnny's woes. It was one thing not to have provided for his sons' tuition, another not to have been able to save them from themselves—from warring tendencies you possessed yourself and had perhaps passed on to them. Johnny's death also forced Waterman to confront the possibility that Bill, whom he had not heard from in eight years, was also gone—if not actually dead, then so deeply estranged he might as well be.

"One of the secret things about Guy," said his oldest brother, Alan, an emeritus professor of electrical engineering at Stanford, "is that for a long time he wouldn't believe either of his boys were dead."

But increasingly it seemed there was much about the world that was too much for Waterman. He described the 1980s as a time when the "gloom about my sons" spread "a darkening shadow over the main currents of my life." Age did not mellow his unease. By 1990, he had stopped rock climbing, and two years later he quit venturing onto steep ice—pastimes that had been his salvation as a younger man. He withdrew from committee work for the Appalachian Mountain Club. He turned his attention to writing articles for baseball journals and completing Twin Firs, the guest cabin. He drew detailed maps of Barra. He and Laura had sold some land, and the homestead now encompassed twenty-seven acres. Guy took the same pains making maps as he did carving the wooden dowels that pinned the hand-hewn logs of Twin Firs. It eased his dour moods to roam Barra's woods, visiting Hop Hollow and Middle Earth, stopping by Sandy Point, the Forest of Arden, or looking in on the graves of his dogs Ralph and Elsa.

In 1997, he began composing his memoirs. Late that year, he asked Doug Mayer, who worked for the National Public Radio show *Car Talk,* if he would bring a tape recorder out to Barra on one of his visits. For "various morbid reasons," he said, he and Laura had been thinking about their funerals, and Guy wanted a selection of music that could be played at his service.

The next summer, in June 1998, his brother Alan and his nephew Dane came for a visit. Guy gave them a copy of his memoirs, all but the pages that appeared to be missing at the end. The text stopped at 178, and then the appendices began at 183.

"Where are the last pages?" Alan asked.

"I haven't written them yet," Guy said.

Had they not been written, or had they been held back until he was ready to explain the plan taking shape in his head? The visit disturbed Dane and his father, though they said nothing to Guy. "My dad and I were both disappointed at how bright and superficial it was," said Dane Waterman. "It has bothered me for the last two years. It wasn't a phony mask Guy was wearing, it was a deflecting of things—of not wanting to get below the surface. I know now we saw him only a few weeks before July 3, when he went out to kill himself."

It was not the first time. Back in 1992, after his sixtieth birthday, he had written but never delivered a note to Laura declaring his intention to commit suicide. He'd drawn up a list of seventeen physical ailments, some of them, such as ingrown toenails, absurdly trivial. When he returned that day in July 1998 from a hike in the White Mountains and confessed that he had thought about taking his life, Laura was dumbfounded. As she later wrote: "My first thought was, as I watched him pace as he was telling me: Am I married to a crazy man? But I knew I wasn't, and I realized how much I loved him, and that the most important thing was to go on loving him as hard as ever I could."

Was Waterman suffering from a physical illness? That same summer he had complained of abdominal pains. He was concerned—his father had died of pancreatic cancer—but he refused to go for tests despite the urging of John Dunn and his wife, Linda, both physicians. "He didn't see any point in it," said Dunn. "If it were a malignancy, he wouldn't have treatment." The Dunns and Mike Young, who was also a physician, kept an eye peeled for symptoms in Guy, but saw none. "He didn't appear to be losing weight," Dunn said. "He wasn't jaundiced, he didn't appear to be anemic. He had a vitamin B_{12} deficiency from his strict vegetarian diet, but his strength was good."

Sick or not, one can only guess what called Waterman back from the brink that summer day. Perhaps it was the conviction that he owed it to Laura to ensure her future when he was gone. Certainly that summer of 1998 marked the beginning of an effort to lay the plans that ultimately concluded on the summit of Mount Lafayette eighteen months later. The Watermans arranged for the eventual transfer of Barra to the Good Life Center, a nonprofit organization dedicated to the homestead philosophy. Barra would be preserved and perhaps provide a livelihood for some young couple who wanted to live simply, cheaply, unhurriedly, and basically.

Perhaps the most pointed sign of Guy's intentions was the property in East Corinth, on which the couple began to build a pretty, machine-cut log house with a view of the Tabor Valley branch of the Waits River. The foundation was poured in February 1999. Guy always referred to the place as "Laura's house," where Laura would live after he was gone. The more he mentioned it, the more his friends began to grasp its implications. After their visit to Barra in late November, Rebecca Oreskes and Brad Ray stopped by "Laura's house" and half-jokingly asked the contractor if he could slow down the construction.

The Watermans celebrated New Year's at Barra with Dan Allen and his wife, Natalie Davis, toasting the new century with glasses of Tang at 7 P.M. (which was midnight Greenwich Mean Time) so Guy could turn in by 9 as usual. In January the coauthors completed a new book, a collection of mountain stories called *A Fine Kind of Madness,* which will be published this fall.

In mid-January Guy had a concert date at the Corinth Town Hall— a final gig he meant to keep. And after that . . . it was just a matter of waiting for one of those spells of killer New England weather. The night temperatures in east-central Vermont that first week of February ranged from the low teens to zero. In the White Mountains, they dropped well into minus figures.

Laura had never been sure of the date, only that it would be sometime that winter. She had come down with the flu the week before, and perhaps that had delayed her husband. When she was well, Guy told her he was ready. They had one last day together, Saturday, February 5. Waterman wrote some final letters. He filled the wood bins.

He told her where he would be and at what time as he was hiking up Lafayette, a mountain he had climbed more than a hundred times. He told her where the authorities would be able to find his body. They agreed that she would wait at least until Tuesday to begin notifying their friends.

On Sunday morning, he gave her the last three pages of his memoir. He told her that if it wasn't cold enough out, he might be back. He suggested that to assuage the anguish after he was gone, she might immerse herself in the ritual of baking bread.

And then he was gone, and she was sitting down with the pages he had given her. She took comfort in the passages he had written. They spoke of his fear of getting old, his regret at the failure of their books to have had more influence. He wished he could have done better, have made more of a difference. He spoke of the depression he had endured, how the last seven years had passed numbly. He had put on the face of genial host and wit, but his real feelings had been off-limits even to his most intimate friends. And he spoke of his family, his father, Johnny, how they embodied the quarrel in himself. "Ariel versus Caliban," Waterman wrote. "As I look at where I have come to, after 66 years of struggling, I see that Caliban has won."

Meticulous as ever, he had crossed out "66" and written in "67."

"The Sad Cure"

He came from the north. It was a trip he had made countless times. He preferred back roads—Route 5 to Wells River, Vermont, then across the New Hampshire state line on Route 10 to Littleton, and then south into Franconia Notch.

It was a beautiful winter day, clear and windy. Eight degrees that morning in Benton to the west of Franconia Ridge; five degrees in the town of Bethlehem north of the mountains. The conditions in the valleys did not approximate those in the higher elevations. The observatory on Mount Washington recorded an average February 6 temperature of three below zero; winds averaged 78 miles per hour, gusting to 130.

He parked his Subaru in the lot across from the trailhead of the Old Bridle Path. He left his snowshoes in the car and tucked the keys in his pocket. He was wearing his plastic double boots, crampons, heavy mittens, and gaiters, and carrying his ice ax, two pencils, and two pens. In his green pack were two water bottles, two flashlights, a tin of anchovies, a can opener, two clocks, and two small stuffed bears. Whenever he and Laura went anywhere, the bears were always with them in the bed.

His 5 P.M. appointment with the summit coincided with sunset at 4:58. He seems to have taken his time climbing up.

A hiker named Marty Sample, coming down from Lafayette that Sunday, posted a note on a website saying that he had seen an older man with a long ice ax headed up the Old Bridle Path, and remembered thinking that it was pretty late in the day to be going up.

The trail ascended through the leafless birch and ragged mountain ash. Higher on, it became a snowy defile through the dark-green curtains of red spruce and balsam fir.

Near the halfway point, it opened on a series of ledges with panoramic views across Walker Ravine, where Waterman had often bushwhacked up to the ridge. Mount Lincoln rose to the south, and hidden on its flanks stood the cairn for Johnny. Farther on, the trail cut up the steep hills known as the Three Agonies for the test given to the AMC hut crews hauling hundred-pound supply packs.

Around forty-two hundred feet the trail reached the frozen bed of Eagle Lake, where the Greenleaf Hut was boarded up for the winter. The icy white dome of Lafayette rose a thousand feet above. People often stopped here and strapped on crampons before venturing up into the hammering west wind. The glassy slopes ahead lay above treeline, except for the dwarf growth of the alpine zone.

From cairn to cairn, up to the summit. He could have checked his clocks or told the time from the slanting sundown light on the Presidential Range to the east. Darkness was pooling in the great basin of the Pemigewasset Wilderness. West in shadow lay the cliffs of Cannon, where his son Johnny had put up a route called Consolation Prize. Behind the long fin of Whitney Gilman Ridge was the Black Dike, which he had climbed with Laura, one of her finest ascents on ice.

Down from the summit, ten minutes in crampons on the gentle grade along the ridge. He stepped into an alcove of rocks just off the trail. In spring the diapensia would be blooming at his feet. He sat down in the snow facing north. In his breast pocket, inside a plastic bag, was a map of Barra, the one he had taken such pains to draw. It showed the streams, the orchards, the gardens, the buildings, the trails, almost the life that he and Laura had choreographed on the homestead. On the back, he'd written a message:

Please: 1. Do not take special efforts to save life. Death is intended. 2. Return pack and VT Subaru (green) in south bound parking lot to Laura Waterman, East Corinth VT, 05040. Thank you. Guy Waterman.

On the same paper he had also scribbled six lines. They were from *Paradise Lost,* Book II. The fallen angel Belial is lamenting the "sad cure" that is the destruction of life, and asks:

> . . . for who would lose,
> Though full of pain, this intellectual being,
> Those thoughts that wander through eternity
> To perish rather, swallow'd up and lost
> In the wide womb of uncreated Night
> Devoid of sense and motion?

It would be sixteen below that night on nearby Mount Washington, and unimaginably more frigid given the winds. It was a matter of hours now. The sweat of ascending wicked away Waterman's envelope of heat. Involuntary shivering begins when a person's body temperature drops below ninety-five degrees. Below ninety-three, shivering stops, and drowsiness and apathy set in as blood rushes to the organs at the core. Below ninety, the heart begins to balk, the breath grows shallow, the eyes dilate, and then, ineluctably, with majesterial indifference, the curtain descends.

When the map of Barra was brought back by the friends who retrieved his body, Laura Waterman imagined that she could see in her husband's shaky hand something of his spirit flaring in a final burst of verse as he waited on his mountain in the cold and wind, with the darkness coming on.

Swan Song

In a way, Waterman was too many people: Caliban, Ariel, Prospero; Melville's Ahab, Prometheus from the Greek canon; Milton's Belial and the Satan of Paradise Lost, who says, "Which way I fly is hell; myself am hell"—a line Waterman never tired of quoting. He had a million literary masks and metaphors to interpose between himself and others. "He could never just be Guy," said his friend Bonnie Christie. "He could not open himself up, even to Laura. The core of him was off-limits."

Not to say there weren't glimpses of it, times when the Hard Man went tender with the innocent joy of his boyhood on the Farm in North Haven. Maybe it was the wild happiness of getting up into a winter storm, or deftly negotiating a long line of rock, or rolling with the cadences of ragtime, something that made life seem like paradise again. . . .

Three weeks before he died, he performed for the last time at the Town Hall in Corinth. He accompanied a local jazz singer named

Danuta Jacob at a fund-raising benefit for the Tabor Valley Players and the East Corinth Fourth of July Parade Committee. Danuta Jacob had been looking for a pianist and was excited to find one as versatile as Waterman. They'd been rehearsing once a week since the summer and were booked for a two-night stand, January 15 and 16, the concluding act of an evening cabaret. Both nights were sold out.

Waterman was keyed up about the show. He paid to have the piano in the Corinth Town Hall professionally tuned and he took the even more extravagant step of renting a tuxedo from College Formals in Lebanon, New Hampshire.

On the evening of the first show, he came into the library at East Corinth and asked if he could change into his tux in the bathroom. "It took him forty-five minutes to put it on," said Janine Moore, the librarian. "He was wringing his hands and pulling the sleeves. Usually he would hold my daughter Daelynn in his arms but this time he felt he couldn't because she might wrinkle the tux."

They had worked out a set of four numbers: "Our Love is Here to Stay"; "I Had Someone Else Before I Had You and I'll Have Someone After You're Gone"; "Body and Soul"; and their closer, "A Good Man Is Hard to Find." All songs Waterman had been playing for almost half a century.

As it happened, a videotape had been made of the final performance. Danuta put it in the VCR. There they were: she on a small riser, swaying in her long brown velvet dress, Guy in his rented tux, hunched over the newly tuned upright, his back to the audience.

His elfin form seemed hardly big enough for the music he was teasing from the keys. When Danuta finished the first song, Guy turned and applauded her. He had a big stomping solo on the next number, but when they had finished, again he clapped for her. It was all over too fast for her—four songs and they were done by 9:30. A photographer got a few pictures. Someone suggested they try out for Garrison Keillor's talent contest. A few days later, a letter from Guy arrived in Danuta's mailbox, expressing his gratitude to her for helping him fulfill a lifelong dream of performing with a singer.

"I was looking at it as our debut," Danuta said. "But he was looking at it as his grand finale. I can only guess that what was going on that night was a celebration of things never completed for him. Maybe he wanted the world to see that side of him one last time."

She dabbed her eyes. On the tape, she and Guy had just finished

"A Good Man Is Hard to Find." The audience was clapping, and Danuta was trying to coax Guy onto the stage to acknowledge the applause. She almost had to tug him up there. It was poignant to see the mix of shyness and happiness when he actually turned and stood before the crowd to receive the sweet balm of their acclaim. It was as if he couldn't believe he had done anything to deserve it. But then maybe he had, and the uncertainty of not knowing made him awkward. Or perhaps it was just the strange textures of the rented tux, and knowing that he was up past his bedtime, and that he had to change and make the hike home to the cabin in the woods. The ovation petered out, and with no further ceremony, he slipped quietly from the stage.

JUNE 2000

A Man's Land

by Rick Telander

W HAT IS A CABIN? What is a piece of land to call your
own? Maybe they are nothing but fear calmed, the flattering of a male ego that craves possessions as a barricade
against the approaching dark. But if they are plainly false, why do they
have such resonance for so many men? I am still surprised at how I
came to have my own, at how inexorable it all seems, at how good luck
is just ruin turned over.

My position coach, Tom Bettis, was a nice man, and so I appreciated
his seeking me out as I headed for chow and telling me Hank Stram
wanted to see me. Old Henry, with his toupee and his rolled-up programs and semimanic smile, was the coach and general manager of
the Kansas City Chiefs. If he wanted to see me, cool.

Coach Bettis, who had spent a fair amount of time trying to help
me understand double-wide formations with trips options, at that
moment had a tenderness in his voice that I recognized only in retrospect. "Oh, and Rick, take your playbook," he said. I'd be happy to,
because Coach Stram would no doubt want to go over some schemes,
since a bunch of guys had already been let go from the team and, as
far as I could tell, only Jim Kearney was ahead of me at strong safety.

It's the damnedest thing, knowing something so well but not seeing
it when it's right in front of your face. Stram cut me, of course. It was
1971. The Chiefs had won the Super Bowl in 1970; they didn't need
me. I'm letting you go early, Stram said, so you can get on to that law
school that's waiting for you.

Law school was bullshit. It was a negotiating ploy I'd used when I'd
talked contract. See, if Stram didn't give me more money—if Lamar
Hunt's almighty Chiefs didn't dig deeper—I'd just head off and
become the attorney I was born to be. I didn't have an agent, and one
of the players I'd met at the East-West Shrine Game had told me this
was a top-notch tactic. What I did instead was return to my college

room in a big off-campus house shared by a million guys in Evanston, Illinois, and proceed to waste away.

Party? Dear God, I remember someone using a bow to fire arrows into a bedroom wall; someone else leaping through a plate-glass window; an ax deployed to chop a dog hole in the back door; a band that cost $10 playing in the beer-splattered front room, led by a singer in a bird mask and a dancing girl wearing a Nazi flag and carrying a bullwhip. I remember drinking a shot of beer every minute for an hour. I remember a lot of things. Others, I don't.

After four months, I got one of my housemates, John Voorhees, a senior middle linebacker on the Northwestern University team and a hometown buddy from Peoria, to drive north with me. It was after Christmas, and I was sick of myself. I had a yearning that wouldn't go away. It had been there in various forms since I was a child. I couldn't describe it then, and I still can't. It's that nameless longing for rootedness, for security, for something real that is not dependent on another man's fancy.

When I was in high school, I had gone with a friend to his family's cottage on Madeline Island, in the Apostle Island chain, off Bayfield, Wisconsin, in Lake Superior. You have to take a ferry to get there. I love water. But in Peoria, water is dark, turbid, shallow, laden with the ebony runoff of the fertile plains. Lake Superior was clear and pure and deep and bottle-green. I nearly swooned. There was a beach on the island where we teenagers would go for bonfires at night, and exotic, sullen, untouchable girls from Minneapolis would lend a transcendence that flamed my love of the place even higher.

Now, John and I were headed north into the snow, vaguely aware that we were prepared to do something permanent. I was twenty-two, John was twenty-one. I had $3,000. He had about the same. My money was my bonus check for signing with the Chiefs, inflated by $500 from management's original $2,500 offer due to my ferocious negotiating stance. John's was a couple of summers' worth of construction-work pay.

We drove out of Illinois, straight up through frozen Wisconsin, and 350 miles later we went to a strip joint in the town of Hurley. We had a few beers and left after a dancer befriended us and I warned John because I noticed she had a beard coming through her makeup. We spent the night in a bunkhouse near a ski area, and in the morning we went east and farther north, into Michigan's Upper Peninsula.

Civilization all but vanished. We drove until we hit the great lake they call Gitche Gumee, the lake of my dreams, flash-frozen white and as jagged as a hurled wedding cake. Along the road were drifts of snow higher than our car. The ice on the lake was blasted into iron blowholes and moon craters. We could go no farther. Now what?

A man was shoveling snow in front of his lakeside house, not far from the Porcupine Mountains. Hello, we said, is there any land for sale around these parts?

The man's name was Knox Jamison, and—what do you know— he was a real-estate fellow, among other occupations, and, yes, there sure was.

We got directions to a spread about five miles from the lake. The snow was so deep it made me think of never-ending winters, of things frozen as hard and silent as granite, forever. The slam of our doors echoed like a sonic boom in the stillness. "Silence, in its way," wrote Mark Slouka in a recent *Harper's* essay entitled "Listening for Silence," "is fundamental to life, the emotional equivalent of carbon." This was silence. This was carbon.

The property owner, a jolly old farmer named Elmer Drow, drove us over the fields on his tractor. John and I sat bone-chilled on the lift-plow in the rear, the dry-as-Styrofoam powder flowing over our pants. We had no idea what we were looking at. Snow and forest went on endlessly in undulations of white.

In short order, I bought forty acres of snow for $2,000. John bought the eighty behind mine for $3,000.

Suddenly, I *had* something. I *owned* something. I could stand in the middle of my forty acres and holler or piss or dig a hole or do nothing at all. No one could cut me. I could not be made to leave. I was a king.

Forget that John and I were four hundred miles from home. That neither of us had jobs. That there might have been quicksand beneath the snow, for all we knew. The yearning had been slaked.

For $100 more, I bought the twelve-by-twenty-four-foot loggers' cabin that was rotting away behind Elmer's tiny house. The cabin was used back in the 1930s, when loggers were on the move in the U.P. It had sixteen-by-sixteen-inch white-pine skids, and in the spring Elmer dragged it to the top of the small hill on my land, and now I was a homeowner, too.

Gradually, I became an actual money-earning freelance writer in

Chicago, which coalesced with my work as a waiter at an Italian restaurant and as the rhythm guitarist in my band, the Del-Crustaceans, and amazingly, as it always seemed to me, I had a steady if small amount of disposable income. John graduated from Northwestern and did go on to law school, but I liked my life and, when I could, I drove my beat-up car to my land and worked at making the cabin habitable. Bringing in electricity four hundred feet from the dirt road was a major expense, but a boom box, a power drill, and a blender for margaritas are things I choose not to live without. Friends would make the eight-hour drive with me at times, and I would put them to work. We were all just kids, and hammering and sawing was a gas.

In 1973, I met a girl at a buddy's wedding, and we started going out. Her name was Judy, she was a great skier, a woodsy gal working on her Ph.D. in psychology, and she would get misty-eyed thinking about her many years as a kid at the Whispering Pines Camp near Mercer, Wisconsin. She came up north with me, too, and—Holy campfire!—here was the Whispering Pines Camp for Young Adults. In the summer of 1974, we stayed so long at the cabin, which now had a potbellied stove, a front porch, a tank for sink water, and a two-hole outhouse, that when we came back to civilization we had no idea Richard Nixon had resigned as president.

We would lie in the field in front of the cabin at night in late summer and watch the Perseid showers, and the streaks of light flaring toward the black-velvet horizon would seem to signal the end of the world. My dog, Leo, a beagle-basset mutt with a voice like a trumpeting elephant and a bulbous black nose scraped pink from mad sniffing, would sit on the blanket, head canted, and test the breeze for news, his wet nostrils pulsing like a shelled bivalve.

The peace was overwhelming. No light but the stars. No sound but the wind. It could reach up instantly with its splendor and its Wordsworthian intimations of mortality and bring me to a state of soft despair that seemed then and now to be sparked by the intuitive knowledge that beauty and loss are inseparable. "Security is mostly a superstition," wrote Helen Keller. I knew that. But this land was mine, and that counted for something. It had to. The despair would pass, and even if it lingered as melancholy, I had the solace of knowing I had found a place that provoked such unrest.

Did I say this was an easy place? I did not. Winter lasts about half the year in the U.P. I have a photo of myself in January 1977, standing atop a drift in Calumet, wearing jeans, a flannel shirt, and a pair of bright yellow boots, casually leaning against the twelve-foot-high eaves of an abandoned building. Summer temperatures can climb into the nineties, and as for the mosquitoes, well, there are T-shirts declaring them Michigan's state bird.

On certain hot July days, the black flies come out of wherever it is they vanish to and chew at your ankles and neck like tiny winged weasels. We call these "fly days," and we have learned not to fight the elements but just to stay inside or take a long drive or hole up in a bar. Fly days have to do with temperature and humidity and barometric pressure and wind, but they also have to do with the mindless evolutionary imperative of living things. Nature isn't sweet. People who come to a place like this and expect San Diego–style outdoor comfort are in trouble. One night I felt my little cabin shaking and heard a strange sawing sound. Terrified, I nevertheless tiptoed outside and shone a light back on the building. A porcupine waddled away. It had been eating the plywood siding. It had been eating my house.

There was a period in the mid- to late '70s when I wasn't certain my land would make the transition with me to full adulthood. Responsibilities kept me from jumping in the car and driving for a day to the cabin. And the thing about cabins is that they exist in places where there is little work and less business. By definition, wilderness is bound up with a lack of access. Maybe this land was a postadolescent lark that needed to be set aside.

Then Knox Jamison or his heirs, I can't remember which, opened up a huge tract of unspoiled, conifered land along Lake Superior, east of the mill town of Ontonagon and about ten miles from my loggers' hut. With another friend, a Chicago hoops pal named Arnie Palder, I bought a parcel that was one thousand feet deep and had three hundred feet of beachfront. It was 1977, and the price was a steep $15,000, but the soaring white pines and balsams and hemlocks made it seem worthwhile. The only way in was via a dirt road that ran two miles off the last little piece of two-lane blacktop. There was no electricity, no sewer, no driveway, no snowplow service. But my God, what a beach! What a view! What solitude! I sold the forty acres and the little cabin for $8,500 and focused on life at the water's edge.

I married Judy in 1980, and then the children came. One, two, three, four: Lauren, Cary, Robin, and Zack. With them came duties and burdens the likes of which this erstwhile romantic Walden-ite boozer had never imagined. Judy and I took the kids to our land, but it was often a nightmare of bugs, thorns, sunburns, and bickering. By 1993, I had decided to chuck it all. The Lake Superior life was a vision, too far away, too unrealistic. Arnie, my financial angel, had never even seen the place. He'd only invested because I had asked him to help me.

Then something amazing happened. While walking through the woods on what I felt might be my family's last foray north, I noticed a neon-orange sticker in the side window of the vacant, rough-milled white-pine cabin on the parcel of land just east of ours. I went closer: SEIZED BY THE U.S. GOVERNMENT, it said. Some drug thing had happened to the owner, and the Feds had snatched the joint.

What if we bought it at auction? What if we had our own permanent shelter just fifty feet from the silent, golden beach—a cozy structure built on a stone foundation and not just a flung-together clubhouse resting on skids, a place where the kids could take their naps, where we could put our stuff, about which we could actually say, "This is our house in the woods"?

I did it. Sixty thousand dollars for the unheated, uninsulated, electricity-free cabin with its crude kitchen, two tiny bedrooms and loft, and 170 feet of beachfront. Then I tracked down, in Arizona, the owner of the 330 feet next to the parcel and for $40,000 bought that piece, too. Now I was land-mad. I had seventeen acres and more than an eighth of a mile of beachfront. I was in debt, having borrowed half the money from Arnie, but I was happy.

My family and I went up in the spring and the summer and the early fall, and we all worked on the house. We painted the inside, flushed the bats out of the chimney and the carpenter ants from the beams, chopped and stacked wood, and planted prairie grass and baby trees in the sandy spaces between the towering pines. I went even further into hock and once again had the electric boys bring in power. I hired a local contractor, an agreeable, bespectacled man who went out on snowshoes to hunt winter rabbits with a handgun, and he built us a dormer on each side of the loft so the place wasn't dark and hotter than hell in the summer. He plumbed our bathroom and put in real windows downstairs and cleared all the mice out of the walls and insulated everything.

The kids suddenly found the U.P. intriguing. They hiked and swam in the sun and played board games on rainy days. They met kids from

Minnesota and Madison, Wisconsin, who camped with their families without amenities a quarter mile to the west. My kids had pop in the fridge and soft beds at night. They brought friends from home with them and eagerly pointed out the northern lights in August and the beaver dams and the fisher tracks and the carnivorous pitcher plants and cranberries in the bog. They pointed out things they'd detested, or had claimed to detest, only months before.

Over time, we all grew more involved with the neighbors. It was the kids who drew us closer, of course. The Schneiders—Dan and Nell— were the patriarch and matriarch of the Wilder, McCarthy, Harrison, and Dercks clans who camped in tents down the beach. The group had been coming to its communal property for years, much as we had, to get away from everything. But our paths had crossed more and more as the boys and girls in our families mingled in the familiar barn dance of pre- and full-blown adolescence. After years of only courteous nods and howdys, the adults realized we had much in common. After all, who but kindred spirits would even come to this place?

There is no desire among any of us for dinner parties or the grating civilities of "normal" society. But the beach volleyball games between girls and boys, teens and geezers, the sober and the Old Style–fueled; the singalongs and the marshmallow roasts under gaping skies—these have become our shared rituals. And what was once an urge, an unexamined whim, an exercise in uncertainty, is now a family heirloom, darn near an estate. The land and the cabin are abruptly a tradition.

Once you have land, tinkering and building can go on forever. Last year, we built a sauna in a stand of trees ten yards from the lake. It has an honest-to-God wood-burning Finnish stove in it and a hand pump that sucks crystal-clear water through a pipe pounded into the floor of Superior. In the winter, we had a fine time heating up and then standing outside in the ever-falling snow, plumes of steam rising from our bodies like little fog banks into the speckled dark. Last summer, we bolted out of the cedar hut and ran like superheated banshees to cool off in the lake.

With the help of a sturdy neighbor from far down the beach, a world-class fast-pitch-softball-pitcher-turned-judge, one of only a couple of year-round residents for thirty miles to the east, I recently sank two thirteen-foot, three-hundred-pound white-pine logs in cemented holes at the head of our dirt driveway. I peeled the bark from each with an antique draw knife—the only kind there is—slathered the wood with preservative, and placed a trimmed, arched, sanded twenty-foot red-pine sapling across their tops. I secured the sapling to the logs with foot-long stove bolts and then lashed everything together with half-inch hemp rope. I know how to lash because I had been a Star Boy Scout on his way to Life when hormones and organized sports kicked in. Another thing I had done as a Scout was to study an anthill for an hour without moving. I plan to do that again next summer, to see once more what happens to social creatures who cannot stand to be away from their brethren.

Three miles down the beach, past both the Firesteel and the Flintsteel rivers, I found a five-foot spar of wave-sanded oak. I carried it home, routed the name "Telander" in the middle, and had each of the kids paint a symbol that reminded her or him of our place. Lauren painted a pine tree. Cary painted the sun. Robin painted the North Star. Zack painted a happy-faced head with sprouting hair and limbs that protruded like sticks from a potato. The sign hangs on chains from the red pine, and it is a joy to see whenever I pass beneath.

A place like mine, like ours, is inconvenient, maintenance-heavy, and probably unsound as an investment. But that misses all the points. Cabin life is different. A crackling, thrashing thunderstorm witnessed up close reminds each viewer that humans dangle in this world by a frayed thread. We learned that lesson too well this past August, when sixty-seven-year-old Dan Schneider—father of four, grandfather of ten, husband of one, and the best damn volleyball line judge on the beach—accidentally tumbled off a fifteen-foot lakeside cliff near Copper Harbor during a family hike and died from massive head injuries.

Our vacations ended early. We beach friends were startled when we saw one another for the first time all shaved and city-proper at the funeral in Milwaukee. Amid the tears, there were vows that soon we would throw off the ties and heels and fears and return to the lake to celebrate Old Man Dan and the things he loved. It was decided that a Lake Superior sunset would still be a fine thing. There is still so much to do.

"I have never seen a woodchuck drink," wrote the great naturalist Edwin Way Teale after he had retired to his beloved Connecticut farm. He theorized that plant juices, dew, and rain provided the animal with all the fluid it needed. But he wasn't sure. And because of that he was going to keep watching woodchucks. He loved the solitude. He loved the action. He wanted to be in the woods, alone with his thoughts, watching the universe. He didn't know what might happen.

Neither do I. But I know that even when I'm not there, my land sustains me. And I need it more each day.

NOVEMBER 1999

Something Wild in the Blood

by Bob Shacochis

H URRICANE DEBBY HAD BROKEN up, humbled by shearing winds into a tropical depression, trailing a steady, bracing suck of breeze that stretched east from Cuba all the way back to the Turks and Caicos Islands, where, on Providenciales, a young islander in swim trunks helped me lug a mountain of gear from my Turtle Cove hotel to his pickup truck. I asked the driver if he was the boatman, too, and he said yes, he was Captain Newman Gray.

"Good. You can tell me where we're going."

"East Bay Cay."

Twenty years ago, when I first came to Providenciales aboard the *South Wind,* a derelict ninety-eight-foot tramp freighter captained by Tay Maltsberger and his wife, Linda, the forty-nine Turks and Caicos were tiny, arid, sunbaked, and mostly useless outposts of the British Crown, still virgin turf for sportsmen, drug runners, and real-estate pioneers.

Now I was looking out the window of Captain Newman's truck at the resorts and casinos crowding Grace Bay, remembering when there was nothing on its austere sweep of beach, when Providenciales did not have a jetport or a store, only an islander-run rice-and-peas shop at its dusty main crossroads and a warehouse stocked with booze, frozen steaks, and a thin collection of building supplies. Nobody was around on the bay then except my wife and me and Tay and Linda. We'd swim from shore to a nearby reef and spear lobsters, perform ballet with eagle rays and sea turtles, and slowly retreat from the tiger shark, big as a sports car, that regularly prowled the formation. At the end of the day, we'd walk carefully back through the thorny island scrub to where Tay and Linda had anchored themselves and were attempting an unlikely enterprise for professional seafarers: Provo's first nursery and landscaping business.

"I know that place," I said to Newman, pointing to the new parking lot and retail office of Sunshine Nursery. I told him there had been a time on Provo when everybody—whites and blacks, and the West Indians especially—knew and loved the couple who started that nursery. But the captain had never heard of my friends the Maltsbergers and made only the smallest grunt of acknowledgment. My memories were beside the point to young Newman, who had migrated from his home on North Caicos to Providenciales to take advantage of the recent economic boom. I was simply the latest job, an American who wanted to be dropped for ten days on some ideal island, the only criterion being that the place have no people, no nothing, except flora under which I could escape the sun.

Within an hour we were aboard the captain's twenty-four-foot cat-hulled reef cruiser, flying toward East Bay Cay, a skinny sidecar that hugs North Caicos's windward side, separated from the mother island by a half-mile-wide channel. I had provisioned myself modestly with rice, beans, fresh vegetables, onions and limes for conch salad, beer, a bottle of rum. Otherwise I planned to fish and dive for my food, which is what one does, happily, on a deserted island in these latitudes.

Captain Newman jutted out his chin to direct my attention to a narrow cut, which I could not yet demarcate, behind a glistening bar mouth between the big island and the cay. "This is the road in," he announced, pointing to a slight taint of turquoise indicating deeper water—perhaps six inches deeper.

We came aground about a hundred feet off a rocky point, the terminus of the shaded white-sand beach I had been watching unwind for twenty minutes. We waded the gear ashore through transparent water, the two of us together hauling the heavy coolers and my main duffel bag, and finally it was done. I saluted the captain good-bye and then turned my back on him and (I hoped) every other human being on the planet for the next ten days.

As his boat receded into the distance, I pulled a celebratory beer from my cooler and sat down to engage myself in what could have been a most illumining conversation about the liberties we finesse for ourselves, but my mind went stone-blank with euphoria and I could only stare at the opulence of color—the blue of jewels, eyes, ice, glass—and the glowing white towers of late-summer cumulus clouds queuing across the wind-tossed horizon.

I was alone, as sooner or later we are all meant to be.

°   °   °

Texas, three days earlier. More than a few years had passed since I'd last bunked with Captain Tay, and this was by far the largest space we had shared: an expansive bed in a dim apartment annexed to the house in San Antonio that had once been his father's and was now his son's.

The captain's one-room apartment had the ambience of an exhibit in some provincial museum—the Explorer's Room—its walls hung with crossed spears, shark jaws, barnacled fragments of sunken ships, intricately carved wooden paddles, yellowed newspaper clippings, and glossy photographs of adventure.

I opened my eyes to stare at the ceiling, the morning sunlight a radiant border around the two makeshift curtains pinned over the windows, and finally called the old captain's name. No answer, and when I nudged him, no response. Captain Tay was a self-proclaimed dying man, an arthritic and half-blind silverback awaiting winter in his bone-strewn lair, and I thought, *Well, that's it for him.* Apparently he had slipped away in the night, fulfilling his chosen destiny by dying in the same bed his wife, Linda, had died in thirteen years earlier.

The night before, the captain had shown me a sketch on a legal pad: the outlines of a human body, front and back, with twenty-eight red *X*s drawing the viewer's attention to a catalog of the physical indignities Tay had suffered over the years: stitches, concussions, animal bites, punctures, cracked ribs, broken bones, and a shrapnel wound he had sustained from a mortar round in the jungles of Colombia while tagging along with his blood brother, a commander in the National Police, on a 1973 raid against guerrillas. Not indicated on the drawing were the recent, less-visible assaults: a bad heart, diabetes, clogged lungs, an exhausted spirit. He had also handed me—one of his designated undertakers—his self-composed obituary, the last line of which read, "He will be buried at sea in the Turks and Caicos," and his desire was that the burial take place over the *South Wind,* the ship his wife's ashes had been scattered over in 1987. As I was leaving for the archipelago after my stopover in San Antonio, I thought it was damned decent of the captain to die with my convenience in mind.

But when I came out of the bathroom a few minutes later, Lazarus was sitting up, pawing the nightstand for his glasses and cigarettes. He was already dressed, because he'd slept with his clothes on. As far as I know he had always done so, ready to leap up at a moment's notice into the god-awful fray.

"I thought you were dead."

"Any day now," said the captain with a spark in his hazel eyes, lying back down to smoke, his shoulders and head propped up with stale pillows. He'd been lying there for six or seven years, a veteran recluse, the lone survivor of all that he had loved, shipwrecked here on this rumpled king-size mattress.

I offered him a respite from the soul-heavy inertia of his retirement, as I'd done annually since he had hunkered down. "Come with me, Tay. Ten days on an uninhabited island. The sort of thing you and Linda used to love. What the hell are you doing lounging around here, waiting to croak?"

This was a bit more irreverence than the captain was accustomed to, and I could hear the growl forming in his throat. "I'm seventy-one years old, I'm an alcoholic, my legs are going out, I've buried all my lovers, and I've done everything a man can do down there where you're going," he barked. "Get it through your head: I want to die."

I tried to imagine him as he had been four decades earlier: a thirty-one-year-old man carrying a briefcase and umbrella, dressed in a Brooks Brothers suit, stepping aboard the commuter train in Westport, Connecticut, riding to Manhattan in the glummest of moods, believing he had traded his "real" life for a half-hearted commitment to virtues that read like a checklist of the American Dream—social status, upward mobility, material comfort—but were somehow entering his system tilted, knocking him off balance. He had married Barbara Rolf, a lithe, sensual blonde from the Ford Modeling Agency, a woman whose face was radiating from the covers of *Life* and *Paris Match* and who had borne him a son named Mark. Tay was natty, lean, dashingly handsome, husband of one of the world's original supermodels, and the father of a towheaded three-year-old boy—all this, and yet he was still a despondent man riding a commuter train from Westport into the city. It wasn't another company job he was hunting for, but a resurrection, some kind of a life in which he could breathe freely again.

He had had that freedom, had pursued it with Hemingwayesque flair—Golden Gloves boxer, three years with the Eleventh Airborne Division during the Korean War, the big man on campus at the University of the Americas in Mexico City, twice elected student-body president. In Mexico City, he had operated his own gymnasium, teaching boxing, judo, bodybuilding. Exciting opportunities had knocked relentlessly at his door. While doing graduate work in industrial psychology, he had led a group of scientists into unexplored regions of British Guiana, Venezuela, and Brazil. There was something wild in his blood that wasn't going to be tamed, no matter how much he muffled it beneath button-down oxfords and dry martinis. Being Texan was likely part of it, he figured. His family had come to Texas just before the Alamo fell, and his great-grandfather had been a civilian scout for the Mormons on their trek to Utah. On both sides, his family lines were heavily saturated with footloose visionaries and hell-raisers and uncontainable spirits.

Stepping off that train in Manhattan, he crossed the platform and caught the next train back to Connecticut. Off came the suit, the briefcase landed in the trash, and he hired on as first mate on a sailboat out of Westport that carried tourists around Long Island Sound. And then he was gone.

"All right, come die in the islands," I told him. "Save me the sorrow of carrying you back there in an urn."

"I'm not moving," the captain snapped, but then he shifted himself upright and his voice became sonorous with care. "You have a good knife?" he asked. "Something that will hold an edge?" He eased up off the bed to rummage around in his moldy piles of gear. "Here, take this knife. I want you to have it."

Ever since I had met Tay and Linda in Colombia in the early seventies—I was fresh out of college, a twenty-two-year-old tadpole who had decided to see the world—the Maltsbergers had seemed intent on teaching me how to take care of myself. I took the knife, just as three months earlier I'd reluctantly taken the pistol he'd been trying to give me for years.

"Any advice, Captain?"

"Keep your matches dry."

Then I held him—this man who had taught me the vocabulary of freedom, schooled me in how it could be seized and harvested and lost, who had made his world so big and then made it as small as you can have it outside a coffin—and said good-bye to him. For all that, I could see that his inner world had never really changed, and that for those of high spirit, a life wish can at times bear a terrifying resemblance to a death wish, and a certain degree of metaphysical disorientation is bound to seep into the program. It was only that the seep had become a flood. You could walk on its banks all day long, throwing lines into the current, but the captain was indifferent to rescue, not dissatisfied with being swept along toward a promise he had made to Linda decades ago:

I will not leave you alone in the sea.

It was January 1971. Meteorologists call the type of storm that slammed into Tay and Linda in the Bay of Biscay, off the northern coast of Spain, an extratropical Atlantic cyclone—an out-of-season, out-of-place hurricane. Trapped in the storm's cataclysmic center, the ten people aboard their boat, the *Sea Raven,* watched in awe and horror for seventy-two hours as the fury doubled and then tripled in intensity. Their efforts to reach port were cruelly defeated by straight-on winds, with the tops of the massive waves humping green over the bow. Force 6 became Force 8 became Force 10. The mainsail blew out, and the captain, unable to steer, ordered the crew to chop the mizzen sail off its mast to bring the ship under control. The pummeling wind and pounding swells vibrated the caulking out of the boards beneath the engine housing, and the ship lost power.

They issued a Mayday, but the answer from the Spanish navy only increased their sense of helplessness and doom. They were going to have to wait in line; ships were in desperate straits throughout the bay, and resources were fully deployed and floundering. Not far from the *Sea Raven's* position, a tanker's castle toppled into the water, taking sixteen men with it. Thirty people were rescued off an American freighter that was going down nearby. A boat put out from the port of La Coruña to respond to the *Raven's* Mayday but had to turn back, heavily damaged. Linda watched the water rise up the hatchway steps as the *Raven* sank lower and lower into the colossal waves.

One summer night eight years before, she'd pulled up in front of Slug's Saloon, an infamous bar and jazz club in Greenwich Village, in a green Porsche coupe. Linda Johnson, a bony doctoral candidate in experimental psychology at NYU, was working in the lab at Albert Einstein College of Medicine. She also was a girl who'd been stuck too long in the convent of her education, and she was beelining from Mary Washington College to Manhattan, the center of the universe, partying like nobody's business and collecting so many speeding tickets in the city that she'd have to sell her beautiful car. She took a seat at the bar at Slug's, where Tay, back after a year in the islands, was running the food concession.

Glamour-wise, Linda was the antithesis of Barbara Rolf. She was a big-toothed, stringy-haired blonde who talked with a corn-pone drawl and a skeptically raised eyebrow. The daughter of a Virginia state senator, she looked like an egghead, her blue eyes blinking behind thick kitty-cat glasses she was always terrified of losing. What Tay saw when he came out of the kitchen that night was . . . brains, an irresistible, exotic quality, given the women he'd been dating. They talked just long enough to recognize themselves in each other: two dreamers in a barely subdued fever of restlessness, possessed with a great need to be on the move away from an ordinary life. She showed up the next night at a party at his loft, and they started seeing each other. She had finally connected with the man who would open the door to the controlling passion of her life: the ocean. When her mother suddenly died in 1965 and left her $20,000 and a Volkswagen, she and Tay hit the road.

"I have left New York—it's true," Linda crowed to a childhood friend four months later in a letter sent from Isla Mujeres, off the coast of the Yucatán. "With only two chapters left to write on my dissertation, eye to eye with a goal that has teased me through sixteen, seventeen, eighteen years of training, I pulled the reins on my job, my Ph.D., my career, all for a little taste of fantasy. After cooping up my spirit for so long in stiff-paged textbooks and overcrowded seminars, when it finally broke free it shook my whole foundation, like waking up with a dream intact, or falling through a keyhole you never thought existed. . . ." She promised her friends and family that she'd be back in several months, but that would never happen. Her jaunt, her waking dream, her infatuation with the questing beast, would last for almost twenty years.

And what exactly was that trip? A very old story, a myth, the type of tale humans have been telling one another for thousands of years: two enchanted lovers, a magical boat called the *Bon Voyage,* harrowing misadventures, a pot of gold—in this case sunken galleons in Cartagena Bay, off the coast of Colombia. They'd been together for five years when in the autumn of 1968 Tay got word that his ex-wife, Barbara, was dying of leukemia; back in the States, ten-year-old Mark needed him. By this time, Linda had fallen in love with Tay to the extent that she could no longer imagine a life without him, and their next few months were a whirlwind of sorrow and happiness: They were married in November, Barbara was dead by January, and before the winter was out, Tay and Linda and Mark were living together in

Dallas, where a network of friends had helped Tay secure a job as foreman of a highway construction crew. But as soon as the three of them reached a level of comfort as a family, the shared lust for adventure churned back into focus. Their recurring dream: to get a bigger, better sailboat and return to Colombia. Linda took classes with the Coast Guard and earned her license as a full navigator, Tay began to cultivate investors, and together they constructed a castle in the air called Sea Raven Enterprises, printed stationery and business cards (CHARTER SERVICE — SEAFARIS — UNDERWATER PHOTOGRAPHY — SALVAGE — CRUISING — MOVIES — TREASURE), and sold shares of stock.

Linda had found the *Sea Raven* in Denmark, frozen solid into a fjord: a 99-ton, 110-foot, gaff-rigged-topsail ketch, a classic Baltic trader built in 1920, as beautiful as any ship ever put to sail. She purchased it for $13,000, and soon Tay and Mark followed her to the Danish coast. The three of them lived on the ship at first, out on the ice; then, when the harbor began to thaw, they set up house in a nearby shipyard and hauled the boat to dry dock for a year of extensive refurbishing.

And then, having sent Mark back to his grandparents in Texas and having welcomed aboard as their captain a former Dutch naval officer named Jaap Stengs, his movie-actress girlfriend (who had never been to sea before), and a crew of six free spirits, they were finally setting sail across the Atlantic, passing first through the Bay of Biscay.

By the fourth day of the storm, the *Sea Raven* was drifting aimlessly in sixty-foot seas and Force 12 winds. The ship's main pumps had ceased to function, and two hundred tons of water had risen four feet above the bilge line. The nearness of death was like a dull pressure somewhere behind the freezing weight of Linda's adrenaline-wracked fatigue, and it translated into a specific dread, which she expressed to Tay: With the *Raven* about to go under, Linda feared they would be separated, and she couldn't bear the terrifying thought of being alone in the sea. Prodding her up the slopes of panic was the image of being tossed around—alone and drowning, with her eyeglasses slapped from her face by the waves, cruelly blinded at the one moment of clear vision. How could she swim to Tay, her one hope for survival, if she couldn't even see him? He calmed her nerves as best he could by roping her to him with an umbilical cord of sheetline. Come what may, he promised, they'd be together.

They waited for the ship to sink or for help to arrive, whichever came first. At last out of the howling gloom a Spanish tanker appeared. With superhuman effort a line was made fast, and the *Raven* was towed into the harbor of Gijón, where according to the official record of the Spanish port authority, "after having moored the *Raven* and put new pumps on board, Captain Jaap Stengs burst out weeping and was not to be calmed down within fifteen minutes. Then he fell asleep."

For five months Tay and Linda remained in Gijón, overseeing the repairs to the storm-mauled ship, but back in Texas the corporation Tay had started was imploding, riddled by infighting and embezzlement. The Maltsbergers' shipyard account was suddenly cut off. To lose a ship in a hurricane was no injustice, but to lose a ship to crooks and double-crossers was an unbearable betrayal.

There's a Jimi Hendrix lyric that poses what perhaps is the only question worth asking: *Are you prepared to be free?* Not free from responsibility, necessarily, but free from external oppression and internal fear. In everyone's life, it seems, there is a season in which this question is addressed or withdrawn, one's habits changed or calcified, one's dreams realized or rejected.

When I was coming of age in the 1960s, in the suburbs of Washington, D.C., my mother took to calling me, disapprovingly, a wandering Jew, implying that I was infected by some disease of waywardness that had the potential to undermine my future and land me in serious trouble. When I graduated from college in the spring of 1973, the gate finally opened on the mystique of other places, other cultures, *otherness* itself, and four months later, instead of securing an entry-level position in my expected career as a journalist, I boarded a flight from Miami to South America. My mother's suspicion was confirmed: At age twenty-two, I was declaring myself a type of hobo, falling from middle-class life into a pit of daily uncertainty.

Flying toward the San Andrés archipelago in the southwestern Caribbean, the cheapest destination available that was technically in Latin America, I was unaware that there were other people like me, people who might think of their urge to travel as an acceptable characteristic of a bona fide lifestyle. Romantics, to be sure; fools, possibly; escapists, probably. Dreamers who pursued irregular but nonetheless intrepid dreams of dubious value to the social order, their minds flaring with extravagant narratives. That's who Tay and Linda were, the first adults I befriended who had decided to step off the well-marked path and keep going.

"I surge into the waves of time, fascinated by the billowing soul of man," Linda wrote a few days before she died, composing her own epilogue. "What imponderable excess baggage we travel with on this trip bound for old bones and flaccid skin. Why ever let it be boring?"

I was grateful for the way she lived; she was the boldest person I ever knew. A life of bravery begins almost by default when you first find yourself oppressed by a low and unforgiving threshold for being bored. The only deliverance for the neurotic, the explorer, and the traveler alike is to throw himself off a cliff into the boiling waters of crisis. And then, to the best of his ability, to have fun.

"You know what's funny about our adventures all those years?" Tay mused as we lay back down together in his bed, smoking cigarettes and watching the Weather Channel play a mindless loop of Hurricane Debby footage. "We never had any money."

A friend, hearing in the Maltsbergers' sad tale a raw need to move beyond the agony of the *Sea Raven,* mentioned he knew an old gringo in Colombia who had a gold mine high up in the Andes and was looking for help. Never especially pragmatic until they were already immersed in challenge or folly, Tay and Linda went off to live in a bone-chilling tamped-earth hut at 11,500 feet, above the jungles of Bucaramanga. Tay and the old man struggled to refine a process for filtering gold out of the large heaps of tailings left centuries earlier by the Spanish conquistadors. They collected seven or eight ounces a week, but it wasn't enough.

After a year and a half the Maltsbergers packed their sea chests and descended the mountains all the way to the coast and beyond, to the San Andrés archipelago, where they had previously chartered out the *Bon Voyage.* This time, they homesteaded on remote Isla de Providencia, its barrier reefs dotted with the seduction of shipwrecks and the promise of treasure. On the edge of Providencia's central town they rented a two-story clapboard building called Lookout House and opened a four-table restaurant, the only thing they knew to do to make a living while they engaged in their treasure hunt. Mark, by then fourteen years old, joined them; he was being home-schooled by Linda and living like a kid in the Swiss Family Robinson, every day a boyhood novel of adventures.

The first time I met them I was a customer in their restaurant, having sat next to one of their partners in fantasy, Howard Kahn, a diving instructor from Chicago, on the flight from Miami to San Andrés. After a fabulous dinner of baked red snapper, Linda offered us drinks on the house and sat down with us, her only customers. I had planned to stay on Providencia for a week, but before the month was out Howard and I had rented a house together down the beach. Soon I was strapping scuba tanks on my back to claw through the ballast stones of the wrecks that Kahn and the Maltsbergers were working, inconceivably, by hand, the salvage operation ill equipped for recovering anything more noteworthy than a few copper nails and coral-encrusted pot-sherds lying half exposed on the bottom. At dinner each evening, Tay and Linda would open their mouths and it was like popping the cork on a magnum of rich stories. A year passed before I tore myself away.

Lookout House was sold out from under them, and they moved to Bottom House, the poorest village on the island, sent Mark back to family and to public school in Texas, and lived on the beach in a hut they nailed together out of hatch covers from a shipwrecked freighter. One day a precartel entrepreneur plying the trade routes between Colombia and Florida sailed his sloop into the island, and the Malts-bergers sailed away with him to the Bahamas, passing through the Turks and Caicos, which looked to Tay and Linda like their kind of archipelago.

On Grand Turk, they opened a restaurant, only to have the newly elected government fire the sole airline that brought tourists to the island. They took to the sea again, with Tay as captain and Linda as first mate of the *Blue Cloud,* a five-hundred-ton freighter that sailed from South Florida to ports throughout the northern Caribbean. But after a year of offering themselves up to every petty bureaucrat in every customs house on the trade routes—imagine bringing a shipload of anything into the wharves of Port-au-Prince and you get the picture—they bought a few acres of scrubland on Providenciales and jumped ship, their long love affair with life on the sea having ripened and burst. I think they meant to start another restaurant on Provo, not a nursery, but they inherited a truckload of pots and pot-ting soil from a bankrupt hotel and that was that. In their fifties, the Maltsbergers finally retired their quest for gold, more emblematic than real anyway, and returned to the fold of property-owning, tax-paying citizens.

My wife and I visited Tay and Linda in Provo whenever we found the time and money, and the last time the four of us drove the road between town and Sunshine Nursery, we stumbled out of the bar at Turtle Cove into the star-smeared island midnight. As we walked toward the nursery's mufflerless old Chevy pickup, Linda tripped on a rock—the roads were unpaved then—and in falling to her hands and knees she lost her glasses, which we promptly found and placed back on her face. The four of us squeezed into the timeworn cab of the truck, Linda behind the wheel. "My God," she exclaimed a few hundred yards down the road, "Bob, you're going to have to drive." She slammed on the brakes. "Tay," she said fiercely in her molasses twang, "I've drunk myself blind. I can't see a fucking thing."

In the morning we solved the mystery of Linda's sudden blindness: When she tripped coming out of the bar, the lenses had popped out of their frames, and they were still there in the dirt when Tay drove back to look for them. But on the road that night, her worst fear had finally materialized: She had lost her precious sight, the ability to see the world. She and I had climbed out of the truck to trade places in total blackness, not a light to be seen anywhere but from a canopy of diamond-bright stars above, with one big one blazing down as we passed each other around the front of the Chevy.

"God damn," she said. "I may be blind, but I saw *that*. Beautiful."

Seven years earlier, after a radical mastectomy, the doctors had given Linda six months to live, and she had lit into them, calling them frauds and swearing she would prove them and their voodoo wrong. She and Tay had been captaining the *Blue Cloud* then, and Linda had started visiting an experimental cancer-treatment center in Freeport and injecting herself daily with a controversial immunological serum she carried everywhere in a dry-ice-filled Thermos. Her cancer had been in remission ever since, but she could sense it was coming back, and it wasn't very long after that night together on the road that they would sell the nursery, which was prospering as the island developed, and Tay would take Linda to the States to die. He brought her ashes back to spread them over the wreck of the *South Wind*, which had proved so unseaworthy that it had been sunk by its owner, a Provo entrepreneur, off the reefs of the island, to be enjoyed forever after by scuba divers.

After the star fell and we started down the road again, Linda, staring blankly into the darkness, surprised us by asking whether we believed in life after death. If there was life after death, Linda wisecracked, Tay had better watch out: Her ghost would come a-chaperoning his liaisons with other women.

But there would never be other women, because grief, too, is blindness, sight fading inward toward memory, and the captain was too
heartsick ever to care to begin again.

"Last chance, Tay. You coming with me?"

No, he wasn't, not today.

On East Bay Cay I savored the exquisite waste of time, time that other
people were using to prosper in the world, time forged by others into
progress and still others into dreams. I dove for lobster and conch,
speared snapper, fly-fished for barracuda just for the violence of the
hookup. Down in the sand I walked for miles, beachcombing in a
daze. I scribbled dry observations in my journal as if it were a ship's
log, and I slept soundly every night, lulled by the constant noise of
nature: the far-off thunder of waves on the reef, the constant hiss and
flutter of wind, the lap of shorebreak. For ten days I did precisely
what I wanted: I read. Great books have made me unemployable; I
can't pick one up without completely shutting down my life. In this
respect Linda's influence continues to inform my days, for it was she
who introduced me to Gabriel García Márquez, she who gave me my
first copies of Peter Matthiessen's *Far Tortuga,* Joshua Slocum's *Sailing Alone on the World,* Graham Greene's *The Comedians.*

I knew what I was doing here on this far-off island—I knew how to
take care of myself, how to enjoy myself—but I couldn't quite explain
to myself why I had come, what I was looking for. Perhaps it was only
a rehearsal for my final voyage with the captain. Or maybe it was an
act akin to a transmission overhaul, lubricating the machinery damaged by life's inevitable grinding down of the romantic dream.

I thought of Captain Tay, back there on the king-sized island of his
isolation, about his influence on how I'd lived my life, and about how I
might measure the difference between us. Technically, at least, we
were two of the most cut-loose people on earth: Americans, white
males, sometimes penniless but possessed of the skills and tenacity
that would always stick enough money in our pockets to get by, with a
powerful and abiding sense of self-reliance and self-sufficiency. We
were doing what suited us and what often made us happy. But Tay's
obstinate disconnection from a world he had formerly possessed with
such ferocious energy had unsettled me. Perhaps I saw myself doing
just that: disconnecting. What is it that finally conquers your appetite
for the world? Fear? Exhaustion? The formerly wild places now sar-

dined with stockbrokers on tour? Paralyzing nostalgia for the way it was? Age and health? Self-pity?

The epiphany of my relationship with Tay and Linda Maltsberger, the revelation that had become as clear and guiding as the North Star, still struck me as the larger truth: Whatever your resources, the world was yours to the exact degree to which you summoned the fortitude and faith to step away from convention and orthodoxy and invent your own life. Tay and Linda knew better than most that there's never a good reason to make your world small.

An image presents itself from aboard the *South Wind,* an abominable vessel with a history as a drug runner, eventually rehabilitated to run fuel between Provo and the Dominican Republic. In 1980, her owner coaxed the Maltsbergers into bringing the freighter down from a Florida boatyard. They hired me on as ship's carpenter to enclose the toilet on the stern of the boat—Linda never did get much privacy in her life with Tay—and to help them deliver the *South Wind* to Provo.

On the fourth day out we entered an armada of vicious squalls in the channel off the Exuma Cays. At midnight I took the helm from Tay, and for the next three wretched hours I fought alone in the darkness to keep the ship on course, waves breaking over the bow and foaming down the deck, lightning strikes erupting on all sides, white rain pelting horizontally into the windshield. Toward the end of my watch Linda awoke, stepped over to the radar screen, and proclaimed that she didn't know where we were, but from the looks of it I had steered too far west and we were about to crash into unseen rocks. Terrified, I changed course twenty degrees, and Linda, storm sibyl, as always so transcendently composed, walked out into the tempest. Sometimes I had to shake my head clear to see her properly. Her physical self, her sense of style—the clothes, the cut of her lank hair, the clunky eyeglasses—seemed so retrograde, so bolted down to the Camelot sixties, as if she still was and always would be some bookish chick from NYU who couldn't quite finish her dissertation on the urban insane.

After the ship's mechanic crawled up out of the engine room to relieve me at the wheel, I went looking for Linda and found her back at the stern. The worst of the storm had passed, and she stood in the cone of illumination under the pole that held our running light, her body swarmed by hundreds of shrieking birds that had sought refuge with us, swirling like snowflakes past the fingertips of her outstretched arms, landing on her shoulders, her head. It seemed for a moment they might carry her away. There was a look of extreme delight on her rain-streaked face, and she turned toward me and nodded as if to say, *How marvelous! How miraculous!* And then she retreated back inside to chart our position and bring us men safely through the night.

DECEMBER 2000

THE LAST TRIP
by Todd Balf

IF THIS WERE A normal Monday afternoon in September in Ketchum, Idaho, Ned Gillette and Susie Patterson would have been at home, together. Around two or three o'clock, they'd likely be returning from a long outing on the Fox Creek loop, a sunbathed, high-ridge trail just behind their house. In their office loft, a rare British Survey map might be lying on the floor after a morning recon of one of the dozen or so remote treks on their active to-do list. Gillette would be eyeing some forbidden range to traverse in Afghanistan, and Patterson would be shaking her head and smiling at her husband's bottomless appetite for adventure. Around sundown, they'd walk out the back door, don climbing shoes, and scale the Gillette-built "Mount Everitt," an impressive bouldering wall named for a tourist trekker's malapropism that Gillette once overheard at Everest Base Camp. The day would probably end with a session in the sauna, just off the edge of an aspen grove. If the phone rang, nobody would pick it up.

Since marrying in 1990, Gillette, the pioneering adventurer and world-class expedition leader, and Patterson, a former U.S. Olympic downhill racer, had fashioned a life that most of us only dream about. Even as they'd be clambering up Ecuadorean volcanoes, they'd have plane tickets waiting for an adventure two months hence to the Patagonia ice cap. They stacked trips on top of trips, thriving on touching down in some remote, rugged, and culturally exotic place. The photographs they took and sold paid their way. They were each doing precisely what they wanted to be doing, with precisely the right person. Patterson thought they were the luckiest people in the world. Sometimes she thought how scary it was to be so close to someone.

Now there are no normal days. On Labor Day, 1998, Susie Patterson is alone, trying to make sense of why her and Gillette's life together was torn apart by two gunmen near a glacier high in the towering Karakoram Range in the disputed Kashmir region between India and Pakistan. Sitting on the porch of the sunny mountain home she and Gillette adored, an uncharacteristically frail-looking Patterson struggles to remember everything that happened. If she can reclaim the details, she believes, she might begin to erase the haunting images of the final night she and her husband spent together. And then she begins to tell the story of how the adventuring world lost one of its giants, and how she and Gillette's family and friends lost "a fine, beautiful, and indescribably important person."

The son of a prominent Vermont businessman, Edward "Ned" Gillette, born in 1945, was an unlikely adventurer. He'd been raised in a conservative New England household, gone to a traditional New England prep school (Holderness), and attended Dartmouth College, where he established himself as a promising economics major and one of the best Nordic skiers in the United States. When he graduated in 1967, he appeared to be destined for modest Olympic glory (this was Nordic skiing, after all) and, then, a career in business. Instead, he walked away from competitive skiing after making the 1968 Olympic team, and he lasted just a single day at the University of Colorado Business School. Soon after, he flung off his rooted New England existence for the vagaries of Yosemite, where he taught Nordic skiing. Yosemite was then, as it is now, a mecca for the country's best, most impassioned climbers and outdoorsmen. Crossing paths with some of the expedition greats of past and present—from Royal Robbins to Yvon Chouinard—the good-looking, smart, and likable Gillette began to see expeditioning as his natural calling.

From his first major outing, in 1972—a three-hundred-mile ski traverse with three Yosemite friends of the Brooks Range in Alaska—Gillette demonstrated an uncommon dedication to accomplishing what he set out to do. The least-experienced member on that trip, Gillette wanted to finish the traverse despite the fact that an early spring melt had transformed the tundra into a slushy quagmire. His teammates outvoted him three to one, but just the same, he returned home already drawing up plans for new forays.

He went on to make an indelible mark. In 1978, he and three others circumnavigated Alaska's Mount McKinley in nineteen days, the first successful attempt since 1903. Five weeks later, Gillette and the adventurer and photographer Galen Rowell became the first to climb the 20,320-foot McKinley in one day. The following year, a Gillette-led expedition made the first ski ascent and descent of 24,757-foot Muztagata, in the Chinese Pamirs (the four expedition members were the first American climbers allowed into China in forty-eight years). In 1980, Gillette, Rowell, and two others traversed the Karakoram Range in winter, ski-hauling 120-pound sleds over three hundred miles of fierce terrain. On that trip, Gillette's first to Pakistan, he became one of the last foreigners to have access to the Siachen Glacier, which was later taken by India during the decades-long border war in Kashmir and has been effectively closed to outsiders ever since. Says Robert Mackinlay, a friend of Rowell and Gillette's who knew well the details of those brutal early trips: Gillette was "one of the original mountain iron men."

In the early 1980s, an increasingly self-possessed Gillette declared that there were no big mountains left to climb, and that the next-generation adventurer was going to have to make his own fun. Then he went on to do just that.

In April 1981, Gillette, his then-girlfriend, Jan Reynolds, and four others completed a three-hundred-mile trek around Mount Everest. Dubbed the Everest Grand Circle, their circumnavigation lasted for more than four months and combined skiing, trekking, and climbing at altitudes varying between seventeen thousand and twenty-three thousand feet.

"It was Ned's signature trip," says Reynolds. By that, she means it featured all of the elements that would turn Gillette into an adventuring legend: It was a first; it was a creative new take on an old story; it drew press attention; and sponsors lined up for it. More than a trip, actually, it was an Event. "There were always two sides to Ned," says Reynolds. "There was the part of him that loved to disappear into the backcountry and ski with best friends. But there was another part that loved the rush of putting together what I called the 'wow!' trip. You know, the whole ride."

Using Everest as a blueprint, Gillette undertook an unprecedented range of "wow!" trips. He tackled mountains, deserts, oceans, and jungles. He completed long, solo overland journeys and daring winter ascents on the planet's most storm-prone and dangerous mountains. He rowed across its most treacherous seas. He veered in and out of politically volatile countries that were either just opening borders or about to close them.

His impact was enormous. A graceful writer and a solid photographer, he recounted his many adventures not only in mountaineering and outdoors publications but also in such popular journals as *National Geographic* and *Esquire*. Within the adventuring community, he proved that it was possible to make a profession of traveling. In exchange for wearing a logo, having a sound-bite-friendly goal, and a guarantee that you'd get the job done, he discovered, you could get someone to subsidize your passion.

Throughout corporate America—long skeptical of gimme-gimme longhaired types—he established credibility. In so doing, he opened the door to a world long closed to adventurers, and hundreds came rushing in behind him. The increased access to sponsors helped extend the boundaries of adventuring by allowing more people to take on more ambitious and inventive trips. Never again would the bulk of expeditioning be scrape-it-together affairs; the modern adventure would be well planned, well marketed, and at least reasonably well financed. In short, Ned Gillette ushered in the era of Expedition, Inc.

Purists called his approach contrived. They argued that he'd sold his soul by associating with the likes of R.J. Reynolds, the tobacco conglomerate that backed the Everest Grand Circle. They sniped that he spent much more time and effort packaging and pitching his adventures than actually *doing* them. Amid all the hoopla, they said, the particulars of the challenge seemed almost beside the point. Many in the Yosemite crowd, with its code of noble understatement and outright anonymity, shunned him. But they were far outnumbered by the legions who were awed and inspired by him. Millions of armchair adventurers passionately followed his career, and countless others set out on their own outdoor odysseys, at least in part due to him.

In 1988, Gillette reached a turning point. He undertook a fourteen-day, six-hundred-mile row in a custom-made, twenty-eight-foot aluminum dory across the Drake Passage from Chile to Antarctica, a stretch of wickedly exposed ocean known for hundred-foot swells and extreme gale-force winds, infamous among mariners as the most dangerous sea passage on the planet. Although he successfully completed the trip (and the endless media and sponsorship obligations afterward), it proved to be the beginning of the end for the classic Gillette-led juggernaut. It had taken five years to pull off and drew on everything he had, mentally and physically. The trip itself was mostly miserable, though Gillette downplayed this fact in public. In the grip of thirty-foot seas for much of the crossing, he and his three-member crew suffered from near-constant nausea, and their self-righting dory capsized repeatedly. Shortly after he returned home, Gillette and Reynolds split up. Vowing to quit leading expeditions and inching toward a marketing and journalism career focusing on the outdoor industry, Gillette headed to Sun Valley in late 1988 as the guest of an old friend, Pete Patterson. An expedition mate on the first telemark-ski descent of 22,834-foot Aconcagua, in Argentina, Patterson hailed from perhaps the best-known skiing family in the valley. He had been a U.S. Ski Team member, and his older brother, Ruff, had coached the U.S. Cross-Country Team. But their attractive, pixie-sized sister Susie was the star—a former national champion and Olympic downhiller who'd finished fourteenth at the 1976 Winter Games and, as a reward, had been given the keys to the city and a lifetime lift pass to Bald Mountain, the Sun Valley Company's 9,150-foot signature peak.

Eleven years younger than Gillette, Susie herself was in transition, an ex–ski queen trying to stir interest in a new investment career. Coincidentally, she was also in the throes of a dying romance.

"Pete introduced us, and after that we didn't see much of him," recalls Patterson. That first weekend was something of a blur. Patterson remembers tooling around town, generally goofing off, and going for a long run with Gillette—who took a shortcut at the end to beat her.

Meanwhile, Pete advised an obviously interested Gillette against getting involved with Susie; she was a handful, he warned. Ruff said the same about Gillette to his sister. "Don't you know who he is?" he asked. "The guy is insane!" But neither paid any attention. "That was part of the attraction," says Patterson. "Everyone was saying, 'Oh, God, not these two.'"

At the weekend's end, Patterson remembers, Gillette said to her, "Come travel with me." Just a few months later, they were standing atop Washington's Mount Rainier, having caused a minor commotion among guides and other climbers as they romped their way to the summit of the heavily glaciated, deeply crevassed giant, unroped and in sneakers. Asked what she wanted to do next, Patterson innocently replied that she wanted to ascend a major peak.

"That's all Ned needed to hear," says Patterson, who'd barely spent even a night in a tent. "He said he knew the perfect mountain." In April of the following year, they were smuggled into Chinese-occupied Tibet to secretly climb Gurla Mandhata, a 25,355-foot peak known locally as Trouble Mountain. They evaded police checkpoints by trekking at night, got lost, ran out of food, and caught a glimpse of a snow leopard. Patterson thrilled to the adventure of it. At 21,000 feet, she was a mile higher than she'd ever been. She decided not to climb on, but she urged Gillette to do so. It was one of the last times they would do anything separately.

On August 18, 1990, on a perfect, blue-sky day in one of the prettiest mountain towns in the world, Gillette and Patterson were married in Sun Valley. The Sun Valley Company, in an unprecedented exception, allowed the couple to hold their reception at the landmark Round House lodge, high on Bald Mountain. A fleet of Suburbans ushered about fifty guests up the hill. Patterson was inclined to hold a more private affair, but she couldn't argue with Gillette's desire to go whole-hog. From the Round House, the view into the surrounding Sawtooths was limitless. "The feeling then, and maybe even more so later," says Patterson, "was that we were two kids playing in this great big world."

In the years immediately following, Gillette and Patterson ticked off dream trip after dream trip. At least one of the outings was vintage Gillette: a high-profile, multisponsored mega-adventure. In 1993, the couple set out to retrace Marco Polo's Silk Road route on a six-month, five-thousand-mile overland journey via camel caravan. They completed the trip, but it fell short of their expectations: Exotic as it seemed, much of the desert travel was tedious, crossing, as it did, vast seas of sand. Upon their return home, Gillette struggled to tell the story. When a major assignment with *National Geographic* fell through, a disappointed Gillette focused again on the reassessment he'd begun earlier. "It was a big transition," says Patterson. "Ned started out on his first trip because it was beautiful and challenging and honest and pure, and then he went through this other stuff that made him what he was. Ultimately, I think, he came to realize he was just missing too much."

The couple began to gravitate toward a new style of travel—a form of hiking and mountaineering they dubbed "ultimate trekking." They trekked where others didn't (or wouldn't) and—traveling super-lightweight and exclusively as a pair—they covered ground faster than most. (Gillette liked to joke that the diminutive Patterson was the perfect partner since she ate little but could go forever. The fact is, both ex-Olympic-level athletes were incredibly fit and mentally tough.)

It was High Romance on two levels. With minimal equipment and no one else to slow them down, the connection to their environment, they felt, was purer. And traveling strictly as a pair meant coming to know each other—and having to rely on each other—to a degree most couples could only imagine. Their new traveling style was also marked by the near anonymity they maintained; even family often didn't know where they were.

Some who knew the couple worried that they were courting disaster. Traveling so fast and so light in such challenging places, without anyone's knowing their specific whereabouts, simply wasn't prudent; the demands it placed on them were too great. But most people admired Gillette and Patterson's style. Says Sun Valley–based adventurer and Karakoram guide Gerry Moffatt, who would occasionally bump into Gillette and Patterson in such faraway crossroads towns as Katmandu or Leh: "I'd joke with Pete, and we'd be like, 'I wonder where friggin' James Bond and the missus are right now?' They were like these secret free agents roaming around Asia. We were all envious."

In the past several years, the couple spent far more time traveling than they did at home. In 1998 alone, they climbed Chimborazo, a twenty-thousand-foot-plus Ecuadorean volcano; crossed the Patagonia ice cap; and trekked in the Kanchenjunga region of Nepal. The ice cap was a particular triumph. Gillette had warned Patterson that due to extreme winds and the exposed terrain, they should be prepared to be pinned down in a tent for up to ten days. But they waltzed across much of the expanse in a matter of hours. "The weather was perfect," says Patterson. "I thought Ned was gonna have a stroke. He was screaming, 'It took Shipton [a famed explorer in the '50s] fifty-two days to cross, and he never saw a thing! Fifty-two days!'"

Even at home, the couple did everything together, almost all of it focused on their love of the outdoors. They ran, hiked, and climbed together, worked on their photo business together, ate virtually every meal together, and planned trips together. Friends said they were never happier.

The trip to the Karakoram was the couple's third to Pakistan. In 1992, Gillette and Patterson traveled to the Chitral region—in the far northwest, near the Afghan border—and came back infatuated with the wild, untraveled, and unrestricted country. In September 1997, they made their first venture to the Karakoram, drawn by the fact that it features the highest concentration of big peaks and long glaciers in the world but is far less touristed than similarly appealing regions, such as neighboring Nepal. The trekking territory they'd planned to cover—the Gilgit region in the Northern Areas—consisted of two parts: Nanga Parbat, the giant 26,260-foot-plus massif anchoring the western end of the Himalayas (about nineteen miles south of the town of Gilgit), and the Haramosh Valley, a little-visited but spectacular route highlighted by the vast Chogo Lungma Glacier (twenty-five miles east of Gilgit).

In keeping with Gillette tradition, the trip had its own unique objectives: The goal was not to go up Nanga Parbat (which had been done many times) but to trek around it via a particularly difficult route—something that few if any Westerners had accomplished. At the crux of that outing, at about the halfway point, was an infrequently traversed, highly technical pass called Khutsu. For the Haramosh Valley trek, the main obstacle was Haramosh La—a sixteen-thousand-foot pass with a deeply crevassed glacier at its eastern doorstep and a treacherous, near-vertical face to the west—one of the toughest crossings in the Karakoram. In 1997, Gillette and Patterson were turned back from both passes, winter having arrived a little early and they a little late. Dispirited, they resolved to return.

Of late, the pair felt an added urgency about going back to the Karakoram; with India and Pakistan once again amping up the border dispute over Kashmir, the entire area could be effectively closed to Westerners at any time. As a result, the 1998 trip was born. This time, the couple was determined not to let bad weather thwart them. They planned to arrive in mid-July, at the heart of the Kashmir/Karakoram summer. Returning was more Gillette's doing than Patterson's. He could never leave a trip undone.

Just prior to their '98 departure, things got shakier than normal in Kashmir. In May, the Indians conducted several much-publicized nuclear-weapons tests, and Pakistan responded with some atomic saber rattling of its own. Since 1947, the region has seen three wars, countless skirmishes, and an escalating level of violent guerrilla activity. After the Soviet pullout from Afghanistan in 1989, many of the mujahideen had flooded into the Northern Areas, including Gilgit, the gateway town to trekking adventures in the Karakoram. Islamic, well armed, and sympathetic to the cause of Kashmiri independence from Indian rule, the mujahideen had been playing hit-and-run with the Indian military for years.

Foreign trekkers were sometimes caught in the cross fire. As early as November 1997, well before the nuclear face-off, the U.S. State Department issued a travel warning cautioning U.S. citizens to defer nonessential travel to Pakistan. Still, despite media reports to the contrary, the areas Gillette and Patterson planned to visit were not considered dangerous. Nowhere in the State Department report was there mention of trouble in those regions, nor, in fact, could anyone recall any reports of violence against Westerners there. American commercial outfitters regularly ran trips through Islamabad, the capital of Pakistan, and through Gilgit.

It's unclear whether Gillette was aware of the State Department's travel warning (if he was, he never mentioned it). Patterson says she checked online but never saw it. In general, the couple didn't shy away from hot spots, but it would be hard to call them reckless. There were many places high on their wish list—Afghanistan and Colombia, for example—where they chose not to go because of an excessively tense political climate. Patterson says she and Gillette discussed the risk of going into Pakistan, especially in light of the nuclear chest-thumping, but they didn't dwell on it. An optimist by nature, Gillette believed Indian security forces would be crawling through Kashmir. If anything, he said, they'd probably be safer than usual.

"We had it wired" is how Patterson describes their strategy for handling the Pakistan transit. They would spend as little time as possible in the cities, where the danger was typically the greatest. On July 16, they flew to Thailand, where they spent several days lounging on the beaches of Phuket to recover from jet lag. From there, they flew to Islamabad, remained in the city for just a day, then went on to Gilgit, where they hired transportation for the brief overland commute to Nanga Parbat. To finish the business they'd started the year before, they'd approach Khutsu from the opposite direction.

Whatever anxiety existed prior to the trip melted away once they arrived by jeep in the lush Astor Valley. Gazing up at the soaring Chongro peaks, the pair realized why they had been so eager to get back. Taking advantage of phenomenal weather, they charged up the sheer Muthat pass in two days, then polished off Khutsu in three more. "It was a fantastic trip," says Patterson. "The Himalayas towering above us, just the two of us, being totally self-sufficient." Having finished Nanga Parbat so quickly meant this as well: They'd have plenty of time to take a second crack at the even more challenging Haramosh La.

*   *   *

The Haramosh Valley offered exactly the sort of trek Patterson and Gillette had come to love. Situated east of Gilgit and slicing across the base of a series of twenty-two-thousand-foot-plus peaks, the Haramosh saw few trekkers. Those who did venture into the area typically hired porters to haul gear and a guide to help negotiate a route across Haramosh La. A normal trip might take ten or eleven days. On July 30, Patterson and Gillette bought enough food and supplies in the gateway town of Skardu for about half that long. As with so many of their recent trips, they planned to complete the route rapidly, then get out.

On July 31, the couple hired a jeep to deliver them to Doko, the head of the trekking route. It took a while for them to get a rhythm going. As beautiful as the towering granite slabs that surrounded them were, Gillette and Patterson couldn't suppress thoughts of busting back to Thailand for some more luxuriating. "On almost every trip, [such thoughts occurred] at the start," says Patterson.

They woke early on August 1 and notched a solid eight-hour day, then camped in the pasturelands near the village of Gareencho. The walking was relatively easy, and the lower glacial regions were lush with trees and flowers. Patterson, usually the weaker of the two at the outset of a trip, was beginning to hit her stride. Late in the day, they caught their first glimpse of the massive Chogo Lungma Glacier. Though unsure about how they would cross the heavily crevassed expanse, they had fallen into a good groove.

A day later, they began making their way along the north margin of Chogo Lungma, asking the occasional porter they encountered for advice about where to cross. Following the locals' recommendation, they skirted the most commonly used crossing (it wasn't the safest way, they were told) and continued up, past the village of Bolocho. That night, they slept near a small miners' camp.

On August 3, Gillette and Patterson were growing anxious about finding a route across the glacier. When they asked for assistance at the mining camp, they received an unnerving reply. The man they approached began barking at them, asking if they had permits, where they were going, and why they were there.

Neither Gillette nor Patterson knew what to make of the incident. Were some in the predominately Shiite Muslim valley hostile to Westerners? Was there a problem because the pair had declined porters and guides, something the town was known for? Patterson, who was sufficiently troubled by the encounter to note it in her journal, told Gillette that she didn't really care if they turned around right then. Gillette thought they were probably overreacting. They decided to carry on.

They opted to take a stab at a crossing by following a trail marked by cairns. "We started across and we were doing fine, and then we just got stopped. The crevasses were huge," says Patterson. The couple dropped their packs and once again thought about turning back. Just as they began to retreat, however, they met a miner named Manzoom who was headed in the opposite direction, toward the village of Arandu, for work. Hailing from Kutwal, a village on the other side of Haramosh La, Manzoom offered Patterson and Gillette guidance on where to cross Chogo Lungma and pick up Haramosh La; following his counsel, Gillette and Patterson crossed the glacier successfully. They were enormously pleased, and that night, at the Laila Base Camp, the couple was eager to ascend the pass.

On the morning of August 4, as the pair set out from Laila, they ran into Manzoom again. He was returning to his village, he said, having been rebuffed by a rival clan in his attempts to work near Arandu. He floated the idea that they'd be better off traveling together over the pass. Gillette and Patterson liked him but said they preferred to travel alone. That was their way, they explained—no offense.

The ascent was one of the most memorable the couple had ever experienced—the skies spectacularly clear, the densest collection of the world's biggest peaks radiating around them as they crested the sixteen-thousand-foot-plus pass. "It was one of those days where you don't feel like you're working at all," says Patterson. "The country was just beautiful."

Unexpectedly, Manzoom was waiting for them at the top. He was sure they didn't know what they were in for. And when Patterson peered down their descent route—a plunging line through massive rockfall—she was grateful that he had stopped. Carefully, the three made their way down: Patterson and Manzoom in the lead, Gillette, with the heaviest pack, behind. Though Manzoom spoke limited English, the trio came to enjoy one another's company. The young, slight Pakistani and Patterson teased Gillette about being clumsy and kicking rocks down on them. When they got to the lower snowfields, the Americans assisted their sparely equipped friend by carving out steps with their crampons and aiding him across the crevasses. Four hours later, by 4 P.M., they were down.

In the green sheepherding fields beyond the runout of the glacier, Gillette and Patterson once more parted ways with Manzoom. The couple wanted to stop and camp there—the spot was magnificent, with sweeping views up to Haramosh peak, a 24,625-foot monster—as they'd done the previous year, before they'd had to turn back. Manzoom, worried about avalanches, wondered if they'd consider continuing down the valley, closer to his village. Patterson and Gillette politely declined. As a rule, they preferred to camp farther from villages; the more conspicuous they made themselves, the more they might attract trouble. Besides, they saw no avalanche risk. They'd see Manzoom tomorrow, they said, when they passed through his village on the way to the Gilgit/Skardu road head.

Out of gratitude for his assistance—and knowing he'd missed a payday in Arandu—the couple gave Manzoom five hundred small rupees (less than $10 U.S. but a significant sum by local standards). Manzoom was elated. He asked if Gillette and Patterson would honor him by stopping at his home and meeting his daughter. The Americans, who'd made lifelong friends all over the world in this way, looked forward to the visit.

That night, the couple was euphoric. They had knocked off the arduous pass and were just a half day from Gilgit. Two days hence, they'd be back in Thailand for a week, simultaneously decompressing and getting jacked up for their next trip, to Nepal, in the fall.

Gillette prepared a simple celebratory dinner of rice, noodles, and biscuits. As darkness fell, he and Patterson sat out under the stars, sipping tea and staring at the moon rising over the Karakoram. Just shy of being full, its glowing, misshapen, crater-scarred form struck Patterson. She'd never seen a moon like that before. Menacing, almost.

Exhausted from the day—the longest, hardest of the trip—the couple climbed into their tent early. They kissed each other good night, quietly exchanged "I love you's," and fell into a deep sleep. The next thing Patterson heard was a gunshot blast.

Then she heard her husband screaming, "Oh, God, my insides! My insides! I think I'm dying. I'm dying!"

It was around midnight. At first, amid the confusion, Patterson had no idea what was happening. "There was nothing I could really see. No blood or anything. I thought Ned was having a bad dream . . . I didn't know." Even in the wan light of the tent, she could see that "Ned had a wild, wild look. His eyes were glazed, then they rolled back into his head and he passed out. I was yelling and shaking him to open his eyes." After what seemed like a long time, but was probably just a few seconds (Patterson can't be sure), Gillette came to. In the next few moments—and without a word from the gunmen—a second and a third shot ripped through the tent lining. The attackers were taking turns firing a twelve-gauge shotgun. Neither blast struck Patterson or Gillette, but Patterson, badly frightened now, pleaded with Gillette to get help, to do something. But Gillette didn't move. "He held me and begged me not to leave him, but I still didn't understand. Things were happening all around us, fast and scary, and I was totally confused and scared to death."

A period of quiet ensued, and the couple decided that—whatever was happening to them—they were sitting ducks in the tent; they'd be better off, they reasoned, if they got out and sought cover.

But as Patterson sat up to put on her boots, a fourth blast erupted. Now she was hit, too. "It felt like a sledgehammer blow," she says. The buckshot sprayed across her back, depositing some eighty pellets into her body, from her shoulder blades to the small of her back. "Oh, no," said Gillette. "They got you, too." It was then that she realized that both she and Gillette had been shot and that they were both seriously injured.

Fighting nausea, barely able to breathe, Patterson crawled out of the tent, followed by Gillette. They scrambled behind their backpacks and huddled tight to each other. Then they waited for the next shot. Or for the attackers—out there somewhere—to say or do something. Nothing.

Five or ten minutes later, Patterson began to shiver from the cold. At roughly eleven thousand feet, the temperature was in the high thirties and dropping. Patterson knew they couldn't stay outside for long, especially given their condition. They had to get back in the tent for warmth. As they crawled toward the entrance, Patterson caught her sole glimpse of their attackers. Incredibly, a large man wearing white clothes was coming at them with a huge boulder hoisted over his head. Things were happening too fast for her to make out much more than his silhouette. The moon, which had lit up the night earlier, was now obscured by clouds. It was difficult to see even a few feet.

Patterson screamed, and Gillette, summoning strength, reached for a rock from their campfire ring and raised it. Stunned, perhaps, or thinking that Gillette held a knife, the assailant retreated into the dark. Gillette's desperate lunge almost certainly saved Patterson's life.

The terror was not over. Sometime later—minutes, maybe even an hour; again, Patterson can't be sure—the gunmen returned to empty two more shells into the tent (their last two, investigators later learned).

"We were crying, 'Please stop, please stop!'" says Patterson.

"'Take whatever you want! We're dying!'"

Still, the gunmen said nothing. The silence held for minutes, then longer. Finally, they were gone.

Gillette and Patterson dismissed the idea of hiking out for help. They were too badly hurt, and, besides, the trail would have been impossible to negotiate in the dark. They decided to sit tight until morning, when, they hoped, help might stumble by.

As they waited for first light, Patterson still didn't understand how badly Gillette was injured. "It seemed like I was actually in more pain than Ned," she says. "I had to keep crawling over his head because I had to throw up. I asked him to help and he'd hold my hand. I think he was in shock."

It's not hard to imagine that Patterson thought Gillette would somehow make it through. He had survived his share of close scrapes. In the early days, for instance, he had arrested a sure fatal fall on Mount McKinley by latching on to an old fixed rope inches from the precipice. People who knew Gillette—and maybe even Gillette himself—held that he had a particularly watchful guardian angel. Whether or not that was true, he was superb at dealing with crises. He never got flustered; he was always in control. In their years together, Gillette and Patterson had been lost without food for three days in the Amazon jungle, and they'd seen their camp ripped apart by a violent high-pass windstorm in Kyrgystan. "I'd be amazed when Ned would describe some near miss we'd had and say how scared he'd been," says Patterson. "If you were with him, you never had the sense he was scared of anything."

But on this night, it was becoming clear, things were different. They said little. "Ned was placid but breathing," she says. "We were conserving energy and focusing on getting through this. At one point Ned said he was worried, but we both had a lot of hope. I still never knew the full [gravity of] the situation. I thought, *We'll get help. A helicopter will come tomorrow.*"

Day broke on August 5. They had survived the night. Now they waited for someone to come up the valley from the villages below. Each took turns crying out softly for help. Several times Gillette managed to sit up, open the tent door, and survey the area in search of assistance.

Early that morning, some eight hours after the attack, it appeared that Gillette would once again cheat death. A trio of shepherds wandered by, and Gillette implored them to get help. They'd both been shot, he told them in English. Somebody needed to get to a phone, to get word to Gilgit and call in a helicopter. Patterson took comfort in the fact that Gillette was acting like his old self: coherent, in charge, knowing exactly what needed to be done. But strangely, the shepherds looked distracted. In fact, they seemed to be laughing at Gillette and Patterson, apparently mocking them for not getting up. "Ned was saying, 'We got shot! We got shot! We got shot six times! Get someone down! We need help bad!'"

Whether the men were confused by the scene or repulsed by it or were somehow "part of the game," as Nazir Sabir, the minister of education for the Northern Areas and one of Pakistan's most distinguished mountaineers, later wondered, nobody is certain. A rumor in Gilgit had it that the shepherds offered to carry Gillette down to their village but that he had refused and insisted they get a helicopter. Others say the shepherds circulated that story to deflect blame. Police cite the language barrier and say the shepherds had little context to assess the situation, since violent crime is rare in the Haramosh. Whatever the case, no rescue party materialized. An hour later, a young shepherd boy arrived at the scene and informed Gillette that nobody had gone for help yet. "He grabbed a handful of rupees, and told the boy to go down now, to go fast. *Now!*" But at that point, Patterson says, "I know Ned lost hope."

Gillette's condition deteriorated rapidly. Patterson placed her hand under his shirt and felt five deep bullet wounds in his stomach. The pellets felt bigger than hers, about as large as her fingernail. "I didn't feel a lot of bleeding, but I felt the shots and felt his heart. It was beating really erratically and his breathing was labored. He felt very hot." Patterson propped up Gillette against a pack and pulled off his fleece to make him as comfortable as possible. She asked him if he wanted his shirt cut open, and he barely managed to say no.

Around midday, Gillette stopped breathing. "After that, I just don't know where I went," says Patterson. "Nothing mattered. I felt like I was gone, too. Or I wanted to be."

For the rest of the day and the ensuing night, Patterson lay alone in the tent, waiting for help. In the period after Gillette died, she lost her ability to think clearly. Finally, a handful of villagers from Kutwal (a little less than two miles away), alerted by the shepherd boy, arrived. They were horrified by what they found. Many feared they'd be implicated in the foreigner's murder. The fundamentalist Muslims were scared to touch Patterson, a lone Western woman, and reluctant to put their hands on anything in the tent—in part because of their strict religious beliefs, in part simply because of the frightening aura of death.

Ultimately, though, the villagers couldn't abandon the distraught Patterson. "You are like a sister, okay?" she recalls one of them saying in halting English. "What is it you need?"

They offered to transport her to their village, or at least to remove Gillette's body. But Patterson only wanted them to stay, to not leave her alone. She hurt too much to move, and she wanted to remain with Gillette. She kept thinking, *This isn't happening to me; it's a nightmare.* Rationally she knew that Gillette was dead, but another side of her believed he'd suddenly move or breathe or say something.

As time passed and the realization sunk in that Gillette wasn't coming back, Patterson agreed to let the villagers wrap her husband's body in his sleeping bag and take him from the tent. It was then that the impact of what had happened hit her. Hidden for hours under Gillette, a grotesque puddle of blood was now exposed. Actually, she now saw, blood was everywhere, and hideous clumps of red-stained down feathers—blown out of his shot-riddled sleeping bag—made the scene even more macabre. Patterson cried out, turned away, and vomited. She thought about how she'd always promised Gillette's mother that she'd bring Ned home safely.

Patterson was overwhelmed by the burning in her stomach, by the weight of what she now knew. Vaguely, she understood she was at a crossroads. She wanted badly to give in—to put an end to her own suffering. But at the same time, something was propelling her to fight.

In retrospect, she says, she might attribute it to an im[?] Ned's spirit, or to knowing how devastated he'd be to [?] sen to check out. But at heart, she says, it was simpler than that. [?] some point, she just decided to live.

By the morning of August 6, it was clear to Patterson that there would be no helicopter rescue. Now, as breathing grew difficult (she would later learn that one of her lungs was filling with blood), and with no real idea of the extent of her wounds, she asked the villagers to get her out. Lashing her sleeping bag and mattress pad across two long branches, several of them formed a makeshift stretcher, hoisted her onto their shoulders, and began the four-hour trek down to Dassu, the road-head town. Gillette's body would follow.

The rocky trail—beginning at the north edge of Mani Glacier (on the Gilgit side of the pass) and passing through the summer sheep-herding villages of Kutwal and Iskere, and then Dassu—was extremely rough, and Patterson suffered enormously. The villagers had tied her in with climbing rope to minimize the jarring, but it didn't help much. She couldn't lie on her back or on her right side because of her wounds. She couldn't rest on her stomach because of her labored breathing. "Have courage," one of the younger villagers told her again and again. "Be strong."

About halfway down, the caravan met up with police coming from Gilgit; apparently, the shepherd boy had reached police headquarters at about 5 P.M. on the previous day. Oddly, the boy didn't mention that the foreigners had been shot. Instead, he said that they were badly injured, perhaps from a fall on the glacier. Police headed for the Haramosh at 5 A.M. on August 6. "He said nothing about it because he was afraid," says Khurshid Alam Khan, the inspector general of the police. "When we saw Susie, that was the first we knew there'd been any shooting." The rescue party included a doctor, who took Patterson's vital signs and assessed her wounds; she was stable but needed to be hospitalized immediately. At Dassu, they loaded Patterson into a jeep for an excruciating three-hour ride to Gilgit.

They couldn't give her fluids for fear it would worsen the buildup in her lung. They also didn't want to give her anything for the pain, because they didn't want her to lapse into unconsciousness. When Patterson couldn't take the agony anymore—with each rock the jeep rumbled over, the pain kicked up a notch—they finally relented and gave her an injection.

At some point on the journey, "all the emotions and the brutality and the physical pain blended together," and Patterson began to drift away again. What she didn't know was that the next five days in Gilgit would be an ordeal unto themselves.

On the morning of August 7, the U.S. embassies in Dar es Salaam, Tanzania, and in Nairobi were ripped apart by bombs planted by Islamic fundamentalist terrorists. The timing of the Patterson-Gillette attack, plus the fact that it had certain execution-style characteristics and that the assailants hadn't attempted to rob the couple, led officials and journalists to speculate about a terrorist link. With many eyes scrutinizing their investigation—including the F.B.I., the U.S. embassy in Islamabad, and the Pakistani government—the local police pursued the case aggressively. Botching it, they feared, could prove deeply embarrassing to them, their region, and their country.

Hours after Patterson reached Gilgit District Hospital, the police were at her bedside, asking for a comprehensive statement, beginning with the moment she and Gillette had touched down in Islamabad. Five policemen guarded her room from the outside; two policewomen were inside. Nobody, other than police and medical personnel, was allowed access.

Over the next five days, the police repeatedly pushed Patterson for her story, forcing her to rehash the episode over and over. When she became emotional, they sometimes rebuked her for not being strong enough. Increasingly, Patterson felt as if she were being interrogated, but for days the authorities kept at it, their suggestion that the couple may have been victims of an international terrorist incident convincing her to continue to fully cooperate.

Gilgit police had first notified the U.S. embassy in Islamabad about what had happened to Gillette and Patterson late on Thursday, August 6. Around 1 A.M. EST on August 7, the embassy notified the respective families. Neither family knew any of the details—they were told only that Gillette had been killed and that Patterson was seriously but not life-threateningly wounded—and their initial attempts to contact Susie were unsuccessful, due to phone problems in Gilgit. Frustrated and painfully aware of how alone and scared Patterson must be, both families took action.

Gillette's sister, Debbie, contacted friends from the San Francisco–

based Geographic Expeditions, one of the foremost U.S. outfitters in Asia, who attempted to call in guide friends from Gilgit to serve as local advocates until family and embassy help arrived. One guide, Amjad Ayub, went directly to the hospital. With security so tight, though, he was refused entry; only when he returned with a fax from the Gillette family was he allowed to enter. Though Patterson knew Ayub only remotely, he was still the first nonstranger she'd seen since the ordeal started.

"I just said words of sorry and she cried for a bit," says Ayub. "Then she relaxed and started telling me about Ned and the kind of adventurer he was, and how very happy he'd been the last couple of years."

In Sun Valley, Patterson's brothers met at the family house. Their first priority was getting Susie out of Pakistan. They decided that Pete, an experienced expedition leader in Asia, would go there, solo. Susie's other brothers, Ruff and Matt, her sister, Barby, and their mother, Joanie, would work the phones and double-check Susie's medical treatment in Gilgit with local physicians. After collecting emergency medical supplies, Pete boarded a plane for L.A., where he obtained a visa and caught a flight to Pakistan.

Gilgit police announced that, on the night of August 8, they'd arrested two suspects, from Kutwal. They'd also recovered the weapon, an ancient twelve-gauge shotgun. According to the police, local villagers, appalled at the crime, had given up the perpetrators. Far from terrorists, the suspects—Abid Hussain and Naun Heshel—turned out to be ordinary farmers. In a signed confession obtained shortly after their arrest, they said they intended to murder Gillette and Patterson, then take their money and gear. They'd never done anything like this before, they said, but they'd had tea that day with Manzoom, whom they had run into after his trek with the couple. Manzoom innocently related the events of the day, including the fact that he'd been paid five hundred small rupees by a well-outfitted (by local measures) Western couple. Hussain, the older of the two, hatched the plan after Manzoom had gone, then convinced Heshel to assist him. Knowing the remoteness of Gillette and Patterson's campsite, the men believed they could kill them and dump their bodies in a crevasse or in a ravine, never to be found. Police said they didn't find it unusual that the assailants hadn't said anything during the attack, or that they hadn't attempted to confront Patterson and Gillette; they were rank

amateurs. When the couple put up a fight—and ultimately survived—the gunmen, who were out of ammunition, simply panicked
and fled.

There were almost no discrepancies between Patterson's statement
and the farmers' confession, but the police ceaselessly attempted to tie
up what few loose ends remained. Patterson was increasingly frustrated that the police wouldn't tell her when she could leave for Islamabad and more-advanced care. Though doctors in Gilgit said she was
going to be okay, she had pain in both lungs and in her kidneys, and she
had difficulty breathing. X rays revealed blood in one lung, but the
local doctors believed it would clear up on its own.

By then, both the Patterson and Gillette families had spoken to Patterson by phone, and they knew she was growing desperate. They began
pressing the embassy in Islamabad to do something to speed her release,
but the embassy had its own headaches. In the wake of the bombings in
Africa and the subsequent arrest of a Pakistani-based suspect, staffers
were gearing for reprisals. (Less than two weeks later, the U.S. State
Department, citing new intelligence, would order the departure of all
personnel in nonemergency positions at the Islamabad embassy. And it
would issue a new warning against all travel in Pakistan.)

Finally, on Sunday, August 9, the embassy sent Consul General
Bernard Alter to Gilgit. With Alter's additional pressure, the local
authorities agreed to wrap up their investigation and have Patterson
on the first flight out of Gilgit on Monday.

Because of Gilgit's location in the mountains, scheduled flights get
out only about 20 percent of the time, and when Monday came and no
flights departed, Patterson was disconsolate. Her brother Pete was
waiting for her in Islamabad, but her fate was now dictated by the
whims of Asian commercial air travel.

Susie implored Alter to start seeking other ways to get her out. But
on Tuesday the flight took off on time, at 7 A.M. Patterson walked off
the plane an hour later in Islamabad. Pete was dumbfounded to see
her disembark under her own power. It has occurred to him many
times, but never more than then, that his sister is one of the toughest
people he knows.

As for Patterson, when she saw her brother, she finally—for the
first time since she'd said good night to her husband eight days earlier—felt safe again. On August 17, Susie Patterson and her brother
boarded their flight home. Connecting through London and San

Francisco, they touched down in Ketchum on August 18. It would have been Ned and Susie's eighth wedding anniversary.

Back in Ketchum, the Labor Day weekend is warm, the last gasp of summer. Tourists, crowded in for the town's Wagon Days festival, are everywhere. Come Tuesday, the town will empty out until ski season and go back to the way the locals like it.

Both in Pakistan and in the United States, the excited talk of conspiracies has all but died. For a time, a story circulated in the U.S. climbing community that Gillette might have been assassinated, perhaps because of his occasional criticism of the political situation in Tibet. The theory was a stretch, especially given Gillette's relative anonymity in recent years, but an American trekker who came across Gillette and Patterson days before the attack helped fuel the rumor. He told his family in a brief phone call from the road that Gillette's relations with villagers in the Haramosh seemed strained. The trekker has since gone into the Tibetan mountains for a six-month journey, but one could speculate that he was around at the time of the mining-camp incident and that that was what he was picking up on.

Investigations by Pakistani police, the U.S. embassy, and the F.B.I. unequivocally conclude that there is no evidence to support claims that the attack was religiously or politically motivated. "You have to understand," says Bernard Alter, "the people in that part of the world who kill people do what they do very well. This was not a hit job. This was an utterly amateurish, ill-thought-out murder-robbery attempt."

In Gilgit there is widespread support for making examples of Hussain and Heshel by publicly hanging them. By press time, the investigation was completed, and the case now rests before the judicial magistrate for the Northern Areas; the men's conviction and death sentence appear to be all but certain. "They have confessed and are ashamed," says Dahira Yasub, a police inspector in Gilgit who was one of the few local authorities to provide some comfort to Patterson. The killers' contrition, of course, is small consolation to the victims' families. "I feel nothing for them," says Debbie Gillette Law. "The senselessness is the hard part."

Others, including Law's son Bryan, are much more openly angry. A twenty-six-year-old rock climber who was strongly influenced by his uncle, Bryan told his mother that if he ran into the killers he would make them suffer as long and torturous a death as Ned had endured. At the time of the incident, Bryan had been climbing a new route on El Capitán in Yosemite, where Gillette's career began. In honor of his uncle, he named the line Ned's Excellent Adventure.

Both in the United States and abroad, there has been a flood of formal and informal tributes to Gillette. Obituaries appeared in major newspapers across the country. Letters and calls poured into the Gillette family homes in Quissett Harbor, Cape Cod, and in Shelburne, Vermont; many came from people Gillette didn't even know but had inspired, from cutting-edge climbers to neophyte adventurers. Gerry Moffatt summed up many people's sentiments when he said, "Ned was a visionary who motivated a generation of us to go out and do wild things."

In Stowe, Vermont, old friends gathered at the Trapp Family Lodge, where Gillette had worked in the early '70s, to eulogize him. One friend, Dudley Root, recounted his adventures with Gillette and credited him with adding "five years to my childhood." Noting the eclectic collection of people and professions represented in the room—from physicians to photographers—somebody remarked that only Gillette could be the ringleader for such a group. Another amended the observation: "Ringmaster," he said.

Undoubtedly the most moving farewell was orchestrated by Pete Patterson. Gillette's wishes were to be cremated, but it's a rare custom in mostly Muslim Pakistan. In fact, in that country only the Hindus practice cremation, and only in the traditional Indian rite of a funeral pyre. Pete recognized that some people back home might see the custom—which, according to Hindu belief, begins a lengthy journey of reincarnation toward the ultimate goal of spiritual salvation—as primitive, perhaps even barbaric. But what he knew—and his sister, consulted in her hospital room, agreed—was that Gillette would not. In fact, for a man whose knowledge of and respect for the customs and belief systems of foreign cultures was as vast as anyone's, the pyre ceremony could not have been more apt.

On August 12, in a little neighborhood square at the southern terminus of the Karakoram Highway in Rawalpindi, Pete Patterson and a small, observant audience of Pakistanis watched as flames leapt from a spectacular bonfire, an enormous sun setting dramatically in the background. The next day, Pete collected Gillette's remains, then drove hours north of Islamabad, to a point on the Indus River where it widens and the crashing whitewater of its upper Tibetan reaches settles into a near-still stretch of honey-colored water. Watching it swirl gently to receive Gillette's remains, Pete knew that this part of the Indus—the only river to cut through the most formidable mountain range in the world—was the perfect resting spot for any adventurer, especially a great one. "It was the only time during the whole thing," says Pete, "that I felt this overwhelming kind of peace, and the sadness was just not there for a while." He said good-bye for everyone.

Susie Patterson's life, since she returned home to Ketchum, has been a challenge. Physically, she's coming around; doctors assure her that the eighty or so pellets, almost all of which remain in her body, don't present a danger to her health, nor should they keep her from resuming the level of activity to which she and Gillette were accustomed. Already, most mornings, she takes her and Ned's old jog on the Fox Creek loop. While the tears erupt each time she reaches the summit overlook, the running feels good.

Psychologically, the picture is murkier. Especially in the mornings—in the time after she wakes up but before she gets out of bed—she's afraid to be alone. Her brothers and sister are taking turns staying with her, helping to answer phones, return mail, and figure out how to work the woodstove. (One of the toughest and somewhat embarrassing things for Patterson to realize is how much Gillette took care of.) But eventually they'll all return to their own lives.

There are questions that nag, too. Each day she reviews a mental checklist, and, though she doesn't want to, she can't help playing the "what-ifs." What if she and Gillette had known about the 1997 State Department warning? Would they have heeded it? What if they had turned around when they got the bad vibe at the mining camp? What if they had agreed with Manzoom's suggestion that they camp closer to Kutwal? What if they had camped somewhere else—anywhere else? What if those shepherds had gone for help? If they had, would Ned be sitting next to her right now? And on . . .

Ultimately, there is one question that bothers her more than the rest: Why—after all that Gillette and she had survived—why did her husband have to die so senselessly? Patterson continues to wrestle with the issue of the killers' motivation. On the one hand, she accepts the official explanation, that she and Gillette were simply the victims of a robbery gone wrong. But a voice in her head says there is something more nefarious at work. "I keep coming back to nothing being stolen," she says. "I can't believe somebody would go crazy the way they did [if all they were after was] to steal some money or crampons or something." In the end, she says, "It's just so sad, I don't really know what to think."

There are images, too, that she can't erase: Ned's wild-eyed look after he was shot . . . the menacing moon that hovered over them that night . . . the tent and the sleeping bag and the packs she left behind, all shot up . . . the pool of blood on the tent floor.

The more Patterson recovers, the more she understands the enormity and the uncertainty of what's in front of her. Yet what's clear, and comforting, is the fullness of the life she led with Gillette. "We had it all and we knew it," she says. "The day before all of this happened, Ned said, 'I don't think a day goes by when either you or I don't say how lucky we are.' I think that's one thing that makes me feel okay. We said everything we needed to say."

Having trained for years at elite levels, Patterson knows the drill for battling adversity: Take charge. Set reasonable goals. Don't look too far ahead. Keep expectations modest. To that end, she limits herself to one significant task a day, whether that's to return a phone call from someone with whom she and Gillette were friends or to look through old pictures of her and her husband's trips.

Patterson is determined to resume in some way the life that she and Gillette started and made flourish. She wants to travel again, soon, and she wants to return to Pakistan. She refuses to harbor animosity for the country. In fact, she credits the villagers in the Haramosh with saving her life.

In their office right now are two airline tickets for the trip the couple was planning to Nepal. The tickets are haunting in a way, but they're also a symbol of hope. Nothing is set just yet, but there is every reason to believe that before long she and, say, her brother Matt will touch down in Katmandu—or maybe even Islamabad—and then walk deep into the mountains.

NOVEMBER 1998

FORTY YEARS IN ACAPULCO

by Devin Friedman

Y OU WAKE IN YOUR dim hotel room to a day just like yesterday and exactly like tomorrow. That's the idea, anyway: that
every day down here be identical. Namely, sunny, with low
humidity and temperatures hovering in the low nineties. This is what
people work their whole lives for, and it's more than you could have
expected. You, a schnook from Poland who came over on the boat in
1920. But these are the facts of life if you're Mort Friedman, known to
some as Mort the Sport, to others as the Window King of Cleveland,
my eighty-nine-year-old grandfather. One full month in Acapulco,
Mexico, every February for the last forty years. You tell everyone: This
is the life, baby.

Wearing only your drawers, you make your way to the window and
throw open the drapes of room 1233 at Acapulco's Continental Plaza
Hotel. And there it is, nearly blinding you: paradise. The high blue sky,
the beach, the deck with its cul-de-sacs of chairs. And right in the
middle, the epicenter of paradise, the Plaza pool, a glowing aqua moat
that smells wonderfully of chlorine even from here on the twelfth floor.
The best goddamn pool in Acapoca (that's how you say it). They've got
fancier hotels up the coast, newer and more expensive. But nobody has
a pool like this, boy. The thought provides no small measure of reassur-
ance, the first in a day spring-loaded with reassuring things.

Your eighty-six-year-old girlfriend, Toby Fishman, is asleep in the
other bed, and you stop on the way to the bathroom and watch her chest
rise and fall, rise and fall. One day, twenty years ago, you woke, dressed,
and nearly left for work before you realized your wife's (my grandmother's) chest was not making this motion. Stroke. Never knew what
hit her, boy. But Toby Fishman is, thank God, alive and well. Not that
you wake her. She doesn't like to be talked to before ten o'clock.

You open the closet and survey your stacks of bathing ensembles.
Thirty pairs of swim trunks with matching tops, each of them brand-
new. This, in the logic of Mort Friedman's Essential Guidelines for

Living, could be called Rule No. 17: You wear a bathing suit once and then retire it forever. Like you told your son (my father) a few months ago, you've always been an A in fashion. Him? C minus.

You slip on a Nautica suit with matching Nautica T-shirt. Then you select from among your shoes, five pairs, all white. Rule No. 14: White is the appropriate color for resort-season footwear. You've got your white loafers, your white sandals, two pairs of white-and-tan saddle shoes, and a pair of unblemished white Adidas tennis sneakers that you pluck from the tree and slip on, sockless.

Dressed, you begin to assemble the necessary pool paraphernalia in the airline tote you take down every day. Toby rouses in the half-light and trudges into the bathroom to put on her face. She applies the foundation, the blush, the lipstick, the three spangly rings, and the heart-shaped necklace cast of platinum and coated in diamonds. At five minutes to ten, you are ready to exit the hotel room and begin your (if you account for thirty-nine years at twenty-eight days, plus, what, ten leap years, plus the fourteen days of this, your fortieth year, you arrive at . . .) 1,116th day of the good life.

Down at the northwest corner of the pool, Adam, the pool boy, is setting out the towels and lining up the chaise lounges for you and the rest of the crew, the dozen or so friends who hold court at the best goddamn pool in Acapoca. At one point, you were one of the young ones. Now you're the oldest guy in the joint. The elder statesman, the ranking member of the pool committee. But to look at you, you're doing pretty good for eighty-nine. Still drive yourself to work every day (you're a general contractor now), still pick up Toby, your girlfriend of nineteen years (what's the point of getting married when everything's perfect the way it is?), for dinner, still come down here to Mexico for a whole month every year. When people hear how old you are, they all say the same thing: Hey, Sport, what's your secret? How do you do it? And chief among the people who want to know your secret is me, your grandson. The bearer of your genes. I have asked you frequently. But you usually shrug, look away (to the left, specifically), and pat your belly. You're not overly verbal.

The only thing you allow has a palliative, rejuvenating effect on you is the yearly pilgrimage to Acapulco. I was in Acapulco once before, about seven years ago, on an ill-fated attempt at college spring break. I stayed at a hotel called, yes, the Copacabana. The highlights of the trip were: (1) getting robbed on the beach; (2) getting slapped by a *chica* at a discothèque; and (3) watching a kid known only as Brick jump from his third-floor balcony into the hotel pool and break his right hip to the applause of the hotel population. Acapulco itself seemed in a protracted state of decline. The old Hollywood-era hotels appeared to have been evacuated, and the new hotels looked like either prisons or beached cruise ships. Having been there, I am no closer to explaining why you return at the same time each year like a Galápagos tortoise preparing to spawn. You're not much help on this account: shrug, look left, pat belly. It occurs to me that, unlike the members of my generation, you do not possess the capacity to find each and every one of your actions endlessly fascinating and worthy of discourse. You do not see yourself as the star of a perpetually filming movie called *My Life*. While this is, in general, one of the reasons it's refreshing to hang out with you, it can become difficult to know exactly who you are, to understand your not-insignificant powers of longevity and happiness.

And now that I am down here recording your behavior like a lab scientist, I have become intimately familiar with the discrete set of rules for living to which you hew religiously. You wake at 9:30; you put on a brand-new bathing ensemble; you wear only white shoes. You fly down on American Airlines on the same date every year; you stay at the same hotel, in the same room, probably sleep on the same mattress (you have been given a "key for life" to room 1233). Before you leave home, you sever all ties, as if you were going off to war or prison. Don't send me letters, you tell my father before boarding the jetliner. Don't call me if the hot-water heater bursts. Someone dies, don't tell me until I get back. That's the essential setup. After that, as far as secrets go, you start by telling me this: Rule No. 36: Breakfast is at ten.

Your table is over by the patio door, next to the decaying piñata. Just like every day, Sol and Charlotte are waiting for you with fresh, hot coffee and a couple of sweet rolls. They are a handsome couple. Sol looks like a regal old seal, with his shiny head and silver mustache and bright white uppers. Charlotte has short, stiff, perfect blonde hair and wears a flowing pool gown patterned with geometric colors. They both have tans so deep they can only be the product of forty years in the Mexican sun. There's something wonderful about being among people not of the SPF generation, people who are, as they call themselves, real sun worshipers.

As you and Toby approach the table, Sol rises. He is wearing one of those Cuban shirts he likes, open all the way down the front. From within protrudes his magnificent round belly. Sol grabs you by the face with his two big hands and kisses you firmly on the cheek. You seize up a second, look left. Your hands make little fists. In the past, this would have been the entirety of your reaction to this kind of behavior. But these displays of affection have become kind of amusing to you now, though you're still a little awkward about initiating them.

You say, These are the Masers. From Chicago. They've been coming down here for forty years.

SOL: That's right.
MORT: Sol runs the biggest goddamn Chevy dealership in America.
SOL: In the world!
MORT: And that's Charlotte, the wife, there.
SOL: Found her fifty-seven years ago. Thank my lucky stars every day.
CHARLOTTE: You better!

Breakfast proceeds apace. The waiters, the busboys, even the omelet guy, know you by name. *Buenos días,* Señor Friedman, they say. Buenadia, you say back. Grease their palms with a dollar or two so they take care of you. You bring a Wet Ones canister stuffed with singles down on the plane with you for this purpose. Rule No. 26: You take care of them, they take care of you.

You order yourself an omelet, real hot. You have always ordered by temperature, and the temperature is invariably *real hot.* The waiter has no idea what you're saying, but neither of you gives much of a shit, and you seem happy with your eggs. Rule No. 13: Asking for what you want is even more important than getting what you want. You've known all these hotel guys forever. José, the waiter, you met when he was twenty; now he's fifty, with a little belly of his own and a slight wheeze as he pours your coffee. But the two of you bring a deep familiarity to your relationship, even an unspoken affection, which is the way you like your affection.

Today is Valentine's Day, a big deal down here. Partly because it's the birthday of Irv Gelden, the patron saint of the Continental Plaza. Irv has been a mythical figure in my family from the time I was a young boy. Irv is rich beyond our wildest dreams. He holds parties, very high-class affairs. Thousands of dollars of lox, you would say, hundred-dollar trays of salami, corned beef, anything you could ever want, which they bring down from California. Rule No. 12: You measure a party by the cost of its meats.

SOL: Gelden happens to be the largest purveyor of meats in the state of California.

MORT: How many butchers he got working for him? A hundred, hundred twenty-five?

SOL: He does all the beef for McDonald's and Burger King on the West Coast. That's a lot of beef, boy.

MORT: The man is a millionaire.

SOL: The man happens to be a multi-, multi-, *multi*millionaire.

But there will be no birthday party this year. A few days ago, Gelden's wife was moving through one of their penthouse suites (Sol: Big as a house) when her high-heeled shoe caught on something (Sol: A doorway, it was) and she fell and broke her hip. Cost them $24,000 to send her home on a private airplane (Sol: Five hundred alone just to send the golf clubs). You say, Can you imagine what would happen if you were just a regular schnook who doesn't have $24,000? You don't want to go to a hospital down here. They're like dungeons, honest to God.

There's a discussion about death. This is to be expected. When I asked who would be in Acapulco this year, you responded, Whoever's still alive. You and Toby and the Masers start to name the people who are no longer here. It's a formidable list. The whole Cleveland Jewish mafia you came with at first, all of them are gone now. You tell me that two people even died when they were already down here. Honest to God. Did you know you have to pay to have the body shipped back? Thousands of dollars it costs you.

There's no sadness to this discussion. The stuff (death) is too goddamned familiar to you to be all spooky and horrific like it is to me. Still, Toby sees it's time to change the subject, and she tells the story of the monkey.

TOBY: Used to be this, what do you call it, chimpanzee at one particular restaurant. You'd take your picture with it.

SOL: They had a cheetah, too.

TOBY: Well, this chimpanzee, he put my sunglasses on. And they took the picture.

You add, This was the best damn picture you ever saw. Everyone who sees it says so. You got the monkey with the glasses, and I'm laughing so hard. You could make a postcard out of it.

But inevitably the conversation boomerangs.

You say, This was nineteen years ago. Of course, the monkey's dead now.

At 10:30, Toby goes upstairs to the room, and you go for your walk on the beach. After the morning workout, you stop at the hotel's outdoor showers, cool yourself off, and head up to the pool, where the *real* hard work gets done. At eleven, you make your entrance. Everyone's there, right down the line. What ensues is not unlike the ceremonial greeting executives get at the office: Good morning, Mort, says Mrs. Weinstock from Michigan. Good morning, you say. Dr. Ruff, a Canadian, waves. Workin' hard, Dr. Ruff, you say, or hardly workin'? He replies, The latter, Mr. Friedman, the latter. Roberta from Jersey says, How's the leg today, Mort? You say, I had a rough one yesterday, baby. But I take a pill. Knock on wood it'll be okay. Roberta says, Don't put weight on it, Mort. Mrs. Weinstock says, Stretch it like this. You see Charlotte and say, Hey, what are you doing? And Charlotte says, A whole lotta nothin'. Just like I like.

The pool is doughnut-shaped. You used to quote how many gallons it holds. (I can't remember the number now, and neither can you.) There are portions of the deck that are crumbling, and the groundskeepers can barely keep the vegetation from encroaching on it, so bounteous are the sunlight and soil down here. You unload the airline tote onto your chair: Vaseline Intensive Care lotion for the skin, Chap Stick for the lips, a box of Kleenex for the nose, a Dennis Lehane book for the brain, and, to claim your territory, you throw the MORT and TOBY signs at the feet of your chairs.

Everyone on the pool committee is of a certain age. Still ambulatory, still full of good cheer. But no longer, maybe, ambitious. All of the men are possessed of great, Sol-like bellies, which they carry around with pride. It's my opinion that the bellies are the product of (1) the psychology born of living through the Great Depression that says, Let's celebrate being well fed; and (2) an overall gravitational settling of the organs (even the nipples are somewhere at the bottom of the rib cage). Rule No. 21: Any shame of physical appearance is ridiculous.

A pervasive feeling of acceptance vibrates among the members of the pool committee. I think you can kind of feel it. You love one another not because of wit or riches (though Irv Gelden is one rich son of a bitch) but because you've known one another for years, because in a world where people with whom you've shared history are dropping like flies, the pool committee is no small thing. Rule No. 9: Breathing is nine-tenths of friendship. Perhaps it is this notion of unqualified accept-ance that allows you to drop almost immediately to sleep. I watch you. All around, books are read, Valentine's hearts are eaten, the decades-old quest for a burpless cucumber is discussed. Important stuff.

Toby talks about what she thought of you before she met you: I didn't want to speak to him. He scared me! He always looked like he was in pain! Walking like this! Or like this! Everyone laughs. Charlotte says, You're the perfect couple. You should never get married. This exchange you've heard before. You sleep on, your face dappled with sun. You missed a patch shaving, on your lip, and there are some wispy white hairs. Your left foot twitches, maybe some kind of dream-triggered response. All around you, the deck is covered in greenery. Things growing at acceler-ated, tropical rates. As you sleep, I think you can almost feel everything growing, moving to erase the hotel and return the whole goddamn place to jungle.

Around 3:45, Sol comes over for a talk. You know, he says, Acapulco ain't what it used to be. There is consensus on this. When you first came, in 1962, there was a little panache to the place. The same high rollers who hit Vegas had villas in the hills. You spent nineteen of the swingingest, most joyous years of your marriage to my grandmother Selma down here with the pool committee. In 1962, you and Selma stood *this* far away from Mr. Kissinger, honest to God. One February, you even whiled away the hours with none other than Mr. Michael Landon. The committee used to hold big parties at night. Fifteen par-ties a year. Fella name of Terry would bring down floor shows from Vegas. It was a real extravaganza, boy. Of course, he's dead now, Terry.

But we love it, Sol says. You say, Yes sir. Sol says, We come here now for the weather and the people. Beautiful people, like Mort and Toby. We'll stick it out.

At four o'clock, everyone gets up and begins preparations for the trip back to their rooms to watch another perfect sunset from their bal-conies. Before they take leave of the pool, though, the committee stands at the fence that lets out to the beach. You all stand there quietly, and Lester from Jersey says, You don't get weather like this in Aruba, you know.

This is one subject of which the whole committee never tires: the perfection of the Acapulco weather. Its dependability, its essential invariability. The place may be going to hell in a handbasket, but you cannot argue weather. There is the frequent incantation of the place-names whose weather isn't as perfect as Acapulco's.

WEINSTOCK: You don't get this in Florida, not in Texas, not in wherever the hell you go in Europe.

BROWN: We've gone on cruises to every island in the South Pacific. This is better.

SOL: Bimini, Bermuda. In all the years we've been here, we got caught in the rain *once*. And one night it was foggy. Remember that? There was supposed to be a party down at the cabanas. But other than that . . .

And he shrugs his shoulders.

Toby says, With weather like this, time stands still. Is it yesterday? Is it tomorrow? Who cares!

Your secret, really, is the schedule. Every moment must be accounted for. I think you don't want any unscheduled cracks into which despair and uncertainty can creep. It's the same when you're at home. You eat dinner at the same place every Saturday night, take a schvitz at the club every Sunday, eat breakfast at the local deli every weekday morning and then drive yourself to work. This is what you brought to my life: inflexibility. And there's no overstating how much good that's done me. What with my parents engaged in multiple divorces, ex-hippie carousing, and a general ecology of uncertainty, inflexibility was practically a forbidden vice. Every Monday, my father and I would have dinner with you, three bachelors exactly thirty years apart. There were no excuses for missing a date. Rule No. 3: No matter what, do not vary the routine. Do not stop driving to work, regardless of eyesight or response time. Do not skip a February in Mexico, even if they have hospitals like dungeons. You want to live? It's an act of willful regularity.

At day's end, you take me upstairs to your room. You show me all the stuff you get special. See that fan, you say. I bet you don't have a fan in your room.

In fact, I don't. You also have a bouquet of flowers and a rolling clothing rack that no one else gets (and probably no one else needs). Rule No. 24: Stay someplace where you're not just a regular schnook. You, Toby, and I discuss the ritual of packing. You begin packing six months before coming down. You keep four or five suitcases open in your special packing room. (When you live alone in a big house, you can afford the luxury of a packing room.) The suitcases are opened sometime in August. They remain open for additions, subtractions, tinkerings, fresh tubes of toothpaste, and new bathing ensembles until a week before departure, when they are sealed, not to be reopened.

MORT: I make a list this long, what I gotta bring down.
TOBY: And he still forgets something every year. I knew you forgot that shirt, Mort.
MORT: I got it down to a science. Four suitcases and one carry-on.
TOBY: Last year, he forgot a shoehorn.
MORT: I check the suitcases at the curb.
TOBY: I gave him a butter knife to use. Instead of a shoehorn. I know how to make do.
MORT: You want something to drink? I'll order you up a Sprite. You like Sprite. They don't have 7-Up.
TOBY: Now he packs a shoehorn, first thing.

You have created a six-month task that takes up a decent amount of time almost every day. Rule No. 2, and it's a primary rule, is: You must always have something you are actively looking forward to, so that hope is scheduled into your life. But there's a corollary to this rule that's even more important.

After we look through the suitcases, we order up some ice cream. Back in Cleveland, your grocery shopping has been refined to a single class of food: snacks. Boxes of mint-chocolate-chip ice cream are stacked in the freezer, and flat-bottomed cake cones are out on the counter; you still dip ice cream skillfully and with a flourish. Boxes of the Nabisco fancy-cookie assortment line the cupboards, along with nuts of various shapes and provenances: smoked almonds and roasted cashews and honey-coated peanuts. On your refrigerator there's a little magnet that says on it NOSH! NOSH! NOSH! (The Friedmans are noshers from way back. One can locate us at any party by heading directly to the hors d'oeuvres table.) The ice cream in Mexico, you say, is particularly good. You like strawberry. When it arrives at room 1233, we unwrap our plastic serving cups silently. You take your wooden spoon and scrape up a bite, looking not unlike a little boy in terms of concentration and facial expression. You then eat the stuff with near-pornographic pleasure. This is Rule No. 1, the most important of Mort Friedman's secrets to life: You must have the capacity to find pleasure in the same things, again and again. Each ice cream cup, each trip to Acapulco, each dip in the pool is actually better, more peculiarly enjoyable, than the last. In your younger days, my family called this stubbornness, rigidity, sometimes (we were so analytical) fear. But now it looks a lot like enlightenment.

JULY 2001

THE BABY GOAT MURDERS

by Larry Brown

I SAW THE SON of a bitch while I was up on my tractor, running the rotary cutter along a wall of green sage grass that was five feet high. It was August in Mississippi, hot, on over in the afternoon but not near sundown. The sky had softened, and the coyote was trotting along in the open like the most unconcerned thing you could imagine. I stopped the tractor when I realized that he hadn't seen me. Or maybe he hadn't registered what I was.

He ambled on across the freshly clipped pasture grass I'd cut the week before, dropped over into a patch of stuff about two feet high, and stopped. I eased back on the throttle, and the Cummins diesel sat there doing its steady chug. I knocked it into neutral, took the PTO out of gear, and heard the *swigswigswig* of the six-foot blade slowing down a little, turning freely, but so heavy and with so much momentum that it would take close to two minutes to finally come to a complete stop. He laid himself down in the grass, and I got off the tractor.

Just for the fun of it, I thought I'd see how close I could get to him if I kept the outline of the tractor behind me and walked in a straight line. I didn't have my gun. It was in the cabinet at the house, and the house was about a quarter mile across the pasture. I didn't think I'd be able to get close to him. But I hated him so bad I wanted to have a better look. I wanted to kill him was what I wanted to do. But the gun was too far away. He'd probably run before I took many steps. But I started taking some anyway.

The glimpse I'd had of him, he didn't look all coyote. He looked about half dog, or coy-dog. He might have been about half malamute, because he had patches of tan and black, and his ears didn't look right. I knew coyotes bred with dogs sometimes and I knew that they ate a lot of dogs, and I knew they ate baby goats, too. I knew that bitterly, and I wished hard for my gun in my hand with each step I took. I took a surprising number of them in a straight line, and he didn't get up and run. I couldn't see him, but my eyes had never left the spot where he'd stopped, even when I was climbing down from the tractor, so unless he'd crawled away, he was still there.

The distance closed from fifty yards to forty to thirty to twenty, and once I got away from the tractor, it didn't make very much noise—the land, or maybe the tall patch of grass I'd been mowing, absorbed the sound somehow. I wouldn't have thought he would have just trotted out across the open like that with me up on the tractor. But I also thought that maybe since I wasn't walking on two legs it messed him up somehow, let him get within shooting distance of a man, a man who, luckily for the coyote, had no gun.

I knew he was still there and I wondered what he would do if I surprised him. Would he run? Would he come at me? I didn't have anything but a pocketknife, but I took it out and opened it up. I started taking baby steps then, looking into that tall grass, and when I got to within twenty feet or so, I could see a brown, mottled form curled and at rest, just a vague glimpse of it through the grass, and I figured he was taking a nap. And how long would he sleep? Would he sleep long enough for me to make it all the way back to the tractor and get on the other side of it and then run bent over behind the wall of sage grass back to the house and get the single-barrel and some buckshot out of the cabinet and then run back? And do this whole sneaking-up thing again until I got close enough for just one damn shot? Just one?

There wasn't anything to do but try. I started backing up, real slow, real careful, watching the spot where he was.

The Immaculate Kid came when we least expected him. I was riding the tractor around one afternoon when I went by Nanette lying in some grass, and there was a little white thing with black spots next to her. You'd have thought I'd gone crazy. I started blowing the horn on the tractor, and whooping and hollering, and they heard me in the yard and came over, and I showed them our first baby goat.

This was before bestial incest crept into the picture.

What happened was that we'd taken Nanette on for a while. My friend Tom had been trying to keep her in his little pasture in Oxford, and it just wasn't working out. But we have more than sixty acres out here, or my wife and her mother, Mamaw, do, and they let me live on it, and my son Billy Ray raises cows on it. All kinds of stuff happens with animals out here. Sometimes things happen that you can hardly believe.

One Saturday, Billy Ray had gone to the sale at Pontotoc. That's one of those big barn deals where they run livestock into the ring—cows, pigs, bulls, heifers, horses and mules, donkeys and burros sometimes—and they've got an auctioneer with a microphone, and he's sitting up there in a booth above the smoke and the sawdust, and once in a while a young pig jumps through the steel pipe ring and maybe shits in somebody's lap. You can sell or buy. Billy Ray bought what he thought was a young goat, but it turned out to be a full-grown pygmy goat. He had Tom's permission to breed Nanette. But when he got that hairy thing home, I said, Forget it, man, he's not going to be able to get up on her. Nanette was a regular-sized goat. We watched him try. She'd just be grazing while he was hunching on her. So we said, Nah, it's not gonna work, and Billy Ray sold the pygmy goat, and I forgot all about it until that afternoon when I found the Immaculate Kid. We called a couple of friends of ours and said, Oh, hey, come over and look at the cute baby goat. They came over, we took pictures and made videos, and my neighbor Joe even got down behind an overturned feed trough with a pig puppet on his hand and messed with the little goat's head, and we had a big time. We celebrated the young goat's life, such as we could. We didn't know then all the trouble that lay down the road. Because when you start screwing around with goats—well, they're not cows. They're goats, and somehow they achieve a realm of even worse nastiness than cows. It's probably hard to believe unless you've witnessed it yourself. But it does occur. It occurs like a motherfucker. I told Billy Ray. He wouldn't listen to me. Even when the baby goats started getting killed at night. Even when they started getting their throats slashed. That's always the problem: He won't listen to me.

But he's tough as hell, can go out and work in all kinds of bad weather, and is already a much better man than I ever thought about being, except that he thinks women ought to stay in their own place. But he's real smart and funny, and he's already twenty-four, and it's only now, at forty-eight, that I can see how much of a boy I was at his birth, when I was twenty-four.

The Immaculate Kid never was good for much. He was too wild to pet, so we didn't get to play with him. After a while we just ignored him, and he and Nanette ranged over the pasture like the cows did, not really soul mates.

Billy Ray's got all kinds of cows, calves, heifers, bulls. And after the new goat had been hanging around for about six months, I began to wonder when those things became sexually active. And would a goat do its mother? I knew dogs would. I knew dogs would in a second. I don't figure big cats would do it. I think their family ties are stronger than that. I didn't know but I went ahead and said something like, Well look, Bud, now, you don't want to let that thing get old enough to where it'd think about screwing its mother before you sell it, okay? And of course he assured me that wouldn't happen. And I went happily on with whatever project I was involved in, either writing something or building something or cutting something down and dragging it somewhere, I'm sure.

And one day I saw him riding her. A goat on its mother. I found Billy Ray and said, Come on, let's get him loaded up and sell him, we don't want to have baby goats born from a mother and son, come on, go catch him. And he did get up and try. He tried for a long, long time. He chased that damn goat all over this place several times, and I don't remember how long it took him to catch it, but I think it was a long time. Eventually the Immaculate Kid got sold, and I hoped Nanette wasn't pregnant.

Fast-forward about three months, and one morning Nanette had three babies about the size of rabbits, with little striped faces and hanging ears, and they were bouncing and bucking around on their new legs, and they were just about the cutest little things I'd ever seen in my life. One was black, one was brown, and one was gray and black. You could pet them. They weren't deformed. They looked pretty normal. I felt a failure to prevent animal incest nonetheless.

But they were just cute as hell. I got them into the heifer pen because I was already thinking about coyotes. The heifer pen is built out of woven wire, and it's right behind Mamaw's house, where Babe, Billy Ray's big Walker hound, sleeps. I figured they'd be safer there. They weren't too hard to catch. They'd run but you could catch them, and they'd bleat—maybe in terror, who knew?—but eventually you could run them down and play with them some. I did it several times.

I made it back to the tractor without him seeing me. I ducked behind it, bent over, and started running. The wall of green sage grass was a couple hundred yards long. It's one of the main pastures and it grows so much grass that the cows can't eat it all, so we have to mow it a few times each summer. That was what I'd been doing that afternoon. I'd mowed a lot of it, but there was still plenty to go. It's probably six or seven acres, maybe more. It's hard for me to look at a piece of land and say how many acres are in it.

So there I was, running bent over. Running bent over, running bent over, running bent over. It's a hard way to run. Man was not meant to run like that. I figured once I got a little ways off from him I could straighten up. But I wasn't going to stop running, not if I had even a slim chance of getting the gun and some shells and making it back up there before he left. I was going to shoot him in the head after what he'd done to my baby goats. He'd come on the place and killed. Over and over. I had the right to defend my livestock. Even if they were already dead.

So I kept running bent over, running bent over, running bent over. I ran bent over for a long time, until I got down under the slight rise of land that lay between us, and then I straightened up and kept jogging back toward the house. I don't remember who was in there. I ran to the gun cabinet and got my Harrington & Richardson single-shot twelve-gauge, scooped up some 00 buckshot and No. 4 steel shot, and jogged back out the door, shells in my pocket, the piece at port arms.

The little goats prospered and grew. Young children were brought out from Oxford to pet them and play with them. They made you just feel good in your heart, by God, to look out there in the heifer pen and see them prancing around, like they had springs under their feet, or all four legs were pogo sticks. They seemed to have limitless energy and enthusiasm. Nanette had a big old bag with fat teats winking from between her legs, and I even thought of milking her but never did.

The little goats got to be the size of big rabbits pretty soon. Their bleats were musical, and Nanette seemed content. She was bad about butting, and Tom's youngest boy had gotten scared of her for that reason, but it never bothered me. Even if she hit you, it wasn't that bad. If she hit me, I'd just get ahold of her horns and wrestle with her for a while. She wasn't mean. She was just a goat.

I couldn't hear the tractor running at all. I said, Shit, it's quit. I was still running and I knew there wasn't any chance of him still being there. Just more wasted effort, just one more thing you spend time doing that doesn't pay off. What difference would it have made anyway? They were dead already. But in a bad way that lives within me, I would have felt better if I could have killed him. No solid proof that he was the one, but he was the only one available and he would do. A sacrificial goat-yote.

When I got back to the wall of sage grass, I bent over again and soon running running running I could hear the murmur of the tractor—odd how that distance swallowed up all the sound—but nothing had changed. I stopped behind the tractor and broke the shotgun open and pulled out some shells. The No. 4 pellets were smaller, but there were more of them. I loaded the chamber and closed the gun and went out front again. I knew he was gone. It had been probably ten minutes, and he wouldn't have lain there for that long. Although with a wild thing you wonder just how they do live, on winter nights when the moon is up and ice hangs from all the trees, and the grass is white and frosted and stiff. What warmth is there for them, and where do they hide? But man has a tough time of it, too. He tries to raise goats for the joy their companionship brings. For the goat songs they sing.

I never did exactly get to be best friends with the little goats. I enjoyed them, but it didn't seem to go the other way. They weren't like dogs, puppies, cats, kittens. They didn't live in the house or even on the front porch, although one time I took one of them over to the patio where the family was cooking out. It didn't really want to go, but I took off my belt and made a loop with the buckle and put the loop around its neck and opened the gate and started leading it out. Nanette got upset. She came after us. The little goat was bleating for her, and she started bleating back, and it just made the little one bleat harder, and before long it started sounding like somebody was murdering them. But I closed the gate and took off across Mamaw's yard with it, the goat kicking and struggling, trying to pull away, and I kept talking to it, and trying to pet it, but it didn't want to calm down, and it took awhile to get it over to the patio. And it didn't like it over there, either. It kept on bleating, and although everybody thought it was cute, it was pretty obvious that it wasn't going to make much of a pet. I took it back to the pen and put it up. Billy Ray came home that evening and opened the gate and let the goats out into the pasture for some reason. The next morning there were only two baby goats.

Billy Ray and I have these little talks sometimes. I tell him how things are going to go if he doesn't do A or B, and then when he doesn't do A or B, it happens, and we have to talk again. And I knew that I had made it perfectly clear to him that Nanette and her babies needed to stay in the heifer pen because of all the coyotes around. We'd shot them. We'd captured them. They were still here. Now we'd lost a baby goat because he hadn't listened to me. I told him, Let's get them back in the pen and let's keep them in there, okay? He said okay.

I got on the tractor while he herded them back toward the heifer pen. I was holding out for hope, praying that maybe it had just gotten separated from Nanette and was wandering around in the pasture, bleating for her. But I made a wide and close sweep right before sundown, and there was nothing. Meat, bones, blood—all gone. But like I said, it wasn't much bigger than a rabbit.

I couldn't tell if he was gone or not. Everything looked the same. The tractor was still running. The wind was still blowing. There were some pieces of rusted tin out on the pasture grass in front, remnants of the '84 tornado that sucked up the barn and spewed it back into thousands of pieces, many of them still lying here and there. Once in a while you'd run over some of it.

I had my shotgun up, ready to aim it. But I didn't see a damn thing to aim it at. I knew I couldn't be that lucky. I knew he was gone.

The place was green and beautiful. The sycamores that lined the creek were in full foliage, and up past the other pond you could see the row of cedars along the fence. More than once I'd mowed a big patch of pasture and kept cutting it into ever smaller circles and seen the rats running, and then watched the hawks fall on them and carry them to the big oaks down in the bottom below the house and eat them, perched on a limb. In long years past I'd fed my father-in-law's cows out of his blue-and-white '67 Chevy pickup, delivered their babies, hauled off the dead carcasses of the ones that hadn't made it. I'd been on this place more than twenty years, had seen it change through weather and wind and snow, had mowed it, fenced it, farmed it, made love and made children from that love on it. I didn't like anything coming on it and taking what it wanted.

Life rocked on. It always does. No matter what happens, you just keep going until the day you can't go anymore. I was saddened by the death of the little goat, even though I hadn't known it very personally, and I was determined that it wouldn't happen again.

But Billy Ray has problems. He has cows and heifers and bulls, and sometimes I don't fully understand every little increment of what's going down because I don't have time to listen to all of it. Nonetheless, I do sit down at night with him sometimes and discuss this cow or that cow. This fence or that fence. This bull or that bull. I know I will never be free of cows. And I know that's what he's interested in, so I try to cheer him along some, though I know already the heartbreak of cow ownership and do not want to sip the wine of its fruits anymore in this life. He let the goats out again for some reason, and another one disappeared.

I got pretty pissed off then. I put the remaining two back in the heifer pen and I kept them in there. But one night, not long after that, the coyote came back. The dogs raised a commotion, some bleating was heard, and the next morning when I went out, Nanette was sitting very still with her horns caught in the woven wire, and the last remaining little baby goat was lying close to the back gate with its throat torn open. It was quite dead. The son of a bitch didn't get to eat it, but he killed it anyway.

The way I saw it, I had failed as a livestock caretaker. I don't think it bothered anybody else as much as it did me. I just couldn't quite reconcile it. It didn't seem fair.

Billy Ray had to haul the last baby goat off. I don't know where he took it. I'm sure wherever it was, some coyotes found it and ate it anyway.

It came as a big revelation to me that he was one of those big brown pieces of tin lying out in the pasture. I only realized it when he stood up and started walking away. I cocked the hammer and put the bead on his shoulder at less than forty yards, and when I touched the trigger I saw his hair fly. But it didn't knock him down, and he only whirled and started running up the hill. I ran with him, sideways, breaking open the gun and fumbling for another shell and loading the gun and shutting it and cocking it again and trying to track him. I couldn't believe the shot hadn't blown him down. How petrified with fear had the baby goats been when he came? At the creep feeder on top of the hill he whirled again, still looking for where the shots were coming from, and I leveled on him and fired, and I knew it was a load of 00 buckshot, and a blast seemed to fan around him, some shock wave that still didn't topple him, and he left running, tail out, streaking low, and I tried to reload again, but it was no use, because he was too fast. He was headed right toward the cows, standing down there in the bottom below the house, as if he knew somehow that I wouldn't shoot in that direction, and he dove among them and exited very fast stage left, ducked into the overhanging creek trees, and was gone.

I stood there looking after the last fleeting image of him, brown, low to the ground and laid out, getting away. Holding the gun like nothing. And feeling so helpless and hating it so bad. He was just an animal, but still he had gotten the best of me. He came, he saw, he ate, he left. And there was not one thing I could do to prevent any of it, given the circumstances of my station and my family and cattle matters that were out of my hands. But still, it hurt. It hurt about as bad as anything had in a while. They were just so goddamn cute. If you could have seen them, you would know what I mean.

We don't have any goats now. Nanette got sick and died. I found her. I don't know if Tom ever told his children or not. But I guess when they grow up they might read this and finally know.

I keep one of Nanette's horns in my desk. There is also a picture of her on a promotional CD for Blue Mountain's *Dog Days*. The horn, hollow and fluted, is a spook, a talisman, a key. I keep it here to remind me of what a man can go through for goats. It reminds me of what is possible in this life in the country, and sometimes what is not.

JULY 2000

4

{ *The*
REPORTING }

ESCAPE FROM KASHMIR
by Sebastian Junger

THE GUERRILLAS APPEARED ON the ridgeline shortly before dusk and walked down the bare hillside into the Americans' camp without bothering to unsling their guns. They were lean and dark and had everything they needed on their persons: horse blankets over their shoulders, ammunition belts across their chests, old tennis shoes on their feet. Most of them were very young, but one was at least thirty and hard-looking around the eyes—"a killer," as one witness said. Jane Schelly, a schoolteacher from Spokane, Washington, watched them come. "There were ten or twelve of them," she says, "and they were dressed to move. They didn't point their guns or anything; they just told us to sit down. Our guides told us they were looking for Israelis." Schelly and her husband, Donald Hutchings, were experienced trekkers in their early forties who took a month every summer to travel somewhere in the world—the Tatra Mountains in Slovakia; the Annapurna massif; Bolivia. Hutchings, a neuropsychologist, was a skilled technical climber who had led expeditions in Alaska and the Cascade range. He knew about altitude sickness, he knew about ropes, and he was completely at ease on rock and in snow. The couple had considered climbing farther east, in Nepal, but had set their sights instead on the Zanskar Mountains in the Indian state of Jammu and Kashmir. For centuries, British colonists and Indian royalty had traveled to the region to escape the summer heat, and over the past twenty years it had become a mecca for Western trekkers who didn't want to test themselves in the higher areas of the Himalayas. It is a staggeringly beautiful land of pine forests and glaciers and—since an Indian-government massacre of thirty or forty protesters in its capital, Srinagar, in 1990—simmering civil war.

The conflict had decimated tourism, but by 1995 Indian officials in Delhi had begun reassuring Westerners that the high country and parts of Srinagar were safe, so in June of that year Schelly and Hutchings headed up there with only the vaguest misgivings. Even the State

Department, which issues warnings about dangerous places (and had Kashmir on the list at the time), will admit that Americans visiting such places are far more likely to die in a car accident than as a result of a terrorist attack. Moreover, a few years earlier, Schelly and Hutchings had decided against going to Machu Picchu, in Peru, because of terrorist activity—but they later met dozens of travelers who had gone there without any trouble. There was no reason to think Kashmir would be any different. The couple hired two native guides and two ponymen (and their horses) and trekked up into the Zanskar Mountains. After ten days, on July 4, they were camped in the Lidder Valley, at 8,000 feet.

The militants, heads wrapped in scarves, secured Schelly and Hutchings's camp, rounded up a Japanese man and a pair of Swiss women who were camped nearby, and then left all of them under guard while the rest of the band hiked farther up the Lidder. Two kilometers away was a large meadow—the "Yellowstone" of Kashmir, as Schelly put it—that was guaranteed to yield a bonanza of Western trekkers. Sure enough, the militants returned to the lower camp two hours later with a forty-two-year-old American named John Childs, his native guide, and two Englishmen, Keith Mangan and Paul Wells. Childs, separated with two daughters, was traveling without his family.

The leader of the militant group, Schelly would learn later, was Abdul Hamid Turki, a seasoned guerrilla who had fought the Russians in Afghanistan and was now a field commander for a Pakistan-based separatist group called Harkat-ul Ansar. He ordered all the hostages to sit down at the entrance to one tent. Childs, nervous, looked down at the ground, trying to avoid eye contact with anyone. He was already convinced that the guerrillas were going to kill him, and he was looking for a chance to escape. A cold rain started to fall, and Turki asked for all their passports. The documents were collected, the militants attempted to read the papers upside down, and then they declared that all the Western men would have to come with them to talk to their senior commander. That was a three-hour walk away, in the village of Aru; they would be detained overnight and released in the morning, said the militants. Schelly was to walk to the upper camp with one of her guides.

"After I left, the men [were told] to lie down and pull their jackets over their heads, and that if they looked up, they'd be shot," says Schelly, who learned these details later from Childs's guide. "The [kidnappers] went through the tents, stealing stuff. And then they took the guys off. By ten o'clock I'd gone to the upper camp and come back down [with the wife and the girlfriend of the Englishmen], and we all piled into one tent because we were still scared. I was awake at four the next morning, and I just kept looking down the trail, thinking they'd be coming anytime now. It was six-thirty, and then seven, and then nine—that's when the knot in my stomach started."

Finally, Childs's guide returned. He had a note with him that he had been instructed to give to "the American woman." It said, "For the American Government only," and it was a list of twenty-one people the militants wanted released from Indian prisons. The top three were Harkat-ul Ansar.

The kidnapped men walked most of the night. They weren't being taken to the "senior commander"—he didn't exist—they were just being led deep into the mountains. The deception reminded John Childs of the tactics the Nazis used to cajole people into the gas chambers, and made him all the more determined to escape. The men walked single file through dark forests of pines and then up past the tree line into the great alpine expanses of the Zanskar Range. It was wild, ungovernable country the Indian Army didn't even attempt to control, and Childs believed that there was no way anyone was going to save them, or even find them. They were on their own. "I was convinced [the militants] were going to shoot us, and so as soon as I heard someone chamber a round into one of those weapons, I was going to take off into the woods," says Childs. "At one point we crossed a stream—it was snow-melt season and the mountain streams were absolutely raging torrents—and I considered jumping in and flushing down to the bottom, but it would have been instant death."

Childs kept his eyes and ears open and waited. A chemical engineer for an explosives company, he was used to solving problems. This was just another one: how to escape from sixteen men with machine guns. There were personalities, quirks, rifts among his captors he was sure he could exploit. He started lagging while he walked, seeing if he could stretch the line out a little bit; he started taking mental notes of the terrain; he started probing for weaknesses in the group. "Escape is a mental thing," he says. "Ninety percent is getting yourself prepared to take advantage of an opportunity or create an opportunity. I knew that, given enough time, I'd get away."

Late that night they came upon a family of nomads at a cluster of three log huts. The head of the family stepped out into the darkness to give Turki a hug, then the militants and hostages all squeezed into the huts and fell into an exhausted sleep. A few hours later, as soon as it was light, Childs sat up and peered through a chink in the wall—alpine barrens and rock, nothing more. Escaping through the forest would have been at least a possibility, but crossing a mile of open meadow would be suicide. He'd be cut down by gunfire in the first twenty steps.

After the hostages were given a quick meal of chapatis, rice, and a local yogurt dish called lassi, they lined up on the trail and started walking again. This would become their routine in the next several days: up at dawn, hike all day, sleep in nomads' huts at night. The militants bought—or took—whatever food they wanted from the nomads and never had to carry more than a blanket and their guns. They told the hostages that they had been trained in Pakistan, near the town of Gilgit, and had come across the border on foot. They'd been in the mountains for months together and were prepared to die for their cause. When Donald Hutchings tried to engage them in talk about their families, one of the militants just patted his gun and said, "This is my family."

India and Pakistan have fought three wars over Kashmir, and Turki's band was the latest permutation in the fifty-year conflict. Harkat-ul Ansar (HUA) is committed to overthrowing Indian (thus, Hindu) rule in Kashmir and absorbing the state into the Islamic Republic of Pakistan. Since 1990, the "militancy," as the rebel movement is known, has been waging a sporadic guerrilla campaign against Indian authority with automatic rifles, hand grenades, and other small arms acquired from Pakistan. Turki called the group he commanded Al Faran, a reference to a mountain in Saudi Arabia near where the Islamic prophet, Mohammed, was born. The first time anyone had ever heard of Al Faran was on July 4, 1995, when they came walking down out of the mountains into Schelly and Hutchings's camp.

The militants led the hostages by day through snowfields and high passes, traveling north. Childs's impression was that they were simply marking time in the high country, avoiding the pony trails in the valleys where they might run into Indian soldiers. As the day wore on, the militants became less worried about being caught, and their vigilance slackened a bit. Turki remained dour and implacable, but the younger ones warmed up to the hostages. They called Don Hutchings "cha-cha," meaning "uncle," and practiced their high-school English whenever they could. Far from being threatening or abusive, they did anything they could to keep the hostages healthy—bandaging their blisters, giving them the best food, making sure they were warm enough at night. Not only did the hostages represent possible freedom for twenty-one separatists rotting in Indian jails, but they were also the only protection Al Faran had from the Indian military. They were a commodity, and they were treated as such.

"It was like a Boy Scout troop with AK-47s," says Childs. "The youngest militant was sixteen or so, a Kashmiri kid who'd been recruited to the cause. He hadn't been issued a weapon yet because he hadn't been through training; he was educated and bright, and his English was good. Turki was dead serious, though, and I didn't let any kind of camaraderie fool me. If he told them to kill someone, these guys wouldn't hesitate for a second; they were too well trained."

By the second day, Childs had noticed an interesting—and horrifying—dynamic. The hostages, all desperately scared, turned to one another for comfort and support. They talked about their families, their homes, and their fears. But they had also been thrown into a ruthless kind of competition. They knew that if the militants were forced to prove their intent, they would shoot one of the hostages. That much was clear—but who would it be? An American? A Brit? A weak hiker? A brave man? A coward? Since the hostages didn't know the answer, they did the next best thing: They tried to make as little an impression on their captors as possible. They didn't complain, they didn't cry, they didn't do anything that might cause them to be noticed. They blended in as completely as possible and hoped that, if the time came to kill people, they'd be invisible to the man with the gun.

Childs quickly realized that he was losing the competition not to stand out. "I was in really rough shape—my boots weren't broken in, and I'd gotten blisters on my heels before I was captured," he says. "The days went on and the skin was rubbed literally to the bone. By the fourth day I was having trouble keeping up." Childs believed that he and Hutchings, the U.S. citizens, were the most valuable hostages, "but you could burn one American and still have one left over."

From time to time the hostages discussed the possibility of trying to escape en masse, but the consensus was that they would be putting themselves at terrible risk. Keith Mangan, in particular, was convinced that the situation would resolve itself peacefully—"Look, these things usually end without any tragedies," he told the others at one point. Childs wasn't so sure. Not only did he believe that Turki would kill them without a second thought, he felt singled out for the first execution. Adding to his misery, he had come down with a devastating case of dysentery. By the end of the first day he was stepping off the trail every hour or so to drop his pants. A militant always gave him a Lomotil pill and followed him, so after a while Childs started relieving himself in the middle of the trail, in front of everyone. Soon they were waving him away in disgust, and he thought, *This is going to be useful. I don't know how, but it will.*

The next time a militant put a pill in his mouth, Childs didn't swallow. He waited until the man looked the other way, then he spit the medicine out onto the ground.

It took six hours for Jane Schelly to hike out to Pahalgam, a jumping-off point for people heading into Kashmir's high country. The entire trekking population of the valley—some sixty or seventy people—was by the end walking out with her, and when they arrived at the Pahalgam police station, utter pandemonium broke out. Schelly informed an officer that her husband had been abducted, and she was taken into a back room and interrogated. "I had to decide whether to give them the note or not," she says, "because it said 'For the American Government only.' I looked over at my guide, and he nodded and I thought, If they're going to help, let's get this show on the road. So I gave it to them, they copied down the names, and then I went to the U.N. post. That was at eight P.M.; they called the [American] embassy, and things were kicked into motion."

The United Nations has had a presence in Kashmir since 1949, after Britain formally relinquished control of its Indian colony and the subcontinent sank into ethnic chaos. The British government's last administrative act was to draw a border between the Muslim majority in Pakistan and the Hindu majority in India, and that sent six million people fleeing in one direction or the other. Hindu mobs attacked trains packed with Muslims trying to cross into Pakistan, and Muslims did the same thing to Hindus going in the other direction. Trains plowed across the border between Amritsar and Lahore with blood literally dripping from their doors.

While half a million people were being slaughtered, the semi-independent state of Kashmir was trying to decide whether to incorporate itself into India or into Pakistan. Kashmir was primarily Muslim, but it was ruled by a Hindu maharajah, and that inspired an army of Pakistani bandits to cross the border and try to take Srinagar in a lightning raid. They were slowed by their taste for pillage, however, which allowed Indian troops to rush into the area and defend the city. War broke out between India and Pakistan, and the nascent U.N. was finally forced to divide Kashmir and demilitarize the border. Fighting continued to flare up for the next forty years, and a surge in Pakistani-backed guerrilla activity again brought the two nations to the brink of war in 1990. This time the stakes were higher, though: India had hundreds of thousands of troops in Kashmir, and both nations reportedly had the capacity to deliver nuclear weapons. Diplomats defused that crisis, but American envoys in Delhi still considered Kashmir to be the world's most likely flash point for a nuclear war.

By the time Jane Schelly and Donald Hutchings showed up in Srinagar, as many as 30,000 locals had been killed since '92, and Kashmir had been turned into a virtual police state. The brutal tactics employed by the Indian Army had brought a certain amount of stability to the area—it was alleged, for example, that security forces machine-gunned every member of a household that had any association with the militants—but the war continued to rumble on in the hills. In 1994, two Brits had been kidnapped by militants and held in exchange for twenty or so HUA guerrillas serving time in Indian jails. The Indian government had refused to bargain, and after seventeen days the militants relented and let the hostages go. They even gave their prisoners locally made wall clocks as souvenirs of the adventure.

Schelly spent her first night out of the mountains at the U.N. post, and the next day she moved to a secure Indian-government compound. High-level British, German, and American embassy officials flew up on the afternoon flight from Delhi, and by July 7 a formidable diplomatic machine was in gear. Terrorism experts—unnamed in the press—were flown in from London, Bonn, and Washington, D.C. Negotiation and hostage-release specialists were made available to the Indian authorities. Surveillance satellites reportedly tried to locate the militants on the ground, and the Delta Force, a branch of the U.S. Special Forces, was in the area being readied for possible deployment. Indian security forces began working their informants in the separatist movement, and Urdu-speaking agents started trying to maneuver between brutally simple parameters for negotiation: no ransom and no prisoner exchanges. Any concession to the guerrillas' demands, it was feared, would only encourage more kidnappings.

Still, there was some hope that Al Faran could be eased toward compromise. Communication was carried out by notes sent along an impenetrable network of local journalists, militants, and nomadic hill people. Hamstrung, on the one hand, by an Indian government that was not entirely displeased with a situation that made Pakistan look bad and, on the other, by a U.S. policy that forbade concessions to terrorists, negotiators found themselves with almost no "wiggle room," as they say. The best they could do was relay messages to Al Faran that pointed out the immeasurable harm the kidnappings had done to the Kashmiri cause; the only way to regain credibility, said the negotiators, was to let the hostages go. To encourage this line of thought, the U.S. government left the negotiating to the Indians—whose country it was, after all—and started pulling strings elsewhere in the Islamic world. They persuaded a Saudi cleric to condemn the kidnappings as un-Islamic, and they tried to massage some of their contacts in Pakistan. "Al Faran was clearly an HUA-affiliated group, and what we know about HUA is that it's not very hierarchical," says a U.S.-government source who closely followed the incident. "It's not at all clear that Al Faran was even interested in communicating with [HUA] headquarters. If we'd had anything suggesting a tightly hierarchical organization, it would have been much easier to negotiate. And they had very poor, unsophisticated decision-making. These were not people with a Plan B."

By the end of the third day, John Childs could barely walk, and the militants seemed to be heading deeper and deeper into the mountains. They were, in fact, just walking in circles, dodging Indian military. To keep himself from sinking into despair, Childs devoted every waking moment to planning his escape. He knew the militants' sole advantage was their incredible mobility; without that, it would be only a matter of time before they were discovered by an army patrol. Which meant that if any of the hostages escaped, the militants wouldn't be able to waste too much time searching; they'd have to look quickly and then get moving again.

"My first objective was to get fifty meters away from them," Childs says. "And then five hundred meters, and then five kilometers. I knew that every bit increased the area they had to search by the square of the distance. And I knew there was no way this guy Turki was going to scatter his crew all over creation looking for me. He couldn't afford to look for me for more than six hours, so if I could stay away from them for that long, my only problem would be not being seen by the nomads."

That meant hiding during the day and traveling at night, which strongly favored an escape after dark. And that was fortunate, because Childs had one ironclad reason for getting up over and over again during the night: Dysentery was still raging through his insides. The militants always posted a sentry after dark, but the hostages weren't tied up when they slept, so the sight of Childs getting up to relieve himself was by now routine. In contrast to Childs, the other hostages seemed to be doing fairly well. The two Brits, Wells, twenty-four, and Mangan, thirty-four, were depressed but physically strong, and Hutchings was fully in his element. When Mangan came down with altitude sickness, Hutchings had him pressure-breathing and rest-stepping as he walked; when the group got lost in a whiteout, he took charge and told them which way to go. At one point, Wells muttered how he would like to grab one of the hand grenades and blow all the militants away, but Hutchings was always personable and helpful—"It's a lot tougher to kill a smiling face," he said. Hutchings had years of psychological training; if anyone could manipulate the situation, he could.

It wasn't until the fourth day, as they were crossing yet another valley, that the militants made their first mistake: They visited a familiar place. It wasn't much, but it was all Childs had.

"We were in the valley that the pilgrims take to Amarnath Cave," Childs says. "And Don knew where we were; he'd been there before. He said, 'Okay, down the valley is Pahalgam and up the valley is the cave.'"

Childs thought about that for the rest of the day. He wasn't going to be able to keep up with the group for long, and Turki wouldn't hesitate to have him shot. Not only would that free up the group; it would also send a message to the authorities, who obviously hadn't given in to the militants yet. If he was going to escape, he'd have to do it soon.

"So, are we going to spend the night here?" Childs asked Turki that afternoon, as they were taking a break. He knew the answer, but he wanted to hear what Turki had to say. "No, too much danger," Turki replied, waving his arm down the valley—Indian military. They wouldn't dare spend much time searching for someone, in other words. That night, the militants made camp along the east branch of the Lidder River, sleeping in a cluster of stone huts generally used by pilgrims on their way to Amarnath Cave. Childs, rolled up in a horse blanket, lay on the dirt floor of a hut, and considered his possible avenue of escape. The camp was at the mouth of two huge valleys that fed into the valley leading to Pahalgam, and Childs's plan was to escape by climbing up, in the opposite direction of what the militants would expect. He'd hide in the snowfields before dawn, stay until dark, and then start down toward Pahalgam. It was a three-day walk, he figured; he had no food, no bedding, and the valley was filled with nomads who might report his location to the militants. It was, at best, a long shot, but it was better than the odds he had now.

And then, exhausted by four days of forced marches, Childs fell asleep.

"There had been other opportunities to escape, but of course you never know if it's the right time," says Childs. "It's not a movie, where you know when it's going to end. You keep asking yourself, 'Is this the best time, or will there be a better time with less risk?' It took a huge effort to focus my thoughts and say, 'Okay, you've got to do this now. You've got to do it when you're tired and not feeling well.'"

Childs woke up in the middle of the night. It was quiet except for the sound of people snoring and the crash of the river. The dysentery was roiling through his system, so he fumbled in the dark and grabbed his hiking boots—knocking over a metal grate in the process—and crept out of the hut. Ordinarily the sentry would greet him and escort him out of camp. But this time no one stirred—the sentry seemed to be asleep. Childs walked out of camp, relieved himself, and then stole back into bed, wondering what to do.

"You can be passive and not make a decision that may save your life," he says, "or you can accept death as a possibility. That was the crux of the whole thing." Childs lay in bed for an hour, preparing himself, and then he got up again. He decided that if anyone stopped him, he'd just claim he was having another bout of dysentery. He thought about waking up the other hostages, but there didn't seem to be any way to do that quietly; the others also lacked his pretext for getting up. Childs stepped out of the hut and waited for someone to say something: silence. He edged out of the firelight into the darkness beyond the huts; more silence. There was always the possibility that someone was watching him surreptitiously—or even had a gun trained on him—but that was a chance he had to take. He stood motionless for a moment, frozen at the point of no return, and then he started to run.

"I thought I was in their crosshairs the whole time," he says. "It was like a dream where you run and run and you're not getting anywhere because your feet are bogging down. I kept expecting to hear a ruckus behind me, but I never saw any of them again."

Childs took off straight up a ridge between the two valleys. He was in his stocking feet, and all he had on was long underwear, Gore-Tex pants, a wool shirt, and a pair of pile pants wrapped around his head. He walked and ran as hard as he could until the ridge got too steep to climb without boots, and then he put them on and kept going. He knew the militants would wake up early for morning prayers, and he had to get as far away as possible before then. He hammered upward for the next three hours, and when dawn came he crept into a cleft in a rock, drew in a few stones to conceal himself, and settled down to wait. As it got lighter he noticed that anyone walking along the ridge would stumble right into him, so he violated his rule against traveling during the day and continued higher up. He was in the snow zone now, really rugged country; the next hiding spot he found seemed perfect, until it became apparent that he was resting on solid ice. He wound up moving to a small patch of moss on a hillside. There were glaciers and peaks all around him, and he was sure no one would follow him up that high; he was at least at 12,000 feet.

By midmorning a drizzling sleet had started to fall, and Childs endured that for a few hours—resting on the moss, dozing from time to time—before starting out for Pahalgam. He was almost down at the bottom of one of the side canyons when he heard a helicopter. The sound of the rotors faded in and out, then seemed to head straight toward him. Since he hadn't heard any aircraft in five days, his first thought was that there must have been a negotiated release of the hostages and now he was stranded in the high mountains with no food and no way to call for help.

"I stood there kind of dumbfounded," he says, "and I started waving my pants around over my head. The pilot circled and I could see there was a soldier in there; he had his gun pointed at me. I was a mess by that point—I hadn't bathed in five days and had mud smeared all over me and looked like a wild man of the mountains. The pilot landed on one skid, I ran up, and [a soldier] said, 'Are you Ger-

man?' I said, 'No, I'm American. I just escaped from the militants.'
He said, 'It's a miracle from God,' and hauled me on board."

The militants, as Childs had thought, had searched down-valley when
they realized he was gone. They didn't find him, but they stumbled
across two other trekkers, Dirk Hasert of Germany and Hans Christian Ostro of Norway—they were subsequently reported missing and
were, in fact, the people the helicopter crew had been searching for.
Rebel sources in Srinagar say that Ostro was belligerent toward the
militants from the start, telling them that what they were doing was
cowardly and un-Islamic; they also claim he was armed with a knife
and had tried to use it. That is impossible to verify, but suffice it to say
that Ostro succeeded in sticking out in the group.

Childs was brought back to Srinagar in triumph and immediately
debriefed in the presence of British and American embassy officials.
It was the first of endless debriefings over the next several days—

"I spent more time in captivity by the State Department than by
the militants," he said later. Childs was then taken to a secure guest
house, where he was introduced to Jane Schelly. For Schelly, the
chance to talk to someone who'd seen her husband only hours earlier
was a relief beyond words.

"Do they have enough food and drinking water?" she wanted to
know. "Do they have enough clothing? Do they know that the women
are okay?"

Everything Childs had to say about the hostages was positive—
they'd suffered no abuse, and the situation seemed similar to the
peacefully resolved kidnappings of a year earlier. The current hostage
team—referred to as "G-4" because the governments of four Western
countries were involved—had no reason to believe that this case
would be different. While Indian security kept up a steady dialogue
with Al Faran, the G-4 team continued to pressure Pakistan to inter-
vene with HUA. (Pakistani officials were stubbornly claiming that the
incident had been staged by India to make them look bad.) A rescue
was deemed to be too risky; even Indian Army patrols were warned
away from areas where the militants might be. Everyone, including
the hostages, was worried that a surprise encounter could erupt into a
firefight.

Childs flew back to Delhi two days after his escape, speaking to
reporters at the airport despite the efforts of officials to bundle him into

an embassy car. A few days later, he stepped off an airplane at Connecticut's Bradley Field, and news crews taped him sweeping his two young daughters up into his arms. He'd gone from the mountains of Kashmir to Hartford in the space of a week, and it rattled him. "Had circumstances been a little different, I'd be dead," he says. "You expect to live out your normal life span, but it could be over in a second. At the time, I thought I'd never see my kids again. Now every breath I take is something I didn't expect."

While Childs was facing the news cameras back home, Jane Schelly was still in Srinagar, working frantically for the release of her husband. "Please let Donald go," she sobbed at a press conference, holding on to Keith Mangan's wife, Julie. "In the name of God, please let our loved ones go." Al Faran responded by passing along a statement that said they had let Childs escape on purpose, but that they would resort to an "extreme step" if India didn't release the HUA rebels. They also sent a photograph of the five hostages sitting on pine boughs in a stone hut, their hands tied behind their backs, their eyes downcast. On an accompanying tape, Don Hutchings said, "Jane, I want you to know that I am okay. But I do not know whether I will die today or tomorrow. I appeal to the American and Indian governments for help."

The G-4 team decided, for security's sake, to move Schelly, the German woman, and the two Englishwomen back to the British embassy's guest house in Delhi. Negotiations remained deadlocked, and one week later some very bad news came in: The militants had supposedly run into an Indian Army patrol near Pahalgam, and two hostages had been wounded in the ensuing gunfight. The Indian government denied that the encounter had taken place, so Al Faran released some photos showing Hutchings lying on the floor of a house with his abdomen wrapped in bloody bandages. There was no blood on his pants, though, and he seemed to be refusing to look into the camera—refusing, perhaps, to cooperate with the deception. The consensus at the U.S. embassy was that the photos had been staged, an opinion Schelly shared.

On an audiotape sent with the photos, Hans Christian Ostro asked the Indian government to give in to Al Faran's demands, pointing out that it was tourist officials in Delhi who had misled him into thinking Kashmir was safe. "I even went to the leader of the tourist office in Srinagar, and he gave me his card and said that if there was anything, I could call him," Ostro said at the end of the tape. "Well, Mr. Naseer, I'm calling you now."

Another week passed, and still there was no breakthrough in the negotiations. Britain's Special Air Squadron and Germany's elite counterterrorism force, the GS-9, had by now joined the U.S. Army's Delta Force in Kashmir, even though an Entebbe-type rescue operation was unlikely; the authorities had no idea where Al Faran was, and there were also delicate sovereignty issues to work out with India. The feeling among the G-4 negotiators was that, as with the previous kidnapping, Al Faran would eventually give in.

They didn't.

On August 14, 1995, "we were at the German ambassador's residence, having lunch with the other families," recalls Schelly. "And during the meal several embassy people were called out of the room, and then more people were called out, and I didn't think anything of it. The German ambassador was called out just prior to dessert. We were eating cherries jubilee, and the next time I looked over, his ice cream had melted all over the place. And then I began to wonder."

While the families retired to a sitting room for coffee, a group of embassy officials talked somberly in a corner. Eventually one of them came over and reported that the body of a Caucasian man had been found in the village of Seer, outside Srinagar, but they didn't know if he was one of the hostages.

In fact, they did know, but they weren't saying. Cars came to pick up the families, the Ostros' car arriving first. After they had pulled away, the German ambassador put his arm around Schelly and said, "It's not your husband." It was not until that moment that Jane Schelly finally accepted the possibility that she might never see her husband again.

The body was that of Hans Christian Ostro. The guerrillas had cut off his head, carved "Al Faran" in Urdu on his chest, and dumped his body by an irrigation ditch. His head was found forty yards into the underbrush, and a note in his pocket warned that the other hostages would suffer the same fate if the HUA prisoners weren't released within forty-eight hours. The families of the remaining hostages were told that Ostro's chest had been carved after he was dead, that he had been "peaceful" when he died, and that he hadn't been killed in front of the other hostages—though how the officials could know that is unfathomable. However peaceful Ostro's death, though, he may have known it was coming: Medical examiners found a goodbye note hidden in his underwear.

The G-4 team—now down to G-3—responded by demanding proof that the other hostages still lived. The militants passed along a photograph of the four holding a dated newspaper and also arranged for a radio conversation between Donald Hutchings and the Indian authorities. At 10:45 on the morning of August 21, a negotiator raised the guerrillas on a military radio, and Hutchings was put on:

"Don Hutchings, this is 108. When you are ready, please . . . tell me 'One, two, three, four, five.'"

"One, two, three, four, five."

"The first message is . . . from your families. Quote, 'We are all staying together in Delhi and we all send our love and prayers. We are helping each other. Be as strong as we are.' Over."

"Okay, I have the message."

"Now, Don Hutchings, there [is] a set of questions for you. You'll have to provide me with the answers because I don't know them. . . . Am I clear to you?"

"Yes."

"What are the names of your pets? I repeat, what are the names of your pets?"

"My pets' names are Bodie, B-O-D-I-E, and Homer."

Hutchings's existence was confirmed. The negotiator continued with personal questions for each of the other hostages and then signed off, telling Hutchings to "have faith in God and strength in yourself." Within days of the radio interview, Al Faran began renewing their threats to kill the hostages, and their tone was so antagonistic that members of G-3 privately admitted that they thought the odds of the hostages' surviving were only fifty-fifty. September crawled by, and then October, and the winter snows started to come to Kashmir. Reports of frostbite and illness among the hostages began to drift in. And then, on December 4, the inevitable happened: Al Faran ran into the Indian Army.

The guerrillas were passing through the village of Mominabad early in the morning when a patrol of a dozen Indian soldiers spotted them from the marketplace and someone opened fire. According to Indian military officials, there were no hostages with them—they were presumably being held nearby—but that's impossible to confirm. The militants jumped a barbed-wire fence, splashed across a shallow stream, and then ran through a patch of scrub willow. They headed across a dry rice paddy, machine-gun fire hammering behind them, the villagers diving into their mud houses and slamming their doors shut. The militants made it across the paddy and took a stand farther upriver, near the small village of Dubrin, and the Indian patrol called for reinforcements. Soon dozens of troops were firing on the rebels, who held off the army for six hours until dark fell, when they left their dead and ran.

Turki was killed, along with four other Al Faranis. Three days after the gunfight, the British ambassador in Delhi received a phone call from a man claiming to be with Al Faran and offering new terms of release: $1.2 million in ransom and safe passage to Pakistan. "You know, you know, we have been treating [the hostages] as our guests for the last five months plus," he complained. "You can expect that we have spent lots of money." The ambassador demanded proof that the hostages were still alive, but the man never called again.

And that was it. From time to time, over the next few months, nomads would report seeing the hostages up in the mountains, but those reports came to be suspect when it was revealed that the nomads were making money both as paid police informants and as messengers and suppliers for the kidnappers. In April 1996, a captured HUA militant claimed that the hostages had been executed about a week after the fight at Dubrin, in retaliation for Turki's death, and that the bodies were buried in a village called Magam. The Indian Army scoured the woods and fields around Magam for weeks without finding anything.

"You want to be optimistic, your heart says be optimistic, but your mind says, 'Sucker, you've gotten your hopes up before,'" says Schelly. "We had a full moon right before Id-ul-Fitr [a feast day at the end of Ramadan], and a friend of Don's said, 'This is the last full moon that's going to pass before Don comes back.' I was so convinced they would release him for Id-ul-Fitr that I packed my bags and got my hair cut. At one point I had to pull the car over on the way home from work and throw up, I was so worked up."

Id-ul-Fitr came and went, as did the one-year anniversary of the kidnappings, without any word from Al Faran. Reports continued to trickle in from the nomads, but nothing could be confirmed. Schelly went back to Kashmir in the summer of 1996 to meet with HUA leaders, and she returned there a few months later to start up a reward program.

Announcements in local newspapers, on local radio shows, and even on the backs of matchbooks offered money to anyone who would come forward with information. The U.S government also offered a reward, and India followed suit.

"It's very difficult to say if the program will be successful," says Len Scensny of the State Department's South Asia bureau. "We haven't had verifiable contact with the hostages in over a year, and we have no current information on their well-being. It's been an ongoing subject of discussion with very senior officials in both India and Pakistan."

Meanwhile, John Childs has resumed his life in America—working, jogging, spending time with his daughters. People who know Childs have made joking references to Rambo, which bothers him, and some even ask why he didn't help the others escape. It's a question that still troubles him. "I rationalize it and say, 'I couldn't have done it any other way,' but without having done it another way I'll never know," he says. "I ask myself constantly, 'Should I have done anything different?' Sitting here in my office it's one thing, but when I actually made the decision to escape I was tired, I was injured, I was miserable, I was terrified. It revealed something about my character, and I'm not even sure if I'm proud of it or not."

And Jane Schelly's hopes are slowly waning. While promoting the reward program in the fall of 1996, she decided to visit the village of Seer, where Ostro's headless body had been found. She talked with the villagers through an interpreter and then walked along a dirt path by the irrigation ditch where, among the rice paddies, two women had spotted the body a year earlier. "It was so incongruous," says Schelly. "The village was on a little pass, and when I was there everyone was harvesting the rice. There [were] stacks of rice straw in the fields and mountain peaks in the distance. It was probably one of the most beautiful spots I've ever seen in my life."

If Don Hutchings is still alive, he's probably looking out at a scene very much like that one—iron-gray mountains, a scattering of mud huts, and a dozen villagers cutting their way across the rice paddies at dusk. One of them, undoubtedly, knows Hutchings is there; one of them, undoubtedly, wonders if telling the army would put his family in jeopardy. He decides to say nothing. And Don Hutchings, peering out through a chink in the wall, watches night come sweeping up his valley one more time.

APRIL 1997

Editor's Note

In August 2001, Jane Schelly received a death certificate for Don Hutchings from the U.S. State Department. On September 15, joined by more than 250 friends, Schelly held a sunset memorial service for her husband at the top of Mount Spokane in Washington, letting go of the search for him and saying a final good-bye. Hutchings's body, and the bodies of his fellow hostages, have not been found.

THE DEATH ZONE
by Peter Wilkinson

DON'T LEAVE ME HERE to die. . . ." Sandy Hill was pleading with guide Neal Beidleman. But Beidleman couldn't walk for her. If Hill was going to get back on a jet to New York City for her son Bo's thirteenth birthday party two Fridays from now, she was going to have to get up off the ice before she froze to death.

"If you can't walk," Beidleman screamed into a fifty-mile-per-hour wind, "then fucking crawl!"

Hill crawled. Fifteen feet, twenty feet . . . no more.

Beidleman looked through the swirling snow at the others. There were ten of them huddled together, in yellow or red or blue down climbing suits, more than twenty-seven thousand feet up on Mount Everest. It was now around midnight, and the group was hours behind schedule and out of oxygen. Charlotte Fox, like Hill, was barely ambulatory, and Yasuko Namba couldn't move at all. Beidleman saw this through his left eye only—snow and ice had scratched the cornea of the other almost blind during the stormy descent from the summit. Somewhere below them—only four hundred yards, as it turned out—lay the tents of Camp 4, hot tea, oxygen, and warmth . . . but in which direction? Within the same radius, toward the Lhotse and Kangshung faces, were drop-offs of nearly forty-eight hundred and ten thousand vertical feet.

Beidleman wasn't the only one shouting.

"Charlotte, move your legs!"

She did not.

"Charlotte, move your legs! Tell me if you're moving your legs! Talk to me!"

That was Tim Madsen, Fox's boyfriend and fellow ski patroller from back home in Aspen. Curled into a ball on the ice, Fox felt her feet freezing into blocks. Death seemed the best option, she was so cold, and she secretly hoped for the warm, hazy feeling that signals the final stages of hypothermia. "Move your arm!" Madsen pleaded.

"Leave me alone!" Fox screamed. "I don't care!"

Above them on the mountain, trapped in the jaws of the storm and the triple-digit windchill, was Beidleman's boss, expedition leader Scott Fischer. A strong climber and one of mountaineering's most experienced guides, Fischer had for some unknown reason fallen far behind the pack.

Scott would be okay, Beidleman thought. At this point he was unaware that Rob Hall, the leader of a second expedition, was also trapped near the summit, tending a critically ill client.

Sometime after midnight, Beidleman realized it would be suicidal to wait any longer. With two of his clients and one of Hall's guides, he set off south into the storm, dead upwind, in the direction, he hoped, of the tents and help. Hill crawled back to huddle with Fox and Madsen, and waited, shivering, for a break in the weather, a rescue team, or unconsciousness.

In the spring of 1996, Everest was not the monumental challenge for the exalted few that it had been in 1980, when Reinhold Messner made his famous North Face solo climb, and far from the mythical monster it had been when Edmund Hillary and Tenzing Norgay made the first verified ascent, in 1953. Since the mid-1980s, when a wealthy American businessman named Dick Bass decided to climb the "seven summits," the highest peak on each continent—and did it—the psychological barrier had been down, and high-altitude commercial guiding was born. Today, if you are fit enough and have the physiological makeup to function at high altitudes—and enough training, Sherpas, guides, bottled oxygen, and money ($65,000 being the norm)—Everest can be bagged.

Summitting is still a punishing physical endeavor that typically takes four to eight weeks in an extremely inhospitable climate. The air on eight-thousand-meter peaks has a third of the oxygen found at sea level. Oxygen deprivation brings on the increased pulse, blue skin, and hallucinatory thinking of hypoxia. Hacking coughs, headaches, vomiting, and severe dehydration are common. Climbers become confused, light-headed, stoned, out of it enough to think they're okay—a trap that can lull them into dying from hypothermia.

Acclimatization is critical. Three camps are made, at progressively higher altitudes above Base Camp, and periods of several days are set aside at each for the body to recover and to let oxygen return to depleted red blood cells. Usually climbers will spend short periods of time at higher camps, retreating to lower camps, as needed, until their systems adjust. When a team is ready, Camp 4 is hastily established at 26,100 feet on the South Col and after a short rest, a fast push to the top is undertaken.

Paying clients, last spring, could choose the businesslike approach of Adventure Consultants, of Christchurch, New Zealand, or the more freewheeling philosophy of Mountain Madness, a Seattle firm. Rob Hall, thirty-five, a founder of Adventure Consultants, had been to the top of the world's highest mountain four times before and had guided more clients—seventeen—to the summit than anyone. He carefully attended to details, like camp setup and oxygen-bottle delivery, and didn't cut his clients a lot of slack. "Rob thought everything through," says Lou Kasischke, a Bloomfield Hills, Michigan, businessman who made the May expedition with Hall. "Options, alternatives, strategies. 'Here's what we're going to do tomorrow and the day after.'"

From its arrival on March 25 in Katmandu, the Mountain Madness expedition had reflected the more free-form style of its leader, Scott Fischer. This was Fischer's fourth trip to Everest, his first leading a commercially guided trip there; he'd summitted once, in 1994, climbing without supplemental oxygen. At forty, Fischer probably understood Everest as well as anybody and was one of those charmed, charismatic risk-takers who dodge trouble by staying completely loose in the face of it. "What was great about Scott," Beidleman says, "was he'd announce, 'Okay, this is it, we're goin', we're doin' it.' And then he'd turn around and say, 'Hey, but we need some food and some equipment. Grab some food. Grab some equipment.' It worked. It's a different style. But Scott was the master at it."

Fischer, offhandedly, would announce to clients, "You need to be at Camp Two today." Other days, "We'd go through the icefall," recalls a client, referring to the treacherous, crevasse-riven Khumbu Icefall, "and Scott would say, 'I'll be right behind you.' He would go back to bed, take another hour of snooze time, and then catch up." If Fischer seemed to be taking Everest a bit for granted, most of his clients seemed to enjoy that approach and, indeed, had opted to make the trip with him because of it. "We had a bunch of very, very independent, strong-willed people," says Beidleman. "We didn't want to take away from their adventure by taking them on a Disneyland ride."

For Fischer, this trip was more a word-of-mouth-building venture than a profit maker. Some clients had demanded deals and paid less than sixty-five grand. So be it. The more people Fischer got up Everest, the better for Mountain Madness. What better way to build a reputation than through Internet coverage and a celebrity client? The latter was Sandy Hill, a forty-one-year-old climber (and occasional *Men's Journal* contributor) who was as adept in the harsh outdoors— she had already scaled six of the seven summits—as she was inside the velvet ropes of Manhattan society.

This was Hill's third shot at the mountain in as many years. In the midst of a divorce from Bob Pittman, her husband of seventeen years and a cofounder of MTV, she arrived at the Manang Hotel in Katmandu having struck an agreement with NBC to send back daily reports via the Internet. Rob Hall's group included the mountaineer and author Jon Krakauer, who planned to write about the climb for *Outside* magazine and also transmit real-time dispatches to a website. Hundreds of thousands of people would follow the ascent and chat with the main characters as the story unfolded. Climbers wishing more private conversations with their families could call home on satellite phones. Starbucks would be serving coffee at Base Camp. By last spring, if Everest wasn't a Disneyland ride, it was a business. "This is something I'm good at; it's what I do," Fischer told *Seattle Weekly* before departure. "And there's a demand for it."

The Fischer and Hall expeditions were among the first of the year, taking advantage of the two-week window of opportunity in May between the unrelenting grip of winter and the monsoon season. Early phases of the ascent, up the easiest, most popular South Col route, passed without major incident: from Base Camp, at 17,500 feet, to Camp 1, 1,600 feet above, at the top of the Khumbu Icefall, and on to Camp 2, four miles above sea level at 21,600 feet. Then, after a pause of several days to acclimatize, it was another 2,250 feet beyond to Camp 3, midway up the Lhotse Face. Fischer was up and down the mountain—even on a rest day—with sick clients and Sherpas, one of whom came down with a serious case of altitude sickness on April 25 and had to be evacuated to a hospital in Katmandu. "Scott did everything that everyone else did, in half the time," says Ingrid Hunt, Fischer's expedition doctor and Base Camp manager.

By the afternoon of May 9, Hall's and Fischer's groups had reached Camp 4, a depressing, rock-strewn lunar wasteland even in the best weather. The spot is also an eerie garbage dump: Besides strips of shredded tents, discarded bright-yellow, green, and red oxygen tanks, spent batteries, empty raisin boxes, and PowerBar wrappers, there is a skeleton or two lying about on the loose shale, still zipped into down suits—grim reminders of the price a moody Everest can exact: 143 lives in forty-three years, most of them in this vicinity. Once in a while, a curious gorakh, a bird more common around Base Camp, wheels overhead, hoping in vain for a raisin, but not even the scavengers linger.

As dusk descended, wind and snow pasted the South Col—as it often does during late spring afternoons. The heavy-duty expedition tents snapped and vibrated. Inside, the teams drank tea or hot chocolate, dressed for the nighttime climb, then lay down around 8 P.M. for a few hours of rest, oxygen-flow regulators turned down low for sleeping. Fischer, apparently somewhat fatigued from tending to a client down below, crawled into his bag and went to sleep immediately.

Twenty-nine hundred vertical feet separate Camp 4 and the summit, a roughly mile-long stretch known as the Death Zone because it is there that the mountain is the least forgiving of mistakes. At this altitude, the human body feeds on itself, dying slowly from cold and lack of oxygen, and the weather can deteriorate rapidly and dangerously. Ambient air temperature at Camp 4 is often twenty degrees below zero at night; factor in the wind, and taking your gloves off for more than a few seconds puts your finger count in jeopardy. Lips stretched by the cold, one begins to resemble a shriveled, skeletal alien. If your body's core temperature dips below ninety-five degrees, hypothermia sets in—uncontrollable shivering first, then, as heat is drawn from the brain, confused thinking, hallucinations, coma, and death.

The biggest worries are high-altitude pulmonary and cerebral edema. Untreated, both can cause permanent damage or kill in a hurry. With pulmonary edema, fluid leaks into the lungs, blood or pink sputum gurgles up, and one dies by drowning. Tim Madsen was stricken with a spot of it at Camp 2, and became lethargic. "It took me twenty minutes to stuff my sleeping bag, then I'd rest for twenty minutes," says Madsen, who descended to Base Camp for a day, and lower for another four, and recovered enough to continue.

Cerebral edema occurs when fluid pools up in brain tissue. It can mess with your head in such a way that you are unaware of your condition. Motor skills fail. You can't walk without stumbling. You have trouble making rational decisions, say crazy things, and can become aggressive and defensive. "How are you doing? You're not looking so good," somebody might say. And you'd reply, "Get away from me! I'm doing fine!" Dealing with cold and altitude on Everest, managing the pain, can be far tougher than the technical aspect of climbing the mountain.

By 7:30 P.M. on May 9, the storm had passed and bright stars hung in the Himalayan sky. Fischer's team awoke anxiously in their tents at 10 P.M., and Neal Beidleman, thirty-seven, told jokes to cut the tension. "Laughter wouldn't come immediately," he recalls. "They'd have to kind of think a minute and then chuckle." Charlotte Fox, like the others, felt a little woozy and slow-witted. Boots on, the team drank tea—fiddling with the stove was a huge effort—and for those who could force down food (loss of appetite frequently occurs at high altitudes), there were candy bars and an easily digestible syrupy liquid called ReLode. "It's going great, isn't it?" said Scott Fischer, who appeared to be fine. "We're gonna pop this thing."

By 11:30, the team had assembled in the dark. Headlamps darted across the sky, creating weird silhouettes. Each climber hooked up to a fresh bottle of oxygen for the ascent and carried a second full one, with the intention of picking up a third on the way down from a stash that Sherpas would create near the South Summit. Each bottle, at a flow rate of two liters per minute, lasted five and a half to six hours. That was at least a sixteen-and-a-half-hour allotment, enough to leave Camp 4, touch the top, and get back before or just after dark the next day.

Above, Fischer noticed the bobbing headlamps of Hall's group making their way up, about an hour out of camp. They, too, were excited. One of Hall's clients, an American postal worker named Doug Hansen, was a second-timer. With Hall as his guide, Hansen had come within three hundred feet of the top in 1995 before bad weather had blown in. On April 10, Hansen had faxed a birthday message to his father, Fabian, back home in Renton, Washington: "I've arrived at Base Camp, strong and healthy. Maybe we can finally get this done with."

Led by guides Neal Beidleman and Anatoli Boukreev, thirty-eight, a renowned Russian climber, the six-client Fischer party moved out, with Fischer, as planned, bringing up the rear. The first formal stopping point out of Camp 4, about a six-hour climb, was the skinny

promontory known as the Southeast Ridge. Here, the climbers actually gained the ridge that led to the top and were treated to a regal
view: Lhotse and Makalu and the Tibetan plains, and in the distant
sky to the west, in a wash of light pink and orange, the umbra—the
shadow Earth makes as the sun shines upon it. Plowing through the
deep, sugary snow here was like climbing a sand dune.

Along the Southeast Ridge, the two teams were intermingled and
the first in a series of time-losing snags occurred. The plan, according
to several expedition members, had been for Sherpas to move out a
few hours ahead, break trail, and fix ropes: critical for any guided
climb, especially crucial for the first expeditions of the season. Ropes
are fixed to make the climb more efficient, faster, and safer. Fischer
indicated early in the trip that he didn't want to fix lines himself.
According to one member of his team, the Sherpas now simply
refused to fix rope as previously agreed; they wanted to climb with the
group. Another team member, less certain, got the impression that no
plan of any sort had been coordinated ahead of time. "Sherpas are
paid to set up camps, fix ropes, but they're not guides," says a friend of
Fischer's who has summitted Everest. "They need someone micro-
managing them. Without a schedule, things don't get done. They're
just standing around. I don't know why these ropes weren't fixed. That
was their job, and they didn't do it."

Finally, Beidleman undertook the job himself, establishing a route
to the top of Everest's South Summit, about one thousand vertical
feet away. In no particular order, the members of the two groups set
off higher. Fischer, behind the scrum somewhere, was supposed to be
pulling sweep: He would decide which climbers would go on and
which, too far behind, would not. "I just figured he was back there
doing his thing," Beidleman says. "I never thought twice about it." It
was a role that Fischer would fail to discharge, for clients and for himself. Some sort of high-altitude malady likely had struck him, compromising his decision making. As a result, Fischer was not catching up to
and reeling in stragglers—he was a straggler himself; the group,
though no one knew it, was effectively without a leader.

Various members of both groups reached the South Summit, about
330 vertical feet below the top, shortly after 10 A.M., and before long a
gaggle of ten or fifteen people formed. Most by now were on oxygen
bottle number three—which meant that they would have less than
originally planned for the descent. Here, Sherpas were to have fixed

ropes across a challenging ridge—the toughest part of the climb—up to the Hillary Step, a rock face forty feet high that marks the start of the final summit stretch. Once again, for reasons still unclear, that did not happen. Fischer's chief Sherpa, Lobsang Jangmu, who'd been to the summit three times before without oxygen, sat down and vomited, for at least the second time since the beginning of summit day. Lobsang apparently had not acclimatized well, perhaps for a reason: The Sherpa who'd developed pulmonary edema a few weeks previously was his uncle. On days when he might have been acclimatizing, Lobsang had been in Katmandu, attending him.

Along with Beidleman, Boukreev, Jon Krakauer, and a Rob Hall guide, Andy Harris, accepted the rope responsibility. "We took it upon ourselves to finally say, 'Well, fuck, we'll do it. What's the problem? Who's got the rope?'" Krakauer reported later in an online dispatch. The four of them finished fixing the final section from the South Summit to the top.

There wasn't quite enough rope, however. A hundred-meter stretch, a dangerous snow ridge with cornices, remained without fixed lines. One client recalls, "That was the first time that I thought, 'Am I really in over my head?'" Climbers slowed and sought good ice-ax placements. By now, some were becoming a little hypoxic; soon, smart people would begin to act stupid and would be unable to smarten up, even if they were aware that the dumbing-down was going on. Climbers forty or fifty feet apart would exist in different orbits. As massive as Everest is, this close to the top the individual climber's universe is small, claustrophobic, personal, with all thoughts centered on summitting and surviving.

"I remember standing there . . . thinking, *My oxygen is running out*," says a client. "But at the same time we were there, and there weren't sufficient impediments to stop us or turn us back." Nor was there a deadline to either summit or turn back. "There were no cutoff times. We never actually discussed cutoff times."

"You don't want to waste an hour up that high," says Charlotte Fox. "But there was no talk of turning around. And we never saw Scott all day."

Boukreev, a veteran of eleven ascents above eight thousand meters without oxygen, pushed on to the summit, followed by Krakauer, Harris, and Beidleman. Krakauer and Harris high-fived, took a few pictures, and headed right back down at about 1:30 P.M. Klev Schoening, a contractor from Seattle, and another Fischer client, Martin Adams, clambered up about twenty minutes later. Some clouds slipped by, but nothing that seemed ominous. Up there at 29,028 feet, at 767 cruising altitude, at the top of the world, the men maneuvered around the ridge to get a full view of five other eight-thousand-meter peaks, across the Tibetan plains, into Nepal and China.

The weather appeared to be holding, but neither of the group leaders was there to judge; only Krakauer remembers an early anxiety about the possibility of bad weather. People kept coming up, presumably waved on by Fischer. This was summit-fever time. Faced with no obvious threats to the climbers' safety, it would be hard for guides to turn back anybody who was so close—and who'd paid so much money. If a 2 P.M. cutoff had been applied, as it sometimes is on commercial Everest expeditions, probably only two Fischer clients would have summitted. As it was, Fox, Madsen, Lene Gammelgaard (another Fischer client), Hall and some of his clients (including Doug Hansen), Hill, and a number of Sherpas, among them the now-recovered Lobsang Jangmu, summitted ten to fifteen minutes apart. Gammelgaard, ecstatic at being the first Danish woman to make the top of Everest, unfurled flags provided by her corporate sponsors and posed for pictures. Charlotte Fox, following summit tradition, pocketed rocks.

Where was Fischer? Beidleman, on the summit for an hour and forty-five minutes—too long—began to pace. Because the ascent had been so slow, the oxygen situation was getting tight. Tim Madsen noticed a plume of clouds approaching and wondered about the weather.

"Scott's not here, but we've gotta get the hell out of here," Beidleman announced at about 3:10. "I was on three, my last bottle," Fox recalls. "Which is the way everyone was." Most clients probably didn't realize it, but they were now close to a zero-tolerance point; any further delays or mistakes could prove fatal.

Headed down, about 650 feet below the summit, Beidleman passed Fischer on his way up; he was moving slowly and looked tired, but not frightfully so. With him was Ming Ho Gau, who is known as Makalu and was the leader of a Taiwanese expedition he had left farther down the mountain. Waves and a few words were exchanged. "I just assumed he [Fischer] would touch the top, instantly turn around, and even before I got back to the South Summit, I totally expected to see him right behind me, helping with people, and all of us going down as a group," says Beidleman. "It just never happened."

Boukreev also encountered Fischer on the way down and saw no reason for concern, but didn't expect to. "Scott had great natural ability. He was very strong," Boukreev says. "One had to know Scott. Everything was always okay with him." Fischer and Boukreev agreed the Russian would descend quickly and be ready to bring oxygen up to other climbers who might be running out, effectively leaving Beidleman to guide Fischer's team down the mountain on his own.

Though his clients were now descending, Fischer continued up, carrying two radios, one to communicate with Lobsang, one to talk with Camp 4 and Ingrid Hunt at Base Camp. For whatever reason— battery failure, extreme cold, line-of-sight problems—it had been nearly impossible for Fischer to reach Base Camp by radio since he'd arrived on the South Col. Now, at the top, he managed to get through.

"Everybody made it, but I'm so tired," he reported.

Uneasy, Hunt radioed back congratulations and said, "Get down the mountain." Then the radio signal broke up again. "I was worried," she says. "Most people who get into trouble get into it during the descent."

Neal Beidleman's group continued to make its way down, more or less together, with Klev Schoening a bit out in front. Below that group, moving faster, were Adams, Harris, and Krakauer, who eyed the sky warily. A stiff wind blew across the ridge, and clouds rolled in to cover the vast west face of Everest. More clouds accumulated below, in the valley known as the Western Cwm. A thunderstorm brewed out over the plains of Tibet, level with Everest's summit. Members of Rob Hall's support staff, looking through telescopes over on Pumori, a nearby peak, could see how bad the weather was getting. But from up on top, it was tough to tell. Whether that information was ever relayed to any of Hall's team is uncertain.

Beidleman's group reached the South Summit, the next step down, at 4 P.M. Late. Of the Fischer clients, only Fox had been this high in the mountains before; people were weary and increasingly hypoxic. Hill, who didn't want to fall behind, called for a shot of dex: They were all carrying, in toothbrush holders, a prepared hypodermic of dexamethasone, a steroid that acts like adrenaline and counteracts the effects of cerebral edema. "If things get bad up there," Ingrid Hunt had said, "just stick yourself with this. It's like a bottle of oxygen." Fox gave Hill the intramuscular jab, and she perked up. Beidleman ordered Lene, whose oxygen bottle was nearly full, to switch with Hill, who had only half of one left. Just below the South Summit, Beidleman glissaded down a section, pulling Hill behind him by her harness. At the bottom, her crampons tore a pocket of his down suit; feathers billowed into the wind. The ragged descent continued, directly into a storm—and catastrophe.

At dusk, around 5:30, shadows reduced the afternoon colors on Everest to black, gray, and white. The wind picked up, the clouds rose higher, and the snow began. Six inches had already fallen on the lower part of the route, though it was impossible to tell that from here, high up the South Col. To avoid the horrifying prospect of getting lost in the dark and having to bivouac overnight here, the group would have to gain the tents of Camp 4 as quickly as possible. A stormy night on Everest is survivable, but it's a desperate gamble.

"Coming down, I sat on the Southeast Ridge, and I saw Scott glissade down this lower section [behind me]," says Tim Madsen. "I could see he was tired. He'd take ten steps, then rest, then ten more steps, then rest. . . . It's not necessarily only the weak people who become exhausted. Maybe the previous days were starting to run him down."

By now, Boukreev had reached Camp 4. "People were already on the borderline [running out of oxygen] at 6 P.M. It was possible that some had enough oxygen [to last] until 8 P.M., depending on who [they were] and how people had used their oxygen. . . . When there is no more oxygen, the person will get lost. . . . It is as if you go up very quickly, vertically, a thousand meters. Everything gets worse very quickly. The person cannot move, cannot walk; people die. You quickly develop cerebral edema or pulmonary edema."

As Beidleman's group neared the end of the last fixed line above Camp 4, the tents were in view, a quarter of a mile to a half mile away. Here, the group bottlenecked with a bunch of exhausted Hall clients. One of them, Seaborn Beck Weathers, a fifty-year-old Dallas pathologist, had spent most of the day on the Southeast Ridge, having trouble with his eyesight, unable to summit. Now, guide Mike Groom had Weathers with him on a short rope. Groom was also trying to assist a Japanese climber, Yasuko Namba, who on this trip captured the last of the seven summits. Namba, her face a mask of frost, was spent; she'd dropped her ice ax and even forgotten to take her sunglasses off.

Another emergency was developing higher up. Doug Hansen, having collapsed at the Hillary Step, could go no farther. He and Hall sat down in the snow. Scott Fischer, somewhere below the South Summit, also sat down, as did a badly hypoxic Makalu Gau. Stricken, perhaps, by cerebral edema, Fischer asked Lobsang to summon a helicopter, which Fischer, in his right mind, would know to be impossible. Lobsang begged his boss to get up. "You have to go down," Fischer said. The Sherpa cut out a little platform for Fischer on the ice and climbed down to save his own life.

Near the tents, close to 6 P.M., the storm hit full force. Krakauer had run into Andy Harris earlier and now saw him approaching Camp 4. "He was acting really strange on the summit ridge, sort of hypoxic and weird. . . . He seemed sort of desperate, his face was all frozen, his nose was frozen, his cheeks were all frosted up. And, he clearly just wanted to get to the tents," Krakauer reported later online. "He was in trouble. He just sat on his butt and slid down blue ice, which is crazy . . . you snag a crampon point, compound fracture." Krakauer watched Harris get within sixty feet of camp and never saw him again. "I think he just walked off the face in the whiteout."

Carrying four bottles of oxygen, Boukreev headed back up the mountain, into seventy-mile-per-hour blasts of wind and snow. With the windchill, the temperature had dropped to around sixty below. Visibility was maybe three feet. Boukreev turned on his headlamp and strapped on an oxygen bottle to speed his ascent. "I could not find the fixed line. I climbed vertically 650 feet. In distance I could not tell, only by the altitude on my altimeter. . . . I found a rope hanging which led somewhere into the clouds." Finding no evidence of climbers, Boukreev was forced to retreat.

Members of both the Fischer and Hall parties staggered on, into snow and dark. Visibility dropped to zero, and the tents disappeared from view. Disoriented, the group spread out. The hard ice flattened, as it does near Camp 4, but there was no sign of the tents. Beidleman came upon someone inert in the snow. Since a few of his clients were a little ahead, he figured the stricken climber was Lene Gammelgaard. He put her on his arm. When he reached to adjust her oxygen mask a while later, he felt a rig he didn't recognize. The climber was Hall's client Yasuko Namba.

Bowed by the storm and joined by Groom, Weathers, and Namba, the group slowed. They were now eleven, including Sherpas. Only three or four headlamps still worked, and it was too windy to go into the packs for spare batteries. The bottled oxygen was nearly gone. The situation was serious now, and if that hadn't dawned on the climbers yet, it may have been that they were too hypoxic to realize it.

The South Col is a rocky saddle about 550 yards wide between the Kang-shung and Lhotse faces. The tents lay in its southeast corner. Coming off the west-southwest side of the Col, the group contoured around to the left, away from the Lhotse Face and a forty-eight-hundred-foot drop-off. Snow zagged in lacerating horizontal planks. It was impossible for any-one to turn their face into the wind or to communicate without scream-ing. Namba, stumbling on her knees, said nothing. The procession continued for an hour, two hours, until Beidleman came to a patch of ice, a rise that seemed to roll downhill, as the ice does just before Camp 4.

A few feet farther was nothingness—probably the Kangshung Face. Beidleman sensed rather than saw it. "It was the void, man," he says. "It was the edge of the earth." The group halted and huddled up to wait out the storm, hoping it would blow over as quickly as the pre-vious night's had.

Beidleman looked at his watch: 10:20 P.M. Everybody lay down on a pack or in the lap of the next person upwind. The stronger climbers whacked the weaker ones to prevent them from falling asleep, a natu-ral and life-threatening consequence of a hypothermic or hypoxic state. Madsen and Schoening took turns as cheerleaders, punching each other and yelling at people who hadn't been heard from in a while. Groom, the only guide from Hall's group still in a position to help, radioed Camp 4 that the group was lost. People there, including Krakauer, shone lights into the sky and banged on pots, hoping Groom and the others might detect the sight or sound. They did not.

Yasuko Namba now seemed close to death. One of the men would grip her arm and shake her, and Namba would squeeze back weakly for an instant before her frozen fingers slipped off. Weathers was silent and virtually blind. For some, the battle against the elements was being lost. "I was completely hypoxic. The cold was just finishing me off," says Fox, who could hear voices but couldn't see anyone, because her eyes were frozen shut. "I crawled up in a ball and tried as hard as I could to die. I'd gotten a lot of great mountains. No regrets. I knew I wasn't going to be able to stay out there all night. I wasn't moving my arms and legs. My body would arc and move on its own, trying to generate heat." Hill coughed uncontrollably.

The ground blizzard raged on, but around midnight the sky became visible and the Big Dipper and North Star winked into view. Beidleman began to be convinced that the time had come for the group to move out again, and almost at that same moment Schoening's voice boomed through the wind: "I know the way!"

Beidleman was skeptical. Using the stars as reference points, Schoening said, he had no doubt. "I've got it figured out. This is it."

"Okay, stand up!" commanded Beidleman. "Get your pack!"

With bones stiff from cold and lack of movement, there was no mad rush. When some climbers stood, their knees buckled, and they tumbled over again like broken dolls. Eventually all started moving, zombielike, except for Namba, who was dragged.

The slim hope that mobilization sparked faded when, after only a few yards, five people sat down again. Beidleman made a fateful decision: He would strike out in the chosen direction, hopefully to locate Camp 4 and send back help to bring the team in. Boukreev was out there somewhere, rested and ready.

Beidleman set off, with Schoening, Gammelgaard, and Groom, walking up a slope, dead into the wind, over a rise and then down. "It was implied that they would go and send help, though nothing was ever said," Madsen says. "Nothing needed to be said." Two Sherpas followed behind.

Hill tried to crawl after Beidleman's party, faltered, crawled a bit, then dragged herself back to the group and began to hallucinate. A teahouse stood on the ice a few feet away, she was sure of it, and a man with dark hair strolled inside, strumming a mandolin. "Don't give up!" Madsen yelled. "You've got your son!"

Beidleman estimates that he covered the quarter mile in fifteen minutes, but he can only guess, because he was so hypoxic by then. There was a headlamp! Or was it just another hallucination? The headlamp came closer: Boukreev, standing outside the tents. Beidleman could hardly talk. He rasped a greeting and gave directions to the others. Schoening, Gammelgaard, Groom, and Beidleman fell into tents and tried to drink some tea, but ended up spilling most of it, so frozen and shaky were their hands.

Before Boukreev set off, between 1:00 and 1:30 A.M., he says, he sought help. He tried waking some members of Hall's expedition. No luck. "It was useless to ask people from other expeditions, because no one in these circumstances risks their life for people they are not responsible for." He tried rousing his own Sherpas. No volunteers. "Nobody could help, not anyone. All climbed into their tents to recover. They climbed into the warmth, put on oxygen. They slept such deep sleep it was as though they had no signs of life." A friend of Fischer's who was in Nepal at the time says, "With the Sherpas, you get the idea these guys are your man Friday, but I don't think they're going to die for the gringo, and I'm not sure they should be expected to. This goes against the myth of the Sherpa, but these guys are going to save their asses first."

Boukreev set off by himself. A short time later, he returned.

Alone.

Beidleman provided better directions. Boukreev plunged back out into the snow. About 350 to 450 yards from camp, he saw a headlamp: Madsen's. Madsen, Fox, and Hill, with Namba and Weathers in the general area, were dozing fifteen yards from the steep descent on the Tibetan side—and a mere fifteen yards from the point at which Boukreev had turned back on his previous rescue foray.

Happy as he was to see the Russian, Madsen was also shocked. "Where is everybody?" he asked. "We need more than one person. There's five of us out here."

"I tried."

Boukreev gave Hill oxygen, grabbed Fox, and vanished into the night.

Weathers was curled up, asleep in the snow. Namba lay on her back on the rocks, a position she'd been in for hours. Suddenly, perhaps in a final, euphoric, precoma stage of hypothermia, Weathers awoke and tried to stand on a boulder. The wind knocked him backward. Twenty minutes passed. Two hours. Madsen wasn't sure how long, and he grew impatient. Boukreev himself might be lost by now or injured. "Enough is enough," Madsen said to Hill, and they both stood up. "We're walking in."

Boukreev reappeared.

He shepherded the two climbers back to camp, between 4 and 5 A.M., and helped the weakest of the survivors off with their crampons, before they collapsed thankfully into their sleeping bags. The Russian says he did not see Weathers, and that by the time he returned after leading in Fox, Namba had died.

"She's dead," said Beidleman, weeping. "But she was so little."

The next morning, as Beidleman took his clients down the mountain—they were still suffering from the effects of the extreme altitude, and Fox's feet were so badly frostbitten that she was eventually evacuated to Katmandu—the magnitude of the tragedy began to take shape and more rescue missions were mounted. Two of Hall's clients had abandoned summit attempts relatively early and made it back to camp. Still alive on the mountain were Fischer, Hall, and Gau; Harris, Namba, and Weathers were presumed dead, and Hansen had died at Hall's side during the night.

Sherpas found Weathers and Namba and reported that they were, indeed, dead. A doctor affiliated with Hall's expedition made a similar determination about the two climbers. Meanwhile, on the other side of the mountain, three members of the Indo-Tibetan Border Police were losing their lives trying to summit from the more challenging North Face. Everest was turning into an open graveyard, and the body count kept rising.

When Sherpas finally reached Fischer and Gau, between 10 A.M. and 1 P.M., the two were scarcely alive. Fischer could not move and was barely breathing. "I think he thought he was Scott, the strongest guy in the world," Fox says, "and it turns out he was only human." Since Fischer would not get up, and the weather hadn't improved much, the Sherpas left him with oxygen and descended with Gau, who they felt could be saved.

Recovered from his missions of the night before, Boukreev went back up the mountain. "I . . . found Scott about 7 [P.M.]. He was dead. I covered his face and secured his body and had to leave him. The winds and cold were as bad as the day before."

Gau, badly frostbitten, was choppered off Everest by Lieutenant Colonel Madan K.C., of the Nepalese military, in one of the highest-altitude rescues ever undertaken. The passenger on Madan's next flight was none other than Weathers. In one of the most memorable moments in mountaineering history, if not the history of man's resolve to live, Weathers had stirred from his grave in the rocks, thought about his family in Texas, stood up, and stumbled back to camp, his arms extended like a mummy's, on the morning after Beidleman and his group were rescued.

Perhaps the most shatteringly poignant moment of all belonged to Rob Hall, who had stayed through the night in a snow hole at the

South Summit with his client Hansen, but was unable to move the next day. He was patched through by radio to his wife, Jan Arnold, in New Zealand, at 6 P.M., before he died. (A rescue mission earlier that day had been forced back by more bad weather a mere two hundred yards from his location.)

"Don't worry about me too much," Hall said to his wife. "If only someone can get up to me and give me a couple Thermoses of tea." Rob and Jan's first child was due in July. Fischer leaves behind two children, Andy, nine, and Katie Rose, five. Hansen is survived by a daughter, Angie, nineteen, and a son, Jaime, twenty-three.

Windburned, hoarse, and twenty pounds lighter, Neal Beidleman is just off the plane from Katmandu, enjoying a quiet, brilliant spring day at home at the base of the slopes in Aspen. The previous few frustrating and sad days were spent closing up camp and haggling with Nepalese officials over Scott Fischer's $4,000 garbage-removal deposit. Fischer was dead. The bureaucrats didn't see a reason to return the money to someone who wasn't a member of Fischer's immediate family.

A weathered barrel of gear sits unpacked on Beidleman's porch. The phone line inside the house is overloading with questions from *60 Minutes, Vanity Fair,* and other magazines and newspapers, local and worldwide. Glad to have her husband back alive, Amy Beidleman says she doesn't mind the intrusions. Beidleman takes the calls and spends hours getting his story out, defending decisions made halfway around the world, fending off hard judgments offered in hindsight. It's not the mountain making him hoarse now.

"We made some mistakes, some little mistakes, along the way, but did we blunder hugely? No, I don't think so," Beidleman says. The record speaks for itself, if not for Fischer's management skills, then of Beidleman's skills as a guide and Boukreev's hardiness. Six of the Fischer clients summitted, and all of them made it home. "Scott's death was really independent of our actions," Beidleman says. "His actions may have affected us, but ours did not affect him."

Rob Hall's group did not fare as well, of course, despite its leader's more meticulous approach. No one knows why Hall elected to stay with Doug Hansen, instead of trying to save his own life. The bodies of clients Namba and Hansen, as well as that of guide Andy Harris, remain on the mountain. Weathers may lose parts of the fingers on his left hand and most of his right hand to frostbite.

And now the future of guided expeditions to Everest is under intense discussion. The primary subject of debate has been whether or not guided clients even belong on high-altitude climbs, whether their mere presence endangers the enterprise for everyone. When, on June 2, Jon Krakauer told *60 Minutes* that Hall and Fischer would be alive today if they had not been guiding clients on Everest, angered survivors were quick to respond.

"Weak people are weeded out by the mountain early on," insists Tim Madsen. "If you expect somebody to take care of you, the mountain knows that and you'll get in trouble early—and not get very far. Climbing on Everest is self-regulating."

Friends of Fischer's also weighed in. "People die on eight-thousand-meter peaks," says Brent Bishop, a guide who summitted Everest with Fischer in 1994. Bishop made it clear that he does not think guiding is the issue. "The good altitude climbers—most of them are dead. Just because people are being guided up doesn't reduce what the mountain can do. That's the allure of it in a lot of ways."

Madsen continues: "Andy Harris, he wasn't baby-sitting people on the descent. And Rob Hall, he sacrificed himself [trying] to save Doug Hansen. The rest of his clients cared for themselves. Everybody went on their own little epic."

Cared for themselves. Their own little epic.

In retrospect, it seems to make sense to question whether clients should ever be on their own in such potentially dire situations; whether a guide should ever let a customer get into a position where a sudden storm would cost him his life. Arguably, a client-to-guide ratio of even two to one wasn't, and isn't, enough on high-altitude climbs such as Everest. When trouble hit, Fischer and Hall were nonfactors, Boukreev was in Camp 4, and Harris had walked off the mountain, leaving Beidleman and Groom to get everyone down.

Historically, the prime directive of adventure-travel guiding has been "Bring everyone back safely." But in the Death Zone, the very concept of guiding changes so much as to be almost invalid. Though some clients in the Fischer and Hall expeditions might not have realized it, everyone that high up must be prepared to save his own life. Even during the thrill of summitting there can be no illusions about that. Life at eight thousand meters is no Class V rapid. No guide, at any price, can muscle back minds or bodies wrecked by altitude sickness.

On a practical level, there are undoubtedly tactics that future guided expeditions may consider that Fischer's and Hall's didn't. They may have more concrete plans for setting fixed ropes. They may arrange for more oxygen to be carried up. And their determination to avoid bad weather may be heightened to the point that fewer groups may actually attempt to summit.

"I don't think you need to be the world's greatest climber to guide Everest," says one client. "You just have to be an organizational nazi." Many experienced mountaineers, though, argue that hard-and-fast rules—including ones like 2 P.M. turnaround times—cannot be imposed on Everest, that the history of climbing is built around improvisation and flexibility.

But no matter how it is approached, Everest has shown that it is not the routine adventure that's been advertised. "Part of summitting eight thousand meters is taking chances," points out Bishop, who was at Base Camp in May. "You've got to throw the dice a little bit. If you get bad luck or any mistakes are made, you're not coming back. I hate to say this, but that's the wonderful thing about it all.

"Everest will always have the last word."

AUGUST 1996

Sunk

by Doug Stanton

O N A WINDSWEPT NOVEMBER morning, Captain Charles Butler McVay III, a 1919 graduate of the United States Naval Academy and a former commander of the World War II cruiser USS *Indianapolis,* wakes and takes stock of his day. He's alone in a drafty bedroom of a Colonial house called Wini-van Farm, near Litchfield, Connecticut. He is seventy years old, in excellent health, with white hair and piercing blue eyes. Always dapper, always self-assured, he dresses in a pressed khaki shirt, khaki pants, and leather slippers, an ensemble that has become a uniform for him, a vestige of his life in the wartime navy.

Ready for the day, he descends the creaking staircase to the kitchen, where he's greeted by the housekeeper, Florence Regosia, who insists on calling him "Admiral," an abbreviation of rear admiral, the rank he received upon his retirement, what's called a "tombstone promotion." McVay, however, usually insists on being addressed as "Captain." Perhaps it seems more honest to him.

He passes through the kitchen, and, outside, he meets Al Dudley, his gardener, and they begin work on the shrubs, binding them with twine and burlap for the long voyage through winter. Men are quick to say about the captain that he is a "man's man"; women find him witty and charming, always a gentleman. So it's easy to imagine him chatting with Dudley, pliers and twine in his hand, as if nothing at all is bothering him.

McVay and the gardener break for lunch, and Dudley trudges back across the road to his own house. Inside, Florence is setting out a sandwich on the dining-room table. McVay's wife, Vivian, with whom he has been speaking less and less, is off somewhere in another room, eating alone. Before sitting down, the captain goes up to his bedroom, ostensibly to change out of his khaki into something suitable for an afternoon of playing bridge at the Sanctum, a gentlemen's club in Litchfield. He closes the door.

Perhaps it's now that some small nerve snaps within McVay, a strand already stretched too far in his life. On the nightstand sits a holster containing a navy-issue .38-caliber revolver. He picks it up.

For all McVay's usual good cheer, Florence has been worried about him. Later, she'll remark that his face had seemed glazed and flushed. A little while later, she walks into the dining room and the captain is nowhere to be found. Upstairs, his bedroom is empty. Then she finds the empty holster on the nightstand. Frantic, she begins rushing through the house.

At about this time, at his tiny house across the road, Dudley is having some weird premonitions—he's sensing that all is not right at Winivan Farm. He hurries back and begins looking for the captain. But McVay himself is nowhere to be seen. Wherever he is, one thing's for sure: He has a gun in his hand. McVay opens the front door and walks through a small wooden entryway onto the front step. Then he lies down, his gaunt face tilted up at a gray sky.

From the yard of Winivan Farm, you can look out at the road heading north into Litchfield and south toward the main arteries leading to the sea. Many of the houses in Litchfield were built by nineteenth-century sea captains, and a number of them still have widows' walks. The village is sunk in a wooded valley, as if the wives of these captains had wanted to drag their husbands as far away from the sea as possible. It's a place people usually come to in peace and prosperity at the end of their lives; it's a place to come and forget things.

The captain brings the barrel of the gun to his head. In his left hand is a set of house keys, and on the key ring is a metal toy sailor, which news reports will later describe as a good-luck charm. Whatever luck the captain has had, it's run out. America doesn't make many men like Charles Butler McVay anymore, men whose sense of duty transcends their sense of self, men who are willing to stand by quietly even as this duty eats them alive. The captain pulls the trigger and blows himself into history.

When word of McVay's death reaches the outside world, major newspapers carry an obituary describing a historic naval career—"Pacific [War] Hero Dies at 70" reads one. In Litchfield, few people know why McVay has killed himself. They also know very little about the life he had lived before moving to the tiny, insular community.

The truth is, Captain Charles Butler McVay was a survivor of the worst disaster at sea in American naval history. This is a dubious distinction, to be sure—one that dogged him throughout the years that followed the tragedy. He never discussed with anyone the nightmarish events that occurred in the early moments of July 30, 1945, when a Japanese submarine torpedoed his ship, the USS *Indianapolis,* killing some 300 men and sending nearly 900 others into the black, churning embrace of the Philippine Sea. When the ship was finally discovered lost, four days later, only 321 of those sailors were still alive. (Four more would die shortly after rescue in military hospitals.)

In the aftermath, two unprecedented things happened: The navy changed the way it tracked ships at sea; and McVay was charged with negligence in his command and court-martialed, ruining his naval career. Of the 400 American captains whose ships went down during WWII—and in the entire history of the U.S. Navy—McVay is the only commander to have been court-martialed for the sinking of his ship during wartime.

In the early '90s, declassified documents that might prove McVay's innocence were discovered. Upon review, however, the navy refused to reconsider its decision; it insists to this day that the verdict delivered by the court-martial was just.

Of the original 317 survivors, 130 are still alive; to a man they contend that Captain McVay was not responsible for the horrific event that changed the course of their lives. In 1999, 14 of them appeared before the Senate Armed Services Committee to gather support for their thirty-five-year-long effort to clear the captain's name—a congressional resolution would declare that the court-martial was "morally unsustainable," and McVay's conviction unjust—and to win a Presidential Unit Citation for their ship. In most history books, the sinking of the *Indianapolis* isn't mentioned, but the disaster haunts the Department of the Navy, and it haunts these men. At night, some of them still reach out from the cage of sleep to grip a bed they are sure is sinking beneath them.

At 4 A.M. on July 16, 1945, Hunters Point dock, in San Francisco Bay, California, is a quiet, deserted place, and it strikes many of the crew of the USS *Indianapolis* as odd. Usually, Hunters Point harbors some fifteen ships, but tonight . . . where the hell is every other ship, and everybody else? It's like the Super Bowl emptying on the night of the game.

The *Indianapolis* is a heavy cruiser, designed to bombard enemy emplacements on land and to blow enemy planes out of the sky. She's 610 feet long, a floating city with enough weaponry to lay siege to downtown San Francisco. She's been at Mare Island Naval Yard for two months for repairs. Four days earlier, however, this respite had been abruptly terminated by orders that the *Indianapolis* stand by to sail immediately.

From out of the fog, two army trucks thunder to a stop, and a detachment of armed marines steps down. The canvas flaps at the rear of the trucks are parted to reveal a black metal canister and a large wooden crate. A cable from a crane aboard the *Indianapolis* snakes down above the crate, which is secured with straps, lifted skyward, and set on the hangar deck. The crate is then placed under strict guard by the marine detachment.

The canister, meanwhile, is taken aboard by two sailors, who carry it up the gangway suspended from a metal pole. It's secured to the deck in the flag lieutenant's cabin and then padlocked. Accompanying the canister are Major Robert Furman and Captain James Nolan, who introduce themselves to the captain as army artillery officers. In reality, Nolan is a radiologist and Furman is an engineer engaged in top secret weapons development.

McVay gives the order to get the *Indianapolis* under way. At about the same time, on an expanse of desert in New Mexico, a tremendous flash fills the morning sky; it's an explosion of staggering magnitude, and the aftershock knocks men off their feet five miles away. It's the first explosion of an atomic device in the history of the world.

Shortly afterward, a marine delivers a message to Dr. Lewis Haynes, the medical officer on Spruance's staff. It is, in essence, a dispatch from President Harry S. Truman, ordering the ship ahead at any cost. McVay informs his staff that in the event of the ship going down, the canister is to be placed in its own raft and set adrift; only after doing this are the crewmen to look to their personal safety.

Lashed to the hangar deck, the large wooden box rides easily as the *Indianapolis* points her bow toward Pearl Harbor. The marines guard the box around the clock; and, during the next nine days, crewmen will constantly shoot the shit about just what the box might contain. Guesses run wild, anywhere from biological weapons to gold bullion.

Beneath them, inside the crate, sit the integral components of the atomic bomb known as Little Boy. Packed in the canister in the admiral's cabin is a large quantity of uranium-235, totaling half the fissile material available to the United States at the time. In three weeks, the bomb will be dropped on Hiroshima. At 8 A.M., McVay clears the harbor and sails past the Golden Gate Bridge into the nuclear age.

Until this moment, McVay's orders have remained sealed in an envelope he's kept locked in his cabin. Now, some distance from land, he tears it open and learns that he is to deliver his secret cargo to Tinian Island, a tiny palm-fringed outpost in the West Pacific. From San Francisco, this is a journey of 6,214 miles, which McVay accomplishes without incident in an astounding 216 hours, including a stop at Pearl Harbor. He rides into Tinian on July 26 at flank speed. A half mile offshore, he drops anchor.

It's unclear if McVay knows the nature of his cargo, but up on the bridge, he is grim-faced and tense; he hasn't been his usual self, the man who likes to describe the *Indianapolis* as a "happy ship." McVay sometimes instigates skeet-shooting sessions on the ship's afterdeck or abruptly announces in port over the ship's PA: "Anyone interested in fishing, join me at the bow." The captain is forty-six, his twenty-six-year career has been stellar, and it's possible he'll make admiral. He may even surpass the accomplishments of his father, an admiral who commanded the Asiatic Fleet during the 1920s.

Standing aboard the *Indianapolis,* McVay sees a flotilla of boats bearing down on him, carrying an impressive gathering of officers from every branch of the military. They board and watch attentively as fitters remove the black canister and the huge crate. The cargo is lowered into a barge and ferried ashore, along with Nolan and Furman, still posing as artillery officers. In less than eleven days' time, Little Boy will be hoisted into the belly of the *Enola Gay,* a B-29 bomber.

McVay and his crew, still unaware of the contents of the crate and the canister, are nonetheless elated by their proficient handling of the mission. The crew lets out a cheer, and a smiling McVay weighs anchor and points the *Indianapolis* toward Guam, 140 miles away.

Arriving at Guam on July 27, McVay reports to the port director for his routing orders; he is about to sail from the Marianas Frontier into the Philippine Frontier. On Guam, this is what surface operations officer

Oliver Naquin knows concerning McVay's voyage along what's called the Peddie/Leyte Route: He knows that Japanese submarines are operating in the area, and that three days earlier the USS *Underhill*, while traveling from Leyte to Okinawa, had been hit by a kaiten—a kamikaze-like torpedo that is piloted by a crewman—and sunk, killing 112 men. Naquin is aware of these things because he is privy to intelligence probably gathered by ULTRA, a top secret code-breaking program; it is part of Naquin's job to "sanitize" ULTRA intelligence so that it can be used by people like McVay without alerting the enemy that its codes have been broken.

Instead of recasting the intelligence in a form McVay can use, however, Naquin's office informs McVay that conditions along the Peddie/Leyte Route are normal. McVay is next given orders to follow a zigzag course at his discretion during daylight hours and at night during periods of good visibility.

Zigzagging is a defensive maneuver used by warships to constantly change course. If a moving target is hard to hit, the thinking goes, then a target moving erratically is even harder. In truth, the maneuver is of negligible value, as several experts will testify at McVay's court-martial, but required by operational regulations. On July 28, McVay is set to sail into a sea he thinks he understands.

Sixty feet below the surface of the Pacific, in the submarine *I-58*, Lieutenant-Commander Mochitsura Hashimoto, the son of a Shinto priest, frets. Incredibly, during his four years at sea, he has yet to sink an enemy ship. He has erected a shrine aboard the sub, and he prays to it for his luck to change. The *I-58* carries nineteen oxygen-powered torpedoes and four kaitens.

Tonight, the kaiten pilots are anxious for the holy kiss of an honorable death, but Hashimoto, peering through the periscope, scans the horizon and finds it empty. Still, he's stationed himself at a critical point on the Peddie/Leyte Route, and he's sure a ship will pass.

Six hundred and fifty miles away, at 9:30 A.M., the *Indianapolis* will pull away from the harbor at Apra, Guam, headed for Leyte.

By the evening of Sunday, July 29, the *Indianapolis* is three hundred miles from the nearest landfall, and a gray scrim of low clouds covers the sky. Sometime between 7:30 and 8:00 P.M., McVay gives the order to cease zigzagging. Besides the worsening weather, what must be on the captain's mind is the latest intelligence report, which has assured him that his route along the Peddie is clear of enemy traffic.

At about 10:30 P.M., McVay steps off the bridge into the cool night air. The captain rarely sees his family, and it's likely he's thinking of Kimo and Charles, his sons by his first marriage, to Kinau Wilder, an actress. Most of all, he's probably thinking of his second wife, Louise Claytor, the niece of a naval captain, who has cast a spell over him.

These few minutes alone away from the bridge are probably the only rest McVay has had all day, and it must be reassuring to feel the ship moving so efficiently—so soundly—beneath him. Because of the high temperatures belowdecks, which regularly exceed 120 degrees, a majority of the men choose to sleep topside, each night traipsing across the deck in search of a cool corner on the ship. Tonight, at least three hundred are scattered about in the dark, under stairways, propped against storage lockers, atop gun turrets. At 11 P.M., the captain retires to his battle cabin. He strips and is shortly asleep.

The officer of the deck in charge of the eight-to-midnight watch has orders to respond to any change in their situation. If, for instance, the visibility improves, he is to resume zigzagging and notify the captain immediately. Captain Charles Butler McVay goes to sleep confident that his ship is in excellent hands.

About three miles away across the Philippine Sea, Lieutenant-Commander Hashimoto sees something up ahead—a blur on the horizon. He's standing in the *I-58*'s conning tower and peering through his binoculars. He can't believe his luck.

He orders the sub to attack depth and creeps ahead at a quiet three knots. He's studying the approaching vessel through the periscope, but he can't make out exactly what type of ship she is. Realizing that a kill shot will be difficult from head-on, Hashimoto swings the sub and falls into position to meet the ship's broadside. From this angle, he can see that she's indeed a large warship—a huge one.

The kaiten pilots are adamant that one of them be launched, but Hashimoto insists that his magnetic torpedoes will be sufficient. One eye pressed to the rubber cup of the periscope, he gives the order to fire.

Each torpedo carries 1,210 pounds of explosive—enough fire-power to level a six-story building—and Hashimoto releases six of them, at three-second intervals, in a widening fan of white lines.

*   *   *

While the torpedoes race toward the *Indianapolis*, her crewmen are playing craps and poker, reading paperback novels, making coffee, sleeping. Marine Private Giles McCoy, nineteen, is guarding two prisoners down in the brig.

Dr. Haynes has just turned in for the night, exhausted after a day of administering one thousand cholera shots. Of those asleep in the tropical heat on deck, many are wearing just T-shirts and underwear, using their shoes for pillows.

At around 12:05 A.M., the first torpedo blows an estimated 65 feet of the bow skyward. The explosion sends a plume of water, lit from within by red streamers of flame, 150 feet into the air, showering the men on deck with foaming seawater, fuel oil, and burning shrapnel. Next, there's a detonation amidships: A second torpedo hits below the waterline and careens through a powder magazine and a tank filled with thousands of gallons of fuel. This explosion is massive. The *Indianapolis* seems to pause for a moment, like a large beast struck between the eyes, and then she continues plowing ahead at twelve knots. With her bow gone, she begins scooping up seawater by the ton. Already, a hundred men are probably dead and the *Indianapolis* is listing to starboard. She has very little time left, and those aboard have even less in which to decide their fate.

All communications and electrical power in the forward part of the ship are disabled, and it's impossible to talk with any personnel in the engine room. The latter situation is catastrophic, because it is now imperative that the engines be stopped. The water rushing in at the bow is punching through auxiliary bulkheads, roaring back through the ship toward the stern and drowning everyone in its path.

Up in his cabin, McVay is thrown from his bed and slammed to the floor. Immediately, he begins collecting himself in a whirlwind of conflicting thoughts. *Have we been hit by a kamikaze? Have we run into a mine? Are we under attack?* McVay now has three things to do immediately: Assess the damage, take care of it, and—if indeed he is in a battle—engage the enemy. Most dreaded of all is the possibility that he'll have to give the order to abandon ship. At this point, he must also get off distress messages detailing the ship's position and condition. Naked, he stumbles from his cabin to the bridge.

"I have tried to stop the engines," the officer of the deck tells him. "I don't know whether the order has gotten through to the engine room." Next, the damage control officer informs him that the ship's forward compartments are flooding quickly, but at this point McVay believes he can still save the *Indianapolis*.

"Do you want to call for abandon ship, sir?" the damage control officer asks.

"Maybe we can hold her. Go back below and take one more look and report back to me immediately."

The man hurries belowdecks to check the damage and seal as many watertight compartments as possible. It's the last McVay will ever see of him. The captain rushes back to his cabin, grabs his khakis, a shirt, and his shoes, then returns to the bridge, where he learns of the ship's worsening situation. His executive officer arrives to tell him that the *Indianapolis* is flooding at an incredible rate. "I recommend," he announces, "that we abandon ship."

McVay is stunned. Peering through the smoke toward the front of the ship, he has been able to see practically nothing. The explosions have ruined the water mains, and fire control has been nonexistent. All power is down, and efforts to reach the engine room have failed.

"Okay," he says. "Pass the word to abandon ship."

Later, the captain will have time to consider this moment, which already he senses is the end of his career. He prepares himself for the inevitable plunge into an inhospitable sea. He begins making his way down from the bridge.

As the order to abandon ship passes like a fever through the crew, as many as four hundred are massing at the port rail near the stern, and they begin jumping, screaming as they drop thirty feet into the sea. The ship's angle is now lifting propellers number three and number four out of the water—and number three is still running. Some of the men drop into the massive, spinning blades and are cut to pieces.

Throughout the ship, men are reacting in a variety of ways. Some rush to their bunks and quickly finish letters home; one man pauses in his berth to clip his toenails; another makes a sandwich and swallows it whole, then drinks a glass of water; yet another is seen running topside wearing just a bathrobe and cradling a bottle of scotch.

The ship is still plowing ahead and now resembles a train careening out of control down its track. Those with knives slash at bags of kapok life jackets and at floater nets stored on the quarterdeck bulkhead. Others begin sliding down the ship's side. Some simply walk off the listing deck as if they are stepping into a swimming pool.

After jumping, the men are scattered in a jagged line that will eventually stretch for twenty miles. A vast, poisonous blanket of black fuel oil pours from the ship's ruptured hull and spreads across the water. It's as sticky as molasses, and the men can't avoid swallowing it as they paddle around in the sea's heavy swells—it coats them and clogs their eyes, ears, and mouths, eating away at the sensitive membranes. As they drift, many of them are in shock, and nothing is visible of their blackened faces except the whites of their eyes.

Those men still on board suddenly find themselves walking on the walls, and some are crushed by falling machinery and equipment. McCoy, standing guard duty in the brig, knows something is terribly wrong, but because there's no smoke or fire in his compartment, it's hard to know what. He has no idea of the terror unfolding in the ship's forward area. Tossed to the floor by the explosion, he thinks at first that they've been rammed by a Japanese destroyer.

Asleep in his private berth in the forward part of the ship at the time of the torpedoing, Haynes is thrown so high from his bed that he lands on his desk. The second explosion knocks him onto the floor, and he hears his hands sizzle on the hot deck. He grabs a life jacket and makes his way through acrid white smoke.

"Open a porthole! For crissakes, open a porthole!" someone is yelling. The doctor finds one open and jams his head through. The relief is instant—he draws in the humid night air with deep breaths. At the same time, something is slapping him in the face, and he realizes that it's a rope and that he might be able to wriggle out the porthole—about twenty inches in diameter—and climb to safety.

He grips the rope and, despite the pain in his hands, grits his teeth, pulls himself up, and is soon standing on the hangar deck. The scene that greets him is horrifying—screaming men in various stages of delirium, some burned beyond recognition. What happens next is almost too much for the doctor to bear. The hangar deck is filled with some thirty stretchers containing his patients. As the ship increases its list, these men begin slowly sliding down toward the sea. They gain speed during their descent and spill over the edge, hitting the water with a splash. Haynes watches one man wearing a leg cast claw at the air and then sink without a sound.

Recognizing that the situation is hopeless, Haynes finally jumps and quickly begins paddling away, afraid, like every man aboard, of being sucked under. When he turns to look back, he can see men standing on the giant, stilled propellers on the port side, riding the ship into the sea.

✿   ✿   ✿

As the *Indianapolis* sinks, distress signals giving her position are broadcast on frequencies monitored by ships at sea and by shore stations: These messages are sent out repeatedly by two men in a pair of radio rooms filling with smoke. Somebody, somewhere, should be receiving them.

In fact, four U.S. vessels will receive SOS messages from the *Indianapolis,* and none will take any conclusive action to determine their accuracy—a response that is more or less pro forma at this point in the war. Japanese forces, hoping to confuse American intelligence and to draw out search vessels, have regularly broadcast bogus distress signals. Earlier in the conflict, such messages might have been investigated, but tonight they're ignored as a possibly deadly prank.

Shortly after the signals have been sent, McVay finds himself walking down the port rail. By all accounts, he is neither scared nor panicked. "I decided that I would attempt to save myself," he later explains. "[But] I must admit that I had the thought that it would be much easier if I go down, [then] I won't have to face what I know is coming after this.

"I was sucked off into the water by what I believe was a wave caused by the bow going down rather rapidly, because I found myself in the water and looked above me and the screws were directly overhead. Within a few seconds, I felt hot oil and water brush over the back of my neck and looked around and heard a swish and the ship was gone."

It had taken just twelve minutes for the ten-thousand-ton *Indianapolis* to vanish. Now completely submerged, the ship lets loose one last tremendous explosion—a resounding *whumphhh.* McCoy feels it penetrate his bones, his gut, the soles of his feet. He's swimming harder than he's ever swum in his life, trying desperately to get away from the ship. As he strokes, he feels a mysterious force reach out and jerk him underwater.

Suddenly, all is silent. He only knows that he's being dragged down. The last thing he remembers is the rush of water past his face and the feeling that his eyes are about to explode from the pressure. And then he blacks out. A short time later, however, he snaps back to consciousness and finds himself rushing toward the surface at great speed, as if he were in an express elevator.

He's not in an elevator, though. He's in an air bubble—a big one— and its dry jaws are clamped around the lower half of his body, so that only his upper body is in the water as he rockets upward. He erupts through the surface with such force that he rises three feet above it.

McCoy has returned to a dismal world of screaming men. For miles, the sea is littered with debris—potato crates, ammunition cans, stray life vests, corpses. He looks around and knows he has one decision to make: *Am I gonna live, or am I gonna die?*

Monday, July 30. As McCoy works his way into a life vest, Haynes, his face and hands badly burned, paddles around the oily soup, yelling for calm. About a half mile away, the captain, blinded in one eye by stinging fuel oil, is clinging to a drifting potato crate.

Coughing up seawater, McCoy is cursing and struggling to regain his wits. Up ahead, he can make out a life raft riding the swells, and he decides it's a far better place to spend the night than dangling alone in his life vest. As he prepares to swim to the raft, a young shipmate slides up to him out of the night. The boy, maybe nineteen or twenty, is in bad shape. He doesn't have a life vest and he's straddling a gunpowder can, which is about the size of a paint bucket. Right now, it's the only thing holding his ass off the cold ocean floor. A body drifts out of the darkness and continues past them. McCoy can't tell who it is—the face is smeared with oil—but he quickly reaches out and pulls the dead man close and cuts off his life vest. The corpse sinks beneath the waves and is gone.

McCoy hands the vest to the sailor and then stares ahead into the darkness. Suddenly, he spots something on the horizon—he can't tell what it is, but it's immense. McCoy becomes convinced that it's a ship, and he's certain that it's coming to rescue them. He reaches down into the water and to his surprise finds his service-issue Colt .45 still in its holster.

He quickly removes the pistol, racks a round, and fires off two shots. What McCoy's looking at, though, is not an American vessel. It's the *I-58*, prowling the kill zone; throughout the war, it's been a practice among Japanese sub commanders to machine-gun a sunken ship's survivors.

Immediately after torpedoing the *Indianapolis*, Hashimoto had begun following the stricken ship on a parallel course, tracking it. By 1:30 A.M., he'd reloaded his torpedo tubes and resurfaced. Hashimoto is certain that a destroyer escort had been accompanying his target, and he worries that he'll be spotted. *Could the warship have sunk?*

With his deck lights turned off for fear of detection, Hashimoto continues his search in the dark. It's impossible to see anything clearly, and he's starting to suspect that he may, in fact, have missed the target. He circles the area for about an hour, and finally, when the risk of being discovered by a destroyer seems too great, he gives up. He will later say that he was looking for wreckage and had no intention of machine-gunning anyone.

He turns the sub north, hoping for a chance to rebuild his life from the ashes of a war he knows his country is losing. Assuming he has sunk the ship, he orders up a celebratory meal of boiled eels and potatoes for the crew. The *I-58* is one of only six large Japanese subs still operational, and this is Hashimoto's last mission. Little does he know that in seven days' time members of his family will be vaporized by a new kind of weapon called the atomic bomb.

The two-mile area over which some nine hundred men are now spread is widening by the minute. Most everyone has left the ship wearing a life jacket or a pneumatic rubber life belt, but within hours the belts begin to fail—their seams corroded by the fuel oil—and the men wearing them begin to drown.

Those in rafts with food are the luckiest. Those clinging to floater nets are the next most fortunate, and those strapped into life vests, like Haynes and his good friend Father Conway, are known as the "swimmers." These are the most wretched of the survivors, and the severely wounded among them begin dying in droves.

The swimmers are separated by several hundred yards of oily sea from the rafters, and scattered between them are smaller groups of men bobbing in life jackets. These number about four hundred, and they're drifting in a mile-long line and losing all orientation. Amid this chaos, Haynes, a man who's never been known as a powerhouse of strength, is emerging as a leader. Like McCoy, he finds himself drawing on seemingly otherworldly sources of stamina. He wants desperately to minister to his men, who, having ingested massive amounts of fuel oil and seawater, are vomiting en masse.

"Many are nauseated, and they retch violently while I, the doctor, look on helplessly," he later recalls. "One commander is so horribly burned that the flesh of his hands is off down to the tendons . . . and he must be supported constantly, his tortured hands and face held clear of the fuel oil and seawater. Almost a dozen men form a circle, men whose own strength is fast ebbing, and they hold him lovingly, defiantly, from the sea that would multiply his suffering."

The commander is Stanley Lipski, and he's been one of Haynes's best friends aboard the *Indianapolis*. That his friend is now dying is breaking the doctor's heart, but he nonetheless turns quickly to the business at hand. Haynes realizes that they must stay together if they're to be spotted from the air come morning, and he begins shepherding those he can reach into larger groups.

Meanwhile, McVay is calmly treading water and formulating a plan for survival. Other than suffering irritation from oil in one of his eyes, he's neither injured nor in great distress. He is, though, completely alone, and for a terrifying moment he believes he's the only one to have made it off the *Indianapolis* alive.

Because he was one of the last to leave the ship, McVay has been cast farthest from the mass of survivors, but as he drifts on the current, he hears voices in the distance. Two life rafts appear out of the darkness, and he strokes over but finds them empty. He climbs aboard one, lashes the other behind, and begins paddling into the gloom. Out of the night comes a yell: "Hey! Anybody out there?"

McVay bears down on his paddle and rows ahead to meet three faces, all of them covered with oil, and he pulls the men aboard even though one of them already seems to be dead. By daybreak, McVay has picked up another floater net and raft with five men clinging to it. Eventually, he'll command three rafts, a net, and eight people—a ragtag flotilla that he intends to lead with fairness and discipline.

Among McVay's contingent is John Spinelli, a spry twenty-two-year-old from Gallup, New Mexico. Exhausted, covered in oil, and scared, Spinelli nonetheless feels a supreme ease under the captain's eye. On board the *Indianapolis*, he'd had little contact with the officer, but now he feels himself swelling with a new sense of pride. "He was like a father to our group," Spinelli says today. "He was just as excited as we were, figuring we were the only ones [left]. We'd looked all around the horizon and we couldn't see anything. All of us felt pretty good."

McCoy swims to a raft floating nearby in the dark, and doing so nearly kills him. Because he can't swim through the oil without choking, he dives deep and claws ahead, rising every ten feet or so to replenish his lungs. By the time he reaches the raft, he's gasping and nearly unconscious. Then he feels somebody grab him by the head and yank him aboard.

The raft is littered with four men. The raft itself is nothing more than a six-by-ten-foot rectangle of balsa wood stretched with gray canvas, and it's been busted to hell by the blast of the torpedoes. McCoy sticks his finger down his throat to make himself vomit, purging his system of the fuel oil and seawater. By the time he's finished, dawn is breaking, and he is limp in a corner of the raft, resting and gathering his strength.

Meanwhile, McVay and his ragged crew begin passing Monday in relative comfort. The fuel oil now makes an excellent sunscreen, and they smear it on their bodies. Determined to save his men, McVay takes an inventory of the rations available and finds several cans of Spam and crackers, a couple of tins of malted milk tablets for thirst, a first-aid kit, flares and a flare gun, a signal mirror, and a fishing kit containing hooks and line—enough, he figures, to last ten days at sea. On scraps of soggy paper he's cadged from the men's wallets, he begins keeping a log of daily activities, and he next orders the crew to stand two-hour watches for rescue planes. By all accounts, he seems glad to be back in command.

Through Monday morning, many of the swimmers have been in relatively good spirits. Having survived the torpedoing, they're overcome by a strange giddiness, at times laughing and shouting over one another's heads like men at a New Year's Eve party: Rescue, many of them feel, can only be a day or two away.

At 10 A.M., they unexpectedly drift free of the oil slick, and beneath them the ocean lights up like an enormous green room. The relief from the stinging oil is instant, but now the men's eyes begin to burn wildly from the glare. Each blink of an eyelid feels like sandpaper being dragged over the cornea. Soon, nearly everyone is blind and suffering from a condition known as photophobia.

And then the sharks arrive, in frenzied schools.

In truth, the sharks have probably been attacking all night, but until now the restless fish have mostly been eating the dead, tearing at the bodies as they cartwheel to the ocean floor. They're likely makos, tigers, white-tips, and blues—some of the oldest predators on the planet. The scene is terrifying for those who can still see. Those who can't can only listen to the screams erupting across the water as the sharks slash at their comrades.

"You know how a bobber on a catfish line floats on the surface above the bait and runs when a fish hits?" Seaman John Bullard will later recall. "The last time I saw this fellow, his head was running like a bobber—a shark had hit him."

Others are snatched off floater nets in midconversation. One sailor is lifted up and carried away while clutching a potato crate he had just scavenged. Of the men adrift in life vests, those who thrash end up dying, and those who play dead survive. Men on the periphery naturally fare worse than those in the middle, and everyone tries to swim to the center. And then, as quickly as they had begun, the attacks stop. The sea is a bloody boil of bits of clothing and badly mauled men. It's a pattern that soon establishes itself as the rhythm of the men's days: The sharks attack in the morning, cruise through the wounded and the dying all day, and then feed again at night on the living and the dead.

Subtler forces are also taking their toll: At this near-equatorial latitude, the Pacific is a steady eighty-five degrees, warm by most ocean standards but still cool enough to induce hypothermia. Dehydration and dementia are also setting in, the first stirrings of a physiological chain reaction that will reach full effect during the next twenty-four hours. At night, the swimmers tie their vests together as the temperature plummets, and eventually all are shivering uncontrollably. One man chews completely through a rope he's placed between his chattering teeth. Soon, the men begin announcing when they have to pee so others can huddle around them.

"It wasn't much," says Seaman Loel Dene Cox, now a rancher in Texas, "but it might warm you up for ten seconds."

Tuesday, July 31. Afloat now without food, water, shelter, or sleep for thirty-six hours, only about 600 of the 1,197 men who had sailed from Guam are still alive—at least 200 more have probably slipped beneath the waves or been eaten by sharks in the previous twenty-four hours.

On Tuesday morning, the situation transmogrifies—the men begin drifting back into some darker place in the brain. Since the sinking, each man has been floating through the hours toward the same hard question: *When do I quit?* "At first, when you get in a situation you abhor," Haynes reflects, "you can't stand it—it's terrible. But you can't get away from it. . . . And then you get so you tolerate it. If you tolerate it long enough, you embrace it. It becomes your way of life." Around sunrise, the men who can't embrace their misery start committing suicide.

Those still lucid enough look on in disbelief as their shipmates calmly untie their life vests and sink without a word. Others suddenly turn from the group and start swimming—maybe they go fifty or sixty feet until a shark inevitably takes them. Some simply slump face-forward and refuse to get up.

Adrift in his half-destroyed raft, McCoy wakes to find a life vest leaning in the corner, its straps still tightly tied. When he peers over the raft's edge, he sees its previous owner floating below the surface. The man hangs motionless until a current catches him and pulls him into the depths. McCoy sits back and starts saying the rosary over and over. Never an overly religious man, he begins a process of what he'll later call his "purification"; he starts asking God to forgive his sins.

McVay's spirits are also wilting. Exhausted and nauseated, his crew is perched on the raft's rails, staring at a burning sky, futilely looking for low-flying planes. The brined canvas of the rafts has chafed the men's already blistering skin—they're bleeding at the elbows and arms—and yet they don't complain. He's now watching them with a growing sense of guilt—do they blame him for the sinking?

When a warship like the *Indianapolis* sets sail, she's constantly tracked on what's called a plotting board. Back on Leyte, shortly before 11 A.M. on Tuesday—the *Indianapolis*'s ETA—such a board is in the port director's office. And amid the clatter of typewriters and trilling of phones, the *Indianapolis*'s course is pointed straight for the board's far edge.

On Monday night, copies of the "Leyte Expected Departures and Arrivals" list had been distributed throughout the command, which means that now at least forty-nine people know that the *Indianapolis* is due in port. The clock on the wall sweeps past noon, and the ship does not arrive. The minutes become hours. Still no one notices.

At the end of the day, the port director's office reacts. And when it does, the last hope of timely rescue disappears. Instead of becoming the object of an intense search, the *Indianapolis* is simply noted as "over-due." Her marker is moved back on the plotting board, giving her a new ETA—Wednesday, August 1.

❖   ❖   ❖

Back out at sea, before the day's close, the situation takes a precipitous turn. With their tongues swelling, throats squeezing shut, and minds unhinging, the men begin drinking seawater. Haynes watches in horror, screaming as he paddles among them, but his pleas are ignored. Finally, he realizes he can only steel himself for the coming physiological apocalypse.

As they drink, the men are setting off a complex series of chemical reactions that will end in hallucinations, seizures, comas, and ultimately death. Their cells shrink, expand, and then explode as their free water is sacrificed in an attempt to dilute the sodium entering the bloodstream. Their bodies are essentially shorting out on salt.

"The guys in our group that drank salt water," recalls McCoy, "looked like they were getting along pretty good. And all of a sudden they just went completely delirious."

At sunset on Tuesday, the men bundle together and drift through a freezing night under a soundless sky. As they do, Haynes senses their anxiety. "High fever grips our shaking bodies," he recounts, "it consumes our reason." Around midnight, the men start killing each other.

"There's a Jap here!" somebody yells. "He's trying to kill me. Get the Jap!" Those with knives still on their belts begin stabbing wildly; others try to drown the closest breathing thing they can find. The death toll in this melee is later estimated at fifty.

Haynes finds himself under attack as two men shove him deep underwater and hold him down. Kicking and punching, he manages to break free and struggle to the surface. He backpedals quickly and swims out into the night, beyond the fringe of the group, certain he will be killed if he's spotted again. Exhausted, he cries out for help. There's a voice in his ear: "Easy, Doc, I've got you." It's his pharmacist's mate, a man he had last seen on board as they both stood on the hangar deck watching their patients slide into the sea. The man hoists the gasping doctor onto his hip. "I've got you," he says. "Nothing's gonna happen to you now, Doc." But Haynes is already out cold.

Wednesday, August 1. As the sun soars into the sky, the men have been afloat for fifty-five hours, and perhaps half of those who survived the boat's sinking are still alive. This means they've been dying at a rate of one man every ten minutes for the past three days. Haynes comes to in the arms of his friend and looks out on a sea of corpses mutilated by sharks. If Tuesday was bad, Wednesday is far, far worse. By midday, their eyes swirling with confusion as they realize no one is coming to rescue them, the men begin hallucinating en masse. Freight trains start pounding along rails ringing the horizon, and hotels spring up on city blocks floating atop the water. Some of the men start checking into the hotels and drown, while others swim to catch the trains. One man—and soon there are dozens like him—sees an island floating nearby, maybe just a hundred yards away, filled with dancing girls, and strokes off to his destiny. Another delirious sailor is seen starting an imaginary outboard motor with furious yanks and then puttering away over the swell.

Twenty-five men decide they're going to swim the six hundred miles to Leyte in a day and a half. They say their good-byes, promising to meet up again back on land, and then kick out over the mirror glass of the sea. They make it only two hundred or three hundred yards and suddenly sink, victims of sharks or exhaustion.

"Everybody would see the same thing," recalls Haynes. "I swam to a row of men and asked them what they were doing. This guy said, '*Shhh*, Doc. There's a small hotel on the island there, and they got one room and you can get fifteen minutes' sleep. Get in line. You'll get your turn.' And I looked at him—there's nothing ahead of him! And then after a little bit I thought I could see something up there!"

The grandest hallucination of all, however, materializes when the *Indianapolis* herself ghosts back to life. At times, the ship is steaming toward the men over the horizon, at others she's drifting fifty feet beneath them, her radar beacons turning dutifully, her flags flying smartly, all the portholes lit and gleaming. Immediately upon spotting her, the men begin diving down to the ship, swimming through the halls, scrambling to the water fountain, where they drink deeply. Eventually they resurface, playfully shooting tall streams of water into the air and gleefully exclaiming to their friends, "I found it—there's fresh water aboard! Come on, fellas, let's go!" And the men take deep breaths and head back down, followed by a half dozen friends, to sit at tables eating ice cream and drinking tall glasses of water until they are dead.

Around nightfall, even Father Conway, who has kept drowning men afloat, praying for them as they die, finally goes insane. The worn-out priest starts thrashing in fits in Haynes's arms, babbling in Latin, keening ancient prayers and blessings, a litany that is other-worldly in its incoherency.

"He got as crazy as a loon before he died," says Haynes. "He kept blessing me, and hitting me—*bang-bang-bang*—in the face." Haynes gathers him close as his friend rides out his frenzy and falls silent.

Back on McVay's raft, the captain and his boys are staying sane by staring at the sky and refusing to give up hope of being rescued. "We managed to get along very nicely during the first two days," McVay remarked later. But "as each hour went by, people became more exhausted from lack of sleep and from the usual tension caused by wondering whether we were going to be sighted or not."

McVay now has the crew in four rafts spread out over seventy-five feet of ocean, in an attempt to make as big a visual target as possible. And by Wednesday at least eight planes have passed overhead. Each time, McVay orders his men to splash at the water, flash their signal mirrors, and wave the long yellow emergency buntings. Grasping their increasingly dire straits, he cuts the men's rations in half, which immediately doubles their putative survival time to twenty days. He doles out one slice of Spam, two crackers, and a malted milk tablet to each man, and then his thoughts turn inward.

The boys listen raptly as the stoic, gray-haired captain confesses, "I'm going to have some explaining to do." On board the Indy, McVay has sometimes talked of becoming an admiral. But now he announces, "I should have gone down with the ship." The boys on the raft disagree.

"I knew there was nothing I could say to them," McVay will later recall. "I thought of many a cocktail hour that you have at home after you have an exhausting day—I thought I would certainly like to repeat some of those evenings. I guess that's what kept a good many people going. They just thought of some happiness that had been theirs and decided they'd stick it out. On the other hand, we know of many people who apparently decided it wasn't worth it."

Over at McCoy's raft, one of the men is repeatedly swimming away in what seems a bizarrely unsuccessful attempt to commit suicide. Others are drifting in and out of consciousness, leaving only McCoy and an Tennessee farm boy named Bob Brundige still functioning. Sometime before nightfall, he and Brundige even start betting with each other as to which of them will die first.

Back on Leyte, the port director's office notes that the *Indianapolis* has once again failed to arrive. Once again, she's dutifully marked as overdue. The thinking in the office is that she'll arrive the next day, Thursday. "They probably missed us on Tuesday and began looking for us today," Captain McVay informs his crew that afternoon. "There's really nothing to worry about, men."

Thursday, August 2. At 9 A.M., twenty-four-year-old navy pilot Wilbur "Chuck" Gwinn and his four crewmen take off from the island of Peleliu, headed north over the Philippine Sea in a Ventura PV-1 bomber. Gwinn has orders today to hunt Japanese submarines along the Peddie/Leyte Route. Two hours into the mission, a navigational antenna breaks free and starts pounding the rear fuselage. Gwinn struggles aft to assess the damage from the gunner's hatch, giving him a view of the sea, three thousand feet below. He pauses to rub his sore neck, and that's when he sees an oil slick. Hurrying back to the cockpit, he turns the plane around, thinking he's probably spotted the remains of a wrecked Japanese sub. He gives orders to get ready to bomb.

Several miles away, Haynes feels the hair stand up on the back of his neck. As the big bomber roars over them at nine hundred feet, most of the survivors think it's a mirage. Up in the air, Gwinn doesn't have a clue what it is he's found. Spotting "little black balls" in the water, he drops the plane to three hundred feet. What he finds blows his mind: about 150 men spread out over a twenty-mile-long strip. Some are thrashing violently, others look dead. But who are they? His crewmen start kicking life vests out the door, and Gwinn hurriedly radios back to Peleliu: "Men in water. Many men in water."

The life vests come tumbling out of the sky and hit the water near Haynes, who can barely paddle to reach them. All around him men begin weeping, tears streaming down their bleeding faces. Overhead, Gwinn is spotting more men every mile, and he quickly radios back to Peleliu: "Send rescue ship." With this dispatch, one of the largest air-and-sea rescues in naval history gets under way. Perhaps 350 men are still alive, and only half of them realize they've just been saved. The rest are too dazed to know.

In a matter of hours, eleven planes and eleven ships are diverted to the kill zone. One of the first to arrive is the *Playmate 2*, a Catalina seaplane piloted by an Indiana lawyer named Adrian Marks. What he sees horrifies him: Legions of sharks have surrounded the sailors, and some are attacking. More men are dying by the minute. Marks starts dropping life rafts, vests, and rations, and then he decides to put down. It's against all orders. The Catalina isn't made to land in open water, and there's a twelve-foot swell—he may die trying. Cutting the throttle, Marks radically lifts the nose of the plane and then sets her down. The *Playmate 2* hits the crest of a wave and is knocked back skyward, then comes down again even harder before finally settling. By nightfall, Marks's crewmen have picked up fifty-six men. Once the plane is full, they stack men on the wings to keep them away from the sharks, wrapping them in parachutes and lashing them down with rope.

As Captain McVay spots the *Playmate 2* circling about ten miles away, he understands two things for perhaps the first time: that he really might be saved, and that he and the boys in his flotilla are not alone. At about midnight, they see a mysterious light burning in the sky. Six miles away, McCoy and Brundige lift their cracked and sunburned faces and see the light, too. When McCoy realizes he's been saved, he promises God he'll do something with his life besides soldiering and killing people. He drops his head and begins to cry.

The searchlight belongs to the USS *Cecil J. Doyle,* a destroyer escort that has been diverted to the rescue scene. The *Doyle* arrives at 11:45 P.M., lowers a motorized whaleboat, and begins off-loading survivors from the *Playmate 2.* At 4 A.M., the *Doyle* catches Haynes in the beam of her searchlight. A cargo net is rolled down the side of the ship, and Haynes is hauled from the sea with a rope tied around his waist. He's naked, burned, bleeding, and half out of his mind. He pushes away the men holding him up, announcing, "I can stand on my own."

Until now, the *Doyle*'s commander has had no idea what ship had been sunk. "Who are you?" he asks. "This is all that's left of the *Indianapolis,*" Haynes whispers. "We have been in the water four days." And then he faints.

By dawn, approximately three hundred men have been rescued. They're fed fruit and water and treated for exhaustion, dehydration, shark bites, saltwater ulcers, shock, and burns. Some of the men, says Haynes, remind him of "cadavers in the dissecting room."

The high-speed transport USS *Ringness,* steaming from Leyte, finds McVay at 10 A.M. on Friday, August 3. Remarkably, the captain manages to walk aboard the rescue ship unassisted. Near dusk, McCoy and his remaining crew of four are found lying semiconscious in their raft. "We looked pretty ugly when they found us," McCoy says. When he steps aboard the *Ringness,* he kisses the deck and bursts into tears. Afterward, he's fed water from a spoon and falls asleep for twenty hours. The search continues until August 9, but following McCoy's rescue no more survivors are found.

On the day of the rescue, McVay composes a message to the command at Guam, including information that he was not zigzagging when the *Indianapolis* was hit.

On Sunday, McVay holds a press conference. "What would be the normal time before you would be reported overdue?" a reporter asks him. "That is a question I would like to ask someone," McVay shoots back. "I should think by noon [on Tuesday] they would have started to call by radio to find out where we were, or if something was wrong. This is something I want to ask somebody myself. Why didn't this get out sooner?" It's as close to a public condemnation of the navy's actions as the captain will ever allow himself to make.

The following morning, the *Enola Gay* drops Little Boy on Hiroshima and 118,000 people are annihilated. Camped out in their hospital wards, the survivors of the *Indianapolis* cheer when they hear the news and then are shocked to learn that the bomb had been their cargo. The next day, Admiral Chester Nimitz calls for a court of inquiry to investigate the sinking of the ship. On August 14, the White House releases a terse bulletin announcing the sinking of the *Indianapolis,* which had been kept secret under wartime censorship rules. Minutes later, President Truman steps into the Rose Garden to announce the surrender of Japan, still staggering under the impact of a second atomic explosion, over Nagasaki. The effect is simple: Either by design or happenstance, the *Indianapolis* disaster is buried under headlines announcing America's victory.

Three days later, the *New York Times* calls the sinking "one of the darkest pages of our naval history." At the same time, the families of the boys who died in the catastrophe begin asking both the navy and the captain for explanations. The navy has few answers, and McVay tries hard to convey his sense of grief and loss in letters he writes to the mothers and fathers of his dead crew.

Soon, however, he's receiving letters of his own. "Merry Christmas!" one of them begins. "Our family's holiday would be a lot merrier if you hadn't killed my son." If Louise doesn't snatch them from the mail, McVay stashes the letters in a drawer in his bedroom, as if wanting to forever remind himself of his guilt. On August 20, 1945, the court of inquiry recommends that he be court-martialed.

As it turns out, the question as to why nine hundred men were left unrescued for five days will not be under the court's consideration. The navy will not be on trial here. This bit of legal sleight of hand is achieved by the navy's careful selection of the charges it brings against the captain: Technically, he's not being prosecuted for losing his ship or for the loss of life that followed but for "hazarding his ship by failing to zigzag" and for "failing to order abandon ship in a timely manner." Of course, had the *Indianapolis* never sunk, no one would be concerned that McVay had quit zigzagging in the first place.

Nimitz disagrees with the inquiry's finding and suggests a letter of reprimand. Chief of Naval Operations Admiral Ernest King, however, presses for the trial, and Secretary of the Navy James Forrestal agrees. McVay has six days to prepare his defense and ends up with an inexperienced lawyer. Before the trial, a reporter asks McVay what he thinks will happen, and he replies, "I was in command of the ship and I am responsible for its fate. I hope they make their decisions soon and do what they want with me."

On December 3, the court-martial commences, attracting national attention when the navy makes the surreal prosecutorial play of flying Hashimoto to Washington, D.C., to testify. Hashimoto tells the lawyers he would have sunk McVay regardless of what course the American ship was making, but after two weeks of testimony, McVay is convicted of "hazarding his ship by failing to zigzag" and acquitted of the charge of "failing to order abandon ship in a timely manner." In view of his outstanding service, King and Nimitz recommend that his sentence be remitted. His naval career, nonetheless, is over.

Today, conspiracy theories abound as the survivors try to explain McVay's court-martial. Some believe King was seeking revenge for a personal insult supposedly inflicted years earlier by McVay's father; still others believe the politically powerful father of a dead crew member successfully lobbied President Truman himself to press on with the trial. Ultimately, though, all that remains is a single question: Was the court-martial just?

The short answer, according to Captain Bill Toti, a former U.S. submarine commander, is no. Toti is one of the few active members of the military who have spoken in support of the survivors' efforts to exonerate McVay. In a careful but biting critique of the navy's treatment of the captain (published last October in *Proceedings,* a publication of the Naval Institute), Toti points out that "here was a man who, because of the unique and absolute nature of the responsibility of command, was culpable for the misfortune that befell his ship. . . . Despite that, there was nothing he could have done to prevent that misfortune, and he should never have been prosecuted in the first place. The lesson here is that a decision can be legally correct and still be unjust."

In the aftermath of the court-martial, Haynes goes on to a successful career in military medicine and later serves in Vietnam before finally retiring in 1978. McCoy becomes an osteopathic doctor and devotes his life to doing "something good for people." As for McVay, he's reassigned to a desk job in New Orleans. He and Louise live a quiet life in a comfortable house. In 1949, after thirty years of military service, he retires and begins selling insurance.

He spends weekends with Louise at a fishing camp on Bayou Liberty, near New Orleans, and his life gradually appears to be tilting toward happiness when suddenly it's rocked again: Louise is diagnosed with cancer and dies.

Within a year, he has impulsively remarried, to Vivian Smith, and moved to Connecticut. One day, his stepson (from Vivian's previous marriage) pauses before the bathroom door in the Litchfield house and hears the captain weeping. He opens the door, and McVay is clutching a letter—more hate mail—and he tells the boy, "I can't take this."

Which is where this story began, on a cold morning in November 1968.

Twenty-eight years later, in a 1996 response to a request by the survivors of the sinking that McVay's court-martial be expunged from his record and that a presidential citation be awarded their ship, the Judge Advocate General of the Navy delivers this pronouncement: "The conclusion reached is that Captain McVay's court-martial was legally sound; no injustice has been done, and remedial action is not warranted."

The living survivors of the disaster, however, vow never to give up their struggle to see Captain McVay's name cleared. At a hearing in September 1999 before the Senate Armed Services Committee, McCoy, now retired, defiantly told a panel of admirals that "Captain McVay's honor has been violated."

After the meeting, says McCoy, one of the admirals "came up, grabbed my hand, and said, 'I want to tell you, Dr. McCoy, you're right.' But then he said, 'Good luck,' and he walked away. I think we won the battle, but we haven't won the war."

If he's less than sanguine about the unresolved struggle to redeem McVay's reputation, McCoy is resigned in his own quest to accept the loss of the *Indianapolis*. Like many of his fellow survivors, McCoy felt shame, dishonor, and rage in the aftermath of the sinking—and anger that the navy could have forgotten them as they fought for their lives.

In Hawaii, in 1990, on the forty-ninth anniversary of the bombing of Pearl Harbor, McCoy also laid to rest his hatred of Mochitsura Hashimoto, whom he had last seen in Washington, D.C., forty-five years earlier, at McVay's court-martial. Through an interpreter, McCoy informed his former enemy, "I forgive you."

"Well, I forgive you," replied Hashimoto.

"Forgive me for what!" shot back McCoy.

"Tell Dr. McCoy," Hashimoto answered, "that I came from Japan to be with him, to pray with him for the losses that I caused on the *Indianapolis*. And I ask him to pray with me for the losses that I suffered at Hiroshima, because I lost my whole family in the bombing."

"I looked at him," McCoy remembers, his voice cracking, "and I thought, *Holy Christ, there's the whole story right there.*"

On November 24, 1999, Lieutenant-Commander Hashimoto, now in his nineties and a Shinto priest like his father, once again entered the lives of the men of the *Indianapolis*. In a letter addressed to Senator John Warner, the chairman of the Senate Armed Services Committee, who controls the fate of the resolution that would exonerate McVay, he stated: "I do not understand why Captain McVay was court-martialed. I do not understand why he was convicted of hazarding his ship by failing to zigzag, because I would have been able to launch a successful torpedo attack against his ship whether it had been zigzagging or not.

"I have met many of your brave men who survived the sinking of the *Indianapolis*. I would like to join with them in urging that your national legislature clear their captain's name. Our peoples have forgiven each other for that terrible war and its consequences. Perhaps it is time your people forgave Captain McVay."

MARCH 2000

Editor's Note

On July 13, 2001, 56 years after the sinking of the U.S.S. *Indianapolis,* the navy exonerated Captain Charles McVay for the loss of the ship and the sailors who died as a result of the ordeal. This exoneration echoed Congressional action taken up earlier in October, 2000, when McVay was declared not culpable "for the tragic loss of the USS *Indianapolis* and the lives of the men who died . . ."

This news was greeted with elation by the survivors, some of whom broke down in tears upon hearing it. Although McVay's court-martial will not be erased from his record, many of his men—including Giles McCoy, who first began the effort to exonerate McVay 37 years ago—feel that in the court of public opinion, their captain's name finally has been cleared. The crew of the *Indianapolis* was also awarded a Unit Citation for their role in the delivery of the components of the atomic bomb Little Boy to Tinian Island. Sadly, this all came too late for Dr. Lewis Haynes, who passed away at his home in Florida, on March 13, 2001, at the age of eighty-nine.

KILLING LIBBY

by Mark Levine

A S U.S. HIGHWAY 2 crosses Montana, it is dotted along its six-hundred-mile length with signposts bearing white crosses. They flicker past like small anonymous advertisements, punctuating the mostly empty road, which stretches across the sparsely populated top of the state—from the wheat fields of Wolf Point in the east, past the wind-scoured town of Chinook, where the plains collide with the Rocky Mountains, skirting the lower fringes of Glacier National Park, and continuing through a claustrophobic corridor of ragged hills. The crosses mark the sites of highway fatalities. Some of them are hung with plastic wreaths; some have names scratched on their surfaces; some are bent by wind and ice; many are rusted.

For a while, as if playing a child's game with myself, I keep a tally of the roadside body count, which lends me the impression that I am being shepherded along my route by specters, that death forms the backdrop of this journey. Near Libby, a hamlet on the northwestern edge of the state, the white crosses begin to multiply, like rogue vegetation. In one innocuous stretch, just outside town, there is a cross every hundred yards or so; a cross stands beside a sign announcing the town limits, in view of the great charred steel skeleton of a former sawmill; yet another one decorates the lawn outside the Libby Area Chamber of Commerce, whose officials have spent the past few years battling the notion that the town, population 2,675, has become, as one resident put it, "America's Chernobyl."

Directly behind the Chamber of Commerce sits a charmless rectangle about the size of a pair of football fields, hemmed in by a chain-link fence. This is Libby's cemetery, adorned with its own bland rows of crosses. Diane Keck knows this place. Until 1954, when she was fifteen and her family moved away, her father was the town undertaker. "In the course of my father's job, he noticed something strange," she says. "A lot of the men who worked up at the mine just outside town were dying young. He made a connection. He told us kids to stay away from the stuff from the mine." Some of that stuff—a micalike mineral of a thousand uses called vermiculite, which is tinged with tremolite, a naturally occurring and particularly virulent form of asbestos—was forever drifting through the air around Libby. The mineral hung in dust clouds over the town and accumulated on the ground at a plant where ore was processed and shipped. "They would dump it into open boxcars and there would be a big poof of smoke," Keck remembers. "And there were big piles of it, like mountains, and we would play blindman's bluff around them."

Ten years ago, Keck started coughing, and she hasn't stopped since. When she hikes in the woods, she gets short of breath. Doctors tell her that she has signs of asbestosis, an incurable lung disease that is caused almost exclusively by industrial exposure to asbestos. A few years ago, Keck learned that most of the children from her old neighborhood had also been diagnosed with asbestos-related lung disease. Her brother has it; so does her nephew, who grew up nearby; so, too, it seems, does nearly everyone in town.

It takes little more than five minutes to drive through Libby, but I have no intention of passing through. The town is the site of a toxic contamination that is unprecedented in American history, and I have followed a trail of white crosses here to meet the people and to hear their stories. Libby has always been remote and rugged, even by Montana standards, and until recently it was a tight-knit, seemingly idyllic community, shadowed by the rough peaks of the Cabinet Mountains, their slopes drenched in blue light. You don't have to hike very far into the hills around town to come upon a chain of secluded lakes, and you can still spend days at those heights without crossing paths with another person. Grizzlies roam the woods, and trout cluster in the shallows of the Kootenai River, which cuts through town. But the fresh, folkloric Rocky Mountain air has become a burden rather than a blessing for many of Libby's residents, who, like Keck, are enduring the effects of a lung-thickening disease and opening their homes to hazardous-waste workers in hooded Tyvek suits who are equipped with respirators and sensitive monitors.

This is the short form of the telling: Just north of Libby stands a hill that once looked like any other hill. For sixty-seven years, the shape of this hill was altered by explosives and earthmovers, and by the labor of men who were brought up the hill on clattering buses. The men came up, and the rock they dug out was brought down, tens of thousands of pounds of rock each hour. It was hard work, removing the top of the hill, but it was good work. It paid well. It supported generations of families. True, the miners died young, but danger was an accepted part of their daily routine; grousing about pain and misfortune was not. Miners kept their suspicions about the vermiculite dust that coated their work clothes to themselves.

Then, in 1990, the hill was vacated by W. R. Grace, the multinational corporation that had operated the mine since 1963. Although the company possessed detailed knowledge of the asbestos hazards to which its workers had been exposed, it had kept that knowledge to itself. State and federal governments had also been aware of the risks. Ironically, Marc Racicot, Montana's attorney general from 1989 to 1993, and its governor from 1993 to 2001, was raised in Libby. But even that didn't compel state officials to inform the community.

By 1995, a few families had noticed that miners' wives were dying of their husbands' ailment, and the miners' children, too, had learned that they often shared it, as if the hazards of the trade were genetically passed on. But not until 1999 did residents begin to notice that asbestosis was showing up in people who had never been at the mine and had never lived with miners. Still, there was no organized outcry about the contamination until the end of that year, when the Environmental Protection Agency began a belated full-scale investigation of the town's legacy of pollution.

The EPA discovered that asbestos has probably shortened the lives of most of the 1,898 workers who toiled at the mine between 1940 and 1990. What's more, the effects are ongoing. An astounding one-third of Libby's residents are believed to have contracted asbestos-related lung disease. "We haven't begun to count the number of people who have been, or will be, killed by this," an EPA scientist, protective of his identity, told me, before adding with disgust, "This was deliberate murder."

Soon after I arrive in Libby, I meet a man named Les Skramstad, whose thin, wavering voice barely rises above a whisper. Skramstad, sixty-four, is grizzled and bowlegged and wears a camouflage cap with a dirty feather stuck in its side. A toothpick often hangs from his mouth when he speaks. Although Skramstad didn't receive a high school diploma until he was in his forties, he is as forceful and eloquent a man as I have met. He has worked as a rancher and a logger and a mechanic. Once, for barely three years, he worked as a miner in

Libby and as a result has full-blown asbestosis. "Full-blown is when you got a death sentence," he says. "You better put your affairs in order." In 1997, Skramstad sued W. R. Grace for personal injury. His was the first of only three cases in Libby to reach a jury, and he won a judgment of $660,000 against the company, which has made him something of a pariah in town. But his victory didn't dispel his bitterness about what he and his community have suffered. "Should a person have to die just because they live in Libby?" he asks.

"It was more or less like a brotherhood at the mine. The first day of work, I got on the bus downtown and they hauled us up on the hill. There was a guy named Tom DeShazer, and I walked over to him and said, 'Here I am,' and he said, 'Yeah, you're going to go be a sweeper in the mill.' He sent me over to the warehouse to get a respirator. I'd never seen a respirator before. A guy named Shorty Welch handed it to me, and I said, 'What am I supposed to do with this?' and he kind of laughed and said, 'Well, wear it if you can.' It was a little aluminum gadget, about the size of your hand, that fit over your nose and mouth.

"I got on the man-lift and rode up to the top floor of that mill, and, my God, I'd never seen anything like it in my life. I guess a guy has seen a dust storm before. The dust was probably three, four inches deep. It was almost like walking on a real plushy carpet. It was so dusty that it was hard to see what the heck was going on.

"I believe I was getting $2.10 an hour. I really wanted that job, so, boy, I started sweeping with all my might. After about fifteen minutes, Jesus, I couldn't breathe. So I threw that respirator off, and it was plugged with dust. I thought I was going to suffocate. Everyone who worked up there looked the same after a few hours. We all looked brown.

"I was beating this dust off myself so I could eat lunch when Tom DeShazer said, 'Oh, don't pay any attention to that. It's just a nuisance dust. It won't hurt you. You can eat a ton of it and it'll never hurt you.'"

— L E S   S K R A M S T A D

I am standing on the porch of a whitewashed house three miles from W. R. Grace's defunct mine. The house is owned by history buff, gentleman farmer, and amateur toxic-contamination expert Mike Powers. Powers, sixty-four, came to Libby twenty years ago and restored a lush turn-of-the-century homestead on the banks of the Kootenai, where he tends his small herd of exotic Swiss cattle and lives in an old farmhouse built from hand-hewn logs.

Once, long ago, Powers's farm played host to the workshop in which the potent dust that helped build and bury Libby was first stirred up. The wizard of Libby, a man named E. N. Alley, who died two years before Powers's birth, slept in the house where Powers now sleeps, and left traces of his handiwork all over the property.

In 1921, Alley ventured into a disused forty-foot-deep shaft that had been dug into a hill near his ranch. He carried a torch to light his way. Before long, he heard a sizzling sound. His flame had roasted some of the loose rock in the tunnel, and the pebbles had puffed up, like popcorn, and drifted before his eyes. Alley had found the world's largest deposit of vermiculite, whose peculiar exfoliating properties are due to the evaporation of water molecules between the rock's layers. Alley staked his miner's claim, came up with the suitably Jazz Age name Zonolite for his product, and christened the mountain after the brand. What he didn't know was that the vermiculite was inextricably braided with asbestos fibers, and that inhaling those fibers—especially in high concentration, especially over long stretches of time—would kill a man.

Zonolite was marketed as a lightweight, nonflammable additive to construction materials, and by 1926 a hundred tons of it were being produced in Libby daily. Its most widespread application would be in home insulation—today, as many as 15 million attics in the United States may contain asbestos-laced Zonolite. A mill was built on top of Zonolite Mountain to separate valuable ore from waste rock. The mill stood ten stories tall, higher by far than any building in Libby, and featured a tangle of grinders, steel screens, conveyor belts, and chutes. Ore would be poured in at the top, and by the time it tumbled to the bottom, being crushed as it fell, it had been sifted into a granular residue. The milling produced plumes of thick, white dust—containing up to five thousand pounds of asbestos each day—that billowed from atop the mountain, settling on the hillside and in creek beds and hovering over Libby like a fog. Children in town would write their names in the dust on sidewalks.

By 1942, when the state of Montana first contacted the Zonolite Company to express its concern about the dust at the mine, there was already ample medical knowledge about the dangers of asbestos. The author of a 1937 article in *The New England Journal of Medicine* did not mince words. "Asbestos," he wrote, "is extremely dangerous and fatal." Such warnings did not deter W. R. Grace, then based in Cambridge, Massachusetts, from buying Zonolite in 1963, or from doubling the mine's daily output—to fifteen thousand tons of ore, containing nine hundred thousand pounds of asbestos—between then and 1990, when the mine closed after mounting signs of a future filled with asbestos-related litigation had become impossible to ignore.

Although Powers never worked in the mine, he recently learned that his lungs are diseased from inhaling asbestos. "My only exposure," he says, "is living here." We tour his farm, and everywhere we go he points out glittering flecks of vermiculite. Standing in the former chicken house, Powers tells me, "The carpenter who helped me work on this building—his lungs are full of asbestos. The guy that worked on the furnace shield has it. The electrician, the plumber—they have it." Powers figures that the property into which he has sunk his savings and his labor is unsalable. "Maybe," he says, "W. R. Grace will buy this farm and turn it into an asbestos theme park." As he talks, Powers bangs on a wall and jolts a puff of vermiculite dust loose into the air.

"Look there," he says. "Strange how it catches in the cobwebs."

"I'd come home from work pretty well laden with dust, and my kids were little at that time, and they'd meet me at the door and grab my legs, and they'd get a blast of it. Then my wife, Norita, would give me a hug at the door, and she'd get a dose of it, too. I contaminated them every single day. If it had just took the lives of us miners, that would have been bad enough. But I carried it home and gave it to my wife and three of our five children. That's a pretty poor percentage. My daughter Laurel, she's got six kids. She's got it. And my boy Brent, he's got it real bad, like me, full-blown. My grandfather lived to be eighty-eight. My dad lived to be seventy-eight. I may not make sixty-eight. Brent, he may not make forty-eight. Any man should look out for his family first, and being that I had a hand in their destiny, that's pretty grim."

— **L E S   S K R A M S T A D**

Chris Weis, a forty-seven-year-old toxicologist, was not, at first, alarmed. Based in Denver, Weis specializes in emergency response for the EPA's Region 8 office, which covers the northern Rockies. Just before Thanksgiving 1999, while attending a meeting in Helena, Montana, Weis was paged by his managers. The agency had seen an inflammatory report in the *Seattle Post-Intelligencer* concerning a small town that Weis had never heard of where close to two hundred deaths and another four hundred cases of fatal illness were being attributed to exposure to mine contaminants.

"Look," he tells me, in the EPA's field office in Libby, "I've got a doctorate in toxicology and a doctorate in medical physiology. My first reaction to the reports was, This doesn't happen."

Weis nonetheless went to Libby to investigate, visiting the former mine and a number of sites where ore was processed and handled. He contacted a pulmonologist in Spokane, Washington, two hundred miles to the west, who had treated hundreds of Libby residents for asbestos-related lung disease, which occurred in town at sixty times the national average rate. He learned of at least nineteen local cases of an invariably fatal cancer called mesothelioma, whose only known cause is exposure to asbestos, and which is so rare that, as Weis says, "one case in a population of a million is considered an epidemic." He spent some time talking to residents. "Libby is a small town," he points out, "so if you talk to forty or fifty people and every one of them has a neighbor or family member with an asbestos-related disease—to say the least, that's unusual." Weis returned to Denver persuaded that Libby had the distinction of hosting "the most severe human exposure to a hazardous material this country has ever seen."

Within two days, the EPA descended on Libby in full force, bringing in a team of scientists, physicians, geologists, and toxic-cleanup experts. None of them were prepared for the dimensions of the disaster they would discover. They learned that W. R. Grace had "pumped so much asbestos fiber into the air shed here, it hung in the center of town in concentrations that were probably twenty times higher than the present occupational-exposure limit," Weis says. They learned that when W. R. Grace left town in 1990, the company had done a sloppy job cleaning up its former properties, which remained highly contaminated. And there was more. "We found disturbing evidence that the material had been readily accessible to the general public in Libby. Ore was often free for the taking. Kids played in it; it was in sandboxes and on ball fields. People would load up their pickup trucks and take it home to use in their gardens as a soil amendment and on their driveways as a surfacing material. When the high school track needed resurfacing in the 1970s, W. R. Grace brought down truckloads of raw ore—almost, in some cases, pure asbestos—and covered the track with it. Kids ran on mine tailings until 1983."

Finally, the EPA called in the Agency for Toxic Substances and Disease Registry, a division of the Centers for Disease Control and Prevention, which invited the residents of Libby and the surrounding valley, past and present, to undergo screening for signs of asbestos-related disease. As Weis recalls, "We anticipated that, given the severity of exposures in Libby, we might see possibly as much as ten or twelve percent of the population come back with scarring on their lungs." Chest X rays were taken of 6,144 people. Preliminary results released this March, representing 1,078 of those examined, revealed that 30 percent showed symptoms of lung disease. "We just weren't prepared for that," Weis says. "What's unprecedented is that so many of these sick people had no known source of exposure to asbestos. They only lived in Libby."

Weis was also shocked to discover that his predecessors at the EPA and other federal agencies had been well informed of the dangers in Libby. "The pieces of this situation were put together in the seventies," he says. "Very detailed studies were done. The results were unequivocal." While it's true that until 1970, when Congress passed the Occupational Safety and Health Act, regulatory oversight of workplaces was severely limited, rarely had a year passed since the mid-fifties in which some government agency did not visit Libby and come back with troubling findings. In 1968, for instance, the U.S. Public Health Service warned W. R. Grace that "the dust concentrations are from ten to one hundred times in excess of the safe limit."

Nonetheless, a series of EPA memos in the early 1980s addressing the health risks at the mine were allowed to languish. At that time, President Reagan, in his first term, was intent on reducing government spending in order to cut taxes. (In a report issued this spring, the office of the EPA's inspector general acknowledged that the "EPA did not place emphasis on dealing with asbestos-contaminated vermiculite due to funding constraints and competing priorities.") It's worth noting that in 1982, Reagan convened a closed-door gathering of advisers to come up with suggestions for where to trim the budget. The group, called the Grace Commission, was chaired by an old friend of the president's, J. Peter Grace, the president and CEO of W. R. Grace.

The EPA is still cleaning up Libby, having spent $12 million on its efforts in 2000, with another $16 million budgeted for 2001. Sixty to seventy percent of Libby's homes are thought to contain vermiculite insulation. Most yards have vermiculite in the soil. At dusk, the streets downtown still glisten with a sheen of powdery ore. Nights at my motel, I often pass hazardous-waste workers in the hallway. They have been brought to Libby by the EPA. By day, they can be seen entering sealed houses around town, beating pillows, vacuuming curtains, and dusting mantels in an effort to measure how much asbestos fiber has worked its way into the fiber of daily life in Libby.

Naturally, the ore that was taken from W. R. Grace's mine did not all stay in Libby for long. It was transported to more than 250 processing plants around the country. The EPA has barely started examining these sites. In Minneapolis, though, the agency tracked down fifty-seven former employees of a factory that had received its share of Libby's vermiculite. Twenty-four of those workers either had died or were dying of asbestos-related disease.

"You can still go to your local Kmart and buy gardening supplies that contain Libby vermiculite," says Weis, who is in charge of gathering and evaluating scientific data on Libby's contamination. "Speaking purely as a toxicologist, I've never seen as hideous a poison as this material."

"Around the last part of 1960, a boss at the experimental lab come down and told us, 'I want you to get in the pickup and go up on the hill and get a load of asbestos.' That was the first time I ever heard the word. I'd seen a lot of it up there, but I didn't know what it was. We got shovels and picks and dug it out of the hill. We brought it down to town, and spread it out as thin as possible in our work area, and put electric heaters on it to dry out. We got on our hands and knees to pick out rocks from it, because we'd been told they wanted 100 percent asbestos. We worked every day on it, all day long, for a couple of weeks. When the stuff got dry, the wind would blow through the door and scatter it all over the building. We didn't want to lose any of it, so we sealed up all the doors with rags. I had no idea what they wanted it for. But like I say, we were just paid to do a job. There was not a peep about it being dangerous."

— LES SKRAMSTAD

Its name comes from a Greek word meaning "inextinguishable," and it endures fire, flood, and frost as fiercely as it clings to a person's lungs. A human hair is well over a thousand times as thick as one of its strands. It can be woven like cotton, which cannot be said of any other mineral. It has been an ingredient in at least three thousand products, common and rare, and, despite the widespread and mistaken impression that it has been banned—efforts by the EPA to do so, in 1989, were overturned on legal technicalities—it remains ubiquitous, not only in insulation but in clutch and brake linings, in pipe and boiler insulation, in wallboard and floor tiles, in oven mitts and plastic pot handles, and in baby powder.

Its advocates and apologists will dispute it, but over the past century, a vast medical literature has exhaustively described the means by which asbestos has killed, according to EPA estimates, 259,000 people in the United States, with another 166,000 deaths anticipated over the next thirty years. Among the proud array of carcinogenic products, natural and fabricated, only tobacco has contributed to a higher death toll. Most of its victims will never know what caused their death, because they are unaware they have been exposed to it, and the lapse between exposure and the onset of illness is typically longer than ten years. In this way, it maims not like a gun, inflicting harm at the moment of contact, but rather like a land mine, which lies dormant for years.

"There's something about this fiber that's not average," says Dr. Brad Black, the director of Libby's new Center for Asbestos-Related Disease. Black's job is not what he bargained for when he opted to be a small-town doctor in a place served by a twenty-four-bed hospital and fewer than ten physicians. Since the "asbestos clinic," as everyone in town calls it, opened last year, Black has seen, he estimates, four or five hundred asbestos-diseased patients, including the construction worker whose chest X ray he has put on display for me.

"See those large patches of white?" Black says, pointing to blocks of washed-out-looking glare that rim the dark crescents of lung. "They wouldn't be there in a healthy lung. It's scarring." Black explains that tremolite asbestos fibers, once inhaled, embed themselves in the lining of the lung—the pleura—like needles, and stay there. The body can't flush them out; medicine can't destroy them; surgery can't cut them out. Surrounding tissue responds to the irritation by calcifying. A healthy pleura is as thick as Saran Wrap; in a person with asbestosis, it may be as thick as an orange peel. Then the lung itself gets covered with calloused tissue; oxygen struggles to find its way into the lung, and carbon dioxide struggles to find its way out. "It's just a progressive scarring," Black explains, "until respiratory or heart failure."

If one were to attempt to devise the perfect suffering, death by asbestosis would come close to fitting the bill. It is slow and incapacitating. It steadily wastes the patient. It brings the patient to the very verge of suffocation and allows him to remain there for months, even years, on end, to reflect on his situation. A typical patient will cough until he vomits. His lungs will fill with fluid. He will feel as if he is swimming in the fluid, drowning.

Just ask Don Kaeding, who survived four years as an artilleryman during the Second World War, but is paying for his twenty-eight months of service on behalf of Zonolite. I find Kaeding yoked by a fifty-foot length of tube to a noisy machine in the corner of his living room. The tubing fits snugly in his nostrils, curls over his ears, runs down his shirt, and snakes its way along the wall to a canister that feeds Kaeding his breath. "God damn, but this is an irritating disease," he says apologetically. "I got these cords to drag around, and they're always in everybody's way. My wife's mother tripped on them one night and broke her arm." Kaeding is seventy-eight. His skin is ashen, his hair waxy, his lips blue. He's been on supplemental oxygen for five years, like a puppet on a life-giving string, and, as he tells me, "ain't no one volunteers for this."

Kaeding—who filed a personal-injury suit against W. R. Grace, only to have his claim dismissed for exceeding the three-year statute of limitations—is one of a cadre of Libby residents being kept alive by mechanical means. Most of them don't leave the house much, because the effort of slipping into a portable oxygen unit, which weighs down a frail body and which gets unpleasantly frosty, tends to consume as much energy as an oxygen-deprived person can muster on a given day. Nonetheless, I spot shoppers resting their air tanks in their carts at the local grocery store. I see an oxygen-outfitted man wheeling a bicycle around town, stowing his gear as others would their Gatorade. And one of my new circle of asbestos-diseased acquaintances tells me the tale of an old woman in Libby who, not long ago, while hooked up to her air supply, put her head beneath her bedcovers, lit a furtive cigarette, and blew herself straight to the next world.

Excerpt from the Deposition of
Earl Lovick, Former Libby Mine
Superintendent, October 27, 1998

Q: And you knew at least by 1962 that your men were being diseased, correct?

A: Yes, sir.

Q: It wasn't at risk of disease, they were in fact being diseased, correct?

A: Some of them, yes, sir.

Q: And they were in fact dying, correct?

A: Some of them, yes, sir.

Q: You had absolute proof that these men had been diseased up there at the mill by 1966 at the latest? Is that true?

A: Yes, sir, that would be true.

Q: And none of the records you had on that were shared with the men. Is that true?

A: Yes, sir.

Q: And so at this point it wasn't just a matter of men being exposed to something that might injure or kill them, these men were already injured and dying, and they were continuing to be exposed every day, is that true?

A: Yes, sir.

Q: And is it fair to say that since you knew that workers were going home with asbestos dust on them, that they were taking home toxic dust?

A: Yes.

Alan Stringer is in a bind. Stringer, fifty-seven, is an engineer of mines, after all, not an engineer of facts, and it turns out that it was an easier job to run an operation that exposed a town to hazard, as Stringer did in Libby from 1981 until the mine shut down, than it is to deal with the emotional, medical, and political fallout. But Stringer is a loyal man, a company man, and when W. R. Grace called on him to be its stand-up guy in Libby once again—dealing with flak from the press and the EPA and the community—he opened an office on Mineral Avenue, downtown, just down the block from the EPA, a few blocks farther from the Center for Asbestos-Related Disease.

"There's no question, it's a sad story," he says. Sadder, too, because W. R. Grace was an excellent record keeper, which only makes

Stringer's job of defending the company tougher. A detailed paper trail demonstrates the company's awareness, even before it purchased Zonolite in 1963, of the asbestos problem in Libby. How to respond to a 1956 report by an inspector for Montana's Division of Disease Control noting that "the asbestos dust in the air is of considerable toxicity"? Or to an internal company memo, from 1967, that refers to "a potentially large group of employees who may already have the beginnings of [asbestosis]"? Or to a 1969 company briefing, marked CONFIDENTIAL and given the subject heading "Vermiculite Report for Mr. Grace," that concludes with the sentence "Tremolite asbestos is a definite health hazard at both the Libby operation and at the expanding plants using the ore"? Well, for Alan Stringer, the response is, "It was another time, another understanding."

Indeed, when times were good in Libby, no one—not workers, nor union representatives, nor politicians in a community in which W. R. Grace was the largest taxpayer—felt pressed to inquire too deeply into the health of miners. Among town doctors, silence was the rule. While the mine was active, W. R. Grace always occupied a seat on the board of the local hospital. As Black remembers, "If you'd have brought up this topic for discussion, you'd have been run out of town as a rabid environmentalist." The company was a pillar of the community. When civic groups were raising funds, the company was there. When the ball field needed new bleachers, the company was there.

But the company also failed to share the results of its own medical-screening program with its employees, even when, in 1969, those tests showed that 92 percent of longtime mine workers were diseased. It would not, it seems, have been cost-effective to acknowledge that working at the mine could make a man terribly sick. A 1968 memo from high-ranking W. R. Grace executive Peter Kostic suggested that thirty-two diseased miners be shifted to less-strenuous work so that "we may be able to keep them on the job until they retire, thus precluding the high cost of total disability." The company failed, as well, to provide workers with on-site showers, an amenity that might have reduced the amount of toxic material miners brought home with them. Another company memo, from 1983—when Stringer was mine superintendent—considered the $373,000 cost of installing such showers in forbidding tones, concluding, "I recommend that no action be taken at this time."

W. R. Grace says that the company complied with ever-changing regulations limiting asbestos exposure, which became more stringent during the 1970s and '80s, and that, alarmed by high rates of lung disease in its workers, it did take steps to reduce dust at the Libby mine. Only in retrospect, the company says, did it become clear that workers and residents had been exposed to harmful levels of tremolite asbestos. Still, the company's files are filled with material that has given Stringer a serious public relations headache.

But slick PR doesn't seem to be a strength at W. R. Grace, which was notably vilified in the book and movie *A Civil Action* for allegedly dumping cancer-causing chemicals in the drinking water of Woburn, Massachusetts. The company's image wasn't burnished any in Libby when, this past April, W. R. Grace filed for bankruptcy under Chapter 11, citing its need for protection from some 325,000 personal-injury claims that had been made against its asbestos-containing products, especially a fire-retardant spray-on insulator called Monokote. By its own account, the pared-down company, which began spinning off its assets in 1995, when it had revenues of $6 billion, did only $1.6 billion in business in 2000, while it forecasts asbestos-related liabilities of $878 million. "Grace cannot defend itself against unmeritorious claims," said Paul J. Norris, the company's chairman, president, and CEO, in announcing the bankruptcy.

Two days after the announcement, I meet with Roger Sullivan, a lawyer in Kalispell, Montana, ninety miles away. About fifteen years ago, a handful of diseased miners in Libby started suing the company, receiving small settlements—generally said to be less than $100,000 each—and agreeing to remain silent about the details of their suits. By the time Sullivan began advocating on behalf of clients in Libby in 1995, settlements had begun to creep up into the middle six figures—still barely enough to cover long-term medical costs. "In the course of developing a few early cases," he tells me, "the circle of victims just kept getting bigger and bigger." Sullivan and his partners, Jon Heberling and Allan McGarvey, have since settled thirty cases against W. R. Grace, have won three trials—including that of Les Skramstad—in front of juries, and have eighty suits pending, representing two hundred individuals.

Of course, these suits have been put on indefinite hold by W. R. Grace's bankruptcy filing, and according to Sullivan, his clients are "frustrated and confused by the chasm between the law and justice." Those with claims pending against W. R. Grace, and those who only recently learned of the harm done to them by the company, now stand a better chance of getting a payoff from gaming machines in local casinos.

"It ought to scare the hell out of the whole town, but it don't. The town looks at us like we're the villains. Like this was a nice little town and we come along and upset the apple cart. A lot of people think we're dreaming this up and taking it out on this poor company. Well, if I strangled a single person—and that's what it amounts to if you've got asbestosis, you suffocate—I'd be in the penitentiary. And yet they do it to families, they do it to kids, and they get away with it."

— LES SKRAMSTAD

Every weekday morning at ten, a group of men, mostly middle-aged or older, meet for coffee and conversation at a grimy little Mexican restaurant in downtown Libby called La Casa de Amigos. The restaurant doesn't open for business until eleven, which suits the members of the coffee klatch just fine. Although they would deny it, their meetings are not open to the public, but are instead the preserve of Libby's dilapidated power elite. Among the regulars who gather beneath faded piñatas and walls hung with threadbare serapes are an assortment of bankers, lawyers, and businessmen, as well as Alan Stringer, the mayor, and a representative to the state legislature. They take wagers on who will pay for their seventy-cent cups of coffee, and they trade gripes about the stigma that has blotted their town. "We're in dire straits," says Mike Munro, who runs a bar and restaurant called Treasure Mountain Casino, "and we've got no way of turning it around. The EPA has brought a different kind of cancer to this town." The men are scornful of the claims of those affected by asbestos-related disease. "There are people in town who are disappointed they haven't been diagnosed," one of them tells me. Another adds, "They thought they'd hit the lottery with this asbestos thing."

Since the EPA arrived in 1999, the town has fractured into a collection of outraged tribes. If Libby was, at one time, divided between blue-collar workers and managers—they lived in different neighborhoods, drank at different bars, prayed at different churches—now it is health, not wealth, that turns neighbors against one another.

Some, like the men in La Casa de Amigos, think the health hazards have been overblown by shiftless residents looking to cash in at the expense of W. R. Grace. Many others have refused to be examined for asbestosis, not wanting to condone the hysteria. Businessmen worry about the local economy: Tales have circulated about out-of-towners calling the Chamber of Commerce to ask if it is safe to drive through Libby, even with the windows rolled up. And there are those who want nothing more from W. R. Grace than acknowledgment in the form of an apology, which has not been forthcoming.

Then there are Libby's sick, who believe they are being persecuted for staining the town's reputation and ruining its economy. According to Laura Sedler, Libby's sole clinical social worker, who runs support groups for people with asbestos-related diseases, "There's an old-fashioned term for what happened to victims in this community: *shunning.*" In 1997, when Les Skramstad took W. R. Grace to court, his suit didn't receive a word of coverage in the local newspapers. The county courtroom was empty of spectators, except for a few widows who wanted to find out what had happened to their husbands. More recently, a woman whose husband had just died of asbestosis stood in the checkout line at the supermarket and listened to the clerk gripe, "I'm sick of hearing about asbestos. We won't be done with this until they all just die off."

But residents in Libby are not only coming to terms with the real-ization that they have been liberally sprinkled with toxic dust; they also seem to be experiencing a childlike sense of abandonment. In the past decade, a prosperous silver mine shut down, and the timber mill that was the largest local employer scaled back its operations by 80 percent. Two thousand jobs have been lost, prompting an exodus of young, able-bodied, and motivated residents. Libby is the seat of what is now the second-poorest county in the second-poorest state in the country. A quarter of the town's population lives below the poverty line; another quarter isn't doing much better.

It's hard not to wonder whether the remoteness of Libby, and the complacency and lack of wealth and lack of influence of its residents—compared, in particular, with that of a onetime Fortune 500 company that donated $764,618 to political campaigns during the 1990s—might have allowed the disaster to occur in the first place. Several hundred sick poor people don't make for much of a political constituency.

Still, the week after W. R. Grace filed for Chapter 11, about two hundred residents air their grievances to a U.S. senator, Max Baucus.

Baucus embraces the role of crusader for Libby's wounded. Facing the
crowd at a local theater, he takes off his jacket, rolls up his sleeves, radi-
ates Clintonesque empathy, and tells the audience, "What happened
here is an outrage. We've got to get you justice. Grace can buy all the
fancy lawyers they want, but I'm going to make sure you will be made
whole." He listens to pleas for health-care facilities, pleas for criminal
action against W. R. Grace, and, toward the end of the meeting, a plea
from a young man, just diagnosed with scarring on his lungs, for Little
League ball fields to replace the contaminated old diamonds. Then,
just as suddenly as he arrived in Libby, Baucus is gone.

I mingle with the crowd after the meeting breaks up. I nod at Alan
Stringer, who sat forlornly through the event in the back corner of the
auditorium with his windbreaker zipped up. I spot Don Kaeding, with
his oxygen tank, and Les Skramstad, in his loudest western shirt.
Diane Keck is there, coughing dryly, and a few feet away stands Mike
Powers, speaking vehemently about the need for aggressive cleanup
of private homes. And I exchange a word or two with Jimmy Racicot,
who has asbestosis and is a relative of the former governor. Or, as he
tells me, in a joking and contemptuous tone, "He's related to me."

When I turn to leave the auditorium, I spot a plaque above the theater entrance, listing the donors who funded its renovation, and I read
the familiar name W. R. Grace.

Excerpt from the Deposition of
Les Skramstad, January 13, 1997

Q: I understand you have had some psychological problems?

A: Yes.

Q: Tell me about those.

A: I have a little problem once in a while justifying my existence on
   this planet.

Q: Since you were diagnosed with asbestosis, have you experienced
   an increase in the frequency of bouts of depression?

A: Somewhat, yes.

Q: And what do you think it is attributable to?

A: Lack of air.

The day before I am to leave Libby, I give myself a tour of the
haunted landscape. I start at the base of Rainey Creek Road, the dirt
road that miners took up Zonolite Mountain for sixty-seven years.

Chris Weis, of the EPA, told me he will no longer drive up the road without wearing respiratory equipment. Yet it remains open to the public. A few days earlier, I saw a young man motor up Rainey Creek on a dirt bike, kicking up a storm of dust. Barely a mile up the road, I pass a clearing littered with beer bottles—and littered, according to recent tests, with asbestos—where teenagers party. Farther up lies a pond, rimmed with high grasses and cattails. Geese float on it. The pond was constructed to capture and neutralize waste from the mine. A hawk glides overhead. Cottonwoods are reflected in the surface of the water. The day is thoroughly still.

Rising above the pond is a reddish brown world of loose rock, hundreds of feet high, striped with late-season snow. This is the waste mountain: millions of tons of discarded ore—slag—brimming with some five billion pounds of asbestos. The state of Montana once gave W. R. Grace an award for reclaiming the mountain, for planting yellow sweet clover and seeding the tailings with grass and speckling it with pine saplings. But as far as I can tell, nothing is growing there.

I drive back down the road, past the site where, for years, ore was sifted into bins and moved across the Kootenai River on open conveyor belts, and then dumped into boxcars of the Burlington Northern Railroad and spread across the country. Then I drive back to town, past the oval track at Libby High School, home of the Libby Loggers. A lone pole-vaulter practices his stride. I continue my drive past W. R. Grace's old expansion plant downtown, where the ore once popped like popcorn. The storage shed is still standing. It looks like the weathered plank barn in an Old West theme park. Part of a rope dangles from a rafter.

If Libby were a fallow kingdom in some obscure myth, a hero would appear to restore the landscape and its people. Libby, being real, has no such luck. When the EPA decides it has scraped W. R. Grace's old facilities clean, it will leave town. But being clean is not the same as being healthy. W. R. Grace says it will cover the medical costs of residents with asbestos-related diseases in perpetuity, but given its bankruptcy proceedings, its word is no longer considered good in this town.

Justice for Libby is a fantasy beneath the western sky. Senator Baucus vows to do his best to convene a congressional inquiry into what happened in Libby and whether anyone at W. R. Grace should be held criminally accountable; perhaps he'll succeed. There is a legal precedent: In 1993, three managers at Film Recovery Systems, a silver-extraction company in Chicago, pleaded guilty to manslaughter charges after a worker died of cyanide poisoning in 1983. But no one in Libby is counting on it. Late this past May, thirty-two townspeople, realizing their efforts to get legal redress against W. R. Grace were futile, filed suit against the state of Montana, saying the state had "conspired with Grace to conceal the results of . . . studies and correspondence" related to the mine. The suit is the stuff of symbolism, which is not in short supply in Libby, and which will have to do for the moment.

Driving out of town the next day, I see a local named Richard Weeks standing on the side of the road, and I stop to say good-bye. Weeks claims to be a prophet—or, more specifically, as he tells me, "the seventh spirit of Moses." He refers me to the texts in the Bible that prove his visionary powers, and that establish Bob Dylan as the prophet Ezekiel. Weeks lives in a red-white-and-blue van parked by the river. He has half a mustache and half a beard, which may be the right look for a town as divided as Libby. "I've been thinking about this asbestos thing," he says. "Dylan has a song about a great flood that will rise up and wash away sin. The flood begins on the Day of Reckoning, which is coming anytime. Look," he says, pointing to the sky, "it's beginning to rain."

Indeed it is. I drive off and leave Weeks standing in the rain, waiting for a cleansing tide to find its way to Libby. I roll down my window and let the rain wash in. It feels good. And the air, the mountain air, tastes good, full of spring. I leave town and take a deep breath and hold it in my lungs. Breathe out. Breathe again.

AUGUST 2001

Editor's Note

At a town meeting in Libby in December 2001, Governor Judy Martz of Montana overcame months of reluctance and announced her support for Libby's designation as a federal Superfund site. The decision will most likely mean that the cost of Libby's cleanup—estimated to be $55 million dollars—will be paid by the state government and the Environmental Protection Agency, rather than by W. R. Grace, which continues to do business despite having filed for bankruptcy protection in April 2001. Meanwhile, the unresolved personal injury claims of sick Libby residents remain stalled in bankruptcy court. Les Skramstad, addressed in Martz's speech as "one of the many great Montanans I have met in my travels," continues to play bass in his country-and-western band, even as his health deteriorates further.

BURIED AT SEA
by Ramsey Flynn

T HE RUSSIANS ARE ABOUT to recover their first dead sailor. It's a stormy predawn on the Barents Sea as a tarp-lined metal basket rises up from the arctic depths and is slowly swung by a crane to the platform of a giant oil-exploration vessel. Workers bracing themselves against the forty-knot gale separate the crane's cables from the dripping basket. "Viktor!" shouts a worker over the screaming wind, summoning his colleague to help him with the door of the examining room. *"Otkrivai!"*—"Open up!"

Once the basket arrives on the gurney inside, the chief medical examiner parts the tarp and views the dead man. The sailor's upper half is so badly burned that there's little left but charred skeleton. The examiner was expecting that much; the would-be rescue divers in August had reported seeing carbon-blackened bubbles when they sprang the crippled submarine's hatch. But what's this down here? The examiner feels the rough surface of a material he wasn't expecting—the sailor's beefy lower half is still clothed in the waterproof shell of a submariner's emergency-escape suit. A few murmurs arise from the small crowd of civilians and military people gathering inside the room. In the aftermath of the tragedy, top officials had sworn the sailors had all died in a few minutes—how had this man found time to put on the extra suit?

The examiner removes the man's blackened woolen socks and marvels at how the cold arctic seawater has preserved the flesh since his expiration more than two months ago. Then he goes through the pockets and feels a bit of oil-soaked plastic material. He draws out the sooty packet and rubs it with his fingers, then notices handwriting. What's this? He had time to write a note? The crowd presses closer, and the chief examiner begins to read: "15:45. It is dark to write here, but I'll try by the feel of touch. . . ."

Thursday, August 10, 2000, 7 P.M. The leviathan *Kursk* floats quietly alongside a loading pier at the ramshackle arctic naval site of Zapadnaya Litsa, taking on armaments for one of the most important military demonstrations in post-Soviet history. Just six years old, the submarine represents a billion dollars of this cash-strapped country's finest technology, a fifteen-thousand-ton predator cloaked in a four-inch-thick layer of black rubber that helps silence her underwater movements. Long as two soccer fields. Five stories high. Sixty feet wide. Twin nuclear reactors. Onboard mascots, including Shilla the cat. A swimming pool. A double hull, with a ten-foot span between the two walls that helps ensure that the enemy can't kill her even with a direct hit. The generous hull gap also makes the perfect space for the launch tubes of twenty-four cruise missiles specially designed to wreck aircraft carriers—or entire cities, if the sailors attach the nuclear warheads. She also can carry twenty-two torpedoes, two new test models of which are being loaded now. As a select few officers and torpedo-factory observers watch, a rusty crane gingerly lowers the prototypes through a portal into the *Kursk*'s front compartment.

Deep inside, the rest of the *Kursk*'s 118 men are casually posted at their battle stations in accordance with torpedo-loading protocol. Toward the stern, an excited Lieutenant Captain Dimitri Kolesnikov—"Dima" to family and friends—rules over a steady hum of preparations. As commander of the state-of-the-art turbine section, Kolesnikov is right where he wants to be. His father was a submariner. Younger brother Sasha, also on the submarine track, has just arrived in the nearby sub-base town of Vidyayevo. And Dima's dearest friend, Lieutenant Captain Rashid Aryapov, commands the sixth compartment, immediately next to his own.

Although from different worlds—Dima hails from Russia's Orthodox Christian north, Rashid from the Muslim south—the young officers have been friends since attending St. Petersburg Naval College together ten years ago. The thickset, redheaded Dima calls his dark-featured friend "Sayeed," or "son of the desert," after a popular Russian movie character, and the pair spent a lot of time watching each other's backs while carousing around the north's Kola Peninsula. But now they're settling down. Both recently got married, and the two couples—along with *Kursk*-mate Lieutenant Captain Sergei Lubushkin and his wife—are bonding into a tight-knit submariners' family. Just last month, the wives joined their husbands for a day on the *Kursk*, where the merry group laughed and played among the hydraulics and wires. When Dima showed off the turbines, he broke into a caricature of himself for his glamorous, henna-haired Olga, barking out military orders as his charges responded smartly: "I say, 'Do that!' The sailor answers, 'Aye!'" Olga performed a string of half-pirouettes through the narrow passageways, and Dima joked at the sight of her approach: "Woman on a boat. Bad sign." All three wives took turns posing with the massive periscope.

Now, Dima and Sayeed take a quick inventory of their personal possessions, including the photos of their wives that both keep taped next to their control panels. In their aft compartments, the sailors are only dimly aware of the torpedo-loading process unfolding above, but they're starting to wonder why it's taking so long. There's talk in the passageways that the two new electrically driven prototypes are leaking explosive battery gas. The captain is, apparently, furious. There've been other rumors that a giant old practice torpedo is leaking fuel through its O-rings into a storage area. Nursing one defective torpedo through an exercise is always tricky. How are they going to deal with three?

From President Vladimir Putin on down, most of the nation's military establishment is approaching the weekend's exercises in a state of high anticipation. To a country with an economy the size of Peru's, the armada now setting out into the Barents represents a key test of the do-more-with-less defense philosophy of Russia's new leader. Much of the Northern Fleet may be rusting at its piers, its rescue systems practically dismantled, but its starring nuclear submarine, the *Kursk,* has its own clever rescue system built in: an escape pod wedged into the fin, capable of whisking ninety sailors safely to the surface. Putin's military advisers actually considered making a mock disaster and rescue part of the exercise, but even without the added theatrics, the event has drawn a crowd of five NATO subs and ships—not that the cold war's end won them an invitation.

As the son of a former submariner, the president has taken a keen personal interest in the exercise. Though he will spend the weekend on a family vacation at the presidential retreat in Sochi, on the Black Sea, he has arranged for several top military men to come along and pass him updates from the Barents. Minding the store from Moscow will be his defense minister, Igor Sergeyev.

And in the Barents, directly overseeing the exercise, will be Northern Fleet commander Vyacheslav Popov, a quintessential Soviet-era admiral. In his fifties, his walrus mustache turning gray, Popov has lately demonstrated his agility in adapting to East-West dynamics by forging a friendship with his nearest NATO counterpart in Norway. Yet Popov couldn't be more imbued with old-style self-reliance and fealty to the Kremlin. As he looks out over the bridge of the nuclear cruiser the *Peter the Great,* Popov knows how much stock his new leader places in the gathering flotilla. Like the rest of his country, Popov doesn't know Putin very well yet, but he's determined not to let the man down.

"Tchert poberi!"—"Damn it to hell!"—mutters *Kursk* captain Gennadi Lyachin, cursing the idiocy of his superiors in Moscow. He's already got one leaking torpedo on board; now he has to take on two more? He's almost of a mind to halt the loading and tell the factory to take these electric nuisances back where they came from. But that would require clearance and a major itinerary change. As it is, the late arctic sunset is dimming the horizon, and the *Kursk* is at risk of failing to make the exercise area by tonight to prepare for tomorrow's cruise-missile firing. Feeling more put-upon than he ordinarily tolerates, the portly sub commander reluctantly boards his vessel.

Prematurely aged after twenty-three years of service—a tenure that entitles him to a salary of $250 a month—Lyachin has seen more than his share of the Russian navy's shrinkage, but takes pride in what he and his crew have been able to accomplish. A year ago, Lyachin's sub sneaked up on a U.S. aircraft-carrier battle group on maneuvers in the Mediterranean, just to prove she could blow them apart if called upon to do so. Later, an embarrassed U.S. vice-admiral had to tell a congressional panel that he'd been forced to divert P3 Orion sub-tracking aircraft from operations over Kosovo just to find the remarkably silent *Kursk.* This brazen exploit helped Lyachin and the *Kursk* crew win recognition as the fleet's finest. It was one more reason his men loved him.

Today's rash of torpedo problems is the latest in a long line of insults to a captain who has been vocal in criticizing conditions in the Northern Fleet. He remembers that during Soviet times they used torpedoes with a stable ignition and fuel system, much like the ones the United States committed to after losing a sub to a suspected torpedo accident in 1968. But the Russian procurement bureaucrats decided that leaner times dictated a shift toward a vastly cheaper system fueled by kerosene and hydrogen peroxide. Loud protests followed in the naval community: Not only was the hydrogen peroxide fuel more volatile, but it had a disturbing habit of leaking, filling cabins with a noxious smell. Finally, the ordnance people began experimenting with new electric torpedoes—which appear to leak only battery gas. Lyachin almost has to laugh at what passes for progress in the Russian navy.

The loading crew backs away, leaving Lyachin with his three sick torpedoes. He hopes his first compartment will know how to handle them. While he has confidence in his men, he's breaking in two new junior munitions men, plus another young guy who's replaced the *Kursk*'s seasoned torpedo coordinator. At least he has the factory specialists lending a hand this weekend, and his twenty-year-veteran first-cabin commander. Lyachin motions to his few charges still topside that it's time to go: *"Davai poyekhali."*

Within minutes, two tugboats move in to escort the *Kursk* away from the pier, at which point Lyachin signals to his men in the turbine compartment. From his upper-deck controls, Dima shouts down to key members of his eight-man team to unleash the juice, and the turbines accelerate with a purring so smooth that Kolesnikov can continue his orders without raising his voice again. The crew feels electrified as the enormous vessel navigates the narrow fjord and tools grandly north along the surface of Zapadnaya Litsa Bay. "Lay north-northwest!" Lyachin barks, and his senior lieutenants relay orders to orient the *Kursk* on a bearing of 345 degrees.

With the course set, Sayeed commands his four-man propulsion team to crank up the reactors, and soon the *Kursk* is approaching its maximum surface speed of sixteen knots. In less than half an hour, she moves out over the continental shelf that fringes the Eurasian landmass and slips into the shallows of the Barents Sea, one of the world's great hornet's nests of East-West submarine games.

The average depth of the Barents is 750 feet, just 245 feet deeper than the *Kursk* is long, leaving little room for adventurous moves. During the more openly contentious years of the cold war, the Barents witnessed at least a half dozen collisions of Soviet and NATO subs, and even post-collapse, there have been a couple of fender benders.

Two U.S. subs arrived here weeks ago to get reacquainted with the Barents's best hiding places. When the *Kursk* arrives in the exercise area, a little after 10 P.M., the NATO vessels track her every move, exploiting the acoustic signature the *Kursk* provided during that Mediterranean stunt last year. Western intelligence is also following her through its extraordinarily extensive surveillance network in the region. Dubbed the Integrated Undersea Surveillance System, this web of underwater cables and listening devices has effectively turned the sea bottom into a 542,000-square-mile echo chamber.

Of course, like everyone else in the Northern Fleet, the *Kursk* crew knows all about the monitoring. In their first major test on Friday, they maneuver the sub into all the right positions and fire one cruise missile—with a low-yield conventional warhead—successfully hitting an empty, rusting target vessel two hundred miles away. When the men bed down for the night, they can take satisfaction in having put on a good show.

Meanwhile, in St. Petersburg, Olga Kolesnikova has taken advantage of her husband's absence to visit with her mother for a couple of weeks, and the two make plans to spruce up Olga and Dima's apartment in Vidyayevo. She tells her mother that when she first laid eyes on the rough dorm-style space, she thought she'd just married "the poorest officer in the whole Russian navy." But she loves her "Mitya" and longs to start a family.

Dima's parents, Irina and Roman, are taking a bus from their home in St. Petersburg to the family's getaway cottage in Estonia. As parents, they're proud of Dima's recent personal turnaround. They'd been worried about the way he'd often link up with certain high school friends when he was home on leave, staying out until the wee hours drinking. When it appeared Dima was jeopardizing his naval career, Roman and Irina convinced him to get treatment. He did, and in December his mother introduced Dima to Olga, who was teaching second grade at the school where Irina works. Olga seemed perfect for Dima, even if she was still recovering from a failed first marriage. Just a few months after meeting her, Dima shocked and delighted his family by announcing their engagement.

Dima has become much better at informing his parents of his activities and has tried to assuage his mother's worries about submarining. Dima wrote home on May 27, "If you don't hear from me, don't worry. Just watch the news on TV. They'll tell you what's going on."

For Khalima Aryapova, Sayeed's departure for the exercise was hard. She's shy and still new to Vidyayevo, and she busies herself with cleaning the apartment while listening to the radio. She has just told her husband she's carrying their first child. Sayeed was happy, of course, but said he was worried about taking on the new addition so early in their marriage, especially given the $50 monthly salary of a lieutenant captain in the Russian navy—and the difficulties of the coming winter in a town where heating and plumbing often fail.

August 12. By early Saturday morning, the *Kursk* crew is gearing up for its pivotal torpedo test. At 8:51 A.M., Captain Lyachin radios to command staff on shore in Severomorsk that he has entered the three-hundred-square-mile exercise area. He takes orders to stage the ambush along a southeasterly course and comes to the periscope depth of sixty feet.

In the *Kursk's* frontmost compartment, the seven members of the torpedo team are excited but anxious to eject these damn leaking torpedoes. They've been ventilating the area and taking extra precautions with everything from the condition of overhead wiring to the way they put down their tools. Even with many of the missiles and torpedoes this weekend bearing low-yield test warheads, there are some twenty thousand pounds of explosives in their compartment alone—a frightening thought when the spark from one dropped wrench could set off the whole lot of it.

Still, experience has taught the men that if they can just get the leaking torpedoes into their firing tubes, the situation should take care of itself. The original plan was for the *Kursk* to fire the two new torpedoes installed two days ago. But Captain Lyachin wants to get rid of the enormous "Fat Boy," whose fuel leak strikes him as more pressing than the irritating new batteries. He radios Admiral Popov, aboard the *Peter the Great,* for permission to substitute the Fat Boy for the first scheduled round. *"Dobro"*—"Proceed"—crackles Popov's voice over Lyachin's squawk box.

On the torpedo cabin's top deck, the crew watches as the conveyor finally eases the thirty-foot-long, two-and-a-half-ton projectile into the right-side torpedo tube. The man in charge of the operation is Senior Warrant Officer Abdulkadir Ildarov, a swarthy, even-tempered forty-year-old compartment commander with a wife and two teenage girls. He last saw them July 26, when his wife was eight months pregnant. He assured her he would be home for the birth in September.

Today's tests also bring the expertise of Mamed Gadzhiev, who, at forty-two, is a veteran designer of torpedoes at Russia's Dagdiesel plant in Dagestan. Earlier in the summer, he told his wife that he was "going on a mission" for two months "up north." He and his close partner Arnold Borisov left in late July. When he's out of town, Gadzhiev normally leaves messages at the plant for his family, because they have no home phone. He called after his arrival, but his wife is worried that there have been no messages so far in August.

The two junior torpedists are young recent graduates of submarine school. Ivan Nefedkov mans the left torpedo tubes. The twenty-year-old, a gifted wrestler, wrote home to his mother in May that he had been selected for the *Kursk* crew. "We endlessly clean her," he wrote, "with soap foam above our knees."

Manning the right-side tubes is Maxim Borzhov. "Mama, you should be proud of me," reads one of his letters home. "I have been taken on such a submarine!" He detailed his excitement about working under the inspiring Captain Lyachin and delighted in being teamed with sub-school classmate Nefedkov, who bunks right next to him. Borzhov will have the honor of preparing the Fat Boy for firing, under the close watch of section commander Ildarov.

In the command-and-control compartment, just behind them, twenty-two-year-old Senior Lieutenant Alexei Ivanov-Pavlov will coordinate his first *Kursk* torpedo test. Ivanov-Pavlov called his parents in July to exult in his new assignment. The parents were thrilled at the rare contact from the boy, who had always distinguished himself as a straight-A student.

With no targets spotted along the area's southern border, the *Kursk* turns and navigates northwest. Shortly after 11 A.M., she slows to twelve knots for a troll. Suddenly, the acoustics and sonar trackers say they've picked something up, about thirty miles to the northwest.

Sonar confirms it's their main "target"—the *Peter the Great* and its battle group. Suddenly, the command center comes alert to the sound of its captain's voice. "Bosun," shouts Captain Lyachin, "helm fifteen degrees!" The sub slows to a stealthier eight knots as Lyachin and Ivanov-Pavlov select coordinates that will make Fat Boy sail right under the *Peter the Great* at a safe distance below its hull.

"Stand by!" crackles Ivanov-Pavlov over the intercom. Ildarov and Borzhov confirm the opening of the tube's front door.

In the control cabin, Ivanov-Pavlov hears Ildarov announce the ready status, receives Captain Lyachin's curt nod, and suddenly barks into the intercom, "TA number one, fire!"

Ildarov pushes the trigger and the Fat Boy begins hissing in its tube as the necessary hydraulic pressure builds to expel the goliath out to sea, where its own engine will take over. "Commander," says Borzhov, according to protocol, "the volley will be fired in five seconds!"

"Volley!" shouts Ildarov into his intercom. In the control and torpedo compartments, excitement blends with anticipated relief. The efforts to stem the fuel leak have worked; one big problem down, two smaller problems to go.

The men await the tremor that comes with an ejection, but it doesn't come. Suddenly there's a louder hiss, then a thunderclap. The men get barely a moment to look at one another's faces before a corona of fire engulfs the torpedo cabin in flame so hot it vaporizes flesh. With a force equal to 550 pounds of TNT, the explosion reshapes the cabin in ways the *Kursk*'s engineers never imagined possible, hammering its rear bulkhead with a power that sends the equipment and the thirty-six men in the second compartment hurtling aftward, rocking the vessel like a brick wall being hit by a fast-moving truck. Amid the chaos, a battered Captain Lyachin frantically orders all hands to attempt emergency surfacing.

The unexploded torpedoes in the cabin in front of him are built to withstand a fire for about two minutes. The heat in the torpedo area is now twelve thousand degrees Fahrenheit.

In the turbine section, Dima Kolesnikov commands his men to give it all they've got, and soon the nine-man team can feel their limping boat accelerating toward the surface, hoping to God it does whatever the captain needs it to do to get them out of trouble. It's 11:29 A.M., and the hundred or so men still alive on the *Kursk* are fighting for their lives.

Aboard the U.S. attack sub *Memphis,* several miles away, the noise is so loud the hydroacoustics men are having a tough time keeping their headphones on. This was obviously not a normal torpedo launch. They can hear the distinct noises of the *Kursk*'s propellers speeding up, amid a rumble of metal on metal and a lot of muffled shouting. Then obvious flooding noises. Holy shit.

More than 180 miles to the northwest, the surveillance people on the USNS *Loyal,* the American surface vessel monitoring the exercise, react with alarm. What the hell was that? The other American submarine, the *Toledo,* has picked it up, too, as have the British sub

HMS *Splendid* and Norway's *Marjatta*. Overhead, Norwegian P3 Orion sub trackers are capturing the noise relayed from air-dropped radio buoys. The NATO observers can't believe the wild spikes on their charts—yet none of them feel free to break radio silence by asking the Russian seamen if they need help.

Some Northern Fleet vessels also know something's up. But on the *Peter the Great,* Popov and his men don't know what to make of the data. They still haven't spotted the Fat Boy's trail. Popov is hoping the explosion came from the target practice of a surface ship. On the other hand, he worries that if his prized *Kursk* is in trouble, it's soon going to be hard to tell. Captain Lyachin is supposed to report his test results within a few minutes, but after that the schedule calls for him to hide silently in the depths until 6 P.M.

On a seismograph mounted in the bedrock of a remote Norwegian hillside 275 miles west, a prominent tracing emerges on the paper, unobserved on this late Saturday morning. It shows what looks like a temblor, 2.2 on the Richter scale.

Water. A surge of it jetting through the broken torpedo tube into the cabin. Lyachin and others in the second compartment know they can't reach the fire, but they hope the seawater will cool the twenty or so remaining warheads before any of them can detonate.

It doesn't. Precisely two minutes and fifteen seconds after the initial explosion, another one rocks the Barents, 125 times stronger than the first. The second blast registers 3.5 on the seismograph in Norway—its most violent tracing ever—and shows up on other seismographs up to thirty-one hundred miles away. Scientists will gauge the blow at the equivalent of around twelve *tons* of TNT, about four times the force of the explosion at the Oklahoma City federal building.

The thirty-six mostly senior-ranking men in the second compartment, including Captain Lyachin and Senior Lieutenant Ivanov-Pavlov, are killed in an instant. The twenty-four men in the third compartment, mostly young officers operating the chart cabin and chemical-control unit, are gone in the next instant. Whichever of the twelve men in the fourth compartment survive are quickly done in by the seawater that cascades through the broken bulkhead, crushing men in its path like the spray from some supernaturally powered fire hose.

The outer hull is split with an eighty-two-foot gash that extends back to the fin and along the fin's right side, eliminating the remaining survivors' prospects of using the front escape hatch or the emergency-evacuation module. The harder inner pressure hull is breached still more extensively, destroying any chance of keeping seawater out.

The blast drives the remaining front bulkheads toward the *Kursk's* fourth compartment, stripping away most of the floor-mounted equipment in their path. An inch-and-a-half-thick torpedo-tube hatch is made to curve inward like a giant bullet and rockets through the fore sections. The heavy steel door of a classified-paperwork cabin is filleted and twisted until it resembles a propeller. The extra-heavy bulkhead hatches guarding the reactors are jammed by the blow, leaving any of the fifteen men in the two nuclear-reactor compartments who are still alive no escape from the arctic seawater that will seep through the imperfect seals. Dima and Sayeed's close friend Sergei Lubushkin is in that tomb.

The explosion sends the sub spiraling downward, causing the reactors to shut off automatically and forcing the lights onto emergency battery power. The terrified sailors in the four aft compartments are tumbled like laundry as the vessel yaws and spins, throwing men and machines against the wall, then the ceiling, then the other wall, then the deck. Many fall on top of one another during the surreal roll, already well bloodied by the levers, clipboards, scraps of furniture, and ladder sections that hurtled into them in the second blow. Outside the vessel, shards of the *Kursk* scatter across the dark seabed—a railing, jagged parts of torpedoes, slices of thick black rubber, stray chunks of hull.

Four minutes after the first blast, the broken *Kursk* slowly glides onto the bottom, leaving a 490-foot trail in the sand before coming to a halt twenty seconds later. It settles in, leaning twenty degrees to its port side and slightly down at the bow, 354 feet deep. The water temperature of the *Kursk's* new neighborhood is thirty-eight degrees.

Amid the confusion and shouts, most of the dazed men still alive in compartments six through eight grab emergency-escape equipment and try to tally emergency supplies: escape suits, some oxygen masks, heavy woolen socks, packets of processed meat and cans of condensed milk, chocolate. They gather up whatever they can and begin crawling back toward the ninth compartment, where, they know, the only escape hatch remains. Thoroughly stunned, many with ears dripping blood from burst eardrums, the twenty-three seal their compartment hatch behind them a few minutes before 1 P.M.

❖   ❖   ❖

In St. Petersburg, it's sublimely warm with a hazy overcast as Olga Kolesnikova excitedly opens a letter from her husband of four months. "I will drown in your eyes," Dima writes in one typically romantic flourish, "like a real submariner, without any sound." In Estonia, Dima's parents are relaxing at a health spa near the cottage. In Vidyayevo, about midday, Khalima Aryapova suspects she's suffering some morning sickness, then hours later notices her heart is beginning to race. In an apartment building nearby, Sergei's wife, Olga Lubushkina, is washing her refrigerator when a particularly annoying song comes on her stereo, satirically celebrating how all submariners die at the same time in a wreck, regardless of rank. She never thought the song was funny, but today for some reason it makes her cry.

In Moscow, the front page of the English-language *Russia Journal* carries a report about Putin's recent visit with officers of Russia's Baltic Fleet, at which he extolled Russia's glorious upcoming return to the world's high seas.

Five thousand miles away in Maryland, electronic eavesdroppers working in the predawn hours at the National Security Agency detect an uptick in the communications traffic of northern Russia. They aren't quite sure what's going on, but the naval exercise there must have hit a snag: The data make it look as if everybody in the Northern Fleet is trying to talk to one another at the same time. Within minutes, word arrives from the USNS *Loyal*. Two major blasts occurred in the area of a Russian submarine, the second of them truly deafening.

The scene at Northern Fleet headquarters in Severomorsk is confused and tense. The huge blast has thrown them for a loop as well. Most of the vessels in the exercise are still communicating, but there's no sound from the *Kursk*. Wasn't there supposed to be a torpedo test?

One P.M. Lieutenant captains Kolesnikov and Aryapov are the Kursk's senior remaining officers. While scrambling into an emergency-escape suit, Dima surveys the terrified men surrounding him in the dimming light of the cramped ninth compartment, normally occupied by just three sailors. Several of his compatriots are wrestling with valves on the emergency-escape hatch above the section's upper deck. One of them is pounding on the hull with a sledgehammer, hoping searchers will hear. Dima looks around, trying to make out the survivors' faces. He and Sayeed crawled here together, but where's

Lubushkin? He'd like to open their hatch and look for Sergei, but it would risk the life of every man in the ninth compartment. Maybe Sergei joined some lucky submariners in the escape module in the fin before the second blow.

Prospects for escape don't look good, but the twenty-three play out their options. Each compartment has its own chemical air-regenerating system capable of supplying oxygen for up to three days—more if they can find the extra "plates" that slow the buildup of carbon dioxide. Some of the men have masks that, if properly supplied, could provide a few more hours. But Dima takes little comfort in these tenuous sustainers of life in the face of the fleet's patchwork rescue system. He knows that the rusting rescue assets are at least twelve hours away in Severomorsk in any case, and that to counter any emergency, the brass is counting on the *Kursk*'s top-mounted escape pod, which is seven compartments from where they sit now.

Impulsively, he searches the wrecked cabin for a pencil and a notepad and begins taking roll. The sailors take a numb comfort in the head count, even though with their damaged hearing the voices all sound like distant mutters. Some of them pray. Some cry. Some crouch on the floor and hold their heads between their knees, hiding their faces from reality. With the compartment's hatch seals compromised, internal pressure is slowly rising and will ultimately bring on excruciating headaches. As the hours wear on, Dima orders the survivors to lie low and stay as quiet as possible to save air.

After taking roll, Dima begins to compose a note to his family. He first greets Olga, using his pet name for her. "Olechka!" he writes. "I love you! Do not suffer too much!"

In a corner, Sayeed is also writing a note, on a page torn out of a detective novel, trying to perform his duty as the vessel's damage-assessment officer. "There is a shortage of belts and individual respiratory kits," he reports. "If we head for the surface, we won't be able to survive the compression."

Onboard the *Peter the Great,* Admiral Popov spends the rest of the afternoon unsuccessfully trying to assuage his anxieties with the idea that the *Kursk* is just remaining incommunicado for its hiding period. Finally, he asks an aide to quietly get in touch with fleet rescue-service chief Alexander Teslenko.

In Severomorsk, Teslenko receives Popov's order around 5 P.M. and is immediately gripped with worry. What if the *Kursk* really is down? He has warned the fleet brass that rescue assets are depleted beyond reason. His "primary rescue vessel," the *Mikhail Rudnitsky,* is, in reality, a civilian floating crane retrofitted to support military mini-subs. Russia's best rescue submersibles have been absent for months, toiling far away south of Greenland, covering their operating expenses by conducting private tours of the newly accessible *Titanic* wreck site. The pair of rescue subs Teslenko has on hand haven't been properly tested in two years. His diving bells are old, and their crews wildly undertrained. Even if the bells make the descent to the Barents's average depth, Teslenko has no deep-sea divers capable of assisting with docking efforts; the deepest his divers can go is about two hundred feet. Ideally, the first thing Teslenko would do once on the scene would be to run an oxygen hose in through a hatch in a bid to buy any survivors more time. But he isn't sure he can get his pressurized-oxygen generator to function. Not that attaching a hose without deep-sea divers is much of an option anyway.

Teslenko feels certain Popov must know most of this, so the rescue chief anxiously tells his crew to gear up as ordered.

Shortly after 5 P.M., one of Popov's officers makes the first attempt to get the *Kursk* to break its radio silence. An hour later, Popov decides to helicopter to his Severomorsk office and wait out the vigil there, instructing his men to tell *Kursk* captain Lyachin he *must* surface and report his status no later than 11 P.M.

Popov's slowness to sound the alarm is not uncommon in a military culture with a long history of reluctance to take bad news to higher authorities. When he finally relents around 11:30 P.M., the word goes to Igor Sergeyev, the top man left back at the Kremlin. The rattled defense minister decides to hold off on ruining the president's vacation until the fears are confirmed.

At 4:35 A.M., the *Peter the Great* reports an "anomaly" on the seabed at a depth of 354 feet. Three hours later, Sergeyev sits in his Moscow office and places the kind of phone call he hates.

At the other end of the line, Putin initially responds to Sergeyev with several seconds of awkward silence. "What is the situation with the reactor?" he finally asks. "What is being done to save the people on board?"

Putin volunteers to fly to Northern Fleet headquarters, but

Sergeyev assures the president that his arrival on the scene would have too little practical effect to warrant breaking off his time away with his family.

Sunday, August 13, late morning. Dark rumors slowly trickle in to Vidyayevo with the return of a few vessels from the exercise. Sergei's wife, Olga Lubushkina, hears the story Sunday morning from some visiting girlfriends. No one seems sure of anything, and she tries to dodge the anxiety by letting the cuffs out of Sergei's pants.

Meanwhile, about eighty-five miles north, in the Barents Sea, the rescue vessel *Mikhail Rudnitsky* has arrived in the exercise area. It will take four hours to anchor and begin searching for the downed sub's exact location, three hours more to prepare its onboard rescue subs, forty-five minutes beyond that to get the first one in the water. By 4:15 P.M. on Sunday—nearly thirty hours after the mysterious Saturday-morning explosions—the Northern Fleet's first-deployed mini-sub is making its way toward the *Kursk* at an underwater speed of two knots.

By 6 P.M., the submersible has homed in on the stricken vessel and gotten the first heartbreaking glimpse of her condition. But before it can do much more, the mini-sub strikes one of the *Kursk*'s surface wings and is forced to make an emergency ascent. Overhead, two NATO sub-tracking turboprops watch from the skies.

Toward evening in Russia, a state-owned television network broadcasts a recording made late the previous day of Admiral Popov proclaiming the remarkable success of the Barents exercise. After seeing the broadcast, Olga Lubushkina calls her parents in Severomorsk to see what they make of it, but they say they haven't even heard the rumors.

While most of a restless Vidyayevo tries to stay calm on Sunday night, Teslenko's *Rudnitsky* sends its second manned submersible toward the *Kursk;* it makes three attempts before giving up a few minutes after 1 A.M. without reestablishing visual contact. The first submersible goes back out, but its batteries die.

With twenty vessels now swarming the rescue site, numerous reports emerge that tapping noises have been heard rising up from the *Kursk.* One vessel says it detects a coded message: "SOS . . . water."

Monday, August 14, 9:30 A.M. In a report on state-controlled radio, a Russian-navy spokesman gently informs his countrymen that a submarine involved in the weekend exercise has suffered a technical malfunction just the day before, and that her captain has decided to descend to the seabed to assess the situation. Rescue vessels have established radio contact with the crew and are supplying air. No casualties have been reported. The broadcast awakens Moscow's increasingly bold independent media outlets, conditioned since the fall of communism to question the government's version of events.

Early Monday, Sayeed's wife, Khalima Aryapova, visits Sergei's wife, Olga Lubushkina, at her job at the Vidyayevo passport office. "Have you heard?" Olga asks. "They say that the *Kursk* is lying on the seabed." At first, Khalima thinks she's joking. Olga tells her she's not but that officials have assured everyone it's just a technical problem.

The midday updates are only slightly more alarming. But watching the news while apartment-sitting for his brother Dima, twenty-two-year-old Sasha Kolesnikov is convinced something is seriously wrong. Though he's just beginning submarine service, even most amateurs know that a nuclear sub like the *Kursk* doesn't descend to the seabed because of "technical faults." Who are these officials to speak such nonsense?

Irina Kolesnikova answers the phone at her vacation cottage. It's her brother on his cell phone. "Something happened to the *Kursk*," he blurts. "Turn on the TV." The Russian reports strike Dima's parents as mild, but when they tune in to a report on the United States' Radio Liberty, the information takes an ominous turn. The *Kursk* is at the bottom, nose down, filling with water. Irina places her faith in the rescue effort, but retired submariner Roman knows the situation is deadly serious. He declines to alarm Irina and pins his hopes on their son's strength and smarts. Can survivors get into escape suits and survive the depths for an ascent? Irina and Roman make plans to catch the first bus out of Estonia at six o'clock Tuesday morning.

Officials at Norway's Defense Ministry see through Russia's clumsy Monday deceits, and they instantly order their top naval officer in the north, Admiral Einar Skorgen, to use his direct hot line to Admiral Popov and assess the crisis as it should be assessed—commander to commander, just neighbors helping neighbors.

Skorgen hesitates a moment before calling. He's been receiving briefings on the news out of the Barents, but until a short while ago he had convinced himself that the situation couldn't be that bad, or Vyacheslav would have called him. Over the past couple of years, the pair has enjoyed a number of unprecedented cross-border visits, emptying bottles of vodka together, sweating in the same *banyas,* joking over military bureaucracy. "Between us sailors," Popov told Skorgen at one point, "we need to forget about what I say in Moscow." Why would Vyacheslav be shy about initiating a call for help? Skorgen picks up the red phone at his office and hits auto dial. A senior aide politely answers at Popov's office in Severomorsk and promptly relays word to the Russian admiral, now back on board the *Peter the Great.* The answer comes back in minutes: Thanks, but no thanks; we've got the situation under control with our own equipment.

Really? thinks Skorgen. For God's sake, they don't even have deep-sea divers anymore! Skorgen suspects Moscow is doing the talking. He calls Oslo and informs them he's putting the Norwegian rescue vessels on standby, just in case.

In Washington, national security adviser Sandy Berger, who has been getting regular updates from the USNS *Loyal* since Saturday, calls his Kremlin counterpart in Moscow. He says he can have divers and equipment on the scene in thirty-six hours. The answer is the same: Thanks, but we can handle it.

Offers from other countries are similarly deflected—from the United Kingdom, from France, from Germany, from the Netherlands, from Italy, from Sweden, from Israel, from Canada, from Japan.

Still, on the Barents, the sounds of tapping continue to rise up: "SOS . . . water."

By 4 P.M. on Monday, Teslenko and his men have maneuvered another submersible to the scene, transported by a floating crane. But the waves are building as the afternoon's weather deteriorates, and the rocking crane can't get the vessel into the water. Teslenko's men decide to send the crane to the nearest shallow area so they can off-load the sub in calmer waters and tow it to the scene from there.

"SOS . . . water."

In the early evening, the image of a harried-looking Admiral Popov is beamed again into TV sets throughout Russia. He acknowledges that it's serious. "I'm not quite sure what happened," he says.

Having received some exterior damage from the rough crane deployment, the backup mini-sub arrives. It dives toward the *Kursk,* but blows a pressure valve halfway down, makes an ascent, then nearly sinks before a quick-thinking crane operator saves it.

"SOS . . . water."

In the *Kursk's* section nine, more than fifty hours after the explosions, the level of poisonous carbon dioxide is rising along with the pressure, worsening the headaches. Oxygen is vanishing. Survivors stay as still as possible, involuntarily taking quick, shallow breaths. There is no energy spared even to write notes. Cold water keeps seeping in, and a slow-burning fire has begun working its way around the compartment—cruelly ignited by oil coming in contact with the extra air-regeneration plates—which further depletes oxygen reserves and adds to the carbon dioxide. Only one sailor is allowed to continue knocking, and he's getting more feeble. Sailor by sailor, brain by brain, consciousness dims. For some, coma approaches.

Sayeed is crammed into a rear corner, the paper containing his status report back in his pocket after being used to provide instructions to the man knocking on the hatch. He has time to dwell on his wife and the afternoon during their recent honeymoon in St. Petersburg when she gleefully threw her coins into the Admiralty Building fountain. According to legend, young marrieds who toss coins there together are destined to return as old couples. Afterward, when she realized her husband had inadvertently given all his coins to her, Khalima fretted superstitiously. Now he has to face never seeing her again or knowing their baby.

Sayeed and Khalima just missed meeting up with Dima and his new bride in St. Petersburg. Sayeed looks now across the crowded compartment at his dear friend and takes comfort in facing the end in the presence of the man he sometimes calls Zoloto—"Golden." It's because of Dima's red hair, but it's also because he always scores top honors on his submarine tests; Zoloto can do no wrong.

"SOS . . ."

Six P.M. On the surface, the low-pressure system spins out swells of up to fifteen feet, toying with the aged rescue equipment.

Pressed for answers about the disaster's cause, Russian naval commander Admiral Vladimir Kuroyedov offers one. He expresses a strong suspicion that the *Kursk* suffered a collision with another vessel—likely a NATO submarine—and the crash set off torpedoes. Given the history, it's certainly a plausible explanation. To key decision makers, it also justifies keeping would-be foreign rescuers from climbing around inside the wreckage of the nation's most state-of-the-art sub.

The Barents storm builds through the night, making further rescue attempts impossible. As dawn breaks on Tuesday, the local print media weigh in, with even the state-controlled organs clucking over the new president's invisibility during the crisis. Illusions about the existence of an oxygen supply and formal communications are shattered. Only the persistent reports of tapping offer hope.

And now, statements begin to emerge that the accident actually happened on Saturday—a day earlier than the government has acknowledged. These rumors combine with another that says that officials in Severomorsk have already ordered the construction of 120 zinc-lined coffins. Zinc is always specified in Russia when the authorities anticipate the need to preserve bodies over long periods of transport to far-off regions.

With the winds abating, Teslenko tries one more time to launch a mini-sub, but it swings wildly from its tethers in the wind, smashing into the mother ship, taking damage to its sonar.

News of the rejected foreign offers circulates on Radio Liberty and in the Russian media. When quizzed about these rebuffs by the gathering journalistic hordes, officials insist their rescue equipment is as good as anything the West has.

As he approaches the sixty-hour mark, Teslenko brings out the old rescue bells. But their primitive mechanical grappling arms are unable to latch on to the *Kursk*'s hatches, and the navy begins to acknowledge that forces beyond its control are preventing successful docking. The officials don't mention one hushed-up new development: The bell operators and other listeners can no longer detect any tapping sounds at all. Among themselves, they try to keep hope alive with the idea that the sailors heard the hatch-contact efforts and are conserving their energy.

In the ninth compartment, the submariners are in various states of advancing stupor. The bulkhead hatch leading into the eighth compartment is now open, as several sailors have sought out the few precious cubic feet of oxygen below the cloud of black smoke from the growing fire. As men lose consciousness, their heads fall into the steadily rising seawater that is filling the compartment, finishing them. The fire steals into the remaining air spaces. With all of the sailors now dead or unconscious, the flames start on the areas of flesh still exposed above the waterline.

Dima Kolesnikov's note, sheathed in protective plastic, is tucked in a pocket just below the water. The handwriting is clear and controlled on one side, where Dima used the dimming last light to greet Olga, her mother, and his family. The other side is awkwardly scribbled, opening with the date of August 12 and the military time, 15:45.

> It is dark to write here, but I'll try by the feel of touch. It looks like there are no chances to get out. 10 to 20 percent. Let's hope at least someone reads this. Here are the names of the compartment's submariners; some will try to escape. Greetings to all. Don't despair. Kolesnikov.

Tuesday, August 15, 11 A.M. As accounts of the failed docking attempts are broadcast around the world, officials in the United States begin hoping the Kremlin will have a change of heart. Defense Secretary William Cohen faxes a letter to the Kremlin, reiterating the offer. Still no deal. Still no public statements or appearances from Putin.

The *Moscovsky Komsomelets* paper is one of the first to bare its fangs over the seemingly nonsensical government position, placing a screaming banner headline on Tuesday's front page: DAMN YOU, DO SOMETHING.

The "Kremlin pool" journalists are finally flown to Sochi, but quickly accept orders not to impose upon their vacationing president by grilling him about the difficulties up north. His published activity schedule shows a few calls to foreign leaders. He takes time for a ride on a Jet Ski.

Out on the balmy surface of the Black Sea, Vladimir Putin is a man off balance. For the first couple of days after the catastrophe, he felt well enough informed by his deputies. But over the past fifty-two hours, as their reports have grown increasingly conflicting, he has begun to question his decision not to fly to the Barents immediately. First, they told him there was little chance of anyone's surviving for more than a few hours after the explosion. Then the reports of tapping. The former KGB colonel is reluctant to ask NATO for anything, but given the condition of the Northern Fleet's rescue equipment, he would have liked to know what his real options were.

But perhaps even more dismaying to the new president is the public outcry over the government's attempts at secrecy. When the people went to the polls in the spring and affirmed his succession of the ailing Boris Yeltsin, it seemed a tacit acknowledgment that without some controls, the free-press free-for-all unleashed by his immediate predecessors would only lead to more chaos. What do the people expect? Television crews on the scene, so the whole world can see the sorry state into which Russia has fallen?

The next morning, tanned and wearing a golf shirt, Putin meets with scholars from Russia's Academy of Sciences. Outside the conference center afterward, he is taking a few questions from the press when a journalist abruptly changes the topic from the country's brain drain to his thoughts about the *Kursk* tragedy. This situation is "beyond critical," says Putin, as calmly as he can. "But all possible efforts to save the crew have been carried out."

That afternoon, President Bill Clinton calls. The two talk for twenty-five minutes, but Putin is noncommittal.

A short time later, Putin tells his men to accept outside help from whatever source they deem most appropriate. Four and a half days after the explosions on board the *Kursk,* the call goes out to Norway and the United Kingdom.

Of all the possible scenarios—terrorist sabotage, friendly fire, a rogue World War II mine—the NATO-sub theory is the clear favorite among Russia's most powerful officials. Now they need to place the criminal sub at the scene. Soon they report that the *Peter the Great* picked up a NATO sub's signal just after the sinking, requesting entry to a Norwegian facility near Bergen.

Late on Wednesday, Russia sends out six search planes in the direction of Norway, hoping for a glimpse of the NATO getaway sub.

In Norway, Admiral Skorgen's men are alarmed by the sight of radar images showing Russian aircraft rapidly approaching Norwegian airspace for the first time since 1996. The Norwegian commander scrambles his own F-16s to mark their airspace. Skorgen gets on the hot line and calls Popov, asking what this is about. Though they're on a first-name basis, Popov's response is all business. "I have information that there has been communication between Western subs," says Popov. "We have reason to believe there's been a collision."

What's so unusual about Western subs communicating while departing the site of an exercise? thinks Skorgen. Somebody's putting him up to this.

But the Russian search planes have gotten what they wanted: They've positively identified a U.S. Los Angeles–class attack sub moving at eight knots toward Norway. They describe it as "limping" toward Bergen "for repairs."

Thursday, August 17. Though they've been informed by now that there are no remaining signs of life from the *Kursk,* the Russian people, even many of the victims' families, still haven't been able to get official confirmation as to who was on board. But the enterprising Russian media are on the case, and they've found a well-placed Northern Fleet officer who's willing to sell the list of sailors' names.

In exchange for a cash payment of $650, made through an anonymous intermediary, a bag is unceremoniously tossed from a moving car to a pair of Russian reporters waiting near a bus stop in the closed military city of Severomorsk.

The names are published Friday morning in Russia's biggest newspaper, *Komsomolskaya Pravda.*

Friday, August 18. The Norwegian and British rescue equipment is among the best in the world. It's also mobilizing from more than a thousand miles away, and neither country can coordinate airlifting the apparatus closer this late in the game. So two ships launch an ambitious and painfully earnest journey to the Barents Sea.

While the rescue effort makes its way toward the *Kursk,* Skorgen continues to use his hot line to Popov to gather info. Initially, intermediaries handle Skorgen's questions, and they're vague regarding proprietary details. Repeatedly, an irritated Skorgen demands to speak directly with Popov.

"Vyacheslav," says Skorgen, "I can't accept waiting until we are in diving position to get this kind of information! You and I know that every minute, every second, counts."

Finally, Popov starts to talk as if his political monitors don't matter to him anymore. He says that the rear hatch offers the best chance. Though there's some damage from the Russian diving bells, the Norwegians and Brits should be able to achieve a seal. Despite the late stage, Skorgen and his men get their first meaningful dose of optimism. Maybe the clever sailors have found some lifesaving air pockets.

Yet late on Saturday, Northern Fleet officials order the rescue vessel carrying the British submersible to hold its position twenty miles away from the wreck site. Only the predominantly Norwegian dive team will be admitted in to assess the worthiness of a rescue effort, and then to call in a rescue sub if appropriate.

By early Sunday afternoon, humans are touching the skin of the *Kursk* for the first time all week. Norwegian diver Paul Dinesson taps the hard rubber with a small mallet, hoping for the telltale signs of air pockets. "Come on, boys," he says into his mask. "Talk to me."

The air-pocket test is not promising, but results from the rear compartments are inconclusive, so divers decide they will attempt to test the hatch valves for air pressure just the same.

At 7:35 A.M. on Monday, August 21, Dinesson frees the outer hatch. A sudden rush of very small bubbles appears, indicating a flooded interior. Dinesson notes that the bubbles have very dark interiors, implying a higher level of carbon dioxide than human beings could possibly generate—usually a sign of fire.

Watching the live television footage of the bubbles surging energetically toward the Barents's surface, Olga Kolesnikova sees them as the liberated souls of her young husband, Dima, and his comrades, soaring heavenward.

By afternoon, the foreign rescuers are departing; Norway's Admiral Skorgen places a call to his friend Popov. He finds Vyacheslav in his Severomorsk office, sounding beaten, even physically sick. Skorgen gently offers his condolences. "*Spaseeba*," Popov thanks him weakly.

They agree to talk later, once the political smoke screens have faded. "Let's hope this never happens again," offers Skorgen, but he senses that Popov is beyond comfort.

By evening, Popov has summoned the strength to make a statement on national television; he does something uncharacteristic of Russian military tradition. He looks into the camera, eyes swollen and red, takes his hat from his head, and apologizes to the Russian people. "Forgive me," he says, "for not saving your men."

Tuesday, August 22. After quietly slipping back into the Kremlin over the weekend, Putin decides it is time to head north. His plane touches down at Northern Fleet headquarters, where he meets with the official fact-finding panel for the disaster. Led by Deputy Prime Minister Ilya Klebanov, the panel is already mulling how the reports of carbon-darkened bubbles at the scene might give the government an opportunity to retake control of the message going out to the public: Wouldn't fire that far back mean all of the sailors had died within minutes? And wouldn't that mean the delaying of foreign rescue offers was moot? A few committee members have even begun looking into alternative explanations for those days-long tapping sounds.

Finding meager solace in these developments, Putin cuts short his meeting with the panel. His government officially pronounced all of the *Kursk* sailors dead just the day before, and he feels his first priority now is to console the families in Vidyayevo, where many of them—including Olga Kolesnikova, Olga Lubushkina, and Dima's father, Roman—are already gathered in a hall awaiting him in various states of surreal denial and reckoning. His elaborate motorcade makes the two-hour pilgrimage from Severomorsk to Vidyayevo, arriving at 8 P.M., still during daylight.

At a meeting in this same simple hall only days before, one mother of a third-compartment submariner became so enraged at a seemingly nonchalant response by Klebanov that she leapt to her feet. "You're swine!" she screamed. "They're dying down there in a tin can for $50 a month, and you don't care! I will never forgive you! Take your medals off and shoot yourself! Bastards!" As medics subdued the woman with a sedative, another outraged mother approached the speechless deputy and began throttling him.

Now, the diminutive Putin steps to the podium, and the crowd strains to hear his remarks. "We have a meeting planned at fleet head-quarters," he says, "but I wanted to see you first. . . ."

"We can't hear you!" shouts a man from the back.

Putin begins again, this time by attempting the difficult task of expressing condolences without offending the members of his audience who refuse to accept that all the men are dead.

"Why didn't they call foreign specialists immediately?" a woman cries. "Why?"

"I can answer that," Putin says firmly. "Because we know we have rescue services and divers. . . ." He's drowned out by a torrent of shouts. "Just a second," he says, louder, but with growing confusion over which of the many lies that have been told—that he himself has been told—he needs to stick to for the sake of consistency. "As soon as foreign aid was offered, on the fifteenth . . ." he says, before being shouted down again by people who have learned too much from the media to accept his revisionist time line.

Frustrated at last, Putin tries a different tack. The fleet's rescue services "broke down," he admits. "There's not a damn thing left. There's not a damn thing left in the country! It's as simple as that!"

For a while, he almost wins them over. The emotional temper of the forum rocks back and forth, with the normally robotic Putin becoming increasingly impassioned and open, letting them see how much the submariner's son in him has been affected by the tragedy. "He got ninety dollars per month!" shouts one woman. "What kind of money is that? For an officer, that's a disgrace!"

"Yes, it's a disgrace," agrees Putin. "Officers must not be thrown off buses because they can't pay for the cost of the journey."

"Right!" say several voices.

Moments later, a woman in the aisle faints and is passed over heads toward the back.

"I am prepared to answer for the hundred days I have been president," Putin says, hoping to wrap up the meeting as the clock rolls past midnight. "For the fifteen years before, I would have been sitting on a bench with you."

But the people on the benches aren't through. "They believed in the state," a woman shouts, "that the state would save them! You don't understand how they believed!"

Caught off guard, Putin falls back on his first impulse. "We invited all the specialists who—"

"You could have saved just five!" one voice interrupts. "Bastards!"

Late October on the Barents Sea. President Vladimir Putin has promised the grieving relatives that Russia will retrieve the bodies of the dead submariners, whatever the expense. And now, an immense oil-exploration platform hovers over the *Kursk*'s wreck site as Russian and NATO divers probe the ship in round-the-clock shifts, hoping for some clue to the cause of the blast, hoping to bring back however many sailors they can safely reach through the manhole-sized openings they have cut in the *Kursk*'s stubborn hull.

The recovery workers expect few big surprises. Over the past two months, Klebanov's fact-finding panel has done a good job of convincing them, and much of the world, that little could have been done to save the *Kursk*'s doomed crew. The plaintive tapping noises are now said to have been nothing more than the expiring sounds of an onboard mechanical device running low on battery power.

During the actual recovery operation, only Russian divers are allowed outside the British submersible. The first to enter the *Kursk*, through holes punched into the eighth and ninth compartments, are

Sergei Shmygin and Andrei Sviagintsev. They've trained for this mission on the *Kursk*'s sister sub, the *Oryol,* walking through the sub in the dark, learning to maneuver by feel. When they first begin touching dead men's bodies, they can tell that some of them are not altogether intact.

Slowly, Shmygin and Sviagintsev maneuver one body into a canvas wrapping and place it in a metal basket for its ascent.

Once the basket is inside the forensic examining room aboard the oil platform, officially inconvenient truths announce themselves in rapid succession. An emergency suit. A note. Then the story the note has to tell. Twenty-three men waited in the ninth compartment, hoping against hope that a more humane new Russia valued their lives above national pride, the protection of state secrets, and whatever other bad habits were left over from the Soviet era.

The facts are excruciatingly simple: We didn't die in minutes, and our desperate tapping was real. We might have had a chance if only our country had asked the right foreigners for help sometime within those first thirty-six hours, instead of waiting four and a half days. This is the Truth According to Kolesnikov, Dima's *pravda.*

It unfolds before more than a dozen witnesses, a number of whom are now weeping, even as the senior officer in attendance considers the devastating political effect of such information becoming public.

Hours later, Northern Fleet vice-admiral Mikhail Motsak bows to the inevitable by reading the Kolesnikov letter, almost verbatim, on national television. The signature headline the following morning: THEY WERE ALIVE.

OCTOBER 2001

Editor's Note

Despite some public criticism over the expense of a recovery operation, President Vladimir Putin stuck to his promise to raise the *Kursk.* All 118 bodies were recovered and identified. Russian military prosecutors probed the wreckage for evidence of a criminal case, especially attentive to any indication that the *Kursk* was hit by a NATO submarine. Chief Russian prosecutor Vladimir Ustinov was among the first to enter the wreck in dry dock, and emerged to declare there was no evidence to support the collision theory. (He also proclaimed all the sailors were dead within eight hours of the blow, an assertion that author Ramsey Flynn plans to challenge in his forthcoming book.) Nevertheless, fourteen senior officers of the Northern Fleet—including admirals Vyacheslav Popov and Mikhail Motsak—have continued to insist they believe the collision explanation.

After prosecutor Ustinov delivered his preliminary findings to President Putin in December 2001—indicating that the *Kursk* should not have been allowed into the exercise with fully armed combat torpedoes—Putin sacked fourteen senior officers of the Northern Fleet, including Popov, Motsak, and rescue chief Alexander Teslenko. Putin added that the case for a collision looked very weak.

At the conclusion of the investigation, in July 2002, Ustinov said that the cause of the *Kursk* disaster was a spontaneous explosion of a defective torpedo.

REBELS OF THE APOCALYPSE

by Rory Nugent

RIEK MACHAR GREETS ME with a smile or a sneer, I'm not sure which. He's a big man with a python grip. He is wearing a flashy red beret, but my eyes linger on his epaulets, as large as legal-sized envelopes and inscribed with the markings of the Sudanese People's Liberation Movement. A pistol rides atop his hip, a convenient resting place for his right hand on those rare occasions when it isn't in motion. His pricey, size twelve Nikes seem out of place; all the soldiers around us are barefoot or wear sandals. Velcroed to Riek's collar tips are strips of fabric with gold bars running through a crimson field. They denote his rank, commander in chief of a thirty-thousand-man rebel army fighting in the world's longest civil war— thirty-seven years and counting. At the moment, it's a two-front war, with Riek's troops battling not only the government of Sudan but another rebel faction as well.

"I'm told that you want to spend a month or two with us," Riek says, shaking his head disapprovingly as he eyes my luggage. "Guerrillas walk thirty miles a day. Can you do that and still carry everything?"

"No problem," I lie, thinking about what I'll jettison. It's not even noon and the temperature is already over a hundred degrees Fahrenheit.

Reik remains several steps ahead of me as we walk through the center of Yuai, the village of twenty-two thousand in the Upper Nile region of southeast Sudan. In the past month it has become a major distribution point for U.N. relief food and supplies. The area was ravaged by the same drought and subsequent famine that drew the world's attention to Ethiopia in 1984. But unlike in Ethiopia, famine still grips the Sudan. The drought has eased lately, but war and world neglect continue. Some estimates are that as many as 3 million Sudanese have died in the last decade from the fighting and lack of food.

Over the next seven weeks I'll see thousands more added to that number as virtually the entire area erupts in war, food supplies are cut off and Riek and I are sent running for our lives.

Seeing us coming now, the women and children of Yuai clear out of
the way. Most of the women refuse to look at us as we pass, but the
children smile and fall in line behind us. Almost every male over fourteen, I soon discover, has enlisted in the rebel army. "I grew up wanting to be a guerrilla. Nothing else, just a guerrilla," one officer tells
me, as if there were other career options for a Sudanese teenager.

As I draw close to Riek, one of his bodyguards taps me on the
shoulder with the barrel of an AK-47. "Not so close," he repeats
whenever I narrow the gap. Off to either side, machine gunners scan
the horizon; to the front and rear, soldiers lug Russian-made grenade
launchers. The weapons are old gifts to the Sudanese rebels from
Mengistu, the benighted Stalinist who ousted Haile Selassie and
dominated Ethiopia until he, too, was deposed in 1992. While he was
in power, though, Mengistu gave generously in the name of communism, sure that a rebel movement of black Christians battling the government in Khartoum, an Islamic thearchy, was worthy of military aid.

"Try to stay with us," Riek admonishes, snapping me out of my
musing. I run to catch up, mindful to stay several yards behind him.
"Remember this," he adds in a loud voice. "If you can't keep up, you
must get out. We have enough problems without adding an American
to the list. Understood?"

There's no arguing with that. The southern Sudan may be the most
troubled place on earth. The smell of death is inescapable across an
area the size of Texas. The U.N. estimates that almost all of the 6.5 million people living here are straddling the line separating life from
death by starvation. A few published reports predict 750,000 Sudanese
will fall victim to war and starvation this year. If that's true, more
people will die in the Sudan than in Bosnia, Somalia, Bangladesh, Pakistan and India combined.

I arrived in the Sudan five days ago, and everyone I've met agrees
that the region is utterly unable to help itself. Millions of people are
alive only because of the generosity of outsiders, and ten of thousands
of others die each year because the outside isn't generous enough.
Everyone is scarred by war, famine and disease, especially children,
all of whom have swollen bellies and rail-thin arms, sure signs of
worms and malnutrition.

When the U.S. Marines landed in Somalia last year, more than
1 million Somalis were believed susceptible to death from famine. In
the Sudan right now, four times that number are at risk. During an

inspection tour last spring, representatives from the Centers for Disease Control in the United States calculated that 80 percent of all children in the southern Sudan were in need of immediate medical attention; a similar survey in Somalia before U.S. intervention there found that 50 percent of children needed medical care.

Relief has not been delivered, in part because of restrictions imposed by the radical Islamic government in Khartoum, and in large part because of all the guns. When bullets fly, relief planes are grounded and U.N. operations are suspended; when armies storm, the traditional society is turned upside down.

Yet beyond international hand-wringing over Khartoum's role as an exporter of fundamentalist extremism, the Sudan receives little of the world's attention. Among the reasons that have drawn me here is to find out why so little is known in the West about what's happening in the southern Sudan. It is not an easy place to enter. The Khartoum government often refuses visas to journalists and threatens them with imprisonment for illegal entry. Even so, I managed to find a way in without much trouble. All it took was money to hire a bush pilot and then to fly over government lines into rebel territory. Over time, perhaps I'll discover other reasons why journalists have stayed away.

Soldiers on lookout snap to attention the moment Riek comes abreast; they return to a slouch as he passes. The men at the perimeter, though well armed, are poorly dressed: Quite a few are naked, with the majority wearing either a pajama top or a U.N. blanket tied like a toga; all are barefoot and trouserless. Only as we near the heart of army headquarters do soldiers start appearing in guerrilla costume. The distribution of fatigues depends on rank and luck. Officers lay claim to booty taken from enemy warehouses; noncoms must rely on battlefield pickings.

"I try not to bury anyone still wearing shirts and shoes," one veteran explains. The soldier turns his back to show me the three holes with burnt edges in the back of his shirt. "Bullets got him, I got the shirt."

A curious-tasting hot drink is brought out to Riek and me. I'm told it's tea. We drink in the shade of a tall acacia tree next to Riek's billet, an inglorious place resembling an eight-foot cube built of straw. His bed, a cot with a moldy piece of foam, nearly fills the space. His clothes and personal property are packed inside two duffel bags. "That's everything I own," Riek says. We sit in chairs "borrowed" from the U.N. There are several lean-tos scattered about, and numerous scraps of plastic lie on the ground. Each piece of plastic is a bed; the lean-tos shelter machine-gun nests.

The cook fire off to our right is the kitchen. The man cleaning a kettle with sand and caramel-colored water is Omai, who has been Riek's personal cook for three years. The rest of the army must fend for itself. The menu revolves around whatever kind of American food-stuff has been lifted that week from the U.N., usually sorghum or unmilled corn.

Only a small percentage of the troops can read or write, and none have been properly trained. Last year Riek's army captured eight of Khartoum's most modern tanks, but since no one could even find the ignition, they were abandoned. "Do you know anything about smart bombs?" Riek asks. I shake my head. "How about regular bombs and guns?" He's disappointed to hear of my incompetence in such matters.

Four men enter the area; Riek informs me that they have come from Ayod. There have been rumors about enemy troops moving toward Ayod. Instead of speaking English, common among officers, they stick to a mix of Arabic and Nuer, but from their serious tone, I sense the rumors are true. However, I can't tell which enemy is threatening the area. It could be troops loyal to Khartoum, or it could be men from the rival guerrilla faction.

The Sudanese civil war started in 1956, a few days after Great Britain merged the separately administered north and south regions into one nation and granted it independence. The north, where Khartoum is located, is peopled by Arabs dedicated to Islam; the south is black, tribal and either Christian or animist. The two regions' languages, customs, laws and traditions are worlds apart. Why the British thought this union would work is anybody's guess, especially since they had fostered animosity between them during their hegemony.

"It was a classic case of divide and rule," Joseph Oduhu told me in Nairobi, Kenya, before I entered the Sudan in early April. Oduhu is in his late sixties, with hunched shoulders and deep-set, penetrating eyes. His round face is almost always creased by an inviting smile. He has been involved in Sudanese politics for the last fifty years and is known affectionately as Uncle for his role in the freedom movement. He was one of the four founders of Anyana, the original rebel organi-zation, which over the next twenty years grew into a forty-thousand-man army. In 1976, under the leadership of Gaafar Nimeiri, the Sudanese government finally sought peace. It reorganized the south, creating three territories, in which freedom of religion was guaranteed. Tax revenue from southerners was at last spent in the south, and locally elected officials were assured relative autonomy.

"I was appointed minister of sports," Oduhu said. "I resigned in a year. I had no power, and the Arabs were pointing at me, saying, 'Look, we're not racists. We have a black cabinet minister.'. . . The fact is they are racists. They see your face, see the color of dirt and start treating you like dirt. And they don't like or trust Christians."

The civil war was reignited in 1983, when Khartoum swung sharply toward fundamentalist Islam. "One day I awoke and heard Nimeiri say we were no longer the Republic of the Sudan; suddenly the Sudan was an Islamic republic. Allah be praised," Oduhu said. All the provisions of the peace were negated. The Koran replaced civil-law books, tax money went north again, and local administrators were stripped of power.

The former leaders of Anyana followed Joseph Kerebeno into Ethiopia. Kerebeno was the army commander in charge of policing the Upper Nile region and led a mutiny of several thousand fellow black soldiers. A few months later another mutineer, John Garang, joined the inner circle. He had studied in the United States and left with a Ph.D. in economics. "We all liked this Garang chap," Oduhu said. "He was smart, well educated, ambitious and a fast talker." Garang convinced the others to abandon the name Anyana for a new one that would appeal to Mengistu's communist sensibilities. So they started calling themselves the Sudanese People's Liberation Army. Since Garang was the only one who got along with Mengistu, he was voted their spokesman and leader.

Under Garang's guidance, the SPLA blossomed. Tens of thousands of volunteers were trained and armed; the guerillas marched from one victory to another. By all accounts Garang was a brilliant leader, dedicated to the fight. Within four years, all but a few southern cities came under rebel control. No one challenged Garang during those years in the mid-'80s, Oduhu said. "We were winning. Always on the move. As things quieted down, I soured on Garang. It was time to stop being only a guerrilla army and become a real movement. You know, elections, a shadow government, a system of checks and balances." But Garang rejected Oduhu's advice. The SPLA was a one-man show, and anyone who disagreed with the boss was jailed.

"I spent eighteen months in an animal cage and two years in solitary confinement for opening my big mouth," Oduhu recalls.

Oduhu said he cheered two years ago when he heard that Riek, Kerebeno and others had banded together to form a new rebel army separate from Garang's. They made their formal announcement in Nasir, a district capital in the Upper Nile region, in the summer of 1991. Approximately twenty thousand troops joined their former SPLA field commanders to establish the Sudanese People's Liberation Movement. The contents of their garrisons became the property of the SPLM. To avoid confusion, the Sudanese call the breakaway group the Nasir faction.

Oduhu believes the Nasir faction can also be useful to the West. In 1989, a coup brought an even more radical government to Khartoum, led by General Omar al-Bashir and his ally Sheik Hassan al-Turabi, leader of the Islamic National Front and a leading figure in spreading fundamentalist Islam throughout the world. Under Turabi's guidance, the government has become an international force in promoting Islamic revolution and sponsoring extremist activities; Muslim radicals with Sudanese passports have been implicated in alleged terrorist conspiracies in the United States. At home, Turabi has imposed one of the severest Islamic social orders in the world. Oduhu considers the Nasir faction the West's frontline troops against the encroachment of Islam into Central Africa.

As I spoke with Joseph Oduhu last April, a new round of peace talks involving both rebel factions as well as Khartoum was due to start in a few weeks. Oduhu would participate as a member of the Nasir delegation. It's a role he has played before, and this time he was not optimistic.

"It's a battle to the end. For us there's no compromising freedom from the north. For Khartoum there's no compromising the greater glory of Allah. For Garang everything can be compromised so nobody trusts or likes him."

Oduhu insisted that only intervention by the West can stop the bloodletting and stem the famine. "We will all blow ourselves to bits until there is a fair vote on establishing a new country. . . . The U.N. can either force Khartoum to allow such a vote or it can sit back and let the dying go on."

I said good-bye to Uncle Oduhu as he packed for a trip to Kongor, where other officers of the Nasir faction were gathering. He was excited because they were to discuss his plan for initiating a shadow government. Sadly, he never presented his program. He was captured and then shot by Garang's troops two days later in Kongor. It's said that the officer overseeing the execution received a hefty reward.

The army rises at dawn. I stay inside my sleeping bag, too bleary-eyed to do much more than listen to the sounds of 125 men starting their day. Radios are on, tuned to the BBC program *Wake Up Africa!*, a mix of news and music. Magazines click in and out of place and firing pins thunk as rifles are given a ritual morning cleaning. Conspicuously absent, though, is the sound of splashing water. We're in the dry season; the rains won't start for another five or six weeks.

A radio operator hands Riek a dispatch. A few minutes later, whistles start blowing. Riek turns toward me and announces that it's time for a walk. Over the week since I joined him, we've established a routine that includes a morning constitutional, but this is different.

I grab my hat and join the parade. The bodyguards, all of whom I've gotten to know, now make room for me next to Riek. As we near the desolate Yuai airfield, he comes to a sudden stop. The bodyguards fan out. I've never seen them so alert. This morning Riek is wearing two pistols. "Garang has attacked Ayod," he says. "The radio reports aren't good. . . ."

Eighteen hundred of Garang's troops are on the rampage. The size of the enemy force, he says, is manageable; he has already ordered two thousand men to reinforce the besieged Ayod garrison. What worries him is fuel. The enemy is highly mobile, riding aboard a fleet of trucks equipped with long-range mortars and heavy machine guns. Riek also has trucks and heavy weapons, but there is less than a barrel of diesel on hand. Without a dime in the treasury, and no way to buy fuel in Ethiopia or Kenya, he has to wait until his border units are able to steal it. Meanwhile, his troops will have to move by foot, the big guns remaining in storage. Complicating everything is an inadequate intelligence network: No one can be sure about the enemy's position. None of Riek's scouts have watches, maps or compasses, making it impossible to sort out the various sightings.

"What about the U.N. compound in Ayod? Is it okay?" I ask Riek.

"I'm told there have been many civilian casualties. . . . The feeding center was the first place they attacked and burned."

We continue our walk in silence.

*   *   *

I had spent four days in Ayod waiting to make connections with Riek.
I slept in the local U.N. complex, a guest of relief personnel. I usually
trailed Dr. Stephen ("Oh, just call me Doc") Collins, a wiry thirty-five-
year-old English physician. In my experience only a few aid workers
answer a calling; most seem to just mark time and somehow feel good
about it. Doc, though, is in his own class, and I finally had to ask him
what led him into relief work. "Rock and roll . . . John Lennon and
Bob Marley had a lot to say about my decision," he said.

On an average night, 150 people walk to Ayod from the surrounding district. Local members of RASS (Relief Association of the Southern Sudan, the humanitarian arm of Riek's movement) record each
name and line up everyone according to which village he or she has
left. Doc moves up and down the lines, shouting instructions: "This
family to the clinics, pronto. . . . Move this group to the feeding
line. . . . Give them all vitamins and double the dosage for her, her,
him, her, and . . ."

One morning I sit next to an emaciated woman and empty my canteen into a gourd, her family's lone utensil. I have to lean into her, my
ear inches from her mouth, to hear her words. She and her four children have been on the road for a week, she says. Their supply of millet
ran out two days into the trek, and they have been living on leaves and
roots. Water came wherever they found it, meaning there were long
stretches of tongue-biting thirst. "This is the closest place for food,"
she says. "We had no choice." She left with fifty-nine other people
from her village close by the Nile; only eighteen made it here. What
happened to the others? She doesn't know. "They stopped walking. We
are Nuers."

Nuers are members of the second largest tribe in the southern
Sudan; only Dinkas outnumber them. They are a tall, handsome
people. The family is the center of their social universe. They accept
food from the U.N. because there's no taboo against gifts from white
people; however, to ask a friend or a neighbor for assistance is to bring
shame on the family. If the family can't help an individual, as in times
of famine, that person is expected to make death a private affair. Usually, the infirm crawl off by themselves to die.

Doc Collins moves the woman and her children to the front of the
food line, and we walk inside the feeding center. It is the size of a football field, crammed with eighteen hundred people waiting for food and

medicine. Another three thousand are camped outside the compound walls, while twelve thousand other villagers rely on the RASS workers for a daily handout of unmilled corn or sorghum. Without the grain, everyone unable to find roots and leaves would starve.

On our last day together, Doc greets me in the morning in a singsong voice. "It's a vitamin-A day. Come together now. We could use your help. Be sure to wear your vest."

The "vest" refers to the shell a Westerner constructs soon after stepping inside a feeding center. It is a mental device that shields the brain and the heart from the screaming horror that bombards the eyes. Almost two thousand starving Sudanese are inside the compound. Their fingers curl around my cuff as I walk among them. Women point to their babies and plead, "Food, please. For her." Often it's hard to tell the dead from the living.

Doc hands me five hundred vitamin-A tablets, with instructions to dispense one to everybody except babies. Blindness is common, affecting almost 10 percent of the population over forty, and it's all due to vitamin-A deficiency. One dose will immunize an individual for six months. I stare at a pill, holding it up to the sun. It is amber colored and tear shaped and rather slippery to handle. I ask Doc if they are expensive. "Nah, a couple of cents a pop."

Most people hold out their palms to take a pill; others are too infirm to do anything but open their mouths. I have to place the vitamins on their tongues and hold the water cup to their lips, catching the pill in midair if they spit it out, coughing, unable to swallow. "I would if I could," a woman says, apologizing because she can't keep the pill down. Her thighs are the size of my wrists, and each rib appears to be embossed on her skin. We try a few more times with no success. Her black eyes stare into mine. "Feed the little ones," she whispers. "I'm too old to care about. This is my forty-first year." Hearing this, I redouble my efforts until she swallows the vitamin.

A few days after learning of the attack on Ayod, Riek counterattacks. His foot soldiers surround and trounce the enemy in a two-day battle several miles south of Ayod. More than 800 of Garang's men are killed. But nothing can vanquish the images from Ayod that haunt me. Civilian casualties are stunningly high: 328 dead, a third of the bodies found among the ashes of the feeding center. I know that Doc Collins and the other relief workers are safe; the U.N. evacuated them and suspended operations the day before I left Ayod. As for the others: "If you couldn't run, you died," an officer returning from Ayod tells me. The death count will continue for weeks. With each supply of food blown up, hundreds more die every day.

One night later that week, Omai serves dinner under the acacia tree. Riek turns on his flashlight and runs the beam over the soupy mix accompanying a plate of boiled corn. "There. There. . . . Dammit, everywhere," Riek gales, pointing out the flies bobbing in the soup.

Omai snags the flies with a piece of straw. Seventeen are picked up and flicked to the ground. He shrugs as Riek stirs the liquid and more carcasses appear. I was tricked earlier in the day by the flies. Walking from Yuai village to headquarters, I noticed a man ahead of me shimmering in the sunlight. His shirt, I thought, must be made from some wildly patterned moiré or sharkskin fabric; perhaps he would trade it for a T-shirt. On closer inspection I discovered that his back was actually covered three deep in flies. "I detest flies," Riek announces to the general agreement of the soldiers around us. "They are the one thing I hate about the Sudan."

The cornmeal has the consistency of white paste and must be scraped off the serving spoon with a finger. Following Riek's example, I pour the soup—swamp water with bits of sun-dried meat—over the tasteless cornmeal to form a gruel. As usual, neither of us will finish our portions.

A gentle wind coaxes the leaves overhead into a dance. The night sky appears to curve in on itself and merge in graceful arcs with the land on all sides. "What do you see when you look at the stars?" I ask Riek. "Millions of green shoots that grow into tall plants that feed the world. I see what can be if we are free."

That's a nice thought, but his answer sounds far too poetic in these circumstances. Riek knows the value of telling journalists what they want to hear. It will take time to break through the sound bites. But if I'm to understand the Sudanese demand for freedom, the engine powering a civil war and famine responsible for millions of deaths, then I must understand Riek.

Riek Machar (pronounced REE-yak ma-CHAR) was born in 1953 in Ler, a town not far from Ayod. He was eight when he first became aware of the civil war. A neighbor returned home from the front with only one arm and made him feel the stub. Two years later Riek was suspended from school for leading his class in a chant for a free southern Sudan. Instead of punishing him for his actions, his mother bought him a new pair of pants. "She said I had become a man," he says.

Riek describes his mother as a modern woman for her time. "Our hut was the first to have screens in the windows," Riek recalls. "We had the first can opener in Ler." His father, on the other hand, had a vested interest in maintaining the old ways. He was the chief of both Ayod and Ler and heir to vast landholdings and herds of cattle. Luckily, Riek says, he was a man with many demands on his time. "My mother was his third wife, and I was the twenty-sixth child. He had thirty-one. . . . Mother had a free hand in raising us."

The average Nuer leaves school after tenth grade; Riek stayed in the classroom until he was thirty-one. He was awarded a doctorate in 1984 from the University of Bedford in England. He recalls gleefully how he turned down lucrative job offers from British insurance companies for a life in the bush as a rebel guerrilla. The civil war had just started up after a seven-year hiatus, and he believed joining the SPLA was the right thing to do. "It was time to fight for freedom from the Arabs," he says. As an undergraduate student at Khartoum University, he had experienced Arab bigotry firsthand. There wasn't a day, he says, that someone didn't slur him for being black; every Friday, the Muslim Sabbath, people would throw rocks at him for not falling to his knees during prayer sessions; and he learned to use the back door when leaving Sunday Mass to avoid Muslim zealots armed with sticks, ready to teach infidels a lesson. "I'm black, so I'm shit to them. . . . The thought of Arabs running my life makes me sick."

He quickly rose through the ranks of the SPLA. Within seven years, he was appointed second in command to Garang. But like Joseph Oduhu, Riek grew to distrust Garang and started asking questions. "Each year, Garang set a date for elections, and each year they were postponed for the following year," he explains. "After a while I wanted to know why, and when I became army chief, I had the information to know he was lying and had been lying all the time."

Riek also matured politically, he says, and started challenging Garang to rework the SPLA platform, which still advocated a return to the federalism detailed in the 1976 peace accord. Garang wouldn't budge, even though Nimeiri was no longer in power, kicked out by men even more dedicated than he to fundamentalist Islam. Riek became convinced that only an independent southern Sudan could guarantee freedom. It wasn't long before his reservations about Garang evolved into compelling reasons to establish the Nasir faction.

Riek doesn't hide his feelings about Garang, and there's no doubt each man feels betrayed by the other. Riek sought out other disgruntled officers. "I was amazed how easy it was to form the army," Riek says.

Critics blast Riek for splintering the rebel movement. Up until the split, the SPLA was on the offensive. The war was draining the Khartoum treasury, and many observers believed the government would be forced to negotiate within a few years. However, since the split, the rebels have spent more energy battling each other than Khartoum. This factional fighting has brought about something northern forces never achieved: the destruction of brigade-size guerrilla units.

Riek listens to these comminations with a smile. He has heard them all before and denies none of them. "People have the right to their opinions," he says smugly. Yes, he wishes the rebel movement were a unified force, and he expects that it will be in the near future. More than five thousand soldiers have left Garang's camp for Riek's in the last six months, he says, including William Nyon, the officer who assumed Riek's place as second in command of the SPLA. Riek is secure in his decisions and predicts rather presumptuously that "history will judge me as the good guy."

Riek is a Nuer, Garang a Dinka. The two tribes share many cultural elements; their languages are similar; both celebrate the cow; they have been at each other's throats for centuries. Riek denies that the factional fighting is merely an extension of ancient tribal rivalries. He points to his bodyguards, his ten most trusted men, and ticks off their tribal affiliations. It's a mix of Dinka, Nuer, Latuka and Shilluk. The majority of the Nasir-faction field commanders are Dinka, and the movement's four-man executive council has only one Nuer. Of the approximately thirty-three thousand men under Riek's command, twenty thousand are Nuer. One reason for fighting for a free southern Sudan, Riek says, is the establishment of a national identity. "It's time to say that we are all southern Sudanese."

Riek may pine for a nation free from tribalism, but I doubt such a dream will be realized in his lifetime. The men of his army seem to get along fine and they all say they can't wait to call themselves citizens of a free southern Sudan, but each soldier proudly wears his tribal scars. The markings can be discerned even in death, the lines and rosettes clearly visible on the skulls of the dead.

* * *

On Sunday, a week after the battle of Ayod, the pounding of drums arrives before the sun. It's the call to mass. Church services start at six to avoid midday heat. Riek grabs his Bible and speeds off to join the Presbyterian choir. Although he neither admits nor denies it, I sense that he privately considers himself a modern crusader battling the Muslim hordes. I visit all three churches in Yuai (Catholic, Presbyterian and Methodist), and each is filled with exuberant parishioners. Spirituality is on the rise in the southern Sudan, with people turning to the Old Testament for guidance. The biblical stories promising redemption after bouts of plague, famine, war and disease have special meaning to the Sudanese, yet few people have totally abandoned the old form of astral association. It's not uncommon for someone to take Communion and have lunch with a witch doctor.

There is still no diesel, and Riek and I are stuck in Yuai until some appears. No one knows when that will happen. "It's not easy fighting a war without money," Riek sighs. While Garang controls the gold mines, which finance much of his operation, Riek controls the oil fields, all of which were blown up years ago. So we wait.

On Friday, there's not a cloud in the sky. Most of the headquarters staff sit chockablock under an acacia tree. It's 105 degrees Fahrenheit, and nobody feels like doing anything more than taking a nap. The crack of a gunshot shatters the calm. We all look westward. Nothing unusual, just a view of stunted and leafless thorn trees appearing to undulate in the hot air.

Two more shots ring out. Riek jumps to his feet, grabs a spare AK-47 and starts jogging toward the sound of the gunfire. I follow with a camera. A burst of small-arms fire brings us all to a stop, and Riek starts shouting orders. Radio operators send out an alert and start packing their gear. The bodyguards circle Riek, as Captain Michael strips him of his beret, epaulets and collar markings. Riek's truck starts up behind us, and the driver revs the engine. A mortar round lands fifty yards away, sending us to the ground. "Stay down," someone yells as I start to stand. A rocket-propelled grenade buries itself within the length of my shadow. Thank God it's a dud.

"Now!" a soldier barks, emptying a clip as I snatch up a bag and run after the slowly moving vehicle, making it to a seat atop the cab. Bullets miss their mark by inches, and I can feel their wind as they rush by or smash into the armor plating. "Hold on!" Riek shouts from inside the truck.

The driver shifts into second and heads for the thorn forest, pedal to metal, small trees be damned. The truck creates its own path. Troops fall in place behind us to set up skirmish lines. The soldier next to me says we're going to Waat. The truck bucks its way through the scrubby thorn trees, moving slowly, allowing me to watch the attack on Yuai.

Most of the enemy troops head directly for the U.N. complex. A series of mortar rounds and grenades land squarely inside the feeding center and clinic, which, being built of straw, go up in flames within seconds. We're downwind, and it's not long before the fetor of burning flesh and hair engulfs us. Earlier in the day, I visited the compound. The U.N. staff was evacuated a few days ago, and it was now run by only a few RASS workers. More than a hundred people were laid out in the medical compound, and another sixteen hundred were living in the feeding center. Horror-struck, I stare at the aid station now as war transforms it into a crematorium. I struggle for a cogent thought; nothing about the attack makes sense. The feeding center has no strategic importance. There are neither arms caches nor soldiers inside, just starving people too weak to hold a gun. From the look of the billowing smoke, it appears that the entire village has been set ablaze. For what? To deprive women and children of shelter? To set chaos in motion?

The sun sets, but tonight, eerily, an orange sky lies to the south. I stare at the cinders corkscrewing to the heavens and wonder how many innocent people have died. Closer to us, women and children running through the forest see the truck's headlights and converge on the ten-wheeler. Riek keeps ordering the driver to stop so the refugees can board. A girl I lift from the ground refuses to let go of me. Even when I try to help others, she won't release her grip. She doesn't say a word; her terror-filled eyes do the talking. When the truck starts up again and I sit, she buries her head in my lap. Her trembling body sends shivers through me, and I hold her tight, able to feel every bone in her skeletal body. Soon there are more than 150 people jammed into the cargo area. Babies wail, and everyone else breathes heavily, gasping as if it's the last breath of life.

In three and a half hours of motoring, we've leveled countless small trees, but we've only gone ten or twelve miles. Yuai still glows on the southern horizon. But it's enough distance to let us rest a bit. Riek sits by himself staring into the darkness. The truck driver dips a stick into the fuel tank; all but the bottom one-eighth of an inch comes up dry.

The wounded are lowered from the truck and put off to one side. I do what I can to help. Omai fetches my medical kit and holds a flashlight. Because I have bandages and medicines, I'm the closest thing to a doctor around, and there's no time to correct perceptions.

The sole army doctor left on a U.N. plane days ago to solicit medicine in Nairobi. I had met Dr. Ochung in Yuai and promptly loaned him my medical kit. He had run out of syringes, alcohol, bandages and every type of pill. A pair of pliers from the motor pool was his only operating tool. He had been using leaves to wrap wounds and amputating limbs with a razor blade and a bayonet; with no painkillers to dispense, a width of tire tread kept tongues in one piece. He called the $6.95 folding saw I brought to cut firewood a "lifesaver," and he meant it. During the battle of Ayod, when U.N. operations were shut, he was the only doctor for six hundred thousand people in an area bigger than England. Right now, there are only four poorly trained medics to deal with the disaster. I wish one of them would show up here.

A mortar round lands nearby, its roar punctuated by the zing of metal shards going every which way. We scramble aboard the truck, and the driver manages to keep us going for another hour until we're out of fuel. Civilians are directed to the nearest footpath to Waat. The rest of us will stay put. There's a chance Commander Nyon's truck has enough diesel to give us a tow; a radio operator is trying to contact him. Someone lays out a piece of plastic for Riek and me to sit on. We talk for the first time since leaving Yuai. "Why the feeding center?" I ask. Hundreds probably died in the blaze, and thousands more will probably die because it's gone.

Riek shakes his head in disgust. He says that he would cashier any soldier of his that did such a thing and that he would send the commanding officer in front of a firing squad. "Has that ever happened?" I ask, knowing that his troops have been accused of atrocities. "Yes, it has happened," he answers, "several times. There is no excuse, and I offer none. My troops know what will happen to them for such crimes."

He bristles when I remind him what he told me earlier in the week: that guerrilla armies make up the rule book, that freedom fighters must be willing to do anything. "Our army has laws!" he shouts. "I believe in a heaven and a hell, and I don't want to go to hell."

"Look around you," I snap. "This is hell."

Riek insists war can be redeeming. What strikes me as madness, he sees as a necessary process. Freedom is a reward that comes with victory, or so he is convinced. Stopping the war for anything short of freedom will cure nothing, in his opinion. In fact, the events in Yuai have only hardened his resolve to become the sole leader of the rebel movement. He calls Garang a devil; the leader must take responsibility for his troops, he says. And I agree: Garang had ample time to discipline his men after Ayod.

Riek insists that if he and his troops don't fight, Garang will be the unchallenged leader of the rebellion. "You're here for two months," he says, "but this is my home, and I want it to be my children's. I fight so my children will never have to fight."

I confront Riek, demanding solutions. He says he's willing to establish demilitarized zones throughout his territory, where U.N. workers can operate safely. Instead of stealing food, soldiers would work for it, building clinics, huts and latrines, digging irrigation ditches and tending crops, reopening schools that have been shuttered for ten years. "We can do these things right away or whenever the U.N. refuses to be bullied by Khartoum," Riek says, referring to the government's capricious rules governing aid operations and the U.N.'s refusal to operate in a country unless it has the approval of that country's government. In the past, Khartoum has closed aid stations, denied relief flights and stymied efforts to combat parasitic diseases.

"How can the fighting be stopped?" I ask.

"The war ends with a vote," Riek says, challenging the world to pressure the Sudanese government. In exchange for a U.N.-supervised referendum on succession by southerners, the Nasir faction is willing to surrender all its weapons and demobilize its army.

"And if the vote is yes, then what?" I ask, reminding him that Garang favors federalism because he doesn't believe that southern Sudan—which has no physical infrastructure, no political parties, no educated middle class, no bureaucracy, not even a money economy—can exist as an independent nation.

Riek advocates a custodial government run by the U.N. that would phase itself out as Sudanese are trained. He foresees national elections to form a government three years after independence. He believes the south has the potential to be rich economically. "Management has been our problem, not resources," he says. The south does have vast reserves of oil, gold and other minerals; the soil is loamy and nutrient filled; the Nile can be tapped; and the climate permits year-round agricultural production. "If the U.N. helps us to our feet, it won't be long before we can take care of ourselves," Riek says, reducing complicated procedures to a simple cliché.

Switching gears, lowering his voice and speaking slowly, Riek says, "My enemy is Khartoum. I have a personal score to settle with Garang, but I want his troops on my side." We both agree that factional fighting should be replaced by finesse, but I doubt Riek has the soft touch needed for such delicate work. This is where someone like Joseph Oduhu could step in and save thousands of lives.

We arrive in Waat around dawn at the end of a towline. I stay near the radio, listening in and trying to make sense of what went wrong. It turns out that the remnants of Garang's army defeated at Ayod never made a full retreat. They headed south until they met up with fifteen hundred fresh troops riding trucks with plenty of fuel and ammunition. Riek's intelligence officers dismissed accounts of enemy trucks heading back toward Ayod and Yuai, positive that the scouts, lacking compasses, had confused north for south, not an uncommon occurrence.

Captain Michael tosses me my bag and gives the order to move out. "They're coming." I race about, checking the Waat feeding center and clinics, all of which are empty. In the distance, soldiers carry the infirm atop jury-rigged litters. After the first bullet flies, my feet don't stop moving until we reach the new headquarters camp five miles east of Waat.

For as far as the eye can see, women and children plod along in single file. In all, over a twenty-eight-hour period, I watch the entire surviving populations of Yuai and Waat, more than forty-three thousand people, walk by me. The weak, the elderly and babies, I'm told, were left behind and presumed dead. "What else could I do? The hut went up in flames. We had to run," a woman from Yuai tells me, four children under seven years of age in her arms or at her side. "I had to leave the baby behind so the others could live."

A young girl walks by carrying her baby brother. She looks to be about eight years old; her brother is no more than two. Flies are four deep where the tears have streamed down her face. She stops, points to my canteen and asks for water. She says her father died last year and her mother died last night, while they were walking from Yuai to

Waat. I search out a RASS worker to take care of her and her brother. I offer the canteen as a gift, but at first she refuses, saying she would be ashamed to take it without giving something in return. She accepts only when she hears that I have two canteens.

The mood is gloomy at headquarters. There's not a drop of diesel; most of the army's food and ammunition was left in Yuai; and once again, no one can pin down the whereabouts of the enemy trucks. Riek can't predict when help will arrive from garrisons in Nasir and Akobo because reinforcements and ammunition must be moved by truck. He looks heavenward and repeats, "Diesel . . . diesel . . ."

Unable to initiate action, Riek's army digs in and keeps watch. The days drag on. Rifles are cleaned two or three times an hour; those who own a needle spend entire afternoons sewing torn garments; otherwise, the men simply sit and navel-gaze.

Five days after the attack, my morning constitutionals turn into graveyard tours. It's impossible to go a kilometer without stumbling upon at least a half dozen bodies. And it only gets worse. On the twelfth day after the attack, with U.N. operations still suspended, I encounter eighty-nine fresh corpses during an hour's walk. It becomes common to see a striped hyena trotting along the grassland carrying a human limb in its mouth. Many vultures are too fat to fly anymore; they hop from one meal to another.

I start accompanying Paul, a RASS worker, as he patrols the area looking for abandoned children. "Anyone over seven knows how to dig for roots and cook leaves, so we look for babies," he says. One day we find eleven children, the next we discover only two. On our fourth day of searching, we pass the corpse of a woman covered with vultures. The stink is enough to keep anyone away, but Paul senses something odd. He scatters the birds, turns over the rotting body and uncovers a pair of infants, both alive. A fingertip of one of the babies, a girl, has been gnawed to the bone by a vulture.

Instead of attacking headquarters, the enemy roam the countryside, rustling cattle and destroying small villages. Their tactical mistake gives Riek time to muster diesel, reinforcements and heavy guns. Thirteen days after the attack on Yuai, several mortar rounds land near the camp. The enemy is preparing a frontal assault at last. So why aren't Riek's men rushing out to confront them? Instead, they gather around cook fires and cows.

"Tradition," Riek explains calmly. They must sacrifice a cow before they go into battle. "There's nothing I can do about it. That's the way it's been for centuries. . . ."

Perhaps the sacrifice worked, or maybe it's important to have troops enter battle on full stomachs, but it isn't long after Riek's men launch their counterattack that the enemy mortars stop. Riek's offensive gains steam. Rolling over enemy positions. His troops are on trucks in their own territory. At last they're mobile. All the what-if-we-only-had-diesel scenarios that Riek prepared go into effect and are surprisingly successful. During the next two days, Garang's troops are routed, leaving behind nearly a thousand dead soldiers. Riek admits to losing ninety-seven troops.

It is a significant victory but not decisive by any means. Once the smoke clears, we go on an inspection tour of the battle sites. Much of the time we walk behind a herd of cattle, what Riek refers to as his bomb squad. Lacking metal detectors, he relies on livestock to clear a path through the land mines.

Ayod and Yuai no longer exist. Not a building stands. Charred circles and squares are all that remain, the sole reminders of once bustling towns. The villages of Pathai and Paguea have been erased from the map, but they will be remembered as massacre sites. In Pathai hundreds of civilians were murdered; scores of them were women who were split in half by a machete, their legs spread apart and sticks from baskets they used shoved up their vaginas. In Paguea I saw thirty-two women laid out in a line, each shot in the head. Riek's troops bury the corpses in foxholes.

Surviving civilians sit by the ashes of their homes and stare blankly at the ruins. The entire region must be rebuilt from scratch. It will not be easy. There is no straw, the basic building material. The rainy season has just started, and the grass won't be suitable for building for another five months. Since the majority of people have no clothes or shelter, thousands will probably die every month from exposure; thousands more will die from disease spawned by the rotting corpses.

Skeletons litter the way. Famine victims are usually found singly under a tree; war casualties are grouped together, their bones picked clean and then bleached by the sun. Finally, seventeen days after the attack on Yuai, the U.N. resumes food deliveries, dispatching a plane carrying corn to the area. I can only guess at the number who died during that two-and-a-half-week period, but with seventy-five thousand people affected in Ayod, Waat and Yuai, one in seven strikes me as a conservative estimate.

Once again no crops have been planted, and the people are totally dependent on shipments of grain from outside. Unless the U.N. can find the necessary donors to increase aid shipments and can brush aside any complaints from Khartoum, there's no doubt that tens of thousands more will die by this time next year.

Riek and I say our good-byes moments before he is to speak to a crowd in Ayod. "What are you going to tell them?" I ask.

"I'm not sure," he says, his eyes roving the landscape for inspiration. All I can see are the ruins of a town and malnourished people. "Something will come to mind. I won't disappoint them."

I linger at the far edge of the crowd. When Riek stands, the assembly hoots, hollers and applauds. People shout out, calling him savior, liberator, champion; several spring to their feet to yell, "Messiah . . . messiah!" The inspiration Riek was looking for has been delivered, and as I turn my back and walk away, he talks about the promised land of a free southern Sudan.

SEPTEMBER 1993

Editor's Note

In January 2002, the rebel leaders Riek Machar and John Garang joined forces, establishing a united Sudanese People's Liberation Army. Later that same month, the SPLA and the Islamic government in Khartoum signed a six-month cease-fire agreement covering the Nuba Mountains region of southern Sudan. The agreement was negotiated in part by John C. Danforth, a former U.S. senator who is now a special envoy to Sudan charged with seeking a peace settlement. Machar has spoken optimistically of the prospects for lasting peace. "With our unity," he said during an interview in February 2002, "we will talk with one voice at the peace table, and it is likely that there can be a breakthrough."

AFTER THE SPILL

by Charles Siebert

BACK IN THE WINTER of 1963, twenty-six-year-old photographer Ross Mullins decided to drop everything and reenact the signature American experience of lighting out for the frontier. He was living in San Francisco when a friend called from the isolated coastal village of Cordova, Alaska, and spoke of the hard-won rewards of a life spent fishing the deep, island-flecked waters of Prince William Sound and living in a close-knit community amid rugged mountains, vast glaciers, abundant wildlife, and free-flowing rivers.

"I decided to come up for a summer, with the idea of returning to San Francisco in the winter," Mullins, now sixty-three, recalled one evening this past September as he and I sat in the cramped kitchen of his seventy-year-old, two-story wood house perched on the side of Eyak Mountain, the lights of the boats in Cordova's harbor flickering gently below us like a fallen constellation. "But I found the fishing engrossing, so I ended up getting involved."

Mullins, who now looks every inch the Alaskan fisherman, with his burly build, a full beard, and denim overalls, bought a secondhand fishing vessel, the boat of a dead man whose wife believed it to be cursed. "The guy had been killed on it," said Mullins. "I made this woman a ridiculously low offer of $8,000. She said, 'If you'll agree never to bring that thing back here, it's yours.'" Mullins fished many good years with the boat and, for a long time after selling it, never had any cause to consider the curse. "I thought I was real lucky," he said.

He poured us each a sip of bourbon and stared at the tall glass jar he'd just placed on his kitchen table. It contained a mass of what looked like molasses-coated marbles, a sample of small rocks that a friend had collected several months earlier while walking the beaches of Sleepy Bay, a sparkling quarter-moon inlet at the northern tip of Latouche Island, seventy miles southwest of Cordova. The bay had been a favorite spot over the years of the Mullins family—Ross, his wife, Sheelagh, and their four children. But its concave configuration also makes it, like a number of Prince William Sound's shoreline nooks, a perfect catch basin. Oil that spills into the sound tends to gather in places like this. Oil that makes it onto the beach intact can coat tiny rocks and, over time, harden into asphalt. Oil whipped by waves into the frothy goo known as "mousse" can seep into the spaces between rocks and get trapped. Mullins handed the jar to me so I could read what was written on the tape fixed to its lid: "Sleepy Bay, Latouche Island, PWS 5/26/98, surface asphalt and mousse from *Exxon Valdez*."

It was ten years ago, early on the morning of March 24, 1989, that the 987-foot supertanker *Exxon Valdez* ran aground on Bligh Reef, just forty miles north of Cordova, spilling 11 million gallons of crude oil into Prince William Sound.

It has been called the worst ecological disaster in history, and whether that label is even quantifiable, the spill certainly was the stuff of mythic tragedy. Start with the crash site, named as it is for *that* Bligh—the infamous British naval officer who explored Alaska's southern coast back in 1778, shortly before taking command of the ill-fated *Bounty*. Then there was the uncanny timing of the spill: Good Friday, twenty-five years nearly to the day since the Good Friday Earthquake, one of North America's most ruinous natural disasters, struck Prince William Sound. There were classic villains, from the so-called "drunken skipper" Captain Joseph Hazelwood to Exxon and Alyeska (the consortium of seven oil companies, including Exxon, that owns and operates the Trans-Alaska Pipeline and its terminus in Valdez), with their woefully ineffective safeguards and spill-response procedures. There were sympathetic victims: nature-loving Alaskans, working-class fishermen, Native Americans, and birds and animals. There was, finally, the spill's backdrop—Alaska—one of the last pristine wildernesses on the planet.

The devastation was on a scale usually assigned to God or Mother Nature. The slick spanned five hundred miles—the equivalent of the distance from the southern tip of Cape Cod to the coast of North Carolina. More than a thousand miles of shoreline were despoiled; hundreds of thousands of birds, marine mammals, and fish were injured or killed.

The spill's symbolic stain spread even farther. As satellites beamed the sickening images of oil-soaked animals around the world, there was suddenly a sense that the spill implicated us all. Eleven million gallons of crude had leaked from their daily, dismissible concealment, and suddenly there was no hiding from the role we had played. It was Judgment Day for our technological sins.

Ten years later, the spill has faded into memory. Oil continues to flow through the pipeline and into tankers, and most of us continue to consume it. Even the chorus of voices calling for protective measures, such as double-hulled tankers, has dwindled to the same vigilant few who were pleading for them before the spill happened.

But anniversaries are natural times to reflect, and a decade is long enough for any lasting effects of the spill to have manifested themselves. So this past September, I set out for Prince William Sound, hoping to discern how, if at all, "the worst ecological disaster in history" had scarred both the environment and the least studied of all the species involved: the one that had caused it.

I started in Valdez, the hemisphere's northernmost ice-free port, as it's often described, and the nearest thing Prince William Sound has to a hub. But Valdez, I quickly discovered, is not really the place to look for damage left by the spill. The fact that the slick never touched its shores notwithstanding, Valdez is an oil town. As the pipeline terminus, it's the shipping-out point for the hundreds of millions of barrels of crude piped out of Alaska's North Slope fields every year. Oil revenues make up some 80 percent of the town's tax base; the vast majority of its workforce is employed by the oil industry. Valdezans, by and large, believe in oil; they profit from its unceasing flow. They don't want spills, of course, but they've accepted a Faustian bargain: The possibility of one is a trade-off for the profits and progress that Big Oil brings. If a spill happens, you clean it up, you do what you can to prevent the next one, and you move on.

Many Valdezans actually benefited from the Exxon accident. In the months that followed, the town received a giant fiscal shot in the arm by serving as the base for the cleanup. Locals made tens of thousands of dollars (in a few cases, hundreds of thousands) by leasing out their boats to Exxon. They became known as "Spillionaires."

"You know what the joke around town is?" a brash barmaid whispered to me one night. "'It's time for another spill.'"

Cordova, on the other hand—eighty miles southeast, the second-biggest town on Prince William Sound—was repeatedly characterized in press clippings I'd read as the place hit hardest by the spill and by a number of Valdezans I met as a community that, in many ways, has yet to recover from the disaster.

The oil never reached Cordova's shores, either, thanks to the prevailing winds and tides and the town's sequestered locale on the sound's craggy coastline. But Cordova and Prince William Sound are essentially one in a way that Valdez and the sound are not. Cordovans live off of and, for months at a time, *on* the water. More than 70 percent of the town's economy is based upon fishing or related businesses—canning, packing, boat repair, net making, and so on.

Standing on the deck of an Alaska Marine Highway Ferry for the five-hour journey from Valdez to Cordova, I spotted Bligh Reef, the peaks of the snowcapped Chugach Mountains rising in the background; bald eagles drifted above the horizon's saw-toothed edge of hemlocks as sea otters basked in the emerald waters, their front paws folded on their bellies like overstuffed vacationers on floating chaise longues. I found myself looking everywhere for some sign of the spill—a stain, a stigmata—but I saw none. There was something almost sacrilegious about the surrounding beauty, as though nature itself had conspired in a coverup with the forces of technology.

I had the same feeling when I debarked in Cordova. There was no obvious evidence that anything untoward had happened there. But it wasn't long before I began to see the cracks in the idyll—the damage Cordova has suffered and the pain that lurks, like the oil on the beaches of Sleepy Bay, just beneath the surface.

Like the Mullinses, a number of people I met in town had jars full of oily rocks or oil—some collected immediately after the spill, others in recent months—which they presented at the slightest prompting. The jars are, in a sense, the townspeople's testaments—evidence not just of the lasting physical presence of the oil and the harm it did to the environment but of the pain and trauma Cordovans suffered. The pain and trauma that comes from witnessing the sullying of a cherished landscape and the deaths of thousands of animals; from the economic and social strife that began during the cleanup and worsened with the collapse of the local fishing industry; from the bankruptcies, the divorces, and the suicides; and from the ongoing struggle over Exxon's refusal to pay the $5 billion in punitive damages awarded by a U.S. district court jury in Anchorage back in 1994 to the fishermen of Cordova and to others the spill affected. The jars of oil, I would come to understand, are the stigmata, the tangible proof of what, in an increasingly technological world, may soon become a tired old maxim: Man-made disasters have their most profound effect upon man.

Cut into the side of Eyak Mountain, overlooking a crowded harbor, Cordova is not quaint or cozy in the way of a New England fishing village. Instead, it has the raw, rough-hewn appearance of the frontier outpost it once was. Life here is hard. The town's twenty-five hundred year-round residents are mostly fishermen—purse seiners and gill netters, crabbers and shrimpers—as well as some timber workers and miners, local merchants, and a smattering of employees of the U.S. Forestry Service and the Alaska Department of Fish and Game. About 18 percent of the population is coastal-Alaskan native.

Along the four-block length of First Street, the town's main "thoroughfare," you'll find a bank, a supermarket, a pharmacy, a souvenir-and-card shop, a couple of restaurants and bars, a historical museum and library, a bookshop called Orca Book and Sound, and, right next door to it, the headquarters of Cordova District Fishermen's United (CDFU). Many of the buildings and the flat, low, utilitarian homes that line the unpaved side streets date back to the early 1900s, when Cordova, not Valdez, was the bustling boomtown of Prince William Sound. Back then, Cordova was a major outlet for copper, brought in by train from the Kennecott Mines, two hundred miles to the northeast.

The mines closed in 1938, but by then Cordova had developed its fishing industry to the point where the town was able to make a relatively smooth transition to quiet waterfront village, cut off from the rest of Alaska by the sound's jagged coastline and the rugged Chugach Mountains. A highway that would have connected Cordova with the rest of Alaska was begun back in the early '60s, but the '64 earthquake obliterated the work in progress and funding was diverted elsewhere. Ever since, Cordova has been, in the local parlance, a "non–road access town." It can be reached only by ferry or by the small prop plane that leaves Valdez once daily. There's been a debate about whether to build a road to the outside world in order to open Cordova to tourist dollars and new business opportunities. It's the debate that, in many ways, defines Alaska—the conflict between the desire for development and increased profits on the one hand and for the preservation of the state's wild environs on the other; between the dependency on oil dollars that characterizes a town like Valdez and the live-off-the-land self-sufficiency of Cordova. To date, Cordova's "no road" faction has held sway.

"Cordova is not a place you can be ambivalent about," Kelley Weaverling, the owner of Orca Book and Sound and the town's mayor from 1991 to 1993, told me one afternoon as we sat in his shop's loft cafe. Weaverling, fifty-two, a gaunt figure with deep-set brown eyes, a long beard, and gray-streaked black hair, came to Cordova with his wife, Susan Ogle, in 1987. They had lived and worked together for years as kayak guides on Prince William Sound and decided to settle in Cordova because it is a town whose economy is based on a renewable, natural resource, set apart from the muck and moil of what Weaverling calls "American mainstream monoculture."

"You either like it here or you're gone," Weaverling continued. "It's not the kind of place where you just drop in, looking for a job. It's not a roadside attraction, it's a destination. It's not an easy one, but it's an awful good one. What gives it its quality is its difficulty."

Cordovans are generally well educated and fiercely independent. "We have a reputation for being real mouthy," Gerald Masolini said one afternoon as I watched him seal freshly packed cans of Copper River red salmon at his cannery on the east end of town. "It's a town of grizzle-heads—you know, hardheads." At the same time, Cordovans are neighborly and giving. The shared rigors of life in such a small, isolated place inspire a sense of community that people in the lower forty-eight normally associate only with disaster relief. People stop in the streets and stores to talk. House-to-house "progressive" dinners are held. There are impromptu group boat-repair parties. In terms of politics, Cordovans mainly vote for what best serves their livelihoods. In terms of religion, they are multidenominational—the town has ten churches.

Whatever their faith, all Cordovans pray for full fishing nets. Cordova is ruled by the seasonal cycles of the catch: herring and halibut in April; in May, king and sockeye salmon; pink and chum salmon all summer; silver orb coho salmon running through to early October; and, finally, crab and shrimp through the winter. During the height of the fishing season, from June to August, Cordova's population swells to more than four thousand, with a small shantytown of transient workers (mostly Mexicans and college kids from the lower forty-eight) springing up on the town's western edge, in Shelter—a.k.a. "Hippie"—Cove.

"It's a lively time," Sheelagh Mullins, a former gill netter herself and a part-time veterinary technician, told me. "All the men are gone and the women basically run the town," she said, laughing. "Then in October, as the season ends, we have these three-day-long parties in the bars to celebrate. After that, it gets real quiet around here."

November begins the down phase, when the population dwindles to its hardened core of year-rounders. There are only four hours of daylight, and the streetlamps stay on around the clock. The snow that covers Valdez, to the north, falls upon Cordova mostly as rain (two hundred inches annually) because of the warming Japanese Current. The fishermen—except, perhaps, for the crabbers and shrimpers—hole up in their houses or go off traveling, their nets folded, their boats in dry dock. A good portion of the population lives off stores of hunted game and smoked fish; the only recreation is skiing, when there's snow, at the ski area on Mount Eyak, adjacent to the center of town, or ice-skating on nearby Lake Eyak.

On the first full weekend in February, Cordova holds its Iceworm Festival, culminating in the procession down First Street of a forty-foot-long stretched-cloth rendition of the tiny annelid that lives just beneath the surface of glaciers. It's an annual sign of spring. Another harbinger: Gene Rossillini, the "Soul of Cordova," would emerge from the cabin he'd built back in the late '60s in the woods above Shelter Cove and once again could be seen strolling down First Street with his ankle-length beard and his knapsack full of rocks, which he always wore to keep himself strong.

Cordova's fishermen are independent contractors; they risk their own money to pursue their trade. Just getting started involves a substantial investment. In 1989, a seining vessel cost as much as $750,000; a single net, $20,000; yearly insurance and fuel, more than $25,000. Forty percent to 50 percent of the season's profits typically go to the crew. There is a finite number of fishing permits for Prince William Sound, and they are traded on the open market, their price determined strictly by demand (you own a permit until you decide to sell it). In 1989, a gill-net permit went for about $160,000 and seining permits for more than $300,000. Fishermen in Cordova could make as much as $500,000 a season, but the majority earned a comfortable middle-class living.

The fishing itself is competitive and dangerous, requiring thorough planning and a sophisticated understanding of the sound's currents, wind patterns, storm systems, and scores of other variables. The Alaska Department of Fish and Game enforces tight regulations, too, determining when, where, and for how long each "opener"—a period of time during which commercial fishing is allowed—will be held, and designating what equipment can be used. Some openers are as brief as twenty-four hours. A few good or bad sets within that time can make or break a season. Still, fishermen willingly abide by the regulations, as they serve both to guard against overfishing and to create a level playing field.

No single concern has drawn Cordovans together over the years more than the prospect of oil tankers bearing crude through the waters of Prince William Sound. There's hardly a soul in Cordova who can't recite the history of the town's battle to keep Big Oil out. As far back as 1971, when plans for the construction of the Trans-Alaska Pipeline were first gaining momentum, Cordovans fought with the oil companies and the federal and state governments to try to get them to consider alternate routes for the transport of North Slope crude. They battled, as well, to get the oil companies to conduct environmental impact studies and a full ecological profile of Prince William Sound, which could serve as the baseline for measuring any damage done in the event of a spill. And they sought laws requiring the companies to implement spill-prevention and -response measures, such as tanker escorts, improved radar tracking, double-hull tankers, and cleanup contingency plans. Ross Mullins and others lobbied intensely and testified before Congress. But despite their efforts, they failed to stop the pipeline route to Valdez, and most of the proposed safety measures were either lobbied away or sidestepped by the oil companies.

The first tankers began departing from Valdez in 1977; by winter of 1989, nearly nine thousand loads of North Slope crude had been shipped out without a major incident. The Trans-Alaska Pipeline was considered a success. Cordovans, however, remained uneasy. Many went to bed at night thinking about the prediction they'd made in a 1971 lawsuit seeking to block construction of the pipeline—that an "inevitable major" oil spill would one day kill countless fish and the town's economy.

March 1989 was a promising time in Cordova. There had been a number of good seasons in a row. Salmon was selling at an all-time average high of more than $1 per pound. For a long stretch through the 1970s and '80s, Ross Mullins had been earning enough to meet his expenses, pay his bills, and even take his family to Hawaii in the winter.

That month, in the last days of the ante-spillian world, Cordova was still very much the town that Mullins had set out for back in '63. The iceworm had made its annual pass along First Street. The shops were stocking up with goods. The Soul of Cordova had emerged from his cabin. With the opening of the herring and halibut seasons a month away, the town was beginning to stir.

"You could feel the buzz in the air," Weaverling told me, looking out his loft window at First Street. "People you hadn't seen all winter were meeting in the street, and the private spotter pilots were getting ready for the first flyovers to locate herring schools. It was great. It was like harvest time."

At 12:04 A.M. on March 24, 1989, that world ended for Cordova with something less than a whimper. The *Exxon Valdez* departed the Alyeska terminal's loading berth No. 5 some three hours before, at 9:21 P.M., freshly topped off with hot North Slope crude. Reports have it that on that particular night, the aurora borealis was more dazzling than it had been in years—a sign, in the lore of Eyak Indians, that misfortune looms. Having cleared the Valdez Narrows, the tanker then steered left out of its assigned shipping lane to avoid ice floes off the Columbia Glacier and was into clear, calm water.

Captain Hazelwood placed the ship on autopilot (he has never explained why; the National Transportation Safety Board report on the accident called the move "extremely inconsistent with normally accepted practice"). For the *Valdez* to pass safely through the sound and out into the Gulf of Alaska, two things had to be done: The autopilot had to be disengaged (a matter of pushing one button), and a ten-degree right-rudder turn had to be executed manually, just before Bligh Reef (two other ships had made similar turns that night).

At approximately 11:50 P.M., Hazelwood reviewed the course change with his third mate, Gregory Cousins. According to Cousins's testimony at Hazelwood's 1989 criminal trial (one of the many criminal and civil cases related to the accident), the captain twice asked Cousins if he felt comfortable performing the ten-degree right-rudder turn, and Cousins twice said he was. Then, at 11:54 P.M.—according to Cousins's testimony and by Hazelwood's own accounts—Hazelwood told the third mate he was going down to his quarters to do some paperwork. He ordered Cousins to phone him when the turn was initiated.

At 11:55 P.M., only a minute after Hazelwood had left the bridge, Cousins ordered his helmsman, Robert Kagan, to execute the ten-degree right-rudder turn. What happened during the next five minutes has never been resolved.

Kagan says he turned the wheel as directed. But, somehow, the ship never responded. Perhaps, as the National Transportation Safety Board (NTSB) report speculated, the autopilot had not been disengaged (despite the fact that both Cousins and Kagan said they recalled it was off), thereby disabling manual steering. Or perhaps Kagan did *not* turn the wheel as directed. Cousins has consistently said that during a minute-and-a-half phone call to Hazelwood (Cousins notified the captain that the turn had been started; Hazelwood acknowledged and said he'd be back on the bridge in a few minutes) and in the three minutes or so afterward, he did not, to his recollection, check that the turn had, in fact, been made. In Hazelwood's criminal trial, it bears noting, the *Valdez*'s chief mate, James Kunkel, testified that Kagan had trouble keeping a ship on course, and that the helmsman had a tendency to oversteer.

Just before midnight, Cousins checked the ship's radar and realized that the vessel's course remained unchanged. He ordered a twenty-degree right-rudder turn, but it was too late. An oil tanker going twelve to fourteen knots takes well over five minutes to change course and some seven miles to come to a full emergency stop. About two minutes later, ship's lookout Maureen Jones appeared on the bridge, shouting that the vessel appeared headed for Bligh Reef. Twice earlier (once just before the ten-degree-turn order was given and then before the twenty-degree order was issued), Jones had matter-of-factly notified Cousins, as part of her routine duties, that the ship was still out of its proper lane. At this point, however, the situation had obviously become serious.

Cousins then gave a hard-right command and called Hazelwood again. "I told him," he testified at Hazelwood's criminal trial, "that I thought we were getting into trouble. He said, 'Where's the rudder?' And I said, 'It's at hard right. . . .' At that point we suffered the first shock."

The *Exxon Valdez*—987 feet long, 166 feet wide, 88 feet high, and with a displacement of almost 240,000 long tons (including the weight of its 53 million gallons of oil)—had crashed into Bligh Reef, its single skin of high-strength steel slicing open on the rocks.

With its rudder stuck at hard right, the *Valdez* pivoted—its stern swinging left toward shore, its bow out toward open water. Cousins, fearing the engine room might get hulled as well, grabbed the wheel from Kagan and turned it hard left to stabilize the ship.

Now back on the bridge, Hazelwood ordered the engines shut down. Choosing not to sound the general alarm for fear of panicking the sleeping crew, Hazelwood sent Cousins and Jones to alert them quietly instead. At 12:27 A.M., from the bridge of the supertanker, came Hazelwood's infamously flat, even-keeled transmission to the coast guard's Valdez Traffic Center: "We've fetched up hard aground on Bligh Reef." He added, almost as an aside, "Evidently, we're leaking some oil."

Chief Mate Kunkel's pronouncement to a crew member was perhaps, in retrospect, more appropriate: "Vessel aground," he told them. "We're fucked."

Eight of the ship's eleven cargo tanks, extending its full length, were ripped open. Radioman Joel Robertson saw oil shooting forty to fifty feet into the air from one of them. Oil was still bubbling up nearly two feet above the water's surface along the tanker's entire starboard side when the vessel was approached by a coast guard cutter shortly after 3 A.M. Within five hours after the *Valdez* went aground, 250,000 barrels of oil—more than 10 million gallons—had already emptied into Prince William Sound.

Unaware of the dark tide gathering to the north, most everyone in Cordova slept. Ross Mullins awoke at 6 A.M. A fan of the newly formed CNN, he turned on the TV as he set about making coffee and heard a report about a potentially major disaster in Alaska—an oil spill in Prince William Sound. Mullins experienced a momentary lapse in comprehension: an Atlanta-based reporter telling him about his worst fears coming true in his own backyard? "I kept saying, 'Jesus Christ, what the hell is this?'" he recalled. "Then I felt this incredible anger. It was like you'd been raped."

Still, no one in Cordova really understood the magnitude of the spill until later in the day, when a group from the town flew to the accident site. "It was devastating," forty-three-year-old Michelle O'Leary, a longtime Cordova fisherman who was on that flight, told me as we sat one morning in the modified A-frame house that she and her husband had built along a jetty on the edge of Orca Inlet. "The amazing thing is that a number of our commercial fishing vessels were part of a spill contingency plan [in 1986, the state of Alaska had mandated that Alyeska develop a plan for a spill of up to 200,000 barrels]. After we made the flyover, we spent the whole day at CDFU trying to get through to Exxon on the phone and say, 'Look, we're sending our boats.' We called Alyeska and they had no idea we were even *in* the contingency plan. It was so screwed up."

Alyeska was primarily responsible for executing the cleanup operation (the coast guard and the state maintained oversight authority). But the spill was far bigger than the contingency plan had prepared for. For that matter, it was beyond the capacity of any of the containment booms and oil skimmers then in use in the United States. Alyeska's spill-response equipment amounted to one barge loaded with boom material, and that barge was in dry dock in Valdez under several feet of snow. The relative remoteness of the spill's location further complicated attempts at an expeditious response effort. The first spill-control equipment didn't arrive until more than ten hours after the tanker crashed.

"The thing I'll never forget on that flyover," O'Leary said, "is seeing these two commercial fishing boats already out there, trying to do something. They had booms stretched between them and no skimmers. Nothing. Just two small boats trying to stem this massive tide of oil."

For three days after the accident, the slick remained in a relatively contained area, just south of Bligh Reef. On Saturday, March 25, Exxon asked for and was given authority to direct the cleanup, in concert with the coast guard and state and federal agencies. As much oil as was in the water already, there were 1,001,900 barrels (four-fifths of the original load) still on board the *Valdez* and in danger of spilling, should the crippled tanker dislodge from the reef and capsize or break apart.

In one of the rare successes of the spill response, Exxon devised a way to transfer that oil to other tankers using submerged pumps. There was also some limited testing of controlled burning and of chemical dispersant (a controversial option because of the dispersant's own potential toxicity) to eradicate the slick.

Back in Cordova, calls went out to Exxon, as they did from all over Prince William Sound, offering assistance from the town's fishing fleet. But the company was rejecting such offers, citing the fear of injury, the lack of workman's compensation, and the unavailability of the necessary booming equipment. The CDFU finally convinced Exxon to fund a small fleet of Cordova's fishing vessels to go out and boom off the waters around the sound's five fish hatcheries. The bulk of the fishermen, however, remained stuck in town.

"There's an image I'll never forget," said Sheelagh Mullins. "It was that first weekend after the spill. I walked out to the end of our road here and looked out over the town, and it was like I didn't know the place. There were people everywhere, darting back and forth frantically, all this activity but with no real purpose. It was like some strange, out-of-control windup toy."

On Sunday evening, a storm hit, and all hope of containing the spill was lost. For three days, winds of up to seventy miles per hour spread the oil full across Prince William Sound and then drove it some four hundred miles south and southwest through the sound, into the Gulf of Alaska. All told, the slick spread over approximately three thousand square miles, enveloping dozens of islands and fouling more than twelve hundred miles of coastline, including three national parks and eight other protected areas.

It was early spring, and creatures everywhere were emerging from the long winter into a lethal veil of darkness (crude oil varies, depending on its place of origin; North Slope crude is a particularly noxious blend). Salmon fry and herring swam by the millions into it. Otters matted with oil went off into the rocks to die. Eagles, sick from ingesting oil-soaked prey, dropped from their perches to the forest floor. Murres, oystercatchers, loons, and ducks dove through the slick, flailed briefly, then foundered. Sea lions, seals, and whales, needing to surface for air, came up breathing and blinking back oil.

Cordovans, meanwhile, were having their own ongoing struggles with Exxon. "The first planeloads of people [they] sent in," said O'Leary, "were all attorneys and public-relations people. The cleanup people came much later. There was this general attitude when it first happened that, well, it's up there in this remote place in Alaska where just a bunch of ignorant fishermen and natives live. It's not going to be a big deal. They thought they could manage it and wound up spending most of their time and effort trying to manage the public's perception. It wasn't spill control so much as spin control."

On Wednesday, March 29, Exxon began hiring fishermen to assist with the cleanup, offering $100 a foot per day for the use of their boats. Those with larger vessels could average $5,000 a day or more for the four to five months the main operation was in effect. One fisherman who had an onboard spray washer, a particularly useful piece of equipment, is said to have made $250,000 a month.

Ultimately, though, the magnitude of the spill would reduce the cleanup operation to absurdist theater. People were wiping rocks with paper towels and being paid by the rock. Until enough skimming equipment was brought in, some of the cleanup workers were using Pampers to soak up the oil. Beaches were scrubbed, many of them steam-cleaned, wiping out all life. Equipment failed to work or broke down. In the attempt to cleanse the beaches, workers actually stomped oil deeper into the ground.

The animal rescue effort was a hollow pantomime, ultimately doing more to assuage people's helplessness and guilt than to save animals. Experts knew from the start that the cause was largely futile; many have said that the cleanup attempts did more harm than good, scaring unsullied otters and birds into oil, traumatizing others from so much handling, and imparting to them various illnesses that would be transferred to other animals.

"It was hell," said Kelley Weaverling, who was sought out by a team from the University of California at Berkeley to direct the bird rescue operation because of his extensive knowledge of the sound. "In some places," he recalled, "the oil was a foot thick on the water. When the tide went out, if the beach had any kind of undulation in it, there'd be pools of oil and we'd frequently find animals by taking little sticks and going in and picking them up and saying, 'I think this little blob is a bird blob.'

"People would break down—fishermen, big, burly, macho dudes, sobbing—and then they'd just shake it off and carry on."

Ross Mullins showed me a tape the night I visited his home. It was of the town meeting held in the Cordova High School gymnasium on Tuesday evening, March 28, four nights after the spill. Nearly the entire population of Cordova was packed into the gym. Behind a podium set up at the front of the room, someone had hung a large picture of the earth from space—the familiar image of the light-blue orb in a sea of blackness having a whole other resonance in this context.

As the session began, the room buzzed, but things quickly settled down as various officials stepped to the podium to summarize, in somber tones, what was known about the spill, what preliminary plans were being made to monitor its progress, and the inevitable damages.

Eventually, Exxon spokesman Don Cornett took the microphone. This was the first opportunity Cordovans had had since the accident to meet face-to-face with a representative of the company. Cornett began by giving his own brief, banal rundown of what had transpired to date. There were a few outbursts from the restless crowd, but, on the whole, the infamously mouthy Cordovans were surprisingly subdued. Everyone seemed to know even then that it was too late, that the damage was done. One woman asked why the pipeline hadn't been shut down and all tanker traffic suspended, thereby subjecting the already-offended citizens of Cordova to the indignity of a lecture from Cornett about the vital importance of Alaska's oil to the rest of the nation.

The remainder of the session was spent talking mostly about the process of filing claims for losses. One fisherman after the next asked how they'd be compensated, but their voices all trailed off in disgust. Trying to put a dollar figure on the economic impact of the damage— let alone on the value of their lifestyle—was unfathomable to them.

In the end, the citizens of Cordova were forced to draw whatever solace they could from the most consoling words Cornett had to offer them: "We will consider whatever it takes," he promised, "to make you whole."

The judge who presided over Joseph Hazelwood's criminal arraignment likened the *Exxon Valdez* oil spill to the bombing of Hiroshima. The comparison may seem hyperbolic, but to Cordovans, it's on the mark. For ten years, the spill has had all kinds of damaging fallout— on the environment, on the economy, and, most of all, on the people. A decade later, Cordovans are anything but "whole." And Exxon, they say, has only perpetuated their suffering.

The spill's final mortality estimates for birds and marine mammals are staggering. Among the fatalities: somewhere between 250,000 and 300,000 murres, loons, grebes, cormorants, petrels, and ducks, and 144 bald eagles, as well as approximately 5,000 sea otters, 300 seals, and 22 killer whales. Today, some animals, such as bald eagles and murres, appear to have rebounded substantially. But many others— harbor seals and certain species of duck, for example—are still struggling to come back.

In all, less than 15 percent of the oil that spilled was recovered. Of the rest, most evaporated or biodegraded. But while the beaches and marshes appear clean, oil, having worked its way deep into the earth, still lingers. No one can say how long it will be before all traces of oil are gone.

Cordova's fishing industry has suffered devastating declines. For a few years, the spill damage wasn't readily apparent. The salmon runs in 1989, '90, and '91 were actually some of the best ever. In fact, 1990 was a record year for pink salmon. It wasn't until 1992 and '93—when the salmon that were fry in the spring of 1989 returned as adults—that the spill's effects became manifest. The returns those years were some of the lowest on record. Herring, especially sensitive to environmental disruptions, were particularly hard hit, as the oil contaminated undersea kelp spawning grounds. The winter crab and shrimp fisheries were all but wiped out.

The natural fluctuations in fish populations make it impossible to determine what changes can be attributed directly to the spill. This much is certain: The combination of the oil's physical effects and the damage the spill did to the reputation of Prince William Sound's catch sent Cordova into an economic tailspin. The same salmon that had sold at $1.15 a pound before the spill was going for twenty cents in '92. The price of a seine-fishing permit dropped by 50 percent that year. Two of the town's five fish-packing plants were closed by '92. Unemployment reached an all-time high. When a school janitor's position came open, there were 170 applications the first day it was posted.

Today, most major fish species have rebounded substantially (herring less so than others). But the fishing industry has not bounced back. During the down years, fish buyers turned to other suppliers in the United States and abroad, and the fishermen of Prince William Sound have yet to regain their market share. Many people believe they may never. The price of a seining permit has plunged to just $28,000, roughly 9 percent of its worth in 1989. Although Cordova's economy is better now than it was in the worst years (one of the fish-packing plants has reopened, though in a limited fashion), its health remains tenuous. Few fishermen earn a comfortable middle-class income anymore. Some Cordovans have packed up and left. Others have been forced to take up new lines of work. For several years, there has even been renewed debate about building the controversial access road to bring in tourists. Thus far, the answer is still no, but the town has reluctantly increased its reliance on tourism. Once a week in the summer, a tour boat now pulls into the town's harbor. Sheelagh Mullins has even started her own walking tour of Cordova's historical sites for the debarking passengers.

The spill brought other unwelcome changes—rifts within the community began to develop. Those who worked the cleanup operation for Exxon felt they were doing the right thing for the environment. And with herring and halibut fishing closed for the season, a paycheck was critical. Others, however, argued that taking money from the accident's perpetrator couldn't be justified. In Cordova, "Spillionaires" had another name: "Exxon whores." By Ross Mullins's reckoning, it wasn't working for Exxon, per se, that caused the worst divisions. That, he believes, was a personal decision. The deeper problem was that some fishermen who worked the spill were then able to afford the newest and best equipment allowed within the state regulations. "A lot of guys felt they were screwed because they didn't get the same opportunity and it put them at a competitive disadvantage," Mullins told me (he worked the spill for a few months but says he didn't make enough money to afford substantial improvements in his fishing setup). "Prior to the spill, it had always kind of been one big happy family. This set fisherman against fisherman."

All these changes bred a host of social problems. Alcoholism, domestic violence, and divorce increased. Rather than going out and socializing, people became more isolated; instead of stopping on the street or at Davis' Super Foods to chat, or hanging out at the Club Bar for a beer and some tunes, they'd go to the grocery store or liquor store and then head straight home. The town's mental-health clinic was overrun. Cases of post-traumatic stress disorder were diagnosed immediately following the disaster and in increasing numbers for several years afterward.

In the spring of 1993, Bob Van Brocklin, the mayor of Cordova during the cleanup, killed himself in bed one night with a pistol shot to the head. Among the woes cited in his suicide note were both his personal economic problems tied to the *Valdez* accident and the stress it had put upon the town. Ever since the spill, Gene Rossillini had been telling people that the damage to the ecology and to his way of life had been weighing on him. A short time after Van Brocklin's death, the Soul of Cordova was found in his cabin with a fatal, self-inflicted stab wound to the heart.

✻   ✻   ✻

When I first arrived in Cordova, I had checked into my room at the Reluctant Fisherman, then walked up the hill to First Street. I'd entered Weaverling's bookshop and started to introduce myself, but had gotten only as far as "I'm writing—" when he'd interrupted: "A story about the tenth anniversary of the oil spill." He'd promptly handed me his jar of oil—he had it right up front, sitting on a wooden display shelf just opposite his cash register.

After the '64 earthquake—which destroyed the boat harbor, impaled half-a-million-dollar fishing vessels on exposed dock pilings, and practically wiped out the entire town—Cordovans quickly bounced back. But the spill is different. It has become an abiding obsession. "The spill," said Ross Mullins, "totally screwed people up, and we're not out of it yet. It's an ongoing nightmare that won't let people get on with their lives."

Steven Picou, Ph.D., a University of South Alabama sociologist who specializes in technological disasters, has been coming to Cordova regularly since the spill, monitoring its effects on people's psyches and upon the community as a whole. There are dozens of reasons why Cordovans' nightmare won't end, Picou told me. For one, their livelihood has been seriously diminished. The loss of income brought on by the collapse of the fishing industry has eroded people's sense of stability. Fishermen are accustomed to weathering lean times, but six depressed years have taken a toll.

The trauma caused by the damage to the environment is another source of lingering pain. Strolling the beach isn't the same when you have to worry about skirting oil mousse. And the images of dead birds and otters still haunt. In general, Cordovans say, the sound feels deflated—a paradise lost.

The fact that oil is toxic, with unknown long-term effects, breeds its own uncertainties. People wonder: Might fish populations plummet again? Is the fish safe to eat? Is the water safe to drink? "That's precisely the opposite mind-set of what's needed for people to recover," Picou said.

"People come back relatively quickly after a natural disaster like an earthquake," he added. "They stop blaming God and then they get together and start rebuilding. But that doesn't happen with a technological disaster. There's this terrible anger because it was preventable." It's particularly galling to many Cordovans that they had been predicting such an occurrence and fighting to prevent it since 1971. Every so often in the course of my conversations with Mullins, he'd burst out in Lear-like fury. "It's like we'd alerted the police," he told me, "and did everything else we could as responsible citizens, and the rape happened anyway."

Worse, there is no "rapist"—no single human face—to bring to justice. The litany of blame invariably begins with Captain Hazelwood. But the investigations by the NTSB and the criminal and civil trials of Exxon and Hazelwood show that the captain was just one of many—Cousins and Kagan, foremost among them—who played a part in the crash. Yes, Hazelwood had put the ship on autopilot and left the bridge, but neither of these actions, improper though many experts consider them, directly "caused" the accident. And it is not clear, despite reports to the contrary, that the "two or three" vodkas Hazelwood acknowledges he'd had between 4:30 P.M. and 6:30 P.M. that day at the Pipeline Club in Valdez meaningfully impaired his ability to captain the ship.

Cordovans have come to realize that myriad others had a hand in the accident, as well—Exxon, Alyeska, the coast guard, the state of Alaska, the federal government, and on. The list goes so far back and points to culprits so big and faceless that it tends to dissolve into abstraction.

The threat of another spill also haunts Cordovans. To be sure, significant changes have been made in the wake of the *Valdez* disaster. An elaborate spill-prevention-and-response network has been established in Prince William Sound, including a pair of state-of-the-art, ten-thousand-horsepower tractor tugs to escort tankers through the sound and an open-ocean rescue tug stationed just south of Cordova, where the sound gives way to the Gulf of Alaska. An advanced radar ship-tracking system is in place. There are seven barges with a combined 818,000-barrel storage capacity for recovered oil, stockpiles of oil-containment and skimming equipment and chemical dispersant, and regularly scheduled drills involving a trained fleet of local fishermen.

Still, for all the progress that has been made, Cordovans and others continue to travel to Washington to lobby on such issues as the long-ago-called-for double-hull tankers. Even today, only a few of the ships passing through the sound are double-hulls. What's more, the oil industry is seeking an extension on a federal regulation passed in 1990 dictating that all tankers transporting oil through U.S. waters be double-hulls by 2015.

"A lot of things have changed since eighty-nine," Weaverling told me. "But essentially the one thing that caused the oil spill has not been addressed: the container. We've still got a wet paper bag with eggs in it. We're being more careful with it, but it's still a wet paper bag with eggs."

A few years ago, Exxon attempted to gain permission from the relevant authorities to bring the *Exxon Valdez*—now fully repaired and renamed the *Sea River Mediterranean*—back to Valdez, something akin to the Greeks announcing to the citizens of Troy that the Trojan horse would be making a return visit as Tony the Pony. Cordovans and other residents of Prince William Sound were outraged; the idea was dropped. But the very suggestion of the vessel's return made Cordovans feel violated all over again.

The subject you are certain to hear about on a visit to Cordova— perhaps the biggest factor keeping people from getting on with their lives—is the continuing legal dispute over the $5 billion in punitive damages (a sum the jury had based upon Exxon's total profits for 1989) awarded back in 1994, in the class-action suit filed by individuals and groups affected by the spill.

Exxon has paid out $1.2 billion to the federal and state governments and other groups and individuals in connection with lawsuits and claims related to the spill. The money has been used to enhance spill prevention and cleanup preparedness, to purchase wildlands to protect them from development, and even to fund the Prince William Sound Science Center in Cordova (its primary mission is to compile the profile of the Prince William Sound ecosystem that Ross Mullins and the CDFU called for back in 1971). That $1.2 billion includes $25.6 million in compensatory damages paid directly to Cordovans.

But Exxon is appealing the $5 billion in punitive damages sought by Cordovans and others, and one hears different estimates of when, if ever, the plaintiffs—sixty thousand of them—might actually see a payout. Brian O'Neill, the plaintiffs' lead trial lawyer, said it should happen within the next year. A fisherman I met in Valdez said his lawyers told him it will be 2010 before any money is paid. In a 1993 essay about the spill in *National Wildlife* magazine, longtime Cordova fisherman Rick Steiner wrote of a chilling phone call from a friend in the oil industry who told him that "lawyers yet to be born will work on this case."

Even if Exxon's appeal fails, the fine will, by some estimates, pose a minimal loss to the company. Five billion dollars is just 17 percent of its 1998 revenues. And while Exxon has been incurring a 5.9 percent annual interest penalty on the settlement (payable if the company loses the appeal), estimates are that it has been earning as much as a 20 percent annual return on the money via investments.

"If they manage to put off paying the settlement until 2001," said O'Neill, "they'll be able to pay out the whole $5 billion on money made from the interest alone."

The lure of the settlement money, combined with the uncertainty of when, or if, they'll get it, creates a debilitating limbo for the Cordovans. "You've got people hanging on by their fingernails," said Mullins. "Waiting for that settlement distorts their ability to make rational decisions about their future."

In postspill Cordova, pathology piles upon pathology. The longer the fight over the settlement drags on, Picou told me, the more Cordovans begin to hear whispers: "Why can't these people get over it? They're just a bunch of lazy fishermen waiting for a handout." At times, Cordovans begin to believe such accusations. Some begin to wonder, in the classic syndrome of the rape victim, if they are somehow responsible for the whole ugly mess. "There are these niggling concerns," Mullins said. "'Could I have done more to prevent this? Did I do something to deserve this?'"

In a sense, Cordovans are at odds with themselves. They seem both angry at the world for not caring more about what's happened to them and yet impatient with their own inability to move on.

"I think the general feeling is that we're tired of it all and we'd like to let it go," said Weaverling. "But to simply try and forget doesn't work. I mean, you can't forget the multiplication tables. You can't forget trauma. Trying to will make you crazier."

Over the years, it's been suggested that the town hold some sort of ceremony—a "Bury the Blues" festival, for example, culminating with the dropping of a casket marked EXXON VALDEZ into the waters of Prince William Sound—to help bring closure.

"What we really need," Weaverling said sarcastically, "is for someone to introduce Prozac into our water supply, or maybe a SWAT team of professional masseuses to keep our shoulders low, or some extra out-of-town bartenders to talk to."

I stayed at Ross Mullins's place well past eleven o'clock the night I left Cordova on the midnight ferry to Valdez. Most of the time we sat in the kitchen, as cramped and cozy as a ship's galley, Mullins having to turn his chair out sideways from the table to make way for his good-sized belly. He said he'd had a particularly hard season and was now on the verge of filing for bankruptcy, just holding on, reciting the fisherman's prayer: "If I can just make it through until next year."

The '98 salmon runs had been good, but they'd been good elsewhere as well, and the glut in supply kept prices at about fifteen cents a pound. As a result, the packing plants had enforced strict limits on what they would buy. Mullins caught 330,000 pounds, but, he said, he could have easily caught a million pounds if he'd had somewhere to sell them. His and Sheelagh's gill-net and seining permits are valued at about one-fifth of what the couple paid for them. His only other assets are his boat and his house.

Sheelagh has her veterinary work and her walking-tour business to try to help make ends meet. Ross told me that Sheelagh incorporates the jar of oily rocks sitting before us on the table into her tours. It struck me as a true act of courage, using a sample of the very stuff that destroyed the town she and Ross had fallen in love with years ago in order to carry on living there now.

On the wall just behind me hung portraits Mullins had taken of his four children. All were once his deckhands, but none appears destined for the fishing life. Richard, thirty-five, is getting his MBA at the University of Washington; Ben, twenty-eight, is a Stanford grad with a degree in political science who works as a recruiter for a high-tech firm in Seattle; Angus, twenty-six, a graduate of the University of Oregon with a psychology and biology degree, works for a computer company; and Meghan, twenty-one, recently moved to New York City to study at the Natural Gourmet Cookery School.

"Ben and Angus were in town this summer helping me on the boat," Mullins said, proud both of the fact that his sons don't need to do that anymore and that they still do.

Mullins continues to fight the oil industry for better safeguards. Recently, he formed the Prince William Sound Fisherman Plaintiffs Committee to keep people better informed of what's going on with the settlement appeals and other developments, and he is working to create a spill-response plan to protect the nearby Copper River Delta, for which no contingency plan currently exists. (Just three years ago a tanker lost its steering in the Valdez Narrows and was two hundred yards from shore when a coast guard crew managed to get it going again.) "But I often find that I can't get as involved as I once did," Mullins said. "I can't deal with these assholes anymore."

I poured us each another sip of bourbon and asked Mullins if he ever thought back to that cursed boat he'd bought when he'd moved to Cordova. He seemed not to hear me. He just stared into that jar as though trying to divine something.

"You ask yourself," he said suddenly, "why do you even bother? You bother because you think maybe it will make a difference, that maybe we'll prevent something from happening somewhere else. But it won't. It's not like what happened here is going to make a difference in other places where they tanker oil. It may have made some difference in this small microcosm. But the corporate culture is going to make the same decisions they made here before the spill in order to get the best bang for the buck. To get a better spill-prevention and cleanup system in Prince William Sound, we had to pay the price."

A short time later, I walked down the hill to the town dock and boarded the ferry back to Valdez. Passing out of Orca Inlet on a clear mid-September night with winter's chill already in the air, I thought back on what Mullins had just said.

Ten years after one of the worst ecological disasters in history, the dark lesson, it seemed clear, is that the victims of such disasters have to learn to live with the consequences forever, while the perpetrators can afford to learn nothing at all.

APRIL 1999

Editor's Note

Contacted for this story, Exxon made the following statements. "The oil spill was a tragic accident which we deeply regret." • The company has apologized to Alaskans and all Americans and has spent $2.2 billion on the cleanup, which the Coast Guard and the state of Alaska declared complete in 1992. • "A broad consensus is developing among scientists . . ." that "the species damaged by the spill and the environment as a whole are healthy and robust." • Exxon has paid $900 million in penalties and damages to the state and federal governments and has voluntarily paid out $300 million in compensatory damages "to individuals, communities, and native corporations . . . in the area of the spill." • The company "is appealing the $5 billion punitive damage verdict because it is unjust and excessive."

In November 2001, the United States Court of Appeals for the Ninth Circuit, in San Francisco, unanimously agreed, remanding the case to Federal District Court in Alaska for reconsideration. The appellate court suggested that the punitive damage should be more in the range of $1.2 billion. But in December 2002, U.S. District Judge Russell Holland ruled that the punitive-damage award should be $4 billion. Exxon, which claims to have paid more than $3 billion in damages and cleanup costs, vows to appeal this latest ruling.

BLACK HAWK DOWN
by Mark Bowden

LATE IN THE AFTERNOON on Sunday, October 3, 1993, helicopters dropped about one hundred elite U.S. soldiers into a teeming market in the heart of Mogadishu, Somalia. They were from Delta Force C Squadron, the secret counterterrorism unit, and the Seventy-fifth Ranger Regiment, the finest light-infantry unit in the world. Their mission was to abduct two top lieutenants of Somali warlord Mohamed Farrah Aidid from a three-story house near the Olympic Hotel, then return to base. It was supposed to take them about an hour.

Instead, the men of Task Force Ranger would be pinned down through a long and terrible night, fighting for their lives. Two of their high-tech helicopters would be shot down. When the force would emerge the following morning, there would be eighteen dead and dozens badly injured. The Somali toll would be far worse. Conservative counts would later number five hundred dead among more than one thousand casualties.

The Battle of Mogadishu is known today in Somalia as *Ma-alinti Rangers,* or the "Day of the Rangers." It was the biggest firefight involving American soldiers since the war in Vietnam.

It was 3:32 P.M. when Chief Warrant Officer Mike Durant, the pilot of the lead Black Hawk, *Super Six Four,* announced the code word for launch ("Irene") over the helicopter's intercom.

—*Fuckin' Irene.*

And the armada lifted off, from the shabby airport on the beach at the south end of Mogadishu, into an embracing blue vista of sky and Indian Ocean. In close formation they flew out across a littered strip of white sand and moved low and fast over running breakers that formed faint crests parallel to the shore. The booted legs of the eager soldiers dangled from the benches and open doors of each bird.

To make room for the Rangers in the Black Hawks, the seats in back had been removed. The men who were not in the doorways were squatting on ammo cans or seated on the flak-proof Kevlar panels laid out on the floor. They all wore desert camouflage fatigues, with Kevlar vests and helmets and about fifty pounds of equipment and ammo strapped to their load-bearing harnesses, which fit on over the vests. All had goggles and thick leather gloves. Those layers of gear made even the slightest of them look bulky, robotic, and intimidating. Stripped down to their dirt-brown T-shirts and shorts, which is how they spent the majority of their time in the hangar, most looked like the pimply teenagers they were (average age: nineteen). They were immensely proud of their Ranger status. It spared them most of the numbing non-combat-related routine that drove many an army enlistee nuts. The Rangers trained for war full-time. With their grunted "Hoo-ah!" greetings, they prided themselves on being fitter, faster, and first—"Rangers lead the way!" was their motto.

In the back of Durant's Black Hawk was a squad of fifteen men, Chalk One, that included Captain Mike Steele and Lieutenant Larry Perino, the Ranger commanders; Corporal Jamie Smith, one of the chalk's best marksmen; and Specialist John Stebbins, until today the company clerk.

So far, *Mog* had been mostly a tease. War was always *about* to happen. Even the missions, exciting as they'd been, had fallen short. The Somalis—whom they called "Skinnies" or "Sammies" (as in "Sommies")—had taken a few wild shots at them, enough to get the Rangers' blood up and unleash a hellish torrent of return fire, but nothing that qualified as a genuine balls-out firefight.

Which is what they wanted. All of these guys. The Hoo-ahs couldn't wait to go to war. They were an all-star football team that had endured bruising, exhausting, dangerous practice sessions twelve hours a day, seven days a week—for years—without ever getting to play a game.

None of the Rangers was more scared, or thrilled, than Stebbins. He couldn't shake the feeling that this was all too good to be true. Here he was, an old-timer in the Ranger company at age twenty-eight, having spent the last four years of his life trying to get into combat, to do something interesting or important, and now, somehow, through an incredible chain of pleading, wheedling, and freakish breaks, he was actually in combat—him, stubby Johnny Stebbins, the company's chief coffee maker and training-room paper pusher, at war!

Stebbins was short and stocky, with pale blue eyes and blond hair and skin so white and freckly it never turned even the faintest shade darker in the sun. Here in *Mog* it had just burned bright pink. He had gone to St. Bonaventure University on an ROTC scholarship, but the army was so flooded with second lieutenants when he got out that he couldn't get assigned to active duty. When Desert Storm blew up, as his luck would have it, his National Guard contract was up. When he reenlisted as a private, the army put him through basic training again, then somebody higher up noticed that his personnel form listed a college degree and, more important, typing ability. He was routed to a desk in a training room at Fort Benning, in Columbus, Georgia.

They told him it would just be for six months. He got stuck there for two years. He became known as a good "training room" Ranger. While the other Rangers were out scaling cliffs and jumping out of planes and trying to break the record for forced marches through dense cover, old man Stebby sat behind a desk, chain-smoking cigarettes, eating doughnuts, and practically inhaling coffee. The other guys would make jokes: "Oh, yeah, Specialist Stebbins, he'll throw hot coffee at the enemy." Ha, ha. When his company, Bravo, got tapped for Somalia, no one was surprised when ol' Stebby was one of those left behind.

"I want you to know it's nothing personal," his sergeant told him, although there was no way to disguise the implied insult. "We just can't take you. We have a limited number of spots on the bird and we need you here." How much more clearly could he have stated that, when it came to combat, Stebbins was the least valuable Ranger in the regiment?

It was just like Desert Storm all over again. Somebody up there did not want John Stebbins to go to war. He helped his friends pack, and when it was announced the next day that the force had arrived in Mogadishu, he felt even more left out than he had two years before as he watched nightly updates of the Gulf action on CNN. Then came a fax from Somalia.

"Stebby, you'd better grab your stuff," his commanding officer told him. "You're going to war."

When he got to *Mog*, there weren't enough Kevlar vests to go around so he got one of the big bulky black vests the Delta Force, or D-Boys, wore. When he put it on, he felt like a turtle. Then he got the news. See, they were glad to have him there and all, but he wouldn't actually be going out with the rest of the guys on missions. His job would be to stay back at the hangar and stand guard. *Maintain perimeter security.* It was essential. Somebody had to do it.

Who else?

He'd suffered guard duty until this morning. As the runner from the command center showed up to shout, "Get it on!," one of the squad leaders strode up with news.

"Stebbins, Specialist Sizemore has an infected elbow. He just came back from the doc's office. You're taking his place."

He would be the assistant for 60-gunner Private First Class Brian Heard. Stebbins ran through the hangar, trading in his bulky tortoise-shell vest for a Kevlar one. He'd stuffed extra ammo in his pouches and gathered up some frag grenades. Watching the more experienced guys, he discarded his canteen—they would be out only an hour or so—and stuffed its pouch with still more M-16 magazines. He picked up a belt with three hundred rounds of M-60 ammo, and just before heading out to Durant's Black Hawk, he stood by the front door of the hangar and sucked on a last cigarette, trying to get his nerves under control. This was it, finally, what he'd been aiming for all this time.

The D-Boys, who had flown in on MH-6s, Little Birds, were already hitting the house where Aidid's lieutenants had been spotted when Durant eased *Super Six Four* down to insert Chalk One. A convoy of Humvees and trucks waited outside the house to transport everyone back to the base. For Durant, this was the most harrowing part of his mission, descending into an opaque cloud of dust to rooftop level over the target building, avoiding poles and wires and squinting down through the Black Hawk's chin bubble into the brown maelstrom to stay lined up while the men slid down ropes to the ground. All Durant could do was hold blind and steady, and pray that none of the other birds flitting around him in the cloud got bumped off course. A complex mission like this one was choreographed as carefully as a ballet, only dangerous as hell. Guys got killed all the time just training for missions like this, much less ducking rocket-propelled grenades (RPGs) and small-arms fire.

After dropping Chalk One, Durant flew out over the desert and went into a holding pattern. He flew long, lazy ovals over the sand, listening to the overlap of voices in his headphones. The first sign that something had gone wrong was the voice of his friend Cliff Wolcott, the pilot of Black Hawk *Super Six One.*

—Six One *going down.*

Wolcott's voice was oddly calm and matter-of-fact. His helicopter had been hit by an RPG. Cameras on the three observation choppers captured the disaster close up and in color for commanders watching TV screens back at the Ranger base. They saw Wolcott's Black Hawk moving smoothly, then a shudder and a puff of smoke near the tail rotor, then an awkward counterrotation as *Super Six One* fell, making two slow turns clockwise, nose up until its belly bit the top of a stone house and its front end was cast down violently, killing the pilot and copilot instantly. On impact, its main rotors snapped and went flying. The body of the Black Hawk came to rest in a narrow alley, on its side against a stone wall, in a cloud of dust.

Abruptly, panic crept into the voices on the command radio net.

—*We got a Black Hawk going down! We got a Black Hawk going down!*

—*We got a Black Hawk crashed in the city!* Six One!

—*He took an RPG!*

—Six One *down!*

—*We got a bird down, northeast of the target. I need you to move on and out and secure that location!*

—*Roger, bird down!*

Durant was ordered to take Wolcott's vacant position over the fight. Moving in fast and low over the city, he caught glimpses of the action through the swirling clouds of smoke and dust beneath his Black Hawk's chin bubble. It was hard to make sense of what was happening below. He could see the general area where Wolcott's bird had gone in, a dense neighborhood of small stone houses with tin roofs in a cross-hatch of dirt alleyways and wide cross streets, but the crashed Black Hawk was in such a tight spot between houses that he couldn't spot it. He caught glimpses of small Ranger columns moving up the alleys, crouched defensively, rifles up and ready, taking cover, exchanging fire with the swarms of Somalis. Durant flipped a switch in the cockpit to arm his crew chiefs' guns, two six-barreled 7.62mm miniguns capable of firing four thousand rounds per minute, but warned them to hold fire until they figured out where all the friendlies were. Durant fell into Wolcott's vacant place in a circular pattern opposite *Super Six Two,* the

Black Hawk piloted by Chief Warrant Officer Mike Goffena and Captain Jim Yacone, and began trying to get in sync with them.

—Six Four, *say location,* Goffena asked.

—*We are about a mile and a half to your north.*

—Six Four, *keep a good eye on the west side.*

—*Roger.*

The idea was to maintain a "low cap," a sweeping circle over the battle area. On the radio, Goffena and Yacone pointed out targets for Durant's gunners, but it was hard to get visually oriented. Durant's seat was on the right side of the airframe, and he was flying counterclockwise, banking left, so mostly he was seeing sky. It was maddening. When he leveled off, he was flying so low and fast that the view through the chin bubble was like peering down a tube. Flashing beneath his feet were rusty tin roofs, trees, burning cars and tires. There were Rangers and darting Somalis everywhere. What with the roar of his engines and the radio din, Durant could not tell if he was being shot at. He assumed he was. He varied his airspeed and altitude, trying to make his Black Hawk a more challenging target.

It was on his fourth or fifth circle, just as things were starting to make sense below, when the grenade hit. It blew a chunk off the tail rotor. Goffena saw all the oil dump out of it in a fine mist, but the mechanism stayed intact and everything seemed to still be functioning.

—Six Four, *are you okay?* Goffena asked.

The Black Hawk is a heavy aircraft. Durant's weighed about sixteen thousand pounds at that point, and the tail rotor was a long way from where he sat. The question came before he had even figured out what happened. Goffena explained that he had been hit by an RPG and that there was damage to the tail area.

—*Roger,* Durant radioed back coolly.

Nothing felt abnormal about the bird at first. He did a quick check of all his instruments and the readings were all okay. His crew chiefs, Bill Cleveland and Tommy Field, were unhurt. So after the initial shock, Durant felt relief. Everything was fine. Then his tail rotor, the whole thing—the gearbox and two or three feet of the vertical fin assembly— just turned into a blur and evaporated. Inside *Super Six Four,* Durant and copilot Ray Frank felt the airframe begin to vibrate. They heard the accelerating high-speed whine of the dry gear shaft in its death throes. Then came a very loud *bang* as it blew apart. With the top half of the tail fin gone, a big weight was suddenly dropped off the airframe's back end, and the Black Hawk's center of gravity pitched violently forward, causing the bird to spin faster than Durant ever imagined it could. Details of earth and sky blurred like patterns on a revolving top. Out the windshield he saw just blue sky and brown earth.

—Going in hard! Going down! Raaaay!

The plummeting helicopter's spin rate suddenly slowed. Just before impact its nose pulled up. Whether for some aerodynamic reason or something Durant or Frank did inside the cockpit, the falling chopper leveled off. With the spin rate down to half what it had been, and with the craft fairly level, the Black Hawk made a hard but flat landing. Flat was critical. It meant there was a chance the men in the helicopter were still alive.

Specialist Stebbins rappelled down from *Super Six Four* outside the target building and heard the pop of distant gunfire. After untangling himself from the 60-gunner, he ran to a wall. He was assigned a corner pointing south, guarding an alley that appeared empty. It was just a narrow dirt path, barely wide enough for a car, that sloped down on both sides from mud-caked stone walls. There were the usual piles of random debris and rusted metal parts strewn along the way, in between outcrops of cactus. He heard occasional snapping sounds in the air around him and assumed it was the sound of gunfire a few blocks away, even though the noise was close. Maybe the air was playing tricks on him. He also heard a peculiar *tchew . . . tchew . . . tchew,* and it dawned on him that this was the sound of rounds whistling down the street. That snapping noise? That was bullets passing close enough for him to hear the little sonic boomlets as they zipped past.

Up the street from Stebbins, Captain Steele spotted a sniper one block west, on top of the Olympic Hotel, the tallest structure around. Steele roared, "Smith!" Corporal Smith came running. Steele pointed out the sniper and slapped his sharpshooter's back encouragingly. Both men took aim. Their target was more than 150 yards away. They couldn't see if they hit him, but after they fired, the Somali on the rooftop was not seen again.

When Wolcott's Black Hawk went down, the ground forces began moving from the target house to the crash site. Most of the force moved on foot. The rest would drive there in the Humvees and trucks. Stebbins ran with the D-Boys, who moved swiftly and confidently from block to block, pausing at each intersection to lay down covering fire as one by one they darted through the open spaces.

Lieutenant Perino and his men had moved down to a small tin shed, a porch, really, that protruded from an irregular gray stone wall. They were only about ten yards from the alley where *Super Six One* lay. Smith was crouched behind the shed, and Perino was just a few feet behind him. They were taking so much fire it was confusing. Rounds seemed to be coming from everywhere. Stone chips sprayed from the wall over Perino's head and rattled down on his helmet. He saw a Somali with a gun on the opposite side of the street, about twenty yards away, behind a tree. Perino saw the muzzle flash and could tell this was where some of the incoming rounds were coming from. It would be hard to hit the guy with a rifle shot, but Smith had a grenade launcher on his M-16 and might be able to drop a 203 round near enough to hurt the guy. He moved up to tap Smith on the shoulder—there was too much noise to communicate any way other than face-to-face—when bullets began popping loudly through the shed. The lieutenant was on one knee and a round spat up dirt between his legs.

Most of the men across the street heard the round hit Smith with a hard, ugly slap. Smith seemed just startled at first. He rolled to his side and, like he was commenting about someone else, remarked with surprise, "I'm hit!" Perino helped move him against the wall. Now Smith was screaming, "I'm hit! I'm hit!" Perino pressed a field dressing into the wound but blood spurted out forcefully around it.

"I've got a bleeder here!" Perino shouted across the street.

Delta medic Sergeant Kurt Schmid dashed toward them across Marehan Road. Together, they dragged Smith back into a courtyard. Schmid tore off Smith's pant leg. When he removed the battle dressing, blood projected out of the wound in a long pulsing spurt. This was bad.

Smith was alert and terrified and in terrible pain. The medic first tried applying direct pressure to the wound, which proved excruciating and obviously ineffective. Bright red blood continued to gush from the hole in Smith's leg. The medic tried jamming Curlex gauze into the hole. Then he checked Smith over.

"Are you hurt anywhere else?" he asked.

"I don't know."

Schmid searched for an exit wound and found none. He could deduce the path the bullet had taken. It had entered Smith's thigh and traveled up into his pelvis. A gunshot wound to the pelvis is one of the worst. The aorta splits in the lower abdomen, forming the left and right iliac arteries. As the iliac arteries emerge from the pelvis, they branch into the exterior and deep femoral arteries, the primary avenues for blood to the lower half of the body. The bullet had clearly pierced one of the femoral arteries. Schmid applied direct pressure to Smith's abdomen, right above the pelvis where the artery splits. He explained what he was doing. He'd already run two IVs into Smith's arm, using 14-gauge large-bore needles, and he was literally squeezing the plastic bag to push sodium-rich replacement fluids into him. Smith's blood formed an oily pool that shone dully on the dirt floor of the courtyard.

The medic took comfort in the assumption that a rescue convoy would arrive shortly. Another treatment tactic, a very risky one, would be to begin directly transfusing Smith, which is rarely done on the battlefield. The medics carried IV fluids with them but not blood. Schmid would have to find someone with the same blood type and attempt a direct transfusion. This was likely to create more problems; Smith could react badly to the transfusion. Schmid decided not to attempt it. What the Ranger needed was a doctor, pronto.

"Oh, shit! Oh, shit! I'm gonna die! I'm gonna die!" Smith shouted. He knew he had an arterial bleed. The medic talked to him, tried to calm him down. The only way to stop the bleeding was to find the severed artery and clamp it. Otherwise it was like trying to staunch a fire hose by pushing down on it through a mattress. He had Smith lean back.

"This is going to be very painful," Schmid told the Ranger apologetically. "But I have to do this to help you."

"Give me some morphine for the pain!" Smith demanded.

"I can't," Schmid told him. In Smith's state, morphine could kill him—after he'd lost so much blood, his pressure was precariously low. Morphine would further lower his heart rate and slow his respiration, exactly what Smith did not need.

The young Ranger bellowed as the medic reached with both hands and tore open the entrance wound. Schmid tried to shut out the fact that there were living nerve endings beneath his fingers. It was hard. He had formed a bond with Smith; they were in this together. But to save the young Ranger, he had to treat him like an inanimate object, a machine that was broken and needed fixing. He continued to root for the artery. He picked through the open upper thigh, reaching up to

Smith's pelvis, parting layers of skin, fat, muscle, and vessel, probing through pools of blood. He couldn't find it. Once severed, the artery had evidently retracted up into Smith's abdomen. The medic stopped. The only recourse now would be to cut into the abdomen and hunt for the severed artery and clamp it. But that would mean still more pain and blood loss. Every time the medic reached into the wound, Smith lost more blood. Schmid and Perino were covered with it. Blood was everywhere. It was hard to believe Smith had any more to lose. "It hurts really bad," he kept saying. "It really hurts." In time his words and movements became slower, labored. He was in shock.

Schmid was beside himself. He had squeezed six liters of fluid into the young Ranger and was running out of bags. He had tried everything and was feeling desperate and frustrated and angry. He got one of the men to continue applying pressure on the wound and conferred with Perino.

"If I don't get him out of here *right now,* he's gonna die," Schmid pleaded.

The lieutenant radioed Captain Steele.

—*Sir, we need a medevac. A Little Bird or something. For Corporal Smith. We need to extract him now.*

Steele relayed this on the command net. It was tough to get through. It was nearly five o'clock and growing dark. The original convoy of vehicles had gotten lost and suffered high casualties. It had returned to the base. Steele learned that there would be no relief for some time. Putting another bird down in their neighborhood was out of the question.

The captain radioed back Perino and told him that Smith would just have to hang on for the time being.

Specialist Stebbins shook with fear. Having his friends around kept him going, but that was about all that did. You could be prepared for the sights and sounds and smells of war, but the horror of it, the blood and gore and heart-rending screams of pain, the sense of death perched right on your shoulder, breathing in your ear, there was no preparation for that. Things felt balanced on an edge, threatening at any moment to spin out of control. Was this what he had wanted so badly? An old platoon sergeant had told him once, "When war starts, a soldier wants like hell to be there, but once he's there, he wants like hell to come home."

Private Heard was beside Stebbins when a burst of rounds hit his M-60, disabling it permanently. Heard now drew his 9mm handgun and fired. Squinting down the alley into the setting sun, Stebbins could see the white shirts of Somali fighters. There were dozens of them. Groups would come running out and fire volleys up the alley, and then duck back behind cover. Over his right shoulder, across Marehan Road and down the alley, Stebbins could hear the rescue guys hammering at the wreck, still trying to free Wolcott's body. The sky was getting darker, and there was still no sign of the ground convoy. Where were they?

Everyone dreaded the approaching darkness. One distinct advantage U.S. soldiers have wherever they fight is their night-vision technology, their Night Observation Devices (NODs), but they had left them back at the hangar. The NODs were worn draped around the neck when not in use, and weighed probably less than a pound, but they were clumsy, annoying, and very fragile. It was an easy choice to leave them behind on a daylight mission. Now the force faced the night thirsty, tired, bleeding, running low on ammo, and without one of their biggest technological advantages. Stebbins gazed out at the giant orange ball easing behind the buildings to the west and had visions of a pot of fresh-brewed coffee out there somewhere, waiting for him.

When shadows fell over the alley, it became easier for Stebbins and Heard to find the Sammies who were shooting at them from windows and doorways. Their muzzle flashes gave away their positions clearly. Stebbins squeezed off rounds carefully, trying to conserve ammo. Heard was shooting now with an M-16 he had gotten from one of the wounded Rangers. He tapped Stebbins on the shoulder and shouted, "Steb, I just want you to know in case we don't get out of this, I think you're doing a great job."

Then the ground around them shook. Stebbins heard a shattering *kabang! kabang! kabang!*—the sound of big rounds smashing into the stone wall of the corner where they had taken cover. He was engulfed in smoke. The wall that had been their shield for more than an hour began to come apart. Somebody with a big gun down the alley had zeroed in on them. After the first shattering volley, Stebbins stepped out into the alley and returned fire at the window where he had seen the muzzle flash. Then he ducked back behind his corner, took a knee, and kept firing rounds in the same place.

Kabang! kabang! kabang! Three more ear-shattering rounds hit the corner and Stebbins was knocked backward and flat on his ass. It was as though someone had pulled him from behind with a rope. He felt no pain, just a shortness of breath. The explosions or the way he had slammed into the ground had sucked the air right out of him. He was dazed and covered with white powder from the pulverized mortar of the wall. He felt angry. *The son of a bitch almost killed me!*

"You okay, Stebby? You okay?" asked Heard.

"I'm fine, Brian. Good to go."

Stebbins stood up, cursing at full throttle as he stepped back out into the alley and resumed firing at the window. To other Rangers watching, it looked like somebody had flipped a switch inside Stebbins. He was a changed man, a wild animal, dancing around, shooting like a madman.

Then there came a *whooosh* and a cracking explosion and both Stebbins and Heard screamed and disappeared in a ball of flame. Stebbins woke up flat on his back again. He had the same feeling as before, like he'd been punched in the solar plexus. He gasped for air and tasted dust and smoke. Up through the swirl he saw darkening blue sky and two clouds. Then Heard's face came swimming into view.

"Stebby, you okay? You okay, Stebby?"

"Yup, Brian. I'm okay," he said. "Just let me lay here for a couple of seconds."

"Okay."

Stebbins figured he'd been hit in the chest by stones flying off the wall, enough to knock him over and out, but not enough to penetrate his body armor and seriously hurt him. Stebbins watched some lights flick on in the distance and was reminded that they were in the middle of a big city, and somewhere life was proceeding normally. There were fires burning back near the Olympic Hotel, where they had dropped in. It seemed like ages ago. He thought that now that it was dark, maybe the Sammies would all put down their weapons and go home, and he and his buddies could walk back to the hangar and call it a night. Wouldn't that be nice?

As darkness fell, the force began to move into a building they had secured earlier. One by one, the men on his corner sprinted across the intersection. Stebbins and Heard waited their turn. The volume of fire had died down. *Okay, the big part of the war is over.* Stebbins then heard a whistling sound and turned in time to see what looked like a rock hurtling straight at him. It was going to hit him in the head.

He ducked and turned his helmet toward the missile, and then he vanished in fire and light.

Super Six Four pilot Durant didn't know how long he was out cold before the two Delta operators showed up. Sergeants Randy Shughart and Gary Gordon had volunteered to go in and try to keep the encircling Somali mob away from the downed helicopter until a rescue convoy could break through. The D-Boys lifted Durant and his crew out of the chopper and arranged them in a perimeter around it. They set the pilot down by himself on one side of the Black Hawk.

Durant still thought things were under control. His leg was broken but it didn't hurt. He was lying on his back, propped against a supply kit by a small tree, using his M-16 to ward off the occasional skinny who poked his head into the clearing. He could hear firing on the other side of the helicopter. He knew Ray Frank, his copilot, was hurt but alive. And there were the two D-Boys and his crew chiefs, Tommy Field and Bill Cleveland. He figured there were probably other members of the rescue team with them. It was only a matter of time before the vehicles showed up to take them out.

Then he heard one of the operators—it was Gordon—cry out that he was hit. Just a quick shout of anger and pain. He didn't hear the voice again.

The other one—Shughart—came back to Durant's side of the bird. "Are there weapons on board?" He asked.

There were. The crew chiefs carried M-16s. Durant told him where they were kept, and Shughart stepped into the craft and rummaged around and returned with both. He handed Gordon's weapon, a CAR-15, loaded and ready to fire, to Durant.

"What's the support frequency on the survival radio?" Shughart asked.

It was then that it dawned on Durant that they were stranded. The pilot felt a twist of alarm in his gut. If Shughart was asking how to set up communications, it meant he and Gordon had come in on their own. They *were* the rescue team. And Gordon had just been shot.

He explained standard procedure on the survival radio to Shughart and listened while Shughart called out.

—*We need some help down here.*

Shughart was told that a reaction force, hastily assembled from reserve Rangers, was on its way. Then he wished Durant luck, took the M-16s, and moved back around to the other side of the helicopter. Durant felt panicked now. He had to keep the Skinnies away. He could hear them talking behind the wall, so he fired into the tin. The voices behind the wall stopped. Then two Somalis tried to climb over the nose end of the chopper. He fired at them and they jumped back. He didn't know if he had hit them or not. A man tried to climb over the wall and Durant shot him. Another came crawling from around the corner with a weapon and Durant shot him. Then there came a mad fusillade on the other side of the helicopter that lasted for about two minutes. Over the din he heard Shughart cry out in pain. Then the noise stopped.

Terror washed over Durant. He heard the sounds of an angry mob. The crash had left the clearing littered with debris, and he heard a great shuffling sound as the mob pushed it away like some onrushing beast. There was no more shooting. The others must be dead. Durant knew what angry Somali mobs could do—gruesome, horrible things. That was now in store for him. His CAR-15 was empty. He had a pistol strapped to his side but he never even thought to reach for it. Why bother? It was over. He was done.

A man stepped around the nose of the helicopter. He seemed startled to find Durant. The man shouted and more Skinnies came racing around. It was time to die. Durant placed the empty weapon across his chest, folded his hands over it, and just turned his eyes to the sky as the mob closed over him. They were screaming things he couldn't understand. A man struck him in the face with a rifle butt, breaking his nose and shattering the bone around his eye. People pulled at his arms and legs, and tore at his clothes. They were unfamiliar with the plastic snaps of his gear, so Durant reached down and squeezed them open. He gave himself over to them. His boots were yanked off, his survival vest, and his shirt. A man half unzipped his pants, but when he saw that Durant wore no underwear (for comfort in the equatorial heat), he zipped the trousers back up. They also left on his brown T-shirt. All the while he was being kicked and hit. A young man leaned down and grabbed at the green ID card Durant wore around his neck. He stuck it in Durant's face and shouted, "Ranger, Ranger, you die Somalia!"

Then someone threw a handful of dirt in his face, which went into his mouth. Someone tied a rag or a towel over the top of his head and eyes, and the mob hoisted him up in the air, partly carrying and partly dragging him. He felt the broken end of his femur pierce the skin in the back of his leg and poke through. He was buffeted from all sides, kicked, hit with fists, rifle butts. He could not see where they were taking him. He was engulfed in a great wave of hate and anger. Someone, he thought a woman, reached out and grabbed his penis and testicles and yanked at them.

And in this agony of fright, suddenly Durant left his body. He was no longer at the center of the crowd, he was in it, or above it, perhaps. He was observing the crowd attacking him. Apart somehow. And he felt no pain and the fear lessened and then he passed out.

Specialist Stebbins had his eyes closed but he still saw bright red when the grenade exploded. He felt searing flames and then he just felt numb. He smelled burned hair and dust and hot cordite and he was tumbling, mixed up with Heard, until they both came to rest sitting upright, staring at each other.

"Are you okay?" Heard asked after a long moment.

"Yeah, but I don't have my weapon."

Stebbins crawled back to his position. He found his M-16 in pieces. There was a barrel but no handgrip. The dust was still thick in the air; he could feel it up his nose and in his eyes and could taste it. He could also taste blood. He figured he'd busted his lip. He needed another weapon. He stood up and started for the door of the courtyard where the D-Boys were holed up, figuring he'd grab one of the wounded's rifles, but he fell down. He got up and took a step and then fell down again. His left leg and foot felt like they were asleep. After falling the second time, he walked, dragging his leg, toward the courtyard.

Air Force medic Tim Wilkinson grabbed hold of Stebbins, who was covered with dirt and powder and dust; his pants were mostly burned off, and he was bleeding from wounds up and down his leg. He was groggy and seemed not to have noticed his injuries.

"Just let me sit down for a few minutes," Stebbins said. "I'll be okay."

The medic helped Stebbins limp into a back room where the other wounded were gathered. It was dark, and Stebbins smelled blood and sweat and urine. The RPG that had exploded outside had briefly set fire to the house, and there was a thick layer of black smoke now hanging from the ceiling about halfway to the floor. The window was open to air things out, and everyone was sitting low. A Somali family of three that had been huddled on a couch moved to the floor so

Wilkinson could ease Stebbins down and begin cutting off his left boot with a big pair of shears.

"Hey, not my boots!" He complained. "What are you doing that for?"

Wilkinson slid the boot off slowly, removing the sock at the same time, and Stebbins was shocked to see a golf-ball-sized chunk of metal lodged in his foot. He realized then that he'd been hit. He had noticed that his trousers looked burned, and now, illuminated by the medic's white light, he saw that the blackened, flaking patches along his leg were skin. He felt no pain, just numbness. The fire from the explosion had instantly cauterized all his wounds. He could see the whole lower left side of his body was burned. Stebbins thrust his hand back into his butt pack for a cigarette and found the pack had been burned as well. Wilkinson wrapped Stebbins's foot.

"You're out of action," he said. "Listen, you're numb now but it's gonna go away. All I can give you is some Percocet." He handed Stebbins a tablet and some iodized water in a cup. Wilkinson also handed him an M-16. "Here's a gun. You can guard this window."

"Okay."

"But as your health-care professional, I feel I should warn you that narcotics and firearms don't mix."

Stebbins just shook his head and smiled.

He kept hearing sounds coming up the alley. But there was no one there. His mind was playing tricks on him. Once or twice he shouted in panic and blasted a few rounds out the window, but it was just shadows. Finally he was left to sit there alone, his pants blown off, clutching his rifle. He realized he had to urinate badly. There was no place to go. So he just released the flow where he sat. It felt great. He looked up at the Somali family and gave them a weak smile.

"Sorry about the couch," he said.

Delta medic Schmid was growing increasingly desperate in his efforts to save Jamie Smith's life. He had relayed an urgent request for blood, but when a Black Hawk risked getting shot down to drop supplies, there was no blood on board. Schmid figured the blood supply must be stretched thin dealing with all the casualties. He had heard on the radio that the docs back at the base were drawing blood from donors to meet the sudden demand.

He kept working on Smith, even though it now felt hopeless. He had Perino and others in the courtyard take turns pressing into Smith's lower abdomen to keep pressure over the femoral artery. The medic had finally relented and given Smith a morphine drip. It had quieted the corporal. He was still conscious, but just barely. He looked pale and distant. He had begun to make peace with dying. He talked about his family. His father, James Senior, had been a Ranger in Vietnam and had lost a leg in combat. His younger brother Mike was planning to enlist and enter Ranger school. Mike's twin, Todd, also wanted to join. Jamie had grown up wanting to be nothing else. He had played football and lacrosse in high school in northern New Jersey, and he had done well enough in his classes to graduate, which was good enough. He hadn't been interested in books or school; he knew what he wanted to be. Nothing could deter him. Not even the scare his father had tried to put in him, speaking to him graphically about the horrors he had seen and experienced in 'Nam. Three years earlier, when he was still in basic training, Smith had written to his father: "Today while walking back from lunch I saw two Rangers walking through the company area. It's the dream of being one of those guys in faded fatigues and a black beret that keeps me going." Smith asked the medic to tell his parents and family good-bye and to tell them that he had been thinking of them as he died, and that he loved them. They said prayers together.

"Hold tight," Schmid told the dying corporal. "We're working on getting you out of here. I'm doing everything I can."

Away from Smith, the medic kept telling Perino: "We need help. He's not going to make it."

But how to convey the urgency with so much else going on? The resupply had delivered more IV fluids, and Schmid pumped those into Smith, but the kid had lost too much blood. He needed a doctor and a hospital. Even that might not be enough to save him. He was just barely alive.

Nobody wanted to write off Jamie Smith. Both of the ground convoys had failed. Commanders back at the base were piecing together a giant rescue effort, but it was taking too much time. So they reconsidered landing a helicopter to take him out with another badly wounded Ranger. The pilots were ready to try it. The officers at the scene of Wolcott's crash were asked if they could adequately secure a landing zone. Lieutenant Perino consulted with one of the veteran

Delta sergeants, who told him they could get a chopper in, but they damn sure wouldn't get it back out.

Captain Scott Miller, the ranking officer on the ground, radioed the answer:

—*We are willing to try and secure a site, but there are RPGs all over the place. It is going to be really hard to get a bird in there and get it out. I'm afraid that we are just going to lose another bird.*

Delta commander Gary Harrell delivered the reluctant verdict from the command helicopter:

—*We are going to have to hold on the best we can with those casualties and hope the ground reaction force gets there on time.*

Not long afterward, Smith started hyperventilating, and then his heart stopped. Schmid went into full emergency mode. He tried CPR for several rotations, compressions and ventilations, then he injected drugs straight into the Ranger's heart. It was no use. He was gone.

It was not until early the next morning that the giant rescue convoy, soldiers from the Tenth Mountain Division, along with Pakistani tanks and Malaysian Armored Personnel Carriers (APCs), fought their way through to the embattled, encircled remnants of Task Force Ranger. After freeing Cliff Wolcott's body from the wreckage, the force was evacuated to a large, decaying soccer stadium in northern Mogadishu.

Stebbins had spent three stifling hours inside a Malaysian APC with other wounded men. He sucked in large lungfuls of fresh air when the hatch of his APC finally swung open. He helped get some of the others off and then a stretcher was lifted on for him. He was dragging himself toward it when a Tenth Mountain sergeant shouted, "Don't make him crawl, boys," and suddenly hands came in from all sides and Stebbins was lifted gently. Essentially naked from the waist down, he was placed among a group of his buddies. Sergeant Aaron Weaver brought him a hot cup of coffee.

"Bless you, my son," said Stebbins. "Got any cigarettes?"

He didn't. Stebbins asked everyone who walked past, without luck. He finally grabbed a soldier from the Tenth by the arm and pleaded, "Listen, man, you got to find me a fucking cigarette." One of the Malaysian drivers walked up and handed him a cigarette. The driver bent down to light it and then gave him the rest of the pack. When Stebbins tried to return it, the Malaysian took it and stuffed it in Stebbins's shirt pocket.

Ranger Sergeant First Class Sean Watson approached.

"Stebby, I hear you did your job. Good work," he said, then he reached down and took a two-inch flap of cloth from Stebbins's shredded trousers and tried to place it over his genitals. They both laughed.

There was little laughter that day or in the days to come. As the force regrouped at the base, the men learned the full extent of their losses. Nearly a third of the Ranger task force was flown out to hospitals. Black Hawk pilot Mike Durant was being held captive somewhere in the city. The bodies of his crew and the two Delta operators who had come to help him were dragged through the streets of the city by jeering Somali mobs, and President Clinton hastily called off Task Force Ranger's mission against the warlord Aidid. The task force arrested twenty-four Somalis that day, among them the two top Aidid lieutenants they were after. But it was a Pyrrhic victory. Horrified by the losses, America would withdraw completely from Somalia.

Delta operators Randy Shughart and Gary Gordon became the first American soldiers to receive the Congressional Medal of Honor since Vietnam. Durant, who was released after eleven days in captivity, was awarded the Distinguished Flying Cross. Specialist John Stebbins, the Ranger company clerk, received a silver star for his heroism.

Nobody won the battle of Mogadishu, but like all important battles, it changed the world. It ended a brief, heady period of post–cold war innocence, a time when America and its allies felt they could sweep venal dictators and tribal hatred from the planet as easily and relatively bloodlessly as Saddam Hussein had been swept from Kuwait in 1991. Whenever America has considered sending troops to troubled spots around the world ever since, the cautionary mantra has been "Remember Mogadishu."

FEBRUARY 1999

THE FIREFIGHTERS

I MET THIS FIREFIGHTER from Delaware on the Saturday after it happened. His name was Don, and he'd driven up right after the towers collapsed. For days, firemen had been coming in from everywhere. All along Chambers Street, in downtown New York, men slept in vehicles bearing the insignia of the Chicago FD, the LAFD, the NOFD, and lots of other FDs whose initials were unrecognizable to me. It was about 7:15 P.M., which meant it was time for the sun to set with a kind of defiant beauty through the smoke of the dead buildings while workmen cranked up the necks of the gawky, powerful lights that were starting to flicker on and make the whole pit look even more like a film set. Don was showing me how, even when they were down the road five hundred feet, he could tell a New York firefighter from the various other FDs that were wandering down West Street, the site of a bizarre street fair of heavy equipment, Japanese TV crews, mountains of donated Evian, and men in every kind of uniform imaginable.

Don didn't really have a solid theory about what gave someone away as FDNY. He'd just point into the gloaming and say "New York" or "Not New York." If I had to pinpoint what was different about them, I'd say the New Yorkers looked as if they'd practically been born in their equipment. They were—and there's no other word for it—brawny. And all of them walked in the perpetual slow motion of the astronaut making his way to the launch pad. Everything about them said: Men with a job to do. Don, the firefighter from Delaware, in his wraparound shades, said simply that these guys were professionals, and he was nearly dumbstruck with admiration.

A steady stream of New York firemen moved in and out of the World Trade Center staging area where they were leading a twenty-four-hour-a-day rescue effort. The crowds hushed as the firemen drew near at 3 A.M., walking through the powdery light in their bunker gear, their Irish and Italian names sparkling in reflective tape at the bottom of their jackets. There was a lot of confusion about what and how to feel in the wake of something that'll take us years to sort through, both physically and mentally. But there was no ambivalence about the firemen. These were the walking angels of the city.

Most of them have been reluctant to talk on the record about what they experienced. There's a strong code of brotherhood-over-individual that seems at once antiquated and impressive, like some ancient culture preserved among us. Some of them decided not to give their last names to the reporters who recorded the stories that follow, because that would make them one particular set of DNA instead of a part of the FDNY. Their plain-spoken response was usually, "We're just doing our job." They are, as Don says, professionals. But remember what they do to collect their salaries. The FDNY practices what they call aggressive interior attack, which means they race into any disaster scene with reckless abandon. It's not that they're especially crazy firefighters; it's that Manhattan is an especially crazy place to put out fires. Practically every alarm is a high-rise fire, which are notoriously unfightable, and because so many people and buildings are packed together it means that any time the department is called, it's possible massive death and destruction will ensue. In the case of the World Trade Center, aggressive interior attack meant that as many firemen as possible ran as fast as they could into the towers and began climbing toward the fires a hundred floors up. In the 136 years that the department has existed, 774 men had lost their lives in the line of duty. And then, in two hours, they'd lost half that many.

In the string of perfect, crystalline autumn days that followed the attack, everyone suddenly remembered where their local firefighters worked. Makeshift memorials sprouted up at every station in the city—doorways were decked with candles and deli flowers wrapped in cellophane, personal notes were taped to the bricks and stuffed into seams in the woodwork (the way people stuff prayers into the Western Wall in Jerusalem). There were big posters that people signed with their well-wishes, like what they do for the high school football team when they go to the state championship. Residents came to the station doors to shake the hands of the firefighters, thank them personally, and drop off donations. The charity fell into roughly three categories: bottled water, baked goods, and socks. Thousands of dollars in Gold Toes and Jockeys and Haneses, in Entenmann's raspberry strudels, Chips Ahoy cookies, doughnuts from all the city's doughnut emporiums. With none of the firemen, apparently, feeling much like eating pastry or changing their socks, the hulking piles sat on tables you could barely squeeze past.

All the New York firemen you saw at those stations, standing around in their duty-blue shorts and T-shirts, folding hose and cleaning boots and waiting to go back to ground zero, were walking stories of incredible luck. There wasn't a man who didn't feel lucky to have a heartbeat. That's part of their story. But if you can call them lucky, they're the unluckiest lucky people in the world. The FDNY were proclaimed as heroes, but they're the kind of heroes no one wants to be. They're heroic in their loss, in their disproportionate death and devastation. That's part of their story, too.

Out on the walls, among the taped flags and sentimental poetry, the notes from the neighborhood kids were the most arresting artifacts. *Thanks for being a hero*, they said. *Thanks for helping find the dead people.* Even, strangely, lots of signs that read, *Thanks for saving the World Trade Center.* On Manhattan's Upper West Side, a girl named Jessica, seven, wrote, *Thanks for going into the World Trade Center.* Then she wrote, *Thanks for saving people's lives,* only that line was crossed out. Then it just said, *Thanks for being firemen.*

— D E V I N   F R I E D M A N

Heinz Kothe
Ladder 12, Manhattan

We were assigned to get people out of the upper floors of the Marriott Hotel. We went up to eighteen and nineteen, knocking on doors, making sure there was no one there. We saw a few civilians, and we chased them out and told them to take the stairs. No one had any idea the towers would collapse, and there was no smoke in the building, so we were just going through as efficiently as possible. There were eight of us up there, and we were on our way up to nineteen and getting ready to walk through the door—and the south tower comes down. We had no idea what had happened. It just rocked the building. It blew the door to the stairwell open, and it blew the guys up near the door halfway down a flight of stairs. I got knocked down to the landing. The building shook like buildings just don't shake.

We just said, "We've gotta get the hell out of here." So we made it down to the fifth floor. There had been no one on the radio, but about then we started getting Maydays. From Ladder 4: "Mayday, Mayday! I'm trapped, and I don't know where I am." We tried to find out where he was. We called the south-tower command post, because we didn't know where Ladder 4 was. But nobody answered. They were all wiped out. There was no one to talk to.

We kept talking to this guy on the radio while we worked on getting out. There were three civilians with us at this point—three men we had chased out of the building—and we flew down those stairs so fast we caught up to them. "I'm losing consciousness. I'm losing consciousness," he was saying on the radio. We told him to turn on his pass alarm, this little alarm on your mask that goes off once it's stationary for thirty seconds. He says, "I'm pinned—I can't turn on my pass alarm."

The two guys who went to go look for him, Angel Juarbe and Lieutenant Petti, are missing. And Mullan, who stayed back at the rubble to show Juarbe and Petti how we'd gotten out—he's missing, too.

So we got through the rubble and found another flight of stairs. They were in terrible shape, and we were trying to get down them, and then we heard this roar. And I thought it was another jet. So I yelled, "Here comes another one! Holy shit!" Turns out it was the second tower coming down. The other guys—there were five of us, plus the three civilians—dove under shit and tried to find something hard, something that was at least connected to something else. I was standing up on the third floor holding on to a pillar, thinking a piece of concrete is going to land on me, a piece of steel is going to take me out. This is taking too long, this is taking too long, I kept thinking—my luck's gonna run out. And then it just stopped. And you could feel the rush of air.

With the amount of dust, I couldn't see my hand in front of my face. I didn't have my mask on, because there'd been no smoke. It was hell trying to catch your breath. Imagine trying to swallow cotton balls. I was spitting out chunks of that white dust. I couldn't see. I must have stood there a minute? I have no idea, I can't put time on anything anymore. I tried to move. Next thing I know I was sliding. I slid on my side, then on my belly; I ping-ponged off things and I stopped only because my feet hit the ground. I don't know how long I fell, but it was long enough for me to scream, "Shit, shit, shit," three times like that.

I don't know if I was inside the building or outside the building. I heard some voices—the guys I was with and the civilians—and I said, "I've fallen and I can't get to you guys. I hurt my foot and I can't get back up." All I could think of at this point was getting out of this build-ing. I was physically, emotionally exhausted. And what was unex-pected for me is that, when the smoke was clearing, there was nothing left. It was absolutely silent. I expected to see bodies. I saw more death going into the building than I saw coming out—from the people jumping, the people in the airplane who looked like they'd been through a meat grinder. There had been limbs, and torsos. And coming out, there was nothing.

I walked 150 yards before I saw anybody. That walk, everything was so quiet. Chunks of concrete, steel, beams just lying around. Crushed firetrucks, civilian cars overturned, smashed police cars with their lights still on, these blue lights sweeping through the dust. There was fire billowing out a window across from the World Trade Center, but you can't hear it, and there's no one there to see it. It was like everyone was just erased. It even crossed my mind that this was a nuclear blast.

My foot started to really hurt, and I stopped walking, and I sat down. That's when I saw other guys staggering out. We were able to calm those three civilians down, get them through the rubble. One of the guys I was with from Ladder 12, Angel Rivera, he was carrying one of them. A cop came up and Angel handed the guy off to the cop. When he went with the cop, the guy turned back and looked at Angel. He had tears streaming down his face, but maybe it was all the dust. He just looked at him, and he didn't have to say anything. It was a look like, "Thank God for you." Angel's having a tough time, and I just keep trying to remind him of that look.

I see now in the newspaper where I was, and what happened to the building. This was the only corner of the building that survived. I'll tell you what, the only hotel I'm ever staying at from now on is a Marriott, fourth floor or lower, the southwest corner. It's a lucky place for me.

Chief John Pritchard
Battalion 41, Brooklyn

I wasn't working. I was jogging with another fireman when the call came. They recalled the whole fire department right after the first tower collapsed. My daughter, Laurie, called me on the cell phone. She was hysterically crying and she asked me to come home right away. I lost my wife recently, and Laurie is an only child and was really worried. She knows what we do and she didn't want me running in there, because she didn't want to be alone. But she understood when

I told her that her mother went through this for thirty-eight years. Now it looks like she is, too. Because that's where I belong.

There are five thousand people missing today. I would venture to say that there were forty thousand people in those two buildings. The way I see it, three hundred firefighters evacuated more than thirty thousand people. And then paid the price—from the probie with six months on the job to our chief of the department. Death is indiscriminate.

From the pictures, it looks like the men are just looking on the surface. But they're crawling into spaces where no human being should even think about going, looking for their brothers, looking for workers. I'm so proud of them. With fire around them and smoke and a beam so hot it's burning them through their turnout coats, they're still looking. There are garbage-can-size holes that open up into forty feet of space, and you can hear the ground rumbling around, and they're crawling in there.

They would do anything that we asked, with unquestionable loyalty. People say it's a quasi-military outfit. It is a *military* outfit. You give an order, it is done. There are never any questions asked about "Why?" or "Where did that come from?" All we do is try and show them the way to go and make sure they don't get hurt. Because they're going to do whatever it takes. We tried to get them to go home and take a rest. But we had ten thousand guys who wouldn't go home.

I can't even explain it. It's not like any job in the world. They don't do it for money. Or fame, politics, whatever. I just wish I could relay that to you, but it's hard. You've got to be part of it to understand. You always hear people saying that the tradition lives on, father and son. This is one of the times you wish it didn't. Because now the fathers are looking for their sons. And the sons are looking for their fathers.

Francisco Cabrera
Ladder 8, Manhattan

What can I say that hasn't been said already? I've only been on the job for, like, less than a year. To be honest, I was scared. I thought the rest of the building was going to fall on me. I lost the officer I was supposed to be with. I was wandering by myself, and I saw a guy with a hose and I could tell he was tired, so I was like, "Let me help you." So he left; I don't know where he went. And I'm there by myself, putting out this geyser of flame with hardly any water. There's barely any pressure. Hoses were ripping apart, leaking.

You're there and you know something could happen to you. But you have to do your job. You want to go and help each other because you live together, you cook for each other, and that guy who could be under the rubble, you've met his wife, and you've seen his kids.

Richie Murray
Engine 205, Brooklyn

I was at home in Staten Island when I saw the fire coming from the north tower. I knew I had to get there immediately, so I ran to my car and drove to pick up two of my guys on the way to our station. We picked up our gear, then six of us—four in the car and two in the open trunk—drove across the Brooklyn Bridge.

We saw our fire engine parked near Liberty Street. Our guys told us that there were people trapped in a Burger King, so six of us made a run down the block to see if we could do anything. That's when the south tower came down on us. I saw a piece of metal the size of a football field coming at us, so me and a buddy dived under a tractor-trailer. There was a volcanic explosion, and everything was filled with hot ash and smoke. Neither of us had brought face masks, and we started losing oxygen, so we held our breath and waited until the smoke started to clear. It seemed like an hour, but it was probably only a few minutes before we ran to find our guys and our engine.

I'm a chauffeur, which means I drive the engine and operate the pumping system. I set up next to the Marriott Hotel and started pumping the water from the river. I stayed there for hours, but my eyes were getting sore from the smoke and ash. This EMT took a look at my eyes and said, "You're coming with me, whether you like it or not." He took me to Cabrini Medical Center, where the doctor diagnosed me with second-degree burns to my eyes. I had to be washed down and decontaminated before they could take me inside the hospital, so they took me to this staging area and told me to take off my clothes. I couldn't see, so I asked the doctor if there were any girls looking. He said that there were nurses there, so I yelled, "Take a look, ladies!" It wasn't until I got home that I realized that I'd been parading around with filthy underwear on.

We're still missing seven guys, and I'd really appreciate it if you'd print their names: Lt. Bobby Regan, Lt. Bobby Wallace, Pete Vega, Joe Agnello, Scott Davidson, Leon Smith, Vernon Cherry.

Lt. Arthur Mezzano
Engine 309, Brooklyn

We got the call at 10:30 and were within a few blocks when the second tower started to collapse. We were driving south on Broadway, about three or four blocks north, and we could see it coming down. So we made a quick left, down toward Water Street, the whole time looking in the mirrors watching this thing fall, and then a ten-story black cloud of debris and dust rushed down all the side streets. It was so much darker than nighttime. Dust is a solid—light doesn't shine through it like it does through darkness. We didn't wait; we just drove slow, very slow.

Finally we parked about three blocks away—it was as close as we could get, because of all the other engines that were there—and made our way on foot. We spent about thirteen hours there, and everything was a really frustrating, slow process. We helped a little with debris removal and then were assigned to establish a water supply, which meant we had to stretch a three-and-a-half-inch hose from the intersection of Liberty and West Streets, the southwest corner of the towers, all the way down to the Hudson River, where the fireboats were, because the hydrants were out of service. We worked on getting the water to two or three different engines. They used it to hose down the debris pile and the surrounding buildings—at that time two buildings still had fires in them. Two buildings just at that intersection. I don't even know what happened at the other three intersections.

Joe
Chicago Fire Department

I woke up Tuesday and I'm in bed with the radio going when I hear a plane's hit the World Trade Center. I even saw the other plane hit on TV, and I couldn't fathom what was going on. And then the first tower goes down and the first thing I think, sitting in my bed, is: We just lost a hundred guys. We just lost a hundred brothers. It was personal. That's why I came here. I mean, if you're a fireman, you're part of a family. I don't care where you're from. So many of us came here because we're all doing the same job—the greatest job in the world. I shit you not.

It took us like thirteen hours to get here from Chicago. My friend drove us in his Suburban, and we got in around 3 A.M. Thursday morning. And we drove right down to the site. This was my first time in New York—I mean, I never even saw the World Trade Center when it was standing. And what we saw that night, the TV does no justice. I went from being sick and wanting to throw up to wanting to cry to being proud that I'm here—every emotion, you know?

The other night, we got in there on the bucket brigades, just these lines of firemen hauling out debris, looking for body parts. I hope we get a chance to get in there again, but it's pretty closed off right now if you're not FDNY. It's frustrating, but I'm not ready to go home yet. I don't know when I will be. I guess I'll just stay here and sleep in my car.

Lt. Vincent Bonura
Ladder 8, Manhattan

I saw something out of the corner of my eye and I turned around and I saw a guy just explode in front of me. And after that, I saw about ten people jumping from the eightieth, ninetieth floors and hitting the pavement like explosions. I saw this guy go through a Plexiglas marquee like a bullet and hit a car. It was just something that you could never forget. He just blew up. I lost it right there. I started screaming. I started crying like a baby. I was like, What am I doing here? That is probably one of the things that will stay in my head for life. I was close enough to see their faces coming down with their eyes wide open.

Tim
The Bronx

By the time we got there, both towers had collapsed. It looked like the Mount Saint Helens eruption. You know, with that fine, white powder covering everything. And it wasn't noisy like you would think because there were no machines there yet. It was like walking on snow. And I'm thinking, the night before I was bitching and moaning about the Giants' *Monday Night Football* debacle. The Giants!

I've been on the pile for the past thirty hours, just on the bucket brigade, creating these holes then going down there and seeing if we can find anyone. And the whole thing is just a mess—huge trucks are lying around like matchsticks. But we go on the mound and dig, with a lot of help from the ironworkers. Ironworkers are like angels on our shoulders. These guys, I tell you—I haven't seen them take a lunch break. Also, the sandhogs, the guys who build the water tunnels—those guys are tough as nails, too. They cut, and the ironworkers cut, and we dig. Then they hook up the cranes and cables. The police are right there with us, too, digging. I mean, they've got their guns on and shit, but they're in here with boots and shovels, crawling in the hole.

You can't tell what's a body part and what's not, because everything is covered in dust. Something lying there, it could be carpeting, it could be a finger or a hand. Once you touch it and it's soft you know. A lot of parts we put in the bucket—we have this location and it gets transferred to a bag. And, you know, any pictures, photographs, we've got a special bucket for that. Them morgue guys—man, I don't know how they do it.

I pulled out seven bodies today. Maybe I know these guys, I can't tell. I've been on the job over twenty years, so I know a lot of people. I saw the list of missing, but I stopped reading it by the time I got to the Ds. I thought I was going to throw up.

So when I find a body, see this flag [he pulls out an American flag folded inside his coat]? I put it over them when I find them. And when they go in the body bag, I take it off and I fold it up, and I keep looking.

Stan Jessamine
Engine 7, Manhattan

The first tower collapsed while I was at the station, and then when we got there, the north tower came down and it just enveloped us. We couldn't see or hear anything, but I guess we really didn't have to. I saw our rig, Number 7, and I knew our guys were inside, and that they were dead—they were all dead. See, we're one of the closest houses to the towers. Our guys were some of the first men in the first tower that was hit, and they were on their way up to put that fire out.

We spent that day just searching, trying to find anybody. I hooked up with a captain from another company and we were walking along West Broadway, coming upon engines that were destroyed and the water was still on—they were still hooked up to the hydrants. By afternoon, we knew the guys were gone, and we were sitting in the station where our truck used to be.

And then they came in. Capt. Dennis Carter first, looking shell-shocked, a very distant look on his face—the whole house could hardly believe it. Guys came in staggering, from all over the place. Like guys that came back from the dead. Covered in the dust, they even *looked* like they were back from the dead.

What happened was, as soon as the plane hit the second building—

and it shook the first tower—our captain thought, Something's wrong, and had the presence of mind to say, "Let's get out of here"—and they all headed back down the stairwell, down thirty flights of stairs, and got out. There are sixty guys in the house. Thirteen were on duty when we got the first alarm. And you know how many are missing? None. Nobody. We used to call ourselves the Magnificent Seven, like in the movie. We had it painted on the rig. But we got a new rig and we just put our new name on it: the Lucky 7.

Michael Kehoe
Engine 28, Manhattan

I don't remember anyone taking my picture, and don't know what floor it was. We were just trying to get up as fast as possible. Inside the north tower, the lobby was a mess. The elevators were blown out, glass was everywhere. People were streaming out. We found the stairwell and made our way up. It was crowded, but everyone was calm. As we went up, people kept saying, "Good luck," "Lots of luck," things like that.

I don't know how long it took, but when we reached the twenty-eighth floor, the whole building shook. Over the radio the chief said, "Everybody evacuate the building now." Later, I learned that was when the second plane hit the south tower. I am not a hero. The heroes are the guys who are still there. I was just doing my job like thousands of other firemen do every day.

John A. Greene
A Psychologist Who Specializes
in Counseling Firefighters

These guys are telling themselves they're going to find some people. But they haven't found a whole body yet. All they're finding is pieces. I talked to a chaplain, and he spent twelve hours blessing body parts. He said everyone was real respectful, letting him do his thing. But, you know, they're only getting hands, feet, and fingers. It'll take this department years to get over. I don't think they're even starting to deal with it yet. They can't. They've all got that thousand-yard stare. There's a thing in psychology called denial in service of the ego. That's what it is. They just keep working and keep going. They haven't processed it, because if they did, they'd melt down and be useless.

I'm on my way to a meeting with the families of the missing fire-fighters to explain support services and benefits to them and, Oh, by the way, bring your husband's fucking toothbrush for DNA identification. I'm not looking forward to it.

Robert Chyriwski
Engine 3, Manhattan

I had heard people talking about jumpers, but I'd never seen it. There's incredible heat, unbearable heat, and I guess they didn't want to get burned alive. Jumping would be a relief to them. I couldn't even look. The chief was announcing over the radio, "Watch out, watch out, there are jumpers." The people were jumping from the front, which is where we were trying to get in. The firefighters and all the other people are standing on the sidewalk. I believe two firefighters were killed by jumpers; I know of one death, personally. Then I start hearing this roar, and that was the noise of the upper floors where the fire was at Tower Two. And I look up and I see debris coming down. I said to myself, Oh, my God, they're all in there. All the firefighters are in there. This can't be happening.

Then it was just a matter of running, running as fast as you can. I was by myself, then I turned the corner and stopped, and then I started back. I was saying to myself, My God, did I just lose my company? I saw a telephone. Tried to call my wife but couldn't get through, so I called my mother and my wife's mother and told them I'm okay. I'm sitting there—I got myself a water—I'm sitting there with my head down and a guy says, "Buddy, are you okay?" I said, "I just lost some guys in my company." He said, "Here's a mask, let's go outside and see if we can find them." Next thing you know, my company is coming toward me. They were looking for me. Where they were, they were lucky to duck inside the parking garage. The door was open, so all the debris just went past them. It was a miracle.

NOVEMBER 2001

REPORTED BY BEN COURT, JOSH DEAN, SEAN FLYNN, TOM FOSTER, DEVIN FRIEDMAN, ALEX MARKELS, MICHAEL REY, AND DAVID WILLEY

FLIERS LIKE MY FATHER

by Stephen Rodrick

I N AN AIRLESS STATEROOM aboard the USS *Kitty Hawk*, I find my dead father.

Somewhere off the Vietnamese coast, the roar of an F/A-18 Hornet launching from the carrier's number two catapult blasts me awake. The crescendo releases me from a nightmare that has intermittently punctured my nights for twenty-three years. In the dream, a young man chases sky and sea off this very same ship. Then, his plane dips imperceptibly, taps the ocean, and disintegrates. All that is left behind is a jagged oil slick and shards from a white helmet floating on the sea.

Still groggy, I hear my roommate, Lieutenant Commander John Mann, a no-nonsense Hornet pilot, shaving just a few feet away. He slips on his flight suit for his first mission of the day and a moment later slams the door behind him. I detect a familiar scent, one that is flinty and masculine. I jump down from the top bunk and open the medicine cabinet. Inside is a blue bottle of Aqua Velva aftershave. I remove the cap and inhale.

And it is May 28, 1979. Upstairs in the master bedroom of a modest four-bedroom house in Oak Harbor, Washington, Commander Peter Rodrick is wearing a white undershirt and briefs. Gray creeps in at his temples. Staring intently into the mirror, he carefully places a small piece of yellow toilet paper near his chin. He always cuts himself there. He slaps on Aqua Velva and winces. In the mirror, he catches his twelve-year-old son peering around the corner. The boy's fingernails are black from folding copies of *The Seattle Times*.

"What's the matter, knucklehead?"

"I don't want you to go."

"Why?"

"I'm scared."

"You've never been before. Scared of what?"

"Scared something bad is going to happen."

His father tousles the boy's hair. "It'll be fine. Now, try and get along with your mom. Don't fight her on everything." He smiles. "Even if you're right."

The boy watches in silence as his father carefully slips into his uniform and trots down the stairs. At the bottom, he kisses his wife, who is grappling with their twenty-one-month-old daughter, trying to be brave. In fifteen years, she has moved six times as her husband has gone from flight school to squadron to staff college and then back to squadron. Over the past six years, she's raised their three children on her own while he's spent 1,200 days at sea. Today, he leaves for a six-month deployment in the Pacific, his third cruise flying an EA-6B Prowler, a radar-jamming plane, aboard the USS *Kitty Hawk.*

The couple's thirteen-year-old daughter, always stoic, throws her father's duffel bags into the Buick station wagon. In the garage, the pilot pauses for a moment and stares at his treasured white MGB. It's already up on blocks and covered with a tarp. A neighbor snaps a family photo in the front yard. Slivers of light flit through the evergreens. Everyone except the boy loads into the car for the fifteen-minute drive to Whidbey Island Naval Air Station. He has papers to deliver. As the car heads away, the boy gives a last wave. His father isn't looking.

After finishing his route, the boy stops by an old water tower. It's at the top of a hill separating two phases of subdivisions carved out of the pines. He tosses his bike down the hill and watches the spokes spin. He's been through this often enough to know what the next six months will hold. A sports and politics junkie living in a house full of females, he will retreat to his room. There, he'll lie on his bed and stare at skiing posters and NFL pennants, and toss an orange Nerf football off the ceiling, constructing an intricate fantasy world of triumphant campaigns and touchdown passes. He will feel alone. At school, he will see "underachiever" and "hyperactive" written on his report cards. There will be lectures about wasting God's gifts. His mother will cry. Every few months, a postcard will arrive from Hong Kong, Okinawa, or some other Shangri-La, exhorting him to do better.

Yet this tour will be different after all. On the Fourth of July, his father's dream will come true. Peter Rodrick will become commanding officer of his own squadron, VAQ-135, the Black Ravens. At the age of thirty-six, he will be one of the youngest skippers in the navy, on the fast track, maybe all the way to admiral. His wife and his mother will travel to the Philippines to attend the change-of-command ceremony.

And in November, the boy will fly to Honolulu and accompany his father back to San Diego aboard the *Kitty Hawk*. Finally, there will be time. Finally, he can come clean about faking sick so he could watch the Red Sox–Yankees one-game playoff last September. After all, the Sox are his dad's team. He'll understand. Finally, he can learn what his father does. He knows he flies jets off carriers, but how? Finally, he can ask him why things seem so hard all the time.

But on November 4, some ninety Americans are taken hostage in the U.S. embassy in Iran. Two weeks later, President Carter sends the *Kitty Hawk* to the Indian Ocean as a show of strength. The boy is unsure what that means. He just knows there will be no trip to Hawaii. His dad calls from a noisy bar in Manila and says he's sorry.

On the morning of November 28, the boy is trying unsuccessfully to skate backward at the Roller Barn for eighth-grade gym class. He can tell you the Electoral College breakdown of the Carter–Ford presidential election and the status of Kenny Stabler's wobbly knees, but when it comes to the things that confer acceptance upon boys— hitting a baseball, building a catapult for Webelos, skating back- ward—he is clumsy. He needs someone to show him how, someone to tell him that it really doesn't matter anyway. But that man is always 8,000 miles away.

So the boy falls on his ass. The burnouts snicker. At first, he is relieved when his gym teacher calls him over, because it stops the laugh- ter. But the teacher's normally exuberant face has gone flat. She points to a man standing by the snack bar. He wears a black uniform, white hat in hand. It is his father's best friend. The boy slowly skates over. The man hesitates, sits down next to him, and puts a hand on his knee.

"Your father has been in an accident."

He says there's hope; the helos are still looking. The boy doesn't believe him. He may be only thirteen, but he's grown up around the navy. If they haven't found him by now, they aren't going to. As the offi- cer drives him home, the world rushes toward him hotter and faster than before. He chokes back vomit. When they arrive at the house on North Conifer Drive, they see the base captain and the chaplain pulling out of the driveway in a black sedan. In the yard, his sisters walk hand in hand. Inside, the wives have already gathered. They smoke Vir- ginia Slims and laugh too loud. A still-hot casserole sits untouched on the table. His mother looks different; she became old the moment the doorbell rang.

That afternoon, it is confirmed that Commander Peter Rodrick and his three crew members, Lieutenant Commander William Coffey, Lieutenant James Brown Jr., and Lieutenant Junior Grade John Chorey are dead. There are no bodies to recover. The men leave four widows and seven children under the age of fifteen. The boy slips into his parents' bathroom. He breathes in deeply. Nothing. He looks in the medicine cabinet, but the bottle, and the smell, are gone.

As much as the triumph of the archers at Hastings or the unveiling of the Gatling gun in the Civil War, the United States navy's victory at Midway, in 1942, was a tectonic change in the history and practice of war. For the first time, a navy defeated an enemy without the fleets ever coming into direct contact, as planes launched from the USS *Enterprise*, the USS *Hornet*, and the USS *Yorktown* sank four of the Imperial Fleet's carriers, crippling Japan's hope for victory in World War II.

When the Cold War ended, however, critics of the navy argued that the aircraft carrier had outlived its usefulness. With smart bombs and long-range land-based bombers, how could anyone justify allocating billions of dollars each year to maintain a fleet of carriers? Then came September 11. The military's ability to strike Afghanistan quickly—without worrying about airstrips in queasy Arab countries—silenced many of the naysayers. From October 2001 to March 2002, Navy pilots flew 7,000 sorties during the war in Afghanistan, and America's twelve strategically placed aircraft carriers remain a linchpin in the country's ability to wage war. In no more than ten days, what the navy brass calls "four-and-a-half acres of American sovereignty" can be within striking distance of any country in the world. The deterrent effect is clear: Piss off Uncle Sam and you're going to have an eighty-plane mobile air base parked off your coast.

But that dominance comes at a price. The 6,900 pilots in the navy each train for hundreds of hours annually, far more than any other pilots in the world. For every hour an Iraqi pilot spends in the cockpit, an American spends twenty-five—launching from and landing on the decks of aircraft carriers again and again, engaging in mock dogfights, making countless simulated bombing runs. Ironically, it isn't just combat that makes a navy flier's job one of the most dangerous in the world, but also the training it takes to be ready for combat. The navy lost seven planes in combat during the Persian Gulf War, and none were lost to enemy fire during Operation Enduring Freedom in Afghanistan. Twenty-four U.S. planes crashed in training accidents during the Gulf War, and in 2000, a year without armed conflict, the navy alone lost twenty planes. It was its fifth-safest year in the past two decades. In all, the navy has endured 656 peacetime crashes in that time, which have killed 275 impeccably trained pilots.

Unlike those who are killed in action, these men are almost never recognized publicly. "Most mishaps occur at sea," says Captain Robert "Brick" Nelson, who works for the Chief of Naval Operations, analyzing how naval aviation can best contribute to the war on terrorism. "There's a small hometown news story and then the boys just don't come home. The public doesn't notice, and we don't expect them to."

Here's an example: The navy has never lost one of its prized EA-6B radar-jamming planes in combat. The Prowler is its official call name, but pilots have dubbed it the Sky Pig for its weight and lack of engine power. Manned by a four-person crew (pilot, navigator, and two radar-jamming officers), it has electronic equipment that is so secret that the pilot in the front seat doesn't have the security clearance to know what the two men in the back are doing. First commissioned in 1968, the Prowler has received several updates, but it still features few of the bells and whistles of the modern jet. As the Pentagon ponders a suitable replacement for the $52 million Prowler, the remaining EA-6Bs are so coveted that each one is accompanied into harm's way by a quartet of fighter planes. But that's battle, not practice. *The Seattle Times* found that 30 aviators have been lost in Prowler accidents since 1980. That number rises to 34 if you count the Prowler that crashed on November 28, 1979. It was my father's.

Peter Thomas Rodrick was raised by devout Catholics in a working-class neighborhood of Brockton, Massachusetts, Rocky Marciano's hometown. He was the oldest son of six children. His mother worked at a VA hospital. His dad was a shipping clerk and a loner who was capable of long, dark moods. There were nods at raising hell—hot rodding in old cars, sneaking out after curfew—but for the most part, he was a quiet kid whose paper route bought his mother her first dishwasher. He was brilliant in mathematics, and in 1960 he was awarded an appointment to the Naval Academy. His mother cried the day he left for Annapolis.

He looked sharp in a uniform, which was good because he had the fashion sense of a Soviet bloc apparatchik. In 1961, he met my mother at a mixer in Norfolk, Virginia, her hometown. It was love at first sight for him, but she took a little longer. They were married two days after Christmas in 1964. My mother, who was a Baptist, converted to Catholicism. Within two years, she had two small children and followed my father from base to base, from Milton, Florida, to Corpus Christi, Texas, to Quonset Point, Rhode Island, to Monterey, California.

His career began to take off in 1973 on the USS *Oriskany*, where he served as officer in charge of a detachment of A-3 Skywarriors. The A-3 was a decidedly unglamorous jet, used for electronic jamming and refueling. Nicknamed the Whale, it had a vast wingspan that provided about a fifteen-foot margin of error when landing on the carrier. My father wasn't a naturally gifted pilot but a grinder who simply worked harder than anyone else. He rose at 3 A.M. to study flight manuals, and at night, when the rest of the squadron would peel off for a few drinks at the officers' club, he would stay behind and plow through paperwork.

A devout Catholic, he was an equally devout sleeper. Every Sunday when he was home, my sister and I would move stealthily around the house, hoping he would sleep through 10:30 Mass. Invariably, he arose at 10:07 and had the entire brood out the door in twenty minutes. Afterward, he would cook waffles and curse at the Red Sox or the Celtics, muttering "son of a biscuit eater." A man of firm moral beliefs, he rarely spanked his kids, but if he saw you littering you'd get a smack and a lecture. If he found one of my newspaper rubber bands in the house, he'd snap it against my neck. Not that he didn't have a wicked sense of humor. At night, he loved to send me out to empty the trash. Then he'd sneak out the back door and scare the bejesus out of me. From time to time, he'd smuggle lobsters back from the East Coast in his plane's tiny luggage compartment.

Although pictures of him in uniform filled our houses, I rarely got a glimpse of his pilot side. When he was on extended leave, the family would pile into the station wagon for long trips all over the country. He thrilled at pushing another forty miles after the gas gauge had hit "empty," particularly in blinding thunderstorms that forced cop cars and 18-wheelers to the side. My mother and I watched in white-knuckle horror. But we never ran out of gas.

After moving the family to Whidbey Island, in the northwest corner of Washington State, in 1974, my father bought a condo in the Cascade Mountains for ski weekends. I was a rotten skier, and I usually gave up by lunchtime. My father, the thrill seeker, always skied the last, icy run, carving down the mountain with the ski patrol.

I waited in the gloaming, petrified he had crashed. Only when I saw the white ball of his ski hat could I relax.

The suburb of Oak Harbor, home to the Whidbey Island Naval Air Station, was a sort of company town for pilots and their families. Death, or the cheating of it, was as common a topic of conversation as the rainy weather. When I was an infant, my father safely parachuted from a T-38 training jet. On a playground in third grade, my friend Timmy Newman told me about his dad's surviving a weak catapult launch on the other side of the world. He ejected and was plucked from the ocean. Just two eight-year-olds talking at recess. On my twelfth birthday, my dad insisted I invite a younger neighbor whose father had just been killed in an A-6 crash. He brought a hastily wrapped stapler as a present. That was my last birthday with my father.

Perhaps because of this painful dynamic, my mother decided she couldn't stay in Oak Harbor after my father was killed, and she moved us to Flint, Michigan. Her sister lived two miles away, and they hoped my uncle could serve as a surrogate father. It never happened; he had two boys of his own. In Michigan, my father haunted a house he had never entered. Models of his planes sat on opposite ends of the mantel like vigilant guard dogs. Every morning, my mother sipped coffee from one of his old squadron mugs. But we avoided talking about him.

It wasn't as if I pushed it. When I was in my late twenties, I asked my younger sister, Christine, two years old when our father died, if there was anything she wanted to know about him. When she said no, I left it alone. For years, his death seemed an abstraction, as if my father were on another cruise, just one that didn't end. Whenever any of my girlfriends broached the subject, I bobbed and weaved my way out of it. To drown out his memory, I poured myself into work and even adopted his nomadic ways, changing cities every year or two.

But in 1998, I got married and began to think about having children. My wife wanted us to stay in suburban Boston so she could keep her job as a reporter at the *Boston Globe*. She also wanted to raise our children in a blissful security neither one of us had had as kids. I resisted. I wanted to live in New York or Los Angeles. Our arguments left me bitterly reflecting on my own childhood. My father had given up nothing for his wife and children. Not his dangerous profession, not his career-climbing. And now, having endured that, I was supposed to be the postmodern man, sinking my own ambitions for a wife and unborn child? It seemed like a cruel joke. At age thirty-five—just a year short of my father's age at his death—I faced some of the hardest decisions of my life. As usual, I felt unprepared and alone. Without knowing my father at all, I could barely get a handle on myself.

Late last fall, after the attacks on September 11, my wife was sent to Pakistan to cover the war. I returned to Michigan for Thanksgiving. The night I arrived, as my mother and sisters watched television, I lay on the couch and felt a physical weight crushing my chest. I stared at the planes on the mantel and my father's portrait on the wall. I wanted to scream, "He died!"

Instead, I went to bed. I woke at 5 A.M. with a fear I had never felt before, even while on dangerous assignments, slogging through jungles with Colombian gangsters or riding in cars with suspected murderers. I stumbled through our neighborhood until dawn, and then told my mother I had to get away. Later, we sat in her car at a gas station and I asked her why we never talked about him. "I thought it would be too painful for you," she said. "People told me we should move on and look forward, not back."

I left an hour later. I wandered the country, visiting friends from Chicago to California. I watched the network news extol the bravery of our pilots as footage of their red taillights heading off to Afghanistan played in the background. I changed the channel.

Then, in February, *Men's Journal* received an e-mail from Lieutenant Brandon Sellers, an F/A-18 pilot based in Atsugi, Japan, asking if a reporter would like to spend a month at sea with his squadron. The e-mail was forwarded to me. I had to sit down when I saw the name of his carrier: the USS *Kitty Hawk*.

I decided that the closest I would ever get to knowing Commander Peter Rodrick—and to understanding why being a navy flier was more important to him than being a husband or a father—was on board this ship, getting to know the pilots who were doing precisely what my father had done twenty-three years ago. Two weeks later, I was on a plane bound for Hong Kong.

The Coyote Cafe is a welcome, if bland, respite for American sailors amid the fish-gizzard takeout shops of downtown Hong Kong. The bar features American-style Mexican food that wouldn't offend an Applebee's patron. Budweiser is plentiful, particularly upstairs, where the men of Squadron VFA-195 gather. The dozen pilots here tonight, ages twenty-five to forty-four, could pass for IBM execs gathering at Hooters. They wear Birkenstocks, shorts, jeans, and polo shirts.

After just two hours, I see something of my father in Lieutenant Commander Klas Ohman. Maybe it's his solemnity in the middle of the revelry. He sips a Coke and smokes a cigar as Lieutenant David Baird, three months removed from bombing Al Qaeda bunkers, gags on Cuervo. The tequila girl is pouring the amber liquid at too steep an angle of descent, and beads of liquor drip down Baird's neck.

"Man, I'm glad those days are over for me," says Ohman, a thirty-three-year-old native of Athens, Tennessee, with a fondness for *Peanuts* and *Baby Blues* comics. "I go home around midnight when everyone stops making sense." Every pilot is assigned a call sign by his colleagues. Ohman's, because of his first name, is Santa. He speaks with a smooth and homey southern accent, choosing his words as carefully as he maneuvers his F/A-18 Hornet through a thunderstorm.

Tonight, Ohman and the other pilots are gathered for a hail-and-farewell party. Baird is off to get married and then plans to attend weapons school in Virginia Beach. His replacement, Lieutenant Junior Grade Daniel Cochran, sits in the corner. He is blond and handsome and talks in the dudespeak of a SoCal surfer. But tonight, Cochran isn't saying much at all, which is exactly as it should be. On the squadron's duty roster, he is listed as FNG, Fucking New Guy. He is to be seen, not heard. Adding to his pain is that his colleagues have decided on his call sign: Coch Ring.

The Chippies—VFA-195's longtime nickname with forgotten origins—have flown for sixty years. Their Korean War exploits inspired the James Michener book *The Bridges at Toko-Ri* and its 1955 movie adaptation. (They're still pissed another squadron was used for the flying scenes.) They're based at Atsugi Naval Air Facility, outside of Tokyo, but they spend half their time on the *Kitty Hawk*, which is the nation's oldest carrier and the only one that is permanently deployed overseas. Normally based in Yokosuka, the ship is in port in Hong Kong as part of a six-week cruise that will also take the Chippies to Singapore and Guam. The squadron is such a regular presence at the Coyote Cafe that the bar features the Chippy Margarita, a sickly sweet concoction featuring an apple liqueur whose green hue matches the squadron's colors.

After toweling himself off, Baird listens as his squadron mates roast him. There's the story of how he spent $700 at a Guam nightclub, in the futile pursuit of a blonde stripper. Then an explanation of how he got the call sign Jumbo (a nude swim followed by a very public shrink-age). Ohman grins and lights another cigar. Eventually, Baird gets his turn. He nods at Commander Kent "Aitch" Aitcheson, the squadron's commanding officer. "To the skipper, I will all my downloaded porn, with appropriate firewalls." Baird then turns to Lieutenant Jason "Nadia" Naidyhorski, a former Wisconsin stock car driver. "To Nadia, I offer the melted-down coins of the crew to give you six more inches on the landing gear; maybe then you can land the plane."

A few nights ago, it took Naidyhorski four tries to land his Hornet on the *Kitty Hawk*. On the third attempt, the Prowler in front of him nearly plowed into the deck, unnerving him further. After landing, an aircraft director, or "yellow shirt," waved him to cut engines and step down, but Naidyhorski shook his head and sat in the cockpit for five minutes, jets flaming, his legs shaking uncontrollably.

The men laugh. Baird goes somber. "Remember your three main responsibilities: Destroy the enemy's stuff, kill the enemy, and sur-vive," he says. He pauses for a moment. Drinks and smokes are put down. "Most important, survive."

This isn't a sentiment that comes up often in the pilots' sweatbox sleeping quarters, or in the ready room, a low-ceilinged space with fake wood paneling and twenty-two pleather chairs anchored to the floor, where they spend most of their time. For the most part, the pilots are sympathetic about my father's death; it's just that death isn't a subject they're eager to dwell on. One evening in the ready room, I ask Ohman how dangerous his job is. "You can just as easily get killed in a car," he insists. "There's a lot of bad drivers out there." I hear dif-ferent versions of the same platitude again and again.

But they never forget the ones who've been lost. Ohman keeps a list of fourteen dead comrades on his Palm Pilot. One of them is Lieutenant Gareth Rietz, a student of his at test-pilot school in Patuxent River, Maryland. One afternoon, Rietz allowed his T-38A training jet "out of parameters," approaching the runway at a fatally steep rate of descent. The plane crashed a half mile short of the runway. "It's a terrible feeling," he says, "when you have to knock on the door of your friend's fiancée."

His story leaves me overwhelmed by memories of my father's memorial service. An hour before the ceremony, a friend of his slipped me a tablet, probably Valium, leaving me with a detached, third-person feel. At the chapel, four caps sat on the altar. Most of the wives were quiet, but Cathy Brown, the widow of Lieutenant James Brown Jr., loudly bled grief, holding their six-month-old daughter. There were no coffins, but there was much talk of a loving God. More than four hundred people sang "Eternal Father," the navy anthem to "those in peril on the sea." Afterward, my family sat mute in our station wagon. A navy friend tried to console my mother. "C'mon, Barbara, you can start a whole new life." Her response was just a whisper: "No."

Ohman's own family life has taken a hit because of his career. His first marriage ended in divorce, which he blames on irreconcilable differences while admitting he was home only a hundred days a year. His seven-year-old daughter, Kelsey, lives in Jacksonville with his ex-wife. Ohman's second wife, Julie, is seven months pregnant. I ask him if he knows any Navy pilots who voluntarily walked away from the game to be with their families. He assures me some have. But he can't think of anyone's name. "I don't feel guilty about my career," he says. "Kelsey doesn't hold it against me. If she did, I'd stop." He gives a shrug. "I've got three pillars: God, country, and family. It's not that I love flying any more than God and my family, but right now it's country. Especially after 9/11."

The next evening, Ohman takes me onto the deck for night landings. As on every carrier, there are four arresting cables stretched across the deck of the *Kitty Hawk* to bring planes to a stop. If a pilot catches the first wire, that means he came in too low, and dangerously close to crashing. The second and third wires are preferred, while the fourth suggests you nearly overshot the deck. Doing this in broad daylight is extraordinarily difficult. Doing it in the dark is treacherous. No other nation asks its pilots to even attempt it.

I hold the back of Ohman's flight suit as we climb steep stairs into the humid, equatorial night. The deck is blacked out, because the glare of lights can blind a pilot at night. There is a relentless sheet of white noise and the stench of jet fuel. A Hornet approaches. As the jet nears, a signal-landing officer gives instructions. The tone of the voice is imperative. Soothing means you're on track; an urgent plea for power means hit the throttle and pull back on the stick so you don't die. We stand maybe thirty feet from where the Hornet touches down and watch the second cable pull it to a stop.

Ohman points at a dim light in the sky. "That's a Hornet. They're so quiet. At night, when you're at 30,000 feet, you feel like you're floating in space." He smiles ear to ear. "There's something just and right about standing on a flight deck at night."

And I feel it. For the next hour, I watch as planes emerge out of the darkness and, somehow, return home to a tiny speck of America in the South China Sea. My eyes fill with tears of pride and regret. The idea that I never had and never will have a conversation with my father about what it's like to land a jet at night on this ship is almost unbearable. I think back to how close I came to spending a week on this ship with him. A week on board as a thirteen-year-old and maybe I would even have followed in my father's footsteps. Would that have made him proud?

When I get back downstairs, I head straight for the bathroom. In the mirror, there are two thin lines of white skin descending from my eyes surrounded by the sweat and filth of the flight deck. I think of what my mother said after his death, that my father was to be rotated off flying and to a staff position within a year. "God took him doing something he loved," she said. "Maybe God knew he wouldn't be able to live without it." For more than two decades, I thought that was unmitigated bullshit. Now I'm not so sure.

A few days later, on a humid, hazy afternoon, I watch with a mix of apprehension and disgust as Ohman burns his Hornet past the deck of the *Kitty Hawk* at 450 knots, a hundred over standard procedure. He banks hard, leaving his wingman far behind. Rookies are told to bank their jets when they are three to four minutes away from the carrier, giving them enough time to line up their approach. Ohman leaves himself between 60 and 90 seconds and still nails the second wire.

A half hour after landing, Ohman walks into the ready room. His green flight suit is ringed with sweat. "Man, you lost me out there," marvels Lieutenant Pete "Boo Boo" Shoemaker, Santa's young flying partner. "That was a shit-hot break." Ohman grins. "In a wartime situation, you never know when you might need to bring a plane in fast," Ohman says. "But mostly, I do it just for fun."

Ohman's nonchalance lights a nerve. An hour after my father took off for his last flight, his plane simply dropped off radar. There was no Mayday, no emergency beacon. The crash had never been fully explained. While navy regulations prohibited Prowlers from flying below 200 feet, pilots had been known to push it down as low as 25 feet, to practice flying at such a perilous level. Laddie Coburn, my father's best friend and his number two on board the USS *Oriskany*, once even suggested to me that he had been flying too low. "Your father was a fanatic about checking off proficiency in different flying situations," he said. "It was a hazy day. If you're moving at 500 miles an hour, it's not hard to lose perspective of where you are. You misjudge your stick a quarter of an inch and that's it."

The possibility that the crash was my father's fault had always been with me. That's the way of the navy. When an accident is unexplained, blame tends to fall on the pilot. But this was different. Quite possibly, my father, the stickler, had been flying at a brazenly dangerous altitude.

Later, over a cup of coffee in the officers' mess, I bring it up with Ohman. I'm not sure what I'm looking for—a kind word, an apology, a nod of understanding. He locks into my eyes and gives my father absolution. "Some of the best pilots I've ever met are dead," he says. "Maybe it was your father's fault, maybe not. We're all walking that line."

On a Sunday afternoon not far from Okinawa, Dan Cochran dips his Hornet into a five-degree descent until the plane hits 1,200 feet. He grins and gives the trigger of his 50mm cannons a quick tug. Firing at a rate of 100 per second, the bullets hit the *Kitty Hawk*'s wake with a fap, fap, fap sound.

On every mission, Hornet pilots work through an exhausting series of training exercises. "Shooting the wake" is not one of them. But for Cochran, it's irresistible. "I love blowing shit up," he tells me one afternoon in the mess hall. "When I was based in Meridian, Mississippi, we'd go out and shoot things with a 20-gauge. One of the guys was getting a divorce, so we blew up all of his wife's birdhouses."

The truth is that Cochran probably would have washed out of my dad's Navy. In his stateroom, he keeps an amp and an electric guitar in a purple velour case. But today, there's room for free spirits who play Andante in A minor on the ax. Still, it gets lonely for Cochran. He often stays in his room watching *The Godfather* and other films on his DVD player. "Some of the guys don't want to hear from the new guy, even at dinner," Cochran says. "You can be having a really bad day, and you've got no one to talk to about it." Fortunately, Cochran's brother, Chris, is a Hornet pilot based at Lemoore Naval Air Station, outside of Fresno, California. There's also his new wife, Kelly, back in Atsugi. They commiserate by e-mail almost daily.

Only a month out of training, Cochran still struggles with the basics of radio communication, keeping his jet at the right altitude, and, mostly, landing it on the ship. "Every time I think I get to the point where I know what I'm doing, I do something stupid and I realize I'm clueless," Cochran says. "Guys like Santa, it's all reflex. I've got to think out everything I'm doing." A grinder, or as close to one as I have found on the *Kitty Hawk*. I tell him that my father was like that and he still became a squadron commander. Cochran looks at me as if I have just tossed him a life preserver. "Really? Sometimes, I just feel like I'm the only one."

A few nights later, Cochran ducks his head through the porthole and emerges onto the *Kitty Hawk's* deck. Sheets of tropical rain immediately soak him. "Shit," he says. "They're gonna make me fly in this?" It is 2100 hours and time for the last launch of the night. Because of a Singapore liberty call and various mechanical problems, Cochran hasn't flown for the past fourteen nights, and he isn't thrilled about this reintroduction. His Hornet is parked all the way at the end of the bow. He runs to his plane, climbs up the ladder, and quickly closes the canopy. Still, all his instruments are soaked. He dries them off, starts his engines, and taxies to the catapult.

Bam. Hornet 412 shoots into the night. But something is wrong. Cochran's HUD, the Hornet's most important instrument, blanks out. The beauty of the HUD is that it displays essentials such as altitude and air speed at eye level, allowing pilots to scan the information without taking their eyes off the horizon. Without it, Cochran has to look down and to his right to monitor the manual instruments. For a rookie, this significantly increases the chance of a "drool cup" crash, in which a pilot fixates on his instruments and loses track of where he is in the sky. Cochran curses and calls the ship.

Down below, Klas Ohman and I walk into the Carrier Air Traffic Control Center (CATCC, pronounced "cat-see"), a labyrinthine room that serves as the *Kitty Hawk's* night-flying nerve center. Constructed in 1961, the coolant center on board the *Kitty Hawk* seems nearly medieval, and most of the crew roasts in the heat. But the CATCC is kept cinema cool to protect its stacks of tracking devices and navigational computers. Enlisted personnel continually write with orange markers on glass chalkboards, keeping track of the location and fuel status of every plane in the air. The orange gives the room a supernatural glow. Officers from each squadron sit on elevated benches like judges in a star chamber. In a long-standing tradition, some wager on which pilots will miss the deck on their first approach.

"Hey, you owe me two bucks," Air Operations Officer Jeff "Squeals" Vielock says to Ohman. "Who do you like tonight?"

"I take Malandrino in the Tomcat and Bibeau in the Hornet," Ohman says.

The mood turns more serious when Captain Michael "Flex" Galpin, head of air operations, arrives. Listening to a weather report, he sighs and says, "This is a big-boy night." He scratches the back of his curly silver hair and studies the board. A wave of planes returns for landing. Sure enough, Malandrino and Bibeau miss. On his second approach, Bibeau overshoots again.

"Goddammit," Galpin says. "Send him off to get some milk." As Bibeau flies back to the tanker to refuel, a phone rings. "Santa, it's for you. It's Cochran."

Ohman takes the phone and his brow furrows. "Well, did you try turning it on and off?" he says. "Give it a kick. Nothing? Okay, hold on." He walks over to the boss. "Can I throw some more bad news your way?"

"No, you cannot," Galpin says curtly. "Sit down, Santa." He picks up another phone and calls the landing officer. "Hey, how you guys doing? Need a wet suit? I can send one down." Then he turns serious. "Okay, get Bibeau in. Work your magic." A few minutes later, Bibeau lands safely, catching the second wire. "They always land after the tanker," Galpin says. "It's like warm milk."

Galpin turns to Santa and asks what's on his mind. Ohman reports Cochran's situation. "I want to offer you the possibility of sending him to Singapore." Diverting Cochran to the nearest landing strip would eliminate the danger of a carrier landing, but would also require Cochran to find Paya Lebar Air Base at midnight. A little navigational error and he'd end up in mainland China. Then, there's the macho factor; sending Cochran to land is an admission of defeat that will ripple up and down the *Kitty Hawk*.

"Shit, he's a fleet guy, bring him in. What's his call sign?"

"Uh, that would be Coch Ring, sir," Ohman says softly. For a rare moment, a room of navy officers is stunned. "But you can just call him Ring."

Up above, Cochran tries to keep calm. His speed drops perilously from 300 knots to 210 while he fiddles with his HUD. Regaining his composure, he decides to leave it alone until he reaches 31,000 feet. He then puts the Hornet on autopilot, circling the carrier. He remembers his mother telling him not to offer God any deal he wasn't willing to keep. "Hey, God, help me out, no strings," he asks.

On the radio, Commander Jeff Rocha, a Hornet pilot with 3,000 hours of experience, suggests Cochran follow on his wing until breaking off for landing. Cochran gratefully agrees. He stays 1,500 feet off

Rocha's right wing until approach. At about a mile and a half, he sees the green landing light of the Kitty Hawk. His speed and descent rate are near perfect. Then, over the radio, a cry of "foul deck, foul deck." The plane ahead of Cochran's isn't clear of the runway.

"Goddammit!" Galpin shouts. Santa quickly approaches him. "Sir, I recommend he fly around by himself this time. It will give him more time to read the instruments." It is a valid point. Riding on Rocha's tail is comforting, but it requires keeping him in sight and prevents Cochran from familiarizing himself with his manual instruments until just before landing.

By now, word of Cochran's difficulties has spread. Kent Aitcheson, the Chippies' commanding officer, is now in the room. Galpin nods in his direction; it's the skipper's call. "Let it ride," Aitcheson says. "He's comfortable with Rocha."

Santa bites his lip and walks away. A few minutes later, Cochran begins his second attempt. This time, he approaches low and momentarily dips below deck level. Cochran overcompensates with too much thrust. His Hornet bounces hard, shooting sparks into the night. His tail hook skips over the four wires. He must go around again.

"Shit," Galpin says. "Tell Rocha to peel off. This time he goes alone."

About three miles above, Cochran prays again. Focusing on the instruments, he comes in hard and fast, but catches the second wire. The plane skids to a stop. Cochran hits full throttle and his engines shoot off a victory torch. In the CATCC, there are handshakes all around. Santa looks beat. "Now, that was fun," he says sarcastically. I also feel spent, overwhelmed at how dangerous and exemplary these men's lives are. For the first time, my father's job seems less a narcissistic indulgence and more like honor.

Down in the ready room, most of the pilots wait for the FNG. Cochran arrives with a broad smile, sweat still beaded on his forehead. The guys shake his hand and pound his back. "Man, I have never been so scared," Cochran says. "I did a no-HUD landing in training and nearly killed myself twice." Later he will e-mail his brother and his parents, telling them about his close call. His mom cries when she reads it.

I leave the *Kitty Hawk* on a C-2 transport plane, wondering whether it was the same catapult that sent my father on his last flight. Walking the oily floors of the *Kitty Hawk*, listening to the rattle of the boiler, sitting in the officers' mess debating the texture of today's ice cream, I felt like I knew who he was. I don't want to leave.

On my return flight to Boston, I have a layover in Detroit and decide not to get back on the plane. I pick up a rental car and drive to my mom's house for the first time since my breakdown at Thanksgiving. I ask her to gather any of my father's belongings she has saved. She retrieves two boxes from the basement. One is filled with photos, a list of personal effects that were returned to us after his death, an application for the space shuttle program, and a letter from the *Kitty Hawk* chaplain mentioning his daily attendance at Mass. The other box holds hundreds of letters dating from 1963 to 1979, letters I never knew existed. I can bear to read only a few of them at a time.

His penmanship was a sloppy mixture of cursive and print that mirrors my own scratch. The pages are filled with pledges of eternal love, pregnancy scares, and complicated plans for meeting in Annapolis. When my father told her he wanted to fly jets, she wrote, more than once, about her fears.

> *I know you must think it is silly me worrying about planes going down. I want you to fly because that's what you want and will be happy doing. I'll just have to have faith that someone greater will watch over you and bring you back to me safe and sound. . . . I love you forever, Barb.*

My parents sometimes exchanged four or five letters a week, but by 1979, he wrote less often, overwhelmed by the responsibilities of command. A few days after his death, a last letter arrived for my mother. Dated 1:15 A.M., November 28, about twelve hours before his final flight, it ran three pages and talked of Christmas presents to be bought and rumors of the squadron's return date. On the back of the envelope, where he usually counted off the days left until he returned home, was a question mark. The letter closed, as always, with a message of devotion:

> *I love you, Barbara, and want to be with you always. I will be with you sometime soon and we will make up for all the days and nights we missed. I am thinking of you constantly and am waiting to hold you in my arms and kiss your wonderful lips and feel your body around me. Just knowing you love me and are waiting*

*for me makes it all worthwhile. Take good care of yourself and
the children and we'll all be together soon. All my love forever,
Pete.*

For the first time, I understand why she never dated again. In
those letters, he was no longer taciturn or elusive. He had two great
passions: flying and his wife. Maybe my sisters and I were a third love.
I only wish he had lived long enough for me to find out.

I make copies of some of the letters and pack them in my bag. The
next day, I drive home to Boston. I'm still not certain I have forgiven
my father. I'm not even sure what I would forgive him for anymore.

A few days after I arrive home, my wife asks for a separation. She
believes that my father's transient life and early death have ingrained
in me a restlessness that will never be salved by children and suburban cookouts. She's probably right.

Meanwhile, the world keeps turning. The Chippies continue to
train on board the *Kitty Hawk*. And in Baltimore, on July 13, Julie
Ohman gives birth to Corinne Elizabeth Ohman, weighing in at
nearly eight pounds. Lieutenant Commander Klas Ohman gets lucky;
he makes it back in time, and manages to spend the next eight days
with his wife and baby before he has to return to the squadron. He
hopes to see his new family for Christmas if war with Iraq doesn't
intrude. "I've had practice leaving my family and little ones," Ohman
says. "It should be easier, but it gets harder every time."

DECEMBER 2002

THE SURVIVORS

by Hampton Sides

WHEN RONNIE CLIFFORD FIRST went to the psychologist, in late September, he presented his case as an enormous engineering project. Here are the problems, he said, here are the elements and fractures and stress points; now put me back together. Ronnie used the metaphor deliberately, for he was trained as an architect and was well versed in the principles of structural engineering. For a decade, he had made his living understanding why buildings stand.

The therapist, a specialist in post-traumatic stress disorder, accepted the project, and the two men went to work, six hours a week. "I was in pieces, just falling apart," Ronnie says in the lilt of his native Ireland. "I was having intense dreams. I couldn't get out of the building. I would jerk myself awake, exhausted. Weird things were happening. I was seeing the number eleven everywhere—like the towers themselves, the way they rose in the sky like an eleven. Whenever I got in the shower, I would scrub and scrub my feet, as if there was something dirty down there and I had to get it off."

Ronnie drives his dark-green Jaguar around the town of Glen Ridge, New Jersey, where he lives and works. It's a rooted place of rambling mansions set in a quilt of woody suburbs seventeen miles from Manhattan. He lives with his wife, Brigid, and their daughter, Monica, in a charmingly fusty shingle-style house with hardwood floors, windows warped by time, and a garage that was once a livery stable. The vintage gaslights that grace the town's streets never turn off.

Ronnie is a fair-skinned man with thinning red hair, thick fingers, and freckled arms. His eyes are blue and squinch into crow's-feet whenever he laughs, which is surprisingly often. Because he didn't leave the family farm in Cork and head for America until he was twenty-seven, his accent is strong. He is forty-seven but sounds like a boy, his voice high-pitched and full of wonder at life's trick connections. He is attentive to the strange atmospherics that have welled up around 9/11, all the coincidences, real or imagined, and the odd numerology of the day.

"Something higher was at work," he says. "When I look at all the things that happened to me and my family that day, I realize that you couldn't design an algorithm to put it all together."

Ronnie, who is a tremendously vivid and empathetic storyteller, wasn't shy about accepting invitations from the media, and he became something of a celebrity in the days after September 11. Eventually, though, the media circuit became overwhelming. He couldn't talk about it anymore. He had to shut off the television and retreat from the world. Everywhere he turned, there it was, an image, a reference, a reminder. Even his friends started to annoy him. The consoling phone calls, the e-mails, the sympathy cards—he wanted it all to stop.

Over a salmon pasta at his favorite restaurant in Montclair, where the waiters all know him, he asks me, almost in a whisper, "Have you ever had anyone close to you die?"

My father, I say. He had a heart attack in his car and smashed into a telephone pole.

"Well," he says, "it would be like if someone said to you, 'Hey, guess what, your dad died. Your dad died. Your dad died.' Every day, every hour, somebody opens it up in your face. Somewhere along the way, I realized, My God, it's never fricking ending, is it?"

That morning, before dawn, Ronnie woke up almost giddy with excitement. There had been a thunderstorm the night before, with power outages across northern New Jersey, but the storm had swept to the east, leaving everything tingly and cool. Ronnie put on a blue suit and a yellow silk tie. He'd bought them special for this day. He wanted to look sharp for a business meeting at the World Trade Center Marriott with a Chicago software executive. The stakes were high: If all went well, the meeting would profoundly change Ronnie's business life, creating a brand-new company that would design Web applications for large corporations. Ronnie's little sister, Ruth, whom he always called on for fashion advice, had helped him pick out the suit, and had been especially fond of the tie. "You always want to stand out," she'd told him.

Ronnie kissed Brigid goodbye, took the commuter train to Hoboken, and then boarded the ferry. The Hudson air was bracing, and the water caught crescents of the morning light as the sun climbed behind the ramparts of Manhattan. "The city was breathtaking," he says. "Before a meeting, it's always important to feel good, and I felt great."

At around 8:45, Ronnie walked into the lobby of the Marriott, which was connected to the lobby of the north tower by a revolving door. As he was checking his yellow tie in a mirror, he felt a massive explosion, followed several seconds later by a reverberation, a warping effect that he describes as the "harmonic tolerance of a building that's shaking like a tuning fork." He peered through the revolving door into the lobby of the north tower. It was filling with haze. People were scurrying to escape what had become a "hurricane of flying debris."

Yet Ronnie remained untouched. It was as though the door were a glass portal to another realm, a world of chaos and soot just inches away. The Marriott lobby was calm, the marble surfaces polished and antiseptic. For a few seconds, the two worlds did not meet.

Then the revolving door turned with a suctioning sound followed by a hot burst of wind, and in came a mannequin of the future. A woman, naked, dazed, her arms outstretched. She was so badly burned that Ronnie had no idea what race she was or how old she might be. She clawed the air with fingernails turned porcelain-white. The zipper of what had once been a sweater had melted into her chest, as if it were the zipper to her own body. Her hair had been singed to a crisp steel wool. With her, in the gust of the door, came a pungent odor, the smell of kerosene or paraffin, Ronnie thought.

Then the mannequin became a person, crying for help. Ronnie had little idea what had happened to her, or where exactly she had come from, but he knew that whoever she was, she was his responsibility now.

Silvion Ramsundar creaks in his black leather sofa, a television remote clutched in his hand, as the jets from JFK Airport whistle overhead. The relentless background keen of the planes has grown so nerve-wracking that he and his wife, Nimmi, have considered moving from their home, in South Ozone Park, Queens. Silvion fingers the bandaged wound on his left shoulder and says, "I hear them all the time, all the time. I can't stand it. Tools of destruction, that's all I can think about. They remind me."

It's not as though Silvion could ever forget, or that he ever truly wants to. He is a head-on sort of person, and he's made confrontation a part of his recovery. In his living room, nailed to the wall for any visitor to see, is a framed pair of photographs of the trade towers, before and after. In the top picture, the metallic duolith gleams in the sun; in the bottom one, there is a smoky void.

"It's part of my history," he says, in a tone that seems to acknowledge that some people might find the photographs oddly blatant.

"I worked there for ten years. Everything that I have in my life happened while I was working there—I bought my first house and my first car, met my wife, had my daughter. Now that the towers are gone, it's like my house burned down."

Silvion will talk about that day, but he refuses to believe that his experiences are beyond what his own personal resources can handle. The best way to get back to normal, he feels, is to start acting as though everything is normal. He steers clear of shrinks, of twelve-step trauma sessions, of appearances on Oprah. One might say that he's in denial of being in denial.

"I've almost displaced the fact that I was there, as if it happened to somebody else," Silvion tells me. His five-year-old daughter, Mariah, wriggles in his lap, careful not to touch his left side. "That's not to say that it's not going to come flooding back someday. But I know this is what's working for me right now. Being home, thinking about other things, not feeling sorry for myself."

Silvion, a genial man in his early thirties, worked for Mizuho Capital Markets, which deals with interest-rate derivatives. Like many denizens of the financial world, he does not succumb easily to melodrama. He speaks in the blunt brogue of the borough of Queens, where he has lived most of his life. But he's a native of Guyana, born of Indian parents, who moved to New York City when he was a boy, seeking a better life. His mother is a devout Muslim, his father Hindu. His black hair is cropped short, his skin a deep bronze. A long, fresh scar tracks across his jaw line.

Silvion was standing on the forty-fourth floor of the south tower, in the Sky Lobby cafe, waiting in the cashier's line with a danish and a cup of coffee. He was making small talk with Christine Sasser, a friend from his office. He had heard a thud of some kind and thought someone back in the kitchen had dropped a large stockpot. Outside, the morning sky swelled with paper, a glittering bulge of confetti. Silvion watched the cloud floating down and wondered what it was. It looked beautiful against the sharp September blue, a trillion motes dancing in the fair light. He squinted out the window for a moment, then proceeded toward the cashier.

He and Christine rode the escalator up to the lounge on the forty-fifth floor, where televisions were blaring. A news show reported that a small commuter plane had crashed into the north tower, but Silvion couldn't see anything out the window. A voice broke over the intercom and announced: "There is a fire in the north tower. Firemen are on the scene. Do not worry. The south tower is secure. You may return to your offices."

Silvion and Christine decided to go on up. How much damage could a commuter plane do? At the very least, it seemed like a good idea to reassess the situation from their office, then place a few calls and collect their belongings.

At approximately 8:50, they pushed the up button for the express elevator. Their office was on the eightieth floor.

The ascent required two separate elevator rides, the first one to the seventy-eighth, and then a second to the eightieth. The doors slid open, and Silvion and Christine walked into their office, only to find that it had been almost entirely evacuated. Only three security guards and a few of the firm's high-level executives remained. Silvion found Charles, a security guard he'd been friendly with for years.

"Where's everybody?" he asked. "It's just a commuter plane."

"No, no, it's big," Charles answered. "An airliner. Look."

Silvion walked around to the far side of the office and gasped. The steel corduroy skin of the north tower had been torn open. Black smoke tendriled through the building's metal grid. Then they saw a man emerge from the hole. He was standing at the edge, looking down, wide-eyed.

Then, the man jumped, and Silvion watched him drop all the way down. That's when he registered the magnitude of the damage across the way, and he pleaded with Charles, "Are you guys leaving? Come on, let's get out of here!"

"In a few minutes," said Charles. "We've got to check up on the place."

"At a certain point," Will Jimeno says, "your house becomes your prison." Will sits at his dining-room table, next to his gun rack, gazing at a deer in his backyard. Ever since he got out of the hospital, in late November, he has sat here—a cop under a kind of house arrest. The view never changes. The TV drones. The deer doesn't move.

In fact, the deer isn't real. It's a target that Will keeps for bow-hunting practice. It's startlingly lifelike, though, a creature comically out of place next to the suburban detritus on the porch. Ordinarily, Will would spend much of the fall in a deer stand in the pine barrens of New Jersey, slathered in camo-scent. But this year he missed the season entirely. For three months he lay in a hospital, his veins coursing with blood thinner. "Next year," he says. "Maybe next year."

Will lives in Clifton, New Jersey, in a modest boxy house clad in green vinyl siding. As we talk, his wife, Allison, bathes their newborn in the kitchen sink, while their older daughter, Bianca, watches *SpongeBob SquarePants* in the other room. Will is a burly man with a round face and black hair cut in a military buzz. He was born in Colombia, but moved to America when he was two and grew up in nearby Hackensack. Before he became a cop for the Port Authority of New York & New Jersey, Will served four years as a gunner's mate in the navy, pulling several deployments in the Pacific on a ship that carried attack helicopters.

Because of the extreme trauma of Will's injuries, his left leg is bound in a formidable-looking brace, and various crutches and walkers are strewn about the house. He wears a PAPD T-shirt, black gym shorts, and a pair of hospital-issue circulation hose. "Aren't those lovely?" he says. "They come in two different colors—black and nude." Today, it's nude. The hose are pulled up nearly to his knees and push firmly against the skin to prevent swelling.

Will has occasional bouts of depression and despair, but by and large he's optimistic. He's had to keep busy, and that's been a godsend. His days have been taken up with a regimen of treadmills, flexes, weights, hydrotherapy, and stretches. Despite skin grafts and extensive reconstruction to repair the damage to his nerves and muscles, his leg is still a mess. "I'll wear a brace the rest of my life," Will says. "But I *will* walk again."

In Will Jimeno I see an iron determination to put the best face on things, and a certain resignation, the look of someone young who has begun to accept the indignities of his condition while feeling stabs of incredulity that this is the new him. If there once was a macho aspect to his personality—proud hunter, sailor, cop—it has been humbled.

The proportions of the tragedy still tax his imagination. The Port Authority lost more police officers that day than any American police force has ever lost in a single day. Thirty-seven PAPD officers died, along with thirty-eight other Port Authority employees. Many of them were his dear friends. Will says, "I don't think I've internalized it, and I'm not sure I ever will."

He motions for me to come closer, turns his left knee outward, and shows me the leg. "It's getting better," he assures me. His knee is swollen, and the thigh is a swirl of ruptured blood vessels. The skin along his leg is cross-hatched with scars. In his thigh there is an orifice left by the surgical removal of flesh, a ropy-skinned hole that's large enough to accept a cork. "For draining," is all he says, and I don't press him further.

Will was working outside the Port Authority Bus Terminal that morning, a rookie cop policing the rush-hour crowds with his Mace and his 9mm Smith & Wesson, when he saw the shadow of a low-flying plane pass over Forty-second Street. A few minutes later, he received an alarm over his radio—a plane had hit the World Trade Center. Immediately, he and nine others boarded a Port Authority bus and sped toward the tip of Manhattan.

When the bus pulled up in front of the towers, everything was coated in a fine gray powder and strewn with chunks of metal and concrete. The carcasses of cars and buses smoldered along Vesey Street. The torched husk of an airplane part was stuck like a harpoon in the side of a building. People lay on the sidewalk, bloody, with paramedics at their sides. Even on the ground, Will could smell the jet fuel. From his years in the navy, he was well acquainted with its sharp stench, and he knew something about how hot it burned.

Senior officers were looking up at the fire with tears in their eyes. Most of the Port Authority policemen had suspected this was a terrorist attack right from the start. Ever since the 1993 WTC bombing, the Port Authority had been an agency steeped in paranoia. The World Trade Center was expressly theirs to protect, and they were trained to be suspicious. "As soon as we pulled up to the site, we knew that this was a combat situation," Will says. "Only we were police officers—we were never trained for war."

While fussing with his equipment, Will kept hearing explosions, one every few seconds, a ragged beat of concussions thudding up and down the street. He turned to look: They were human bodies, dropping from above, blowing up on impact. They sent up aerosol clouds of blood and left divots in the sidewalk. The ground became littered with body parts and personal effects—watches, high-heeled shoes, PDAs, a briefcase. "I've heard experts say the people were dead before they hit the ground," Will says. "But you could tell they were conscious. They saw what was coming."

∗   ∗   ∗

With no medical training, Ronnie Clifford scarcely knew what to do with the helpless woman who stood before him. He sat her down on the cool marble floor, then dashed into the bathroom and ran water into a clean black garbage bag that he found. He hurried back out and dribbled the contents over her body.

Then he sat down on the puddled floor and tried to comfort her. Despite her condition, she was lucid. He took out a pen and notepad and jotted down her information. Her name was Jennieann Maffeo. She was Italian-American, from Brooklyn, single, forty years old. She worked for USB PaineWebber. She was an asthmatic, she said, and had an extreme intolerance to latex. She could not adequately describe what had happened to her. She had been standing outside the north tower next to a man she knew, waiting for a bus, when she heard a loud crash above. In an effort to protect them from falling debris, a security guard herded everyone inside the tower's lobby. Suddenly, she told Ronnie, something bright and hot enveloped her, a vapor maybe. She thought it could have dropped down the elevator shaft. She was worried about the man who'd been next to her. Surely he was dead, she feared.

Periodically Ronnie yelled for a paramedic, but no one came. People were streaming through the revolving doors now and scattering. Ronnie didn't know what to do, what to say. His new suit was soaking wet, and wisps of skin clung to it. He sat close to Jennieann, but didn't think he should hold her, for he feared that the germs on his hands would cause a fatal infection. He thought about his strong-willed sister, Ruth, and wondered how she would have handled this. She had once run a European day spa in Boston and had made skin health her professional and personal concern. She knew what vitamins to take, what salves to daub on burns, and she always coached Ronnie to take care of his skin. She would have known what to do.

Jennieann turned to Ronnie and looked beseechingly at him through her half-closed eyelids. "Sacred heart of Jesus, pray for us," she said.

Sitting in a pool of water, alone in the swirling stampede, he whispered the Lord's Prayer in her ear.

Anxiously, Silvion and Christine rode the elevator back down to seventy-eight. More than a hundred people were there waiting for express cars, tapping their feet, cutting nervous jokes. Christine tried to make a call from her cell phone but couldn't get a carrier. "This elevator better come soon, or we'll have to take the stairs," Silvion said.

A few seconds later, at 9:06 A.M., Silvion glimpsed a brilliant flash of milky light out of the corner of his left eye. There was a boom and a terrific concussion of air. The entire wall to his left ripped open, and a pressure wave hurled him ten feet across the lobby.

As he tumbled through the air, he felt debris piercing his body. He landed on his back. His briefcase was tossed in the opposite direction. A miscellany of tiles and Sheetrock landed on him. He could smell what he later learned was jet fuel, and there were fires all around.

Silvion wasn't sure if he could move. He had cuts everywhere. He was bleeding from his ears and had a long laceration across his jaw, with the skin hanging loosely from his chin. He was having trouble breathing. Something hard and sharp was embedded in his upper chest, and the wound was pulsing dark blood, a red coin growing on his shirt. His left arm dangled lifelessly.

He lay dazed for a few moments, with no idea what had happened. The only thing he could imagine was that an explosion from the other tower had somehow carried over. He studied the wound on his chest long enough to ascertain that whatever had entered his body was significant, about the size of a deck of cards. He could neither lift his arm nor move his shoulder. Nerves and muscles had evidently been severed. He worried that the projectile had struck a major artery.

Then he realized that a man was lying across his legs. He sat up and struggled to roll him off. When he saw the man's face, Silvion knew he was dead.

Will Jimeno raised his hand to volunteer when Sergeant John McLoughlin, a Port Authority veteran who knew every rivet of the building, asked for men to accompany him into the north tower and start rescuing victims. The group quickly assembled. The four men were preparing to venture into the tower when the second crash came, the United Airlines jet. Because of the speed and angle of the impact, this second explosion was much more massive than the first. The shock wave worked its way down the building, like a thrum in a bell.

Even so, Will and his three comrades gathered their equipment and pressed into the World Trade Center.

*   *   *

Ronnie Clifford was still whispering the Lord's Prayer in Jennieann Maffeo's ear when the second plane hit. The whole edifice rumbled and groaned and swayed, then the floor beneath him buckled hideously and seemed to raise him off his feet. Pieces of the building began falling around him. Ronnie knew then that they absolutely must get out.

"Jennieann," he said. "Can you stand up?"

"I'll try," she answered.

Ronnie removed his new suit coat and draped it over her front so that she wouldn't have to walk out of the building naked. A nurse who worked for the Marriott arrived with a bottle of oxygen and a mask, which she held over Jennieann's mouth as they shambled across the hotel's crowded lobby. Drawing closer to the door, Ronnie heard someone say, "A plane hit the tower," and then someone else say, "A second plane hit the other tower," which was the first time he had an inkling of what had happened. He was growing more frustrated and alarmed. The crowds weren't moving fast enough through the bottleneck at the door. Jennieann was in excruciating pain. Finally, Ronnie held her arm and pushed impatiently through the throng.

"Out of the way!" he screamed in a voice he didn't know he had. "Make way!" When people turned to look, they shrank in horror, and suddenly Ronnie and Jennieann were able to file straight out, as though the waters were parting before them. "It was like I was taking Frankenstein out of the building," Ronnie says.

When they emerged onto the street, Ronnie looked up and saw a lady plummeting toward the ground, clutching her purse. "I keep thinking about that," he says. "I can't get the image out of my head. Why was she worried about her purse?"

Even in her state, Jennieann was self-conscious about her nakedness. Ronnie understood that his suitcoat wasn't enough. Then, out of nowhere, a huge gentleman appeared with a clean white tablecloth and gently wrapped it around Jennieann, like a shroud. It was as though he had foreseen her predicament. The man smiled and helped Ronnie get her down the steps.

A fireman was standing on the street corner, grimacing at the burning buildings, which were breaking apart. Ronnie could hear the sound of them cooking, the sound of rivets popping, the sighs steel girders make when they bend. With wild gesticulations, the fireman screamed at the lingering crowds, "Run, run! I'm telling you, just run."

"Can you run, Jennieann?" Ronnie asked.

"I think so," she said. She looked at her feet. The rubber soles of what had once been her running shoes were melted to her feet.

"Let's try, then," Ronnie said. He took her arm, and in a tentative, shuffling gait, they ran.

On the seventy-eighth floor of the south tower—or, rather, what had formerly been the seventy-eighth floor but was now an upheaval of fuel-splattered wreckage—Silvion Ramsundar tried to shake off the shock. The heat was intense, and flames were engulfing the mangled corridors. Is it over? he thought. Am I going to die right here? What happened just now? He peered through the thickening smoke and realized that the majority of the hundred or so people who had been waiting for the elevator were now dead. At least they weren't moving.

Silvion scanned the lobby for his friend Christine and spotted her some thirty feet away, stunned and injured but still alive. She had lacerations on her arms and face, and her left ankle was bleeding profusely. Silvion managed to stand. Picking his way among the bodies, he hobbled over to Christine. She slowly registered his presence. She saw the red stain blooming on his white shirt and said, alarmed, "You're bleeding bad."

"I think I can move," he said. "How about you?"

Christine nodded and struggled to her feet. Silvion remembered that there was a stairwell somewhere near the elevator bank. It was the only way out. They fumbled along the wall, blind, until Silvion grabbed what felt like a handle with his right hand. He gave it a jerk, but it wouldn't turn.

Now the black smoke was so dense along the ceiling that they had to creep on the floor. Not far from the first door, they found another. Silvion gave it a try, and this time the latch turned. The heavy fire door swayed open—it was the emergency stairwell he'd been looking for. The buckled stairway was hot but relatively clear of smoke. Silvion brightened for a moment, then hesitated. He wasn't sure he could make seventy-eight floors. His breathing was shallow and labored, and he was growing weak.

For a brief moment, Silvion gazed back through the smoke. He heard choking, coughing, the cries of the injured. He thought about his friend Charles, the security guard, and realized he must be dead.

Silvion turned back toward the stairs. He leaned against Christine, and they began walking down in the sodium glare of the emergency lights, on steps marked with fluorescent tape. They settled into a pace that was comfortable for him, stopping occasionally so that he could catch his breath. More people filled the stairwell. Some were hyperventilating and removing clothing in response to the heat. Occasionally Silvion had to step around people who could go no further.

Somewhere in the high sixties, they reached a landing that was obstructed by a massive beam. Two large men managed to shift it just enough so that the file of evacuees could crawl through, then resume their descent.

As they walked, people could plainly see that Silvion was critically injured. One man applied his handkerchief to the wound as a compress. Later, a woman removed her slip and cinched it around Silvion's shoulder to stanch the blood. They kept walking.

Silvion kept his mind fixed on the numbers—sixty-two, sixty-one, sixty, fifty-nine—and tried as best he could not to consider his wound.

Will Jimeno had spent only nine months on the job as a cop, and although he had undergone an intensive six-month training course at the police academy, he was thoroughly unprepared for the situation in which he now found himself. He had spent most of his brief career on duty at the Port Authority Bus Terminal, a vast and shabby complex in midtown Manhattan. Up until this moment, his most challenging situations had been a shooting incident involving an emotionally disturbed person and the case of a homeless man with advanced AIDS who perished on a bus.

Now, the officers were down in the concourse, not far from the Gap, at a point almost equidistant from the two towers and just beneath the famous bronze globe, a sculpture designed to symbolize world peace through world trade. The concourse level was ordinarily a bustling shopping mall, but now it was desolate, and the tile floors ran cold with water from the firefighters' hoses.

The men opened an equipment closet and rummaged for gear: flashlights, crowbars, gloves, first-aid kits, and self-contained breathing apparatuses known as Scott Air-Paks. Their radios, tuned to Port Authority frequencies, blew a constant gale of staticky screams.

Among the group of cops, now numbering five, were a veteran named Christopher Amoroso and two other rookies, Dominick Pezzulo and Antonio Rodrigues. Pezzulo and Rodrigues were close buddies of Will's from his police-academy class. Thirty-six years old, Pezzulo was a funny Italian from the Bronx, a weightlifter who, Will says, was "built like Jean-Claude Van Damme." He had a beautiful wife and two kids, and loved to fish for blues in Long Island Sound. Rodrigues, whom everyone called A-Rod, was a colorful bald guy with a thick Portuguese accent. A gifted artist, Rodrigues was always doing caricature sketches of the other cops.

The younger men never questioned Sergeant McLoughlin's judgment. A highly decorated veteran of the department, he had won a medal for his valor in the evacuation following the 1993 Trade Center bombing. Will says, "If he asked me tomorrow, I'd follow him into that building again."

The five men tossed the paraphernalia into a canvas cart and hustled toward the north tower.

Running from the buildings, Ronnie Clifford and Jennieann Maffeo found an ambulance beside a green knoll across West Street, near the World Financial Center. He spirited her, still wrapped in a table linen, into the hands of the paramedics and gave them the notes he'd scribbled that described her vital facts. Then the ambulance took off for the Weill Cornell Burn Center, uptown.

Ronnie called Brigid, his wife, from a pay phone. "I'm all right," he told her in a voice she would later describe as "close to panic." There was a long pause. "I've just gone through something terrible," he said. "I'm alive. I'm okay. I love you."

Ronnie hung up and tried to get his bearings. He turned to look again at the towers. The infernos were raging even more fiercely than before. People were still occasionally leaping from above, while firemen were marshaling in large numbers and marching into the buildings.

He tried to call his sister, Ruth, in Connecticut, but couldn't get through. Ruth lived in an old mansion beside a lighthouse on Long Island Sound. But then Ronnie remembered that she wouldn't be home. She was on a trip to Los Angeles to take her four-year-old daughter, Juliana, to Disneyland and to attend a seminar by the New Age self-help author Deepak Chopra. Her best friend, Paige Farley-Hackel, was coming along. Ronnie was certain they were in California by now. Whatever Ruth was doing, he hoped to God she wasn't watching CNN.

Ronnie wasn't sure what to do next. He felt he ought to try to help people evacuate, or volunteer at a hospital. Then he thought about Monica, his daughter. He remembered that it was her birthday and that they'd planned to have a celebratory dinner that night.

She was turning eleven.

Dusted in gray flour, Silvion Ramsundar and his friend Christine shuffled out of the south tower around 9:50 A.M. Christine needed stitches for her multiple lacerations, but the paramedics were gravely concerned about Silvion's condition. They went to work on him immediately. His left lung had collapsed, his pulse was faint, he'd lost a dangerous amount of blood, he was dehydrated, and he was in shock. A photographer for the New York Post snapped his picture, a portrait that would become one of the more arresting images of the day. His wound had become unbearable. "My body sort of relaxed," Silvion says. "I had a sense of relief—okay, I made it, seventy-eight floors. And that's when the pain really kicked in."

It was only when Silvion was hurtling toward Saint Vincent's Hospital in an ambulance that he learned what had happened. "A second plane?" His mind reeled at the implications. The plane had struck the very floor where he had been standing; the gas he'd smelled was jet fuel. It couldn't have been an accident. He was having trouble absorbing this. But by then, the morphine had begun to take over.

Reversing his course from earlier that morning, Ronnie Clifford boarded the ferry to Hoboken. The ferry operators weren't even bothering with tickets; they were simply ushering people aboard. During the ride across the Hudson, Ronnie stood at the stern of the boat and watched the buildings burn. His begrimed jacket was slung over his shoulder, a memento of a business meeting that was not to be.

Then, at 9:59, just as he reached the creosoted piers of New Jersey, the south tower collapsed. In a terrific, thunderous implosion, the eleven became a one.

The Port Authority officers were directly beneath it all. Within seconds, Will Jimeno and his four partners were assaulted by concrete, tile, marble, and a hail of glass shards. There was a tremendous snarling roar, which Will could feel more than hear. Sergeant McLoughlin pointed toward a safe place, behind a massive concrete pillar. As they dashed toward it, the tower came down on them. Will momentarily lost track of everyone else. He ran until the world became dark and close and his body could no longer move.

He couldn't catch his breath. He couldn't see. It felt as though someone had poured hot sand down his throat. His whole left side and his right foot were pinned by something large, as if the weight of the towers was bearing down on him. He was coated in a puree of insulation, Sheetrock, fabrics, fibers, papers, paints, plastics, wiring—all the substances of society, the mingled grounds of the modern world. It got in his ears, his lungs, his mouth. Even now, six months later, Will can smell it. He calls it "the smell of World Trade Center."

Finally the cloud began to dissipate, and a tiny shaft of light slanted in. Will couldn't see the sky, but there was just enough filtered light for him to make out shapes. He was in what amounted to a tiny cave, trapped by a piece of an elevator shaft. Various fires flickered in pockets and folds all about him. His radio was out of reach.

Will called for Pezzulo. "Dom, you all right?"

"Yeah, I'm here." Pezzulo was also pinned. He lay only a few feet away from Will. Once the dust settled a little more, they could see each other.

They heard McLoughlin somewhere in a void below. The sergeant was gasping in pain, trapped in the fetal position. He couldn't see a thing, nor could the other men see him. By the sound of things, the sergeant was in worse shape than Will. "Somebody relieve the pressure!" McLoughlin yelled. "I can't stand it."

"A-Rod? Chris?" Will called out for the two others, but he got no response.

Then they were assailed by a horrible chirping sound, incessant and shrill, like a dozen car alarms going off. It was the Air-Paks, strapped to the men's backs. An Air-Pak has an attached motion detector; if its wearer doesn't move within one minute, an alarm is triggered. The signal is incredibly harsh and loud so that rescuers can locate a fallen or trapped comrade. But now so many Air-Paks were sounding off all around the World Trade Center that there was little hope of locating any one. The alarms were canceling each other out by their sheer numbers. It sounded like a field of crickets.

Ronnie Clifford took the commuter train home from Hoboken. Next to him sat a lady who was deep into a bottle of booze. The cars were overcrowded with people on cell phones bawling to their spouses. Someone nearby had a BlackBerry, a wireless Internet device, and was receiving chilling updates on the tiny screen. *Another one's hit the Pentagon. Another one's down in Pennsylvania. Another one's heading for the White House.*

As the train hummed and clacked west toward home, Ronnie's thoughts drifted back to Jennieann. It seemed that she had saved his life, just as he had saved hers. If he had remained in that building much longer, perhaps helping other people, he'd be buried now. If the horrified crowds in the lobby hadn't instantly made way for them, he might still be trapped. In the queer way fate had worked, Jennieann had been his ticket out. He prayed for her.

Just minutes after the south tower fell on Will Jimeno, his buddy Dom Pezzulo managed to free himself from the rubble. Pezzulo thought about crawling toward the hole to seek help, but decided to try to extricate his friends instead. It soon became apparent that the cause was hopeless, but he clawed at the debris with his bare hands for about a half-hour, struggling with blocks of concrete ten times his size. The Air-Paks shrieked relentlessly.

Then Will heard another noise, another rumble in the distance, like the wrath of a volcano. Pezzulo backed up a few feet and braced himself for another collapse. "Oh, my God," Will said. "Here we go again." The north tower came down around them. It was 10:28.

From above, a jagged block of concrete fell through the hole and tumbled into their crawl space. Will watched as the slab struck Pezzulo and "laid him down like a rag doll." Pezzulo withered in pain. He made a wisecrack to the sergeant, something about requesting permission to take a coffee break. He was losing a lot of blood. He turned and said, "I love you, Will."

Will said, "I love you, buddy."

"Don't forget," Pezzulo added. "Don't forget I died trying to save you guys."

Then Pezzulo unholstered his 9mm sidearm, pointed it up toward the hole, and fired off a single round. "It was like a last-ditch effort," Will says, "as if to say, We're down here, come find us."

Will watched as Pezzulo slumped back and gasped for air. His gun fell to his side.

John McLoughlin, unable to see anything down in his black hole, shouted through the pain, "What's going on up there?"

"Sarge—it's Dom. He's gone. I just saw him pass."

A team of plastic surgeons at Saint Vincent's sutured Silvion Ramsundar's chin back together. Then they went to work on his chest. His shoulder blade was broken, and the piece of shrapnel was lodged dangerously close to his aorta. The doctors worried that if they weren't extremely careful in removing the object, they could paralyze his arm for life. Once they dug out the gobbet with their surgical tools and examined it, the doctors decided it was a shard of metal from the airplane that had crashed into his floor. Silvion wanted to keep it—a piece of that day once embedded in his body—but later an FBI agent arrived with a Ziploc bag, marked it EVIDENCE, and carried the artifact away.

When Ronnie Clifford arrived home in the late morning, he embraced Brigid and then climbed upstairs straightaway for a shower. More than anything else, he wanted to rinse off the residue of his morning. At least he had his daughter's birthday party to look forward to. He paused to think about what this would mean for Monica as she grew up, to have turned eleven on September 11, 2001. Monica was across the street at school—innocent, for now, of what had transpired in the city.

Ronnie, it turned out, was innocent, too. He had assumed it was only fair, after witnessing so much, after doing his part as a good Samaritan, that he should sail away on the Hoboken ferry, unscathed. But then he received a piece of news by phone from his brother-in-law that, with a bit of work on the Internet, he confirmed. Among the ticketed passengers on American Airlines flight 11, the first plane, the one that hit the north tower, had been Paige Farley-Hackel, his sister Ruth's best friend and a close friend of his. A little later in the afternoon he was able to verify an even more devastating fact: Ruth and her four-year-old daughter, Juliana, had been on the second plane, the United Airlines flight from Boston.

Ronnie had somehow lost track of when Ruth and Juliana were supposed to fly to Los Angeles. He thought they'd gone out the day before. Paige took American, Ruth took United, but they both ended up in the hands of hijackers, friends in separate missiles aimed at the same target.

Ronnie tried to imagine Ruth's last moments on the plane. Most likely, Ronnie thought, she would have been sitting calmly in her seat as they banked low over the Hudson. And in the seconds before the plane hit, she would have been holding little Juliana, and singing a song in her ear.

Will Jimeno and Sergeant McLoughlin were the only ones left. Amoroso, Rodrigues, and now Pezzulo were all dead. The two men waited for hours for something to happen. Occasionally fireballs floated down into the hole and were extinguished in the wreckage. One of them must have landed near Pezzulo's Smith & Wesson and heated it up. The gun went off, and bullets ricocheted around the hole. "You're not going to believe this. We're getting shot at!" Will yelled to McLoughlin.

They talked to each other a lot during the afternoon, the veteran sergeant and the rookie. They talked about their families, about life and death, about their buddies who lay buried about them. Both men were in agony, squirming under the pressure, their arms and legs swelling. But they were lucid. With his free hand, Will tried to chip away at the concrete with his handcuffs and a spare magazine of his gun. It was useless. Every couple of minutes, he would yell out, "PAPD 813!" which is Port Authority code for "officer down." But as midday stretched into late afternoon, his calls began to lack enthusiasm.

Then, from the hole above, Will heard a voice. Someone was frantically shouting a name, then, "Are you down there? Are you down there?"

Will couldn't catch the name, but he shouted back, "Sergeant McLoughlin and Officer Jimeno are here!" He was ecstatic. But then the voice left and never returned.

Will began to talk to himself out loud, a stream of dire thoughts. He thought about Allison, his wife, who was seven months pregnant. "At that point I pretty much accepted death," he says. "I asked God to watch over Allison and my little four-year-old and the new baby girl. I wanted to see the baby, just once."

At around 8 P.M., Will was roused by another voice. "United States Marine Corps, can anybody hear me?"

Will yelled back, "Don't leave us! The last guy left."

Then a marine trained his flashlight into the hole and spotted him. "I'm not leaving you," he said.

Soon the paramedics came, and firemen and cops and Port Authority officers, a long trail of men harnessed to one another, clambering over the pile. For three hours they dug and scraped and sawed, pulling away rebar, widening the hole. They used their bare hands, welding torches, buzz saws, and the Jaws of Life. Finally, they reached Will. They feared they would have to amputate his left leg, but at last budged the pillar just enough to slip him free.

They would get to McLoughlin, but first they slid Will into a basket and hauled him out. It was 11 at night, thirteen hours after the south tower had collapsed. Will looked around at the devastated site, a smoky panorama of harsh lights and humming generators and flickering welders' sparks.

"Where is everything?" he asked.

One of the officers leaned over and said to him, "There's nothing left, kid. It's all gone."

Later in September, Ronnie Clifford went to visit Jennieann at the hospital. She was wrapped in gauze from head to toe, save for narrow slits for her eyes and her mouth. Although Jennieann was heavily sedated and could not talk, her sister said she was aware of visitors. Ronnie sat with her for a while, and urged her to be strong. Before he left, he placed his yellow silk tie on the pillow beside her, the tie he'd been wearing on the eleventh, the one Ruth had coached him to wear. Ronnie wasn't sure why this gesture had occurred to him. He just wanted her to have something to remember him by. Something that stood out.

Jennieann was in the hospital for forty-one days, drifting in and out of consciousness. The mounting infections, the skin grafts, the side effects of her medications—it was all too much for her system. On October 21, she died of kidney failure.

That same day, workers at ground zero located Ruth's remains. The family had already held a service for her and Juliana a month earlier. More than twelve hundred people had showed up. There had been long, bittersweet remembrances and a Celtic bagpiper. Ronnie organized a huge party afterward on Ruth's front lawn.

As soon as he got home from the funeral, Ronnie collapsed in exhaustion. "My emotions were swimming around," he says. He was a nervous wreck. One time, Monica and a friend were horsing around on the hardwood floor and made a sharp thumping sound. Ronnie lost it. All he could think of was falling bodies, the woman with her purse. He couldn't get the images out of his head.

Finally, recognizing that the problem was "far greater than anything I could deal with," Ronnie went to a psychologist's office. Doug, the therapist, sat back in his reclining chair and invited him to talk about his life. He asked Ronnie to keep a journal of his dreams. He put him under mild hypnosis and had him relive every sight and smell and sensation of that horrible day. What started out as six hours a week has since fallen away to one hour every other week. The engineering metaphor has proved apt.

Mostly, Silvion Ramsundar misses the views. The way electrical storms scudded out to the Atlantic, the sunsets that went on forever, the morning sun lighting up the clustered spires of lower Manhattan, the Statue of Liberty standing sentinel at his feet.

Silvion spent two weeks mending in the hospital, followed by months of physical therapy to restore his shoulder. The arm still tingles and throbs, and it bothers him in countless little ways. As he talks, he twists and flexes his arm. "They say it's never going to be 100 percent," he says. "It gets all locked up. I can't pick Mariah up the way I used to, to take her up to bed. But they say, just be grateful you can use your arm at all."

When he arrived home from the hospital, Silvion didn't relive the incident, exactly, but he had bad dreams: He kept finding himself trapped in a fire, smashing up his car, being chased. Then he started having anxiety attacks whenever he drove over a bridge. In daydreams and reveries, Silvion can still summon the sight of the Sky Lobby with sickening vividness. That he survived the blast through nothing more than dumb luck, an accident of positioning, troubles him. "There was only one quadrant on that floor that was safe from the plane, and it happened to be where I was standing," he tells me, with fresh amazement. "If I'd been standing ten feet to my left, maybe I wouldn't be sitting here. Had I been a foot to my right, maybe the debris would have hit my heart. Why me? Why not the guy who was standing next to me? How come *I* was in the right place?"

In the past few months, Silvion has logged some serious quality time with his family. Chores around the house, countless trips to Home Depot. For ten years, he lived at the speed of Wall Street. These days, he doesn't bother getting up until nine. Sometime in the spring, Silvion plans to return to work at Mizuho Capital Markets and get back into the derivatives game.

In a very real sense, Silvion has been Americanized, secularized, confirmed in the high church of pluralism and the mutual fund—the very things, of course, that make the terrorists burn. And yet one of the odd twists to the whole event, for him, is that because he is of Indian descent, dark-skinned and raven-haired, he sometimes gets the look, the double take of suspicion. Who are you, where are you from, what's hidden in your shoe? "It's justifiable," he reasons. "Until this threat is completely gone, I have to expect it."

As he talks, he sits beneath his before-and-after diptych of the trade towers and assures me, with a kind of provisional confidence, that he's okay. He has one modest request, though. If he has a choice, he prefers not to work in a high-rise. "I'm good on the ground floor," he says.

Will Jimeno has no idea where the rumor started, the beautiful, fantastic rumor. In the hours after they were discovered in the rubble, he and Sergeant McLoughlin became the subject of an incredible story repeated so often that the national media reported it as confirmed fact: A Port Authority cop, in some accounts several, was said to have "ridden the wave" of debris down from the eightieth floor and survived with barely a scratch. It was the kind of legend that springs up in the chaos of a catastrophe—a wildly untrue story that reflects a true hope. All around the world, people were praying that more victims would be pulled alive from the ruins. If a man could ride down that mighty wave and live, then there was still a chance.

When he got to Bellevue Hospital, Will was assaulted by a green army of surgeons. He didn't understand why, with a tragedy of such mammoth proportions, he should get such solicitous treatment. He didn't understand that, at that point, there were no other survivors. He was the survivor—he and his sergeant and a handful of others. The green army rolled him into the operating room and set to work. He had a condition known as compartment syndrome. The wracking pressure in his leg had built up so powerfully that, when the doctors cut it open that night, blood and backed-up fluids sprayed the walls like a Jackson Pollock canvas.

In twelve days, Will had eight operations to excise the dead tissue and relieve pressure. The doctors worried about blood clots and kidney failure and gangrene. When they suctioned out his upper airway, the vacuum ticked and chattered with the sound of grit. At one point, Will saw a rock sliding up through the tube.

All those weeks in the hospital, Will thought about his comrades day and night. He still does—especially Pezzulo and Rodrigues. He can't get them out of his head. He's commiserated with their wives, described their bravery. Sergeant McLoughlin, who was pulled out of the rubble eight hours after Will, was released from the hospital in January, after kidney dialysis and some two dozen operations. He's improving gradually. "One day at a time," Will says. "Like me, he's trying to get by."

Will has decided to remain with the PAPD, maybe working at the pistol range. "I have moments where I'm not happy, where there's mental anguish," he says. "But right now I'm at peace with this. I didn't live through all this just to quit."

Before 9/11, Will and Allison knew they were having a baby girl, but they had bickered over the name. Will wanted Alyssa. His wife wanted Olivia. When they found him in the rubble that night, he asked someone to call Allison and tell her to name the baby Olivia. "If I didn't make it," he says, "I didn't want her to feel guilty about going with the name she wanted."

Now Will is holding his newborn, a beautiful three-month-old with a full head of hair. She was born November 26, which is also Will's birthday. He was there at the hospital at Allison's side, crying in his wheelchair. Now he lifts her up and holds her high over his head and smiles up into her eyes. She smiles back.

Her name is Olivia.

The first time Ronnie went out sailing after September 11, it was as though he'd never been on the water before. He's been a sailor ever since he was a boy in Cork, and in recent years he's kept a twenty-six-foot fiberglass boat in a slip in the Bronx. Now, though, he was unsteady, indecisive, skittish. He was reluctant to heel her over in strong winds. He was nervous about every piece of the rigging.

Whenever the boat made a shudder, his heart raced. At what seemed like his lowest moment ever, he found himself looking across Long Island Sound, struggling to comprehend the gap in the skyline.

But Ronnie kept at it. Every weekend, he was out there on the Sound. As the fall progressed, the winds grew stronger and he began taking more risks. One day, he was out in twenty-five-knot winds and he realized something extraordinary was happening: He was smiling.

Even the hole in the skyline ceased to prey on him as it had before. He scarcely even noticed it.

Sitting in the library of his house in Glen Ridge, I ask Ronnie if he thinks he'll ever find meaning in September 11—the day his daughter turned eleven, the day his sister and niece smashed into a building at the very moment he was reciting the Lord's Prayer into the ear of a horribly burned stranger. "Meaning?" he says, turning the word over in his mind. "It was so horrible, so horrendous, there's got to be goodness afterward. To me, the trade towers represented positive and negative. Before and after. Good and evil. Two ones."

Outside, in the broad daylight, I can see the vintage gaslights flickering up and down the street.

"For me," Ronnie says, "the meaning is the rest of my life."

APRIL 2002

CONTRIBUTORS

Scott Anderson is a journalist and novelist whose most recent books are *Triage* and *The Man Who Tried to Save the World* (which was excerpted in *Men's Journal* in May 1999), an investigation into the mysterious disappearance of an American relief worker in Chechnya. Anderson divides his time between New York City and a cabin in the Catskills.

Todd Balf, a *Men's Journal* contributing editor, has reported on, written about, and sometimes participated in expeditionary adventures for fifteen years. He is the author of *The Last River: The Tragic Race for Shangri-La*. His new book, *The Darkest Jungle*, about maverick explorer Isaac Strain's attempt to discover a shipping route through the jungles of Panama, will be published by Crown in 2003.

John Balzar is the author of *Yukon Alone*. He covered adventure, war, and politics as a correspondent for the *Los Angeles Times* for twenty years and now writes a column for the paper. He lives in southern California.

Rick Bass is the author of sixteen books of fiction and nonfiction, including the novel *Where the Sea Used to Be* and *The Hermit's Story*, a collection published by Houghton Mifflin. He lives in northwest Montana.

Roy Blount Jr. is the author of sixteen books, including *Be Sweet, If Only You Knew How Much I Smell You,* and *Roy Blount's Book of Southern Humor. The Main Stream,* a documentary about his wandering down the Mississippi River, appeared on PBS in 2002. He lives in New York City and in Massachusetts.

Mark Bowden is a correspondent for *The Atlantic Monthly* and a columnist for the *Philadelphia Inquirer,* where he was a staff writer for twenty-two years. His book *Black Hawk Down* was an international bestseller and a finalist for the National Book Award in 1999. He is also the author of *Bringing the Heat, Doctor Dealer, Killing Pablo,* and, most recently, *Finders Keepers,* published by Atlantic Monthly Press.

Chip Brown is a *Men's Journal* contributing editor, and has written for more than thirty other national magazines. He won the National Magazine Award for feature writing in 1989, and was a finalist in 1990 and 1994. He is the author of *Afterwards, You're a Genius: Faith, Medicine and the Metaphysics of Healing.* He expanded his *Men's Journal* piece on Guy Waterman into a book, *Good Morning Midnight,* published by Riverhead. He lives in New York.

Larry Brown was born in Oxford, Mississippi, in 1951. He served two years in the United States Marine Corps and was a firefighter in his hometown for sixteen years. His essays and short stories have been published in many magazines, and he is the author of eight books of fiction and nonfiction, the most recent being *Billy Ray's Farm.* He lives with his family on a farm near Oxford.

Tim Cahill is the author of seven books of nonfiction, including *Pass the Butterworms: Remote Journeys Oddly Rendered,* and is the coauthor of three IMAX screenplays, including *Everest.* A contributing editor at *Men's Journal,* he also writes for *Rolling Stone, National Geographic,* and *The New York Times Book Review.* His new book, *Hold the Enlightenment,* was published by Ballard Books. He lives in Montana.

Philip Caputo is a *Men's Journal* contributing editor who served in the United States Marine Corps in Vietnam from 1964–1967. He won the 1973 Pulitzer Prize for investigative reporting, and was a finalist for the 1981 National Book Award for *Horn of Africa.* He is the author of nine other books of fiction and nonfiction, including *In the Shadows of the Morning,* a collection of his travel writing, and *Acts of Faith,* a novel set in contemporary Sudan, published by Alfred A. Knopf.

Ramsey Flynn won the National Magazine Award for Reporting in 1988 and has been awarded many other writing and editing honors. His work has been anthologized in *Nonfiction for the 1990s.* While researching the *Kursk* disaster for "Buried at Sea," Flynn made three trips to Russia, conducted over two hundred interviews, and reviewed thousands of reports. His book about the *Kursk* will be published in 2003 by HarperCollins. He lives outside Baltimore.

Devin Friedman is a former senior writer for *Men's Journal*. His work has appeared in *GQ, Esquire, The New Yorker, The New York Times Magazine,* and *Rolling Stone,* among others.

Charles Gaines, a *Men's Journal* contributing editor since the premiere issue, has written fifteen stories for the magazine. He has published twenty-three books, including *Pumping Iron,* a national best-seller, and *Stay Hungry,* a finalist for the National Book Award. His latest book is *Leaper,* a collection of the best writing on Atlantic salmon, published in the United States by Lyons Press. He lives with his wife, Patricia, two hunting dogs, and a Yorky in Alabama and Nova Scotia.

Jim Harrison is the author of twenty-four books, including *Legends of the Fall* and *Wolf: A False Memoir,* which he also adapted into a screenplay. A *Men's Journal* contributing editor since 1998, his latest book is *Off to the Side,* a memoir published by Atlantic Monthly Press.

Sebastian Junger, a contributing editor at *Men's Journal,* is the best-selling author of *The Perfect Storm* and an award-winning journalist, reporting on such issues as war, terrorism, and human rights from war-torn regions across the world. Winner of the National Magazine Award for Reporting in 1999, Junger is a frequent contributor to *Vanity Fair.* His most recent book is *Fire,* a collection of his magazine work. Junger is based in New York City.

Mark Levine is a *Men's Journal* contributing editor who has also written frequently for *The New Yorker.* He is the author of two award-winning books of poems, *Debt* and *Enola Gay.* He teaches poetry at the Iowa Writers' Workshop and divides his time between Iowa City and Brooklyn.

Thomas McGuane is the author of nine novels, three collections of essays, and one collection of short stories. His most recent novel, *The Cadence of Grass,* was published by Random House. He resides with his wife and family in Sweet Grass County, Montana.

John McLaughlin is a New York–based freelance writer specializing in international politics, sports, and travel. His work has appeared in *Travel & Leisure,* the *New York Times, Harper's Bazaar,* and *The Village Voice* in the United States, as well as in the *Daily Mail* and the *Daily Telegraph* in the United Kingdom.

Jonathan Miles is a contributing editor at *Men's Journal* and *Field & Stream.* His work has also appeared in *The New York Times Book Review,* salon.com, *Food & Wine, The New York Times Magazine, Gray's Sporting Journal,* and other magazines, and has twice been selected for the annual *Best American Sports Writing* anthology. He lives in New York.

John Paul Newport, a native of Fort Worth, Texas, is a senior contributing editor at *T&L Golf* and the author of *The Fine Green Line,* a chronicle of his year-long odyssey playing on the professional golf mini-tours. He has written feature articles for *Men's Journal, Golf, Golf Digest, Sports Illustrated,* and many other national publications. He lives with his wife and daughter in Nyack, New York.

Rory Nugent, whose piece "Rebels of the Apocalypse" was nominated for a National Magazine Award for Reporting in 1993, has searched for dinosaurs in the Congo (and maybe saw one), and has looked for the most elusive duck in the world. His third book, *The Docks,* will be published by Pantheon in 2003.

P. J. O'Rourke is a *Men's Journal* contributing editor and a correspondent for *The Atlantic Monthly.* He is the author of ten books, including the bestselling *Eat the Rich,* and, most recently, *The CEO of the Sofa* (Grove-Atlantic). He lives in New Hampshire and Washington, D.C.

George Plimpton is the editor of *The Paris Review* and the bestselling author of seventeen books, including *Paper Lion, Shadow Box, The Curious Case of Sidd Finch,* and, most recently, *Shackleton.* He is the Honorary Fireworks Commissioner of New York City.

David Roberts writes primarily about adventure, archaeology, history, and literature. He is the author of thirteen books, the most recent being *True Summit: What Really Happened on the Legendary Ascent of*

Annapurna. In his twenties and thirties, he led or co-led thirteen mountaineering expeditions to Alaska and the Yukon, making many first ascents. He lives in Cambridge, Massachusetts.

Stephen Rodrick is a contributing editor for *Men's Journal* and *Philadelphia Magazine.* He lives in New York and Philadelphia. His work has appeared in *The New York Times Magazine* and *ESPN Magazine,* and in the 1999 and 2000 edition of *The Best American Sports Writing.* He is at work on his first novel.

Bob Shacochis's collection of stories, *Easy in the Islands,* received the 1985 National Book Award for first fiction, and his first novel, *Swimming in the Volcano,* was a finalist for the 1993 National Book Award. *The Immaculate Invasion,* a chronicle of the U.S. military's invasion of Haiti, was named a *New York Times* Notable Book, and was a finalist for *The New Yorker* Book Award for Best Nonfiction in 1999. His nonfiction book on the Himalayas, *Kingdoms in the Air,* will be published in 2003 by Grove/Atlantic. He teaches creative writing in the MFA programs at Florida State University and Bennington College, and lives in Florida and New Mexico.

Hampton Sides, a native of Memphis, Tennessee, is the author of the *New York Times* bestseller *Ghost Soldiers.* His work has appeared in *The New York Times Magazine, DoubleTake, The New Republic,* and the *Washington Post,* and on NPR's "All Things Considered." His collection of Americana pieces will be published in late 2003 by Anchor Vintage. He is at work on a narrative history about the conquest of the Navajo Nation. He lives in Santa Fe, New Mexico.

Charles Siebert was born in Brooklyn, New York, where he currently resides. He is the author of the memoir *Wickerby: An Urban Pastoral* and the novel *Angus.* He is currently at work on another memoir, *A Man After His Own Heart,* to be published by Crown.

Doug Stanton, a *Men's Journal* contributing editor, is the author of the *New York Times* bestseller *In Harm's Way: The Sinking of the USS Indianapolis* and the extraordinary story of its survivors. The book has been translated into seven languages and will be made into a movie to be directed by Barry Levinson. Stanton received an MFA from the Writers' Workshop at the University of Iowa, and lives in northern Michigan with his wife and two children. He is at work on a book about U.S. Special Forces in the war in Afghanistan, to be published by Little, Brown.

Rick Telander is a sports columnist for the *Chicago Sun-Times*. He is the author of six books, including the recently published children's novel *String Music*. He lives in suburban Chicago with his wife and four children.

Peter Wilkinson has been a contributing editor at *Rolling Stone* since 1990, and a contributing editor at *Men's Journal* since it was launched in 1992. He lives in Manhattan with his wife, Jane, and his daughter, Alice.

Charles M. Young grew up in Madison, Wisconsin, and presently resides in Manhattan, New York. Over the years, he has written for numerous publications, including *Rolling Stone, Playboy,* the *New York Times,* and *Men's Journal.* He is currently writing a history of the Butthole Surfers.

Permissions

**All of the essays in this book were previously published in
Men's Journal.**

Scott Anderson: "As Long As We Were Together, Nothing Bad Could
 Happen to Us" (August 2000)
Todd Balf: "The Last Trip" (November 1998)
John Balzar: "Far North" (February 1999)
Rick Bass: "Creatures of the Dictator" (April 1994)
Roy Blount Jr.: "Blunder Road" (May/June 1992)
Mark Bowden: "Black Hawk Down" (February 1999)
Chip Brown: "Much About This World" (June 2000)
Larry Brown: "The Baby Goat Murders" (July 2000)
Tim Cahill: "The Most Dangerous Friend in the World" (November
 2000)
Philip Caputo: "Alone" (August 1998)
Ramsey Flynn: "Buried at Sea" (October 2001)
Devin Friedman: "Forty Years in Acapulco" (July 2001) and "The
 Firefighters" (November 2001)
Charles Gaines: "The Cajun Road" (November 1998)
Jim Harrison: "Starting Over" (February 2000)
Sebastian Junger: "Escape from Kashmir" (April 1997). Reprinted by
 permission of the Stuart Krichevsky Literary Agency, Inc. This
 article appeared in the book *Fire* by Sebastian Junger, published by
 W. W. Norton & Co.
Mark Levine: "Killing Libby" (August 2001)
Thomas McGuane: "Cutting Horse Road" (August 1999)
John McLaughlin: "The Hour and the Glory" (August 1995)
Jonathan Miles: "The Big Game" (May 2002)
John Paul Newport: "They Might Be Giants" (July/August 1993)
Rory Nugent: "Rebels of the Apocalypse" (September 1993)